Composition at Virginia Tech

Composition at Virginia Tech

A Rhetoric and Reader for Good Writing

macmillan learning
curriculum solutions

bedford/st.martin's ▪ hayden-mcneil ▪ w.h. freeman ▪ worth publishers

Additional Content taken from:

Patterns for College Writing: A Rhetorical Reader and Guide, Thirteenth Edition
by Laurie G. Kirszner and Stephen R. Mandell
Copyright © 2015 by Bedford/St. Martin's

Practical Argument: A Text and Anthology, Second Edition
by Laurie G. Kirsszner and Stephen R. Mandell
Copyright © 2015 by Bedford/St. Martins

The EasyWriter, Fifth Edition
by Andrea A. Lunsford
Copyright © 2014 by Bedford/St. Martins

Technical Communications, Eleventh Edition
by Mike Markel
Copyright © 2015 by Bedford/St. Martins

Joining the Conversation: A Guide for Writers, Second Edition
by Mike Palmquist
Copyright © 2014 by Bedford/St. Martins

Copyright © 2017 by Bedford/St. Martin's

1 0 9 8 7 6
f e d c b a

For information, write:
Macmillan Learning Curriculum Solutions
14903 Pilot Drive, Plymouth, MI 48170
www.macmillanlearning.com

ISBN: 978-1-319-06978-0

Acknowledgements
A special thank you to the graduate teaching assistants and instructors who were instrumental in writing the questions that accompany the readings. Jonathan Adams, BeeJay Silcox, Jared Gibbs, Kristin Colonna, Colleen Correll, Elizabeth Dellinger, Matthew Denton-Edmundson, Matthew Hall, Katie Brooks, Courtney Colligan, Daniel Lawrence, Travis McDonald, Matt Prater, Jessica Hill, Adam Sandlin, Patrick Siebel, Maegan Stebbins, Czander Tan, Julie Mengert, Kevin West, Abbey Williams, Ana-Christina, and Acosta Gaspar de Alba.

Acknowledgments and copyrights can be found at the back of the book on page 476, which constitutes an extension of the copyright page.

Contents

An Introduction to First-Year Writing at Virginia Tech

Welcome

Whether you are a new student, a transfer, or a seasoned Hokie, welcome to First-Year Writing at Virginia Tech. While most people with experience in higher education may not be able to tell you much about all the courses they took, they usually remember their First-Year Writing or Freshman English composition course. Even though I have been teaching for more than twenty-five years, I still remember the first essay I wrote for my Freshman English class. At the time, it didn't occur to me to think about the class as part of a larger picture; it was a required course. In hindsight, however, the course helped to familiarize me with and to prepare me for the writing that I would be doing during my matriculation through the university.

Much of what is considered a first-year writing course and how it is taught has changed since I took my Freshman English course, yet the *need* to express ideas clearly and concisely, think and read critically, and understand and apply the appropriate conventions of academic writing has not changed. While what is considered "effective" communication is contextual, the process of communicating effectively is crucial. With that said, the overall goal of our first-year writing sequence and of this textbook is to help you understand communicative needs and contexts and effectively address them.

We approach this task of thinking and communicating through writing with a series of outcomes. Our programmatic outcomes are derived from the Council of Writing Program Administrators (WPA) Outcomes Statement[1] that was revised and approved in July 2014. While not focused on a specific university or course, the statement articulates the following:

> ...the writing knowledge, practices, and attitudes that undergraduate students develop in first-year composition, which at most schools is a required general education course or sequence of courses. This Statement therefore attempts to both represent and regularize writing programs' priorities for first-year composition, which often takes the form of one or more required general education courses. To this end it is not merely a compilation or summary of what currently takes place. Rather, this Statement articulates what composition teachers nationwide have learned from practice, research, and theory. It intentionally defines only "outcomes," or types of results, and not "standards," or precise levels of achievement. The setting of standards to measure students' achievement of these Outcomes has deliberately been left to local writing programs and their institutions. (1)

---

[1]Full WPA Outcomes are located in the back of this book.

These outcomes have been adapted more locally, and what follows is a detailed description of Virginia Tech's outcomes, requirements, instructional materials, and readings for our first-year writing program.

Our first-year writing program consists of three composition courses:

- English 1105: First-Year Writing: Introduction to College Composition
- English 1106: First-Year Writing: Writing from Research
- English H1204: First-Year Honors English

Outcomes for First-Year Writing

Fundamentally, these outcomes are developed and built upon all our first-year writing courses; however, each course also has a specific focus and requirements related to the work of university writing. Since we have multiple sections of three courses, we use the explanation and practice of these outcomes throughout this textbook, as a way of providing multisectional continuity. That doesn't mean that you and your roommate, with different teachers and in different sections, will have the same exact assignments. But these outcomes and textbook create a framework and support materials for both of you to work toward the same goals through shared course objectives and texts. What follows is a description of the outcomes that are the foundation of our writing program.

I. Rhetorical Knowledge

Effective communication begins with an awareness of the rhetorical dimensions of writing and speaking. After completing the first-year writing curriculum, students should be able to use their awareness of rhetorical situations to both critically engage texts and produce original compositions.

II. Critical Thinking, Reading, and Writing

We use writing to communicate with others, of course, but writing can also be the beginning of inquiry, allowing reflection on the material one is reading or researching. After completing the first-year writing curriculum, students should be able to critically use writing and reading to learn and communicate, and they should understand the intimate connection between language and knowledge.

III. Writing Processes

Writing is a process: When producing a text, a writer may go through a process or series of processes. While not everyone works the same way, it is important to understand writing as both a process and a product. After completing the first-year writing curriculum, students should understand the common features of writing processes, and they should be aware of and able to use the processes that work best for them, and help them create the best possible writing products.

IV. Knowledge of Conventions

Of course, every good writer knows that it is important to pay attention to conventions of spelling, grammar, and punctuation. Conventions go beyond these concerns, however. Different rhetorical situations call for different kinds of texts and ways of addressing audiences. After completing the first-year writing curriculum, students should understand basic spelling, grammar, and punctuation conventions and the relationships among conventions, rhetorical situations, and genres.

V. Writing in Electronic Environments

Today, we are constantly adapting to emerging technologies. These technologies themselves have rhetorical dimensions and are often valuable composition tools. After completing the first-year writing curriculum, students should understand the relationships among rhetorical situations and electronic environments, and they should be comfortable using such environments in all parts of the writing process.

VI. Visual Literacy

The visual dimension of writing reaches beyond examining visual texts. After completing the first-year writing curriculum, students should possess the skills to use visuals as a means of composing and communicating. They should also understand the relationship between visuals and the texts in which they appear and the importance of attending to a composition's appearance—to its visual design.

VII. Effective Oral Presentation Skills

In both our academic and professional careers, it is important to feel comfortable speaking in front of an audience. A piece of writing is not the same as its oral delivery, and it is important to understand the advantages and constraints of both communication methods. After completing the first-year writing curriculum, students should be aware of strategies for feeling comfortable speaking in front of an audience. They should also understand the relationships among rhetorical situations and written and oral communication.

First-Year Writing Course Descriptions

English 1105: First-Year Writing: Introduction to College Composition

Learning Objectives

By completing English 1105, students will:
- Gain knowledge of composition's rhetorical dimensions
- Use writing as a tool for critical thinking and reflection

- Practice writing as a process by using various brainstorming, invention, revision, and editing strategies
- Write in several genres that utilize analysis, reflection, narrative, critique, and argument skills
- Practice using the conventions of written, spoken, and visual composition
- Practice writing and creating in digital environments

Course Requirements

- A *minimum* of three papers for formal grading. Major papers in English 1105 tend to be four to ten pages in length, depending on the topic and the task.
- A *minimum* of twenty pages of informal writing, such as journal responses, discussion board postings, blogs, and proposals.
- *At least* one group oral presentation including the use of visual elements (Many instructors include individual presentations as well.)

One goal of English 1105 is to help you understand writing as rhetorically situated. As such, your course may have numerous writing assignments focused on rhetorical analysis. These writing assignments and the readings that accompany them will allow you to focus on how to "take apart" a text and look at each aspect of it in relation to the whole. The readings in the English 1105 section vary in "form" and represent a range of genres. **Chapter 1, "Reading and Writing Rhetorically,"** written by Jessica Hill, provides you with a framework for understanding how to rhetorically analyze written texts—analyzing the rhetorical choices a writer makes when creating a text to meet the communicative needs of a rhetorical situation. Similarly, **Chapter 2, "Analyzing Visual Texts,"** with an introduction by Jessica Hill, gives you a framework for understanding how to rhetorically analyze visual texts.

In English 1105 you will encounter a range of texts, and you will also be expected to compose a range of texts. Many English 1105 assignments focus on you as the writer, treating everything you encounter in the world around you as text. Because your teacher may assign personal or expository writing, we have included **Chapter 3, "Narration,"** with an introduction written by Sean Conaway. This chapter will help you effectively use narration in your essay assignments.

You may also be assigned essays focused primarily on argument or persuasion. Although most good writing has a clearly discernable position or thesis, it can be argued that not all writing is persuasive. Even within the range of persuasive genres, the degree to which the author is seeking to accomplish a focused position or argument is also rhetorically situated. **Chapter 5, "Developing an Argument,"** written by Hannah Baker, comprehensively walks you through the process of developing and writing a persuasive essay and/or argument.

Presentations (both individual and group) are part of the curriculum for all first-year writing courses. While you may find the process of presenting your ideas or research, or even working in a group to present an understanding to the class, a bit daunting, presentations are a critical part of knowledge dissemination. Although we can't give you a magic potion to make it easy or carefree, **Chapter 9, "Presentations,"** provides you with a range of practical skills that may help the process go more smoothly.

English 1105 Readings

The readings chosen for English 1105 fall into three categories: *Writing and Language, Narratives and Personal Essays,* and *Rhetorical Analysis and Argument.* The essays in the Writing and Language section focus mainly on writing as process and on the processes involved in how we use language. Specifically, Donald Murray's essay "The Maker's Eye: Revising Your Own Manuscripts" and Anne Lamott's "Shitty First Drafts" help us see how even experienced writers use processes that involve good and bad attempts. Paul Roberts's "How to Say Nothing in Five Hundred Words," Casey Miller and Kate Swift's "Who's in Charge of the English Language?" Alleen Pace Nilsen's "Sexism in English: Embodiment and Language," and Shelly Branch's "One Term Says It All: 'Shut Up!'" explore a range of issues connected to language, from academic writing to what is considered "correct" language usage. The other readings in the English 1105 section are designed to function as source materials for rhetorical analysis and argument (like Deb Aronson's "The Nurture of Nature" and Taylor Clark's "Meatless Like Me") and as inspiration (from Nancy Mairs's "On Being a Cripple" to Chang-rae Lee's "Coming Home Again") for the required writing in English 1105.

Chapter 4, "Knowledge of Conventions: Grammar and Style," by Julie Mengert, and **Chapter 6, "Critical Thinking and Reading,"** by Natalie Richoux and Steve Oakey, provide instruction and practice in areas that do not apply to a specific semester. Permeated throughout all composing that is done in your first-year writing class is the concept that composing is a process. Knowledge of the conventions associated with a specific communicative situation or genre is key to writing effectively. As explained in the WPA outcomes and reiterated in our own outcomes, "[s]uccessful writers understand, analyze, and negotiate conventions for purpose, audience, and genre, understanding that genres evolve in response to changes in material conditions and composing technologies and attending carefully to emergent conventions" (See page 474). Critical thinking is also a necessary skill for any first-year writing course. The WPA Outcomes Statement articulates this point by stating the following:

Critical thinking is the ability to analyze, synthesize, interpret, and evaluate ideas, information, situations, and texts. When writers think critically about the materials they use—whether print texts, photographs, data sets, videos, or other materials—they separate assertion from evidence, evaluate sources and evidence, recognize and evaluate underlying assumptions, read across texts for connections and patterns, identify and evaluate chains of reasoning, and compose appropriately qualified and developed claims and generalizations. These practices are foundational for advanced academic writing. (2)

English 1106: First-Year Writing: Writing from Research

English 1106 builds on the skills learned and practiced in English 1105. As its name implies, however, English 1106 is also an introduction to writing with sources, both primary and secondary. For example, you may be asked to find and cite sources from the library and on the Internet, but you may also be asked to conduct primary research—or "fieldwork"—using tools such as interviews, observations, and surveys.

In addition to practicing research skills by searching for and collecting primary and secondary sources, you will practice synthesizing elements of research into coherent wholes. Successful synthesis of research requires that you understand and interpret your sources and put them in conversation with each other. This work also emphasizes correctly documenting and attributing your sources.

Learning Objectives

By completing English 1106, students will:

- Continue to practice writing as a process, using multiple invention and revision strategies

- Write in several genres that require paraphrase, synthesis, analysis, evaluation, argument, and documentation skills

- Practice writing from primary and secondary research, developing different types of research projects that use fieldwork, library, and online research methods

- Demonstrate knowledge of the conventions of bibliographic citation

- Demonstrate an understanding of the uses of source material of all types, taking care to always distinguish between source material and one's own work

Course Requirements

- A *minimum* of three graded papers written from sources. Major papers in English 1106 tend to be five to fifteen pages in length with proper citations.

- A *minimum* of twenty pages of informal writing, such as journal responses, discussion board postings, blogs, and proposals.

- *At least* one individual presentation including the use of visual elements (Many instructors include group presentations as well.)

English H1204: First-Year Writing: Honors English

Honors English is open to all Virginia Tech students whose entrance scores indicate that they qualify for the course. As English H1204 is an honors-level course, students can expect to work both with close analysis and research, including traditional library research, online research, and fieldwork. The reading in Honors English is chosen to deepen one's critical reading, writing, and thinking skills. Students should expect reading and writing assignments to be at an advanced level, reflecting this course's honors designation.

Learning Objectives

Honors English reviews the content of English 1105 and focuses on the work of English 1106 at the honors level. See the learning objectives for those courses.

Course Requirements

- A *minimum* of three graded papers written from sources. Major papers in Honors English tend to be five to twenty-five pages in length with proper citation.

- A *minimum* of twenty pages of informal writing, such as journal responses, discussion board postings, blogs, and proposals.

- *At least* one individual presentation including the use of visual elements. (Many instructors include group presentations as well.)

The primary focus of both English 1106 and H1204 is writing from sources or research writing. **Chapter 7, "Preparing to Write the Research Paper,"** written by Jared Gibbs, and **Chapter 8, "Writing the Research Essay,"** written by Beejay Silcox, walk you through the process from generating ideas and conducting research to writing and revising your final paper.

English 1106/H1204 Readings

The readings in this section have been divided into two categories: *Advanced Rhetorical Analysis and Argument and Research Writing*. While in English 1105 you worked with rhetorical analysis primarily focused on a single, often shorter text, in English 1106, you will be rhetorically analyzing longer text, working across texts and using outside sources to support your rhetorical analysis. English 1106 assignments will require you not only to think carefully about the decisions you make as a writer but also to find outside sources and use them to support your arguments or raise additional issues. The readings in this section are designed to provide you materials for analysis and inspiration, along with many examples of texts that use both primary and secondary sources in a range of formats. In fact, most of the authors in this section use some sort of research in the process of creating their writing.

Final Thoughts

I began this introduction welcoming you to this course and this textbook. I want to end with a few thoughts about why I think first-year writing courses stay with us. My speculation on this idea of the staying power of first-year writing is that the course asks us to share our writing and thinking with a class, often much smaller than our other general education courses. Because the class is smaller, we often get to know those around us. Also, because the teachers have fewer students, they are often more invested in the individual student—providing more feedback and often conferencing beyond office hours. While **Chapter 10, "Where Do You Go for Help?"** written by Jennifer Lawrence and Julia Ferrar, describes a range of support services for any challenges you may face, do not hesitate to get to know your teacher and your fellow students. We are all invested in your success. I am confident that you have landed in a wonderful program with outstanding teachers—many of whom thoughtfully and skillfully authored the chapters in this textbook. I am also confident that if you do your part to have a successful semester, you will become a better student, and perhaps in ten, fifteen, or even twenty years, when asked about the course you remember from your undergraduate career, you too will say "I can remember my First-year Writing/Freshman English/Composition course."

I wish you all the best, and I hope you have a great semester.

Sheila Carter-Tod, Ph.D.
Associate Professor of Rhetoric and Writing
Director of Composition
Department of English
Virginia Tech
Blacksburg, VA

Chapter 1

Reading and Writing Rhetorically

Written texts can hold the power to influence our emotions, incite our action, and even change the way we think about things. Through the composition of words on a page, a careful writer can tear down, build up, reveal, obscure, name, or elide nearly anything. This is called rhetoric. The study of rhetoric is the study of how language functions in society. This involves how you read pieces of writing, view commercials and visual displays, and produce your own written and visual texts. Rhetoric can be found in any use of language, which means that learning to be a careful rhetor (producer of rhetoric) and a careful rhetorician (critical consumer of rhetoric) applies to every kind of writing in your life, from your online persona on social media to your college essays. To read rhetorically is to pay attention to the rhetorical strategies an author uses to achieve his or her purpose for his or her **audience**. Reading rhetorically can help you understand texts, make judgments about information, and recognize the influence of a situation on that text. Reading rhetorically can also give you examples for your own writing.

Audience the targeted reader of a piece of writing, which may include a specific person or people, or the kind of person who is likely to read a given publication

1.1 What Is Rhetoric?

We often hear the term *rhetoric* used to describe empty promises, political subterfuge, and outright trickery, as though rhetoric is a kind of fancy clothing we put on our ideas to convince people to believe or buy something they wouldn't otherwise. This view of rhetoric can be traced all the way back to the fourth century BCE, when Plato claimed that rhetoric was a way of hiding the truth and avoiding responsibility. However, Plato's student Aristotle convinced many people that rhetoric was a way of exploring different ideas and points of view. Aristotle's idea of rhetoric is a key component of democracy and impacts American social values of equality and difference. According to Aristotle, rhetoric is "the faculty of observing in any given case the available means of persuasion." His definition of persuasion was not a form of tricking people, but of speaking effectively in order for your ideas to be heard and considered. Since Aristotle's time, other scholars have suggested that rhetoric not only allows us to explore reality but also actually creates reality. For Lloyd Bitzer (See page 13), rhetoric is a way of acting in the world—persuading people, inciting them to action, and demonstrating points of view—which means that language creates society, rather than merely revealing society. In practical application, we apply rhetoric when we think about how to communicate our message, and we apply rhetorical analysis when we think about how others are trying to communicate.

1.2 Rhetorical Analysis: Determining Why and How a Piece of Writing Is Effective

Analyzing the way a writer arranges his or her text can reveal information about the purpose and effect of that writing. A writer's **purpose** might be to persuade, to inform, or to entertain, but these purposes are often more complex than they sound. For example, essayist Nancy Mairs writes compelling personal narratives that are designed to confront social issues. While her work is entertaining and provides information about a topic or issue, her ultimate purpose is to persuade readers to view others in more empathetic ways. This is Mairs's way of confronting social issues.

In her piece "On Being a Cripple" (p. 275) Mairs shares her experiences with the disease multiple sclerosis as a way of addressing the way we talk about and treat people with disabilities. Mairs writes that "like fat people, who are expected to be jolly, cripples must bear their lot meekly and cheerfully. A grumpy cripple isn't playing by the rules" (para. 18). In this sentence Mairs breaks several cultural rules of politeness, using the labels *fat* and *cripple*. In fact, this sentence taken out of **context** might appear to be rude and hurtful. However, Mairs uses this language purposefully. Let's examine this excerpt and see what Mairs does in her writing.

Speaks bluntly from her own experience

Sarcasm and self-deprecating humor

Terms that are not only politically incorrect, they are potentially hurtful

In our society, anyone who deviates from the norm had better find some way to compensate. Like fat people, who are expected to be jolly, cripples must bear their lot meekly and cheerfully. A grumpy cripple isn't playing by the rules. And much of pressure is self-generated. Early on I vowed that, if I had to have MS, by God I was going to do it well. This is a class act, ladies and gentleman. No tears, no recriminations, no faint-heartedness.

Directly addresses the readers

Anytime you read a text, go ahead and mark it up. What do you notice? What stands out for you? What is the author doing and why? Annotation is simply a method for beginning your analysis of a written work. You can underline words and phrases, circle them, or write your notes in the margins. Once you've marked your initial impressions and observations, it's time to begin thinking critically about the way the text operates within a situation and group of people. This is called the rhetorical situation.

Writer the person or persons who created the text

Purpose the reason the text was created

Context the time and place, culture, and political or social issues surrounding a piece of writing

The Rhetorical Situation

The purpose, context, people, and strategies associated with a given piece of language are important in determining how the writing affects and persuades the audience. This is known as the rhetorical situation. Conducting a thorough rhetorical analysis begins with the basic annotation shown above, but it is much more systematic. Once you know the kinds of elements to identify, the function of a piece of language will become clear. Knowing the rhetorical situation can shed light on what the author wants the audience to think, feel, or understand, and how well the author accomplishes this. In addition, knowing the rhetorical situation of any writing task can help you create texts that are more likely to be successful in achieving your purpose. Aristotle, one of the earliest and most important contributors to the art of rhetoric, considered rhetoric to be an integral part of sharing ideas and considering topics. He created the rhetorical triangle, which asks you to consider the relationships among the author or speaker, the audience, and the subject.

Figure 1.1 The Rhetorical Triangle

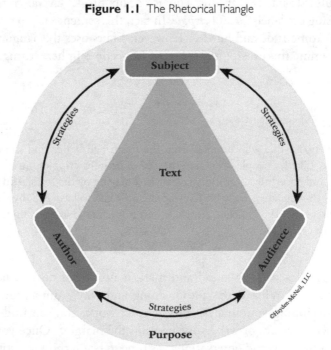

The nature of the audience—including their expectations, tastes, and attitudes—is important in determining the effect a particular piece of rhetoric creates. The nature of the author—including his or her credibility, charisma, and attitude—also has a profound effect on the way a piece of rhetoric is received. In Nancy Mairs's essay, for example, the rhetorical situation is important in elucidating her seemingly offensive statement and showing how her writing is actually addressing social issues, rather than contributing to them. Consider how you would respond to Mairs's writing about physical impairments in such a brusque way if she were able-bodied and unimpaired. How would you receive her writing if she had a condescending attitude? Does your own set of physical abilities and limitations affect how you respond to her writing? In addition to the relationship between author and audience around a given subject, the author's purpose plays an important role in defining how the text functions. Aristotle referred to this by the Greek work *telos,* which simply means object or aim. However, the purpose of a text always relates to the people and time in which the text is created. A work cannot be completely understood when removed from its context, because the context lends meaning. Context is established through not only the author's point of view and intent but also the selection of words that are culturally available to use and the point of view of the audience.

The rhetorical situation is more complex than merely examining the author, audience, subject, and purpose of a message. Many theorists have argued about what belongs in the rhetorical situation, and by examining these arguments we can see that the context in which a piece of rhetoric is placed plays a crucial role in shaping its message. Aristotle added the Greek term **kairos** to his definition of the rhetorical situation. *Kairos* refers to the timeliness and appropriateness of the rhetoric and how it affects the message. This means that the time and place a piece of rhetoric is circulated (published, broadcasted, or tweeted, for example) affects the message itself. If the rhetor acts too late, he or she misses the ideal moment for sharing his or her message. But in addition to speaking or writing at just the right moment, *kairos* also means that a piece of rhetoric must fit a given situation or context. In contemporary terms, we might talk about the way a text is situated within the contexts of culture, media, political climate, religious beliefs, or current trends in the economy.

Lloyd Bitzer believes that rhetoric is any form of language that is adapted and applied to a context. Therefore, he defines the rhetorical situation as the relationship among three specific elements: **exigence**, audience, and constraints. The exigence refers to the need or demand for something. To determine the exigence, you must consider what in the situation requires the writer or speaker to intervene. **Constraints** can be anything in the situation that affects what can or should be said. For example, you might not be able to call your boss by his or her first name without risking repercussions. This kind of constraint is one that you may or may not choose to observe, based on the consequences. Other constraints might be outside of your control, such as those of a given medium. For example, it is impossible to write a tweet that is more than 120 characters long or to include your facial expressions in a handwritten letter. Many rhetorical strategies are created as a way of dealing with constraints, such as using text as part of an image attached to a tweet, or using emojis in written communication.

Kairos the timeliness and appropriateness of a piece of communication

Exigence the time and place in which the piece is written or spoken, the social situation in which it is created and shared, and the pressing need or problem it addresses. Identifying the exigence can help you answer the question "Why was this piece written?"

Constraints aspects of the situation, medium, genre, culture, or audience that place boundaries around what can or should be communicated

In addition to this focus on time and place that we learn from Bitzer, Kenneth Burke is interested in rhetoric as an act of identification. Rejecting Plato's idea of rhetoric as tricking people, Burke builds on Aristotle's idea of rhetoric, defining persuasion as simply asking people to examine and identify with your point of view. Thus, rhetoric can showcase a point of view in a way that helps the reader see and understand it. Burke also considers rhetoric to be a kind of drama—he says that communication is made up of a relationship among agents, acts, scenes, purposes, and agency, much like a play is made up of scenes, actors, and the audience. Burke was concerned not only with where the rhetoric takes place but also with how it takes place, and how the relationships among audience, author, situation, and strategies shape the message an audience receives.

When analyzing a piece of written, spoken, or visual language, it is important to take all these definitions of the rhetorical situation into consideration. The figure below can help you fill in the basic elements of the rhetorical situation.

Figure 1.2 The Rhetorical Situation

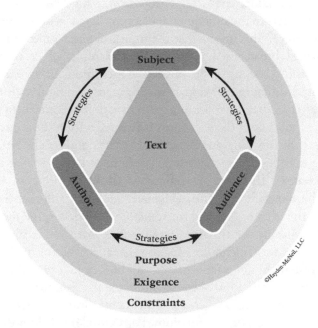

Let's consider the rhetorical situation for Mairs's essay "On Being a Cripple." If you examine the publication information at the bottom of page 477, you will see that Mairs's essay was published in 1986. This is the same year that the abbreviation

PC was first used in print to refer to the term *politically correct*. In American culture in the 1970s, the term *politically correct* was already being used to criticize token attempts at understanding different perspectives on identity traits such as gender, race, and sexuality. By the 1980s the term *politically correct* had begun a debate about politeness, self-interest, and whether or not political uses of language could be considered genuine.

With growing attention to individuals with disabilities in American culture at this time, groups began introducing new terms for physical impairments, designed to respect and understand difference. As Mairs herself describes, these terms range from *handicapped* to *disabled* to *differently abled*. And as our reactions to Mairs's text might reveal, the term *crippled* has been reduced to a slur. This context is important, because Mairs uses her **ethos** as a disabled woman to explain her feelings about these terms, and even to use terms that many assume are insulting. Writing at a time when debates were raging about respect and truthfulness, Mairs describes her feelings about the way such terms shape people's perceptions of her and about how language can limit, belittle, or showcase her own experiences and loss. She writes the following about the term *cripple*:

> I like the accuracy with which it describes my condition: I have lost the full use of my limbs. "Disabled," by contrast, suggests any incapacity, physical or mental. And I certainly don't like "handicapped," which implies that I have deliberately been put at a disadvantage, by whom I can't imagine (my God is not a Handicapper General), in order to equalize chances in the great race of life. (275)

Ethos a person's credibility or identity within a given situation

In the following passage Mairs not only reveals her feelings about these terms but also shows the way language can hide certain uncomfortable realities that we need to face. She writes:

> Most remote is the recently coined euphemism "differently abled," which partakes of the same semantic hopefulness that transformed countries from "undeveloped" to "underdeveloped," then to "less developed," and finally to "developing" nations. People have continued to starve in those countries during the shift. Some realities do not obey the dictates of language. (275)

By placing Mairs's text within the time and place she is writing, we can see the way she is responding to an exigence, by drawing attention to a problem in society. The way she responds at this moment in time is also important, because her claims have larger implications about how individuals (and America as a nation) treat or ignore people different from themselves simply based on the language we use. Because our understanding of words comes from the way they are used in society, no language is entirely neutral.

The Construction of Strategies and Appeals

The strategies an author uses to convey his or her message are integral to the rhetorical situation and help define the success of a piece of communication. Aristotle referred to these strategies as appeals. Aristotelian appeals include *ethos, pathos,* and *logos.* These ancient Greek terms refer to the way a writer or speaker gives his or her audience a reason to listen or believe.

Ethos refers to the credibility of the writer and is the root for our modern word *ethics.* In rhetoric, *ethos* refers to how credible and believable an author is. Rather than saying that an author does or does not have *ethos,* in rhetorical analysis the aim is to understand the nature of that *ethos* and how it affects the text. For example, Mairs is not a medical expert on multiple sclerosis; however, she is an individual with personal experience. As a physically impaired woman who has struggled with the effects of multiple sclerosis on her mobility, Mairs offers a credible perspective on what it feels like to be defined by terms such as *crippled, disabled,* and *differently abled.* As an author, Mairs has experiences that create a particular kind of *ethos* for her readers.

Pathos and *logos* are appeals that call for readers to engage in a particular way, by using their emotions or their minds. You might recognize the root of the word *pathetic* in *pathos,* because the term *pathos* refers to sadness and tragedy. An author who uses *pathos* writes in a way that appeals to his or her readers' emotions. In one paragraph, Mairs lists all of the positive activities she was once able to perform, ranging from holding her children to marching in rallies and demonstrations. After this extensive list, Mairs describes her decline and the tests she underwent before receiving the diagnosis of multiple sclerosis. The force of this description of her abilities followed by her decline appeals to her readers' emotions, calling for their empathy and even their anger over her situation. *Logos* is the Greek root for the word *logic.* *Logos* refers to reasoning, planning, and logic. An author who uses *logos* appeals to readers' sense of logic and reasoning.

These appeals are used in a variety of ways, never in isolation. An author might switch between them or even use several appeals at once. Immediately following Mairs's description of her physical decline and the battery of tests that were part of her search for an answer, she writes a paragraph in which she gives a succinct and unemotional definition of multiple sclerosis. She begins the paragraph very impersonally, with the sentence "Multiple sclerosis is a chronic degenerative disease of the nervous system" (para. 7). Mairs goes on to explain how the disease functions. This appeal to logic allows her readers to understand the severity of her disease in a very different light from her personal experiences. Emotional appeals alone might not be enough to convince her readers of the severity of her disease, since emotions are subjective. By pairing her emotional experience with a logical definition, Mairs adds credibility to her experience, engaging her readers' minds to support their emotional reactions.

Pathos an appeal to the audience's emotions

An author can apply a variety of linguistic tools to construct these appeals, suiting them to a particular audience, time, and place. For example, Mairs draws in her audience and asserts credibility or *ethos* through a combination of informative and personal writing, by using language that communicates her experiences mixed with formal vocabulary associated with medical diagnoses.

Linguistic features that help formulate appeals and create particular effects include:

- Vocabulary
- Sentence structure
- Sentence length
- Style
- Organizational patterns
- Metaphors and similes

1.3 Why Rhetorical Analysis?

While you may not be asked to conduct a formal rhetorical analysis in many situations outside of your writing courses, you will be asked to accomplish tasks that require rhetorical skills. These skills include:

- Careful reading of text
- Argumentation
- Providing evidence in support of your claims
- Understanding or presenting different perspectives
- Responding effectively in a variety of situations

Rhetorical analysis is a way to learn the expectations readers have for a piece of writing, as well as the possibilities for creating a variety of effects within and against those expectations. Rhetorical analysis is a foundation for effective reading and writing.

Comparative Rhetorical Analysis

Comparing the rhetoric of multiple texts can offer a glimpse into the way writing functions for a particular audience and within a given situation. This kind of comparative analysis can reveal information about a particular genre of writing, about how rhetorical strategies help an author fulfill the purpose of a text, and about how a writer can adapt to a particular audience or genre to accomplish his or her purpose.

For example, danah boyd's essay "Inequality: Can Social Media Resolve Social Divisions?" (p. 419) has many themes and strategies in common with Amanda Hess's essay "Why Women Aren't Welcome on the Internet" (p. 367). boyd and Hess both write about the way social groups deal with difference and about the nature of discrimination that can take place in virtual social worlds. However, Hess is a journalist who writes about sexuality and boyd is a media scholar. These writers take similar approaches to educating their audiences and incorporating primary sources and first-hand accounts into their work. They share a variety of rhetorical strategies, with some variation, but their work indicates that they are trying to achieve slightly different goals with their writing. Similar to the analysis of a single text, a comparative rhetorical analysis begins with an exploration of the rhetorical situation.

Common components of comparative rhetorical analysis include:

- Analysis of the rhetorical situation

- Attention to genre

- Exploration of rhetorical strategies

- Comparison and contrast

- A thesis or argument about the similarities or differences

Examining Genres. Comparative rhetorical analysis can reveal information about the way a particular writer engages with a genre, and it can also provide information about the common features of a genre that you might need to learn how to write. At their most basic, genres are categories of texts or objects that have been sorted by their features. You might be familiar with the term *genre* when it is used to describe music or movies. For example, a movie in the action genre will have scenes of intense action, such as car chases, shootouts, or other forms of violence; action movies will rarely be slow explorations of a person's feelings or their budding love. Written genres work in much the same way. When your supervisor asks you to write a memo, he or she is not expecting you to write an elaborately detailed exploration of your feelings, but rather a specific kind of writing that is brief, focused, and uses vocabulary common to your company.

Of course many texts blur the lines between genres, merge genres together, and even create new genres. This is because genres are not finite categories; they are common ways of communicating. In fact, genres can be considered ways of achieving goals by using common forms of language. For example, if you want your coworkers to understand the importance of your analysis, you will likely use a kind of report writing to communicate with them. This is because the report genre showcases information in a particular way, and because your readers know that a report will help them understand the implications of that analysis. Genres begin with purpose, and their features are simply the ways people accomplish these purposes. We call these features of a genre **conventions**, because they are commonly used and help readers understand how to orient themselves to a particular text.

Conventions the spoken or unspoken rules that determine what is acceptable in a given situation

Any place of business, discipline of study, or social group will have its own rules or conventions for speaking and writing, which affect the rhetorical decisions they make within the expectations of a genre. The term **discourse community** refers to these groups who share particular kinds of language, genres, and rhetorical conventions.

Discourse Community any group of people with their own set of vocabulary or practices for speaking and writing

■ **Activity 1.1**

> The rhetorical strategies writers choose relate to both the genre in which they are writing and the audience they are writing for. Consider the scenario below:
>
> A startup soda company has just launched a new drink called Punch in Your Face! To generate interest they are offering a sweepstakes. You grab a bottle on your way to class and inside the cap is the winning code. You've just won an all-expense paid cruise on the Mediterranean. You leave Friday night and there's so much to do.
>
> You will miss a week of class, including a test, for this cruise. Write an email to your professor to try to get your test rescheduled.
>
> You want your best friend to come with you, but if he or she can't, you'll ask your roommate instead. Write a text or Facebook message to each of them to determine who will be available to come without hurting anyone's feelings.
>
> You're scheduled to work Saturday morning and will need someone to cover your shift. Write a note or text to a coworker and ask them to swap shifts with you.

Now consider the differences among your messages. How did the audience change the way you wrote your messages? How was the goal different for each message? How did you write to accomplish your goal? What does this reveal about the genres of text messages and emails? How do they differ and why? Does the audience change how you approach the conventions of each genre?

Comparison and Contrast. The foundation of comparative rhetorical analysis is comparing two or more texts to learn about the situation, the writing, or the writer. You can begin a comparative analysis with a variety of goals, such as learning more about a genre you will have to write or exploring the way multiple authors approach a common topic.

Comparative rhetorical analysis is best accomplished when you examine each text individually and then compare them. Use **brainstorming** to begin with a list or diagram of the similarities and differences. You might begin your brainstorming with content, and then move through the elements of the rhetorical situation. Let's examine danah boyd's essay "Inequality: Can Social Media Resolve Social Divisions?" and Amanda Hess's essay "Why Women Aren't Welcome on the Internet."

Brainstorming a problem-solving technique that involves the spontaneous generation of ideas

Read and annotate each essay, examining your own impressions and each element of the rhetorical situation described above. Next, make a list of similarities and differences. You might begin this comparison with general impressions and themes.

Venn diagram
a graph employing
closed circles which
represent logical
relations between
propositions by the
inclusion, exclusion,
or intersection of the
curves

For example, Amanda Hess and danah boyd both write about gender and issues of equality, use firsthand accounts, show examples of written communication from a social media platform, and share passionate, even hateful, language as an example of the kind of discrimination people encounter through digital communication. boyd, however, writes about situations encountered by others, while Hess writes of her own experiences of being stalked and harassed. boyd examines online and offline life, interviewing and observing others, while Hess blends online and offline life to explore the impact of stalking through social media. boyd writes about social discrimination that is based on class, ethnicity, and race, while Hess writes of discrimination based primarily on gender and sexuality. A simple **Venn diagram** can help you begin your comparison and contrast.

Figure 1.3 A Venn Diagram

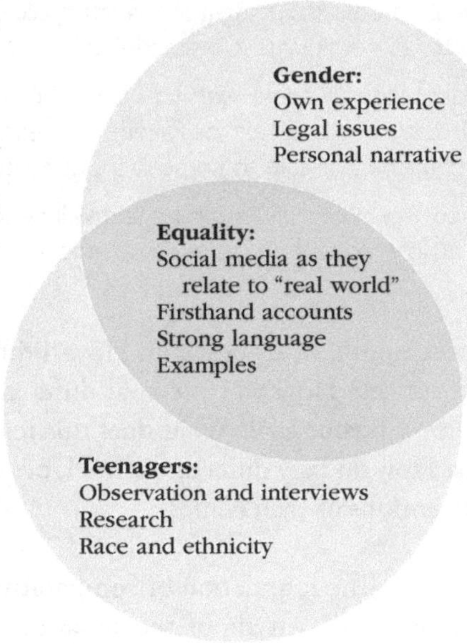

Gender:
Own experience
Legal issues
Personal narrative

Equality:
Social media as they
   relate to "real world"
Firsthand accounts
Strong language
Examples

Teenagers:
Observation and interviews
Research
Race and ethnicity

Comparing Elements of the Rhetorical Situation

Once you have identified some basic similarities and differences, move through the elements of the rhetorical situation and fill out a list or diagram with the similarities and differences in each category. Table 1.1 shows how you might compare elements of the rhetorical situation.

Table 1.1: Rhetorical Situation

	Text 1	Text 2
Writer/designer		
Reader/audience		
Purpose		
Context		
Exigence		
Constraints		
Appeals		
Rhetorical strategies		

After you have identified and compared the elements of the rhetorical situation, you need to examine the way they work together. For example, Hess uses examples of bold hate speech from her stalkers combined with a discussion of how a lack of understanding about technology and an unequal distribution of gender in law enforcement fault the Web user. Hess directs her reader's attention to the problem of victim blaming and the need for changes in the way we police behavior on the Web. When we examine the way these strategies work together to fulfill Hess's purpose, we can compare them to boyd's rhetorical strategies to understand subtle differences in their purposes. For example, boyd uses primary research to explore the link between face-to-face social interactions and Web interactions. Her examination of social interactions in teenagers emphasizes exonerating Web technology from blame. The bibliographic information on page 476 shows that boyd's essay was first published in her book titled *It's Complicated: The Social Lives of Networked Teens,* a text that exposes the myth of technology destroying the social skills of teenagers. By examining the way elements of the rhetorical situation work together in a text, you can see that these authors have slightly different goals for writing their essays.

Below are some questions that can help you move forward when you get stuck:

- When you've identified content, ask: How? For what purpose? What's the point?

- When you've identified rhetorical strategies, ask: What is the effect? How do they serve the author's purpose? What exactly does the author do?

- When you've identified the effects of strategies, ask: So what? How does this relate to audience and purpose?

- When you've identified the effectiveness of these strategies in serving the writer's purpose, ask: How can I prove this? How often does the author do this? How can I show how she does this? Why is it effective?

- When you've identified interesting comparisons, ask: Do these strategies work with or against one another?

Generating a Thesis or Argument. The biggest question to ask yourself when discussing the similarities and differences of two pieces of writing is "So what?" Whether you set out with a specific purpose or simply choose to explore some interesting texts, you need to consider why the results of your analysis matter to anyone. When you write an essay describing your analysis, your readers need to be able to identify the purpose of your comparison. Perhaps the writer's argument impacts the action readers might take. Or maybe you found that the *ethos* of the author has implications for the way he or she conveys purpose in a piece of writing. In essence, your thesis is an argument for your reading of a text that suggests implications for other writers, readers, or texts.

The three keys for developing a thesis are:

1. Pick a focus

2. Answer the question "So what?"

3. State your point clearly

Ways to Focus

You may choose to focus your argument on the strategies each author uses, their purposes in writing, the topics they choose to address, or the effects of their strategies on the reader. Consider the following ways to focus your paper:

Compare or contrast the way the two authors write about the same **topic:**

- What is the purpose or desired outcome for each text?

- How do the authors use strategies to deal with this topic?

- Does the *ethos* of each author have any bearing on how they address this topic?

Compare how the two authors use the same **strategy:**

- Are the purposes the same?

- Are the effects the same?

- Does the *ethos* of each author have any bearing on how or why those strategies are used?

- Do these strategies create a specific effect together?

Contrast how the two authors use different **strategies:**

- Are the purposes the same?

- Are the effects the same?

- Does the *ethos* of each author have any bearing on how or why those strategies are used?
- Do these strategies create a specific effect together?

Compare or contrast the way the two authors create an **effect** with their writing:
- Do these effects serve the same purpose?
- Are they created through similar or different strategies?
- What role does the author's *ethos* play in creating the effect?
- What role does the genre play in creating the effect?
- What is the impact of the effect on the audience?

Compare or contrast the way authors achieve their **purpose.**

You will likely find many interesting similarities and differences between these two pieces of writing. As you develop your thesis, consider whether all of your findings belong in your paper or not. You won't be able to discuss everything you notice in your comparison if you want your readers to understand your own purpose for your essay.

Consider the following paper by Tim Radford. This student writer began with an exploration of the differences in Amanda Hess's and danah boyd's approaches to their topics in the essays discussed above. As he continued his rhetorical analysis, Tim found that the writers were actually making parallel arguments in their essays. Several of Tim's classmates disagreed with his reading, creating the need for a compelling essay with lots of evidence for his reading of these texts.

Tim Radford

ENGL 1106

12 September 2016

Comparative Rhetorical Analysis of "Inequality:
Can Social Media Resolve Social Divisions?" and
"Why Women Aren't Welcome on the Internet"

Introduction situates the analysis within the context of the rhetorical situation.

When the Internet was initially created, its purpose was simply to exchange information. As the Internet has evolved over decades, this exchange of information has become much more elaborate. Researcher danah boyd explains that when social media Web sites were developed, many people predicted that they would be the end of racism and other prejudices because of how connected users would be. Social media has done the exact opposite by allowing online users to demonstrate subtle prejudice or even send death threats directly to someone and everything in between. "Inequality: Can Social Media Resolve Social Divisions?" by danah boyd is an informative essay written to prove that social media build higher walls of social division. Amanda Hess writes "Why Women Aren't Welcome on the Internet" to expose a harsher side of technology and prove these sites encourage biases, especially against women.

The commonalities of these two essays provide significance for the contrast.

Despite having different tones and coming from different sides of the same topic, boyd and Hess use similar rhetorical strategies to argue that the Internet and technology have significant negative effects on social biases.

Both of these authors talk about negative effects social media has on users, though they tailor their arguments in different ways. boyd writes to shed light on the biases that social media create whereas Hess writes to expose the dangers that social media can pose to women. Each of these authors writes within a given context. The unique perspective of each author shapes the audiences they wish to reach and the ways they adopt their rhetorical strategies for their readers. In

"Inequality: Can Social Media Resolve Social Divisions?" boyd is writing to an audience that would be comprised of high school students, college students, and those who frequent social media sites such as Facebook, Twitter, or Instagram. Her audience could very well be those who don't use social media, such as older generations, and need to be warned about these sites. In "Why Women Aren't Welcome on the Internet," Hess could be focusing on an audience of those who are unaware of the abuse that women suffer through the Internet, specifically on free-speech social media sites such as Twitter. These two authors define their audiences through exigence and purpose and appeal to them through language and logic.

Exigence is the necessity in society or in their personal lives that has given these authors a reason to write what they are writing. Purpose is how the author intends to address this necessity or problem. For example, the author's purpose may be to instill a sense of awareness or invoke a change in a particular audience. These two pieces share a similar exigence of prejudice through the Internet and other emerging technologies, giving the two writers similar purposes for writing their respective pieces. boyd writes to prove that social media has not resolved any social divisions despite predictions made in the early 2000s. She proves this through personal interviews with users of social media during their emergence, the ideas of modern sociologists studying this field, and by following the early history of social media Web site development. Hess seeks to spread her opinion that even though women have made great progress in civil rights in the near past, the Internet is a new frontier in which women are treated like second-class citizens or worse.

Because these two writers have similar purposes in writing such pieces, their strategies in delivering their messages are similar. For example, both boyd and Hess use unconventional language in the form of quotes from interviewees or

This paragraph begins with a claim about the two authors' use of rhetorical strategies. It then follows with an explanation and examples from one of the texts. The paragraph then concludes with an explanation of the significance of this example, which supports Tim's thesis.

from personal attacks through social media. In "Inequality: Can Social Media Resolve Social Divisions?" boyd cites a Web site called "notaracistbut.com" in which users anonymously deliver hate speech. One comment on the Web site reads, "Not to be a racist, but I'm starting to see that niggers don't possess a single ounce of intellect" (Boyd 424). This Web site encourages users to formulate and share racist thoughts simply for the sake of being racist. This site may be seen as humorous by many, but in this case the site serves no other purpose than to grow a hatred for people who are different. boyd inserts this evidence to show that some places on the Internet have no positive effect on destroying biases. boyd also cites critics of popular movies who have used similar hostile language to prove that it is not only popular social media Web sites that are providing opportunity for prejudice but also popular culture.

Works Cited

boyd, danah. "Inequality: Can Social Media Resolve Social Divisions?" *Composition at Virginia Tech: A Rhetoric and Reader for Good Writing*. Boston: Bedford, 2016. 419–435. Print.

Hess, Amanda. "Why Women Aren't Welcome on the Internet." *Composition at Virginia Tech: A Rhetoric and Reader for Good Writing*. Boston: Bedford, 2016. 367–378. Print.

Chapter 2

Analyzing Visual Texts

Rhetoric is not confined to written and spoken words but is used in all forms of communication, including images and videos. In our society we are surrounded by visual media of all types, and applying the basic principles of rhetorical analysis and the rhetorical situation can allow you to critically engage with these media. While advertisement analyses are the most common visual analysis assignments, you can analyze and design any kind of printed or digital communication.

When you are rhetorically analyzing an image, you are looking for a message, but you are also looking at how that message is communicated. By examining how a visual text functions, you can learn more about how the creator wants to persuade his or her viewers to think or feel differently. Sometimes visual analysis can reveal rhetoric in Plato's sense of trickery, as in an advertisement trying to convince viewers of an item's quality, but it can also show the way designers help viewers understand a particular perspective on a concept.

Activity 2.1

Select an image of your choice and examine the rhetorical situation. Just as with written texts, start by exploring your main impressions of the message through annotation or freewriting to identify the rhetorical situation. Answer the following questions to help guide your analysis:

Author

What company, organization, or individual created this image? What are their affiliations, values, or known intentions? Who is sharing this image? What are their affiliations, values, or known intentions?

Audience

What audience was this text originally designed for? How can you tell? Are there additional audiences the text was designed for? What are the affiliations, values, or known intentions of each audience group? Who is this text being shared with now? How can you tell? What are their affiliations, values, or known intentions?

Purpose

What is the creator trying to get the audience to do or understand? What outcomes do you think they anticipate?

Exigence

What need or demand is the creator trying to fill? What problem are they trying to solve?

Context

What is the cultural, political, or regional situation in which this text appears?

Strategies

What clues in the image lead you to your answers above? What about the image do you find compelling?

2.1 Principles and Elements of Design

Just as written and spoken text make use of grammatical and stylistic strategies within the rhetorical situation, there are principles and elements of design that are important to consider in both analysis and production of visual texts.

Design elements are the building blocks of an image. These include such things as lines and shapes, the size of those lines and shapes, and the colors that are used. Principles of design govern how the elements are arranged to create an effect. These principles include such things as balance, contrast, and repetition. For a basic list of design elements and principles, see Table 2.1.

Table 2.1: Design Elements and Principles

Design Elements	Design Principles
Color	Balance
Direction	Emphasis
Repetition	Movement
Line	Pattern
Shape	Rhythm
Size	Unity
Texture	Contrast
Value	

Design in Focus

Examining the way design elements and design principles are applied to an image can reveal information about the rhetorical function of the text. Consider each of the components below and try to locate them within an image.

Emphasis.   Various elements of an image can be emphasized for the viewer, and this emphasis can be achieved by increasing the weight of the element, placing it in a central location, or using contrasting colors. For example, shapes, lines, and images can have a visual weight, which simply means that they attract your eyes and appear to be stronger or more important than other portions of the image. Visual weight can be achieved by making an item larger or darker in color. By giving an item visual weight, a designer is communicating that the image is more important, significant, or stronger.

Organization and Directionality.   When you look at an image, there is often a seemingly natural path for you to follow. This path is designed by placing lines for your eyes to follow and using the visual weight of objects to direct your eyes. Your eyes will naturally fall on the item with the most emphasis. From there, the eyes travel along the lines or planes of each shape, seeking out the nearest item with visual emphasis. Repetition of colors can also create this path, drawing your eyes through the image.

Colors.   The colors used in a given image are important in terms of the ways they relate to one another. These colors can create a mood, suggest a particular quality, and even draw your attention to certain portions of the image. The type of colors chosen and the relationships among those colors are important in determining the moods or styles being evoked.

Complementary Colors:	Each color has another color that is its exact opposite. Several examples include yellow and purple, orange and blue, red and green, and black and white. Complementary colors create the strongest form of contrast when placed next to each other.
Analogous Colors:	Analogous colors are simply colors that are next to one another on the color wheel. For example, green, blue, and purple are analogous colors. Analogues can also include multiple shades of the same color, such as a yellow green, a primary green, and a blue green. Analogous color schemes are pleasing to the eye and do not draw attention to difference the way complementary colors do.
Warm and Cool Colors:	Just as a writer can choose between active and passive voice, a designer can select colors that are active and passive as well. Warm colors—reds, pinks, oranges, and yellows—create emphasis and excitement and attract a viewer's attention. In many cultures these colors are associated with warnings and danger. Cool colors—blues, purples, and greens—create a more calming or natural effect. In American culture, green is associated with positivity and forward motion and is also a strong signifier of nature.

Consider these components of design in the following section on visual arguments. These elements and principles are strategies for creating visual messages. As you analyze visual arguments, examine the way these design elements and principles allow the creator to assert his or her argument through the appeals of ethos, pathos, and logos.

2.2 Thinking Critically about Visual Arguments[*]

A **visual argument** can be an advertisement, a chart or graph or table, a diagram, a Web page, a photograph, or a painting. Like an argumentative essay, a visual argument can take a position. Unlike an argumentative essay, however, a visual argument communicates its position (and offers evidence to support that position) largely through images rather than words.

When you approach a visual argument—particularly one that will be the subject of class discussion or writing—you should do so with a critical eye. Your primary goal is to understand the point that the creator of the visual is trying to make, but you also need to understand how the message is conveyed. In addition, you need to evaluate whether the methods used to persuade the audience are both logical and fair.

Visual Texts versus Visual Arguments

Not every visual is an argument; many simply present information. For example, a diagram of a hunting rifle, with its principal parts labeled, tells viewers what the weapon looks like and how it works. However, a photo of two toddlers playing with a hunting rifle could make a powerful argument about the need for gun safety. Conversely, a photo of a family hunting trip featuring a teenager proudly holding up a rifle while his parents look on approvingly might make a positive argument for access to guns.

2.3 Using Active Reading Strategies with Visual Arguments

Being a critical reader involves responding actively to the text of an argument. Active reading strategies—*previewing, careful reading, highlighting,* and *annotating*—can also be applied to visual arguments.

When you approach a visual argument, you should look for clues to its main idea, or message. Some visuals, particularly advertising images, include words (sometimes called body copy) as well, and this written text often conveys the main ideas of the argument. Apart from words, however, the images themselves can help you understand the visual's purpose, its intended audience, and the argument that it is making.

---

[*]"Decoding Visual Arguments is taken from Laurie G. Kirszner and Stephen R. Mandell, *Practical Argument: A Text and Anthology*, Second Edition, Chapter 3, pp. 74–87.

Comprehension Clues

- The individual images that appear
- The relative distance (close together or far apart) between images
- The relative size of the images
- The relationship between images and background
- The use of empty space
- The use of color and shading (for example, contrast between light and dark)
- If people are pictured, their activities, gestures, facial expressions, positions, body language, dress, and so on

Appeals: *Logos, Pathos,* and *Ethos*

As you study a visual argument, you should consider the appeal (or appeals) that the visual uses to convince its audience.

- An ad produced by Mothers Against Drunk Drivers (MADD) that includes statistics about alcohol-related auto fatalities might appeal to logic (*logos*).
- Another MADD ad could appeal to the emotions (*pathos*) by showing photographs of an accident scene.
- Still another ad could appeal to authority (*ethos*) by featuring a well-known sports figure warning of the dangers of drunk driving.

When you have studied the visual carefully, you should have a good general sense of what it was designed to communicate. Look at the image on the next page.

This visual uses the image of a young child holding a mutilated teddy bear to make an emotional appeal to those concerned about children's exposure to TV violence.

The visual includes three dominant images: the child, the teddy bear, and a giant TV screen projecting an image of a hand holding a knife. The placement of the child in the center of the visual, with the teddy bear on one side and the knife on the other, suggests that the child (and, by extension, all children) is caught between the innocence of childhood and the violence depicted in the media. The hand holding the knife on the TV screen is an extension of the child's actual arm, suggesting that the innocent world of the child is being taken over by the violent world of the media.

Figure 2.1 This illustration by Todd Davidson first appeared in the *Age* newspaper, Melbourne, Australia, on March 22, 1998.

To emphasize this conflict between innocence and violence, the teddy bear is set against a dark background, while the TV, with its disturbing image, is paradoxically set against a light background. (The image of the child is split, with half against each background, suggesting the split between the two worlds the child is exposed to.) The child's gaze is directed at his mutilated teddy bear, apparently the victim of his own violent act. The expression on the child's face makes it clear that he does not understand the violence he is caught up in.

Because it treats subject matter that is familiar to most people—TV violence and children's vulnerability to it—this visual is easy to understand. Its powerful images are not difficult to interpret, and its message is straightforward: TV violence is, at least in part, responsible for real-world violence. The visual's accessibility suggests that it is aimed at a wide general audience (rather than, for example, child psychologists or media analysts).

The visual's purpose is somewhat more complex. It could be to criticize the media, to warn parents and others about the threat posed by media violence, or to encourage the audience to take action.

Now, turn your attention to the following graph. This graph appeals to logic by using statistics as evidence to support its position. In so doing, it makes a powerful visual argument about the relationship between violent video games and crime. The visual uses accessible graphics and has an open, inviting design; its format is designed to make its information clear to most people who will look at it. The main idea that it conveys might be summarized as follows: "Although video games have become more and more violent, the number of crime victims has actually declined."

This idea is likely to come as a surprise to most people, who might assume a causal relationship between violent video games and violent crime. But as the graph shows, in 1972—when video games did not exist—the crime rate was considerably higher than it was in 2004. Because the information in the graph is intended to contradict its audience's probable assumptions, it seems to have been created to convince people to change the way they look at video games. In other words, it is an argument (and, in fact, it is structured as a **refutation**).

Figure 2.2 United States Department of Justice, Crime Victims per 1,000 Citizens

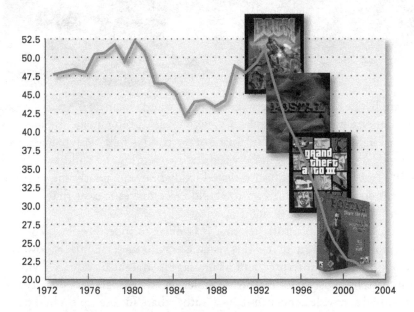

Activity 2.2

Look at the visuals that follow, and then answer the questions on page 40.

Figure 2.3 Bill Watterson, *Calvin and Hobbes*, "Graphic Violence in the Media"

©1995 Watterson/Dist. by Universal Press Syndicate

Figure 2.4 Parenthood Library, Distribution of Language, Sex, and Violence Codes in PG-Rated Movies.

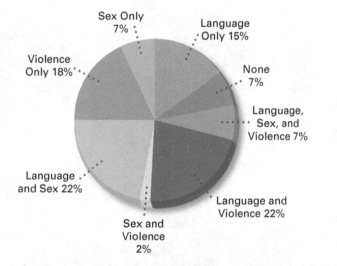

This chart is from "Protecting Children from Harmful Television: TV Ratings and the V-chip," parenthood.library.wisc.edu/Nathanson/Nathanson.html

Figure 2.5 Netwellness.org, Homicides per 100,000 Population

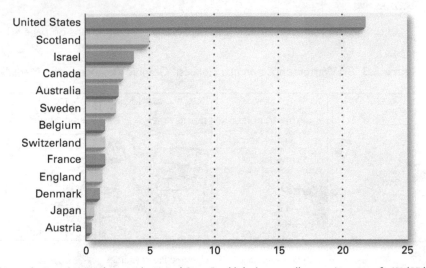

This graph appears in "Violence in the United States," published at netwellness.org/question.cfm/31497.htm

Figure 2.6 Boy Shooting Plastic Gun

Figure 2.7 Robert Mankoff, Killing It: Murders in *New Yorker* Cartoons (by decade)

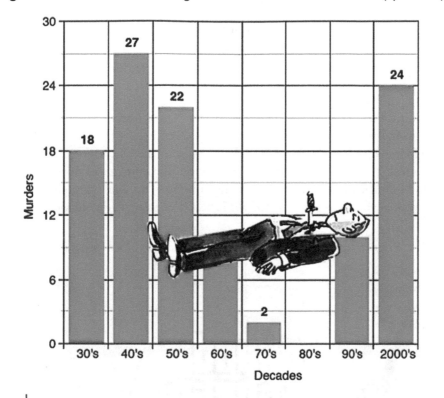

Identifying the Elements of a Visual Argument

1. Are all of the visuals on pages 35–36 arguments, or do you think some were designed solely to present information? Explain.

2. What main idea does each visual communicate? State the main idea of each visual in a single sentence.

3. What elements in each visual support this main idea?

4. If the visual includes words as well as images, are the words necessary?

5. What purpose does each visual seem designed to achieve?

6. What kind of audience do you think each visual is aimed at?

7. Does the visual appeal primarily to *logos*, *pathos*, or *ethos*?

8. Do you think the visual is effective? That is, is it likely to have the desired effect on its intended audience?

2.4 Highlighting and Annotating Visuals

Now, it is time to look more closely at visuals and to learn how to *highlight* and *annotate* them. Unlike highlighting and annotating a written text, marking a visual text involves focusing your primary attention not on any words that appear but on the images.

Begin by identifying key images—perhaps by starring, boxing, or circling them—and then consider drawing lines or arrows to connect related images. Next, go on to make annotations on the visual, commenting on the effectiveness of its individual images in communicating the message of the whole. As in the case of a written text, your annotations can be in the form of comments or questions.

The following image shows how a student, Jason Savona, highlighted and annotated an advertisement for *Grand Theft Auto IV,* a popular violent video game.

Figure 2.8 Rockstar North, Advertisement for *Grand Theft Auto IV*

Top of gun = taller than tallest building

Huge lone figure looking down on city

"Liberty City" skyline (looks like NY)

Hazy yellow sky

Dark image stands out against lighter background

Name of game centered; large type in contrasting black and white for emphasis

Activity 2.3

Look at the following visual, and then highlight and annotate it to identify its most important images and their relationship to one another. When you have finished, think about how the images work together to communicate a central message to the audience. What argument does this visual make?

Figure 2.9 Mediaviolence.org, *The Top Games of 2011*

According to CNBC, the Top Games of 2011 include:
Rage
Bulletstorm
Max Payne
Twisted Metal
Deus Ex 3: Human Revolution

Activity 2.4

Interview a classmate about his or her experiences with video games—or with actual violence. Does your classmate see any links between the kinds of videos that are watched by friends and family members and the violence (or lack of violence) that occurs in his or her community? Write a paragraph summarizing your interview.

2.5 Responding Critically to Visual Arguments

A **critical response** analyzes the ideas in a text and expresses your reactions to them. When you respond in writing to a visual argument, you should rely on your highlighting and annotations to help you understand the writer's ideas and see how the words and images work together to make a particular point.

As you prepare to write a critical response to a visual argument, you should keep in mind questions like those in the following checklist.

QUESTIONS FOR RESPONDING TO VISUAL ARGUMENTS

✔ In what source did the visual appear? What is the target audience for this source?

✔ For what kind of audience was the visual created? Hostile? Friendly? Neutral?

✔ For what purpose was the visual created?

✔ Who (or what organization) created the visual? What do you know about the background and goals of this person or group?

✔ What issue is the visual addressing?

✔ What position does the visual take on this issue? How can you tell? Do you agree with this position?

✔ Does the visual include words? If so, are they necessary? What points do they make? Does the visual need more—or different—written text?

✔ Does the visual seem to be a *refutation*—that is, an argument against a particular position?

✔ Is the visual effective? Attractive? Interesting? Clear? Convincing?

When you write a critical response, begin by identifying the source and purpose of the visual. Then, state your reaction to the visual, and examine its elements one at a time, considering how effective each is and how well the various elements work together to create a convincing visual argument. End with a strong concluding statement that summarizes your reaction.

The critical response that follows was written by the student who highlighted and annotated the advertisement for *Grand Theft Auto IV* on page 38.

Response to *Grand Theft AUTO IV*

Jason Savona

The advertisement for *Grand Theft Auto IV* presents a disturb- 1
ing preview of the game. Rather than highlighting the game's
features and challenges, this ad promotes the game's violence.
As a result, it appeals more to those who are looking for video
games that depict murder and other crimes than to those who
choose a video game on the basis of the skill it requires.

The "hero" of this game is Niko Bellic, a war vet- 2
eran from Eastern Europe who has left his country to build
a new life in the fictional Liberty City. Instead of finding peace, he has found a new kind of war. Now, trapped in
the corrupt world of organized crime, Bellic is willing to
do whatever it takes to fight his way out. His idea of justice is vigilante justice: He makes his own rules. The ad
conveys this sense of Bellic as a loner and an outsider by
showing him as a larger-than-life figure standing tall and
alone against a background of the Liberty City skyline.

In the ad, Bellic holds a powerful weapon in his huge hands, 3
and the weapon extends higher than the tallest building behind
it, dominating the picture. Clearly, Bellic means business. As
viewers look at the picture, the dark image of the gun and the
man who holds it comes to the foreground, and everything else—
the light brown buildings, the city lights, the yellow sky—fades
into the background. In the center, the name of the game is
set in large black-and-white type that contrasts with the ad's
hazy background, showing the importance of the product's name.

This image, clearly aimed at young players of violent 4
video games, would certainly be appealing to those who want
to have a feeling of power. What it says is, "A weapon makes
a person powerful." This is a very dangerous message.

Margin annotations:
Identification of visual's source

Reaction to visual

Analysis of visual's elements

Concluding statement

■ **Activity 2.5**

Write a one-paragraph critical response to the visual you highlighted and annotated in Activity 2.3 on page 39. Use the following template to shape your paragraph.

Template for Responding to Visual Arguments

A visual posted on the site mediaviolence. org shows_____ .

_____ .

This visual makes a powerful statement about _____ .

The central image shows _____

_____ .

The background enhances the central image because _____

_____

_____ .

The visual includes words as well as images. These words suggest _____

_____ .

The goal of the organization that posted the visual seems to be to _____

_____ .

The visual (is/is not) effective because _____

_____ .

■ **Activity 2.6**

Consulting the one-paragraph critical response that you wrote for Activity 2.5, write a more fully developed critical response to the visual on page 39. Refer to the highlighting and annotating that you did for Activity 2.3.

Narration

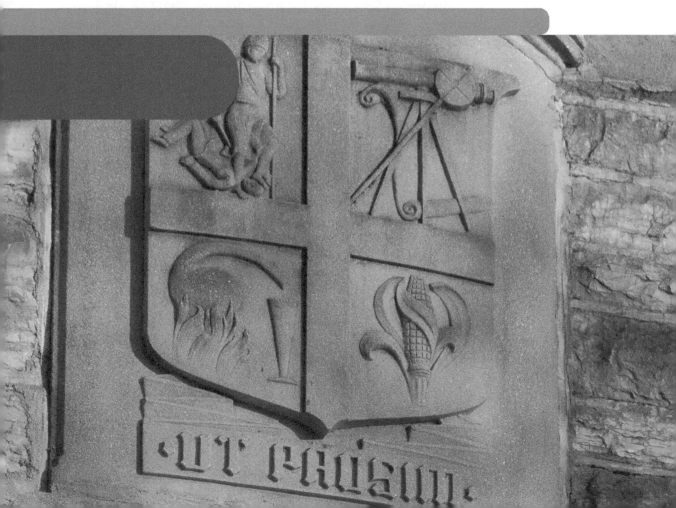

Narration, or the act of telling a story, is one of the fundamental modes of discourse. The ability to tell a story is a distinctly human endeavor. It can be argued, in fact, that the act of narration is what makes us human. We use narratives daily and incessantly to make decisions and make sense of the world and of ourselves. Narratives help us decide where we want to eat dinner and which candidate gets our votes. Narratives tell us who we are and where we're from and point us to where we should hope to go and how to get there. We use stories to create our identities and to figure out where we fit in the world.

3.1 An Introduction to Narration

Although narrative is certainly one of the fundamental modes of discourse you will study in your freshman composition courses, it isn't relegated to the English class-room. You'll rely on narration throughout your coursework at Virginia Tech, regard-less of your major, and in your careers as well. Simply put, a narrative is a causally linked chain of events told for a particular purpose. Imagine, then, how a biologist might explain the process of photosynthesis, or how a political scientist would map the rise in popularity of a particular party, without engaging in narrative. A systems engineer utilizes narrative to explain how a factory might become more efficient, while a nutritionist needs it to describe why a particular diet will optimize your metabolism. Narrative is necessary for communicating everything from the orbits of solar systems to why you were late for class this morning.

Narrative isn't our only mode of discourse, but even the components of a well-told narrative inform other types of writing. What we call "the point" of a story is another way of saying the thesis of an argument. Just as a well-told narrative of-fers concrete and sufficient details and evidence to support the point, an argument about gun-control legislation or carbon-reduction initiatives relies on the same sorts of evidence to prove the thesis. And in that same argument the writer might employ a variety of anecdotes—narratives—to engage the reader and illustrate the signifi-cance of a particular set of facts. Also, because narrative relies on a logical and clearly linked chain of events, the ability to shape narratives informs how we structure other modes of writing, such as laboratory or history reports and any set of instructions.

While you'll use narrative techniques in many ways in your freshman com-position courses, one of your major assignments in English 1105 will be the per-sonal essay—a narrative pulled from your own life experiences. You may be asked to write about formative experiences in your education, how you view yourself as a writer, or a particular facet of your community. Some instructors may ask you to explain how you came to hold a particular fundamental belief or how your family life shaped your ambitions and goals. All these assignments will require you to tell stories, to cast the people in your life—and yourself—as characters that a reader can understand and believe. You'll need to ground these characters and their actions in a realized setting, evoking the reader's senses with concrete details that prove your story took place in the real world. And you'll need to think hard about and reflect upon the significance of these experiences to prove that these events are meaningful, that they've shaped you in some way.

Before you question the value of writing a personal essay, consider the importance of being able to reflect upon and draw meaning from your experiences. Sometimes it seems that much of our lives, and our beliefs and values, go unexamined. We act and react without paying much attention to why and don't take the time to consider what can be learned from these actions and how they affect us. A personal narrative essay is an opportunity to turn your critical gaze on yourself, to use reflection as a tool for exploring the events that shape your worldview, your goals, and your principles. What events and which people have affected who you are and how you see the world? How can you narrate these formative events in a way that connects to other people's lives, so that they might gain insight?

To help you answer these questions, we've included a helpful guide to writing and revising your own narratives, written by Laurie G. Kirszner and Stephen R. Mandell. This guide introduces you to the basics of writing narratives and provides useful advice that you should take advantage of throughout the writing process, from planning to drafting to revising. This section covers the global concerns of narrative writing, such as developing and supporting a meaningful thesis and consistently maintaining a clear narrative structure, as well as the local, sentence-level concerns like the importance of concrete details and sensory imagery and how to address common grammatical mistakes when revising and editing your narrative.

To illustrate the importance of revision, Kirszner and Mandell provide two narratives written by students in a writing course similar to yours. Many students in college composition classes are afraid that they don't have anything important to say about their experiences. These student samples demonstrate that what we might assume at first glance to be mundane or ordinary becomes meaningful, engaging, and instructive when written reflectively and with close attention to detail. Make sure to read the commentary after each essay, which highlights some of the choices each writer made to craft an effective piece and the changes they made during revision.

Finally, the Readings section of this book includes several personal narrative essays from a variety of professional writers. Our goal when compiling these was to offer a diverse set of exemplary options—different backgrounds, subject matter, styles, and voices—to illustrate the many ways experienced writers go about mining experience for meaning. Included at the end of each essay are discussion questions to help you identify the various strategies and techniques each writer employs. Answering these questions, whether through informal writing or in classroom discussion, will help you begin to appreciate the thoughtfulness and craft this genre requires and to brainstorm ideas for your own personal narrative.

3.2 What Is Narration?*

Narration tells a story by presenting events in an orderly, logical sequence. In the following paragraph from "The Stone Horse," essayist Barry Lopez recounts the history of the exploration of the California desert.

<table>
<tr><td>**Topic Sentence**</td><td><u>Western man did not enter the California desert until the end of the eighteenth century, 250 years after Coronado brought his soldiers into the Zuni pueblos in a bewildered search for the cities of Cibola.</u> The earliest appraisals of the land were cursory, hurried. People traveled *through* it, en route to Santa Fe or the California coastal settlements.</td></tr>
<tr><td>**Narrative traces development through the nineteenth century**</td><td>Only miners tarried. In 1823 what had been Spain's became Mexico's, and in 1848 what had been Mexico's became America's; but the bare, jagged mountains and dry lake beds, the vast and uniform plains of creosote bush and yucca plants, remained as obscure as the northern Sudan until the end of the nineteenth century.</td></tr>
</table>

Narration can be the dominant pattern in many kinds of writing (as well as in speech). Histories, biographies, and autobiographies follow a narrative form, as do personal letters, diaries, journals, and some of the content on personal Web pages or social networking sites. Narration is the dominant pattern in many works of fiction and poetry, and it is an essential part of casual conversation. Narration also underlies folk and fairy tales and many news reports. In short, anytime you tell what happened, you are using narration.

3.3 Using Narration

Narration can provide the structure for an entire essay, but narrative passages may also appear in essays that are not primarily narrative. In an argumentative essay supporting stricter gun-safety legislation, for example, you might devote one or two paragraphs to the story of a child accidentally killed by a handgun. In this chapter, however, we focus on narration as the dominant pattern of a piece of writing.

Throughout your college career, many of your assignments will call for narration. In an English composition class, you may be asked to write about an experience that was important to your development as an adult; on a European history exam, you may need to relate the events that led to Napoleon's defeat at the Battle of Waterloo; and in a technical writing class, you may be asked to write a report tracing a company's negligent actions. In each of these situations (as well as in many additional assignments), your writing has a primarily narrative structure, and the narrative supports a thesis.

---

*"Narration" is taken from Laurie G. Kirszner and Stephen R. Mandell, *Patterns for College Writing: A Rhetorical Reader and Guide,* Thirteenth Edition, pp. 97–122.

The skills you develop in narrative writing will also help you in other kinds of writing. A *process essay*, such as an explanation of a laboratory experiment, is like a narrative because it outlines a series of steps in chronological order; a *cause-and-effect essay*, such as your answer to an exam question that asks you to analyze the events that caused the Great Depression, also resembles a narrative in that it traces a sequence of events. Although a process essay explains how to do something and a cause-and-effect essay explains why events occur, writing both these kinds of essays will be easier after you master narration.

3.4 Planning a Narrative Essay

Developing a Thesis Statement

Although the purpose of a narrative may be simply to recount events or to create a particular mood or impression, in college writing a narrative essay is more likely to present a sequence of events for the purpose of supporting a thesis. For instance, in a narrative about your problems with credit card debt, your purpose may be to show your readers that college students should not have easy access to credit cards. Accordingly, you do not simply tell the story of your unwise spending. Rather, you select and arrange details to show your readers why having a credit card encouraged you to spend money you didn't have. Although it is usually best to include an explicit **thesis statement** ("My negative experiences with credit have convinced me that college students should not have access to credit cards"), you may also imply your thesis through your selection and arrangement of events.

Including Enough Detail

Narratives, like other types of writing, need to include rich, specific details if they are to be convincing. Each detail should help to create a picture for the reader; even exact times, dates, and geographic locations can be helpful. Look, for example, at the following paragraph from the essay "My Mother Never Worked" by Bonnie Smith-Yackel:

> In the winter she sewed night after night, endlessly, begging cast-off clothing from relatives, ripping apart coats, dresses, blouses, and trousers to remake them to fit her four daughters and son. Every morning and every evening she milked cows, fed pigs and calves, cared for chickens, picked eggs, cooked meals, washed dishes, scrubbed floors, and tended and loved her children. In the spring she planted a garden once more, dragging pails of water to nourish and sustain the vegetables for the family. In 1936 she lost a baby in her sixth month.

This list of details adds interest and authenticity to the narrative. The central figure in the narrative is a busy, productive woman, and readers know this because they are given an exhaustive catalog of her activities.

Varying Sentence Structure

When narratives present a long series of events, all the sentences can begin to sound alike: "She sewed dresses. She milked cows. She fed pigs. She fed calves. She cared for chickens." Such a predictable string of sentences may become monotonous for your readers. You can eliminate this monotony by varying your sentence structure—for instance, by using a variety of sentence openings or by combining simple sentences as Smith-Yackel does in "My Mother Never Worked": "In the winter she sewed night after night, endlessly.... Every morning and every evening she milked cows, fed pigs and calves, cared for chickens...."

Maintaining Clear Narrative Order

Many narratives present events in the exact order in which they occurred, moving from first event to last. Whether or not you follow a strict **chronological order** depends on the purpose of your narrative. If you are writing a straightforward account of a historical event or summarizing a record of poor management practices, you will probably want to move directly from beginning to end. In a personal-experience essay or a fictional narrative, however, you may want to engage your readers' interest by beginning with an event from the middle of your story, or even from the end, and then presenting the events that led up to it. You may also decide to begin in the present and then use one or more **flashbacks** (shifts into the past) to tell your story. To help readers follow the order of events in your narrative, it is very important to use correct verb tenses and clear transitional words and phrases.

Using Accurate Verb Tenses.   **Verb tense** is extremely important in writing that recounts events in a fixed order because tenses indicate temporal (time) relationships. When you write a narrative, you should be careful to keep verb tenses consistent and accurate so that your readers can follow the sequence of events. Naturally, you need to shift tenses to reflect an actual time shift in your narrative. For instance, convention requires that you use present tense when discussing works of literature ("When Hamlet's mother *marries* his uncle..."), but a flashback to an earlier point in the story calls for a shift from present to past tense ("Before his mother's marriage, Hamlet *was...*"). Nevertheless, you should avoid unwarranted shifts in verb tense; they will make your narrative confusing.

Using Transitions.   **Transitions**—connecting words or phrases—help link events in time, enabling narratives to flow smoothly. Without them, narratives would lack coherence, and readers would be unsure of the correct sequence of events. Transitions indicate the order of events, and they also signal shifts in time. In narrative writing, the transitions commonly used for these purposes include *first, second, next, then, later, at the same time, meanwhile, immediately, soon, before, earlier, after, afterward, now,* and *finally*. In addition to transitional words and phrases, specific time markers—such as *three years later, in 1927, after two hours,* and *on January 3*—indicate how much time has passed between events.

3.5 Structuring a Narrative Essay

Like other essays, a **narrative** essay has an introduction, a body, and a conclusion. If your essay's thesis is explicitly stated, it will, in most cases, appear in the **introduction**. The **body paragraphs** of your essay will recount the events that make up your narrative, following a clear and orderly plan. Finally, the **conclusion** will give your readers the sense that your narrative is complete, perhaps by restating your thesis in different words or by summarizing key points or events.

Suppose you are assigned a short history paper about the Battle of Waterloo. You plan to support the thesis that if Napoleon had kept more troops in reserve, he might have defeated the British troops serving under Wellington. Based on this thesis, you decide that the best way to organize your paper is to present the five major phases of the battle in chronological order. An informal outline of your essay might look like this.

Sample Outline: Narration	
Introduction:	Thesis statement—If Napoleon had kept more troops in reserve, he might have broken Wellington's line with another infantry attack and thus won the Battle of Waterloo.
Phase 1 of the battle:	Napoleon attacked the Château of Hougoumont.
Phase 2 of the battle:	The French infantry attacked the British lines.
Phase 3 of the battle:	The French cavalry staged a series of charges against the British lines that had not been attacked before; Napoleon committed his reserves.
Phase 4 of the battle:	The French captured La Haye Sainte, their first success of the day but an advantage that Napoleon, having committed troops elsewhere, could not maintain without reserves.
Phase 5 of the battle:	The French infantry was decisively defeated by the combined thrust of the British infantry and the remaining British cavalry.
Conclusion:	Restatement of thesis (in different words) or review of key points or events.

By discussing the five phases of the battle in chronological order, you clearly support your thesis. As you expand your informal outline into a historical narrative, exact details, dates, times, and geographic locations are extremely important. Without them, your statements are open to question. In addition, to keep your readers aware of the order of events, you must select appropriate transitional words and phrases and pay careful attention to verb tenses.

3.6 Revising a Narrative Essay

When you revise a narrative essay, pay special attention to the items on the following checklist, which apply specifically to narrative essays.

REVISION CHECKLIST: NARRATION

✔ Does your assignment call for narration?

✔ Does your essay's thesis communicate the significance of the events you discuss?

✔ Have you included enough specific detail?

✔ Have you varied your sentence structure?

✔ Is the order of events clear to readers?

✔ Have you varied sentence openings and combined short sentences to avoid monotony?

✔ Do your transitions indicate the order of events and signal shifts in time?

3.7 Editing a Narrative Essay

When you edit your narrative essay, focus on the grammar, mechanics, and punctuation issues that are particularly relevant to narrative essays. One of these issues—avoiding run-on sentences—is discussed next.

Grammar In Context: Avoiding Run-Ons

When writing narrative essays, particularly personal narratives and essays that include dialogue, writers can easily lose sight of sentence boundaries and create **run-ons**. There are two kinds of run-ons: *fused sentences* and *comma splices*.

A **fused sentence** occurs when two sentences are incorrectly joined without punctuation.

CORRECT (TWO SENTENCES):	"The sun came out hot and bright, endlessly, day after day. The crops shriveled and died" (Smith-Yackel 124).
FUSED SENTENCE:	The sun came out hot and bright, endlessly, day after day the crops shriveled and died.

A **comma splice** occurs when two sentences are incorrectly joined with just a comma.

COMMA SPLICE:	The sun came out hot and bright, endlessly, day after day, the crops shriveled and died.

Five Ways to Correct These Errors

1. **Use a period to create two separate sentences.**

   The sun came out hot and bright, endlessly, day after day. The crops shriveled and died.

2. **Join the sentences with a comma and a coordinating conjunction (*and, or, nor, for, so, but, yet*).**

   The sun came out hot and bright, endlessly, day after day, and the crops shriveled and died.

3. **Join the sentences with a semicolon.**

   The sun came out hot and bright, endlessly, day after day; the crops shriveled and died.

4. **Join the sentences with a semicolon and a transitional word or phrase (followed by a comma), such as *however, therefore, or for example*.**

   The sun came out hot and bright, endlessly, day after day; eventually, the crops shriveled and died.

5. **Create a complex sentence by adding a subordinating conjunction (*although, because, if,* and so on) or a relative pronoun (*who, which, that,* and so on) to one of the sentences.**

   As the sun came out hot and bright, endlessly, day after day, the crops shriveled and died.

EDITING CHECKLIST: NARRATION

✔ Have you avoided run-ons?

✔ Do your verb tenses clearly indicate time relationships between events?

✔ Have you avoided unnecessary tense shifts?

✔ If you use dialogue, have you punctuated correctly and capitalized where necessary?

A Student Writer: Literacy Narrative

In the following essay, student Erica Sarno traces her development as a writer. Her assignment was to write a **literacy narrative**, a personal account focusing on her experiences with reading and writing.

Becoming a Writer

Introduction

I used to think that writing was just about filling pages. Composing an essay for school meant getting the job done and checking it off my to-do list. During my last two years of high school, however, my attitude started to change. Several experiences helped me understand that writing is not a skill that some people are born with and others are not. If I wanted to write, all I needed was a desire to express myself to others and a willing audience. Realizing that there was someone on the other side of the page, eager to listen, helped me develop into a more effective writer.

Thesis statement

Narrative begins (junior year)

My first real lesson in my development as a writer took place in Mrs. Strickland's junior English class. Mrs. Strickland was hard to approach. She dressed as if she expected to be giving a press conference at the White House. She wore tan suits and silk scarves, and she had a helmet of dyed blonde hair. We seemed to disappoint her just because we were high school students. Maybe I saw her lack of interest in us and our work as a challenge because, one day, I took a risk and wrote a very personal essay about losing my aunt to cancer. When I got the paper back, Mrs. Strickland had written only, "Did you read the instructions?" I could not believe it. For the first time, I had actually written about what was important to me rather than just filling the pages with words, and she had not even read past my introduction! Still, I knew then that I had something to say. I just needed someone to listen.

Narrative continues (senior year)

The next year, I had Dr. Kelleher for senior English. My year with Dr. K profoundly changed the way I see myself as a writer (and as a reader). Finally, a teacher was paying

1

2

3

attention to what I had written. His only rule for writing was "Don't be boring!" I rewrote sentences, hoping for an exclamation point or one of Dr. K's other special marks in the margin. Dr. K had a whole list of codes and abbreviations, like "BTH" ("Better than Hemingway") or "the knife" (when the writer slayed the opponent in an argument). I also relied on Dr. K to tell me when I was falling into my old habit of just filling the page. He would write a funny comment like, "Come back! Log out of Facebook!" Then, he would give me a chance to try again. Trusting him to be a generous reader and an honest critic helped me develop my voice and my confidence as a writer.

Meanwhile, I started to become a better reader, too. I could tell when a writer was writing to me, wanting me to understand. I could also tell when a writer was writing just to get the job done. Instead of just skimming the assigned reading, I got in the habit of writing in the margins and making notes about what I thought. I underlined ideas that spoke to me, and I wrote "Really??" next to ideas that seemed silly. Instead of assuming a reading would be boring, I gave every assignment a chance. Whether I liked a book or not, I felt that I could explain my reasons. I was finally seeing for myself that writing is just another way for people to talk to each other.

4   *Narrative shifts to focus on reading*

Eventually, in the spring of my senior year, I experienced what it feels like to connect with a broader audience. I suggested a column about "senioritis" to the school paper, and even though I had never written for the public before, the editor loved my idea. I knew what I wanted to say, and I knew I could collect plenty of stories to help me illustrate my ideas. What I did not predict was how much I would learn from the experience of writing those six columns. Knowing that hundreds of people would be reading my pieces, I revised them over and over again. When Dr. K read one of my last columns aloud to our class, I got to see how my work affected people. Watching the expressions on my classmates' faces and hearing them

5   *Narrative moves outside the classroom*

Conclusion

> laugh at the funny parts helped me understand what good writ-
> ing is. In that moment, I truly connected with my audience.
>
>   Although I still have a lot to learn, I now understand how   6
> important the relationship between the writer and the reader
> is. When I write, I am writing to be heard. When I read, I
> am reading to understand. The communication may not be per-
> fect, but I know I am not alone in my task. And even though
> I am not in Dr. K's class anymore, I still sometimes imagine
> that he will be reading what I have written. Thinking about
> him reminds me that someone cares about what I have to say.

Points for Special Attention

Assignment. Erica's assignment was to write a literacy narrative. At first, she considered writing about her favorite childhood books or about how she learned to read, but in the end she decided to focus on more recent experiences because she could remember them more clearly (and, therefore, could include more specific detail).

Thesis Statement and Title. Because her focus was on her development as a writer, Erica was careful to include the words *develop* and *writer* in her thesis statement. Her thesis statement also clearly explains the key factor that encouraged her development—the presence of an interested reader.

Structure. In her essay's first two body paragraphs, Erica discusses her junior and senior English classes. However, instead of just contrasting the two teachers, she explains how she herself changed as a result of their different approaches. In paragraph 4, she explains the connection between her reading and her writing, and in paragraph 5, she recounts her development into a reader writing for a wider audience.

Topic Sentences. To move her narrative along, Erica was careful to include transitional words and phrases—*The next year, Meanwhile, Eventually*—in her topic sentences to show the movement from one stage of her development to the next.

Working with Sources. Erica's assignment made it clear that although other assignments in the course would be source-based, this narrative essay should be based solely on her own memories and reflections.

Focus on Revision

When she reread an early draft of her essay, Erica immediately saw a problem: she had written a comparison-and-contrast essay instead of a narrative. Instead of focusing on her development as a writer, she had simply compared her junior- and senior-year English classes. This problem was revealed by her draft's thesis statement—"The difference between junior and senior year of high school was the difference between being ignored and being heard"—as well as by the topic sentences of her first two body paragraphs:

First Body Paragraph: Mrs. Strickland was an uninspiring teacher.

Second Body Paragraph: Unlike Mrs. Strickland, Dr. Kelleher encouraged me as a writer.

Erica also noticed that her entire essay dealt with classroom style, further highlighting the contrast between her two teachers. Realizing that her development as a writer had also taken place outside the classroom, she condensed her discussion of the two English classes and added material about reading (para. 4) and about writing for her school paper (para. 5).

When she wrote her next draft, Erica was careful to include transitions and topic sentences that signaled her focus on her development over time, not on the differences between two classes or two teachers. Finally, as she reviewed her draft, she noticed that her original summary statement—"Knowing that there was someone on the other side of the page made me a better writer"—could be expanded into an appropriate and effective thesis statement.

A Student Writer: Narration

The following essay is typical of the informal narrative writing many students are asked to do in English composition classes. It was written by Tiffany Forte in response to the assignment "Write an informal essay about a goal or dream you had when you were a child."

My Field of Dreams

When I was young, I was told that when I grew up I could be   1   Introduction
anything I wanted to be, and I always took for granted that
this was true. I knew exactly what I was going to be, and I
would spend hours dreaming about how wonderful my life would
be when I grew up. One day, though, when I did grow up, I   Thesis statement
realized that things had not turned out the way I had always
expected they would.

   When I was little, I never played with baby dolls or   2   Narrative begins
Barbies. I wasn't like other little girls; I was a tom-
boy. I was the only girl in the neighborhood where
I lived, so I always played with boys. We would play
army or football or (my favorite) baseball.

Almost every summer afternoon, all the boys in my neighborhood and I would meet by the big oak tree to get a baseball game going. Surprisingly, I was always one of the first to be picked for a team. I was very fast, and (for my size) I could hit the ball far. I loved baseball more than anything, and I wouldn't miss a game for the world.

3

My dad played baseball too, and every Friday night I would go to the field with my mother to watch him play. It was just like the big leagues, with lots of people, a snack bar, and lights that shone so high and bright you could see them a mile away. I loved to go to my dad's games. When all the other kids would wander off and play, I would sit and cheer on my dad and his team. My attention was focused on the field, and my heart would jump with every pitch.

4

Even more exciting than my dad's games were the major league games. The Phillies were my favorite team, and I always looked forward to watching them on television. My dad would make popcorn, and we would sit and watch in anticipation of a Phillies victory. We would go wild, yelling and screaming at all the big plays. When the Phillies would win, I would be so excited I couldn't sleep; when they would lose, I would go to bed angry, just like my dad.

5

Key experience introduced (paras. 6–7)

It was when my dad took me to my first Phillies game that I decided I wanted to be a major league baseball player. The excitement began when we pulled into the parking lot of the old Veterans Stadium. There were thousands of cars. As we walked from the car to the stadium, my dad told me to hold on to his hand and not to let go no matter what. When we gave the man our tickets and entered the stadium, I understood why. There were mobs of people everywhere. They were walking around the stadium and standing in long lines for hot dogs, beer, and souvenirs. It was the most wonderful thing I had ever seen. When we got to our seats, I looked down at the tiny baseball diamond below and felt as if I were on top of the world.

6

The cheering of the crowd, the singing, and the chants   7
were almost more than I could stand. I was bursting with enthusiasm. Then, in the bottom of the eighth inning, with the
score tied and two outs, Mike Schmidt came up to bat and hit
the game-winning home run. The crowd went crazy. Everyone
in the whole stadium was standing, and I found myself yelling and screaming along with everyone else. When Mike Schmidt
came out of the dugout to receive his standing ovation, I
felt a lump in my throat and butterflies in my stomach. He
was everyone's hero that night, and I could only imagine
the pride he must have felt. I slept the whole way home and
dreamed of what it would be like to be the hero of the game.

The next day, when I met with the boys at the oak tree,   8   Narrative continues
I told them that when I grew up, I was going to be a major
league baseball player. They all laughed at me and said I
could never be a baseball player because I was a girl. I told
them that they were all wrong and that I would show them.

In the years to follow, I played girls' softball in a com-   9   Analysis of childhood experiences
petitive fast-pitch league, and I was very good. I always
wanted to play baseball with the boys, but there were no mixed
leagues. After a few years, I realized that the boys from the
oak tree were right: I was never going to be a major league
baseball player. I realized that what I had been told when I
was younger wasn't the whole truth. What no one had bothered
to tell me was that I could be anything I wanted to be—as long
as it was something that was appropriate for a girl to do.

In time, I would get over the loss of my dream. I found new   10   Conclusion
dreams, acceptable for a young woman, and I moved on to other
things. Still, every time I watch a baseball game and someone hits a home run, I get those same butterflies in my stomach and think, for just a minute, about what might have been.

Points for Special Attention

Assignment.   Tiffany's assignment was to write about a goal or dream she had when she was a child. As a nontraditional student, a good deal older than most of her classmates, Tiffany found this assignment challenging at first. She wondered if her childhood dreams would be different from those of her classmates, and she was somewhat hesitant to share her drafts with her peer-editing group. As it turned out, though, her childhood dreams were not very different from those of the other students in her class.

Introduction.   Tiffany's introduction is straightforward, yet it arouses reader interest by setting up a contrast between what she expected and what actually happened. Her optimistic expectation—that she could be anything she wanted to be—is contradicted by her thesis statement, encouraging readers to read on to learn how things turned out and why.

Thesis Statement.   Although the assignment called for a personal narrative, the instructor made it clear that the essay should have an explicitly stated thesis that made a point about a childhood goal or dream. Tiffany knew she wanted to write about her passion for baseball, but she also knew that just listing a series of events would not fulfill the assignment. Her thesis statement—"One day, though, when I did grow up, I realized that things had not turned out the way I had always expected they would"—puts her memories in context, suggesting that she will use them to support a general conclusion about the gap between dreams and reality.

Structure.   The body of Tiffany's essay traces the chronology of her involvement with baseball—playing with the neighborhood boys, watching her father's games, watching baseball on television, and, finally, attending her first major league game. Each body paragraph introduces a different aspect of her experience with baseball, culminating in the vividly described Phillies game. The balance of the essay (paras. 8–10) summarizes the aftermath of that game, gives a brief overview of Tiffany's later years in baseball, and presents her conclusion.

Detail.   Personal narratives like Tiffany's need a lot of detail because the writers want readers to see and hear and feel what they did. To present an accurate picture, Tiffany includes all the significant sights and sounds she can remember: the big oak tree, the lights on the field, the popcorn, the excited cheers, the food and souvenir stands, the crowds, and so on. She also names Mike Schmidt ("everyone's hero"), his team, and the stadium where she saw him play. Despite all these details, though, she omits some important information—for example, how old she was at each stage of her essay.

Working with Sources.   Tiffany's essay is very personal, and she supports her thesis with experiences and observations from her own childhood. Although she could have consulted sources to find specific information about team standings or players' stats—or even quoted her hero, Mike Schmidt—she decided that her own memories would provide convincing support for her thesis.

Verb Tense.   Maintaining clear chronological order is very important in narrative writing, where unwarranted shifts in verb tenses can confuse readers. Knowing this, Tiffany was careful to avoid unnecessary tense shifts. In her conclusion, she shifts from past to present tense, but this shift is both necessary and clear. Elsewhere she uses *would* to identify events that recurred regularly. For example, in paragraph 5 she says, "My dad *would* make popcorn" rather than "My dad *made* popcorn," which would have suggested that he did so only once.

Transitions.   Tiffany's skillful use of transitional words and expressions links her sentences and moves her readers smoothly through her essay. In addition to transitional words such as *when* and *then*, she uses specific time markers—"When I was little," "Almost every summer afternoon," "every Friday night," "As we walked," "The next day," "In the years to follow," and "After a few years"—to advance the narrative and carry her readers along.

Focus on Revision

In their responses to an earlier draft of Tiffany's essay, several students in her peer-editing group recommended that she revise one particularly monotonous paragraph. (As one student pointed out, all its sentences began with the subject, making the paragraph seem choppy and its ideas disconnected.) Here is the paragraph from her draft:

> My dad played baseball too. I went to the field with my mother every Friday night to watch him play. It was just like the big leagues. There were lots of people and a snack bar. The lights shone so high and bright you could see them a mile away. I loved to go to my dad's games. All the other kids would wander off and play. I would sit and cheer on my dad and his team. My attention was focused on the field. My heart would jump with every pitch.

In the revised version of the paragraph (now paragraph 4 of her essay), Tiffany varies sentence length and opening strategies:

> My dad played baseball too, and every Friday night I would go to the field with my mother to watch him play. It was just like the big leagues, with lots of people, a snack bar, and lights that shone so high and bright you could see them a mile away. I loved to go to my dad's games. When all the other kids would wander off and play, I would sit and cheer on my dad and his team. My attention was focused on the field, and my heart would jump with every pitch.

After reading Tiffany's revised draft, another student suggested that she might still polish her essay a bit. For instance, she could add some dialogue, quoting the boys' taunts and her own reply in paragraph 8. She could also revise to eliminate **clichés** (overused expressions), substituting fresher, more original language for phrases such as "I felt a lump in my throat and butterflies in my stomach" and "felt as if I were on top of the world." In the next draft of her essay, Tiffany followed up on these suggestions.

Peer-Editing Worksheet: Narration

1. What point is the writer making about the essay's subject? Is this point explicitly stated in a thesis statement? If so, where? If not, can you state the essay's thesis in one sentence?

2. List some details that enrich the narrative. Where could more detail be added? What kind of detail? Be specific.

3. Does the writer vary sentence structure and avoid monotonous strings of similar sentences? Should any sentences be combined? If so, which ones? Can you suggest different openings for any sentences?

4. Should any transitions be added to clarify the order in which events occurred? If so, where?

5. Do verb tenses establish a clear chronological order? Identify any verb tenses that you believe need to be changed.

6. Does the writer avoid run-on sentences? Point out any fused sentences or comma splices.

7. What could the writer *add* to this essay?

8. What could the writer take out of this essay?

9. What is the essay's greatest strength? Why?

10. What is the essay's greatest weakness? What steps should the writer take to correct this problem?

Chapter 4

Knowledge of Conventions: Grammar and Style

The fourth WPA outcome is Knowledge of Conventions. Conventions in composition refer to the guidelines and rules we follow when writing. Examples of these conventions include grammar, style, MLA and other documentation formats, and editing.

In your writing course, then, you will learn how to cite a source in MLA format, how to correct a comma error, and how to write in a more concise manner.

Before beginning to understand these conventions, first think about how you will present yourself as a writer. If you submit a formal assignment that is full of grammatical or stylistic errors, how will your writing be perceived? Will your instructor take your argument or main point seriously?

As discussed in Chapter 1, also consider your personal *ethos*: To present yourself as a credible writer, you should edit and proofread your work according to these writing conventions. Think of a book or article you read that was poorly written: How does that affect how you perceive the author?

Because they affect how you present yourself and are perceived as a writer, knowledge of conventions is important in any writing you do in your course.

4.1 Parts of Speech

To best understand how grammatical rules work, learning the underlying principles and terms, such as the parts of speech (see Figure 4.1), will help you identify errors and then correct them on your own.

There are, of course, many different errors that we could discuss, but the errors below are the ones most often seen in first-year writing courses.

Figure 4.1 Parts of Speech

Nouns
Words that answer the questions of who and what; a person, place, thing, or idea.

Pronouns
Words that take the place of nouns.

Verbs
Words that denote action or a state of being.

Prepositions
Words that work in combination with a noun or pronoun to create phrases that convey spatial, temporal, or directional meaning and that modify verbs, nouns/pronouns, or adjectives.

Adjectives
Words that modify/clarify nouns and pronouns by giving more information and answering the questions "What kind?" or "Which?" or "How many?"

Adverbs
Words that modify, or further describe, verbs and adjectives. Many, though not all, adverbs end in -*ly*.

Conjunctions
Words that join two independent clauses, or sentences, together (*and, but, for, or, nor, so, yet*).

Articles
Words that precede a noun or a noun phrase in a sentence (*a, an, the*).

An **independent clause** can stand on its own because it doesn't depend on anything else to complete a thought. Essentially it is a complete sentence, because it contains a **subject** and a **verb**.

> He listened to music while he studied.

Notice the use of a subject and verb in this sentence.

A **dependent clause**, however, cannot stand alone, as it depends on another clause to complete a thought.

Keep these two types of clauses in mind as you begin to learn about punctuation.

Coordinating conjunctions are the seven words that join two independent clauses. You can remember them by the acronym FANBOYS: *for, and, nor, but, or, yet, so.*

> Peter likes to go running outside every day, but when it rains he runs on the indoor track.

Pronoun-Antecedent Agreement

Pronouns are words that substitute for nouns; common pronouns include *he, she, it,* and *they.* **Antecedents** are the words that the pronouns refer to; pronouns and their antecedents must agree in number and gender: Both must be singular or both must be plural.

> No one studied for his or her test last night.

OR

> The students did not study for their tests last night.

4.2 Commas

It's hard to go through a day without encountering directions of some kind, and commas often play a crucial role in how you interpret instructions. See how important the comma is in the following directions for making hot cereal:

> Add Cream of Wheat slowly, stirring constantly.

That sentence tells the cook to *add the cereal slowly.* If the comma came before the word *slowly,* however, the cook might add all of the cereal at once and *stir slowly.*

Setting Off Introductory Elements

In general, use a comma after any word, **phrase**, or **clause** that precedes the subject of the sentence.

However, health care costs keep rising.

Wearing new running shoes, Julie prepared for the race.

To win the game, players need both skill and luck.

Fingers on the keyboard, Maya waited for the test to begin.

While her friends watched, Lila practiced her gymnastics routine.

Some writers omit the comma after a short introductory element that does not seem to require a pause after it. However, you will never be wrong if you use a comma.

Separating Clauses in Compound Sentences

A comma usually precedes a coordinating conjunction (*and, but, or, nor, for, so,* or *yet*) that joins two independent clauses in a compound sentence.

The climbers must reach the summit today, or they will have to turn back.

With very short clauses, you can sometimes omit the comma (*She saw her chance and she took it*). But always use the comma if there is a chance the sentence will be misread without it.

I opened the junk drawer, and the cabinet door jammed.

EDITING FOR COMMAS

Research shows that five of the most common errors in college writing involve commas.

- ✔ Check that a comma separates an introductory word, phrase, or clause from the main part of the sentence.

- ✔ Look at every sentence that contains a coordinating conjunction (*for, and, nor, but, or, yet,* or *so*). If the groups of words before and after this conjunction both function as complete sentences, use a comma before the conjunction.

- ✔ Look at each adjective clause beginning with *which, who, whom, whose, when,* or *where* and at each phrase and appositive. If the rest of the sentence would have a different meaning without the clause, phrase, or appositive, do not set off the element with commas.

✔ Make sure that adjective clauses beginning with *that* are not set off with commas. Do not use commas between subjects and verbs, verbs and objects or complements, or prepositions and objects; to separate parts of compound constructions other than compound sentences; to set off restrictive clauses; or before the first or after the last item in a series.

✔ Do not use a comma alone to separate sentences.

Use a semicolon rather than a comma when the clauses are long and complex or contain their own commas.

> When these early migrations took place, the ice was still confined to the lands in the far north; but eight hundred thousand years ago, when man was already established in the temperate latitudes, the ice moved southward until it covered large parts of Europe and Asia.
>
> —Robert Jastrow, *Until the Sun Dies*

Setting Off Nonrestrictive Elements

Nonrestrictive elements are word groups that do not limit, or restrict, the meaning of the noun or pronoun they modify. Setting nonrestrictive elements off with commas shows your readers that the information is not essential to the meaning of the sentence. **Restrictive elements**, on the other hand, *are* essential to meaning and should *not* be set off with commas. The same sentence may mean different things with and without the commas:

> The bus drivers rejecting the management offer remained on strike.

> The bus drivers, rejecting the management offer, remained on strike.

The first sentence says that only *some* bus drivers, the ones rejecting the offer, remained on strike. The second says that *all* the drivers did.

Since the decision to include or omit commas influences how readers will interpret your sentence, you should think especially carefully about what you mean and use commas (or omit them) accordingly.

Restrictive   Drivers *who have been convicted of drunken driving* should lose their licenses.

In the preceding sentence, the clause *who have been convicted of drunken driving* is essential because it explains that only drivers who have been convicted of drunken driving should lose their licenses. Therefore, it is *not* set off with commas.

Nonrestrictive   The two drivers involved in the accident, *who have been convicted of drunken driving*, should lose their licenses.

In this sentence, however, the clause *who have been convicted of drunken driving* is not essential to the meaning because it does not limit what it modifies, *The two drivers involved in the accident*, but merely provides additional information about these drivers. Therefore, the clause *is* set off with commas.

To decide whether an element is restrictive or nonrestrictive, mentally delete the element, and see if the deletion changes the meaning of the rest of the sentence. If the deletion *does* change the meaning, you should probably not set the element off with commas. If it *does not* change the meaning, the element probably requires commas.

Adjective and Adverb Clauses.   An adjective clause that begins with *that* is always restrictive; do not set it off with commas. An adjective clause beginning with *which* may be either restrictive or nonrestrictive; however, some writers prefer to use *which* only for nonrestrictive clauses, which they set off with commas.

Restrictive Clauses

> The claim that men like seriously to battle one another to some sort of finish is a myth.
> —John McMurtry, *"Kill 'Em! Crush 'Em! Eat 'Em Raw!"*

The adjective clause is necessary to the meaning because it explains which claim is a myth; therefore, the clause is not set off with commas.

> The man⌄ who rescued Jana's puppy⌄ won her eternal gratitude.

The adjective clause is necessary to the meaning because it identifies the man, so it takes no commas.

Nonrestrictive Clauses

> I borrowed books from the rental library of Shakespeare and Company, *which was the library and bookstore of Sylvia Beach at 12 rue de l'Odeon.*
> —Ernest Hemingway, *A Moveable Feast*

The adjective clause is not necessary to the meaning of the independent clause and therefore is set off with a comma.

An adverb clause that follows a main clause does *not* usually require a comma to set it off unless the adverb clause expresses contrast.

> The park became a popular gathering place,⌃although nearby residents complained about the noise.

The adverb clause expresses contrast; therefore, it is set off with a comma.

Phrases.   Participial **phrases** may be restrictive or nonrestrictive. Prepositional phrases are usually restrictive, but sometimes they are not essential to the meaning of a sentence and thus are set off with commas.

Nonrestrictive Phrases

The singer's children, refusing to be ignored, interrupted the recital.

Using commas around the participial phrase makes it nonrestrictive, telling us that all of the singer's children interrupted.

Appositives.   An **appositive** is a noun or noun phrase that renames a nearby noun. When an appositive is not essential to identify what it renames, it is set off with commas.

Nonrestrictive Appositives

Savion Glover, the award-winning dancer, taps like poetry in motion.

Savion Glover's name identifies him; the appositive *the award-winning dancer* provides extra information.

Restrictive Appositives

Mozart's opera *The Marriage of Figaro* was considered revolutionary.

The phrase is restrictive because Mozart wrote more than one opera. Therefore, it is *not* set off with commas.

Separating Items in a Series

He has plundered our seas, ravaged our coasts, burnt our towns, and destroyed the lives of our people.

—Declaration of Independence

You may see a series with no comma after the next-to-last item, particularly in newspaper writing. Occasionally, however, omitting the comma can cause confusion.

All the cafeteria's vegetables—broccoli, green beans, peas, and carrots—were cooked to a gray mush.

Without the comma after *peas*, you wouldn't know if there were three choices (the third being a *mixture* of peas and carrots) or four.

Coordinate adjectives—two or more adjectives that relate equally to the noun they modify—should be separated by commas.

The long, twisting, muddy road led to a shack in the woods.

In a sentence like *The cracked bathroom mirror reflected his face*, however, *cracked* and *bathroom* are not coordinate because *bathroom mirror* is the equivalent of a single word, which is modified by *cracked*. Hence they are *not* separated by commas.

You can usually determine whether adjectives are coordinate by inserting *and* between them. If the sentence makes sense with the *and* added, the adjectives are coordinate and should be separated by commas.

> They are sincere *and* talented *and* inquisitive researchers.

The sentence makes sense with the *and*s, so the adjectives should be separated by commas: *They are sincere, talented, inquisitive researchers.*

> Byron carried an elegant ~~and~~ pocket watch.

The sentence does not make sense with *and*, so the adjectives *elegant* and *pocket* should not be separated by commas: *Byron carried an elegant pocket watch.*

Setting Off Parenthetical and Transitional Expressions

Parenthetical expressions add comments or information. Because they often interrupt the flow of a sentence, they are usually set off with commas.

> Some studies have shown that chocolate‚ of all things‚ helps prevent tooth decay.
>   ^   ^

Transitions (such as *as a result*), **conjunctive adverbs** (such as *however*), and other expressions used to connect parts of sentences are usually set off with commas.

> Ozone is a by-product of dry cleaning‚ for example.
>   ^

Setting Off Contrasting Elements, Interjections, Direct Address, and Tag Questions

> I asked you‚ *not your brother*‚ to sweep the porch.

> *Holy cow*‚ did you see that?

> Remember‚ *sir*‚ that you are under oath.

> The governor did not veto the bill‚ *did she*?

Setting Off Parts of Dates and Addresses

Dates.   Use a comma between the day of the week and the month, between the day of the month and the year, and between the year and the rest of the sentence, if any.

On Wednesday, November 26, 2008, gunmen arrived in Mumbai by boat.
       ∧   ∧   ∧

Do not use commas with dates in inverted order or with dates consisting of only the month and the year.

She dated the letter 5 August 2013.

Thousands of Germans swarmed over the wall in November 1989.

Addresses and Place Names.   Use a comma after each part of an address or a place name, including the state if there is no ZIP code. Do not precede a ZIP code with a comma.

Forward my mail to the Department of English, The Ohio State
University, Columbus, Ohio 43210.   ∧
        ∧   ∧

Portland, Oregon, is much larger than Portland, Maine.
       ∧   ∧   ∧

Setting Off Quotations

Commas set off a quotation from words used to introduce or identify the source of the quotation. A comma following a quotation goes *inside* the closing quotation mark.

A German proverb warns, "Go to law for a sheep, and lose your cow."
                      ∧

"All I know about grammar," said Joan Didion, "is its infinite power."
                    ∧   ∧

Do not use a comma following a question mark or an exclamation point.

"Out, damned spot!/" cries Lady Macbeth.

Do not use a comma to introduce a quotation with *that* or when you do not quote a speaker's exact words.

The writer of Ecclesiastes concludes that/ "all is vanity."

Patrick Henry declared/ that he wanted either liberty or death.

Avoiding Unnecessary Commas

Excessive use of commas can spoil an otherwise fine sentence.

Around Restrictive Elements.   Do not use commas to set off restrictive elements—elements that limit, or define, the meaning of the words they modify or refer to.

I don't let my children watch movies/ that are violent.

The actor/ Joaquin Phoenix/ might win the award.

Between Subjects and Verbs, Verbs and Objects or Complements, and Prepositions and Objects.   Do not use a comma between a subject and its **verb**, a verb and its **object** or complement, or a **preposition** and its object.

Watching movies late at night/ allows me to relax.

Parents must decide/ what time their children should go to bed.

The winner of/ the prize for community service stepped forward.

In Compound Constructions.   In compound constructions other than compound sentences, do not use a comma before or after a coordinating conjunction that joins the two parts.

Improved health care/ and more free trade were two of the administration's goals.

The *and* joins parts of a compound subject, which should not be separated by a comma.

Mark Twain trained as a printer/ and worked as a steamboat pilot.

The *and* joins parts of a compound predicate, which should not be separated by a comma.

In a Series.   Do not use a comma before the first or after the last item in a series.

The auction included/ furniture, paintings, and china.

The swimmer took slow, elegant, powerful/ strokes.

4.3 Grammatical Rules

Parallel structure is ensuring that you use the same pattern of a word or phrase throughout a sentence. The main goal is to ensure that you do not mix structures or forms.

The students are completing their homework, finished their studying, and plan to go to bed.

In this example, verb forms are mixed throughout the sentence.

Better: The students completed their homework, finished their studying, and went to bed.

Notice here how all of the verbs are in past tense.

One of the more serious errors you can make in your writing is a **sentence fragment**; this is when your sentence is missing either a complete subject or verb.

The dog ran outside into the rain. Which resulted in his owner getting soaked.

In this example, the fragment can be combined with the sentence before it with a comma.

Better: The dog ran outside into the rain, which resulted in his owner getting soaked.

People eating outside.

In this example, a main verb is missing, and the addition of *are* before *eating* would make this fragment a complete sentence.

Better: People are eating outside.

Comma Splices

A **comma splice** occurs when a comma incorrectly joins two independent clauses.

The snow is supposed to begin at midnight, however, that looks unlikely to happen.

The lines at the dining hall are very long, Sally will likely miss her next class.

You can correct a comma splice in the following ways:
- Join the sentences with a semicolon (usually the easiest and most grammatical correction).
- Use a period to create two separate sentences (grammatically correct but can result in choppy flow).
- Join the sentences with a comma and a coordinating conjunction.
- Join the sentences with a semicolon and a transitional word or phrase (followed by a comma), such as *however, therefore,* or *for example*.

Using the examples shown above, here are two corrections:

The snow is supposed to begin at midnight; however, that looks unlikely to happen.

The lines at the dining hall are very long, so Sally will likely miss her next class.

Run-on/Fused Sentences

A **run-on**, or fused, sentence happens when two sentences are fused together with no punctuation between them.

The homework was very difficult I stayed up all night trying to complete it.

The dog barked most of the night it made sleeping nearly impossible.

You can correct a run-on sentence in the following ways:

- Join the sentences with a semicolon (usually the easiest and most grammatical correction).

- Use a period to create two separate sentences (grammatically correct but can result in choppy flow).

- Join the sentences with a comma and a coordinating conjunction.

Using the examples above, here are two corrections:

The homework was very difficult; I stayed up all night trying to complete it.

The dog barked most of the night, and it made sleeping nearly impossible.

Semicolons

A semicolon is a modified period. It functions in the same way that a period does—it connects two independent clauses—but it's not as strong a punctuation mark as a period.

A simple rule to remember is that a semicolon must have an independent clause (a complete sentence) on either side of it.

The furniture will be delivered this afternoon; someone will need to be home to receive it.

Sarah and Benjamin worked on their fieldwork papers all day; they are going to see a movie in the evening to take a break.

You can also use semicolons to separate items in a series that contain commas or that are complete sentences.

The work for next week includes the proposal, which is two pages long, and is due on Monday; the report, which is ten pages long, and is due on Wednesday; and the presentation, which is five minutes long, and is due on Friday.

Colons

Colons are used to introduce material or to offer an explanation; they are also commonly used before a list. When you use a colon, an independent clause should precede it.

Next week, the conference will be scheduled in four cities: Blacksburg, Charlottesville, Richmond, and Norfolk.

Colons are also used after a salutation in a business letter, when telling time, or in certain titles.

Dear Dr. Thompson:
11:17 a.m.
Writing Is Fun: The Importance of Being Concise

4.4 The Top Twenty

Some of the errors discussed above are included in the following list of the top twenty errors most often seen in students' writing. However, not all of the top twenty errors are covered above. Make sure to review the errors below to help improve your writing.

1. Wrong Word

                             precedence
Religious texts, for them, take ~~prescience~~ over other kinds of sources.
                                ^

Prescience means "foresight," and *precedence* means "priority."

                        allergy
The child suffered from a severe ~~allegory~~ to peanuts.
                         ^

Allegory is a spell-checker's replacement for a misspelling of *allergy*.

                                   of
The panel discussed the ethical implications ~~on~~ the situation.
                                        ^

Wrong-word errors can involve using a word with the wrong shade of meaning, using a word with a completely wrong meaning, or using a wrong preposition or another wrong word in an idiom. Selecting a word from a thesaurus without knowing its meaning or allowing a spell-checker to correct spelling automatically can lead to wrong-word errors, so use these tools with care. If you have trouble with prepositions and idioms, memorize the standard usage.

2. Missing Comma after an Introductory Element

Determined to get the job done, we worked all weekend.
                                        ^

Although the study was flawed, the results may still be useful.
                                    ^

Readers usually need a small pause—signaled by a comma—between an introductory word, phrase, or clause and the main part of the sentence. Use a comma after every introductory element. When the introductory element is very short, you don't always need a comma, but including it is never wrong.

3. Incomplete or Missing Documentation

                                                                    ” (263).
Satrapi says, "When we're afraid, we lose all sense of analysis and reflection."
                                                                            ^

The page number of the print source for this quotation must be included.

                                                            ("100 Best").
According to one source, James Joyce wrote two of the five best novels of all time.
                                                                            ^

The source mentioned should be identified (this online source has no author or page numbers).

Cite each source you refer to in the text, following the guidelines of the documentation style you are using. Omitting documentation can result in charges of plagiarism.

4. Vague Pronoun Reference

Possible Reference to More Than One Word

Transmitting radio signals by satellite is a way of overcoming the problem of scarce

                                    the airwaves
airwaves and limiting how ~~they~~ are used.
                            ^

In the original sentence, *they* could refer to the signals or to the airwaves.

Reference Implied but Not Stated

                            a policy
The company prohibited smoking, ~~which~~ many employees resented.
                                    ^

What does *which* refer to? The editing clarifies what employees resented.

A pronoun should refer clearly to the word or words it replaces (called the *antecedent*) elsewhere in the sentence or in a previous sentence. If more than one word could be the antecedent, or if no specific antecedent is present, edit to make the meaning clear.

5. Spelling (Including Homonyms)

Ronald ~~Regan~~ **Reagan** won the election in a landslide.
^

~~Every where~~ **Everywhere** we went, we saw crowds of tourists.
^

The most common misspellings today are those that spell-checkers cannot identify. The categories that spell-checkers are most likely to miss include homonyms, compound words incorrectly spelled as separate words, and proper nouns, particularly names. After you run the spell-checker, proofread carefully for errors such as these—and be sure to run the spell-checker to catch other kinds of spelling mistakes.

6. Mechanical Error with a Quotation

"I grew up the victim of a disconcerting confusion, " Rodriguez says (249).
^

The comma should be placed *inside* the quotation marks.

Follow conventions when using quotation marks with commas, colons, and other punctuation. Always use quotation marks in pairs, and follow the guidelines of your documentation style for block quotations. Use quotation marks for titles of short works, but use italics for titles of long works.

7. Unnecessary Comma

Before Conjunctions in Compound Constructions That Are Not Compound Sentences

This conclusion applies to the United States/and to the rest of the world.

No comma is needed before *and* because it is joining two phrases that modify the same verb, *applies.*

With Restrictive Elements

Many parents/of gifted children/ do not want them to skip a grade.

No comma is needed to set off the restrictive phrase *of gifted children,* which is necessary to indicate which parents the sentence is talking about.

Do not use commas to set off **restrictive elements** that are necessary to the meaning of the words they modify. Do not use a comma before a coordinating conjunction (*for, and, nor, but, or, yet, so*) when the conjunction does not join parts of a compound sentence (error 13). Do not use a comma before the first or after the last item in a series, between a subject and verb, between a verb and its **object** or object/complement, or between a **preposition** and its object.

8. Unnecessary or Missing Capitalization

Some ~~Traditional~~ ^{traditional} Chinese ~~Medicines~~ ^{medicines} containing ~~Ephedra~~ ^{ephedra} remain legal.

Capitalize proper nouns and proper adjectives, the first words of sentences, and important words in titles, along with certain words indicating directions and family relationships. Do not capitalize most other words. When in doubt, check a dictionary.

9. Missing Word

The site foreman discriminated ^{against} women and promoted men with less experience.

Proofread carefully for omitted words, including prepositions, parts of two-part verbs, and correlative conjunctions. Be particularly careful not to omit words from quotations.

10. Faulty Sentence Structure

~~The information which high~~ ^{High} school athletes are presented with ~~mainly includes~~

information on what credits ~~needed~~ ^{they need} to graduate, ~~and thinking about the college~~

which ~~athletes are trying~~ ^{colleges to try} to play for, and ^{how to} apply.

A sentence that starts out with one kind of structure and then changes to another kind can confuse readers. Make sure that each sentence contains a subject and a verb, that subjects and **predicates** make sense together, and that comparisons have clear meanings. When you join elements (such as subjects or verb phrases) with a coordinating conjunction, make sure that the elements have parallel structures.

11. Missing Comma with a Nonrestrictive Element

Marina, who was the president of the club, was first to speak.

The clause *who was the president of the club* does not affect the basic meaning of the sentence: Marina was first to speak.

A nonrestrictive element gives information not essential to the basic meaning of the sentence. Use commas to set off a nonrestrictive element.

12. Unnecessary Shift in Verb Tense

Priya was watching the great blue heron. Then she ~~slips~~ and ~~falls~~ into the swamp.
<small>slipped</small> <small>fell</small>

Verbs that shift from one **tense** to another with no clear reason can confuse readers.

13. Missing Comma in a Compound Sentence

Meredith waited for Samir, and her sister grew impatient.

Without the comma, a reader may think at first that Meredith waited for both Samir and her sister.

A compound sentence consists of two or more parts that could each stand alone as a sentence. When the parts are joined by a coordinating conjunction, use a comma before the conjunction to indicate a pause between the two thoughts.

14. Unnecessary or Missing Apostrophe (Including *Its/It's*)

Overambitious parents can be very harmful to a ~~childs~~ well-being.
<small>child's</small>

The library is having ~~it's~~ annual fund-raiser. ~~Its~~ for a good cause.
<small>its</small> <small>It's</small>

To make a noun **possessive**, add either an apostrophe and an *-s* (*Ed's book*) or an apostrophe alone (*the boys' gym*). Do *not* use an apostrophe in the possessive pronouns *ours*, *yours*, and *hers*. Use *its* to mean *belonging to it*; use *it's* only when you mean *it is* or *it has*.

15. Fused (Run-On) Sentence

Klee's paintings seem simple, they are very sophisticated.
<small>but</small>

~~She~~ doubted the value of meditation, she decided to try it once.
<small>Although she</small>

A **fused sentence** (also called a *run-on*) joins clauses that could each stand alone as a sentence with no punctuation or words to link them. Fused sentences must either be divided into separate sentences or joined by adding words or punctuation.

16. Comma Splice

I was strongly attracted to her, she was beautiful and funny.
<small>for</small>

We hated the meat loaf/ the cafeteria served ~~it~~ every Friday.
<small>that</small>

A comma splice occurs when only a comma separates clauses that could each stand alone as a sentence. To correct a comma splice, you can insert a semicolon or period, connect the clauses with a word such as *and* or *because*, or restructure the sentence.

17. Lack of Pronoun-Antecedent Agreement

All students   uniforms.
~~Every student~~ must provide their own ~~uniform.~~
  ^   ^

                       its
Each of the puppies thrived in ~~their~~ new home.
                            ^

Pronouns must agree with their antecedents in gender (male or female) and in number (singular or plural). Many **indefinite pronouns**, such as *everyone* and *each*, are always singular. When a singular antecedent can refer to a man or a woman, either rewrite the sentence to make the antecedent plural or to eliminate the pronoun, or use *his or her*, *he or she*, and so on. When antecedents are joined by *or* or *nor*, the pronoun must agree with the closer antecedent. A collective noun such as *team* can be either singular or plural, depending on whether the members are seen as a group or as individuals.

18. Poorly Integrated Quotation

                        showed how color affects taste:
A 1970s study of what makes food appetizing "Once it became apparent that the
                                        ^

steak was actually blue and the fries were green, some people became ill"

Schlosser 565).

    According to Lars Eighner,
  "Dumpster diving has serious drawbacks as a way of life" (~~Eighner~~ 383). Finding
  ^
edible food is especially tricky.

Quotations should all fit smoothly into the surrounding sentence structure. They should be linked clearly to the writing around them (usually with a signal phrase) rather than dropped abruptly into the writing.

19. Unnecessary or Missing Hyphen

This paper looks at fictional and real-life examples.
                                    ^

A compound adjective modifying a noun that follows it requires a hyphen.

The buyers want to fix⁄up the house and resell it.

A two-word verb should not be hyphenated.

A compound adjective that appears before a noun needs a hyphen. However, be careful not to hyphenate two-word verbs or word groups that serve as subject complements.

20. Sentence Fragment

No Subject

Marie Antoinette spent huge sums of money on herself and her favorites.

Her extravagance
~~And~~ helped bring on the French Revolution.
∧

No Complete Verb

was
The old aluminum boat sitting on its trailer.
∧

Beginning with a Subordinating Word

where
We returned to the drugstore*/*, ~~Where~~ we waited for our buddies.
∧

A **sentence fragment** is part of a sentence that is written as if it were a complete sentence. Reading your draft out loud, backwards, sentence by sentence, will help you spot sentence fragments.

TAKING A WRITING INVENTORY

One way to learn from your mistakes is to take a writing inventory. It can help you think critically and analytically about how to improve your writing skills.

- ✔ Collect two or three pieces of your writing to which either your instructor or other students have responded.

- ✔ Read through these writings, adding your own comments about their strengths and weaknesses. How do your comments compare with those of others?

- ✔ Group all the comments into three categories—*broad content issues* (use of evidence and sources, attention to purpose and audience, and overall impression), *organization and presentation* (overall and paragraph-level organization, sentence structure and style, and design and formatting), and *surface errors* (problems with spelling, grammar, punctuation, and mechanics).

- ✔ Make an inventory of your own strengths in each category.

- ✔ Study your errors. Mark every instructor and peer comment that suggests or calls for an improvement, and put all these comments in a list. Consult the relevant part of this book or speak with your instructor if you don't understand a comment.

✔ Make a list of the top problem areas you need to work on. How can you make improvements? Then note at least two strengths that you can build on in your writing. Record your findings in a writing log that you can add to as the class proceeds.

■ Activity 4.1

Look at a paper your instructor has graded and identify the errors you made the most. Using the principles discussed in this chapter, correct your errors and see how the corrections improve your writing.

■ Activity 4.2

Correct the following sentences:

1. The snow is falling quickly it will begin to pile up soon.
2. A good writer will edit their work before submitting it.
3. My laptop beginning to crash.
4. I really enjoyed the movie's plot, and that it wasn't very long.
5. Reading is one of my favorite hobbies it's a good way to spend a rainy day.
6. When my phone rang I stopped the DVD to answer it.
7. The contractors are quickly building the house and it should be ready by the holidays.

■ Activity 4.3

Find a blog post on a topic that interests you. Look for errors discussed in this chapter. What errors do you notice? Do the errors have an impact on how you read the author's work? If so, what is the impact?

4.5 Style

You may have heard that someone has a great "style" in his or her writing. There are many stylistic preferences that instructors have for writing. Below we will discuss a few areas of style that can help you become a stronger writer. Remember too that the more you write, the better writer you become, and these stylistic rules will soon become easy to follow. Reading effective pieces of writing, such as the essays assigned in this book, will also help you become a better writer because these readings demonstrate the stylistic principles you should emulate in your own writing.

Using Specific Language

The words you choose have specific meanings, and you want to make sure that your readers understand these meanings as you do.

The following words are inherently vague and should be avoided when possible:

thing	this	that	it
society	good	bad	etc.

Do not use these words to begin a sentence or in the thesis statement of your essay.

This was a fascinating book to read.

Improved: *Harry Potter and the Sorcerer's Stone* was a fascinating book to read.

Using specific words makes your writing clearer and ensures your audience is correctly interpreting your meaning.

Avoiding Passive Voice and "To Be" Verbs

Whenever possible, you should use concrete, specific verbs. Doing so will make your writing more descriptive and accurate. Reliance, on the verb "to be"—*is, am, are, was, were*, and so on—weakens your writing and places less emphasis on the action of the sentence.

Passive voice is another style issue that weakens your writing. In some disciplines, passive voice is preferred because it places less emphasis on the subject and hides what is really going on. However, in English classes, you want to use **active voice** as much as possible to have clear subjects in your sentences. When the subject of your sentence is continually hidden, your points may potentially seem less important, resulting in comprehension issues.

To identify passive voice, look for a "to be" verb followed by a verb in past tense:

Passive Voice: The message was written on the blackboard.

Active Voice: The teacher wrote the message on the blackboard.

Passive Voice: The ball was thrown at the last second of the game.

Active Voice: The basketball player threw the ball at the last second of the game.

Passive Voice: The report was developed over four weeks.

Active Voice: The group of students developed the report over four weeks.

Being Concise While Also Varying Your Sentences

When you start to write, it can be difficult to simply get your ideas out. By trying to meet the length requirement for an assignment, you also may write long sentences and paragraphs. To avoid wordiness, choose strong nouns and verbs that convey your point in as few words as possible. Don't pad or add "fluff" to your sentences by using excessive qualifiers (for example, *so very*, *always*); once you have made your point, move on.

> **Wordy:** Throughout history, advertising has been a part of our fascinating and ever-changing culture.
>
> **More Concise:** Advertisements have an impact on the American culture.
>
> **Wordy:** Writing a long paper can be so difficult, and I always have a very hard time getting started, especially writing introductions.
>
> **More Concise:** Writing a long paper is difficult, and it's especially hard to write an introduction.

Writing shorter, more concise sentences is important, but be sure to also vary your sentences: Some sentences should be short and some should be long. If your paragraphs contain only very short sentences, the flow of your sentences will be choppy overall. Conversely, if your paragraphs contain only long sentences, your meaning can get lost. Choose your words and phrases deliberately, as all of the words and phrases in your papers should relate back to your main idea or thesis and aid in the overall development of that idea.

Avoiding Clichés

Some students rely heavily on clichés—phrases that are overused and that can make your writing trite or redundant. For example, notice how the clichés used in the following paragraph impede the meaning of the words. How many clichés can you find in this example?

> I'm sitting down to write a personal narrative, but I'm dog tired. It's hard when you're busy as a bee to find time to write, and I'd like to receive an A on the paper, but that's putting the cart before the horse. To write an effective personal narrative, one must air dirty laundry and perhaps reveal some skeletons in the closet, but that may seem like I have an ax to grind. I'm at my wits' end as I sit to write this, but I'm hoping my teacher will be all ears. After all, there's a fat chance that I'm going to write in depth about a family affair and push the envelope, so my teacher will have to read between the lines when all is said and done. I'm hoping she's not waiting for the other shoe to drop with my writing, but I suppose that's the way the cookie crumbles.

Transitions and Flow

Transitions are like bridges in your papers. They help smooth the flow of thought between sentences and paragraphs. Without proper use of transitions, your papers will have a choppy flow, and your audience may have difficulty following the sequence and development of your ideas.

Sometimes, the flow *between two sentences* can be choppy. In that case, it's usually best to add a transition to help improve the flow.

> It is cold outside. Children should make sure to wear a warm coat to school in the morning.

> It is cold outside, so children should make sure to wear a warm coat to school in the morning.

When the flow *between paragraphs* needs improvement, add transitions as "hook" words or phrases that connect two ideas, and therefore paragraphs, together. You can also think of these transitions as "echo" words.

> **First Paragraph:** …Therefore, being concise in your writing is one of the most important style principles.

> **Second Paragraph:** Because of the importance of being concise in writing, instructors should teach how to write effectively early in the semester.

Here, the words *importance, concise,* and *writing* help connect the paragraphs together, with these words from the first paragraph echoed in the second sentence.

Use the following list to help choose transitional words or phrases:

Adding or Showing Time (helpful in narratives):
and, also, next, too, then, first, second, third, finally, in addition, moreover, immediately

Comparing (helpful in argumentative writing):
however, nevertheless, on the other hand, as stated previously, although, others may argue

Concluding (helpful for writing a conclusion to any paper):
finally, in conclusion, in summary, to sum up, to conclude, as stated, as explained

Giving Examples (helpful in writing with sources):
for example, as previously explained, for instance, to illustrate, to state, to explain

Showing Exception (helpful in argumentative writing):
nevertheless, on the other hand, however, in contrast, despite, contrary to previous findings

■ **Activity 4.4** **Being Specific**

In a nearly finished draft of your paper, circle every vague word. Change these words to be more specific, particularly vague words that begin sentences.

■ **Activity 4.5**

Write a paragraph of about 250 words describing your classroom, without using any of the following words: *this, that, it, thing, you, I, we,* and *us.* After writing the paragraph, analyze how difficult it was to write and how you could apply these principles to all your writing.

■ **Activity 4.6** **Passive Voice and "To Be" Verbs**

In a nearly finished draft of your paper, circle every verb. Identify "to be" verbs and those that create passive voice in your paper.

■ **Activity 4.7**

Write a 250-word paragraph about yourself without using any passive voice or "to be" verbs. What kinds of verbs did you have to use instead? Was this a difficult task? Why? How can you apply what you've learned here to your other assignments?

■ **Activity 4.8** **Transitions and Flow**

Read a paper you've previously submitted to your instructor backward: from the conclusion up to the introduction. Does the paper make sense? Are there areas where you could have inserted stronger transitions to make the parts better fit together?

■ **Activity 4.9**

Before your next major assignment is due, read your work aloud to catch errors you may miss on the computer screen and to identify choppy flow. How can you better improve the flow of your paper? Do you need to insert transitions between sentences and paragraphs? What transitional words or phrases work best?

Chapter 5

Developing an Argument

K nowing how to effectively and professionally develop an argument is an important skill in college and beyond. Until this point, you've probably considered the basic papers and presentations from high school to be "arguments," with little function beyond proving to teachers that you understand how to present your ideas clearly. But arguments have important purposes outside of the classroom, and in the college setting you'll frequently be asked to develop arguments for real-world scenarios. After you graduate, you may need to write speeches or articles to persuade others; to create and develop a persuasive proposal for a project; or to enact change in your community, government, or job. Informally, you may need to use the strategies of argumentation when discussing issues in a committee, solving problems in a team setting, or effectively resolving disagreements among coworkers or employees. The goal of this chapter is to gradually develop your ability to effectively compose arguments. With practice, you will begin to internalize different strategies, allowing you to draw on the skills reflexively when necessary. Whether you're writing a research paper, developing a senior capstone project, or composing a speech or presentation, the strategies and activities that follow should provide you with a clear sense of where and how to begin.

5.1 What Is an Argument?

Before we can discuss what argument is, we must acknowledge what it isn't. Most of us have engaged in an "argument" at some point, but we need to recognize the difference between argument and what could be better termed a "fight" or a "debate." Argument may seem to share a similar context, but it is neither of these things.

Argument Isn't a Fight

The word *argument* brings to mind verbal disagreement. Think of how you have used the term *argument* in this way: "I got into a huge argument with my mother," or "My roommate and I had a big argument last night." When we hear argument used in this context, we associate it with anger, hostility, raised voices, and slamming doors. We think of angry talk-show hosts and guests, trolling *YouTube* commenters, or righteously outraged politicians.

But this confuses *arguing* with *fighting*. Argument does not imply anger or heated verbal discussion, and is not intended to rile up, offend, or frustrate. An argument is not about winning or losing but about productive discussion and creative problem solving. When well constructed and developed, arguments should leave audiences curious, inspired, reflective, and motivated to learn more. When you think of argument, instead of imagining heated disagreements, envision a round-table discussion: reasonable individuals who disagree conversing in an attempt to find common ground, to learn from and instruct one another. Keep this image in mind as you move through this chapter, as you will be asked in your first-year writing course to enter a conversation with your own argument.

Argument Isn't a Debate

Because argument is not about winning or losing, you must move beyond thinking of argument as a *debate*. Debating is a useful, skill-building tool, encouraging you to anticipate counterpoints and develop skillful rebuttals. But it also creates the context of winners and losers, of two opponents (audience and author) competing with one another. As the author of an argument, you might be tempted to think of your goal as winning by overwhelming your audience with skillful rhetoric.

But you need to take a different approach. Argument is about inquiry and discovery, about creatively solving problems through productive conversation. Imagine sitting at a table and having a conversation, with the goal of winning against the others seated around you. You see them as antagonists and opponents, and they are keenly aware of this. When they present views you disagree with, you don't listen rhetorically; instead, you leap into the fray, countering their arguments and research with your own views. Eventually the conversation ends, and everybody leaves the room mildly disgruntled and with the same views they entered with, some even more deeply rooted than before. Nothing productive has occurred.

This is the key weakness of debate: It fails to *persuade*. It may occasionally bump a neutral audience off the fence, but it cannot shift the positions of those who already hold opposing views. And this is the ultimate purpose of argument: to *persuade* audiences to revisit or reconsider their current positions. When we take our seat at the table, it should be with a willingness to understand our audience and with the goal of persuading them not to capitulate, but to re-envision, reflect, or reconsider. Debaters in a courtroom or in politics may cleverly employ *pathos* by inciting fear, anger, hopefulness, or pride in agreeing audiences in order to claim victory, but appealing to those who already agree is not persuasion; it is unlikely debaters will effectively *persuade* those who disagree. And although persuasion is certainly evident in the closing arguments of a trial that attempt to sway a neutral jury, or in a political speech that tries to win undecided voters through sentimental visions of a better future, this is not the philosophy of argument we are discussing here. When rhetorically sound, based on reason, and performed responsibly with the common goals of truth seeking and persuading, an argument can be a productive and team-building act, as "opponents" gradually move closer toward understanding and consensus.

But if argument isn't about fighting or debating, then how do we approach it?

Argument Is about Truth Seeking and Persuading

As we move toward greater understanding of what an argument is, it's important to know the context in which you should construct arguments. Even before you begin developing an argument, you must have two accepted goals to be successful: to seek the truth and to persuade. As you listen to current voices and opinions in a particular conversation, it's important that you try to listen *rhetorically*, moving beyond your knee-jerk reactions to understand not only what others are saying but why they might feel the way they do. This is key to ensuring you establish a truth-seeking frame of mind as you begin to develop ideas. Once you've listened, evaluated carefully, and researched further, you'll be ready to establish your own argument. Your first goal should always be to find the truth by listening to and engaging with the current conversation (the process); your second goal is ultimately to persuade a resistant audience based on your findings (the product). Balancing these two goals and modes will strengthen your *ethos* with the audience, demonstrating your focus on inquiry and discovery and your willingness to listen to the views of others even as you persuade. This can be a difficult line to walk, but when executed well, such arguments can be strongly persuasive even with resistant audiences. In later sections, we'll address specific strategies to employ as you develop your argument, but for now, remember that before you can *argue* you must first *understand*.

Don't mistake the "truth-seeking" purpose for identifying "Truth" (or, as we call it, "Capital T Truth") and forcing an audience to accept this presumed truth. Argument is about engaging in conversation with others, combining viewpoints and knowledge to seek truth in collaboration with other voices. Rather than thinking of truth as static, fundamental, or inarguable, think of it as evolving. You contribute to the current argument, allowing our understanding of truth to grow. Others will then also contribute, adding new angles of vision and knowledge, expanding the issue further. Don't approach your argument with the view that you will discover the one and only valid opinion on the issue. Truth seeking should be the goal of everyone who has participated or will participate in the conversation.

Argument Is about Shining a Light on the Issue

To avoid presuming your argument is the one and only truth, approach your issue with the goal of shining a light on different aspects of the controversy. Rather than reviewing others' arguments, trying to find holes in their assertions, or immediately rebutting claims you disagree with, think instead about why others might hold the views they do. What experiences, values, and beliefs could influence their current views? What context likely contributed to the development of those viewpoints? What experiences, values, and beliefs influence your response to their ideas? What context are you starting from? What might they be missing about the issue? What might you be missing? Combined together, shining a light and seeking truth should guide you toward an understanding of argument as communal, purposeful. You and others participating in the argument (whether they hold views in agreement with or in opposition to yours) are seeking answers together. Question others' views, but question your own as well.

5.2 The Purpose of Argument

As mentioned above, arguing is not about winning. Don't think of your argument as unsuccessful if it doesn't change everyone's mind on the subject. Arguments aren't necessarily sound simply because they've persuaded large numbers through fear or anger. Instead, focus on your argument as part of an ongoing process, a conversation among individuals who are concerned about the issue. Your argument is not a chance to *win*; it is a chance to *learn*.

A Process and a Product

Your final argument, whether communicated in written, spoken, or visual form, is the *product* you place in the current *process* as your contribution to current discourse. Essentially, your argument is first a *product* of the conversation and, once completed, it then becomes a part of the *process*. This relates directly to argument's truth-seeking purpose—your argument is not the finale but simply another step in a never-ending process, as those engaged in the conversation continuously seek answers to their questions on the issue.

A Contribution to Current Discourse

The duality of argument (as process and product) can be difficult to grasp initially. To clarify, the simplest (and most accurate) way to think of argument is as a conversation. If we assume an argument is meant to be a fight or a debate, we end up developing products that struggle to contribute to current discourse. Our ideas exist in a vacuum, with no anticipation of a response that should be heard. In previous chapters, you learned the importance of the rhetorical situation: Arguments don't occur in a void free of context. When developing an argument, you want to consciously insert yourself into this context by identifying current discourse on a controversial issue, determining a point of entry, and contributing to the conversation. Recognizing the current conversation is vital to avoid developing an argument that adds little or nothing beyond what others have already said and to ensure you can move discourse forward (like a conversation). Arguments you compose, whether in writing, a video, or a public speech, must have significance for the issue and audience. This is what Chapter 1, "Reading and Writing Rhetorically," identified as exigence or, in the language of rhetorical appeals, *kairos*, and it is essential to developing a strong and significant argument.

You've likely already dipped your toes into an informal mode of critical discourse. When you read an editorial in the *Collegiate Times*, or listen to a *YouTube* personality review a new video game, these authors are telling you something about their worldviews. They might explain to readers the course of action they think best, the ethics of a particular belief or behavior, the problems they hope to solve, how to define something, or why they believe something has value. When you read, listen to, or view these arguments, you inevitably begin to generate an opinion in response to theirs. But you're not alone. Scroll through the comments section of an online article or blog, or those on a *YouTube* video, and you'll find others reacting to the author's opinions and voicing their own. A conversation is taking place!

Now imagine that you, propelled by your gut response but curious to learn more, leave this site and search through Newman Library's Summon databases for other opinions, Google facts and information about the issue, or even develop and administer a survey to see if others share your current views. You gradually expand your understanding of the issue and the broader conversation surrounding it. The information and opinions you encounter even (ideally) begin to refine your viewpoint; you agree in part with writer X, but the data you found make you inclined to think part of writer Y's position has merit. Your own view on the issue begins to develop complexity and nuance. Inquiry has happened! Discovery is happening! A contributive argument is developing! Understanding the conversation, listening to others' viewpoints, inquiring, and discovering are all parts of your *process* as you develop your final argument (your *product*). Remember not to think of your argument as a static product. Once it becomes part of the greater process (the conversation), others might respond, contribute, and move the conversation forward. Your views might begin to evolve further in reaction to the inquiry and discovery of others. Your argument, then, is always in some ways a *process*.

5.3 Arguments Can Take *Explicit* or *Implicit* Forms

We tend to think of arguments (within conversations) in their standard form: *explicit* arguments that present a controversial claim supported by stated reasons and evidence. But arguments can also be *implicit*, in written, spoken, and visual forms of composition. Explicit arguments directly and overtly state their positions and rationale, while implicit arguments take a less straightforward approach. Consider some implicit arguments you might encounter on a daily basis: memes, images on advocacy advertisements, product advertisements, or a story told passionately by a speaker or writer. A meme featuring a well-known politician might contain an implicit argument about the individual's views on a particular issue; an advocacy advertisement depicting a helpless child in a third-world country implicitly tells the audience they should care and provide help; advertisements for popular fragrances implicitly argue that these products will make audiences more appealing, and they might also implicitly argue what the audience should want to be (more traditionally masculine/feminine, more sexually appealing to the opposite sex). A story or narrative about the emotional and physical tolls experienced by a military veteran could implicitly be arguing for greater support and resources for military personnel. Implicit arguments can be powerful for persuading certain audiences, shifting views with subtle rather than overt techniques.

In the early stages of developing an argument, it is helpful to consider which strategy or combination of strategies will work best for your rhetorical context, as discussed in Chapter 1, "Reading and Writing Rhetorically." Don't assume you can simply construct an argument implicitly or explicitly based on your personal preference. Instead, think of the strategies you will use to construct the most persuasive argument within the argument's rhetorical context. Below are guidelines and questions to consider as you determine the best approach for your audience and argument.

Consider Message

Arguments always have an intended purpose or goal, and it's important to remember they exist on a spectrum between truth seeking and persuading. When deciding whether to use explicit or implicit constructions for your argument, first determine your ultimate goal. Some arguments are designed to improve understanding between two or more opposing groups, with the ultimate goal of encouraging both sides to reconsider certain positions, or understand the validity of each position's existence. Other arguments hope to shift the audience's point of view or position closer toward that of the author, while still others seek common ground and compromise. It's always important to think about the ultimate goal of your particular argument, as this will allow you to develop a better understanding of what you need to do to persuade successfully.

Questions to Ask about Message

- What conversation are you entering? How controversial is this conversation?
- What do the opposing sides disagree about? What might motivate these disagreements? How does each side tend to argue about the issue? What do they say?
- Where does this conversation or discourse take place?
- What is your position on the issue?
- What do you hope to add to the conversation?
- Where will your argument be read, heard, or seen?
- What do you want the audience to *do* or *think* after reading, hearing, or seeing your argument?

Consider Audience

Extremely resistant or sensitive audiences may respond more positively to an argument made using implicit strategies, while neutral, skeptical, or moderately resistant audiences will respond well to an explicit claim and reasons.

Questions to Ask about Audience

- What position does your audience currently hold?
- What underlying assumptions or values motivate this point of view?
- What past experiences may have influenced their current position?
- How aware of the issue's context (its position in current discourse) might they be?

Consider Author

Remember that you are authoring this particular argument, and your audience's response to the argument will be influenced by their perception of you—your positions, your approach, your *ethos*. Consider how you might need to present yourself to a given audience, based on what you know about them from the "Question to Ask about Audience" above.

Questions to Ask about Author

- What are your strengths as author of this argument?
- What is your position on the issue?
- What *ethos* do you currently have?
- What biases do you bring to the argument?
- What experiences, values, and beliefs influence your current view?
- How will you ensure you approach the issue with the goal of shining a light and truth seeking?
- Where have you acquired most of your knowledge on this issue?
- What research will you need to conduct to strengthen your *ethos* with this audience?
- How will your audience view you as an author?
- How should you present yourself to this audience, given what you know about their values, assumptions, and experiences?

5.4 Strategies for Development

Developing an argument successfully requires knowledge of different processes, strategies, or tools. These processes build your argument gradually, and in the next few pages we'll discuss and practice each strategy to help you internalize these stages.

Developing the Content

Many students who are new to writing try to begin drafting their papers with the introduction and thesis. They determine their topic and point of view, draft a general introduction, and state their opinion. Supporting ideas develop in subsequent paragraphs as they come up with the ideas. This makes sense if we think of writing as existing, from the beginning, in product form. If you use this approach, it's usually because you assume the best arguments are developed in linear fashion, transitioning immediately from thought to finished product. This approach might work with shorter, simplified projects or school papers, but for the longer and more complex works expected in your 1105, 1106, and H1204 courses, this strategy is prohibitive and frequently results in poorly constructed, rhetorically deficient arguments.

Instead, think of arguments as building in several stages, with each stage utilizing several proven processes to strategically and successfully develop arguments.

Synthesizing Current Discourse

The first step in developing your argument's content is to acquire a broader understanding of the conversation you wish to enter. The simplest place to start this process is to seek out a current voice in the conversation and compare it to other voices writing and conversing on that topic. This step is part of the stage we refer to as synthesis. Synthesizing allows you to compare and contrast current arguments, internalize the key points of concern or disagreement, and begin to generate questions for further inquiry.

5.5 Strategies for Synthesis

Conducting a Rhetorical Analysis of Others' Arguments

In earlier chapters you were introduced to the basics of rhetoric and practiced analyzing arguments using these basics, identifying how well arguments in different media use specific rhetorical appeals to persuade their intended audiences. The chapters on writing rhetorically and analyzing rhetorical appeals have given you the tools to evaluate the potential effectiveness of others' arguments. As you progress toward developing your own argument, it's important to continue using these skills, as you both evaluate other voices in the argument and determine the best rhetorical choices for your argument. Analyzing the arguments of others can help you begin to determine possible openings in the conversation. If a writer relies heavily on personal experience for supporting evidence, then you may find weaknesses or gaps through which to enter with stronger evidence. If they fail to anticipate and address a counterclaim or question from their audience, you have room to enter the conversation and strengthen the argument. Using rhetorical analysis allows you to identify where these weaknesses might be, and whether you agree or disagree with the argument, you can find your point of entry and contribute to the conversation.

Questions for Rhetorical Analysis

- What is the message/purpose of the argument?
- Who is the author?
- Who is the intended audience? What is their position on the issue?
- What is the context of the author's argument, its *kairos*?
- Where does the author use *pathos* to persuade the audience?
- Where does the author utilize *ethos*? *Logos*?

Responding to Current Discourse

After you've analyzed a current argument rhetorically (whether it be an editorial, essay, article, or blog post), you can begin to participate in the conversation by responding to the author's arguments. This step is key in determining your current point of view, recognizing your own biases, and developing a sense of where you might need to conduct further research to fully synthesize the current conversation. At this stage, freewriting is one of the most useful strategies for generating ideas.

Questions for Freewritten Response

- Which of the author's points do you agree with? Why?
- Which do you disagree with? Why?
- What do you think the author is missing about the issue?
- What ideas or possibilities does the author fail to consider?
- Why are these potentially important?

Asking Questions

At this stage it might be tempting to immediately establish your own position and determine whether you agree or disagree with the author's ideas. Instead, first ask critical questions to help you maintain the truth-seeking purpose at this early stage.

Questions for Inquiry

- Has the *kairos* of the conversation changed? How?
- What questions do you have about the issue itself? The facts surrounding the situation?
- What types of evidence does the author rely on? How recent are the author's sources? What type of evidence might be more reliable?
- What information do you need to determine your own position's validity?

Common Pitfalls

Many young writers initially struggle making the leap from analysis to argument. When asked to join a conversation with others in a multisided argument (an argument that enters a current conversation on the chosen topic, rather than presenting a non-contributive thesis), some writers will analyze the argument, instead of contributing to it. Here are some common ways writers do this:

- The writer focuses on describing or summarizing the arguments of others rather than explaining how their own opinions will contrast or build on the ideas of others.

- The writer focuses on explaining the strengths and/or weaknesses of the others' arguments, rather than emphasizing their own argument and contribution to current discourse.

- The writer focuses on undermining or rebutting the views of others, rather than moving the conversation forward.

- The writer focuses on supporting why the others are correct (rearguing the original authors' points), rather than adding something the other writers missed or didn't address.

- The writer focuses on developing a "compare and contrast" of several different articles or essays, rather than synthesizing voices and establishing a thesis that adds to the conversation.

Activity 5.1

Read William Zinsser's "College Pressures" (pages 385–390). Examine the differences between analyzing this essay as opposed to responding to it and contributing to the conversation. Then, work in your group to identify the key differences and transitions from analysis to response and inquiry. This will help you begin to internalize the processes necessary to synthesize ideas, preparing you to do so independently in later activities and assignments.

Directions: In your group, nominate a speaker, reader(s), and a recorder. The speaker should be prepared to share answers, and the recorder will be responsible for writing down your answers and handing them in after class. Your reader(s) will read the three sections (Rhetorical Analysis, Response, and Questions for Inquiry) to improve group comprehension. Read along as your readers read the sections aloud.

Then, work together to answer the following questions:

- What are the main differences you see in writing a rhetorical analysis as opposed to developing a response and questions for inquiry?

- In what ways does the role of the writer differ the most when conducting an analysis as opposed to responding and inquiring?

- Review the three sections again. Which ideas from the rhetorical analysis connect to the writer's points of response? Which parts of the analysis and response inspired the questions for inquiry?

Rhetorical Analysis of Zinsser Excerpt

Purpose

- Zinsser's purpose is to persuade his audience to consider the stress students are under in college and to ultimately reconsider how they approach and understand the purpose of college.

Audience

- Zinsser appears to address an audience comprised of current college students and possibly parents and university administrators as well.

Kairos

- Zinsser indicates that events of the decade in which he's writing (1970s) have contributed to some of the problems and pressures students face.

Logos

- Zinsser supports his reason that students will *need* to break the circles they're trapped in by providing a quote from Carlos Hortas, identifying the seriousness of the circles' impact on students' experiences in college.

- Zinsser supports the idea that students should not just select their major based on the highest pay scale post-college by providing a hypothetical example in which the students' lives might become ones of "colorless mediocrity" (para. 33).

Ethos

- Zinsser demonstrates his *ethos* to students in the audience, building a bridge to them by identifying his concern for their futures.

- Zinsser demonstrates his authority on the issue by citing Hortas, the dean of Branford College at Yale.

Pathos

- Zinsser uses evocative language to characterize the current situation of students in college— "violence is being done" (para. 32), "their parents' dreams" (para. 31), and "their classmates' fears" (para. 31)—to create an emotional response in the audience.

Response to Zinsser Excerpt

- My own experience with college is similar to what Zinsser describes, but it's slightly different. I've felt under a great deal of pressure, but I've never felt that my parents were pressuring me into a particular field of study. They've just been supportive and encouraged me to find something I like that will be marketable after college.

- I think Zinsser might be wrong in believing that students should take risks in college. Many friends I know, as well as myself, are concerned about how much college costs and how they will find jobs after college to pay it off. It might be wise for students to seriously consider the average salaries in their major when selecting a course of study.

- I'm not sure I agree with Zinsser that students are the only ones who can break this circle they're trapped in. I think they *need* to, but I don't think they're ultimately capable of doing this on their own without others' support. My own experience might support this: My parents' support helps alleviate a lot of the pressure I sometimes feel.

Questions for Inquiry

- Zinsser wrote this article in the 1970s: Is the economic situation today comparable to that in the 1970s?

- Zinsser worries that students shouldn't focus on marketability of their degrees because it could lead to "colorless mediocrity" (para. 33). Do people who choose their degree based on marketability have less job satisfaction than those who are excited about their studies? Those who studied liberal arts?

Activity 5.2   Practicing Synthesis

Read Thomas H. Benton's article "The Seven Deadly Sins of Students" (pages 326–329) to practice the skills of analysis, response, and inquiry, allowing you to begin synthesizing your views and current discourse on the issue of college students' behavior.

Step 1: Analyze Rhetorically

- Which two audiences can we assume Benton is writing for? Why? Consider where the article was published. Who likely reads the *Chronicle of Higher Education*?

- How are the two audiences' concerns different?

- What does Benton's message or purpose appear to be?

- What conversation is he entering? Why is the message relevant? (*kairos*)

- Where does Benton use *pathos* to persuade the audience?

- Where does he utilize *ethos*?

Review the paragraph where Benton addresses the sin of "lust" (para. 8) using the questions below to evaluate the *logos* of the claim.

- What are two examples Benton gives as evidence of this sin?
- According to Benton, whom should we blame for this sin?
- What assumptions/values does the audience need to share in order to agree with Benton's ideas?

Step 2: Respond to the Argument

- Which "sins" have you observed students committing (or committed yourself) in college?
- Do you agree with Benton about the seriousness of each sin?
- Before reading Benton's article, had you considered these behaviors problematic?
- What do you find logical or troubling about Benton's assumptions regarding the motivations for certain student behaviors?

Step 3: Develop Questions for Inquiry

- Based on your response, what facts do you need to verify to support your current position?
- What questions do you have about Benton's claims?
- Which points or assertions are you skeptical of?
- What information do you need to broaden your understanding of the issue?

Bringing It All Together

To complete the synthesis stage, use your questions for inquiry to find additional information about or related to the issue. You might use these questions to seek out further articles on the subject, verify facts, and strengthen your understanding of the issue's context and the views/experiences of those affected (searching for or conducting studies, surveys). With this additional information, you can synthesize and begin to establish your own contribution to the conversation.

Sample Synthesis

Below is a hypothetical student's synthesis paragraph. After reading Benton's article "The Seven Deadly Sins of Students," Jane Student chose to develop a critical research essay that argued in response to these types of views. Below is the completed synthesis that she used to construct her contribution to the conversation.

Jane's Synthesis

Although I recognize that many students do, in fact, commit the sins Benton presents in his article, the one that most concerned me was his argument about the sin
of "lust." I agree with Benton that female professors frequently suffer under the gaze
of male students, and Benton rightly places the blame on the students, arguing that
they see an attractive female faculty member as somehow entertaining or more interesting to "look at" during a boring lecture. But Benton shifts the blame in a very
problematic way when he points out how female students commit the sin of lust.
Rather than arguing that they too participate in objectification by perhaps ogling
attractive male professors, he instead argues that female students dress provocatively,
encouraging the objectifying gaze of their fellow students and professors. I believe
this argument is damaging to female students because it creates a hostile environment and strays close to victim blaming. Basically, Benton says that when female
faculty members are objectified, it's the fault of their male college students, but
when female students are objectified (by other students, by faculty) it's their own
fault because of the way they dress.

I think Benton's ideas might be representative of a larger problem that female
students face on campuses. In fact, a study conducted by Rachel M. Calogero at the
University of Kent and published in *Psychological Science* found that women who
faced frequent objectification "had a decreased motivation to challenge gender-based
inequalities and injustices." I hope to argue that faculty judgment and objectification
of female students create problems not just for the students but also for the university
because it might deter young women from taking a more active role in changing society. This should be of particular concern at Virginia Tech, where we pride ourselves
on serving communities and creating meaningful change. I hope to survey female
students and faculty about their experiences with gender-based injustices or socially
constructed expectations, and to survey male students as well about their perceptions
of female students and faculty. Hopefully, this data will help me connect the issue's
significance to an audience of faculty and students at Virginia Tech.

Assessment

Jane's synthesis begins with a specific point she wants to address from Benton's
article—his arguments about the student sin of "lust." She responds to this, saying
she disagrees and explaining why his view might be problematic. But she doesn't
stop at response. Instead, she tries to take it further, using the information collected
during her inquiry step to move the conversation forward and connect it directly to
her anticipated audience.

The tentative argument she sets up in her synthesis allows her to enter a current ongoing conversation (one Benton was also participating in) and ensures that
she begins to move that conversation forward by contributing something new (she
wants to look at the ramifications of judging female students in this way, and how

that might be affecting Virginia Tech). Her argument is still in its early stages, with plenty of room for the thesis to be refined and qualified, but she is no longer writing a basic school paper. Instead, she's beginning to develop a contribution to current critical discourse, one that might be printed in the *Collegiate Times*, presented at a research conference for undergraduates, or published online. Her argument is the *product* of what she learned from the current *process* (the conversation), and once finished, she can enter it into that *process*, allowing others to respond and move the conversation forward once again.

■ **Activity 5.3**   **Process Activity: Completing the Synthesis Process**

Required Materials: Any freewritten response to a reading—the facts, opinions, and information—you have created to answer your questions for inquiry.

Directions: Briefly review your freewritten response and the facts, opinions, and information you gathered to answer your questions for inquiry. Use the prompts below to synthesize this information with the ideas of the original author, drafting one to two paragraphs using the prompts as a guide for organization and content.

- Which key point(s) did you agree or disagree with in the original article? Why?

- Compare and contrast the information you collected to the arguments made by the original author—do the facts, opinions, and information support, disprove, agree, or disagree with the original author's arguments?

- What do you think the original author is missing about this issue? What do you hope to add to the conversation? Why are your ideas important? How will you connect your argument to the values and concerns of the audience?

5.6 Constructing the Framework of the Argument

Synthesizing current voices and information with your own ideas gives you a jump start on refining your thesis. Now you're ready to begin creating the framework for the body or bulk of your argument—its supporting reasons, articulated assumptions, anticipated points of rebuttal, and necessary concessions to opposing research and views. To do this, you'll need to begin developing possible supporting reasons for your tentative thesis.

Once again, we'll break this process of framing or outlining your argument down into several strategic steps.

The Seven-Minute Paper

Many students struggle to develop their arguments because they suffer from the initial writer's block—they may wish their arguments to be fully formed before committing them to paper or refrain from writing down supporting reasons until they've completed their research and thought their arguments through in their entirety. But developing an argument isn't about perfection in every step of the process, or even in the first draft. Instead, it's about taking small steps that allow you to watch your argument build and your ideas shift and change as you discover new research and sometimes even change your own point of view. This allows you to enter the development stage with a strong truth-seeking purpose—your goal is inquiry and discovery of the truth, even as you consider how best to persuade the audience to accept the truth you've uncovered. This can certainly feel intimidating and unfamiliar, which is why the gradual, step-by-step approach can make development more manageable.

One strategy that many students find extremely helpful at this early stage is to write the "seven-minute paper." Essentially, this is the freewritten, "this-paper-is-due-in-seven-minutes-what-do-I-say" version of your argument. It's flawed, potentially repetitive, sometimes clear to no one but you; but it puts all of your current thoughts in one place, allowing you to determine potential supporting reasons and points you will need to bring into the conversation.

Guidelines.   The seven-minute paper should be freewritten, with little breaks in writing, even if you feel you're repeating thoughts. If you feel at a loss for words, write a short filler sentence, even if it's simply, "I have no idea what I'm talking about right now." Try to keep your pen or pencil moving for the full seven minutes: You never know when the lightbulb of inspiration will flicker on.

Jane's Sample Seven-Minute Paper

If I'm going to argue that objectifying or allowing the objectification and judgment of female students is damaging, then I'll need to make sure I'm clear on what I mean by objectifying. Obviously someone like Benton doesn't think he's doing anything wrong or overtly damaging by saying female students in athletic gear are committing some sin of "lust" but that might just be a sign of the underlying problem being so common—or maybe socially acceptable? So I need to explain how the judgment or evaluation of some behaviors is in itself possibly objectifying. Then I'll argue how this has negative fallout for the students themselves. I mean, if female students feel that their professors are judging them based on apparel and attire, they may become much less comfortable around those professors. And this means professors can't really fulfill their purpose if they're focused on judging their students' appearance rather than their work, or if those students who would normally have questions or concerns they would bring to their professor fear some type of objectification or judgment simply because of how they've dressed. But is this also a problem that moves beyond the classroom? I mean if students are unaware that they might be judged, then the problem isn't going to be as immediate, it might instead create an atmosphere that female students struggle to function in as productively as possible. Basically another version of disempowerment even if they're unaware of it. If this is combined with other barriers they face, like assumptions about their biological capacity for learning or excelling in certain areas, or their ethos on subjects, then it might create a situation where they're influenced by those views and judgments even if they're not consciously aware of it. So how does this affect VT? VT has a few clubs that focus on engaging female students in STEM fields, creating connections and support systems. They clearly care about the broader issue of few women in these fields but they might be missing one of the key underlying causes that Benton's article unintentionally reveals. If VT promotes support for female scholarship but doesn't educate students and faculty about how to make this an inclusive environment, then they might not be able to successfully reach their goals for equipping all students to serve and improve their communities. Maybe they aren't focused enough on improving the VT community? What have other schools done to accomplish this? Have any other schools looked at this specific issue and tried to fix it?

Assessment.   Jane's paper is simply one long paragraph at this stage. It's imperfect, it has some repetition and some areas where she goes off on a tangent, but she's begun to put her current thoughts to paper, collecting them in one place where she can extract the most useful ones to include as supporting reasons. Perhaps her supporting arguments will shift and change again as she continues building the argument in each subsequent step, but she's found a starting point to begin constructing the framework.

■ **Activity 5.4** **Individual Process Activity**

> **Directions:** Review your own synthesis paragraph(s). Take out a spare sheet of paper. Write your current tentative thesis at the top. Set a timer for seven minutes, and put on some classical music to help you relax and focus.
>
> Draft a freewritten argument supporting your position on the issue. Write down all your current thoughts on the subject, arguing for why you believe your view is important, why it's justified, and why you think audiences need to address this issue, and any questions you have or hope to answer.

Identifying Supporting Reasons in the Freewrite

The seven-minute paper is highly beneficial for putting jumbled ideas in an accessible place, but now you need to consider how to move from that freewrite to a more cogent outline. After drafting ideas in one place, conduct a scavenger hunt for possible supporting reasons or points, carefully evaluating the content you've developed, determining which ideas should be kept and which should be rejected or set aside for the time being.

Activity 5.5   Group Practice

Directions: Review Jane Student's seven-minute paper. Identify at least five possible supporting reasons or points within her freewrite, placing a star beside each one you find. Compare notes with your group members, using the questions below to evaluate your progress with this step.

- Did you find similar points?

- Jane's tentative thesis (from her synthesis) asserts that judging female students for their attire can create problems for both the students and the university. How do the points you found in her seven-minute paper begin to support this?

- Are there any points or ideas you find confusing?

- Are there any points that don't immediately appear connected to Jane's thesis?

- How should she reword/clarify her points to strengthen their persuasiveness?

- What questions could she answer to help you understand her reasoning?

Activity 5.6   Individual Practice

Directions: Review your own seven-minute paper. Identify several possible supporting reasons or points you made in the freewrite. Every time you think you've presented a new idea, place a star beside it.

Activity 5.7   Pair

Part I Directions: Exchange the starred seven-minute paper with a classmate. Review your peer's tentative thesis at the top, and read through their seven-minute paper, paying close attention to the points they've starred. Answer the questions below to provide them with feedback for further development and refinement.

- Do the starred points appear to support your peer's tentative thesis?

- Are there any points or ideas you find confusing?

- How should your peer reword or clarify points to strengthen their persuasiveness?

- What questions could they answer to help you understand their reasoning?

Part II Directions: Reconvene with your peer.

As the reader: Explain your evaluation of the writer's seven-minute paper, asking your peer questions for clarification and explaining where you were confused and how they might clarify.

As the writer: Answer your reader's questions, and try to explain your ideas further. Ask your reader to clarify if you're unsure of where they're confused or why. Take notes on their suggestions for rewording and clarification and on the questions they think you might answer to develop further.

Framing the Supporting Reasons and Identifying Underlying Assumptions

Structuring the content of arguments can be difficult, particularly when you have a large amount of freewritten notes and ideas. Transferring those ideas into a more manageable, literal frame is a helpful way to organize and create a potentially mobile outline. Storyboarding, a strategy used in writing narratives, can be part of your process of developing arguments as well. The content of the frame is simply different in purpose.

The frame will not only contain your supporting reasons but will also ensure you identify and articulate the underlying assumptions of your ideas; this is vital in developing an argument with consistently strong *logos*.

About Underlying Assumptions.   There are several terms that can be used to reference underlying assumptions. Philosopher and rhetorician Stephen Toulmin referred to these as "warrants," but they are simply ideas (usually unspoken) that the audience must accept in order to find your reason persuasive. Like the iceberg that destroyed the *Titanic*, it is frequently the underlying assumptions that have the most damaging effect on your argument's persuasiveness. Essentially, your reasons might appear logical and sound to you and to an agreeing audience, but if the intended audience doesn't share your values and assumptions, they won't find your reasoning logical or persuasive.

The Basics of Underlying Assumptions

- All reasons rely on particular assumptions and values.

- Sometimes our audiences will share these assumptions and values with us, but frequently they will need us to provide evidence for why they should accept our values.

- In the early stages of developing an argument, it's important to articulate the underlying assumptions for each of our reasons. This allows us to determine which underlying assumptions an audience might share and which they will question.

- Articulating underlying assumptions is the first step in strengthening the *logos* of our arguments and identifying places where further development will be necessary.

Articulating Basic Underlying Assumptions.   The underlying assumptions for basic reasons can be easily identified by determining what the audience presumably views as important.

For example:

You shouldn't text and drive because you could die.

The reason (*because you could die*) assumes that the audience values this concept (*dying would be bad/I'd rather not die*).
    Therefore, the underlying assumption is simply: *Dying would be bad* or *It's important to avoid death.*

Articulating More Complex Underlying Assumptions.   Some reasons are more complex in their construction, but you can still identify their underlying assumptions by determining what the audience must value in order to find the reason persuasive.

For example:

Orcas shouldn't be in captivity because captive spaces restrict space for them, preventing the same levels of exercise (both mental and physical) they would experience in the wild.

The reason (*because captive spaces restrict space for them*) assumes the audience believes that animals should experience life similar to their natural habitats.
    Therefore, the underlying assumption is: *Orcas should experience the same levels of exercise they would in the wild.*

Using the "X & Y Formula" to Articulate Underlying Assumptions. Some writers find it helpful to put ideas into a formula or word problem to identify underlying assumptions. The basic formulas used are simple fill-in-the-blank phrases:

- "If X, then I should do Y"
- "I should do Y because X is good/bad"

For example:

Thesis:	You should adopt pets from shelters instead of purchasing from breeders.
Reason:	*Because pets in shelters are more in need of a home.*

Underlying Assumption (as XY Statement): *If one animal needs a home more than another, then I should get the one in greater need.*

Regardless of which strategy you use, articulating underlying assumptions is an important step in developing a strong, persuasive argument for your audience.

Articulating underlying assumptions can frequently be difficult, and it requires intense critical thinking about what the reason assumes about its audience's values and priorities. It's important to practice articulating assumptions with your peers and the class as a whole. This will gradually strengthen your ability to identify assumptions and articulate them clearly for others.

■ **Activity 5.8**   **Group Practice: Articulating Assumptions**

Group Directions: With your peers, review the thesis you were assigned. For each supporting reason, collaboratively try to articulate the underlying assumption. Remember: Underlying assumptions usually answer the question "What does the audience believe or value in order to find the reason persuasive?" Use any of the strategies discussed above to help you articulate the assumptions together.

Thesis #1: We should pass laws to criminalize inhumane practices such as declawing of cats.

Reason 1: Declawing prevents natural behaviors like marking territory through scratching, which causes the animals stress.	Underlying Assumption
Reason 2: Declawing can negatively affect behavior and personality in the cat, leading to withdrawal or timid reactions to humans.	Underlying Assumption
Reason 3: Declawed animals are in greater danger if they get loose outside the home, as they won't be able to defend themselves.	Underlying Assumption

Thesis #2: It is unethical to keep large predators in zoos for casual observation/ entertainment.

Reason 1: Animals in restricted spaces suffer from a lack of exercise, which can lead to physical health problems, such as muscular atrophy, and mental-health issues, such as increased aggression.	Underlying Assumption
Reason 2: Zoos remove the practical need/ opportunity to hunt, which deprives animals of acting on natural instincts.	Underlying Assumption
Reason 3: Zoos inevitably put human trainers/zoo workers in proximity to naturally dangerous predators, which could lead to serious injury or death among workers.	Underlying Assumption

Thesis #3: Schools should encourage students to practice meditation to help them alleviate stress during college.

Reason 1: Meditation can improve the quality and consistency of sleep, ensuring students are more likely to be well rested.	Underlying Assumption
Reason 2: People who practice certain types of meditation are able to relax more easily in high-stress situations than those who do not.	Underlying Assumption
Reason 3: Meditation can help improve focus and concentration, similar to the effects of soporifics such as Adderall but without the potential for abuse.	Underlying Assumption

Thesis #4: We should decriminalize marijuana at the federal level.

Reason 1: Marijuana is currently categorized as a Schedule I drug (along with heroin, LSD, and ecstasy), but it does not fit the parameters of Schedule I drugs. This category is reserved for drugs with the most dangerous psychological effects and likelihood for addiction/abuse.	Underlying Assumption
Reason 2: Marijuana does not fit the parameters for the next category either, Schedule II drugs (which include meth, cocaine, and oxycodone).	Underlying Assumption
Reason 3: Marijuana's effects and potential for abuse make it more similar to alcohol than to the drugs on Schedules I and II of the Drug Enforcement Administration (DEA).	Underlying Assumption

Constructing Your Own Framework

At this stage, you've developed tentative supporting reasons, and you've practiced articulating underlying assumptions for several sample thesis statements. Now it's important to begin storyboarding your reasons and underlying assumptions, creating a framework on which to build the argument further. The following is an example of an Argument Frame, a tool frequently used by writers as a way to organize ideas onto one manageable page, with ideas in boxes that can be cut out, moved around, and used as a storyboard for an argument.

Table 5.1: Tentative Thesis

Reason 1 Evidence	Underlying Assumption Evidence
Reason 2 Evidence	Underlying Assumption Evidence
Reason 3 Evidence	Underlying Assumption Evidence
Reason 4 Evidence	Underlying Assumption Evidence
Reason 5 Evidence	Underlying Assumption Evidence
Possible Counterarguments/Research from Audience	Concede, Qualify, or Rebut?
Questions Your Audience Might Ask?	
Necessary Terms to Define/Facts to Establish?	

■ **Activity 5.9** **Individual Activity: Developing the Argument Frame**

Directions: Create your own argument frame, either on a spare sheet of paper or in a Word document. Write down your tentative thesis at the top. In the two columns that follow, include the supporting reasons you developed from the seven-minute paper and refined with your peers. Leave space to identify underlying assumptions and necessary evidence for each. Include boxes at the end for anticipated counterarguments/research, audience questions, or terms that will need to be defined.

■ **Activity 5.10** Individual Activity: Articulating Underlying Assumptions

> **Directions:** Review the reasons you've written in the left-hand column of your argument frame. Beside each reason, try to articulate the underlying assumption it relies on. What must the audience value or believe in order to find your reason persuasive?

Understanding the Audience: Anticipating Audience Questions, Unshared Assumptions, and Counterarguments

When you construct an argument, it's tempting to think of your audience as an antagonist. But it's important to remember that you're not debating or fighting the audience, but actively trying to persuade them. When dealing with resistant audiences that need a persuasive argument, you need to view them not as antagonists but as potential allies you've yet to acquire. Remember: Argument is about combining truth seeking and persuasion. To do this successfully, you need to focus on understanding your audience's concerns and the context that created their views and influenced their values and beliefs.

This approach allows you not only to anticipate counterarguments from your audience but also to identify which underlying assumptions to support with evidence, and the questions, concerns, and misconceptions the audience might need addressed in order to be persuaded.

Approaching arguments this way allows you to build a bridge to the audience, strengthening *ethos* and using argument to create and strengthen community rather than build walls or create "sides."

In order to do this, you must first develop a strong understanding of the audience you intend to persuade.

■ **Activity 5.11** Individual Activity: Audience Analysis Questions

> Use the questions below to begin analyzing your audience. Several questions might require you to conduct further research to fully understand your audience's values, concerns, and beliefs.
>
> - What age range does your audience encompass? How does this influence their current views on the issue?
>
> - What socioeconomic class are you targeting? How does this influence their values and concerns?
>
> - What region(s) is your audience from? Will this have a significant impact on their views?
>
> - What position does your audience already hold on the issue? What assumptions do they have about the issue's significance?

- What does your audience value? What influences these values?

- What are the discernable beliefs of your audience (political, religious, moral)?

- What concerns your audience (what might trigger them to feel discomfort, sadness, uncertainty)?

- What type of experience does your audience have with the issue? Will they have positive or negative associations with the issue?

- What knowledge does your audience have about the issue? What background or foundational information will you need to establish?

- What questions do you need to research further to understand this audience?

Identifying Shared versus Unshared Assumptions

Audience analysis is an important resource when determining which underlying assumptions you'll need to support and which the audience will accept without evidence. With your completed audience analysis in hand, you can review your argument frame, identifying assumptions you'll need to explicitly develop and support in your essay, and those you can leave stated without evidence or simply unstated.

■ **Activity 5.12**   **Individual Activity**

> **Directions:** Review your answers to the audience analysis questions in Activity 5.10, and the reasons and underlying assumptions in your argument frame. Based on your analysis of the audience, which assumptions will they share with you? Which assumptions will need additional support in order for the audience to accept them? Place stars beside the underlying assumptions you think need to be supported with evidence or explained to the audience. Place an X next to any assumptions you believe the audience will simply accept unstated. This identifies the assumptions you will need to articulate or develop with evidence in your paper (stars) and those you can exclude (Xs).

Identifying Supporting Evidence for Reasons and Underlying Assumptions.   Persuasive arguments are frequently based on finding common ground with your resistant audience, through evidence you know they will find persuasive or arguments they will find the most motivating. Although this can be effective, it is not the only way to persuade an audience, and frequently it will limit the progress you're able to make with a resistant audience that has little in common with you.

   In these cases, finding ways to support the underlying assumptions the audience does not currently share can go a long way toward crafting an argument they will find unexpectedly persuasive. In the sample reasons below, the writer is trying to support the following thesis: *Except in rare cases for conservation and research purposes, large marine mammals should not be held in captivity.*

Each reason is intended to support this thesis, but because the audience is resistant to the idea of imposing stricter laws on marine parks, the writer must encourage them to share the underlying assumptions.

Reason:	Captive spaces restrict space for orcas, preventing the same levels of exercise (both mental and physical) they would experience in the wild.
Necessary Evidence:	Information identifying the difference between tank sizes and natural roaming areas of orcas in the wild.
Underlying Assumption:	Orcas should experience the same levels of exercise they would in the wild.
Necessary Evidence:	Evidence showing that restricted space has harmful effects on the animals (supporting that it is unethical to keep them in captivity)
Reason:	Tanks do not permit socialization in family groups due to size restrictions and control over reproduction.
Necessary Evidence:	Data on socialization opportunities in marine parks; evidence that parks need to control reproduction
Underlying Assumption:	Orcas should be able to socialize in family groups and not have reproduction artificially controlled.
Necessary Evidence:	Evidence identifying the negative effects (mental and physical) of restricting natural socialization and removing animals from family groups

■ **Activity 5.13** **Group Activity: Identifying Necessary Evidence**

Below is an additional reason from the above writer's argument. With your group, identify the type of information and evidence necessary to support both the reason and the underlying assumption. What might persuade the resistant audience to share the writer's values?

Reason: Placing orcas in artificially created social groups is damaging to their emotional and physical health and well-being.

Necessary Evidence:

Underlying Assumption: The health and well-being of orcas should be our priority.

Necessary Evidence:

■ **Activity 5.14**   **Group Practice Activity: Identifying Necessary Evidence**

> **Directions:** Review the stock thesis assigned to your group from Activity 5.8 (on pages 106–108). Together, review each supporting reason and underlying assumption. Confer with your group to determine the evidence needed to support or verify each supporting reason and underlying assumption. Note: Some underlying assumptions may require the same type of evidence. We'll address what this means in later activities.

■ **Activity 5.15**   **Individual Activity: Identifying Necessary Evidence**

> **Directions:** Review the reasons and underlying assumptions in your argument frame. Under each, identify the information and evidence you would need to persuade the audience to (1) accept that your reason is grounded in fact and (2) share the reason's underlying assumption. At this stage, your necessary evidence is simply a short description of the information you need to find.

Note: In later chapters you'll find detailed walk-throughs for how to develop research questions and find necessary sources and information. For now, simply write notes about the information you'll need to search for. Then utilize the information in later chapters to acquire the necessary information.

Anticipating Audience Questions and Counterarguments.   At this stage, you should have the basic framework of your argument established. You have a tentative thesis, supporting reasons with their underlying assumptions, and a sense of the evidence you might need to support these arguments.

It would be tempting to stop here, but remember that you're writing for an audience you hope to eventually persuade. They aren't static or passively reading, but potentially part of the conversation you've entered. Your argument should acknowledge the audience as a participant in the conversation, one who's influencing your arguments and whose concerns, questions, and counterarguments you hope to address sufficiently.

Strategies for Anticipating the Audience: Elbow's Believing and Doubting Game

The rhetorician Peter Elbow developed what he called the "believing and doubting game" to help writers of arguments develop a stronger understanding of their audiences and to give them the tools to anticipate concerns, questions, and counterarguments the audience might bring up when reading their arguments.

■ **Activity 5.16** **Individual Activity: Believing and Doubting Game**

Directions: The game has two parts, and you must complete both in order to strengthen your argument fully.

As a believer: First, review your argument frame and play the role of a "believer." Pretend you are someone who wholly agrees with the ideas you've outlined. Write down all the reasons why someone would agree with you and the experiences or evidence they might offer as further support. Playing the believer of your own ideas can seem silly at first, but it can help you identify ways to develop your argument further and offer potentially persuasive explanations for your point of view.

As a doubter: Review your argument frame again, this time with a critical eye, and play the role of the "doubter." Put yourself in the shoes of an audience who disagrees completely with all your ideas. Be argumentative and critical, playing devil's advocate to argue against your own ideas. Write down all the reasons why someone would disagree with you, the counterarguments they might present, and the evidence or experiences they might use as support for their counterclaims. Consider the ways they might find fault with your reasons and your underlying assumptions. Consider as well the questions they might skeptically present about your argument's implications and the assumptions they might hold that run counter to your own. Playing the doubter of your own ideas can be uncomfortable, but it's a crucial step in development, allowing you to begin anticipating the audience and identifying key concerns, questions, and counterarguments that you might need to address.

■ **Activity 5.17** **Individual Activity: Assessment**

Directions: Review your doubting portion of the previous activity. Then, use the prompts below to assess the information you gleaned from the game and integrate it into your argument frame.

- What questions did you raise as the doubter?

- What concerns would a doubting audience have?

- What counterarguments might they present? Write these down at the end of your argument frame.

- How could you respond to these questions? Assuage concerns? Will you need to concede to their counterarguments? How will this affect your argument? What further evidence and information will you need to respond effectively to the potential concerns, questions, or counterarguments?

Strategies for Anticipating the Audience. Using Your Writing Community.   The believing and doubting game is an effective strategy, but don't rely on yourself alone for developing the argument. Remember that as a member of the first-year writing course at Virginia Tech, you're part of a writing community. Your fellow classmates, tutors at the writing center, and your instructor are all part of the same community and are there to help you develop and refine ideas. It's always beneficial to seek out a fresh pair of eyes to help you anticipate what an unknown reader's concerns, questions, and counterarguments might be.

■   **Activity 5.18**   **Group Activity: Round Robin Response**

Directions: Organize your group in a small circle. Take out your argument frames, completing the activity below as both a writer and reader.

As the writer: Pass your argument frame to the person to your left.

As the reader: Review your peer's tentative thesis. Then begin reading through their reasons and underlying assumptions. Put yourself in the mind-set of a resistant audience. After reading their first reason or underlying assumption, write down a concern, question, or counterargument you think a resistant audience might have. Pass their frame to the next person in your circle. Repeat with the next frame passed to you.

Note for readers: Try to add a concern, question, or counterargument for a reason or assumption that others in the group haven't addressed yet. The goal is to provide your peer with as many potential places as possible to anticipate their audience. To avoid repeating the same response as others, skim through the responses from others in the group before writing down your own.

As a group: After everyone has provided a comment on each group member's frame, reconvene, and make sure each member of the group has their own argument frame in hand again. Go around the circle, allowing each writer to ask questions about the responses they received. Help the writer understand your concern, question, or counterargument, discussing the response as a group to strategize ways to address that response in the writer's argument.

■   **Activity 5.19**   **Individual Activity: As the Writer**

Take notes on your peers' explanations and suggestions. Based on their responses, determine the concerns, questions, and counterarguments you might need to address in your argument. What type of information and evidence would you need to adequately address these anticipated responses?

Chapter

Critical Thinking and Reading

In addition to being the second WPA outcome of first-year writing, good critical thinking and reading skills are fundamental to academic success. Additionally, critical thinking through reading and writing is described in the WPA outcomes as the following:

...the ability to analyze, synthesize, interpret, and evaluate ideas, information, situations, and texts. When writers think critically about the materials they use—whether print texts, photographs, data sets, videos, or other materials—they separate assertion from evidence, evaluate sources and evidence, recognize and evaluate underlying assumptions, read across texts for connections and patterns, identify and evaluate chains of reasoning, and compose appropriately qualified and developed claims and generalizations. These practices are foundational for advanced academic writing.[1]

But what do we mean when we talk about critical thinking in a first-year writing course and how do we develop and hone these skills or behaviors?

6.1 Critical Thinking

In college, nothing will contribute to your success more than your ability to "think critically." But because it's an everyday activity, we may not have consciously considered how this thinking process works. With every decision we have to make, however minor, we find ourselves breaking down information, by various methods, that influences a reasoned decision about how to proceed next. Critical thinking instructs our decisions about what type of car to purchase, what foods to eat, and what classes to take. You may wonder how these examples relate to critical thinking. Let's look at how a student's decision in choosing a class is informed by a process of critical thinking.

When you coordinate your plan of study for your undergraduate education, you meet with an academic advisor and discuss the classes you can take to become more competent and knowledgeable. For example, a computer science major may want to take classes in fine art because of her interest in developing photography and illustration software. She wants a fuller and richer understanding of her potential users, who have a strong appreciation of art. She hasn't chosen this class based just on enjoyment, though that's important; she's also critically evaluated why this class benefits her in a tactical way. She asked herself questions about why the class is meaningful; and made conclusions based on how the class can enhance her future knowledge and skills.

On the surface, this example seems nothing more than a choice typically made by a college student, but viewed with a critical lens, it shows a process of a decision making that has been carefully considered. Intelligent individuals are aware that "thinking about thinking" through a *questioning*, speculative mind-set is a

---

[1]http://wpacouncil.org/positions/outcomes.html

conscious, controlled process that resists examining things in a passive, disinterested way. This example demonstrates how critical thinking is an ordinary but important action we constantly engage in, and that it encompasses many analytical processes, such as questioning, testing, creating, and interpreting.

When considering the process of critical thinking, it's important to understand that the term *critical* is often associated with "criticism" or unnecessary cynicism, but educators do not view the word in a negative way. The word *critical* actually has its root in the Latin *criticus*, which means "fit or suitable for deciding; capable of judging, decisive." As the root of the word implies, this tradition of thoughtfulness is an eminently practical goal to embrace in any dimension of school life. In your classes, therefore, your teachers will help you practice thinking skills that require you to examine and re-examine points of view in order to understand and challenge many perspectives, including your own assumptions and biases, and to arrive at a reasoned and well thought out position. When you practice critical thinking, you avoid taking something at "face value," however authoritative a writer or source appears: Critical thinkers by nature are skeptical and try to avoid simplistic views of the world (they also regularly adjust and concede their positions with humility when new facts and data are established).

Critical Thinking and Analysis

At this point, you may ask how critical thinking relates to analysis. There's much overlap between these terms, of course, so it's important to make a brief distinction between the two.

Analysis is the process of breaking down information. It is a step-by-step method to interpret a problem and to arrive at an answer or solution. Analysis can be described as perceiving something through a particular context, much like the specific assignments you'll experience in your composition classes. For example, your teacher may ask you to analyze a source using rhetorical knowledge to interpret how the text functions and persuades its audience of an issue. To do this, you'll use analysis to support your claims, breaking the text down in a specific way related to the criteria given in the assignment. Critical thinking, on the other hand, is characterized by careful, nuanced evaluation and judgment based on conscientious reflection. Analysis can be applied, to a degree, to any text that perhaps only skims the surface of something, but when you use "critical analysis," you engage in a process in which you make claims and observations that go beyond the obvious and familiar. In doing so, you may even contribute to knowledge itself.

There are many dimensions to and descriptions for critical thinking when it comes to problem solving. Broadly speaking, when you think critically, you:

- Summarize—extract and restate the material's main message or central point
- Analyze—break things down into their component parts

- Synthesize—bring parts together in a coherent way
- Evaluate—make judgments, based on sound reasoning, evidence, and reflection

It's important to note that critical thinking includes a combination of skills defined in many ways according to different knowledge and belief systems. Despite these varied definitions, we should all practice engaged inquiry and reflection throughout our professional and civic lives, as critical thinking leads to informed and empathetic choices that will benefit our standing and that of others in the world. These skills are important in every profession and in everyday life. If you make critical thinking a habit, you'll perceive your environment in stimulating ways and the learning process as endlessly rewarding.

In your composition courses, you'll begin to see the essential connection between critical thinking and reading and how these analytical tools relate to your writing. If you learn, for example, how to structure an argument, judge the credibility of a source, or make a decision using the methods explained in this chapter, it will not be hard to apply these principles to the many other writing contexts you will engage in: The thinking and writing skills we teach in this book are "transferable" to the *actions* of your everyday lives.

Useful Critical Thinking Questions

The following prompts can help guide the critical thinking process for any text or activity.

1. Does this information make sense?
2. What does my intuition, experience, and education tell me about this information?
3. What are the strengths and weaknesses of this information?
4. What sources can be believed? What sources can be discarded?
5. How can I best summarize this information?
6. Are my assumptions about this information valid? If so, why? If not, why not? Do I need to investigate with more facts and data?
7. What's a solution to this problem?
8. Did I ask enough questions? Did I ask the right critical thinking questions?
9. Does the conclusion I've reached make sense?
10. Does my research and information support the conclusion reached? Did I reason my position based on good reasons and sound evidence?

■ **Activity 6.1** **Individual Activity 1**

> A key component of critical thinking involves asking strong questions and appreciating the contexts that surround a text, issue, or idea. Write down a list of questions you could ask about a reading, an assignment, or an essay you are currently examining. Develop at least five questions, and then in a group, explain why and how you arrived at these questions.

■ **Activity 6.2** **Group Activity 2**

> Working in a group, choose a problem you've encountered (in a class reading, in an assignment from your instructor, in an issue having do with your course theme). Compile a list of questions that best address and solve this problem. For example: What's the source of the problem? Do you have the data available to solve the problem?

■ **Activity 6.3** **Individual Activity 1**

> In class, talk about the importance of distinguishing fact from opinion in the critical thinking process. Facts are verifiable; opinions, although they may be based on fact, are not. Facts and opinions are not opposites, nor is one better than the other. They are simply two kinds of statements. Examine some statements in class, and determine if they are statements of fact or opinion. For example, "Studies suggest a correlation between violent video games and adolescent behavior." Is this a statement of fact or opinion?

■ **Activity 6.4** **Group Activity 2**

> Identify the important traits of critical thinking and how these traits might be used in your writing assignments this semester.

■ **Activity 6.5** **Individual Activity 3**

> Reflect on a moment when you used critical thinking skills for an effective piece of writing you've composed.

6.2 Critical Reading

In your composition courses, your teachers will assign readings that come in many forms. These readings help define and explain much of the content of your course theme. You will be assigned readings for comprehension and understanding, and this reading process is key for learning how to gauge what experts have to say in their fields of inquiry. (Note that we practice distinct modes of reading depending on the discipline: scientific, legal, literary.) But we read for profound reasons other than gaining information and understanding central ideas, important as they are. Most fundamentally, we read for *meaning, discovery,* and *knowledge,* and this process plays out in multifaceted ways.

In this section, then, we discuss a more active way of reading—critical reading, a practice parallel to critical thinking that requires a deeper and more fulfilling engagement with the text. Generally, critical reading is a process of **analyzing, interpreting,** and **evaluating**. A critical reader applies certain strategies, models, questions, and theories that enhance the clarity and comprehension of a given text or issue. When we read critically, we use our critical thinking skills to question both the text and our own comprehension of it, resulting in an informed position or opinion.

6.3 Critical or Active Reading Strategies

Critical reading, as opposed to reading, is a more active way to comprehend a text. When we read a text on a straightforward level, our purpose is to gain a basic understanding of the reading, such as what the text says, what information the text uses, where the text is published, what the topic and thesis are, and so on. But when we read critically, we use specific questions and contexts to understand the text and for richer interpretations that can guide our thinking and inform our rhetorical analysis and writing.

When we read closely, we try to understand not only what a text says but also *why* a text says what it does and *how* it argues and functions. We make judgments about the text, analyzing, for instance, how the language works in a source and what types of reasoning and evidence the author uses. Effective critical readers can also question a text's assumptions and arguments when necessary in a particular context.

There are three modes of analysis that you should use when approaching a text with a critical and active lens:

- Analyzing what a text does
- Evaluating what a text says
- Interpreting what a text means

Following are questions you can ask to help you analyze, evaluate, and interpret texts.

For Analysis: Breaking down a text into its component parts to look for patterns of meaning.

- What's the purpose or exigence of the text?
- What's the thesis of the text? What does the text say?
- What's the author's voice, tone, and stance?
- What evidence and examples are used in the text?
- What rhetorical appeals (to emotion, logic, authority) and strategies (of narration, argumentation, evaluation) are used in the text?
- What illustrations, graphs, or other visual information are used in the text? What is their function? Do they support an argument, provide background or contextual information, and/or clarify a concept that is difficult to communicate through language alone?

For Interpretation: The way something is explained or understood.

- In what cultural and historical contexts does the argument take place? How do the cultural and historical contexts of the author influence the argument?
- What methods of analysis are employed in the text? (Psychological, sociological, legal, scientific.) What theories are employed in the text?
- What's your reaction to the text? How do you feel about the argument expressed in the text? Do your biases affect your comprehension of the text? If so, how?

For Evaluation: The systematic assessment of the value, worth, or merit of a process or object.

- Are the sources in the text reliable?
- How well does this text contribute to the discipline? Is the logic used in the text reasonable? Is the argument logical? Consistent?
- How well does the text use different methodologies (statistics, graphs, questionnaires)?
- Are theories well explained and integrated clearly in the text?
- What are the strengths and weaknesses of the theories in the text?
- Are counterarguments adequately considered in the text?

There are several strategies for becoming a successful critical and active reader that will help you gain further insight into a text and draw deeper conclusions and understandings of that text. These include previewing text and vocabulary, reading with a purpose, marking text, and summarizing.

Previewing Text and Vocabulary

Before reading, you should look at any titles, introductions, subheadings, charts, graphs, and captions and attempt to make predictions about what the text is about. Additionally, you should scan the text to find words or phrases that are new or confusing, and be sure to understand this vocabulary before diving into a text. Look at the structure of the text: Is it funny, sad, realistic? How do you know? Is it fiction? A poem? A story? How do you know? Is it nonfiction? A letter to someone or a newspaper article? How do you know?

Reading with a Purpose

To be a critical reader, you should fully understand why you are reading a text and know what you want to gain from it. You can read closely in search of humor, the author's purpose, use of literary devices (such as foreshadowing, imagery), facts, confusing passages, arguments, biases, and limitations. Rereading is also a crucial part of the critical reading process. For the assignments you work through, examine the piece several times until you are satisfied that you understand the text fully for meaning and your argument.

Trope the use of figurative language—via word, phrase, or even an image—for artistic effect such as using a figure of speech

Marking Text

Marking or annotating a text is an invaluable tool for a critical and active reader. Annotating a text can help you understand confusing passages, point out tropes, identify elements of the text, see patterns in the author's writing, and so much more. Annotations include circling words, phrases, names, and dates that stand out, and underlining an author's claims and important information connected to those claims. Annotating helps you make connections both within the text and external to the text. Use the margins of the pages to write notes and to ask questions that you can reference later.

Summarizing

Finally, if you have successfully and actively read a text, you should be able to write a brief summary of the text (four to six sentences). Always practice critically and actively reading a text before writing a summary. If the summary is difficult to write, reread the material and be sure to identify and understand the author's thesis and claims.

Activity 6.6

As you read a text critically, make a list that incorporates:

- Three to five things you already know about the subject
- Three to five things you want to know about the subject

After you finish reading, make a list of three to five things you learned. How has this process aided your thinking about the topic, and why is this important as you proceed to provide a solution to or an opinion about the subject?

Activity 6.7

While reading an assignment or essay, ask and write down your answers to the following strategic questions:

- What are the larger implications of this text for the course and the assignments I will be doing later?
- Why did I underline, highlight, or circle a particular word or passage?
- What is the thesis of this text, and how is it demonstrated and supported throughout?
- What idea do I most like in the text and why?
- What question would I most like to answer for the author and why?
- What part(s) of the text make most sense to me and why? What part(s) of the text do not make sense to me?
- If I take the main arguments of this text seriously, what are the implications of this reading, and vice versa?
- What's the most interesting or provocative statement in the text and why?

Activity 6.8

Test your reading comprehension in increments as you read. Set a timer, and read for half an hour. When the timer goes off, write down the key points of the text you read. After you write down the key points, reread the text and fill in what you missed before. What does this reading process tell you about yourself and the text? How has this reading process aided your discovery of an issue, theme, or idea?

6.4 Applied Critical Reading and Thinking

Critical reading and thinking are vital to your writing because they allow a deeper understanding of texts that you can use as evidence in later arguments you write. However, evidence cannot stand on its own; evidence requires your interpretation and presentation to support the argument you make in your writing. By critically reading arguments made within texts, you develop a well-reasoned and supported response that acknowledges the arguments of others and the implications they have for your own writing of the subject. The following is an example of how a student critically read a source and used the argument within that text to support her own position in response to an argumentative essay prompt.

Essay Prompt and Response

In her English 1105 class, Natalie Richoux gives an assignment that requires students to use their personal experiences and readings from the semester to create an argument that either supports or opposes the issue presented within the following prompt:

> For quite some time, "college" has stood, more or less, as a synonym for success. However, the fact that college has stood as a synonym for success has pushed graduating high school students to enter college (roughly 45% of graduating high schoolers enrolled in college courses in 1965, compared to 65% in 2013) and dynamically changed the structure and atmosphere of the university. Based on your own experiences and readings from this semester, formulate an argument that either supports or opposes the notion that college is a synonym for success.

This essay question requires critical and active reading and writing in multiple ways. First, the prompt asks students whether college is a synonym for success, which requires them to move beyond conventional notions of success and to define what success means to them (money, power, health, family). Then the prompt asks students to do two things: (1) form their own opinions, which requires critical thinking based on experiences and (2) form an opinionated stance that is situated within other people's writing and acknowledges the arguments that both support and oppose the issue.

Acknowledging arguments that both support and oppose an issue requires a counterargument, which anticipates a position someone might take against what you have to say. With this counterposition acknowledged, you then provide a rebuttal as to why this counterargument may be wrong. In order to provide a counterargument, it isn't enough to know what the text says on a surface level; you must engage with your reading on a deeper level by using the critical reading methods discussed in this chapter. Critical readers go beyond the facts in order to understand the complexity and perspective of the argument and to present a response that showcases their own understanding of the topic. As you read the following student essay, you'll see how Priscilla Gyamfi uses her critical thinking and reading skills to acknowledge both sides of the issue and to present her perspective on how college success should be defined.

Student Example by Freshman Priscilla Gyamfi

Priscilla Gyamfi
Mrs. Richoux
English 1105, Essay 3
December 12, 2016

College Success

I cannot recall a time when the idea of attending a four-year college was not going to be the next stage in my life after high school and how college would give me success later in life. I believe the reasoning behind that is due to a shift in American values so that chasing your dreams could include going to college. The thought process is that college equals a diploma, which means a career that further leads to a comfortable lifestyle of financial security, nice houses, fancy cars, and expensive clothes. In short, college has come to equal success. Growing up, I easily believed that college meant success, but I did not realize how many people were just as eager to take hold of the same dream. With more individuals going to college and entering the workforce, the chances of finding a job that will become a career begin to dwindle rapidly. Although college can provide people with the tools and experiences necessary to be successful, it is only the student that can guarantee personal success through their accomplishments, work ethic, and willingness to grow as an individual.

Colleges had previously lost monetary support from the government, as state funding was cut because students had chosen alternative avenues such as the military or vocational trade schools. The drop in funding forced colleges to compensate by increasing tuition to even out costs. The impact left negative repercussions on everyone, especially students who could barely afford college in the first place. I presume universities tried to alleviate this situation by admitting more students to make up for the lost funds while also appearing more

accepting. In admitting more students, colleges have also lowered their academic standards; allowing more individuals to
achieve higher education is a positive initiative, but not if
this decision was predominantly based on the desire to increase
revenue and state funding. It appears that colleges held standards comparable to Ivy League universities but have softened
their hearts to widen their pockets. Despite popular opinion,
I don't believe carrying high standards as a university is a
bad trait. These standards protect people who are not mentally
prepared for college. Students who made it through high school
by the skin of their teeth generally do not survive college
because they may lack the motivation, focus, and work ethic
to do well and commit the seven sins of college students.

Here, Priscilla tactically selects an assigned reading from her English 1105 class. While the reading addresses the inherent flaws that lie with college students, Priscilla approaches the text through a critical lens and finds a deeper meaning within Benton's essay that supports her argument: College doesn't guarantee success; rather the determination and motivation of the student determine success.

Thomas H. Benton, author of "The Seven Deadly Sins of
Students," discusses the ultimate sins that students commit at
universities. He outlines the sins as sloth (procrastination—
the inability to manage time), greed (students pursue degrees
that will make them wealthy, and that don't reflect their pas-
sions), anger (about grades they receive and the "unfairness"
of it), lust (students show up barefoot, in pajamas), gluttony
(one word—alcohol), envy (cringing at the success of others and
resigning your own), and pride (students think they're better than, well, everyone). While Benton is outlining the attitude of students today and the climate of a university, I
see these as reasons why college does not stand as a synonym
for success. College provides students with the opportunities to equip themselves with tools that can make them successful individuals in the future, but students have to be willing to adjust themselves, their attitudes, and their thinking
to take advantage of all a university offers them; they need
to be willing to put in the hard work and have the determination and motivation to become successful. A diploma doesn't just
hand you success; it means you've been afforded the opportunity
to become successful with all college can offer you, but you

have to take advantage of the situation, unlike my brother.

When my older sister and I were growing up, we made it a mission to please our parents through our grades, and this determination was instilled in my younger sister. My older sister recently graduated from Penn State and currently works for a large firm in D.C. My younger sister is only in the eighth grade, but is taking advanced language arts. She is also in the National Junior Honor Society. We have all continuously strived for excellence and have always held ourselves accountable for our failures—something my brother has never learned to do. My brother is the reason why the stereotype that women value education more continues to thrive. For example, he is fully aware of his poor academic performance and offers no explanation for this performance because he simply does not care. I would've been in trouble with my parents had I not been able to answer a simple question like, "Why is this F on your report card?" But I digress. My mother and I recently had an honest conversation about my brother's future, and I told her he wasn't ready for university schooling because he is irresponsible and lacks determination. People like my brother cower and run away when faced with adversity, so why waste time and money when it isn't necessary? College cannot hand anyone success; it is what a student does with their time in college that will equip them to be successful in the future, but the student has to be responsible and determined to chase that success.

While the ratio of less driven to driven people in college is substantial, there is a greater imbalance between the number of students entering universities and the number of professors available to teach at these universities, and the professors commit seven sins as well. Following Thomas Benton's article discussing the sins of students, he penned "The Seven Deadly Sins of Professors," which illustrates the sins of professors within higher education. Benton argues there is sloth (professors pretend to be busy to not spend time and effort on

Throughout Priscilla's essay, she points to the notion that students achieve success by working diligently and seeking out opportunities that will help them pave a path to success; further, Benton points out how students are squandering these opportunities through sins. Priscilla illustrates critical thinking and reading and its relation to writing as she connects her argument and Benton's argument to her own evidence about her brother's lack of academic determination and motivation.

Priscilla further demonstrates the importance of critical and active reading by tying in a second reading from her English 1105 course, another essay by Benton. Priscilla takes Benton's notion of the sins of professors and through active reading connects it within her essay, contenting that college is not a synonym to success in part due to the atmosphere of professors in large lecture halls and the reliance of teaching aids and helpers. Further, she connects Benton's argument to her position and then tactfully provides evidence for both arguments through firsthand experiences at Virginia Tech. She reaches deeper than the surface of Benton's work, which discusses the flaws of professors, making connections to show how the flaws are inherent in students' lack of success and motivation.

teaching and students), greed (for status and recognition among their peers), anger (against fellow peers who seem inferior or wrong), lust (adultery and affairs that occur and leave lingering hostility), gluttony (one word again—alcohol), envy (institutional hierarchies where everyone wants to be on top), and pride (professors believing they know all). While different from students' sins, these sins still showcase faults in higher education and why college will not, even cannot, stand as a synonym for success. These faults are egregious in professors, but not all professors. Students have to be willing to hunt down the professors who haven't let the sins rule their lives and can become good mentors. This entails more work, determination, and motivation on the student's part, but it can lead to many invaluable opportunities to become a student who achieves success one day. And in today's climate of academics, finding those professors is becoming increasingly difficult.

The idea of intimate class sizes where students can take advantage of the situation to get to know a professor, one who might care and doesn't commit sins, has become all but obsolete as colleges create sizable buildings to cram hundreds of students into a single room. Classrooms are no longer conducive to an appropriate learning environment for the students or the professors who have to lecture 300 people in a single course. Instead of hiring more professors or, heaven forbid, admitting fewer students, many universities are having graduate students teach introductory level courses. Too many colleges have allowed greed to get the better of them by exposing students to instructors who are not as qualified as someone with a master's degree or doctorate. Many of the individuals that fill these rooms are freshmen, like me, who have probably never truly experienced college life and feel constantly overwhelmed. We are adjusting to an incredible amount of challenges, some of which seem to be working against our desires to excel academically. Although academic excellence is primarily attributed to a student's will, a portion of the blame can be placed on how the material is taught. Virginia Tech, along with many other universities, has adopted academic spaces such as the Math Emporium, a place where students go for quizzes and tests. However, many students find themselves dropping classes at the Math Empo because they are either failing or simply do not understand the material. The first time I went there for my elementary calculus orientation, my instructor reassured us by stating we did have an actual teacher, but throughout the semester I have found this hard to comprehend. She might be a teacher, but only on paper. I learned the material on my own. The Math Empo hires students to help with the math, but they are just that: helpers. Like the rest of the school, the number of students exceeded the number of helpers. Convenience does not replace quality. Giving a student online lecture notes does not make the lessons any easier to understand, and I believe the university knows this as well and decided to offer alternative resources so students could receive additional aid. The lack of resources further highlights that college is not a synonym for success but merely an opportunity for success, as students have to be willing to seek out those opportunities.

While various resources have been set in place for students, colleges can neglect to prepare students for the competition that awaits them in the workforce. Businesses and companies want to hire people who are resourceful, determined, and intuitive. A bachelor's degree is supposed to ensure a job with a higher pay grade than for someone with only a high school diploma. However, students misunderstand the fact that a bachelor's degree does not guarantee anything except the opportunity to apply for a good job. The degree itself has become commonplace, which has unfortunately brought more difficulty to applicants. When so many other people have the same golden ticket, what makes you stand out? After busting your butt through college, and putting in work every semester to make the dean's list, it stings knowing that other people have done the same thing, and it is frustrating. So what does that mean for you? It means applying to all the internships you possibly can, using your vacations to study abroad, spending more money to obtain a graduate degree—all of which are opportunities colleges offer you, but you have to take advantage of them. A bachelor's degree does not prepare you at all for the competition that awaits you in the workforce; it does not even open your eyes to the fact that it exists. All it really does is take your money and abandon you in a cold world with nothing except a piece of paper and mountains of student debt.

Here Priscilla offers the counterargument of her essay. She elevates her own arguments and demonstrates her critical thinking skills by carefully anticipating and thinking through how someone might counter her argument; consequently, she provides a rebuttal to this claim. A counterargument vitally demonstrates critical thinking because it goes beyond your own opinions and limitations to approach the issue from a different perspective.

I acknowledge that there are many students who know how to handle the demands that are present in college and, despite competition in the foreseeable future, would make excellent candidates within their respective fields of work. Some of these individuals spent their entire high school careers pulling all-nighters and holding weekly study sessions to get into a good college and probably intend to work twice as hard to get onto a good career path. A number of these people might also be first-generation students who understand how important attending college is for their family. In both scenarios, these are generally the kinds of students that will take advantage of every possible opportunity and resource to ensure their academic success. Unfortunately, no university, no matter how prestigious, is completely filled with these types of students. I did not entirely understand why people who paid thousands of dollars in tuition would not even bother to come to class on a regular basis. However, at one point, I found myself in this category of students. Even though I spent my time at the Chemistry Learning Center (CLC) receiving help for my lab reports, I remember thinking I didn't care about my Biochemistry First Experience class because I had matched all of the requirements to do well. Since I used that class time for education, I began making excuses for other people who did not attend class regularly. Sometime after, I had an epiphany and came to the conclusion that students who skip class, including myself, do so because they are not invested in the subject matter. We chose classes that we might not have cared about to fulfill the requirements of a major we might not have been passionate about because it will lead to a diploma and ensure wealth. Society has determined financial standing as a sign of an individual's success, and this philosophy has been ingrained in our minds since the beginning of time. I differ in this ideology and proclaim that having a successful life means that you have maximized every opportunity to create the best possible version of yourself. There is a unique and insurmountable joy that comes from embracing experiences that you never imagined for yourself, ones that cannot be bought with money.

Priscilla shows her understanding of the definition of success, which is a demonstration of her critical thinking skills in relation to her assignment prompt.

While college experience does provide access to future opportunities, having a degree does not automatically ensure success, as a large quantity of students in college do not take it seriously and do not excel academically in college. Some of the blame can be placed on the crowded classrooms, limited staff, or how material is taught, but most of the blame should be placed on the students. Even though additional resources are offered, very few students actually take advantage of these. Many students do not realize that competition awaits them when they leave college. They simply do not understand that a bachelor's degree can only take them so far and that it is up to them to make up the rest. I hope to be at a place in my life when I can say confidently, "I never dreamed about success, I worked for it" (Estee Lauder).

Works Cited

Benton, Thomas H. "The Seven Deadly Sins of Students." *The Chronicle of Higher Education. 14* Apr. 2006. Web. 2 Dec. 2015.

Benton, Thomas H. "The Seven Deadly Sins of Professors." *The Chronicle of Higher Education.* 12 May 2006. Web. 2 Dec. 2015.

Final Thoughts

Priscilla Gyamfi's essay illustrates the importance of reflection in developing a purposeful way to think about the essay prompt through engaging questions. In this example, Priscilla needed to define how she conceptualized success and use this definition throughout her essay, exploring and contesting any biases and limitations that were expressed in the articles she cited and from her own knowledge about the subject. Additionally, she provided two forms of evidence in support of her argument: personal experience and critical essays. Therefore, Priscilla approached the prompt in a critical way to solidly negotiate her argument and demonstrate her stance on the issue.

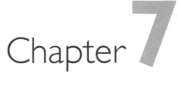

Chapter 7

Preparing to Write the Research Paper

What is research? Research is taking place at colleges and universities across the country, but it can refer to a remarkable range of activities, including:

- Running a tightly controlled experiment in a lab

- Observing a physical place or object

- Surveying or interviewing fellow students

- Searching for journal or other periodical articles using a library database

- Surveying social media posts related to a specific topic or viewpoint

- Modeling the response of a particular structure to a particular environment

- Transcribing a 200-year-old handwritten manuscript

- And, of course, reading a book

As the above list suggests, *research* means many different things for different disciplines. But what do we mean by research in the first-year-writing classroom?

Your specific research-writing task for English 1106 or H1204 will depend on your instructor. In general, though, research-writing assignments usually have a couple of key features in common. First, your assignment will approach research writing as critical thinking. A research project is a formalized, methodical approach to a subject. It is a highly organized means of critiquing a particular topic or answering a specific critical question. Second, your assignment will ask you to think about audience; it will require you to critically consider whom you are writing for and how your audience will help shape your research and writing process.

In Chapters 7 and 8, we will assume that we are writing a researched article about a subject or question on which we are *relative* experts, and that we must express ourselves clearly and effectively to a general, educated audience.

7.1 So You Have to Write a Research Paper?

So you have to write a research paper? But what does that mean—what's your task? All students in English 1106 and H1204 are required to produce some sort of writing from research, but what that writing looks like will vary from section to section. So before you go any further into this chapter's discussion of research, you should take stock of your task, making sure you know precisely what is being asked of you.

So what *is* your task? Or, to use the terminology in Chapter 1, what is your rhetorical situation? Ask yourself the following:

- For what purpose are you writing?

- For what audience are you writing?

- What constraints are placed on your writing task?

To answer these questions, carefully review your assignment sheet for the following details:

- Are you free to choose your own research topic, or is a topic provided for you? Are you required to choose a topic within certain boundaries? How much freedom do you have?

- Is your audience identified for you? If not, how will you determine your audience (other than your instructor, of course)? Audience is something to carefully consider, because whom you write for helps to shape how you write. You would not write about mushrooms for a general audience in the same way that you would for an audience of mycologists. So if an audience hasn't been explicitly identified for you, clarify this with your instructor.

- Finally, what sort of constraints do you face? Consider formal constraints, like length, formatting, number of required sources, and due dates. Then, consider external constraints, like other coursework and responsibilities that may compete with this research project for your time and energy. How will you balance these demands and still produce the best work you can?

To know precisely what an assignment asks of you, you must understand its language. Essay assignments use specific verbs to tell you what actions are required of you. But if you are unfamiliar with the verbs or with how they are used in an academic setting, you may fail to successfully complete the assignment. Table 7.1 includes examples of common essay assignment verbs.

Table 7.1: Essay Assignment Verbs

Simple		Complex	
account	give a reason for; explain	*analyze*	break into separate parts and discuss, examine, or interpret each part
identify	point out and describe	*criticize*	make judgments; evaluate comparative worth; support your judgment with evidence and careful reasoning
outline	describe main ideas, characteristics, or events; emphasise structure, leaving out minor details	*interpret*	comment on; give examples; describe relationships; explain meanings; describe, then evaluate

■ **Activity 7.1** **Know Your Essay Verbs**

Carefully read your assignment sheet, and identify the key verbs that are used to explain your task. How many did you find? Which verbs are simple and which are complex? In your own words, rewrite the assignment instructions as you understand them.

Let the Action Begin

Once you've carefully studied your assignment sheet and considered your rhetorical situation, it's time to get started. Later in the chapter, we'll discuss the research processes leading up to the initial drafting of your paper, including developing a research topic, proposing a research project, finding and evaluating sources, and planning your first draft. Chapter 8, "Writing the Research Essay," continues the discussion, working through writing processes from beginning to middle to end, and addressing specific writing concerns, like appropriate tone and style, flow, and structure.

7.2 Beginning Your Research

Developing a Critical Approach

Before you begin hunting for sources, you need to have a research topic. But a topic itself is not enough. Effective research writing comes not so much from having a compelling or exciting topic—space travel, or *Sharknado*—as from having a provocative or novel *approach* to a given topic. In fact, it is somewhat misleading to refer to a research topic when what is really required is some sort of critical research question.

It's fine to have a general topic in mind when you begin a project, but you quickly need to narrow your focus. Looking for sources with only a general topic—like wolves—in mind, is like beginning a trip with only a direction— like north—in mind. Knowing you want to go north eliminates three-quarters of your possible paths, but much remains up in the air: Where is your exact destination? From where precisely are you beginning? And why do you want to go north in the first place—what's the purpose?

In order to work out an approach, consider the following chart:

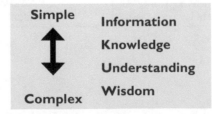

One can easily fall into the trap of thinking about research as just finding information. But as this chart suggests, *information* is just the beginning. Calling the search for information research is like looking up a restaurant's online menu and calling *that* research.

Knowledge is the next step—after all, a primary goal of research at the university level is the creation of new knowledge. But for our purposes, knowledge alone is not enough. Facts are useful to know, of course, but what a general reader wants, and what an effective research paper should provide, is a way to think about facts, which brings us to the next term: *understanding.*

An effective research paper does more than relate facts or data; it offers the reader a way to *understand* specific facts and data. For instance, data from the **Bureau of Labor Statistics** tell us that Americans' real wages have been essentially flat for fifty years. But what should a reader do with this fact? It isn't enough to simply acknowledge it or remember it. The reader needs to make some meaning from it, to put it into context to understand it and perhaps do something with it.

Striving for understanding means asking specific types of research questions. When developing an approach to your research topic, avoid questions with pat answers, ones that can be found simply by retrieving pertinent information. And avoid questions to which you (think you) already know the answers, unless you're willing to ask the questions in a new way. Such questions too often lead researchers to assume that connections and conclusions are obvious and require little support, when from a reader's perspective, they require ample evidence and vigorous explanation and analysis.

A research question should lead to *more* questions, such as "Why?" or "How?" Using the fact discussed earlier—that Americans' real wages have been flat for fifty years—the following "Why?" or "How?" questions can be asked about it:

- Why have Americans' real, inflation-adjusted wages remained flat for the past five decades?

- How have flat wages affected Americans' standard of living over the last fifty years?

- Why is it a cause for concern that Americans' real wages haven't risen in fifty years?

- How can Americans' wages be made to grow faster than they are now?

To answer these questions, you must ask additional, related questions—there are no pat answers here. Using the last question as an example, to understand what might be done to make wages grow faster, you should ask many related questions, like these:

- What forces usually cause a country's wages to rise?

- Are any of these forces present today in the United States?

- When wages rose quickly in the past, what caused that rise?

DeSilver, Drew. "For most workers, real wages have barely budged for decades." *Pew Research Center.* N.p., 9 Oct. 2014. Web. 15 Dec. 2015. <http://www.pewresearch.org/fact-tank/2014/10/09/for-most-workers-real-wages-have-barely-budged-for-decades/>

- How do wages in the United States compare with wages in other developed countries?

- Have other countries' real wages risen over the past fifty years, while Americans' wages have remained flat?

- If so, what differences exist between the two countries that might explain the wage disparity?

These are just some of the questions you might have to ask to find an answer to how Americans' wages might be made to grow faster. The list is not exhaustive, nor does it include all the questions that *have* to be asked. The list merely illustrates the point made above: A good research question generates more questions. By answering those additional related questions, you begin to develop an answer to the larger research question.

So what you want is a research *question*, not a research topic. And you want a research question that invites not pat answers—mere information or factual knowledge—but one that suggests a critical *approach*, and that aims at *understanding*.

Table 7.2 summarizes this discussion, using a new research subject.

Table 7.2: Simple to Complex: American Gun Violence

Basic Thinking	*Information*	*Topic:* "Guns"	Gives both researcher and reader no real direction. Invites decontextualized facts and data ("Siri, tell me something about guns."). Provides no clear focus, ignores context, and makes it difficult to distinguish among useful and useless sources.
Intermediate Thinking	*Knowledge*	*Basic Question:* "What number of Americans die each year from gun violence?"	Provides some direction, but invites a simple answer—a basic fact or definition. Does not implicitly invite analysis, explanation, or additional questions. May be useful as part of a larger, more nuanced research question, but is insufficient by itself.

Complex Thinking	*Understanding*	*Critical Question:* "How can American gun violence be reduced while preserving citizens' Second Amendment rights?"	Gives both researcher and reader a clear critical approach to a particular subject or problem. Allows researcher to clearly distinguish among useful and useless sources. Considers context, explicitly or implicitly. Leads to additional, related questions. Requires a nuanced discussion, including ample evidence, analysis, and explanation.
Guru	*Wisdom*	*Critical Mind-set and Experience*	Usually requires a critical, questioning mind-set, time, and broad experience. Not a feasible research goal. Cannot be rushed; cannot be achieved merely through hard work or cleverness alone. Sometimes confused with understanding, knowledge, or information, often by people with little or narrow experience. (See: Silicon Valley.)

As Table 7.2 shows, in order to move from a general topic to a focused, critical research question, you must move from basic thinking to complex thinking.

Approaching a research project in a critical manner takes *work*. But such critical thinking is also a skill that can be practiced and honed over time. So don't let initial challenges discourage you; if you're having trouble doing more than asking basic questions about your topic, for instance, a little focused practice can help you see more clearly how to develop the critical questions most useful for a research paper. The following activity, as well as those below, will help you do this sort of focused practice.

■ **Activity 7.2** **Moving from Basic to Complex**

> Look at Table 7.2 and replace the examples in the third column with your own
> material. First, add your general research topic. Next, see how many basic ques-
> tions you can ask about your topic. Finally, using the table as a model, see what
> sort of critical research questions you can ask about your topic. How many can
> you come up with?

Preliminary Thinking and Research

What if you *have* started with a general topic in mind—like *poverty*—but are struggling to find your way to a focused, critical research question? A good way to begin,
even before doing preliminary research, is to consider your topic through different
contextual *lenses*. How might you think about poverty through the lens of religion,
for example, or politics, or economics? Or you might consider even more limited
contexts, such as health care, food and nutrition, housing, or transportation.

What matters is not necessarily what context you choose, but that you do
choose a context and use it as a lens to carefully consider your general topic. Once
you start thinking this way, you will discover that you already have one or more
contexts in mind, even if you haven't previously recognized how they may shape
your thinking about a topic. When you say you want to write about poverty, what
you really mean is that you want to write about poverty in political and economic
contexts; you want to look into what is being done by the government to help those
in poverty, and find out what economic forces may be affecting the ability of poor
Americans to find gainful employment.

■ **Activity 7.3** **Considering Context**

> Contextual lenses are powerful tools for focusing and deepening a research
> project. Practice identifying such lenses using the following outline:
>
> I.   Choose a research topic. (You can use the topic you're considering for
>   your actual project, but any topic will do. In fact, doing this activity using
>   different topics will present you with varying intellectual challenges,
>   which will strengthen your critical thinking skills.)
> II. List as many possible contexts as you can for this topic (e.g., politics,
>   religion, culture, history, economics). Don't worry about contexts over-
>   lapping—just list as many as you can.
>   a. Choose two or three specific contexts from your list, and use them
>   to think about your topic. What sort of issues, questions, or prob-
>   lems do you come across when using a particular context as a
>   critical lens?
>   i.   For an extra challenge, choose a context that seems far-
>   fetched to you, and see if you can use it to find a workable
>   critical approach to your topic.

Note: Some informal online research may be useful when completing this activity.

 b. Here's a brief example to get you started:

  i. <u>Topic:</u> Woodworking

  ii. <u>Contexts:</u> Economic, Cultural, Religious, Labor/Employment, Natural Resources, Environmental

  iii. <u>Using a Contextual Lens:</u>

   1. Natural Resources: Thinking about woodworking in terms of natural resources leads you to think about wood as a resource. What sort of wood products are used in woodworking, and how are they supplied? How do you distinguish among superior and inferior wood resources? How are these resources supplied, and what sort of limits exist to how much can be supplied, or how much can be *sustainably* supplied? How have wood products changed over time—how is the type and selection of lumber and other wood products available today different from that available fifty years ago, or one hundred years ago? What accounts for these differences?

    • Note: There's obviously some contextual overlap here with *Environmental.* This overlap is OK. What matters is that you find a context that aids your critical thinking. Here, the general topic of woodworking is approached through the lens of natural resources, without focusing specifically on environmental concerns. But someone else may find it more helpful to approach the topic through the lens of environmental concerns. Such differences are normal. Again, what matters is that you find a contextual lens that works well for you, that stimulates your own critical thinking about your research topic.

   2. Religious: At first, it may seem that nothing useful can come from thinking about woodworking in a religious context. But there's some potential here. The Shaker community, for instance, developed a particularly influential and iconic approach to furniture design that persists to this day. You might explore the relationship between Shaker furniture design and the community's overall religious beliefs. You might also think in terms of production methods. Some religious communities place specific limits on the types of tools and technologies its members may use, which will obviously influence the type of products these communities both purchase and manufacture. How might such restrictions affect woodworking practices?

Preliminary research is also useful in moving from a general topic to a critical research question. The goal is to familiarize yourself with the topic, with at least some of its history, and with the way it is currently being addressed (if it is being addressed at all) in public discussions, through news media, social media, elected officials, and so on. In short, some general reading on your topic can help you find where the good research questions are, and whether or not anyone is asking them. And don't lock yourself into a particular research question or critical approach too quickly. Use your preliminary reading to explore new ground related to your topic.

Completing Activity 7.3 is useful here, as it will help you identify different ways to search for information on your topic. A search for "poverty [and] religion" will return quite different results from a search for "poverty [and] politics," for instance.

Preliminary research will also help you answer the "So what?" question about your topic, and answering that question is vital to your paper's ultimate success (the "So what?" question will be discussed further in Chapter 8). Your topic matters to you, or you wouldn't have chosen to write about it. But why should it matter to anyone else? Doing preliminary research on your topic can help you find this out; reviewing the current public discussion of your topic will help you determine both how it's being discussed and why people care about it. Then you can use this new knowledge to craft a critical approach to your topic. You might also discover an "in" for your discussion—a critical hole in the way a topic or issue is being talked about. Or you might even end up addressing the "So what?" question by saying, "This matters, but not for the reasons you think." In either case, preliminary research can help you to answer the "So what?" question early on.

After considering context and performing some initial research, you should begin trying to work out your research question. Sometimes this step will come easily—after all, you have already spent a fair amount of time thinking about your topic. Other times, though, you will need to continue working at your question. Here are some activities that can help you with that work.

■ Activity 7.4   Detail versus Big Picture

As you try to come up with an effective research question, it is helpful to know whether you are a detail-oriented person or a big-picture type of person. Figuring out where you are on a detail-oriented/big-picture spectrum is a way to acknowledge your own tendencies as a critical thinker. It can also help you acknowledge and address a particular weakness.

If you know that you are a person who tends to focus on details ("What is the average VT classroom size, in cubic feet?"), then you'll have to make a conscious attempt to broaden your critical perspective. But if you know that you tend to ask very broad, philosophical questions ("What *is* education, really?"), then you can expect to have to narrow your scope a bit.

On a scale of one to ten, one being the most detail-oriented, and ten being the biggest of big pictures, where do you see yourself? What's your number?

- This activity works best when done in small groups, or even as a whole class, where you have others with which to compare yourself.

Activity 7.5   Issues Tree

This activity should be done both in small groups and individually.

An "issues tree" (also known as a "logic tree") is a systematic and graphical approach to problem solving that breaks a complex question down into its component parts. The premise is simple: Write your research question on the left side of your page, and then make a list of all the questions you need to answer in order to answer your research question. Then, repeat this process with each of your sub-questions.

Here's an example, using our previous question about Americans' wages:

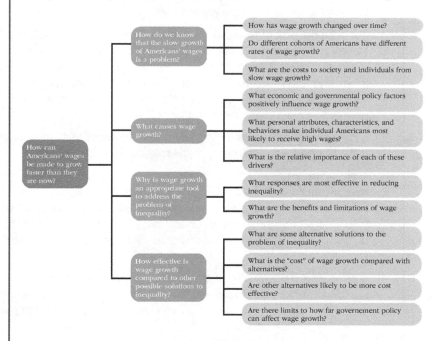

Notice how the questions branch off from one another to create a sideways "tree."

To be effective, your issues tree needs to follow three basic rules:

1. Your tree will come to an abrupt stop if the questions you include are easily answered with yes or no answers. Avoid questions that start with *is* and use questions that start with *why, how, when, where,* and *what.* And remember, you don't need to be able to answer these questions now.

2. Your completed tree should contain all the issues that need to be resolved, but they should not double up, overlap, or leave any gaps. This requirement is commonly expressed with the acronym MECE: Mutually Exclusive and Collectively Exhaustive. Creating a tree where every question is self-contained is difficult and will take time and creativity, but it is worth the effort. The more time you spend on planning your questions, the more straightforward and clear your thinking will become.

3. Each layer of sub-questions should be focused on the same level of detail, moving from big to small picture as you move from left to right. The left side of the page considers big-picture, "conceptual" thinking; the right side of the page outlines the smaller concrete details.

There are many reasons why this structured approach to thinking through your question is useful as you begin your research project:

- It breaks down your question into manageable parts: A good research question is complex, but complex problems can be big and daunting to think and write about. Breaking your question down into issues and sub-issues results in smaller questions that are easier to answer.

- It is a simple way of testing if your research question is going to work, because you'll have a visual representation of the complexity of your challenge. If you generate hundreds of sub-questions, your present research question is probably too broad to be answered in a single, focused paper. If you can barely think of any sub-questions, your research question is probably too narrow to sustain a long piece of analytical work.

- It can provide insight into missing issues and sub-issues that are necessary to make a strong argument, but that you may not have considered.

- It helps you work smarter and plan your research and writing. Once you have identified all the sub-questions you'll need to answer, you will have a clearer sense of what research and evidence you need to find. You will also have a sense of how to sequence and prioritize your work—that is, which questions need to be answered first and which require the most intellectual engagement.

- It provides a clear visual map that shows how each piece of your research fits into the whole, and allows you to share your plan with other people (like your classmates or your instructor) to explain what you are doing and to receive help and feedback.

Now, try creating an issues tree for your own topic. Recreate the chart on the previous page, but fill it in with your own topic and questions.

7.3 Writing a Proposal

Why write a proposal? By the time you get to the point where you can write a proposal, you've probably been working on your project for some time, in one way or another. So why not skip the formal proposal and just get on with your research?

Even if you've dutifully completed all of this chapter's activities, your thinking and writing about your research project are still scattered across several different documents. And if you haven't completed these activities to guide you in developing a research project, then your thinking about the project is likely only that—thinking. Your approach may seem clear to you, but you can't be sure of its value until you've articulated it in writing, allowing it to be read and critiqued by your peers or your instructor. Writing a formal proposal is important precisely because it forces you to clearly and concisely articulate what you'll do, how you'll do it, and why it matters.

More practically, a proposal is a common form of writing, and you are almost guaranteed to have to write one at some point in your professional career, whether you go into business, remain in the academic world, or pursue public service.

Common Features

Let's look at some common features of a formal proposal. Table 7.3 identifies such features and briefly explains their significance.

Table 7.3: Common Proposal Features

Description	A brief but precise explanation of the project. A sort of elevator pitch: If you had only one or two minutes to explain your project to another person, how would you do that? What about your project is most important to know, and what can be left out? Similar to the *abstract* that accompanies most journal papers; may even be called an abstract.)
Purpose	A clear discussion of the research project's specific goals. Often both articulates a project's particular aims and addresses their perceived significance (identifies goals and explains why those goals matter).
Methods	An explanation of how a project's goals will be pursued. What will research look like—what will the researcher(s) be *doing*? Often states how the approach is different from or better than previous approaches to the research problem.
Timeline	A detailed statement of the planned schedule for the project's completion. Usually broken into different sections that correspond to different stages in the research or writing process.
Resources	A brief description of the resources required to successfully complete the project. May be included in the "Methods" section, or may be a separate, supplemental discussion that addresses specific resources (e.g., treatment of animal or human subjects). Often also addresses specific financial or other resource needs, though these may be outlined in a separate section.

Your assigned proposal, and those you may have to write in the future, may not correspond precisely to the table above—specific labels and sectional divisions will vary, for instance. But there will be similarities among them. And some features almost always appear in a proposal in one form or another, such as the purpose statement and discussion of methods.

The following activities, which focus on comparative analysis, will help you begin thinking critically about the proposal genre. Working through these tasks carefully can help you not only in your present proposal assignment but also in your future proposals.

■ **Activity 7.6**   **Comparative Analysis**

1. Go to the "Sample Applications and Summary Statements" Web page for the National Institute of Allergy and Infectious Diseases (NIAID) at: https://www.niaid.nih.gov/researchfunding/grant/Pages/appsamples.aspx

2. Select two of the sample applications provided.

3. Review either the "Research Plan" or "Full Application" for each sample, and *write an analysis* that compares the documents with Table 7.3.

   a. Carefully lay out the similarities and differences among the sample applications and Table 7.3. For example: Do the features outlined in the table appear in the samples? Are their labels the same or different? Does each feature have a dedicated section, or are some features combined into a single discussion?

   b. Consider specifically the differences among the table and the sample applications you've selected. What accounts for these differences? (In other words, why do you think the NIAID grant application is structured the way it is?)

■ **Activity 7.7**   **Assignment Comparison**

1. Go to the "Strategy to Write the Research Plan" Web page for the National Institute of Allergy and Infectious Diseases (NIAID) at: https://www.niaid.nih.gov/researchfunding/grant/strategy/pages/3stratplan.aspx

2. Write a brief essay that compares your proposal assignment with the strategic guidelines provided by the NIAID. Identify similarities and differences and discuss their significance.

   a. For example, notice that the NIAID's "Strategy to Write the Research Plan" begins with a reminder to "Know Your Audience." Might this remark signal that the NIAID's strategy is an explicitly rhetorical one?

7.4 Finding Sources

Once you've chosen your topic, developed a workable research question, and composed a formal proposal, you're finally ready to begin the task that we usually associate with the term *research*—you're ready to begin collecting sources.

Be Strategic

Begin your search for sources with a clear plan. A carefully considered research strategy will save you time and energy, and it will help make your search more fruitful. Access to information is not generally a problem today. The problem is knowing where to find the information you need and how to distinguish among source types and qualities. In short, finding sources today is all about sorting, selecting, and evaluating.

In this chapter, you have already spent some time thinking about ways to focus your research project. Such focus has the happy side effect of helping to limit the volume of information you'll have to sort through when selecting sources. But it is also useful to develop a specific strategy for finding your sources, to work out a method for breaking down your search for material into logical, manageable chunks.

Your specific method will depend, of course, on your particular research project. A good basic strategy to begin with is to think in terms of needs: What do you need as the researcher and writer? And what does your reader need? Table 7.4 addresses these questions.

Table 7.4: Thinking in Terms of Needs

Your Needs	Basic Facts/Data/ Information	Answers to basic, discrete questions (e.g., "How do wages in the United States compare with wages in other developed countries?"), which will help to answer your overall research question.
	Critical/ Conceptual/ Contextual Sources	Material that helps to explain and support your *approach* to your research project. May range from basic historical or contextual information to explanations of special theories or ideologies. Often also helps to address the "So what?" question.
Reader's Needs	Reason to Invest	Material that draws the reader in both intellectually *and* emotionally.
	Proof That It Matters	Convincing arguments or illustrative examples that answer the "So what?" question, showing why anyone should care about the topic or your approach to it.
	Examples and Explanations	Illustrative examples and respectful explanations of complex, esoteric, or idiosyncratic concepts, theories, or technical processes.

Table 7.4 is a useful way to conceptually break up the task of finding sources, helping to identify different limited, specific goals for our research. But the divisions suggested by the table aren't hard and fast; there is some overlap among the categories. For instance, the examples and explanations your reader may need are likely to overlap with your own need to explain and support your approach to your research project. Nevertheless, developing a research strategy like the one above can be an effective tool for making your search for information as efficient and successful as possible.

■ **Activity 7.8** **Develop a Research Strategy**

> Using Table 7.4 as a starting point, develop a chart for your own particular research topic. What basic facts or data do you need to find? What historical or critical contexts do you need to explain to your reader, and what sources will you use to do that? How will you give your reader a reason to invest in your research paper—how will you "hook" them? Use the basic categories in Table 7.4, flesh them out, and identify specific research needs for your own project.

Where to Find What You Need: University Libraries

Virginia Tech has multiple library branches, but for simplicity's sake, the singular *library* is used throughout this section.

While much of your writing and research work now happens online, libraries remain indispensable to research. **Virginia Tech's library** is an invaluable resource for your research work in this class and beyond, providing access to databases, books and periodicals (both print and electronic), and other media that you might not otherwise be able to use. In addition, the library remains a vital gathering place for students doing all kinds of work, such as organizing group projects, practicing presentations in a classroom setting, or getting research advice from a librarian with experience in a pertinent discipline.

For a full overview of the library's resources, see Chapter 10, and visit the library Web site at http://www.lib.vt.edu. Below are a few key ways that the library can aid your research.

Summon.   Summon is the library's Google-like search engine. It connects you not only to the library's catalogue but also to pertinent databases and other resources related to your search terms. As Figure 7.1 shows, it is a very powerful research tool. For more information, visit http://www.lib.vt.edu/help/summon/index.html, or see Chapter 10, "Where Do You Go for Help?"

Figure 7.1 How to Use Summon

Databases.   Databases are indispensable tools for finding both journal and general audience articles, and they can be accessed directly through the Virginia Tech library Web site, at http://www.lib.vt.edu. Some databases are general-interest databases, indexing articles from newspapers, magazines, and even scholarly journals. While these databases can be useful when beginning your research, once you've focused your research topic, you'll need to use subject databases, which primarily index articles from more specialized scholarly and technical journals.

The difference between scholarly journal articles and other articles is important. Articles found in popular journals or magazines are often published widely and usually address a general audience, meaning they are useful for introductory or background information on a topic. Scholarly journal articles, on the other hand, are typically both written and published by academic researchers, are filled with more specialized information, and are most useful once you have narrowed your topic and developed specific research questions.

Interlibrary Loan (ILLiad).   Despite the university library's vast collection of materials, you will sometimes still need to find a source that you cannot access by visiting the library or using its online databases. In such cases, you can often get the source you need by using interlibrary loan, or ILLiad. For more information, see Figure 7.2, and visit http://www.lib.vt.edu/ill/index.html.

Figure 7.2 ILLiad: Interlibrary Loan

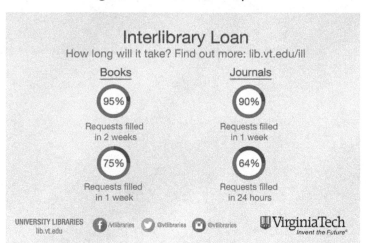

Special Collections.   Despite its location—the first floor of Newman Library, right next to the café—Special Collections is regularly overlooked by students. But it is a valuable and singular space in the library, providing access to manuscripts, rare books, architectural drawings, historical photographs and maps, as well as Virginia Tech's archives. And as discussed later in this chapter, these materials can figure into research projects in ways you might not expect.

For more information, visit http://spec.lib.vt.edu, or check out the Special Collections introductory LibGuide at http://guides.lib.vt.edu/specialcollections/basicintroduction.

Types of Sources

The volume and variety of information available today is so vast that any attempt to address all possible types of sources would be foolish. But what we *can* do is look at some common ways to categorize sources, as well as consider a helpful strategy for thinking about sources in relation to your research project.

Table 7.5 looks at some basic ways to break down the types of sources now available.

Table 7.5: Categorizing Sources

Traditional Publications	Traditional materials (both print and electronic) that are still most commonly associated with the term *publishing*, such as books, magazines, newspapers, journals (trade and academic), and government reports and publications.
Publications Subject to Editorial or Peer Review	Books and articles that are subject to an oversight process *intended to maintain specific standards of quality and veracity.* General audience publications tend to have editorial oversight, while journals, especially academic, tend to rely on peer review.
Personal Web Sites/Blogs	Personal writing not usually subject to oversight. Quality depends in part on whether such writing is done by an expert, as well as whether the writer sticks to subjects related to her or his field of expertise. Prolonged reading experience is sometimes needed to gauge value. Two strong examples: • Paul Krugman (economics) at: http://krugman.blogs.nytimes.com • Tom Murphy (physics) at: http://physics.ucsd.edu/do-the-math/
Social and Opinion Media	Not generally considered a source of reasoned discourse with verifiable, carefully supported claims. Can be a valuable resource, depending on its use—helpful for projects looking at public opinion, subcultural thought, etc.
Primary versus Secondary	*Primary* sources are firsthand experiences or accounts (e.g., diaries or interviews), while *secondary* sources are those at least one step removed from direct experience (e.g., historical nonfiction).

Special Collections and Archives. As mentioned above, Special Collections offers unique resources to researchers. Archival and primary documents generally can be quite valuable to a research project. For example, say that you are developing a research project on NASA and the value of space exploration. Such a project could be greatly enriched by your holding, experiencing, and using primary documents, such as Charles Lindbergh's letter to Michael Collins following the first moon landing or the original flight plan for the *Apollo 11* mission. These documents and others are available for your use through Virginia Tech's Special Collections, which serves as home for the Archives of American Aerospace Exploration (AAAE).

Or perhaps you are doing a project exploring how women's place in the professional world has changed over time. Then documents from the International Archive of Women in Architecture (IAWA), also housed at VT's Special Collections, may be of particular value to you.

Resources like these enrich a research project, helping to give it a depth and perspective difficult to achieve using only recently published online materials. So get to know Special Collections. Check out the introductory LibGuide or get in touch with the Special Collections staff, who can help you find resources for your current project. Special Collections offers you a unique research experience, one that you don't want to miss out on.

■   **Activity 7.9**   **Reflecting on Sources**

Review the areas that Special Collections actively collects in (see LibGuide), or is particularly strong in, and find an artifact (text, manuscript, or other item) that relates to one of your interests.

Once you have found an artifact that interests you, work through it by answering, in paragraph form, the reflection questions below. Conclude your reflection by discussing how the artifact you've chosen might fit into a larger research project. What other sorts of sources might your artifact be paired with in a larger research project? What research question might your artifact help answer, or what topic might it illuminate?

Document Reflection Questions

Initial Response

- What sort of "gut reaction" do you have to this text, and why do you think you have that reaction? What connections do you immediately make, and why do you think you make them? Also, what do you wonder? That is, in what ways does this text make you ponder or ask questions about history, human relations, the meaning of life?

Close Reading

- What is known? What can we know just from the text itself?
- What is unknown? What can't we know—what questions do we have that cannot be answered by the text alone
- What can be inferred? What can we responsibly infer from the text alone?

Rhetorical Context

- Who created the text?
- Why did they create it—what is the text's purpose?
- For whom was the text created—who is its audience?

Other Contexts

- What other contexts might have bearing on the way we understand the text? Can we understand the text as responding to, or influenced by, a particular context (e.g., historical, cultural, religious, political, class, racial)?

Fieldwork.   Specific kinds of fieldwork vary widely from discipline to discipline. In the writing classroom, fieldwork refers to the ways of directly accessing experience, knowledge, or opinion: the creation of primary sources.

So what does such fieldwork look like? Table 7.6 lays out some ways that fieldwork, generally speaking, may figure into a research project.

Table 7.6: Fieldwork Possibilities

General Research Topic	Fieldwork Possibilities
College Student Thought and Behavior	*Interview* individual college students regarding their experiences.
	Survey many college students regarding their experiences.
	Record direct observation of or experience with other college students.
A Specific Architecture or Design Movement	*Interview* faculty or other experts in the architecture and design fields.
	Record direct observation of or experience with a building or artifact that exemplifies the design movement you're studying.
Local Food Production	*Interview* individuals involved in local food production, either as producers or consumers.
	Survey a representative sample of the local population regarding their awareness of and/or consumption of locally produced food.
	Record direct observation of or experience with local food being produced or sold.

For more detailed information on fieldwork, see the following section on primary research.

■ **Activity 7.10**   **Fieldwork: Local History**

> Find documents in Special Collections related to a specific building on campus or in the local community (e.g., Burruss Hall, War Memorial & Chapel, The Lyric Theatre, the Post Office building on Main St.). Learn basic information about the building, such as when it was built and any notable events in its history. Then observe and experience the building yourself. Interview students and locals about the building, especially if they are there when you visit.
>
> Write a narrative account of your archival research and fieldwork, including personal critical reflection on both experiences.

7.5 Conducting Primary Research

Although the library and the Internet offer a wealth of authoritative information, in the workplace you will often need to conduct primary research because you need new information. There are eight major categories of primary research: analysis of social-media data, observations and demonstrations, inspections, experiments, field research, interviews, inquiries, and questionnaires.

Analysis of Social-Media Data

Every hour, people post about 30 million comments, about 7 million photos, and some 453 years of video footage on social media[1]. A torrent of information is continuously coming online, and many organizations are working hard to sift through it to find useful insights.

■ **Activity 7.11**   **Document Analysis**

Evaluating Information from Internet Sources

The following blog post appears in the FAQ section of the Climate Change Truth File section of the Web site of the Committee for a Constructive Tomorrow. The questions below ask you to consider the guidelines for evaluating Internet sources.

1. This portion of the site is called "Climate Change Truth File." Does this title make you more likely or less likely to consider the information authoritative?

2. If you were considering using this source in a document you were writing, what information would you want to discover about the site and the organization that publishes it? How would you locate it?

3. The bulk of this passage is devoted to two prominent scientists who have changed their minds on the question of whether human-caused global warming is a serious threat. If the claim about the two scientists is true, does the case for human-caused global warming collapse?

---

[1] McCaney, K. (2013, June 18). Energy lab team explores new ways of analyzing social media. GCN. Retrieved June 26, 2013, from http://gen.com/articles, 2013/06/18/Energy-lab-new-ways-analyzing-social-media.aspx

How can you ignore thousands of scientists who say manmade global warming is a serious threat?

The idea that there is a "scientific consensus" does not hold up. Scientists who are skeptical about "dangerous manmade climate change" have been speaking out for years. Just this year, two prominent former believers in man-made global warming announced they were reconsidering the science.

"Gaia" scientist James Lovelock had been "alarmist" about climate change for years. Now he says "The problem is we don't know what the climate is doing. We thought we knew 20 years ago."

German meteorologist Klaus-Eckart Puls also reversed his belief in man-made global warming in 2012 and called the idea CO_2 can regulate climate "sheer absurdity." "Ten years ago I simply parroted what the IPCC told us," he said. "One day I started checking the facts and data. First I started with a sense of doubt, but then I became outraged when I discovered that much of what the IPCC and media were telling us was sheer nonsense and was not even supported by any scientific facts and measurements. To this day, I still feel shame that as a scientist I made presentations of their science without first checking it."

In 2010, a report documented that More Than 1000 International Scientists Dissented Over Man-Made Global Warming Claims. Many of them were former IPCC scientists. Climate scientist Mike Hulme dismantled the "thousands of scientists agree" claim put forth by the United Nations and news media. Claims that "2,500 of the world's leading scientists have reached a consensus that human activities are having a significant influence on the climate" are disingenuous, Hulme noted. The key scientific case for CO_2 driving global warming, like many others in the IPCC reports, "is reached by only a few dozen experts in the specific field of detection and attribution studies; other IPCC authors are experts in other fields." Other scientists are excluded or not consulted.

Dr. William Schlesinger agrees with the UN climate view but has admitted that only 20% of UN IPCC scientists deal with climate. In other words, 80% of the UN's IPCC membership are experts in other fields and have no dealing with or expertise in climate change as part of their academic studies.

Source: Committee for a Constructive Tomorrow, 2013: www.cfact.org/issues/climate-change/climate-change-truth-file/. Reprinted by permission of Committee for a Constructive Tomorrow, www.CFACT.org.

Businesses are spending the most time on social-media research, trying to figure out what customers like and dislike about their products and services, learn what they want, and reinforce brand loyalty. Take the case of Nielsen, which for fifty years has been monitoring the TV viewing habits of Americans by distributing questionnaires and attaching devices to their TVs, and then selling the data it collects to TV networks and producers, who use the information to determine how much to charge advertisers. The problem at Nielsen is that many people don't watch TV on TV or they don't watch shows when they are broadcast. Now Nielsen also uses social-media analysis: gathering data by monitoring social media to listen in on what people are saying on Twitter, Facebook, and other services about different TV programs.[2]

But organizations other than businesses are analyzing social-media data, too. For instance, the U.S. Geological Survey created the Twitter Earthquake Detector (TED), a program to monitor Twitter for the use of the word *earthquake*. Why? Because they realized that when people experience earthquakes, a lot of them tweet about it. The Centers for Disease Control, a U.S. federal agency, analyzes keywords on social media to monitor the spread of diseases, such as the H7N9 flu virus, in the United States and around the world. According to one scientist, "The world is equipped with human sensors—more than 7 billion and counting. It's by far the most extensive sensor network on the planet. What can we learn by paying attention?" (McCaney, 2013).

One more example: In 2008, an article in a medical journal suggested that lithium might slow down the progression of ALS, a condition sometimes called Lou Gehrig's Disease. But the study reported on only a small number of patients with ALS. When other people with ALS heard about the article, they suggested gathering data from people with ALS across the country. Some 596 patients volunteered: some who were already using lithium, some who were not, and some who started using it (with the approval of their doctors). Although studies such as this do not replace controlled double-blind experiments (in which neither the patients nor the researchers know whether the patients received the therapy), they are much faster and cheaper, and they can help researchers determine how to use their limited experimental resources wisely. According to the director of the ALS study, "sometimes the alternative is not our way or the old way. It is our way or it is not studied at all."[3]

How do you perform social-media data analysis? There are many software programs that can help you devise searches. Among the most popular is Hootsuite, which includes tools for listening in on what people are saying about your company on social media such as Twitter, Facebook, LinkedIn, and many other services. In addition, Hootsuite helps you monitor and manage your company's social-media presence and provides analytics: demographic data about who is following your company, their attitudes, and their behaviors. Figure 7.3 shows a Hootsuite dashboard, the screen that lets you view and manage all the information.

---

[2]DeVault, G. (2013). Market research case study. Nielsen Twitter TV rating metric. Retrieved June 26, 2013, from http://marketresearch.about.com/od/market.research.social.media/a/Market-Research-Case-Study-Nielsen-Twitter-Tv-Rating-Metric.htm

[3]Marcus, A.D. (2011 April 25). ALS study shows social media's value as research tool. *Wall Street Journal*. Retrieved June 26, 2013, from http://www.wsj.com/articles/SB10001424052748704489604576283010994997034

Figure 7.3 A Hootsuite Dashboard (courtesy of Hootsuite).

Like other similar tools for managing social media, Hootsuite enables you to keep your personal and business social media separate. Here we see a portion of a person's personal social-media feed.

You set up "streams," which are filters that enable you to see only those tweets and other media that meet certain criteria. For instance, "News Feed" filters out everything that is not news. "News Feed—Photos" shows only news items that include photos. "Mentions" shows only those items in which you are mentioned.

Observations and Demonstrations

Observation and demonstration are two common forms of primary research. When you *observe*, you simply watch some activity to understand some aspect of it. For instance, if you were trying to determine whether the location of the break room was interfering with work on the factory floor, you could observe the situation, preferably at different times of the day and on different days of the week. If you saw workers distracted by people moving in and out of the room or by sounds made in the room, you would record your observations by taking notes, taking photos, or shooting video of events. An observation might lead to other forms of primary research. You might, for example, follow up by interviewing some employees who could help you understand what you observed.

When you witness a *demonstration* (or *demo*), you are watching someone carry out a process. For instance, if your company was considering buying a mail-sorting machine, you could arrange to visit a manufacturer's facility, where technicians would show how the machine works. If your company was considering a portable machine, such as a laptop computer, manufacturers or dealers could demo their products at your facility.

When you plan to observe a situation or witness a demo, prepare beforehand. Write down the questions you need answered or the factors you want to investigate. Prepare interview questions in case you have a chance to speak with someone. Think about how you are going to incorporate the information you acquire into the document you will write. Finally, bring whatever equipment you will need (pen and paper, computer, camera) to the site of the observation or demo.

Inspections

Inspections are like observations, but you participate more actively. For example, a civil engineer can determine what caused a crack in a foundation by inspecting the site: walking around, looking at the crack, photographing it and the surrounding scene, examining the soil. An accountant can determine the financial health of an organization by inspecting its financial records, perhaps performing calculations and comparing the data she finds with other data.

These professionals are applying their knowledge and professional judgment as they inspect a site, an object, or a document. Sometimes inspection techniques are more complicated. A civil engineer inspecting foundation cracking might want to test his hunches by bringing soil samples back to the lab for analysis.

When you carry out an inspection, do your homework beforehand. Think about how you will use the data in your document: Will you need photographs or video files or computer data? Then prepare the materials and equipment you'll need to capture the data.

Experiments

Learning to conduct the many kinds of experiments used in a particular field can take months or even years. This discussion is a brief introduction. In many cases, conducting an experiment involves four phases.

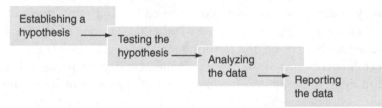

- **Establishing a hypothesis.** A hypothesis is an informed guess about the relationship between two factors. In a study relating gasoline octane and miles per gallon, a hypothesis might be that a car will get five percent better mileage with 89-octane gas than with 87-octane gas.

- **Testing the hypothesis.** Usually, you need an experimental group and a control group. These two groups should be identical except for the condition you are studying: in the above example, the gasoline. The control group would be a car running on 87 octane. The experimental group would be an identical car running on 89 octane. The experiment would consist of driving the two cars over an identical course at the same speed—preferably in some sort of controlled environment—over a given distance, such as 1,000 miles. Then you would calculate the miles per gallon. The results would either support or refute your original hypothesis.

- **Analyzing the data.** Do your data show a correlation—one factor changing along with another—or a causal relationship? For example, we know that sports cars are involved in more fatal accidents than sedans (there is a stronger correlation for sports cars), but we don't know what the causal relationship is— whether the car or the way it is driven is the important factor.

- **Reporting the data.** When researchers report their findings, they explain what they did, why they did it, what they saw, what it means, and what ought to be done next.

Field Research

Whereas an experiment yields quantitative data that typically can be measured precisely, most field research is qualitative; that is, it yields data that typically cannot be measured precisely. Often in field research, you seek to understand the quality of an experience. For instance, you might want to understand how a new seating arrangement affects group dynamics in a classroom. You could design a study in which you observed and shot video of classes and interviewed the students and the instructor about their reactions to the new arrangement. Then you could do the same in a traditional classroom and compare the results.

Some kinds of studies have both quantitative and qualitative elements. In the case of classroom seating arrangements, you could include some quantitative measures, such as the number of times students talked with one another. You could also distribute questionnaires to elicit ratings by the students and the instructor. If you used these same quantitative measures on enough classrooms, you could gather valid quantitative information.

When you are doing quantitative or qualitative studies on the behavior of animals—from rats to monkeys to people—try to minimize two common problems:

- **The effect of the experiment on the behavior you are studying.** In studying the effects of the classroom seating arrangement, minimize the effects of your own presence. For instance, if you observe in person, avoid drawing attention to yourself. Also, make sure that the video camera is placed unobtrusively and that it is set up before the students arrive, so they don't see the process. Still, any time you bring in a camera, you cannot be sure that what you witness is typical.

- **Bias in the recording and analysis of the data.** Bias can occur because researchers want to confirm their hypotheses. In an experiment to determine whether students write differently on physical keyboards than on touch screens, a researcher might see differences where other people don't. For this reason, the experiment should be designed so that it is *double blind*. That is, the students shouldn't know what the experiment is about so that they don't change their behavior to support or negate the hypothesis, and the data being analyzed should be disguised so that researchers don't know whether they are examining the results from the control group or the experimental group. For example, the documents produced on keyboards and touch screens should be printed out the same way.

Conducting an experiment or field research is relatively simple; the hard part is designing your study so that it accurately measures what you want it to measure.

Interviews

Interviews are extremely useful when you need information on subjects that are too new to have been discussed in the professional literature or are too narrow for widespread publication (such as local political questions).

In choosing a respondent—a person to interview—answer three questions:

- **What questions do you want to answer?** Only when you know this can you begin to search for a person who can provide the information.

- **Who could provide this information?** The ideal respondent is an expert willing to talk. Unless there is an obvious choice, such as the professor carrying out the research you are studying, use directories, such as local industrial guides, to locate potential respondents.

- **Is the person willing to be interviewed?** Contact the potential respondent by phone or in writing and state what you want to ask about. If the person is not able to help you, he or she might be willing to refer you to someone who can. Explain why you have decided to ask him or her. (A compliment works better than admitting that the person you really wanted to interview is out of town.) Explain what you plan to do with the information, such as write a report or present a talk. Then, if the person is willing to be interviewed, set up an appointment at his or her convenience.

When you wish to present the data from an interview in a document you are preparing, include a transcript of the interview (or an excerpt from the interview). You will probably present the transcript as an appendix so that readers can refer to it but are not slowed down when reading the body of the document. You might decide to present brief excerpts from the transcript in the body of the document as evidence for points you make.

Guidelines: Conducting an Interview

PREPARING FOR THE INTERVIEW

Follow these suggestions for preparing for and conducting an interview—and for following up after the interview.

- **Do your homework.** If you ask questions that have already been answered in the professional literature, the respondent might become annoyed and uncooperative.

- **Prepare good questions.** Good questions are clear, focused, and open.
  - **Be clear.** The respondent should be able to understand what you are asking.

Unclear	Why do you sell Trane products?
Clear	What are the characteristics of Trane products that led you to include them in your product line?

    The unclear question can be answered in a number of unhelpful ways: "Because they're too expensive to give away" or "Because I'm a Trane dealer."

  - **Be focused.** The question must be narrow enough to be answered briefly. If you want more information, you can ask a follow-up question.

Unfocused	What is the future of the computer industry?
Focused	What will the American chip industry look like in 10 years?

  - **Ask open questions.** Your purpose is to get the respondent to talk. Don't ask a lot of questions that have yes or no answers.

Closed	Do you think the federal government should create industrial partnerships?
Open	What are the advantages and disadvantages of the federal government's creating industrial partnerships?

- **Check your equipment.** If you will be recording the interview, test your voice recorder or video camera to make sure it is operating properly.

BEGINNING THE INTERVIEW

- **Arrive on time.**

- **Thank the respondent for taking the time to talk with you.**

- **State the subject and purpose of the interview and what you plan to do with the information.**

- **If you wish to record the interview, ask permission.**

CONDUCTING THE INTERVIEW

- **Take notes.** Write down important concepts, facts, and numbers, but don't take such copious notes that you can't make eye contact with the respondent or that you are still writing when the respondent finishes an answer.

- **Start with prepared questions.** Because you are likely to be nervous at the start, you might forget important questions. Have your first few questions ready.

- **Be prepared to ask follow-up questions.** Listen carefully to the respondent's answer and be ready to ask a follow-up question or request a clarification. Have your other prepared questions ready, but be willing to deviate from them if the respondent leads you in unexpected directions.

- **Be prepared to get the interview back on track.** Gently return to the point if the respondent begins straying unproductively, but don't interrupt rudely or show annoyance. Do not say, "Whoa! I asked about layoffs in this company, not in the whole industry." Rather, say, "On the question of layoffs at this company, do you anticipate…?"

CONCLUDING THE INTERVIEW

- **Thank the respondent.**

- **Ask for a follow-up interview.** If a second meeting would be useful, ask to arrange one.

- **Ask for permission to quote the respondent.** If you think you might want to quote the respondent by name, ask for permission now.

AFTER THE INTERVIEW

- **Write down the important information while the interview is fresh in your mind.** (This step is unnecessary, of course, if you have recorded the interview.) If you will be printing a transcript of the interview, make the transcript now.

- **Send a brief thank-you note.** Within a day or two, send a note showing that you appreciate the respondent's courtesy and that you value what you have learned. In the note, confirm any previous offers you have made, such as to send the respondent a copy of your final document.

Figure 7.4 is from a transcript of an interview with an attorney specializing in information technology. The interviewer is a student who is writing about legal aspects of software ownership.

Figure 7.4 Excerpt from an Interview

Interview Transcript, Page 1

Q. Why is copyright ownership important in marketing software?

A. If you own the copyright, you can license and market the product and keep other people from doing so. It could be a matter of millions of dollars if the software is popular.

Q. Shouldn't the programmer automatically own the copyright?

A. If the programmer wrote the program on personal time, he or she should and does own the copyright.

Q. So "personal time" is the critical concept?

A. That's right. We're talking about the "work-made-for-hire" doctrine of copyright law. If I am working for you, anything I make under the terms of my employment is owned by you.

Q. What is the complication, then? If I make the software on my machine at home, I own it; If I'm working for someone, my employer owns it.

A. Well, the devil is in the details. Often the terms of employment are casual, or there is no written job description or contract for the particular piece of software.

Q. Can you give me an example of that?

A. Sure. There was a 1992 case, *Aymes v. Bonelli*. Bonelli owned a swimming pool and hired Aymes to write software to handle record keeping on the pool. This was not part of Bonelli's regular business; He just wanted a piece of software written. The terms of the employment were casual. Bonelli paid no health benefits, Aymes worked irregular hours, usually unsupervised—Bonelli wasn't a programmer. When the case was heard, the court ruled that even though Bonelli was paying Aymes, Aymes owned the copyright because of the lack of involvement and participation by Bonelli. The court found that the degree of skill required by Aymes to do the job was so great that, in effect, he was creating the software by himself, even though he was receiving compensation for it.

Q. How can such disagreements be prevented? By working out the details ahead of time?

A. Exactly. The employer should have the employee sign a statement that the project is being carried out as work made for hire and should register the copyright with the U.S. Copyright Office in Washington. Conversely, employees should try to have the employer sign a statement that the project is not work made for hire and should try to register the copyright themselves.

Q. And if agreement can't be reached ahead of time?

A. Then stop right there. Don't do any work.

The student prompts the attorney to expand her answers.

The student responds to the attorney's answers, making the interview more of a discussion.

Inquiries

A useful alternative to a personal interview is to send an inquiry. This inquiry can take the form of a letter, an email, or a message sent through an organization's Web site. Although digital inquiries are more convenient for both the sender and the recipient, a physical letter is more formal and therefore might be more appropriate if the topic is important (concerning personnel layoffs, for instance) or related to safety.

If you are lucky, your respondent will provide detailed and helpful answers. However, the respondent might not clearly understand what you want to know or might choose not to help you. Although the strategy of the inquiry is essentially that of a personal interview, inquiries can be less successful because the recipient has not already agreed to provide information and might not respond. Also, an inquiry, un-like an interview, gives you little opportunity to follow up by asking for clarification.

Questionnaires

Questionnaires enable you to solicit information from a large group of people. You can send questionnaires through the mail, email them, present them as forms on a Web site, or use survey software (such as SurveyMonkey).

Unfortunately, questionnaires rarely yield completely satisfactory results, for three reasons:

- **Some of the questions will misfire.** Respondents will misinterpret some of your questions or supply useless answers.

- **You won't obtain as many responses as you want.** The response rate will almost never exceed 50 percent. In most cases, it will be closer to 10 to 20 percent.

- **You cannot be sure the respondents are representative.** People who feel strongly about an issue are much more likely to respond to questionnaires than are those who do not. For this reason, you need to be careful in draw-ing conclusions based on a small number of responses to a questionnaire.

When you send a questionnaire, you are asking the recipient to do you a favor. Your goal should be to construct questions that will elicit the information you need as simply and efficiently as possible.

Asking Effective Questions   To ask effective questions, follow two suggestions:

- **Use unbiased language.** Don't ask, "Should U.S. clothing manufacturers protect themselves from unfair foreign competition?" Instead, ask, "Are you in favor of imposing tariffs on men's clothing?"

- **Be specific.** If you ask, "Do you favor improving the safety of automobiles?" only an eccentric would answer no. Instead, ask, "Do you favor requiring automobile manufacturers to equip new cars with electronic stability control, which would raise the price by an average of $300 per car?"

Table 7.7 explains common types of questions used in questionnaires.

Include an introductory explanation with the questionnaire. This explanation should clearly indicate who you are, why you are writing, what you plan to do with the information from the questionnaire, and when you will need it.

Table 7.7: Common Types of Questions Used in Questionnaires

Type of Question	Example	Comments
Multiple choice	Would you consider joining a company-sponsored sports team? Yes _____ No _____	The respondent selects one of the alternatives.
Likert scale	The flextime program has been a success in its first year. strongly disagree __ __ __ __ __ strongly agree	The respondent ranks the degree to which he or she agrees or disagrees with the statement. Using an even number of possible responses (six, in this case) increases your chances of obtaining useful data. With an odd number, many respondents will choose the middle response.
Semantic differentials	Logging on to the system simple __ __ __ __ __ __ difficult The description of the new desalinization process interesting __ __ __ __ __ __ boring	The respondent registers a response along a continuum between a pair of opposing adjectives. Usually, these questions measure a person's feelings about a task, an experience, or an object. As with Likert scales, an even number of possible responses yields better data.
Ranking	Please rank the following work schedules in order of preference. Put a 1 next to the schedule you would most like to have, a 2 next to your second choice, and so on. 8:00–4:30 _____ 9:00–5:30 _____ 8:30–5:00 _____ flexible _____	The respondent indicates the priority of a number of alternatives.

Type of Question	Example	Comments
Short answer	What do you feel are the major advantages of the new parts-requisitioning policy? 1. _____ 2. _____ 3. _____	The respondent writes a brief answer using phrases or sentences.
Short essay	The new parts-requisitioning policy has been in effect for a year. How well do you think it is working? _____ _____ _____ _____ _____ _____	Although essay questions can yield information you never would have found using closed-ended questions, you will receive fewer responses to them because answering them requires more effort. Also, essays cannot be quantified precisely, as data from other types of questions can.

Testing the Questionnaire   Before you send out *any* questionnaire, show it and its accompanying explanation to a few people who can help you identify any problems. After you have revised the materials, test them on people whose backgrounds are similar to those of your intended respondents. Revise the materials a second time, and, if possible, test them again. Once you have sent the questionnaire, you cannot revise it and resend it to the same people.

Administering the Questionnaire   Determining who should receive the questionnaire can be simple or difficult. If you want to know what the residents of a particular street think about a proposed construction project, your job is easy. But if you want to know what mechanical-engineering students in colleges across the country think about their curricula, you will need a background in sampling techniques to identify a representative sample.

Make it easy for respondents to present their information. For mailed questionnaires, include a self-addressed, stamped envelope.

Figure 7.5 below shows a sample questionnaire.

Figure 7.5 Questionnaire

September 6, 2016

To: All employees
From: William Bonoff, Vice President of Operations
Subject: Evaluation of the Lunches Unlimited food service

As you may know, every two years we evaluate the quality and cost of the food service that caters our lunchroom. We would like you to help in our evaluation by sharing your opinions about the food service. Please note that your responses will remain anonymous. Please drop the completed questionnaires in the marked boxes near the main entrance to the lunchroom.

1. Approximately how many days per week do you eat lunch in the lunchroom?
    0 _____   1 _____   2 _____   3 _____   4 _____   5 _____

2. At approximately what time do you eat in the lunchroom?
    11:30–12:30 _____   12:00–1:00 _____   12:30–1:30 _____   varies _____

3. A clean table is usually available. ┝━━━━━━━━━━━━━━━━━━━━━━
    strongly disagree _____ _____ _____ _____ _____ _____ strongly agree

4. The Lunches Unlimited personnel are polite and helpful.
    strongly disagree _____ _____ _____ _____ _____ _____ strongly agree

5. Please comment on the quality of the different kinds of food you have eaten in the lunchroom.
    a. Daily specials
       excellent _____   good _____   satisfactory _____   poor _____
    b. Hot dogs and hamburgers
       excellent _____   good _____   satisfactory _____   poor _____
    c. Other entrées
       excellent _____   good _____   satisfactory _____   poor _____

6. What *foods* would you like to see served that are not served now? ┝━━━━━━
    _____
    _____
    _____

7. What *beverages* would you like to see served that are not served now?
    _____
    _____
    _____

8. Please comment on the prices of the foods and beverages served.
    a. Hot meals (daily specials)
       too high _____   fair _____   a bargain _____
    b. Hot dogs and hamburgers
       too high _____   fair _____   a bargain _____
    c. Other entrées
       too high _____   fair _____   a bargain _____

9. Would you be willing to spend more money for a better-quality lunch if you thought the price was reasonable?
    yes, often _____   sometimes _____   not likely _____

10. On the other side of this sheet, please provide whatever comments you think will help us evaluate the catering service.
    _____

Thank you for your assistance.

Likert-scale questions 3 and 4 make it easy for the writer to quantify data about subjective impressions.

Short-answer questions 6 and 7 are best for soliciting ideas from respondents.

Presenting Questionnaire Data in Your Document   To decide where and how to present the data that you acquire from your questionnaire, think about your audience and purpose. Start with this principle: Important information is presented and analyzed in the body of a document, whereas less-important information is presented in an appendix (a section at the end that only some of your audience will read). Most often, different versions of the same information appear in both places.

Typically, the full questionnaire data are presented in an appendix. If you can, present the respondents' data—the answers they provided—in the questionnaire itself, as shown here:

1.   Approximately how many days per week do you eat lunch in the lunchroom?

0 **12**   1 **16**   2 **18**   3 **12**   4 **9**   5 **4**

2.   At approximately what time do you eat in the lunchroom?

11:30–12:30 **3**   12:00–1:00 **26**   12:30–1:30 **7**   varies **23**

Selected data might then be interpreted in the body of the document. For instance, you might devote a few sentences or paragraphs to the data for one of the questions. The following example shows how a writer might discuss the data from question 2.

Question 2 shows that 26 people say that they use the cafeteria between noon and 1:00. Only 10 people selected the two other times: 11:30–12:30 or 12:30–1:30. Of the 23 people who said they use the cafeteria at various times, we can conclude that at least a third—8 people—use it between noon and 1:00. If this assumption is correct, at least 34 people (26 + 8) use the cafeteria between noon and 1:00. This would explain why people routinely cannot find a table in the noon hour, especially between 12:15 and 12:30. To alleviate this problem, we might consider asking department heads not to schedule meetings between 11:30 and 1:30, to make it easier for their people to choose one of the less-popular times.

The body of a document is also a good place to discuss important nonquantitative data. For example, you might wish to discuss and interpret several representative textual answers to open-ended questions.

Ethics Note: Reporting and Analyzing Data Honestly

When you put a lot of time and effort into a research project, it's frustrating if you can't find the information you need or if the information you find doesn't help you say what you want to say. Your responsibility as a professional is to tell the truth.

If the evidence suggests that the course of action you propose won't work, don't omit that evidence or change it. Rather, try to figure out why the evidence does not support your proposal. Present your explanation honestly.

If you can't find reputable evidence to support your claim that one device works better than another, don't just keep silent and hope your readers won't notice. Explain why you think the evidence is missing and how you propose to follow up by continuing your research.

If you make an honest mistake, you are a person. If you cover up a mistake, you're a dishonest person. If you get caught fudging the data, you could be an unemployed dishonest person. If you don't get caught, you're still a smaller person.

7.6 Evaluating Sources

Source evaluation discussions often boil down to labeling sources as either acceptable or unacceptable, good or bad, trustworthy or biased. Such firm categories of course are sometimes useful, but when writing, it is better to think about a source's value in a slightly different way.

Earlier in the chapter, we addressed the value of thinking in terms of needs when searching for sources. Similar questions are equally useful when evaluating sources:

- How do I need or want to use this source?

- Can I use it in that way?

- Might this source be more valuable if used another way?

When we ask, "Is this source acceptable?" we're usually looking for a yes or no answer. But the most appropriate response is often this: "That depends on what you are trying to do with it." Even biased, false, or misleading material can be useful, depending on how a researcher puts it to use.

For instance, say that you're writing about a particular historical event, and you come across a biased account of that event in a magazine article. If your purpose is to write a brief but accurate description of the event in question, then this biased account is of little use to you. But what if your purpose is to write a critical analysis of the ways in which misleading media coverage of an event has influenced the public's perception of what happened? Suddenly the biased account becomes much more useful to you as a specific example of the media coverage you wish to analyze.

A source's value, then, depends on your purpose for it. Labeling a source as good or bad, truthful or misleading, doesn't indicate its value to you as a researcher and writer; truthful sources can be used poorly, and misleading ones can be used effectively. What matters is whether the source is fitted to your purpose for it.

Let's look at this approach in a larger context. Table 7.8 illustrates how sources can be broken down by purpose and type for a research project related to traffic and parking on Virginia Tech's campus.

Table 7.8: Source Type and Purpose

Purpose	Source Type
Introduction	*Direct Experience*: A firsthand account can illustrate the present traffic and parking circumstances, as well as raise specific problems/concerns (personal, or via interview).
Present Context	*Facts and Figures*: Specific data can help to support and articulate the problems/concerns raised in the introduction (research/survey reports, journal articles, etc.).
	Official Account/Opinion: A statement on the problems/concerns by a university/public official is an important part of the present context (interview, or pull from existing articles).
Student Interests	*Fieldwork*: Allows direct expression of students' understanding of, and opinion on, problems/concerns (interview or survey).
	Organizational Position(s): Offers a different student perspective (interview, or pull from existing articles).
University Interests	*Official Account/Opinion*: Additional and perhaps more in-depth expression of university officials' understanding of, and opinions on, problems/concerns (interview, or pull from existing articles).
	University Publication: Provides the university's official, published position on problems/concerns (institutional plans, reports, or promotional materials that specifically address the problems/concerns).
Environmental Concerns	*Facts and Figures*: Specific data can help to place the problems/concerns within a larger environmental context, especially in terms of the environmental impact of infrastructure/transportation.
	Expert Opinion: Provides expert judgment on how the problems/concerns in question should be addressed in an environmentally responsible way (interview [e.g., VT faculty], pull from existing newspaper, magazine, or journal articles).
Conclusion	*Case Studies*: One or two examples of responses to similar problems/concerns can help build a strong ending. What do the results tell us about how we should act? (magazine or journal articles)

As you can see, Table 7.8 considers sources in terms of type and purpose, which helps to ensure that the researcher will evaluate potential sources in the proper terms: What is she or he looking for, and how does she or he plan to use it? But such a plan isn't exhaustive, of course, nor is it final. As you work through your research, be flexible, responding to what you actually find. You may find unexpected sources that you'd like to include in your paper, or you may discover a new way to use an existing source. Whatever the case, you should be willing to adjust your plan depending on what you find.

■ **Activity 7.12** **Planning by Source Type and Purpose**

> Using Table 7.8 as a template, create a chart for your own research project that identifies the different types of sources you expect to use, as well as their specific purpose within your paper. This activity will help you find and evaluate new sources, as well as review the sources you already have and clarify your purpose for them.

■ **Activity 7.13** **Analyze Another Author's Plan**

> Using Table 7.8 as a template again, create a chart for one of the research readings in the textbook. Choose a reading where outside material is explicitly identified—for example, Lee Ann Fisher Baron's "The Influence of 'Junk Science' and the Role of Science Education" (p. 448) or Nicholas Carr's "iGod" (p. 452)—and then sort that material according to type and purpose.
>
> Then, write a brief analysis that considers how the author uses each source and that evaluates how well each source fits the purpose you identify.

The Annotated Bibliography

You will likely be asked to compile an annotated bibliography as part of your research project. But why do you need to write one? Far from being busy work, writing an annotated bibliography is an excellent way to make serious progress toward your final research paper. Provided your bibliography is sufficiently detailed, it can have many benefits: It ensures that you know your sources thoroughly; it allows you to identify key quotes for use in your final paper; it can catalyze the synthesis process by highlighting important relationships among your sources; and it helps you to identify holes in your research—questions you've yet to answer, connections you've yet to make, and evidence that needs additional support. In short, an annotated bibliography is a great way to take stock of what you have, how you plan to use it, and what else you need to get.

The following is an example of an annotated bibliography assignment.

Annotated Bibliography and Comparative Analysis

> Write an annotated bibliography that takes stock of the sources you have so far, examining them with an eye toward how well they will fulfill your intended purpose for them, and how well they work together.

The bibliography should be arranged in alphabetical order, as is standard, and the entry for each source should have three parts:

Part 1: Bibliographic Entry

This section gives the publication information: author, date, title, book or journal, volume page numbers, etc. [MLA Format; Bold Print]
Example:

Weiner, Lois. "Teachers and Cops." *Jacobin* 28 Dec. 2014. Web. 3 Jan. 2015.

Part 2: Summary

This section articulates an objective summary of the reading. It should convey precisely what the author states in the source.

1. It should distill the original article or source.

2. It should trace the main points of the author's argument or discussion.

3. It should reference particularly important examples/outside sources used to support the argument or discussion.

4. It should use selective quotation.

5. It should be only one paragraph long.

Part 3: Quotes

This section directly quotes two or three statements the author made in the article that you feel exemplify its claims or interpretations. Or you will choose passages that directly relate to and support an important point in your own paper. You can also choose sentences that you feel the author expressed exceptionally well. Include the page number(s) where you found the quote (use paragraph numbers in the absence of separate pages). Place quotation marks around the chosen passage and make sure that you cite the passage verbatim.

Following the last bibliographic entry, include a brief reflection essay (one to two pages) that critically compares all the sources you've gathered so far with an eye toward the role they will play within your final research paper. In other words, you should answer the questions "What do I have?" and "How will I use it?" After working through all your sources for the bibliography, how well do the sources fit together? Do you still think that your sources fit their purpose within your project?

Do you find any spaces in your research that need to be filled—sources that need additional support, purposes that still lack a source? Use this reflection to take stock of what you have and identify what else you need to do.

7.7 Planning and Progress

Write an Essay Plan

If you've been dutifully completing all of this chapter's activities, then you've already done a fair amount of planning for your research paper. And you may already have something that will work quite well as an essay plan.

In the previous section, for instance, we looked at a strategy for evaluating your sources based on your purpose for them within the research paper. Activity 7.12 asked you to outline your planned essay, identifying major sectional divisions, listing the sources needed for each section, and explaining how you planned to use each source within your paper. Such an outline can work well as an initial essay plan.

Or, earlier in the chapter, Activity 7.5 asked you to create an issues tree for your research topic, helping you to develop an appropriately focused research question. An issues tree, if fully developed, can also work well as an initial essay plan.

If you've yet to write anything resembling an essay plan, or if you wish to create a new one that is more precise and detailed than your previous ones, here are a few guidelines to direct your planning efforts:

- Make sure you have organized your project using a clear research question and critical approach.

- Know what subsidiary questions must be addressed in order to satisfactorily answer your research question.

- Create a basic outline for how you will structure your discussion. Identify major structural divisions.

- Anticipate your readers' needs and plan to address them. What will they want to know? How will you get them to invest in your paper? How will you hold their interest?

- Identify clear, specific purposes for each of your sources (both those you already have and those you still need to find).

- Identify a specific way to address the "So what?" question.

■ **Activity 7.14**   **Make a Plan**

> Using the guidelines above, and borrowing a basic template from a previous activity (e.g., Activity 7.5), write a plan for your research essay. Make it as comprehensive as possible.

Write a Progress Report

Many instructors require their students to write a progress report at some point during the research process. While its form will vary, a progress report's purpose is fairly consistent: Assigning a progress report creates an intermediate deadline by which you must have completed part of their research and perhaps drafted part of your paper as well. In addition, the report allows you to revisit your initial research and essay plans and to make necessary adjustments. Research projects often must be adapted to research results, assimilating new or unexpected sources or responding to changes in external constraints. In fact, change is generally expected, and if your approach to your project has not shifted through the course of your research, then you could have a problem. Let your research lead you, and be careful not to subconsciously filter your sources to get the results you want or expect.

■ **Activity 7.15**   **Write a Progress Report**

> Write a progress report that answers these three basic questions:
>
> 1. What have you completed?
>
> 2. How has your project changed and why?
>
> 3. What do you have left to do, and when will you do it? (include a precise timeline)
>
> Be sure to provide specific supporting evidence and examples as part of your answer to each question.

How Do You Know When You're Done?

When writing a research paper, or any kind of researched writing for a general audience, at some point you'll probably ask yourself: What is "enough" research?

Research paper assignments usually help to answer this question by including specific requirements for number and type of sources. But these sorts of limits, useful as they may be in a classroom setting, aren't present in the "real world." We need to address how to determine what counts as enough research.

Instead of asking, "How do I know when I'm done?" ask, "How do I know when I have enough research to begin writing?" This is a much more practical question, because it acknowledges that the research and writing processes overlap; you don't finish your research and then begin writing, dividing the work into two totally separate tasks. The process of finding and evaluating sources is likely to run through to the end of your writing process, as you can never be sure how your sources will fit in a paper until you begin writing it.

So, how do you know when to begin writing? The answer is that it depends on who you are; some people need to write in order to figure out what they think and where they're going, while others prefer to work out their paper mentally before they begin any sort of draft. Everyone's process is different, and you should use the one that works best for you. A good rule of thumb is to begin writing when you know you have something to say, when you have moved beyond just knowing about your topic and have a definite argument to make about it.

Chapter 8

Writing the Research Essay

8.1 The Writing Process

If you Google "How to Write a Research Essay" you'll find thousands of near-identical step-by-step guides, which suggests that writing is a straightforward and linear process. It's not. While there are certainly identifiable tasks and stages you will need to go through to produce an essay (and which this chapter will review), the writing process is often recursive (circular) and messy, and you may find yourself revisiting earlier stages as your understanding of your subject increases. For example, it may not become clear until you start writing that you need to find more sources, or that your topic is too broad or too narrow, or even that you have changed your mind about your topic and want to argue a different position. Don't be disheartened; this is evidence you are developing as a researcher, thinker, and writer.

Knowing Your Audience

To produce an effective essay you need to appeal to your audience. As discussed in Chapter 7, being clear about the identity of your audience is crucial. It helps you to decide:

- What information you need to include and exclude in your essay

- What assumptions and biases may be at work

- Which jargon or terminology you can or should use

- Which key terms or ideas need to be explained or defined

- Where and how you can make the greatest intellectual contribution

- What kinds of arguments, approaches, or ideas are likely to be most accepted (or conversely, most controversial)

- How to structure your information (tell your story) for maximum impact

- Which writing conventions apply (e.g., citation rules)

- What tone and point of view are most appropriate in your writing

So then, who is the audience for an academic research paper?

While your instructor is the person who will grade your work, he or she is not your *sole* audience. One of the purposes of a research paper is to make a contribution to a broader academic community. Think about the type of audience that would be interested in, and benefit from, your research—this group is your audience (unless you've specifically been assigned another one, of course).

Defining Key Terms

Regardless of their academic background, you can assume that the audience for your paper is articulate, educated, and intelligent. As a consequence, it is not necessary to define commonly understood words, but it may be important to define "key terms" in your essay to make sure you and your audience are having the same conversation. The kinds of words or ideas that benefit from definition are those that are central to your topic or question and that can be interpreted or understood differently in different contexts or disciplines.

Defining key terms is a powerful way to tailor your essay question and demonstrate your own intellectual contribution to a topic. A clear definition signals to your audience that you know what you're talking about and can successfully negotiate uncertainty; it also minimizes misunderstanding by providing a common frame of reference.

A Quick Note on Tone and Point of View

Academic writing should be "formal." In this context, formal means serious and accurate, a tone that signals respect for your audience and your task. In general, formal writing:

- Uses a firm, confident, and dispassionate (unemotional) voice

- Employs straightforward rather than highly descriptive language

- Avoids colloquial (conversational) expressions—including slang, hyperbole, abbreviations, clichés, and contractions

- Avoids emotive punctuation (e.g., exclamation points)

- Uses accurate grammar, syntax, and spelling

- Has highly structured and logically organized content

- Demonstrates familiarity with key terminology

- Cites references throughout the text to support all assertions and properly acknowledge external sources

Formal academic papers are often written in third-person point of view, because this perspective encourages readers to consider the logic of the case you are building rather than emotional factors. There are instances when first person may be considered appropriate or acceptable, so—as always—it is vital to be clear about questions of purpose and audience (see Table 8.1).

Table 8.1: Points of View in Academic Writing

Point of View	Impression	Usage	Pronouns
First Person	Informal, subjective, personal, conversational, intimate, emotional, and biased.	For autobiographical writing or for tasks where your personal opinion is relevant or important (e.g., college essays, email).	*I, me, my, mine, we, our, ours, us*
Third Person	Formal, impartial, objective, distant, unemotional, unbiased, considered, professional, and serious.	The default for most formal academic writing—research essays, lab reports, and proposals.	*he, she, it, they, him, her, them, his, her, hers, its, their,* and *theirs*

There is a common perception that formal language requires highly elevated and complicated vocabulary, as well as long complex sentences. You might be tempted to go through your draft and systematically upgrade your writing with more sophisticated words and phrasing. Avoid this temptation! It is important not to confuse the complexity of your ideas with the complexity of your writing—**expressing an idea simply does not mean that it is simplistic**. Sentences that are clear, straightforward, and plain do a much stronger job of communicating your intelligence and contribution than sentences that are dense, verbose, and full of thesaurus words. Focus on the depth of your thinking, rather than the sophistication of your vocabulary.

While the guidelines for formal tone and viewpoint are indeed valuable, they are not set in stone. In fact, these rules are frequently broken by experienced writers of formal prose. (One rule was even broken in the previous paragraph. Which rule and why?) But this doesn't mean that you should take the rules lightly. Learning to write in different styles, appropriate to different situations, takes time and practice—immersion in a certain style is usually required before you can begin to bend the rules expressively and intuitively. Guidelines are valuable precisely because they speed up your ability to internalize a style, to become familiar with its most common characteristics. So respect such rules, but also recognize their limitations.

■ **Activity 8.1** **Formal to Informal**

- Write a short paragraph (approximately five sentences) in an informal first-person point of view that expresses your opinion on a subject you care about. Now swap your paragraph with another member of your class, and rewrite each other's paragraphs in a formal, academic third-person point of view.

- Apart from changes in pronouns, what adjustments did you need to make to formalize your peer's writing? What difficulties did you face? What are the strengths and weaknesses of both styles? When you compare your original paragraph with the rewrite, which passage strikes you as more effective? Why?

8.2 Getting Started

Good writers are good thinkers. If you don't know what you think, you'll have trouble working out what to write. Most people who get stuck during the writing process have misdiagnosed the problem; it's not writer's block, it's thinkers block.

If you find yourself bogged down, take some time away from your draft to work out exactly what message you are trying to convey—focus on your *content* before your execution. A useful technique is explaining what you want to write to a friend or family member.

Your ideas are the most important part of your research project, which is why a clear and detailed **essay plan** is incredibly helpful (see Chapter 7). But at the very least, you shouldn't start drafting unless you are clear about your **research question** and your thesis.

Taking a Stance

Even if your essay question or topic has been assigned, there is *always* room for you to take control of your paper and adapt the question to show independent thought and creativity. One way is through your interpretation of the question and definition of key terms; another is through the *position* you take on the topic—your **stance**, or thesis.

In some papers, you may be explicitly asked to argue for or against a particular proposition (argumentative/persuasive essay), while in others, you may simply be expressing your interpretation of ideas or information (exploratory/analytical essay). Regardless of the task, you are expected to take a stance or position to approach your topic critically but personally.

A common way to communicate your stance is with a thesis statement. A thesis statement is often (but not always) a single, clear, and concise sentence that outlines your stance early in your writing. Strong academic writing generally states the thesis explicitly in the introductory section of the paper (within the first page) and then returns to it throughout the paper.

Your thesis should be made clear at the beginning of your paper so that your reader understands the purpose and focus of your paper. It is the job of the rest of your paper to gather and organize evidence to persuade the reader of the logic of your position. In travel terms, your thesis tells the reader where you are going and why the journey matters.

Your thesis also serves as a sort of touchstone, helping you to determine what material is pertinent to your writing task. Keep your thesis in mind as you draft to make sure all of your points are relevant. A strong thesis also provides a clear way to assess how successful you have been in achieving the goal you set for yourself—in travel terms, again, it helps you judge if you've reached your destination and whether you've communicated the journey's meaning.

While there is wide agreement that a thesis statement is useful and necessary, it is surprisingly difficult to define what an effective one looks like. In fact, it is almost easier to explain thesis statements in the negative.

An effective thesis statement is not:

- The essay question, restated

- A topic statement

- Your conclusion

- A blanket assertion of fact

- Your step-by-step plan for your essay

Look at the essays in the "Readings" section to see how other authors have communicated their theses. What works? What doesn't? What can you learn from them for your own writing?

■ **Activity 8.2** **Writing Thesis Statements**

1. Choose another class member as your peer.

2. Write a paragraph that explains your position: What is your topic? Why does it matter? What are you arguing? Why?

3. Now swap your paragraph with your peer, and try writing three thesis statements based on their position.

4. Trade your paragraphs again. Which statement is the most effective and why?

Remember, your topic and stance may change as you write, so it may be necessary to revisit your thesis statement after you finish drafting to make sure it reflects the content and focus of your paper. If the content of your thesis statement does not match the content of your paper, it will give your reader the impression that you have set yourself one task, but completed another.

One final note on the thesis statement: You may have been told that there are rules about where in your introduction your thesis statement *should* appear. While it is important that your introduction make your position clear, as you will see below, there are no strict rules for where in the introduction your thesis statement should go.

8.3 Introductions

Introductions and conclusions are difficult to write. They are also the most important and memorable sections of your paper. What a reader encounters at the beginning of an essay influences how they approach the entire piece of work. Think of your introduction like a pair of glasses—it is there to help the reader see the world in a particular way. If your introduction is well executed, your reader will be focused and see clearly; if not, they'll be fumbling in the dark.

What you choose to say in your opening paragraph(s), and *how* you say it, conveys **explicit** and **implicit** information to your readers, including:

* Your familiarity with the discipline

* Whether you are clear about your topic, and your position toward it

* What you are seeking to achieve

* The quality and confidence of your writing

* Whether you put effort and thought into your work

* Whether the essay as a whole is likely to be interesting and well executed

Ideally, after reading your introduction, your reader will actually want to finish reading your paper. Accordingly, it is worth paying extra attention to your introduction to ensure you start off strong and capture the attention and interest of your audience. You only have one chance to make this vital first impression.

Your introduction does *not* have to be the first section you write. Many writers use the process of writing as a form of intellectual discovery, as a way to gain clarity about their thinking. For example, they might not know exactly what they are going to argue until they start to put their ideas on the page; alternatively, they might find that their opinions change as they begin to flesh out their arguments. For these discovery writers, it makes sense to write the introduction last so that it reflects and reinforces the content of the paper. Other writers have trouble getting started unless they write an introduction—the introduction is like a road map, and they don't know where they are going until they have one. For these road-map writers, it makes sense to write a tentative, placeholder introduction to get the writing process started and then return to it once the draft is complete to make sure it is still strong.

You may have been told that there is a specific formula for writing introductions. There isn't one. An introduction can drop the reader right into the fray with a few sharp sentences or ease the reader into the topic over the course of two or three paragraphs. There are many effective ways to start a research paper, including but not limited to:

- A question or series of questions
- A provocative or thoughtful quote
- An anecdote or event
- A specific example or problem
- A hypothetical situation
- Interesting or unusual statistics

Generally, an introduction will include information about what your topic is, why it matters, your stance (your thesis), and how you will approach your analysis. But how each of these elements is drawn out is up to you, and there is extensive room for variation. What is important is that your introduction is confident, useful, purposeful, and interesting. Introductions written to a formula seldom meet these criteria.

■ **Activity 8.3** **A Terrible Introduction**

- The following introduction is terrible. Seriously. Individually read and annotate (mark up) the introduction, identifying all the common but ineffective strategies it employs. Identify problems that you have found in your own introductions.

- In a small group, compare your notes. What does the introduction do wrong? Why is it ineffective?

Since the dawn of time, mankind and womankind alike has struggled with violence. Violence is defined by the World Health Organization as "the intentional use of physical force or power, threatened or actual, against oneself, another person, or against a group or community, which either results in or has a high likelihood of resulting in injury, death, psychological harm, maldevelopment, or deprivation." There are many different kinds of violence, from petty schoolyard fights, to the horrors of war and genocide. In today's modern society, no type of violence is more prominent or frightening than international terrorism. Recently, the rise of ISIS has been of particular note with more and more countries turning their attention the spread of this barbaric death cult. Do media representations of this issue change how it is perceived and understood? This essay will consider media representations of ISIS and concludes that the spread of ISIS has been of great concern in the media.

■ **Activity 8.4** **Introduction Copycat**

Working in a group, select four essays that you have not read from the "Readings" section of this book. For each one, consider:

1. Where does the introduction stop? How did you know?

2. What is the author's thesis? How effective is it?

3. What do you think the rest of this essay is about based on the section you read? How confident are you in this assessment? How does the author signal to the reader both where the discussion is going and why it matters?

4. How well does the introduction communicate the author's stance on the topic?

5. Look at the introduction sentence by sentence. How has the author constructed the introduction? What are the main component parts (e.g., anecdote, questions, direct statements of argument)? How has the author tried to engage your interest?

6. Consider the similarities and differences among the introductions. If you were to write a list of five rules for effective introductions, what would they be?

Then, on your own, think about which two introductions were the most effective. Why?

Using these effective introductions as models, write two alternative openings to your own research essay, mimicking their structure and tone.

8.4 Middles

When writers talk about paragraphs, they often focus on mechanical construction (e.g., the number and type of sentences) rather than purpose and content. If you approach paragraphs like a formula, you will end up with an essay that is formulaic—uncreative, repetitive, simplistic, and superficial. The standard "five-paragraph essay" structure that you may have been taught in high school is straightforward and easy, but college-level thinking is neither of those things.

Dedicate the time and space you need to introduce, develop, and interpret each of your main ideas. A strong paragraph can be a few sentences or a whole page—the complexity of the paragraph depends on the complexity of the idea. You'll often hear instructors say they are looking for paragraphs that are well developed and well written, but what does that mean?

A **well-developed** paragraph exhibits:

•   **Purpose:** The reader should be clear about the main idea of your paragraph and how it relates back to your thesis.

- **Focus:** As a basic rule of thumb, one idea = one paragraph. If you are detailing a complex idea that comprises many sub-points, each new point within that idea should have its own paragraph.

- **Evidence and support:** The claims you make to support your idea should all be substantiated. Evidence is a broad term that can include (depending on your discipline) real and hypothetical examples, expertise, data and statistics, and interviews.

- **Unity:** All the sentences in your paragraph should relate to the main idea of that paragraph.

- **Coherence:** The information in your paragraph should be well organized, logically ordered, and easy to follow.

- **Synthesis:** The information in your essay looks for connections *among* sources in order to develop your arguments.

A **well-written** paragraph exhibits:
- **Energy:** The paragraph should have momentum and interest so that readers feel compelled to keep reading.

- **Narrative:** Each paragraph is a mini-story with a beginning, middle, and end.

- **A strong start and finish:** Just like your essay as a whole, the start and finish matter. Pay particular attention to your opening and closing sentences.

- **Clarity:** Keep your language plain and simple so that your reader can understand and appreciate your ideas

Transitions

Transitions are the bridges of your essay. When used well, they create strong logical connections between your paragraphs to improve flow and focus. When used poorly, they waste time and space and make your argument seem thin. A strong transition tells your reader what to do with the information you have just provided so that the next step in your paper seems logical—in other words, it synthesizes. A weak transition merely tells your reader what you did, and what you are going to do next it only summarizes.

You can tell if your transitions need work by focusing on how well your essay flows. Your essay should have a strong internal "narrative," which is a fancy way of saying that it should tell a story. Think about how you tell anecdotes to your friends and family—for your story to make sense to your listener, each event in the story leads to the next. Your essay should work the same way—each idea or argument should lead into the next one. If your essay has weak transitions, your instructor may mark it with words like *choppy, mucky, jumpy, unrelated,* and *abrupt* or you will be asked for "better **signposts**." If you are getting these kinds of comments on your work, or if you like to write an essay in sections and then combine them at the end, you should pay particular attention to transitional sections.

Signposts an indication to readers that an author is making a transition

If you find yourself spending too much time on transitions in your paper, consider whether your argument is strong and logical and if you have enough content. In complex papers, you may be able to use subheadings to cut down on the need for transitions—check with your instructor.

Activity 8.5 Paragraphs and Transitions

Select an essay from the reader and look at its body paragraphs. In small groups, consider a single paragraph of the essay (each group should take a different paragraph—try to cover all of them) and answer the following questions:

- What is its purpose? How do you know?

- What is its main claim?

- What support does it provide for this claim?

- How does it relate to the thesis of the essay?

- How does it relate to the paragraph that came before it?

- How does it relate to the paragraph that comes after it?

As a class, discuss the paragraphs in sequence. What trends do you notice?

Individual work: Before you write your transitional phrases, summarize in a sentence how the next point you're transitioning to fits into your analysis as a whole. This activity should help you see the connections among your ideas more clearly, and may even help you find a more logical order of your content if you are struggling to sequence your ideas.

Writing with Sources

In a research essay you are being asked to draw heavily on *other* people's research in order to support your *own* original work. It's a complicated proposition and one that can seem inherently contradictory. It helps to think about your research paper as an invitation to a dinner part—you are being asked to join an existing conversation but to bring your own opinions to add something new and fresh. While you need to listen to the experts already sitting at the table, you shouldn't let them dominate the conversation and you don't have to agree with them—you can add your own ideas and use your own language to express them. A great conversation draws contributions from everyone at the table and—through discussion and dissent—you leave with a deeper and more nuanced understanding about a topic. That's what good research does too—it extends (or even changes) the academic conversation.

Synthesis versus Summary

Research writing is more than cutting and pasting together other people's ideas. Good writers *synthesize* the material they use, which is a fancy way of saying that they look for connections *among* sources in order to develop their own arguments. Summary is a necessary foundation for synthesis, but be careful not to construct a "Franken-essay" from a series of summaries. Remember, your sources provide evidence for *your* thesis.

Table 8.2 breaks down some key differences between summary and synthesis.

Table 8.2: Summary versus Synthesis

Summary	Synthesis
Demonstrates comprehension and understanding	Demonstrates critical and creative thinking and insight
Collates information	Compares and contrasts information
Restates key points	Interprets key points to make new meaning
Looks within a text	Looks for connections and relationships among texts
Treats sources as distinct entities	Combines bits and pieces of sources for own purpose
Provides overview of content	Interprets content
Requires simple reading and thinking skills	Requires complex reading and thinking skills

Quoting versus Paraphrasing

One of the most effective ways to use your sources is by incorporating their words into your work. A common mistake that new students make is to overuse quotes and create a patchwork essay of other people's voices—**don't let other voices drown out your own**. It is important to be strategic in the quotations you include, and it is essential that every external voice or idea you include is explained or analyzed—a quote does not speak for itself.

A crucial skill you will develop as you practice writing is judging when to use a direct quotation and when to paraphrase. First, what's the difference between the two? You have no doubt used direct quotation in your writing at some point, repeating someone else's idea verbatim within your paper and placing that idea within quotation marks, "like this." Another way to insert outside ideas into your writing is to paraphrase them, or restate them using new language. If you are asked to rewrite something using your own words, then you are being asked to paraphrase.

Writers often paraphrase outside ideas for the sake of brevity or in order to communicate them more clearly. Paraphrasing also allows a writer to maintain her or his own voice to keep the writing style as consistent as possible. This benefit can be especially useful when a writer is drawing on multiple sources at once.

Table 8.3 explains the differences between quoting and paraphrasing.

Table 8.3: Quoting versus Paraphrasing

Quotations must be identical to the original, using a narrow segment of the source. They must match the source document word for word and must be attributed to the original author.	Paraphrasing involves putting a passage from source material into your own words. A paraphrase must also be attributed to the original source. Paraphrased material is usually shorter than the original passage, taking a somewhat broader segment of the source and condensing it slightly.
You should use a quote...	**You should paraphrase...**
<ul><li>To show that an expert or authority supports your position.</li><li>To provide evidence for a claim of fact.</li><li>To include historically significant language.</li><li>When a source presents their idea in a particularly striking, moving, or unique way.</li><li>To serve as a passage for analysis, comment, or critique (e.g., to set out a position with which you wish to agree or disagree).</li><li>To support your definition of a new or unfamiliar term or phrase.</li><li>When you want to distance yourself from the original source to make it clear that the statement is not your own.</li></ul>	<ul><li>When what you want from your source is the idea, not the language used to express it.</li><li>If you can state the point of the source more succinctly by eliminating irrelevant information (be careful not to manipulate the meaning of the passage by doing so).</li><li>To explain or simplify a passage that may be difficult to understand.</li><li>If a quote would break the flow of your paper. (Too many quotes can make an essay choppy and difficult to follow.)</li><li>To communicate statistics and numerical data.</li><li>When you are combining the information from the source with your own analysis or other data (synthesizing).</li></ul>

How to Quote

Here are three quotation strategies to help you more effectively incorporate external research into your own writing. A passage from one of the readings—Anne Lamott's "Shitty First Drafts" (p. 262)—is used to demonstrate each approach.

Model One: My Idea—Your Idea—My Explanation/Analysis

Introduce a quote using a complete sentence ending with a colon:

> Here is one of Anne Lamott's most important points: "Very few writers really know what they are doing until they've done it."

Now provide *your* explanation of why this quote matters—show the reader *why* this is one of Lamott's most important claims.

Model Two: My Idea <u>and</u> Your Idea—My Explanation/Analysis

Merge a quotation with your own introduction, separating your writing and the quote with only a comma, or perhaps no punctuation at all (use whatever punctuation is necessary grammatically). This style is more fluid than the first model.

> One of Lamott's most important points is that "[v]ery few writers really know what they are doing until they've done it."

Now provide *your* explanation of why Lamott's claim matters.

Model Three: Ideas and Explanation and Analysis and Quotes (It's All Happening at Once)

Weave your own writing together with the material you want to quote. (This method is similar to paraphrasing, which requires you to restate a passage in your own words and sometimes includes fragmentary quotations from the original text). This style is more fluid than the other styles, but it also requires the most skill. It has the considerable advantage, though, of allowing you to make the text your own; this style lets you incorporate outside texts but maintain your voice, your personal tone as a writer.

> Lamott uses her own writing experience to challenge the mythology that professional writers produce "elegant first drafts." It is an important observation, because the blank page can be intimidating, and new writers are often discouraged. Writing instructors should therefore make it clear that "[v]ery few writers really know what they are doing until they've done it."

This model is quite a bit longer than Models One or Two, because those models' examples are quotations without explanation or analysis. All quotes must be explained, analyzed, elaborated on, argued with—they must be dealt with in some way. Don't assume that your reader will interpret your quote the way you do. In Models One and Two, the explanation and elaboration should follow the quote. In Model Three, the quote is integrated with the explanation and analysis.

■ **Activity 8.6** **Quotation Style Practice**

Choose a passage from two of your sources, preferably passages you intend to reference in your paper. Practice writing about both passages using the three quotation models above. If you find yourself struggling to follow Model Three, think carefully about the analysis and explanation you'll need to provide your reader for them to understand the quotation's significance.

How to Paraphrase

1. **Focus on ideas** and on understanding the paper or passage as a whole, rather than skimming for specific phrases.

2. **Put the original text aside** when you write so you aren't overly influenced.

3. **Restructure the idea** so that it reflects the way *your* brain works.

4. **Change the words** to reflect your language and tone. Think about how you would explain the idea to someone unfamiliar with your subject (your mother, your roommate, your sister).

■ **Activity 8.7** **Paraphrase Practice**

Choose several passages from one of this semester's readings that have stuck with you. Practice paraphrasing them, following the guidelines above. Or select several quotations that you plan to include in your research paper. Practice paraphrasing them, following the guidelines above.

8.5 Implications

The "So What?" Question

What distinguishes an exceptional essay from a good one is engagement with the "So what?" question. Compelling essays consistently consider the *implications* of their observations so that the reader feels its claims are significant, that they *matter*. As Caroline Eisner explains:

The "So What" question is about giving your readers enough information so that they will want to, will feel compelled to, keep reading, rather than continually, or even once, asking themselves, "Why should I care about this?" Will your reader care about your argument, perspective, and topic, or will your reader ask, "So what? Why should I care about this and keep reading?[1]

---

[1]http://www.academiccoachingandwriting.org/academic-writing/academic-writing-blog/-approach-the-so-what-question

Make sure you actively engage with the matter of meaning: Try to ensure that your reader won't even consider asking the "So what?" question.

■ **Activity 8.8** **The "So What?" Game**

> (adapted from http://writingcenter.unc.edu/handouts/conclusions/)
>
> If you feel like your essay isn't saying anything original or interesting, ask a friend to read it with you. Read it out loud and instruct your friend to stop you and ask "So what?" or "Who cares?" or "Why is that important?" every time they hear you make a definitive statement—get them to channel their annoying inner child that just keeps asking questions!
>
> Answering these "So what?" questions will push the sophistication of your thinking and increase the amount of original content in your paper.
>
> You can also use this strategy on your own, asking yourself "So what?" as you develop your key ideas. Useful places in your draft to ask this question are at the end of paragraphs, where you bring each idea to a point of closure.

Conclusions

Like introductions, conclusions have a disproportionate impact on how your paper is received. A poor conclusion can sink a solid paper. Conversely, a strong conclusion can elevate a weak paper. Your conclusion is your chance to have the last word, but more crucially, it is the place where you have a chance to synthesize *your* ideas, demonstrate the scope of your critical contribution, and impress your reader by helping them see the topic, issue, and world differently in some fundamental way. You may have been told that your conclusion should simply summarize what you have already said and finish by restating your thesis and main point, but this formulaic approach is a missed opportunity to answer the big "So what?' questions.

While your conclusion should not introduce entirely new content, it should consider the implications of what you have discovered, beyond the scope of your essay topic. Ask yourself the following questions:

- How will my conclusion affect people's lives?

- Were my results surprising or confronting?

- Is this issue more complex than it looks?

- Does the standard approach to this topic need to be challenged, qualified, or changed?

- What now? Can I offer a solution to a problem? Are there behaviors or ideas that I think need to be changed?

- What will happen in the future if things don't change now?

- What are the implications for future research? Are there any tensions or questions remaining that need to be investigated?

- What broader phenomenon can we understand better by studying this smaller one?

The Turn

It can help to think about conclusions using the idea of "the turn." In a poem, a piece of fiction, or even an argument, the turn is a point at which things suddenly shift, where the reader finds herself on a new path, or sees an idea from a fresh perspective.

Turns are often key moments in literary works, serving as emotional high points, as climaxes. They are the moments in a book or poem where you read twice. They are the moments that slow you down, that require renewed attention and focus to follow the sudden shift. They are the moments that make you say, "Whoa!"

What better way than this to think of a conclusion? Such a turn renews readers' interest, broadens their perspectives, and invites them to make connections and consider implications they might earlier have overlooked. In short, the conclusion as a turn helps open readers to the possibility of being affected by your writing, of finding themselves still pondering your ideas long after they've finished reading your paper.

■ **Activity 8.9** **Conclusion Copycat**

Working in a group, return to the four essays you used in Activity 8.4, and for each one, consider:

- Is there a turn? If so, where is it?

- Where does the conclusion begin?

- Look at the conclusion sentence by sentence. How has the author constructed the conclusion? What are the main component parts (e.g., anecdotes, questions, direct statements of argument)?

- How has the author tried to engage your interest?

- Compare the conclusion with the introduction. How are they similar, and how are they different?

- Does the author try and answer the big "So what?" question? If so, what is the answer?

- Consider the conclusions together. What are their main similarities and differences?

- Which conclusion(s) did you consider to be the most effective? Why?

- Which did you consider the least effective?

Then, on your own, using two effective conclusions as models, write two alternative conclusions to your own research essay, mimicking their structure and tone.

Table 8.4: Conclusions

Should	• Synthesize (not summarize) the content of your paper. • Consider all your material and arguments together, and answer the big "So What?" question so that your reader is left with no doubt as to why your arguments and observations matter. • Provide the reader a sense of closure by *demonstrating*, not stating, that you achieved what you set out to do. • Leave a strong and interesting final impression—it's the last thing that's read, and (along with the introduction) the part of your paper that's most remembered.
Can	• Consider the broader implications of your argument, or place the issues you have considered within a broader context (e.g., social, historical, scientific, ideological). • Consider your main points collectively, and draw connections among them. • Elaborate on the significance of your findings or argument. • Return to the theme(s) of your introduction with fresh eyes. • Include a provocative or illustrative insight or quotation. • Finish with a question, series of questions, or a challenge to your reader. • Finish with an anecdote that illustrates the key claim of your paper. • Propose a particular course of action or a solution for a problem identified in your paper. • Suggest a new definition for a key term or a new approach that might change the way your issue is considered. • Suggest where scholars should direct further study, or what they've been doing wrong all along.

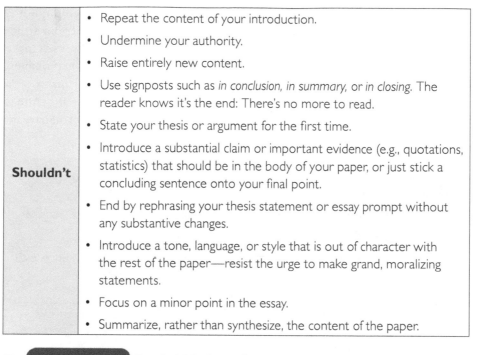

Shouldn't	• Repeat the content of your introduction.
	• Undermine your authority.
	• Raise entirely new content.
	• Use signposts such as *in conclusion, in summary,* or *in closing.* The reader knows it's the end: There's no more to read.
	• State your thesis or argument for the first time.
	• Introduce a substantial claim or important evidence (e.g., quotations, statistics) that should be in the body of your paper, or just stick a concluding sentence onto your final point.
	• End by rephrasing your thesis statement or essay prompt without any substantive changes.
	• Introduce a tone, language, or style that is out of character with the rest of the paper—resist the urge to make grand, moralizing statements.
	• Focus on a minor point in the essay.
	• Summarize, rather than synthesize, the content of the paper.

■ **Activity 8.10**   **Break ALL the Rules**

Using Table 8.4, write the worst possible conclusion for your essay. How many fatal mistakes can you build in? Are you capable of true dreadfulness? Share your abomination with your classmates. Who did the best worst job?

8.6 From Draft to Final: Revision, Editing, and Proofreading

If you haven't yet read it, now is the time to check out Anne Lamott's "Shitty First Drafts." Lamott argues that "Almost all good writing begins with terrible first efforts" (para. 8). Even if you planned every single part of your paper before you started writing, putting "pen to paper" (or fingertip to keyboard) is a process of discovery, and you simply won't produce your best work in your first draft. That's okay—what's important is just getting the ideas down. The first time around, focus on quantity, not quality. The more you write, the more material you'll have to use as you revise your "shitty first draft."

The terms *revision, editing,* and *proofreading* are often used interchangeably, but they mean very different things (see Table 8.5). All three processes are necessary to produce a quality final paper, but their sequencing is crucial. You can't work on all three processes at the same time. You have to work first at the global/structural level (revision) and get that settled, and then move to the next level down (editing). It is pointless to become preoccupied with single paragraphs or sentences if your structure is not firmly established. It is possible that some of these paragraphs won't make it into the final draft. Revision also creates more editing and proofreading problems, and you will waste valuable time if you focus on fixing minor problems only to create more. Imagine your essay is a house. You want to make sure the structure is strong before you make it pretty. There's no point scrubbing the floor if you have no doors and windows.

Table 8.5: Revision, Editing, and Proofreading

Sequence	Process	Focus
1st	**Revision** "Re-visioning" your paper	*Content* at the paper, and then paragraph, level
2nd	**Editing** Correcting clumsy or unclear expression	*Execution* at the sentence level
3rd	**Proofreading** A final check for mechanical errors and compliance with assignment requirements	*Accuracy* at the sentence/word level

■ Activity 8.11 **Reverse Outline**

(adapted from http://writingcenter.fas.harvard.edu/pages/revising-draft)

Develop a "reverse outline" for your paper to check its organizational logic:

- Identify the main idea(s) in each paragraph and then rank their importance in advancing your thesis.

- Now rearrange your points in order of importance, and consider how each point relates to the one before and after it. Does each point need to be there? Is there anything missing?

- You now have a tool for restructuring your argument, removing redundant information, and expanding your content.

Some general tips for polishing your essay:
- Don't treat your draft as sacred. Be willing to substantially change it to substantially improve it. Be brutal to be better.
- Plan to leave yourself some time between finishing your draft and starting your revision so you can approach your writing with clear eyes. Sleep on your draft—things will always look different in the morning.

- Enlist other people to help you compensate for your writing weaknesses. If you're a big-picture thinker, get a detail-obsessed friend to proofread for errors. If you are a detail-obsessed person, find a big-picture thinker to read for structure and organization.

- When you ask someone to read your work, be clear about *why* you need them to read it—directing their focus will help you get more useful feedback.

- It may take several passes to finalize your revisions—once you play with one structural element, other necessary changes will become apparent.

- You may find you do a better job working on a hard copy rather than on a computer screen.

- Read the text aloud. You will hear problems your eyes will miss.

- The more you can imagine yourself as a reader looking at your paper for the first time, the easier it will be to spot problems.

Activity 8.12   **Revision Question Race**

> Revision is sometimes described as a dialogue, because the writer asks a series of questions about what their paper has achieved, and the answers help them identify what needs to happen to improve their draft. Practice this idea as a group:
>
> In five minutes, come up with as many revision questions as you can, starting with the phrase "Does my paper_____?"
>
> For example:
>
>> Does my paper answer the research question?
>>
>> Does my paper even have a research question?
>
> The person who comes up with the most questions wins!
>
> Go around the room and compare your answers. Compile a master list and use it as a guide as you begin revising your work.

Editing

Expression and tone problems often fall into one of these categories:

1. **Unclear or lazy:** The language is vague or imprecise, a problem that often reflects a lack of clarity or effort on behalf of the writer. If you're unsure about what you want to say (and why), you are unlikely to express yourself clearly.

Prominent Examples

This/that: Two of the worst offenders. If you are starting a sentence with *this* or *that* (e.g., "so this means," "what this shows is that," "that is a mistake,") make sure it's to *what* you are referring. When you do, you'll most often see that *this* or *that* is unnecessary and the sentence can be rewritten far stronger without it.

Very/really: These words—and many others that are commonly added for emphasis or description (*beautiful, clever, thing*)—don't add anything to the meaning of a text. How can you rewrite the sentence to say what you mean with evocative specificity? Rather than simply describing the phenomenon or idea, be clear about its effects, or draw an analogy that illustrates your point.

***Clearly/obviously/undoubtedly/common knowledge* (and other generalizations):** These expressions are most often used when the opposite is true, but the writer doesn't know how to make their point convincingly. Instead of working out the logic, the writer simply states their conclusion with a word like *obviously*, when in fact, it is not obvious at all.

2. **Redundant:** fluff and waffle. The writing is full of words and phrases that take up space but don't actually say or add anything. Be brutal and ask yourself if every sentence in every paragraph is doing something important *and* unique. Then ask yourself if every *word* in every sentence is necessary. Think about your writing like a racehorse—a fat racehorse isn't going to win. It is slow going at first, but with practice you'll become adept at stripping back your writing to its most lean and powerful form.

   Prominent Examples:
   Clichés: "Clichés offer prefabricated phrasing that may be used without effort on your part. They are thus used at the expense of both individuality and precision, since you can't say just what you mean in the mechanical response of a cliché." Thomas Pinney: *A Short Handbook and Style Sheet.*

   Take heed of this advice by Jack Lynch: *They're not clever, they're not funny, they're not memorable, they're not convincing.*

   At the end of the day; in any way, shape, or form; playing the race card; as you can see.

3. **Emotive and judgmental:** The language is emotional and often carries with it explicit or implicit moral judgment and superiority. The writer substitutes the emotional weight of the language for the intellectual weight of thinking. The writing becomes a polemic, rather than a logical argument or measured discussion. Emotive writing can also stray into *ad hominem* territory—attacking the character of a person or institution rather than their ideas. There is minimal scope to using emotive language in an essay, but avoid directing it *at* someone; instead use it to describe (particularly your *own* feelings), rather than deploying it in an argument.

Prominent Examples: *Bad/good* (and all versions of this split—e.g., *terrible/dreadful/awful, amazing/great/wonderful*), *wrong/right, stupid/dumb/pathetic/annoying.*

4. **Overcomplicated:** The meaning of the piece is overshadowed or obscured by "thesaurus writing"—but big is not always better. And simple is not the same as simplistic. Complex ideas do not benefit from complicated expression. Say what you mean as clearly and simply as possible. Rely on the power and sophistication of your ideas, not the impressiveness of your faux SAT word vocabulary.

5. **Inconsistent:** The tone varies wildly throughout the piece. Most commonly the piece will start informally, become businesslike in the middle, and then go back to being informal and emotive again at the end. While there is some room in the introduction and conclusion for experimentation and looseness, your essay should read as a smooth and consistent document, not seesawing between styles.

Proofreading

Proofreading is the final stage of the editing process and consists of a final, detailed sweep through your paper with an eye for errors. It may sound straightforward, but it can be difficult to focus on what you've actually written in your paper because you know what you *meant* to write. A great technique to avoid error blindness is to proofread your essay from the bottom up so you are not considering your sentences in context and only considering their technical accuracy.

8.7 Finishing Up

One of the final and most crucial stages in polishing an essay is ensuring you cited and documented your sources appropriately. It is not only direct quotes that need citations; you must also cite other people's *ideas*—for example, areas where you have paraphrased. You also need to cite facts, figures, ideas, or any other information that is not common knowledge. Your reader should be able to immediately tell from your citations alone which parts of your essay are original and which parts are drawn from others. When in doubt, be safe and cite.

Citation formatting is one of those technical issues that academics make a big fuss about. Why do we care so much? Here are five reasons why citations matter:

1. Ideas are "the currency of academia," and citations give credit to the hardworking authors whose works you have used—it's the right thing to do.

2. They provide a "paper trail" so others can locate the materials you consulted to extend or evaluate your research.

3. They provide evidence of your research effort and competence.

4. Their *absence* signals where you have made your own contribution.

5.   They provide solid evidence that you have not plagiarized, and keeping track of them offers a strong strategy for avoiding plagiarism.

If you're not careful with citations, your reader will assume you haven't been careful with your work, and it can sway them against you—the same as if your paper was full of spelling mistakes. There is an assumption that lazy formatting = lazy thinking. Citation mistakes will lose you points. Being accurate will absolutely make the difference between a B+ and an A−…and those are easy points to keep!

Citation rules exist to bring consistency to academic work so that the most important information is always present and in the same order. These rules can be frustrating because each academic discipline has its preferred citation method, and they're all subtly different. Most styles ask for the same pieces of information (author[s], title, date of publication, publisher, place of publication, and page numbers where applicable), and all styles ask for in-text citations throughout your paper, in *addition* to a list of all the sources you used at the end.

Styles differ in the order information is presented. Each discipline uses a different style because each has a different *priority* for information. Table 8.6 shows the difference in priorities among the three most widely used styles: APA, MLA, and *Chicago*.

Table 8.6: Styles and Priorities

Style	Context	Priorities
The American Psychological Association (APA)	Preferred style for most social sciences	Privileges the most up-to-date research and is most interested in the currency of sources—the date a source was published.
Modern Language Association (MLA)	Preferred style for literature and humanities	Privileges authorship and provides the information readers need to locate a text.
Chicago Manual of Style	Preferred style for history	Privileges readability and gives the option of footnotes at the bottoms of pages rather than citations in text.

Detailed information about citation styles can be found through the library's Web site at http://www.lib.vt.edu/find/citation/index.html. You may also save time and energy if you use citation management software (like EndNote or Zotero). And if you are contemplating a career in an academic discipline, it is worth learning the formatting rules of your chosen discipline, because you'll refer to them again and again.

If you're not given formatting instructions, or you're not clear about what's required, ask your instructor. Whatever you do, choose a single style and stick to it. Consistency is key.

Letting Go

How do you know when you're done and it's time to hand your paper in? The philosophical answer is: You're never really done—the process of learning never ends, and there will always be ways to improve your expression or expand your ideas. The practical answer is: You're done when:

- You are confident that every paragraph in your essay, every sentence in every paragraph, and every word in every sentence are doing something useful (and doing it well).

- You have checked to make sure you've complied with the assessment instructions—that you've answered all parts of the assignment question *and* also complied with its mechanical requirements (i.e., fonts and margins, coversheets, citation styles, word limits).

If you've reached this point, congratulations! You've written a research essay.

Presentations

9.1 How Can I Make an Oral Presentation?

Writers are often asked to make a presentation, lead a discussion, or share their thoughts through speaking rather than writing. The ability to present your ideas through an oral presentation is an important skill that you'll use not only in your courses but also throughout your professional and personal life.

Making an effective oral presentation involves much more than simply taking what you've written and reading it aloud. When you're physically present to share your ideas, your ability to connect personally with your audience is affected by your choice of words, your physical appearance, your use of gestures and other forms of nonverbal communication, your ability to maintain eye contact, and variation in your tone of voice. In addition, your connection with your audience is affected by their ability to follow your line of argument. As you prepare your presentation, remember that most people find it more difficult to understand complex information, ideas, and arguments when they hear them than when they can read them (and reread them). Therefore, be sure to focus on how you can help your readers follow your points and see you as a credible presenter.

Consider Your Purpose, Role, and Audience

When you make an oral presentation, your most important goals are engaging your audience and keeping them interested in your ideas. As you plan your presentation, ask what you want to accomplish, what your audience expects to hear, and how you can balance your purpose with their needs and interests. The answers to these questions will shape everything in your speech from language choices to visual aids.

Narrow Your Scope

It is important to consider how much your audience knows about your topic. With their knowledge and expertise in mind, focus on a few key points and decide how much detail you'll need to provide to help them follow your line of argument. If you have already drafted a written document, use it as the basis for your presentation, but don't try to cover every point and every piece of supporting evidence you've included in your document.

Draw on your thesis statement, reasons and evidence, and conclusions to create a brief overview of your presentation that you can use in your introductory remarks. This "preview statement" will help your audience understand your line of argument and the organization of your presentation right from the start.

Create a Bare-bones Outline

Once you've developed a focus for your presentation and determined its main point and general organization, you can create an outline. It's a good idea to begin with a basic outline that includes the following:

- An opening line that captures the attention of your audience

- A statement of your main point—typically in the form of a thesis statement

- A sentence establishing your credibility and purpose so that your audience can see that you care about and understand the issue, either through personal experience or through research, and that they can trust what you have to say

- Two to four key points

- Evidence to support your key points

- Transition statements to guide your audience through your talk

- A conclusion that reinforces your audience's understanding of the main ideas they should take away from your talk

- A closing line or an invitation to ask questions that makes it clear to your audience that you have finished your presentation

Think about Language

In an oral presentation, you'll use spoken language to connect personally with your audience. Through your choice of words, metaphors, imagery, and turns of speech, you'll engage your listeners in your argument and ideas. Keep your purpose and role in mind as you decide how to address your audience. For example, if you are attempting to solve a problem, your goal might be to engage your audience personally with the problem. You might talk about how the problem affects "us" and ask them to consider what "we" should do to address it.

As you consider your language choices, keep in mind that spoken language is usually more casual than written language. If you adopt the formal tone of your academic research essay, you might sound stiff and unnatural. Remember as well the power of repetition in oral presentations. You'll help your audience follow your line of argument by stating important points more than once and in different ways. Finally, consider the role of emotional appeals in your presentation. To connect personally with your audience and to engage your audience with your issue, you should explore the use of vivid descriptions, surprising statistics, and humor. Don't rely heavily on emotional appeals, however. To maintain your credibility, you'll want to balance emotional appeals with logic by presenting sound reasoning and support for your argument.

Prepare Speaker's Notes

Although many speakers write their presentations word for word, this strategy usually does not produce outstanding results. It's better to develop a set of speaker's notes to prompt yourself as you present your points. Using notes, instead of a word-for-word speech, will force you to speak directly to your listeners. Many seasoned speakers use note cards for their speaker's notes, as they are easy to hold in one hand and are not as distracting as fluttering paper. As you prepare your notes, make sure that they are easy to read so that you can view your next point with a quick glance. Your speaker's notes should include the following information:

- Your opening line, written out in full, to get you started in case your mind goes blank because of nervousness

- Your preview statement

- Any statements that you need to give word for word, such as carefully worded statements about a controversial point or clear descriptions of a complex concept

- Your supporting points and reminders of important evidence, including direct quotes, statistics, and names of important people

- Transition sentences from one part of the presentation to the next

- Memory prompts for any parts of your presentation that you've found yourself forgetting as you practice

- Reminders to use a visual aid, such as a chart

Engage with Your Audience

When you give an oral presentation, *how* you say something is almost as important in getting your message across as *what* you say. The following techniques will help you polish your delivery:

- **Maintain eye contact with your audience.** Eye contact communicates that you know your topic and that you care about making sure the audience understands your arguments.

- **Vary the pitch of your voice.** Speaking in a monotone is the fastest way to put your audience to sleep. When you mention a startling statistic, raise your pitch. To demonstrate weight and importance, go to a lower register in your voice. Practice using vocal variety to make sure that it sounds natural.

- **Speak loudly.** You might feel as though you're yelling, but the audience will let you know (by looking surprised) if you are too loud. Speakers rarely are.

- **Articulate every word clearly.** Consonants are often dropped in casual conversation, so try to make them clearer than you would in normal speaking.

- **Slow down.** Most presenters speak too quickly. Slow down your normal rate of speaking to give the audience time to process your words. As you practice, note where you tend to speed up, and add a comment (such as "Slow down!") to your speaker's notes.

View Speaker's Notes

The following speaker's notes are from an oral presentation on the use of steroids by adolescent girls involved in sports.

1. Intro
    Barry Bonds, A-Rod, Marion Jones, Lance Armstrong—what do all of these big names have in common? (**pause, wait for audience response**)

    - All accused of using performance-enhancing drugs

    - Used to seeing athletes break records, find out later about steroid use

    - Happening for younger athletes—including young women

Include nonverbal cues in your note cards as a reminder to interact with your audience.

Use short phrases to cue your thoughts

2. Establish credibility & preview

    - My background as an athlete

    - Explain why I care about the topic

    SLOW DOWN!

    Preview:

    (1) First, I am going to talk about the positive impact that competitive athletics can have on young women.

    (2) Then, I'll go over some of the negative consequences of competitive athletics on these young women, including steroid use.

    (3) Finally, I want to talk about what parents and coaches can do to help create a positive athletic experience for these young women.

Use brief reminders about nonverbal communication. Format your nonverbal cues in a different color so you don't accidentally speak them out loud..

Write your preview statement word for word in your notes.

(*Continued on next page*)

3.   Positive impact of competitive athletics on young women

- President's Council on Physical Fitness and Exercise—ways sports impact young athletes

For the body:

- Less risk of heart disease and certain cancers as adults

- Improves:
  - Immune system
  - Posture
  - Strength
  - Flexibility
  - Endurance

Internal transition: Also improves mental health

Include your source citations. Refer to your sources to establish your credibility.

Use internal transition cues to provide time for you to switch to your next note card as your audience thinks about the point.

CHECKLIST FOR PREPARING AND DELIVERING ORAL PRESENTATIONS

✔ Determine the presentation's purpose.

✔ Narrow your presentation's scope to between two and four key points.

✔ Write a preview statement.

✔ Choose supporting evidence for your key points.

✔ Create a basic outline of your presentation.

✔ Prepare speaker's notes that you can read easily and quickly.

✔ Consider how the size and physical arrangement of the room will affect your ability to interact with your audience.

✔ Practice your presentation, and ask for feedback from your practice audience.

✔ Arrive early to ensure adequate time for setup.

✔ During the presentation, observe and respond to your audience.

✔ Vary the pitch of your voice, speak loudly, and clearly articulate your words.

9.2 How Can I Create a Multimedia Presentation?

As a student, you've probably seen more than a few multimedia presentations. You've probably also become far too familiar with how easily these kinds of presentations can go badly. If so, you're not alone. Search the Web for phrases such as *death by PowerPoint* and *PowerPoint boredom*, and you'll find thousands of pages that discuss—often quite humorously—efforts to ban the use of programs such as PowerPoint and Keynote.

Fortunately, PowerPoint boredom is a curable condition. Whether you are speaking in front of a group, presenting a recorded talk online, or simply sharing a set of slides, you can create multimedia presentations that engage your audience and might even bring them around to your point of view. With care and planning, you can use multimedia presentation tools to illustrate points using more than spoken words alone, allowing your audience to follow your argument more easily and better understand complex ideas.

Consider Your Context, Audience, Purpose, and Role

During a multimedia presentation, slides containing text or graphics are projected on a screen, and in some cases, audio, video, or animations are played. Multimedia presentations can also include links to the Web and embedded applications, such as spreadsheets. As you consider whether and how you might use multimedia during a presentation, focus in particular on the setting in which your audience will see your presentation. Most often, multimedia presentations are made in person, typically in lecture halls or meeting rooms that are equipped with projection equipment and public address systems. At other times, though, these presentations are given in more intimate settings where the presentation is viewed on a laptop screen or using a portable LCD projector. In some cases, multimedia presentations are created for delivery via the Web, allowing a larger audience to access the presentation. Web-based multimedia presentations can be designed so that the speaker either appears in a smaller video window next to the presentation slides or provides a voice-over for each slide. More often, however, Web-based presentations consist only of the slides, and no audio or video is provided.

A strong multimedia presentation does one of two things. If it is used to accompany an oral presentation in front of a group of listeners, it should highlight your points without stealing the show. If it serves as your only point of contact with your audience—that is, if it will be viewed on a computer, tablet, or smartphone—your presentation needs to stand on its own. In this sense, context—and in particular the setting in which your presentation is delivered and any time limits you might have to work within—has important implications for how you pursue your writing goals and meet your audience's expectations.

Once you understand the context for your presentation, consider how it will shape your efforts to achieve your purpose, adopt your role, and meet the expectations of your audience. If you are giving a talk as you make your presentation, you can use many of the techniques that are used during an oral presentation, such as observing and responding to your audience, varying the pitch and loudness of your voice, using gestures, and establishing eye contact with members of the audience.

You can also invite questions and encourage discussion among members of your audience. If you are preparing a presentation that will be viewed on the Web, put yourself in the place of someone who will be encountering your ideas for the first time. Ask yourself what you'd find confusing, surprising, or interesting. Better yet, ask some friends to read a draft of your presentation. Observe their reactions to each slide, and ask them how you might improve the presentation.

Develop Your "Talking Points"

Regardless of the setting in which your presentation will be delivered, you'll need to consider how you'll convey your main point to your audience. Much as you would do with other genres, you'll need to develop a series of key or supporting points and choose evidence to support them. Unlike in written genres, such as articles and multimodal essays, you'll need to make your points quickly. You'll also need to repeat them often enough to get your ideas across clearly, yet not so frequently that you begin to bore your audience. Striking this balance is the key to connecting with your audience. Fortunately, multimedia presentations can make use of some powerful tools for creating that connection.

The distinguishing feature of a multimedia presentation is the wide array of sources you can use to engage with your audience. A presentation on recent changes in education policy, for example, might include video clips in which students, teachers, parents, and community members discuss the effects of those policies or the reasons leading to their development. A presentation on social networking might include links to social-networking sites, a chart illustrating the growth in use of such sites over the past decade, or screenshots showing a range of purposes for which such sites are used.

The sources you choose should support your points or allow you to distinguish your ideas from those advanced by others. If your presentation slides are intended to accompany an oral presentation, your sources should complement rather than compete with what you have to say. You've probably seen more than your fair share of presentations in which speakers have read their slides aloud and offered little or nothing beyond the words on the slide. It is far more effective to use your slides to expand on or illustrate—not simply repeat—what you are saying out loud. If, however, you expect your audience to view your presentation online without a recording of what you are saying, you might create some slides that convey your key points clearly and concisely in writing.

As you choose sources to support your talking points, make sure they will be consistent with any time limits you might face. A video clip might be compelling and highly persuasive, but if it is too long, it will crowd out other points you want to make.

As you might do with a multimodal essay, consider how the differences among various types of sources—such as images, audio clips, video clips, tables, and charts—can help you achieve your purpose. An image projected on a screen while you talk is more likely to complement your words than will a video clip, particularly one that has a sound track. On the other hand, a video clip can convey far more information than can most images. If you are developing a presentation that will be viewed on a computer, tablet, or smartphone, the video clip might be more effective in getting your points across to your audience.

As you decide which sources to include in your presentation, keep in mind the needs, interests, knowledge, experiences, and backgrounds of your audience. Choose sources carefully. Images and video clips that one audience might view without a great deal of concern could be offensive to another. If your subject matter requires exposing your audience to disturbing images or explicit language, as might happen if you are addressing issues such as gun violence or censorship, warn your audience. If you are uncertain about the potential impact of a source, consult your instructor, a librarian, or a friend or classmate who might be similar to the audience you are trying to reach.

Choose Composing Tools

The program you choose to create your multimedia presentation will have a strong effect on its organization and design. Conventional multimedia presentation programs, such as Apple Keynote, Google Slides, Microsoft PowerPoint, and Open-Office Impress, organize presentations as a collection of slides ordered in a linear sequence from a cover slide to a closing slide. If you don't specify a particular layout, these programs use default slides consisting of a heading and a bulleted list. In contrast, a multimedia presentation program such as Prezi (prezi.com) allows you to create "zooming" presentations that can be useful for creative purposes such as digital storytelling, while Capzles (capzles.com) arranges slides along a timeline, which works well when your points have a chronological or sequential structure.

Your choice of composing tool will affect not only how you conceptualize your presentation but also the kinds of multimedia sources you can include and how they will appear. Conventional programs such as PowerPoint offer the greatest flexibility in the types of sources that can be included in a presentation. They also offer a wide range of tools for linking to sites and various types of media on the Web. If you decide to use a less conventional program, however, you need to consider not only that program's capabilities, which might surprise and intrigue your audience, but also its limitations in handling various types of sources.

You'll also find that some multimedia presentation programs provide features that can help you during a presentation. The "presenter view" tools in conventional presentation programs allow you to see information that is not projected on the screen, such as notes on the current slide and small images of upcoming slides. These tools can remind you of important ideas that are related to but not displayed on the slide and can help you keep track of where you are in your presentation. Essentially, they serve the same function as the speaker's notes you might use during an oral presentation (see p. 207).

Figure 9.1 Presenter View in PowerPoint

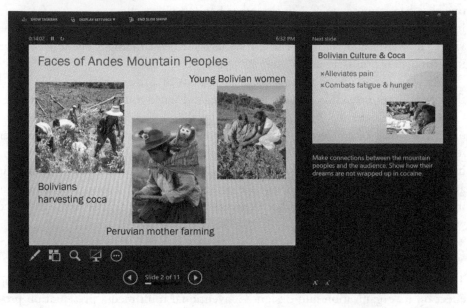

Develop a Consistent Design

Over the past two decades, audiences in settings ranging from business meetings to lecture halls seem to have been subjected to more poorly designed multimedia presentations than there are drops of water in the ocean. Perhaps you, too, have been at some of these presentations. If so, you'll be aware of the benefits of the following design guidelines:

- Choose a color scheme that reflects the purpose and tone of your line of argument. Use bright colors, for example, for a lighthearted topic. Use neutral colors for a serious presentation.

- Be consistent in your choice of fonts, colors, and page layout.

- Use readable fonts, such as 44-point Corbel for headings and 28-point Calibri for body text. Avoid elaborate script fonts, which are often unreadable from a distance, or overly playful fonts like Curlz, which can come across as unprofessional.

- Keep text to a minimum: A general rule is six words per bullet point, six bullet points per slide, and no more than six slides of all text in a row.

- To enhance the readability of slides, use either a light background with dark text or a dark background with light text, and a minimum of text effects (such as shadows or flashing text).

- Use audio, video, and animation with moderation. Generally, clips should run no longer than one minute each.

- Avoid the use of slow or overly complex transitions between slides.
- Avoid the use of distracting sound effects on slides or during slide transitions.

Organize Your Presentation

The organizing pattern you select for your presentation should help you achieve your purpose and meet the expectations of your readers. It should also be consistent with your line of argument. If you are giving a presentation to an audience, as opposed to creating a presentation that will be read in digital form, you should consider other factors as well, such as your audience's inability to refer back to what you've already presented if they get confused or can't recall something you said earlier. As a result, you might find it useful to summarize key ideas or information at various points in the presentation, to forecast what you'll be talking about in the next part of your presentation, to be open to questions from the audience, and even to ask for questions at particular points.

Practice and Revise Your Presentation

Even experienced presenters find it useful to practice their presentations. They understand how difficult it can be to get everything right the first time. Practicing allows you to ensure that you don't leave out important information and ideas, that the embedded media and links you've included in your presentation display properly and function as expected, and that any animations and other special effects work as intended.

Practicing in front of a group of classmates or friends also allows you to determine whether your overall line of argument makes sense, whether you've organized your reasons and evidence effectively, and whether the sources you've chosen are appropriate. It can also help you learn whether your equipment is working properly and whether your presentation will fit within any time limits you've been given.

Give or Distribute Your Presentation

If you are making a presentation to an audience, you can draw on the same set of techniques used in effective oral presentations, including maintaining eye contact, varying the pitch of your voice, speaking loudly enough to be heard clearly, and slowing down so that your audience can follow your argument (see p. 206). In addition, make sure that you can advance your slides easily—either by using a slide clicker, which is similar to a computer mouse, or by standing close enough to your computer or tablet to advance the slides manually—and that you are facing your audience. In case your equipment fails—for instance, if a laptop loses power or an LCD display fails to work properly—be sure that you have a backup plan. You could bring printouts of your presentation, for example, or create a handout summarizing your points.

If your presentation will be viewed in digital format, make sure that you've removed any notes that you don't want your audience to see; ensure that the format in which you've saved the file can be read on a wide range of computers, tablets, and smartphones; and choose a means of distributing the file. You can distribute a file by placing it on a Web site, uploading it to a blog or social-networking site, attaching it to an e-mail message, sharing it through a service such as DropBox, or saving it on a flash drive and giving it to people you want to view it. If you've uploaded the file, open it and check its appearance. If necessary, revise the presentation, save it to a new file, and replace the file you uploaded. Do the same with files that you plan to attach to e-mail or put on a flash drive.

View a Presentation

The following figures show slides from a multimedia presentation designed by Elizabeth Leontiev, a first-year student who had worked on a writing project that addressed the role of coca leaves and tea in Bolivian daily life.

This is formatted in a clear, eye-catching font.

The name of the presenter is clearly identified.

Coca Is Not The Enemy

Presented by:
Elizabeth Leontiev

Faces of Andes Mountain Peoples

Fonts are large and easy to read.

Bolivians harvesting coca

Peruvian mother farming

Bolivian women harvesting

Photographs personalize the presentation.

Captions for each photograph help the audience understand the issue.

Drinking coffee for Americans

Chewing coca leaves and drinking coca tea for Bolivians

Photographs and captions help explain the role of coca leaves and tea in Bolivian daily life.

The speaker uses the slides to support her presentation, rather than take its place.

Morales's Plan

A photograph personalizes Morales for the audience.

- •Maintain traditional way of life
- •Work with farmers

A brief, bulleted list conveys key elements of Morales's plan.

CHECKLIST FOR CREATING MULTIMEDIA PRESENTATIONS

✔ Consider your context, audience, purpose, and role.

✔ Create an outline of your presentation, focusing on the line of argument you want to present to your audience.

✔ Identify points that would benefit from multimedia illustrations.

✔ Collect and work with sources that will illustrate or support those points.

✔ Choose a multimedia presentation program that is consistent with your context, audience, purpose, and role.

✔ Follow effective design principles regarding color scheme, fonts, and page layout, paying particular attention to the following:

· consistent use of fonts, colors, shading, borders, and rules

· readable fonts for headings and subheadings

· a readable body font designed for viewing on a screen

· if used, transitions between pages (dissolves, page flips) that are quick and not distracting

· if used, background images and sounds that are chosen to enhance rather than obscure the elements on each page

✔ Use multimedia elements in moderation.

✔ To ensure that your slides are readable and well designed, preview your presentation on a screen similar in size to the one you will be using during your talk.

✔ Face your audience as you make your presentation.

✔ Use multimedia elements to advance your line of argument, pointing out important information and illustrations on slides.

✔ Create a backup plan in case your equipment fails. Consider using slide printouts or a handout as a backup.

✔ If you are distributing your presentation in digital format, ensure that it displays properly on computers, tablets, and smartphones.

9.3 How Can I Work on a Group Presentation?

Group presentations have become common not only in writing and writing intensive classes but also in business, nonprofit, and government settings. The extent of collaboration can vary widely: Each member of the group might be assigned to work on a different section of the presentation, or the whole group might work together—electronically or in person—to plan, design, draft, polish, revise, and edit the entire presentation. To prepare to work collaboratively on a group presentation, become familiar with the purposes, processes, and potential pitfalls of working with a team. Learning how to work together while you are a student can help you succeed on projects long after you've completed your degree.

■ **Activity 9.1** **Working Together: Develop Guidelines for Group Work**

Most writers can look back at a group project and find something they didn't like about the experience. They might have been in a group dominated by an ineffective leader. They might have had to do far more than their fair share on a project. At the last minute, they might have been left in the lurch by someone who failed to deliver a critical part of the project. Whatever the reason, some writers prefer to work alone. Yet group work can be productive and satisfying, and most experienced writers can point to a wide range of situations in which working with other writers significantly improved their work on a writing project.

To get ready to work with other writers, reflect on your experiences with group work. Then, working with the members of your group, develop a set of guidelines that would improve the quality of group work. To carry out this activity, follow these steps:

(Continued from previous page)

1. Individually, spend five minutes brainstorming or freewriting about your experiences with collaborative work. List both positive and negative experiences.

2. As a group, discuss your experiences. Each person should note the advantages and disadvantages of collaborative work.

3. As a group, identify the most significant challenges to working together effectively.

4. As a group, create a list of guidelines that would address these challenges.

Once you've completed the activity, share your guidelines with other groups in the class. As a class, create a list of guidelines for collaborative work in your course.

Understand the Purposes of Working in a Group

Asking a group to work together reflects a set of beliefs about the value of collaboration. In corporate settings, for example, working together might be a means not only of ensuring that a project results in useful work but also of building a sense of togetherness and commitment among team members. In an academic setting, a group project allows students to carry out a project that a single student would find difficult to produce alone, helps them learn more about a subject, and familiarizes them with the collaborative processes they might encounter in their professional lives. In this sense, collaborating on a project might be as important as—or even more important than—making a presentation or producing a document.

Understand Potential Problems and Develop Solutions

Recognizing—and taking steps to avoid—potential pitfalls can increase the likelihood that a collaborative project will succeed. Common problems encountered during group work range from individual concerns about participating in a group to behaviors that undermine the group's effectiveness. If you want to collaborate successfully, be aware of these problems and learn how solve them.

- **Some people prefer to work alone,** and they make those feelings all too clear, often to the point of insulting their classmates. Remind such people of the reasons the group is working together and the danger their attitude poses to the long-term success of the project.

- **Some people worry about losing a sense of individual worth.** Assure them that their contributions not only are important but also will be recognized as such—if not formally, then by other members of the group.

- **Some individuals will try to dominate a group,** perhaps believing that the project will fail unless they take control. To avoid this problem, make sure at the outset of the project that everyone's ideas are heard and respected, and explain that developing a plan for the project is not a process of arguing for the superiority of a particular set of ideas so much as it is the synthesis of useful ideas.

- **Some members will find it difficult to schedule or attend group meetings.** Ensure that meeting times and locations accommodate everyone's needs. If you can't do so, have the group discuss the problem with the instructor.

- **Some members of a group will use meeting time unproductively**—at least in the eyes of other members of the group. This can cause problems, particularly when it is difficult to find time to meet or if meeting time is limited. To address this issue, be sure the group establishes and sticks to an agenda for each meeting.

- **Some group members will want to work only on what they feel capable of doing well.** In nonacademic settings, where a strong emphasis is often placed on the effectiveness of the final document, this is usually not a problem. In academic settings, however, where the goals of most collaborative projects include learning new skills and acquiring new knowledge, it is important that all members of a group take on new challenges.

- **Some members of a group won't contribute as much as others—and some won't contribute at all.** In collaborative projects for a class, you'll find that some members refuse to participate. Perhaps they assume that they can't make much of a contribution, or perhaps they're trying to save time by not participating. Regardless of their intentions, their lack of participation causes hurt feelings and might affect the overall quality of the project. To avoid these problems, establish ground rules about how to address unequal participation.

- **Some members of a group will resent the extra time required to coordinate work on a project.** Remind these people of the reasons for working together and the benefits of doing so.

- **As the group works on a project, disagreements will arise.** As you develop ground rules for working together, consider how you'll address disagreements. Strategies include voting, discussing until consensus emerges, and seeking guidance from an instructor or a supervisor.

Establish Ground Rules

At the beginning of a project, spend time discussing potential difficulties and establishing ground rules. These can include guidelines for:

- Selecting meeting times and places

- Conducting discussions
- Resolving disputes
- Determining individual contributions to the project
- Ensuring equitable contributions from group members
- Defining the consequences for inadequate participation

Ground rules can take various forms, ranging from an informal agreement among group members to a detailed statement signed by each member.

Activity 9.2 **Working Together: Establish Ground Rules for a Group Project**

In your writer's notebook, develop a set of ground rules for your group by responding to the following prompts. Share your responses with the members of your group, and agree on a formal set of rules.

1. Meetings will be held at [location] on [dates and times].

2. Discussions will be [moderated by the same person at each meeting, moderated by a different person at each meeting, unmoderated], and notes will be taken by [the same person at each meeting, a different person at each meeting].

3. When disagreements arise, they will be resolved by _____.

4. The following members of the group will take the lead on the following activities: [list names and activities].

5. To ensure equitable contributions by each group member, we will _____.

6. Group members who do not contribute equitably will face the following consequences: [list consequences].

7. Group members who drop out of the project will face the following consequences: [list consequences].

Create a Plan

Once ground rules have been established, develop a plan for completing the project. Plans do not have to be highly detailed, particularly at the beginning stage of the project. However, they should define the overall goals of the project and identify key steps that must be taken to achieve those goals. An effective plan will define deadlines for the completion of each step, identify who is responsible for specific activities associated with completing a given step, and suggest strategies for carrying out those activities.

Where Do You Go for Help?

We are excited that you have chosen Virginia Tech as the place where you want to live, learn, and grow. You are not on this journey alone; there are plenty of services that can help you along the way. This chapter lists some of the support services that can help you be successful in your academic courses and as you face challenges during your undergraduate career.

10.1 Virginia Tech Writing Center

Figure 10.1 Students in the Writing Center

The Writing Center provides undergraduate students, graduate students, faculty, and staff free writing support through one-on-one consultations with a trained writing coach. The Writing Center coaches assist students with all stages of the writing process, from brainstorming to editing. They can help with writing and reading assignments from any course in the university and with writing projects that are not linked to classes. Writing instruction in English is always available and sometimes in other languages as well.

If you would like to work with the same coach at the same time each week, you can request a writing partner. Meeting with the same coach each week is a great way to help you meet your writing goals.

See the Writing Center Web site for more details about their services.

Writing Center

Location
Newman Library, 2nd Floor
Regular Hours
Monday, Tuesday,
Wednesday: 9 a.m.–10 p.m.
Thursday, Friday: 9 a.m.–5 p.m.
Sunday: 7 p.m.–10 p.m.
Other times and locations often available.

Web Address
http://www.composition.english.vt.edu/
writing center
Phone Number
(540) 231-5436

10.2 Virginia Tech CommLab

The CommLab strives to create a comfortable learning environment that provides Virginia Tech students and faculty members access to constructive feedback and practical resources for improving oral presentations. By visiting CommLab, clients are able to gain valuable presentation-related insight and develop their public speaking skills.

Location
Newman Library, 2nd Floor
Regular hours vary by semester
Web Address
http://www.commlab.vt.edu
Phone Number
(540) 231-9280

Figure 10.2 CommLab

10.3 Newman Library

The main Virginia Tech library is your go-to place for help with research resources. The library subscribes to extensive information resources that are available to you as a student. See the graphic on the following page for how to get started.

Figure 10.3 University Libraries Are Here to Help

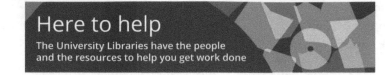

Here to help
The University Libraries have the people
and the resources to help you get work done

PEOPLE

ASK A LIBRARIAN
ONLINE CHAT

lib.vt.edu/help/ask.html

YOUR LIBRARIAN

lib.vt.edu/instruct/clprg.html

Each college has its own librarian.
Get in touch with yours for specialized help.

REFERENCE DESK

Need help with research
or using the libraries?
The reference desk is on
the second floor of
Newman Library, near
the Circulation Desk.

RESOURCES

SUBJECT GUIDES

guides.lib.vt.edu/subject-guides

Subject Guides are organized by
discipline and can help you
navigate our many databases.

SUMMON

vt.summon.serialssolutions.com/

Summon is a good starting place for
research. Use the Summon search
box on the library homepage to
search for books, ebooks, articles,
multimedia, and more.

HOMEPAGE

lib.vt.edu

OFF-CAMPUS
SIGN IN

Sign in with your
PID and password
to access library
resources
off campus.

UNIVERSITY LIBRARIES   Ⅲ **VirginiaTech**
Invent the Future®

Librarians are happy to support you at any point in the research process, including developing an initial research topic, strategizing your process, navigating specific resources, and understanding and evaluating different kinds of information. You might have a workshop with a librarian to work on these and other aspects of research—often, as part of or as a replacement for class. Contact a librarian for personalized help at the Reference Desk, by email, or by online chat on the library's Web site.

To learn more about library spaces and resources at Virginia Tech, you can take a self-guided audio tour. Visit the Circulation Desk on the second floor of Newman Library to get started. More details are available at http://www.lib.vt.edu/instruct/toursked.html.

Newman Library Hours
Sunday: open 9:00 a.m.
Monday–Thursday: open 24 hours*
Friday: closes 8:00 p.m.
Saturday: 9:00 a.m.–8:00 p.m.
*During 24-hour operation, a valid Hokie Passport is required to access or remain in the library between midnight and 7:30 a.m.

10.4 The Virginia Tech InnovationSpace

The Virginia Tech InnovationSpace is a multimedia computer lab that provides assistance through free and open access to software, hardware, and specially trained staff. At the InnovationSpace you will find video editing stations, Macintosh- and Windows-based computers, scanners, tutorials, classes, and loaner equipment to assist you with your multimedia projects.

Figure 10.4 The Virginia Tech InnovationSpace

Location
1140 Torgersen Hall
Regular Hours
Monday–Wednesday: 10:00 a.m.–8:00 p.m.
Thursday–Friday: 10:00 a.m.–6:00 p.m.
Sunday: 1:00 p.m.–8:00 p.m.
Web Address
http://www.is.vt.edu
Phone Number
(540) 231-4826

10.5 Virginia Tech Information Technology Support (4Help)

The mission of Virginia Tech's Information Technology Support unit (4Help) is to enhance the University's missions of teaching, learning, research, and outreach by providing centralized computing and telecommunications support services to Virginia Tech students, faculty, and staff.

Information Technology Support (4Help) is comprised of two operational units delivering two levels of support: the Virginia Tech Operations Center (VTOC) and University Computing Support. VTOC is able to reset passwords and provide assistance with navigating the online help resources. Call Center operators are available at (540) 231-4357. University Computing Support provides a second level of support during regular business hours (Monday–Friday, 8:00 a.m.–5:00 p.m.), including walk-in appointments in the Student Services Building. See the Web site http://computing.vt.edu/content/4help for details.

10.6 The Student Success Center

Figure 10.5 The Student Success Center

The Student Success Center offers undergraduate students a variety of services and academic support, including tutoring, academic coaching, workshops on topics related to academic skills and behaviors, and college success strategies courses. The center supports undergraduate learning from enrollment to degree completion by offering programs and services that can help you become a more effective learner.

Be aware that instructors may also contact the Student Success Center on a student's behalf, using an academic referral. Instructors use the VT Early Academic Referral System (EARS) to express concerns about a student's excessive absences, missing assignments, poor academic performance, or other academic issues. If referred, students are encouraged to meet with a Student Success Center representative for help in cultivating strategies for success.

Location	**Web Address**
110 Femoyer Hall	http://www.studentsuccess.vt.edu
Regular Hours	**Phone Number**
Monday–Thursday: 8:00 a.m.–8:00 p.m.	(540) 231-5499
Friday 8:00 a.m.–5:00 p.m.	

10.7 Undergraduate Academic Advising

Every new student at Virginia Tech is assigned to an academic advisor for help with making responsible academic and career choices. To determine the name of your academic advisor, log into Hokie Spa and click on the link for "General Student Information." Academic advising is viewed as a collaborative process between the student and advisor, with both individuals committed to student success. Specific responsibilities of the university, advisor, and ultimately the student are outlined at http://www.advising.vt.edu.

10.8 Student Services/University Offices

Below is an abbreviated list of some useful phone numbers.

In case of immediate emergency, call VT Police/ Virginia Tech Rescue	(540) 231-6411
Cook Counseling Center (for psychological concerns), Monday-Friday, 8:00 a.m.–5:00 p.m.	(540) 231-6557
After hours/weekends	(540) 231-6444
Suicide prevention	(540) 231-6557
Environmental Health and Safety Services	(540) 231- 6411 (via campus police)
Dean of Students Office (advising and accessing university resources)	(540) 231-3787
After hours/weekends	(540) 231-6411 (via campus police)
Schiffert Health Center, Monday–Friday 8:00 a.m.–5:00 p.m.	(540) 231-5313
After hours/weekends	(540) 231-6444
Women's Center at VT (for education, prevention, counseling, and advocacy services)	(540) 231-7806
Services for Students with Disabilities (assists with academic accommodations)	(540) 231-3788
Campus Alcohol Abuse Prevention Center	(540) 231-2233

10.9 Useful Links

Below is an abbreviated list of some useful Web sites related to writing.

Writing Support Pages

Virginia Tech Library's "Introduction to Academic Research"	http://www.lib.vt.edu/info/ugrad.html#id140120-3
Purdue OWL	http://owl.english.purdue.edu/
Strunk's *Elements of Style*	http://www.bartleby.com/141/
Grammar Girl	http://grammar.quickanddirtytips.com/
TESL Journal	http://iteslj.org/

Virginia Tech Library's Guide to Citation and Style Manuals

http://www.lib.vt.edu/find/citation/index.html
http://www.lib.vt.edu/find/citation/z-generators.html

Research-Related Government Sites

Library of Congress	http://www.loc.gov/index.html
U.S. Census	http://www.census.gov

Readings

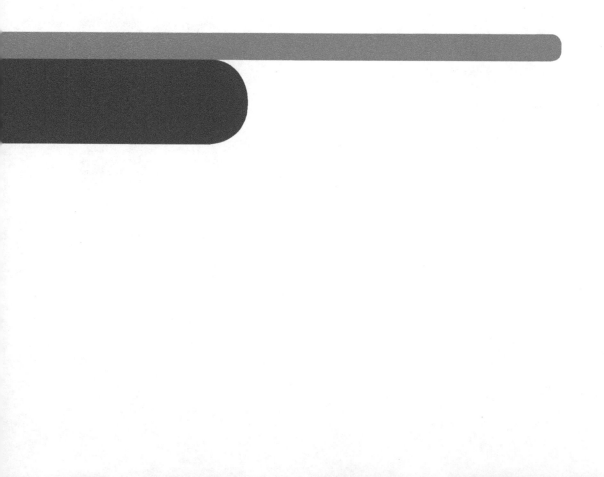

Writing and Language

Paul Roberts [1917–1967]

How to Say Nothing in Five Hundred Words

California-born **Paul Roberts** received his B.A. from San Jose State College and his M.A. and Ph.D. from the University of California at Berkeley, where he taught for fourteen years after serving in the merchant marine during World War II. Writing in a down-to-earth, often humorous style, Roberts published several books on English composition, including *Understanding Grammar* (1954), *English Sentences* (1962), and *Modern Gramma*r (1954). He died in Rome in 1967.

"How to Say Nothing in Five Hundred Words" is from Roberts's best-known book, *Understanding English* (1958), and is representative of his clarity and wit. Roberts recommends that composition students check their tendency to state the obvious and instead strive for interesting content backed by concrete examples.

NOTHING ABOUT SOMETHING

It's Friday afternoon, and you have almost survived another week of classes. You are just looking forward dreamily to the weekend when the English instructor says: "For Monday you will turn in a five-hundred word composition on college football."

Well, that puts a good big hole in the weekend. You don't have any strong views on college football one way or the other. You get rather excited during the season and go to all the home games and find it rather more fun than not. On the other hand, the class has been reading Robert Hutchins in the anthology and perhaps Shaw's "Eighty-Yard Run," and from the class discussion you have got the idea that the instructor thinks college football is for the birds. You are no fool, you. You can figure out what side to take.

After dinner you get out the portable typewriter that you got for high school graduation. You might as well get it over with and enjoy Saturday and Sunday. Five hundred words is about two double-spaced pages with normal margins. You put in a sheet of paper, think up a title, and you're off:

WHY COLLEGE FOOTBALL SHOULD BE ABOLISHED

College football should be abolished because it's bad for the school and also bad for the players. The players are so busy practicing that they don't have any time for their studies.

This, you feel, is a mighty good start. The only trouble is that it's only thirty-two words. You still have four hundred and sixty-eight to go, and you've pretty well exhausted the subject. It comes to you that you do your best thinking in the morning, so you put away the typewriter and go to the movies. But the next morning you have to do your washing and some math problems, and in the afternoon you go to the game. The English instructor turns up too, and you wonder if you've taken the right side after all. Saturday night you have a date, and Sunday morning you have to go to church. (You shouldn't let English assignments interfere with your religion.) What with one thing and another, it's ten o'clock Sunday night before you get out the typewriter again. You make a pot of coffee and start to fill out your views on college football. Put a little meat on the bones.

WHY COLLEGE FOOTBALL SHOULD BE ABOLISHED

In my opinion, it seems to me that college football should be abolished. The reason why I think this to be true is because I feel that football is bad for the colleges in nearly every respect. As Robert Hutchins says in his article in our anthology in which he discusses college football, it would be better if the colleges had race horses and had races with one another, because then the horses would not have to attend classes. I firmly agree with Mr. Hutchins on this point, and I am sure that many other students would agree too.

One reason why it seems to me that college football is bad is that it has become too commercial. In the olden times when people played football just for the fun of it, maybe college football was all right, but they do not play football just for the fun of it now as they used to in the old days. Nowadays college football is what you might call a big business. Maybe this is not true at all schools, and I don't think it is especially true here at State, but certainly this is the case at most colleges and universities in America nowadays, as Mr. Hutchins points out in his very interesting article. Actually the coaches and alumni go around to the high schools and offer the high school stars large salaries to come to their colleges and play football for them. There was one case where a high school star was offered a convertible if he would play football for a certain college.

Another reason for abolishing college football is that it is bad for the players. They do not have time to get a college education, because they are so busy playing football. A football player has to practice every afternoon from three to six, and then he is so tired that he can't concentrate on his studies. He just feels like dropping off to sleep after dinner, and then the next day he goes to his classes without having studied and maybe he fails the test.

(Good ripe stuff so far, but you're still a hundred and fifty-one words from home. One more push.)

Also I think college football is bad for the colleges and the universities because not very many students get to participate in it. Out of a college of ten thousand students only seventy-five or a hundred play football, if that many. Football is what you might call a spectator sport. That means that most people go to watch it but do not play it themselves.

(Four hundred and fifteen. Well, you still have the conclusion, and when you retype it, you can make the margins a little wider.)

These are the reasons why I agree with Mr. Hutchins that college football should be abolished in American colleges and universities.

On Monday you turn it in, moderately hopeful, and on Friday it comes back marked 5 "weak in content" and sporting a big "D."

This essay is exaggerated a little, not much. The English instructor will recognize it as reasonably typical of what an assignment on college football will bring in. He knows that nearly half of the class will contrive in five hundred words to say that college football is too commercial and bad for the players. Most of the other half will inform him that college football builds character and prepares one for life and brings prestige to the school. As he reads paper after paper all saying the same thing in almost the same words, all bloodless, five hundred words dripping out of nothing, he wonders how he allowed himself to get trapped into teaching English when he might have had a happy and interesting life as an electrician or a confidence man.

Well, you may ask, what can you do about it? The subject is one on which you have few convictions and little information. Can you be expected to make a dull subject interesting? As a matter of fact, this is precisely what you are expected to do. This is the writer's essential task. All subjects, except sex, are dull until somebody makes them interesting. The writer's job is to find the argument, the approach, the angle, the wording that will take the reader with him. This is seldom easy, and it is particularly hard in subjects that have been much discussed: College Football, Fraternities, Popular Music, Is Chivalry Dead?, and the like. You will feel that there is nothing you can do with such subjects except repeat the old bromides. But there are some things you can do which will make your papers, if not throbbingly alive, at least less insufferably tedious than they might otherwise be.

AVOID THE OBVIOUS CONTENT

Say the assignment is college football. Say that you've decided to be against it. Begin by putting down the arguments that come to your mind: it is too commercial, it takes the students' minds off their studies, it is hard on the players, it makes the university a kind of circus instead of an intellectual center, for most schools it is financially ruinous. Can you think of any more arguments just off hand? All right. Now when you write your paper, *make sure that you don't use any of the material on this list.* If these are the points that leap to your mind, they will leap to everyone else's too, and whether you get a "C" or a "D" may depend on whether the instructor reads your paper early when he is fresh and tolerant or late, when the sentence "In my opinion, college football has become too commercial," inexorably repeated, has brought him to the brink of lunacy.

Be against college football for some reason or reasons of your own. If they are keen and perceptive ones, that's splendid. But even if they are trivial or foolish or indefensible, you are still ahead so long as they are not everybody else's reasons too. Be against it because the colleges don't spend enough money on it to make it worth while, because it is bad for the characters of the spectators, because the players are forced to attend classes, because the football stars hog all the beautiful women, because it competes with baseball and is therefore un-American and possibly Communist inspired. There are lots of more or less unused reasons for being against college football.

Sometimes it is a good idea to sum up and dispose of the trite and conventional points 10 before going on to your own. This has the advantage of indicating to the reader that you are going to be neither trite nor conventional. Something like this:

> We are often told that college football should be abolished because it has become too commercial or because it is bad for the players. These arguments are no doubt very cogent, but they don't really go to the heart of the matter.

Then you go to the heart of the matter.

TAKE THE LESS USUAL SIDE

One rather simple way of getting interest into your paper is to take the side of the argument that most of the citizens will want to avoid. If the assignment is an essay on dogs, you can, if you choose, explain that dogs are faithful and lovable companions, intelligent, useful as guardians of the house and protectors of children, indispensable in police work—in short, when all is said and done, man's best friends. Or you can suggest that those big brown eyes conceal more often than not, a vacuity of mind and an inconstancy of purpose; that the dogs you have known most intimately have been mangy, ill-tempered brutes, incapable of instruction; and that only your nobility of mind and fear of arrest prevent you from kicking the flea-ridden animals when you pass them on the street.

Naturally, personal convictions will sometimes dictate your approach. If the assigned subject is "Is Methodism Rewarding to the Individual?" and you are a pious Methodist, you have really no choice. But few assigned subjects, if any, will fall in this category. Most of them will lie in broad areas of discussion with much to be said on both sides. They are intellectual exercises, and it is legitimate to argue now one way and now another, as debaters do in similar circumstances. Always take the side that looks to you hardest, least defensible. It will almost always turn out to be easier to write interestingly on that side.

This general advice applies where you have a choice of subjects. If you are to choose among "The Value of Fraternities" and "My Favorite High School Teacher" and "What I Think About Beetles," by all means plump for the beetles. By the time the instructor gets to your paper, he will be up to his ears in tedious tales about the French teacher at Bloombury High and assertions about how fraternities build character and prepare one for life. Your views on beetles, whatever they are, are bound to be a refreshing change.

Don't worry too much about figuring out what the instructor thinks about the subject so that you can cuddle up with him. Chances are his views are no stronger than yours. If he does have convictions and you oppose them, his problem is to keep from grading you higher than you deserve in order to show he is not biased. This doesn't mean that you should always cantankerously dissent from what the instructor says; that gets tiresome too. And if the subject assigned is "My Pet Peeve," do not begin, "My pet peeve is the English instructor who assigns papers on 'my pet peeve.'" This was still funny during the War of 1812, but it has sort of lost its edge since then. It is in general good manners to avoid personalities.

SLIP OUT OF ABSTRACTION

If you will study the essay on college football in [the "Nothing about Something" section], 15 you will perceive that one reason for its appalling dullness is that it never gets down to particulars. It is just a series of not very glittering generalities: "football is bad for the colleges," "it has become too commercial," "football is a big business," "it is bad for the players," and so on. Such round phrases thudding against the reader's brain are unlikely to convince him, though they may well render him unconscious.

If you want the reader to believe that college football is bad for the players, you have to do more than say so. You have to display the evil. Take your roommate, Alfred Simkins, the second-string center. Picture poor old Alfy coming home from football practice every evening, bruised and aching, agonizingly tired, scarcely able to shovel the mashed potatoes into his mouth. Let us see him staggering up to the room, getting out his econ textbook, peering desperately at it with his good eye, falling asleep and failing the test in the morning.

Let us share his unbearable tension as Saturday draws near. Will he fail, be demoted, lose his monthly allowance, be forced to return to the coal mines? And if he succeeds, what will be his reward? Perhaps a slight ripple of applause when the third-string center replaces him, a moment of elation in the locker room if the team wins, of despair if it loses. What will he look back on when he graduates from college? Toil and torn ligaments. And what will be his future? He is not good enough for pro football, and he is too obscure and weak in econ to succeed in stocks and bonds. College football is tearing the heart from Alfy Simkins and, when it finishes with him, will callously toss aside the shattered hulk.

This is no doubt a weak enough argument for the abolition of college football, but it is a sight better than saying, in three or four variations, that college football (in your opinion) is bad for the players.

Look at the work of any professional writer and notice how constantly he is moving from the generality, the abstract statement, to the concrete example, the facts and figures, the illustration. If he is writing on juvenile delinquency, he does not just tell you that juveniles are (it seems to him) delinquent and that (in his opinion) something should be done about it. He shows you juveniles being delinquent, tearing up movie theatres in Buffalo, stabbing high school principals in Dallas, smoking marijuana in Palo Alto. And more than likely he is moving toward some specific remedy, not just a general wringing of the hands.

It is no doubt possible to be *too* concrete, too illustrative or anecdotal, but few inexperienced writers err this way. For most the soundest advice is to be seeking always for the picture, to be always turning general remarks into seeable examples. Don't say, "Sororities teach girls the social graces." Say, "Sorority life teaches a girl how to carry on a conversation while pouring tea, without sloshing the tea into the saucer." Don't say, "I like certain kinds of popular music very much." Say, "Whenever I hear Gerber Spinklittle play 'Mississippi Man' on the trombone, my socks creep up my ankles."

GET RID OF OBVIOUS PADDING

The student toiling away at his weekly English theme is too often tormented by a figure: five 20 hundred words. How, he asks himself, is he to achieve this staggering total? Obviously by never using one word when he can somehow work in ten.

He is therefore seldom content with a plain statement like "Fast driving is dangerous." This has only four words in it. He takes thought, and the sentence becomes:

In my opinion, fast driving is dangerous.

Better, but he can do better still:

In my opinion, fast driving would seem to be rather dangerous.

If he is really adept, it may come out:

In my humble opinion, though I do not claim to be an expert on this complicated subject, fast driving, in most circumstances, would seem to be rather dangerous in many respects, or at least so it would seem to me.

Thus four words have been turned into forty, and not an iota of content has been added.

Now this is a way to go about reaching five hundred words, and if you are content with a "D" grade, it is as good a way as any. But if you aim higher, you must work differently.

Instead of stuffing your sentences with straw, you must try steadily to get rid of the padding, to make your sentences lean and tough. If you are really working at it, your first draft will greatly exceed the required total, and then you will work it down, thus:

> It is thought in some quarters that fraternities do not contribute as much as might be expected to campus life.

> Some people think that fraternities contribute little to campus life.

> The average doctor who practices in small towns or in the country must toil night and day to heal the sick.

> Most country doctors work long hours.

> When I was a little girl, I suffered from shyness and embarrassment in the presence of others.

> I was a shy little girl.

> It is absolutely necessary for the person employed as a marine fireman to give the matter of steam pressure his undivided attention at all times.

> The fireman has to keep his eye on the steam gauge.

You may ask how you can arrive at five hundred words at this rate. Simply. You dig up more real content. Instead of taking a couple of obvious points off the surface of the topic and then circling warily around them for six paragraphs, you work in and explore, figure out the details. You illustrate. You say that fast driving is dangerous, and then you prove it. How long does it take to stop a car at forty and at eighty? How far can you see at night? What happens when a tire blows? What happens in a head-on collision at fifty miles an hour? Pretty soon your paper will be full of broken glass and blood and headless torsos, and reaching five hundred words will not really be a problem.

CALL A FOOL A FOOL

Some of the padding in freshman themes is to be blamed not on anxiety about the word minimum but on excessive timidity. The student writes, "In my opinion, the principal of my high school acted in ways that I believe every unbiased person would have to call foolish." This isn't exactly what he means. What he means is, "My high school principal was a fool." If he was a fool, call him a fool. Hedging the thing about with "in-my-opinion's" and "it-seems-to-me's" and "as-I-see-it's" and "at-least-from-my-point-of-view's" gains you nothing. Delete these phrases whenever they creep into your paper.

The student's tendency to hedge stems from a modesty that in other circumstances 25 would be commendable. He is, he realizes, young and inexperienced, and he half suspects that he is dopey and fuzzy-minded beyond the average. Probably only too true. But it doesn't help to announce your incompetence six times in every paragraph. Decide what you want to say and say it as vigorously as possible, without apology and in plain words.

Linguistic diffidence can take various forms. One is what we call *euphemism*. This is the tendency to call a spade "a certain garden implement" or women's underwear "unmentionables." It is stronger in some eras than others and in some people than others but it always operates more or less in subjects that are touchy or taboo: death, sex, madness, and so on.

Thus we shrink from saying "He died last night" but say instead "passed away," "left us," "joined his Maker," "went to his reward." Or we try to take off the tension with a lighter cliché: "kicked the bucket," "cashed in his chips," "handed in his dinner pail." We have found all sorts of ways to avoid saying *mad*: "mentally ill," "touched," "not quite right upstairs," "feeble-minded," "innocent," "simple," "off his trolley," "not in his right mind." Even such a now plain word as *insane* began as a euphemism with the meaning "not healthy."

Modern science, particularly psychology, contributes many polysyllables in which we can wrap our thoughts and blunt their force. To many writers there is no such thing as a bad schoolboy. Schoolboys are maladjusted or unoriented or misunderstood or in need of guidance or lacking in continued success toward satisfactory integration of the personality as a social unit, but they are never bad. Psychology no doubt makes us better men or women, more sympathetic and tolerant, but it doesn't make writing any easier. Had Shakespeare been confronted with psychology, "To be or not to be" might have come out, "To continue as a social unit or not to do so. That is the personality problem. Whether 'tis a better sign of integration at the conscious level to display a psychic tolerance toward the maladjustments and repressions induced by one's lack of orientation in one's environment or—" But Hamlet would never have finished the soliloquy.

Writing in the modern world, you cannot altogether avoid modern jargon. Nor, in an effort to get away from euphemism, should you salt your paper with four-letter words. But you can do much if you will mount guard against those roundabout phrases, those echoing polysyllables that tend to slip into your writing to rob it of its crispness and force.

BEWARE OF THE PAT EXPRESSION

Other things being equal, avoid phrases like "other things being equal." Those sentences that come to you whole, or in two or three doughy lumps, are sure to be bad sentences. They are no creation of yours but pieces of common thought floating in the community soup.

Pat expressions are hard, often impossible, to avoid, because they come too easily to be 30 noticed and seem too necessary to be dispensed with. No writer avoids them altogether, but good writers avoid them more often than poor writers.

By "pat expressions" we mean such tags as "to all practical intents and purposes," "the pure and simple truth," "from where I sit," "the time of his life," "to the ends of the earth," "in the twinkling of an eye," "as sure as you're born," "over my dead body," "under cover of darkness," "took the easy way out," "when all is said and done," "told him time and time again," "parted the best of friends," "stand up and be counted," "gave him the best years of her life," "worked her fingers to the bone." Like other clichés, these expressions were once forceful. Now we should use them only when we can't possibly think of anything else.

Some pat expressions stand like a wall between the writer and thought. Such a one is "the American way of life." Many student writers feel that when they have said that something accords with the American way of life or does not they have exhausted the subject. Actually, they have stopped at the highest level of abstraction. The American way of life is the complicated set of bonds between a hundred and eighty million ways. All of us know this when we think about it, but the tag phrase too often keeps us from thinking about it.

So with many another phrase dear to the politician: "this great land of ours," "the man in the street," "our national heritage." These may prove our patriotism or give a clue to our political beliefs, but otherwise they add nothing to the paper except words.

COLORFUL WORDS

The writer builds with words, and no builder uses a raw material more slippery and elusive and treacherous. A writer's work is a constant struggle to get the right word in the right place, to find that particular word that will convey his meaning exactly, that will persuade the reader or soothe him or startle or amuse him. He never succeeds altogether—sometimes he feels that he scarcely succeeds at all—but such successes as he has are what make the thing worth doing.

There is no book of rules for this game. One progresses through ever-lasting experiment 35 on the basis of ever-widening experience. There are few useful generalizations that one can make about words as words, but there are perhaps a few.

Some words are what we call "colorful." By this we mean that they are calculated to produce a picture or induce an emotion. They are dressy instead of plain, specific instead of general, loud instead of soft. Thus, in place of "Her heart beat," we may write "Her heart *pounded, throbbed, fluttered, danced.*" Instead of "He sat in his chair," we may say, "He *lounged, sprawled, coiled.*" Instead of "It was hot," we may say, "It was *blistering, sultry, muggy, suffocating, steamy, wilting.*"

However, it should not be supposed that the fancy word is always better. Often it is as well to write "Her heart beat" or "It was hot" if that is all it did or all it was. Ages differ in how they like their prose. The nineteenth century liked it rich and smoky. The twentieth has usually preferred it lean and cool. The twentieth century writer, like all writers, is forever seeking the exact word, but he is wary of sounding feverish. He tends to pitch it low, to understate it, to throw it away. He knows that if he gets too colorful, the audience is likely to giggle.

See how this strikes you: "As the rich, golden glow of the sunset died away along the eternal western hills, Angela's limpid blue eyes looked softly and trustingly into Montague's flashing brown ones, and her heart pounded like a drum in time with the joyous song surging in her soul." Some people like that sort of thing, but most modern readers would say, "Good grief," and turn on the television.

COLORED WORDS

Some words we would call not so much colorful as colored—that is, loaded with associations, good or bad. All words—except perhaps structure words—have associations of some sort. We have said that the meaning of a word is the sum of the contexts in which it occurs. When we hear a word, we hear with it an echo of all the situations in which we have heard it before.

In some words, these echoes are obvious and discussable. The word *mother*, for example, 40 has, for most people, agreeable associations. When you hear *mother* you probably think of home, safety, love, food, and various other pleasant things. If one writes, "She was like a mother to me," he gets an effect which he would not get in "She was like an aunt to me." The advertiser makes use of the associations of *mother* by working it in when he talks about his product. The politician works it in when he talks about himself.

So also with such words as *home, liberty, fireside, contentment, patriot, tenderness, sacrifice, childlike, manly, bluff, limpid.* All of these words are loaded with favorable associations that would be rather hard to indicate in a straightforward definition. There is more than a literal difference between "They sat around the fireside" and "They sat around the stove." They might have been equally warm and happy around the stove, but *fireside* suggests leisure, grace, quiet tradition, congenial company, and *stove* does not.

Conversely, some words have bad associations. *Mother* suggests pleasant things, but *mother-in-law* does not. Many mothers-in-law are heroically lovable and some mothers drink gin all day and beat their children insensible, but these facts of life are beside the point. The thing is that *mother* sounds good and *mother-in-law* does not.

Or consider the word *intellectual*. This would seem to be a complimentary term, but in point of fact it is not, for it has picked up associations of impracticality and ineffectuality and general dopiness. So also with such words as *liberal, reactionary, Communist, socialist, capitalist, radical, schoolteacher, truck driver, undertaker, operator, salesman, huckster, speculator*. These convey meanings on the literal level, but beyond that—sometimes, in some places—they convey contempt on the part of the speaker.

The question of whether to use loaded words or not depends on what is being written. The scientist, the scholar, try to avoid them; for the poet, the advertising writer, the public speaker, they are standard equipment. But every writer should take care that they do not substitute for thought. If you write, "Anyone who thinks that is nothing but a Socialist (or Communist or capitalist)" you have said nothing except that you don't like people who think that, and such remarks are effective only with the most naïve readers. It is always a bad mistake to think your readers more naïve than they really are.

COLORLESS WORDS

But probably most student writers come to grief not with words that are colorful or those 45
that are colored but with those that have no color at all. A pet example is *nice*, a word we would find it hard to dispense with in casual conversation but which is no longer capable of adding much to a description. Colorless words are those of such general meaning that in a particular sentence they mean nothing. Slang adjectives, like *cool* ("That's real cool") tend to explode all over the language. They are applied to everything, lose their original force, and quickly die.

Beware also of nouns of very general meaning, like *circumstances, cases, instances, aspects, factors, relationships, attitudes, eventualities*, etc. In most circumstances you will find that those cases of writing which contain too many instances of words like these will in this and other aspects have factors leading to unsatisfactory relationships with the reader resulting in unfavorable attitudes on his part and perhaps other eventualities, like a grade of "D." Notice also what "etc." means. It means "I'd like to make this list longer, but I can't think of any more examples."

Questions

1. How does Roberts use subheadings to organize his essay? If you only read the headings, what would you know about Roberts's argument?

2. Roberts offers nine rules of writing. Which rules are you most guilty of breaking? How and why?

3. Roberts's essay was originally published in 1958. In small groups, identify and be prepared to discuss which assumptions the essay appears to be making about its intended audience. How many of these assumptions hold true for college students today, and which ones do not? In what ways has the author's expected audience changed since 1958, and how does this alter the effectiveness of his argument?

Donald Murray [1924–2007]

The Maker's Eye: Revising Your Own Manuscripts

Donald Murray, an acclaimed novelist, poet, and journalist, was born in Boston, Massachusetts. He graduated from the University of New Hampshire, where he later worked as an English professor. Murray is considered an expert on the writing process, and he has written several composition textbooks and sourcebooks. These works include *A Writer Teaches Writing: A Complete Revision* (1985), *Learning by Teaching* (1982), and *Write to Learn* (Seventh Edition, 2004). Murray's editorials in the *Boston Globe* won him the Pulitzer Prize in 1954. He died from heart failure on December 30, 2007.

In his essay "The Maker's Eye: Revising Your Own Manuscripts," Murray emphasizes that writers can only rely on themselves to bring their work to success. While stressing the importance of revising and rewriting, Murray challenges writers to be their own critics, to review their work as if they were seeing it for the first time, and to rework their writing through multiple drafts. In the essay, he outlines the steps necessary to "edit oneself" in order to yield the most polished work possible.

When students complete a first draft, they consider the job of writing done—and their teachers too often agree. When professional writers complete a first draft, they usually feel that they are at the start of the writing process. When a draft is completed, the job of writing can begin.

That difference in attitude is the difference between amateur and professional, inexperience and experience, journeyman and craftsman. Peter F. Drucker, the prolific business writer, calls his first draft "the zero draft"—after that he can start counting. Most writers share the feeling that the first draft, and all of those which follow, are opportunities to discover what they have to say and how best they can say it.

To produce a progression of drafts, each of which says more and says it more clearly, the writer has to develop a special kind of reading skill. In school we are taught to decode what appears on the page as finished writing. Writers, however, face a different category of possibility and responsibility when they read their own drafts. To them the words on the page are never finished. Each can be changed and rearranged, can set off a chain reaction of confusion or clarified meaning. This is a different kind of reading which is possibly more difficult and certainly more exciting.

Writers must learn to be their own best enemy. They must accept the criticism of others and be suspicious of it; they must accept the praise of others and be even more suspicious of it. Writers cannot depend on others. They must detach themselves from their own pages so that they can apply both their caring and their craft to their own work.

Such detachment is not easy. Science-fiction writer Ray Bradbury supposedly puts each 5 manuscript away for a year to the day and then rereads it as a stranger. Not many writers have the discipline or the time to do this. We must read when our judgment may be at its worst, when we are close to the euphoric moment of creation.

Then the writer, counsels novelist Nancy Hale, "should be critical of everything that seems to him most delightful in his style. He should excise what he most admires, because he wouldn't thus admire it if he weren't...in a sense protecting it from criticism." John Ciardi, the poet, adds, "The last act of the writing must be to become one's own reader. It is,

I suppose, a schizophrenic process, to begin passionately and to end critically, to begin hot and to end cold; and, more important, to be passion-hot and critic-cold at the same time."

Most people think that the principal problem is that writers are too proud of what they have written. Actually, a greater problem for most professional writers is one shared by the majority of students. They are overly critical, think everything is dreadful, tear up page after page, never complete a draft, see the task as hopeless.

The writer must learn to read critically but constructively, to cut what is bad, to reveal what is good. Eleanor Estes, the children's book author, explains: "The writer must survey his work critically, coolly, as though he were a stranger to it. He must be willing to prune, expertly and hard-heartedly. At the end of each revision, a manuscript may look...worked over, torn apart, pinned together, added to, deleted from, words changed and words changed back. Yet the book must maintain its original freshness and spontaneity."

Most readers underestimate the amount of rewriting it usually takes to produce spontaneous reading. This is a great disadvantage to the student writer, who sees only a finished product and never watches the craftsman who takes the necessary step back, studies the work carefully, returns to the task, steps back, returns, steps back, again and again. Anthony Burgess, one of the most prolific writers in the English-speaking world, admits, "I might revise a page twenty times." Roald Dahl, the popular children's writer, states, "By the time I'm nearing the end of a story, the first part will have been reread and altered and corrected at least 150 times....Good writing is essentially rewriting. I am positive of this."

Rewriting isn't virtuous. It isn't something that ought to be done. It is simply something 10 that most writers find they have to do to discover what they have to say and how to say it. It is a condition of the writer's life.

There are, however, a few writers who do little formal rewriting, primarily because they have the capacity and experience to create and review a large number of invisible drafts in their minds before they approach the page. And some writers slowly produce finished pages, performing all the tasks of revision simultaneously, page by page, rather than draft by draft. But it is still possible to see the sequence followed by most writers most of the time in rereading their own work.

Most writers scan their drafts first, reading as quickly as possible to catch the larger problems of subject and form, and then move in closer and closer as they read and write, reread and rewrite.

The first thing writers look for in their drafts is *information*. They know that a good piece of writing is built from specific, accurate, and interesting information. The writer must have an abundance of information from which to construct a readable piece of writing.

Next writers look for *meaning* in the information. The specifics must build to a pattern of significance. Each piece of specific information must carry the reader toward meaning.

Writers reading their own drafts are aware of *audience*. They put themselves in the 15 reader's situation and make sure that they deliver information which a reader wants to know or needs to know in a manner which is easily digested. Writers try to be sure that they anticipate and answer the questions a critical reader will ask when reading the piece of writing.

Writers make sure that the *form* is appropriate to the subject and the audience. Form, or genre, is the vehicle which carries meaning to the reader, but form cannot be selected until the writer has adequate information to discover its significance and an audience which needs or wants that meaning.

Once writers are sure the form is appropriate, they must then look at the *structure*, the order of what they have written. Good writing is built on a solid framework of logic, argument, narrative, or motivation which runs through the entire piece of writing and holds it together. This is the time when many writers find it most effective to outline as a way of visualizing the hidden spine by which the piece of writing is supported.

The element on which writers may spend a majority of their time is *development*. Each section of a piece of writing must be adequately developed. It must give readers enough information so that they are satisfied. How much information is enough? That's as difficult as asking how much garlic belongs in a salad. It must be done to taste, but most beginning writers underdevelop, underestimating the reader's hunger for information.

As writers solve development problems, they often have to consider questions of *dimension*. There must be a pleasing and effective proportion among all the parts of the piece of writing. There is a continual process of subtracting and adding to keep the piece of writing in balance.

Finally, writers have to listen to their own voices. *Voice* is the force which drives a piece 20
of writing forward. It is an expression of the writer's authority and concern. It is what is between the words on the page, what glues the piece of writing together. A good piece of writing is always marked by a consistent, individual voice.

As writers read and reread, write and rewrite, they move closer and closer to the page until they are doing line-by-line editing. Writers read their own pages with infinite care. Each sentence, each line, each clause, each phrase, each word, each mark of punctuation, each section of white space between the type has to contribute to the clarification of meaning.

Slowly the writer moves from word to word, looking through language to see the subject. As a word is changed, cut, or added, as a construction is rearranged, all the words used before that moment and all those that follow that moment must be considered and reconsidered.

Writers often read aloud at this stage of the editing process, muttering or whispering to themselves, calling on the ear's experience with language. Does this sound right—or that? Writers edit, shifting back and forth from eye to page to ear to page. I find I must do this careful editing in short runs, no more than fifteen or twenty minutes at a stretch, or I become too kind with myself. I begin to see what I hope is on the page, not what actually is on the page.

This sounds tedious if you haven't done it, but actually it is fun. Making something right is immensely satisfying, for writers begin to learn what they are writing about by writing. Language leads them to meaning, and there is the joy of discovery, of understanding, of making meaning clear as the writer employs the technical skills of language.

Words have double meanings, even triple and quadruple meanings. Each word has its 25
own potential of connotation and denotation. And when writers rub one word against the other, they are often rewarded with a sudden insight, an unexpected clarification.

The maker's eye moves back and forth from word to phrase to sentence to paragraph to sentence to phrase to word. The maker's eye sees the need for variety and balance, for a firmer structure, for a more appropriate form. It peers into the interior of the paragraph, looking for coherence, unity, and emphasis, which make meaning clear.

I learned something about this process when my first bifocals were prescribed. I had ordered a larger section of the reading portion of the glass because of my work, but even so, I could not contain my eyes within this new limit of vision. And I still find myself taking off my glasses and bending my nose toward the page, for my eyes unconsciously flick back and forth across the page, back to another page, forward to still another, as I try to see each evolving line in relation to every other line.

When does this process end? Most writers agree with the great Russian writer Tolstoy, who said, "I scarcely ever reread my published writings, if by chance I come across a page, it always strikes me: all this must be rewritten; this is how I should have written it."

The maker's eye is never satisfied, for each word has the potential to ignite new meaning. This article has been twice written all the way through the writing process....Now it is to be republished in a book. The editors made a few small suggestions, and then I read it with my maker's eye. Now it has been re-edited, re-revised, re-read, and re-re-edited, for each piece of writing to the writer is full of potential and alternatives.

A piece of writing is never finished. It is delivered to a deadline, torn out of the type-   30
writer on demand, sent off with a sense of accomplishment and shame and pride and frustration. If only there were a couple more days, time for just another run at it, perhaps then....

Questions

1. What are Murray's major points about revision? How does he reinforce these points?

2. Describe your own revision process. How many of Murray's revision points do you currently make use of? Which of Murray's suggestions might you use to make your writing better?

Casey Miller & Kate Swift [1919–1997, 1923–2011]

Who's in Charge of the English Language?

Born in Toledo, Ohio, **Casey Miller** earned a B.A. in philosophy at Smith College in 1940. From 1943 to 1946, she served in the U.S. Navy in Washington, D.C., in naval intelligence. From 1947 to 1954 she worked on the staff at Colonial Williamsburg and then became the curriculum editor of Seabury Press for a decade. In 1964 she turned to freelance editorial work, merging her talents with those of her editorial partner, Kate Swift, in 1967. Together, they wrote "Desexing the English Language" for *Ms.* Magazine in 1971, followed by *The Handbook of Nonsexist Writing* (1980) and numerous other articles and books that promoted nonsexist language and ultimately changed standard English language usage. **Kate Swift** was born in Yonkers, New York, and graduated with a B.A. in 1944 from the University of North Carolina. During World War II, Swift served in the U.S. Army. She was employed as a science writer by the American Museum of Natural History from 1954 to 1965 and then served as news director for the Yale School of Medicine from 1965 to 1970. Her editorial partnership with Casey Miller began in 1967 with the publication of a high school sex education manual for Seabury Press. Swift's freelance career began in 1970.

In "Who's in Charge of the English Language?" originally delivered as a speech at the annual meeting of the Association of American University Presses in 1990, Miller and Swift make a plea to university press editors that they diligently impress upon their authors the necessity of precision when choosing gendered terminology. Employing Douglas Hofstadter's linguistic metaphor of "the slippery slope," Miller and Swift deplore our culture's resistance to change its tendency to marginalize women in the English language through male-biased pronouns and outdated gender-specific suffixes.

In order to encourage the use of language that is free of gender bias, it's obviously necessary to get authors to recognize gender bias in their writing. The reason that's so difficult is that our culture is steeped in unconscious attitudes and beliefs about gender characteristics, a condition reflected in our use of words.

Every human society has recognized the relationship between power and naming: that the act of naming confers power over the thing named. In the Book of Genesis, Adam named all the animals and was given dominion over them, and then, later, the story says "Adam called his wife's name Eve." Those who have the power to name and define other things—animals, wives, whatever—inevitably take themselves as the norm or standard, the measure of all things.

English is androcentric because for centuries it has been evolving in a society where men have been dominant. They were the ones in charge of the major social institutions: government, law, commerce, education, religion. They shaped the course of history and were the subjects of history. It's natural that the languages of patriarchal societies should come to express a male-centered view. That's basic anthropology. Anthropologists know that the single best way to understand the culture of any society is to study the lexicon of its language: a people's words reflect their reality. But the question is: Whose reality? The English language still reflects a world in which the power to define gender characteristics is a male prerogative.

We all know that English contains a variety of words that identify and emphasize difference between the sexes. A number of English words actually express polarization of the sexes. Never mind that beyond having one or the other set of biological features necessary for reproduction, every individual is distinct in personality, combining in a unique way those polarized qualities called "masculine" and "feminine." Never mind that virtually no one fits the mold at either pole. It remains a cherished precept of our culture, semantically underlined in our lexicon and embraced by the purveyors of every commodity imaginable, that the sexes must be thought of as opposite.

FEMALE-NEGATIVE-TRIVIAL

This linguistic syndrome can be described as "female-negative-trivial" on the one hand, and   5 "male-positive-important" on the other. If that strikes you as overly exaggerated, consider for a moment a group of people who are *not* in charge of the English language—that is, lexicographers—and the definitions they have come up with for a pair of words which relate to gender—the words *manly* and *womanly*. These definitions are from the most recently updated edition of *Webster's Third New International Dictionary* (copyright 1986).

> **Manly** 1. a: having qualities appropriate to a man: not effeminate or timorous: bold, resolute, and open in conduct or bearing…b. (1): belonging to or appropriate in character to man [*and they give as examples*] "manly sports," "beer is a manly drink," and "a big booming manly voice." (2): of undaunted courage: gallant, brave [*and among the quotations they give as examples*] "it seemed a big manly thing to say" and "a manly disregard of his enemies"…

Now compare the same dictionary's definition of *womanly*, remembering that lexicographers base their definitions on hundreds of examples of usage that have appeared in print.

> **Womanly** 1: marked by qualities characteristic of a woman, esp. marked by qualities becoming a well-balanced adult woman [*and their examples are*] "womanly manners" and "womanly advice." 2: possessed of the character or behavior befitting a grown woman: no longer childish or girlish: becoming to a grown woman [*and their example is from Charles Dickens*] "a little girl wearing a womanly sort of bonnet much too large for her" 3: characteristic of, belonging to, or suitable to women: conforming to or motivated by a woman's nature and attitudes rather than a man's. [*The first example here is*] "convinced that drawing was a waste of time, if not down-right womanly, like painting on China." [*And another example*] "her usual womanly volubility."

What are these two supposedly parallel entries telling us? They're saying that in addition to defining characteristics appropriate to a man, like vocal pitch, *manly* is synonymous with admirable qualities that all of us might wish we had. "Bold, resolute, open in conduct or bearing; of undaunted courage, gallant, brave." And where is the list of comparable synonyms for *womanly*? There aren't any. Instead, *womanly* is defined only in a circular way—through characteristics seen to be appropriate or inappropriate to women, not to human beings in general. And the examples of usage cited give a pretty good picture of what is considered appropriate to, or characteristic of, a well-balanced adult woman: she's concerned with manners, advice, and hat styles (as distinguished from sports and beer, which are felt to be manly); she wastes time in trivial pursuits like painting on china; and she talks too much.

THE SLIPPERY SLOPE

Most writers and editors today recognize that the female-negative-trivial syndrome is clearly evident in the use of so-called feminine suffixes with nouns of common gender. In 1990 no publishable author would identify someone as "a poetess," except in ridicule. (Adrienne Rich says the word brings out the "terroristress" in her.) But respectable writers are still using *heroine*, *suffragette*, and *executrix* when referring to a hero, a suffragist, or an executor who is a woman.

These words illustrate what Douglas Hofstadter calls "the slippery slope" of meaning. In his book *Metamagical Themas*, Hofstadter shows diagramatically how the slippery slope works. A triangle represents the idea of, let's say, a heroic person. At one base angle of this triangle is the word *heroine*, representing the female heroic person. At the other base angle is the word *hero*, representing the male heroic person. And at the apex is the generic word, again *hero*, encompassing both. But because the *hero* at the apex and the *hero* at one base angle are identical in name, their separate meanings slip back and forth along one side of the triangle, the slippery slope. The meanings blend and absorb each other. They bond together on the slope. And *heroine*, at the other base angle, remains outside that bond.

Another word that comes to mind in this connection is *actress*. It's our impression that women performers in the theater and films today are tending more and more to refer to themselves and one another as "actors." It may be deliberate, conscious usage on the part of some. Considering that their union is called Actors Equity, and that they may have trained at Actors Studio, and performed at Actors Playhouse, they simply accept that the generic word for their profession is *actor*. But when this word appears in juxtaposition with *actress*, the generic meaning of *actor* is absorbed into the gender-specific meaning, and women are identified as nonactors, as being outside or marginal, in de Beauvoir's phrase, as "the other."

Many people will undoubtedly go on feeling that *actress* is a term without bias, but we   10 would like to suggest that it is on its way to becoming archaic, or at least quaint, simply because people it has identified are abandoning it by a process that may be more visceral than cerebral. In a sense it's their word, it has defined them, and, whether intentionally or not, they are taking charge of it, perhaps dumping it. We'll see.

Because linguistic changes reflect changes in our ways of thinking, a living language is constantly being created and re-created by the people who speak it. Linguistic changes spring from nothing less than new perceptions of the world and of ourselves.

Obviously we all know that over time the "rules" of grammar have changed, and we know that words themselves change their meanings: they lose some and acquire others; new words come into existence and old ones disappear into that word heaven, the *Oxford English Dictionary*. Nevertheless, most people resist change, especially, it seems, changes in grammar and the meanings of words. What we tend to forget—or choose to forget—is that the only languages which don't change are the ones no one speaks any more, like classical Greek and Latin.

Take the narrowing process that turned the Old English word *man* into a synonym for "adult male human being." As long ago as 1752 the philosopher David Hume recognized how ambiguous that word had already become: "All men," he wrote, and then added, "both male and female." And you are probably familiar with the numerous experimental studies done in the last few years, primarily by psychologists and sociologists rather than linguists, which show that most native speakers of English simply do not conceptualize women and girls when they encounter *man* and *mankind* used generically. In fact the narrowing process is felt so strongly, at least at an existential level, that a growing number of women today strongly object to being subsumed under those male-gender terms. "We aren't men," they're saying; "we're women, and we're tired of being made invisible."

Yet despite women's objections, and despite the slippery, ambiguous nature of generic *man*, lots of people, especially formally educated people, have a hard time giving it up. They forget, it seems, that words have a power of their own—the power of taking over meaning. A writer starts out talking about the species as a whole and, more often than we'll ever know, ends up talking about males. Listen to this well-known author, for example, who was discussing aggressive behavior in human beings—all of us, *Homo sapiens*. "[M]an," he wrote, "can do several things which the animal cannot do....Eventually, his vital interests are not only life, food, access to females, etc., but also values, symbols, institutions."

RESISTANCE TO CHANGE AND THE PROBLEM OF PRECISION

It's probably helpful, once in a while, to look back at the way some of the most familiar and 15 accepted words in use today were greeted when they were newcomers.

Back in 1619, for example, the London schoolmaster Alexander Gil described what he called "the new mange in speaking and writing." What he was deploring was the introduction of newly coined, Latin-derived words to replace older English ones. According to him, the "new mange" included such terms as *virtue, justice, pity, compassion*, and *grace*. And he asked, "Whither have you banished those words our forefathers used for these new-fangled ones?" Alexander Gil was headmaster of St. Paul's school at the time, and it might be noted that one of his students was an eleven-year-old named John Milton who—fortunately—was not persuaded to reject Gil's "new-fangled" words.

And how about old terms that have lost favor, like the once-accepted use of the pronoun *they* with a singular referent, as in "If a person is born of a gloomy temper, they cannot help it." That was written in 1759 by none other than the very correct, well-educated British statesman, Lord Chesterfield. However, since most academics are not yet ready to revive that convenient usage—despite precedents ranging from Shakespeare to Shaw—it still isn't surprising to come across a recently published book about, let's say, the psychology of children, in which the distinguished author uses *he* and its inflected forms as all-purpose pronouns, leaving readers to guess whether a particular problem or development applies to boys only or to children of both sexes. We submit that such writing is not just unfortunate. It's inexcusable.

These days more and more writers acknowledge that *he* used generically is, like *man* used generically, both ambiguous and insidious, and they take the time and trouble to write more precisely. But sometimes, even after several polite but probably exhausting battles between author and editor, all the author will agree to do is add a disclaimer. Disclaimers can be helpful, of course (for example, those providing guidance as to what a writer of some previous century may have meant by a now-ambiguous term). More often, however, they are nothing but excuses for sloppiness.

There is also an element here which we don't think should be ignored: the deep if often unacknowledged psychological impact of the grammatical "rule" mandating masculine-gender pronouns for indefinite referents. As long ago as the 1950s, Lynn White Jr., then the president of Mills College, described with great perception the harm that rule can do to children when he wrote:

The penetration of this habit of language into the minds of little girls as they grow up to be women is more profound than most people, including most women, have recognized; for it implies that personality is really a male attribute, and that women are a human subspecies.... It would be a miracle if a girl-baby, learning to use the symbols of our tongue, could escape some unverbalized wound to her self-respect; whereas a boy-baby's ego is bolstered by the pattern of our language.

Obviously many literate men (and some literate women) must find the truth of White's perception difficult to accept, or we wouldn't still be battling the generic use of masculine-gender pronouns. But since accuracy and precision are what we're talking about today, let us ask this question: what is one to make of a scholar—a professor of communications with a special interest in semantics, as a matter of fact—who dismissed the problem of sexist language as follows: "I tend to avoid 'gender-exclusive' words," he wrote, "except when in so doing, I would injure the rhythm of a sentence." 20

Has it never occurred to him that in writing a sentence, any sentence, he must choose both its words and the way those words, in their infinite variety, are put together? That the choice isn't between exclusionary language on the one hand and rhythm on the other? (Surely it's possible to write with style and still communicate accurately what it is you want to say.) The choice is between settling for an ambiguous or inaccurate term because it "sounds good"—and finding the exact combination of words to convey one's message with clarity and precision. It seems to us that editors have every right to expect nothing less than the latter.

English is a vigorously alive tongue, and it reflects a vigorously alive, dynamic society that is capable of identifying its ills and thereby trying to cope with them. Neither the term *sexism* nor the term *racism* existed fifty years ago—which, as you know, isn't the same as saying that the attitudes and practices they define didn't exist before; of course they did. But those attitudes and practices came to be widely examined and questioned, and finally to be widely acknowledged within the dominant culture, only after they were put into words.

Without precision, language can betray everything we stand for. As George Orwell put it in his essay "Politics and the English Language," we must "Let the meaning choose the word and not the other way about." And Orwell went on, "In prose the worst thing you can do with words is surrender to them."

With George Orwell giving us courage, may we be so bold, in closing, as to adapt his wisdom to the occasion by adding this final thought? In publishing, the worst thing you can do is surrender to some tyrannical author who lets the word choose the meaning rather than the other way about.

Questions

1. Why does gendered language matter? Think of examples of where you have seen, heard, or read gendered language. What impact did it have on you as the audience?

2. In discussing the politics of gendered language, the authors make several references to George Orwell, specifically his admonitions about word choice and the need for writers to control it. When and how do you consider word choice in your own writing? How do you know when you've chosen the right word for a situation—aesthetically, logically, and politically?

Alleen Pace Nilsen [b. 1936]

Sexism in English: Embodiment and Language

A Professor of English Education at Arizona State University, **Alleen Pace Nilsen** specializes in preparing secondary school educators to teach English language skills and literature written for children and young adults. She received her B.A. from Brigham Young University in 1958 and her M. Ed. from American University in 1961. She earned her Ph.D. at the University of Iowa with a doctoral dissertation that examined the ramifications of sexist language in children's literature, and subsequently took a teaching position at Arizona State University in 1973. Nilsen edited *Sexism and Language* (1977) and wrote *Changing Words in a Changing World* (1980). Co-authored with her husband, Don L.F. Nilsen, her publications include *Encyclopedia of 20th Century American Humor* (2000), *Vocabulary Plus K–8: A Source-Based Approach* (2004), and *Vocabulary Plus High School and Up: A Source-Based Approach* (2004). Her collaborative work with Ken Donelson, *Literature for Today's Young Adults* (2005), is now in its ninth edition.

"Sexism in English: Embodiment and Language" is an updated chapter of Nilsen's original 1972 contribution to the collection *Closer to the Ground: Women's Classes, Criticism, Programs*, edited by Nancy Hoffman. Nilsen traces her emergence as a feminist in the 1970s through her investigation of the roots of sexism in the English language. Amassing shoe boxes of file cards filled with her notations of gender-related linguistic curiosities drawn from a desk dictionary, most biased *against* women, Nilsen substantiated her theory that sociological observations of sexism in American culture could be corroborated by linguistic evidence.

During the late 1960s, I lived with my husband and three young children in Kabul, Afghanistan. This was before the Russian invasion, the Afghan civil war, and the eventual taking over of the country by the Taleban Islamic movement and its resolve to return the country to a strict Islamic dynasty, in which females are not allowed to attend school or work outside their homes.

But even when we were there and the country was considered moderate rather than extremist, I was shocked to observe how different were the roles assigned to males and females. The Afghan version of the *chaderi* prescribed for Moslem women was particularly confining. Women in religious families were required to wear it whenever they were outside their family home, with the result being that most of them didn't venture outside.

The household help we hired were made up of men, because women could not be employed by foreigners. Afghan folk stories and jokes were blatantly sexist, as in this proverb: "If you see an old man, sit down and take a lesson, if you see an old woman, throw a stone."

But it wasn't only the native culture that made me question women's roles, it was also the American community within Afghanistan.

Most of the American women were like myself—wives and mothers whose husbands were either diplomats, employees of USAID, or college professors who had been recruited to work on various contract teams. We were suddenly bereft of our traditional roles. The local economy provided few jobs for women and certainly none for foreigners; we were isolated from former friends and the social goals we had grown up with. Some of us became 5 alcoholics, others got very good at bridge, while still others searched desperately for ways to contribute either to our families or to the Afghans.

When we returned in the fall of 1969 to the University of Michigan in Ann Arbor, I was surprised to find that many other women were also questioning the expectations they had grown up with. Since I had been an English major when I was in college, I decided that for my part in the feminist movement I would study the English language and see what it could tell me about sexism. I started reading a desk dictionary and making note cards on every entry that seemed to tell something different about male and female. I soon had a dog-eared dictionary, along with a collection of note cards filling two shoe boxes.

The first thing I learned was that I couldn't study the language without getting involved in social issues. Language and society are as intertwined as a chicken and an egg. The language a culture uses is telltale evidence of the values and beliefs of that culture. And because there is a lag in how fast a language changes—new words can easily be introduced, but it takes a long time for old words and usages to disappear—a careful look at English will reveal the attitudes that our ancestors held and that we as a culture are therefore predisposed to hold. My note cards revealed three main points. While friends have offered the opinion that I didn't need to read a dictionary to learn such obvious facts, the linguistic evidence lends credibility to the sociological observations.

WOMEN ARE SEXY; MEN ARE SUCCESSFUL

First, in American culture a woman is valued for the attractiveness and sexiness of her body, while a man is valued for his physical strength and accomplishments. A woman is sexy. A man is successful.

A persuasive piece of evidence supporting this view are the eponyms—words that have come from someone's name—found in English. I had a two-and-a-half-inch stack of cards taken from men's names but less than a half-inch stack from women's names, and most of those came from Greek mythology. In the words that came into American English since we separated from Britain, there are many eponyms based on the names of famous American men: Bartlett pear, boysenberry, Franklin stove, Ferris wheel, Gatling gun, mason jar, sideburns, sousaphone, Schick test, and Winchester rifle. The only common eponyms that I found taken from American women's names are Alice blue (after Alice Roosevelt Longworth), bloomers (after Amelia Jenks Bloomer), and Mae West jacket (after the buxom actress). Two out of the three feminine eponyms relate closely to a woman's physical anatomy, while the masculine eponyms (except for "sideburns" after General Burnsides) have nothing to do with the namesake's body, but, instead, honor the man for an accomplishment of some kind.

In Greek mythology women played a bigger role than they did in the biblical stories of the Judeo-Christian cultures, and so the names of goddesses are accepted parts of the language in such place names as Pomona, from the goddess of fruit, and Athens, from Athena, and in such common words as *cereal* from Ceres, *psychology* from Psyche, and *arachnoid* from Arachne. However, there is the same tendency to think of women in relation to sexuality as shown through the eponyms "aphrodisiac" from Aphrodite, the Greek name for the goddess of love and beauty, and "venereal disease" from Venus, the Roman name for Aphrodite.

Another interesting word from Greek mythology is *Amazon*. According to Greek folk etymology, the *a-* means "without," as in *atypical* or *amoral*, while *-mazon* comes from "mazos," meaning "breast," as still seen in *mastectomy*. In the Greek legend, Amazon women

10

cut off their right breasts so they could better shoot their bows. Apparently, the storytellers had a feeling that for women to play the active, "masculine" role the Amazons adopted for themselves, they had to trade in part of their femininity.

This preoccupation with women's breasts is not limited to the Greeks; it's what inspired the definition and the name for "mammals" (from Indo-European "mammae" for "breasts"). As a volunteer for the University of Wisconsin's *Dictionary of American Regional English* (*DARE*), I read a western trapper's diary from the 1830s. I was to make notes of any unusual usages or language patterns. My most interesting finding was that the trapper referred to a range of mountains as "The Teats," a metaphor based on the similarity between the shapes of the mountains and the women's breasts. Because today we use the French wording "The Grand Tetons," the metaphor isn't as obvious, but I wrote to mapmakers and found the following listings: Nipple Top and Little Nipple Top near Mount Marcy in the Adirondacks; Nipple Mountain in Archuleta County, Colorado; Nipple Peak in Coke County, Texas; Nipple Butte in Pennington, South Dakota; Squaw Peak in Placer County, California (and many other locations); Maiden's Peak and Squaw Tit (they're the same mountain) in the Cascade Range in Oregon; Mary's Nipple near Salt Lake City, Utah; and Jane Russell Peaks near Stark, New Hampshire.

Except for the movie star Jane Russell, the women being referred to are anonymous— it's only a sexual part of their body that is mentioned. When topographical features are named after men, it's probably not going to be to draw attention to a sexual part of their bodies but instead to honor individuals for an accomplishment.

Going back to what I learned from my dictionary cards, I was surprised to realize how many pairs of words we have in which the feminine word has acquired sexual connotations while the masculine word retains a serious businesslike aura. For example, a callboy is the person who calls actors when it is time for them to go on stage, but a callgirl is a prostitute. Compare sir and madam. *Sir* is a term of respect, while *madam* has acquired the specialized meaning of a brothel manager. Something similar has happened to master and mistress. Would you rather have a painting "by an old master" or "by an old mistress"?

It's because the word *woman* had sexual connotations, as in "She's his woman," that 15 people began avoiding its use, hence such terminology as ladies' room, lady of the house, and girl's school or school for young ladies. Those of us who in the 1970s began asking that speakers use the term *woman* rather than *girl* or *lady* were rejecting the idea that *woman* is primarily a sexual term.

I found two hundred pairs of words with masculine and feminine forms; for example, *heir-heiress, hero-heroine, steward/stewardess, usher/usherette*. In nearly all such pairs, the masculine word is considered the base, with some kind of a feminine suffix being added. The masculine form is the one from which compounds are made; for example, from king/queen comes kingdom but not queendom, from sportsman/sportslady comes sportsmanship but not sportsladyship. There is one—and only one—semantic area in which the masculine word is not the base or more powerful word. This is in the area dealing with sex, marriage, and motherhood. When someone refers to a virgin, a listener will probably think of a female unless the speaker specifies male or uses a masculine pronoun. The same is true for prostitute.

In relation to marriage, linguistic evidence shows that weddings are more important to women than to men. A woman cherishes the wedding and is considered a bride for a whole year, but a man is referred to as a groom only on the day of the wedding. The word *bride* appears in *bridal attendant, bridal gown, bridesmaid, bridal shower,* and even *bridegroom.* Groom comes from the Middle English *grom,* meaning "man," and in that sense is seldom used outside of the wedding. With most pairs of male/female words, people habitually put the masculine word first: *Mr. and Mrs., his and hers, boys and girls, men and women, kings and queens, brothers and sisters, guys and dolls,* and *host and hostess.* But it is the bride and groom who are talked about, not the groom and bride.

The importance of marriage to a woman is also shown by the fact that when a marriage ends in death, the woman gets the title of widow. A man gets the derived title of widower. This term is not used in other phrases or contexts, but widow is seen in widowhood, widow's peak, and widow's walk. A widow in a card game is an extra hand of cards, while in typesetting it is a leftover line of type.

Changing cultural ideas brings changes to language, and since I did my dictionary study three decades ago the word *single* has largely replaced such gender-specific and value-laden terms as *bachelor, old maid, spinster, divorcee, widow,* and *widower.* In 1970 I wrote that when people hear a man called "a professional," they usually think of him as a doctor or a lawyer, but when people hear a woman referred to as "a professional," they are likely to think of her as a prostitute. That's not as true today because so many women have become doctors and lawyers, it's no longer incongruous to think of women in those professional roles.

Another change that has taken place is in wedding announcements. They used to be 20 sent out from the bride's parents and did not even give the name of the groom's parents. Today, most couples choose to list either all or none of the parents' names. Also it is now much more likely that both the bride and groom's picture will be in the newspaper, while twenty years ago only the bride's picture was published on the "Women's" or the "Society" page. In the weddings I have recently attended, the official has pronounced the couple "husband and wife" instead of the traditional "man and wife," and the bride has been asked if she promises to "love, honor, and cherish," instead of to "love, honor, and obey."

WOMEN ARE PASSIVE; MEN ARE ACTIVE

However, other wording in the wedding ceremony relates to a second point that my cards showed, which is that women are expected to play a passive or weak role while men play an active or strong role. In the traditional ceremony, the official asks, "Who gives the bride away?" and the father answers, "I do." Some fathers answer, "Her mother and I do," but that doesn't solve the problem inherent in the question. The idea that a bride is something to be handed over from one man to another bothers people because it goes back to the days when a man's servants, his children, and his wife were all considered to be his property. They were known by his name because they belonged to him, and he was responsible for their actions and their debts.

The grammar used in talking or writing about weddings as well as other sexual relationships shows the expectation of men playing the active role. Men *wed* women while women *become* brides of men. A man *possesses* a woman; he *deflowers* her; he *performs*; he *scores*; he *takes away* her virginity. Although a woman can *seduce* a man, she cannot offer him her virginity. When talking about virginity, the only way to make the woman the actor in the sentence is to say that "she lost her virginity," but people lose things by accident rather than by purposeful actions, and so she's only the grammatical, not the real-life actor.

The reason that women brought the term *Ms.* into the language to replace *Miss* and *Mrs.* relates to this point. Many married women resent being identified in the "Mrs. Husband" form. The dictionary cards showed what appeared to be an attitude on the part of the editors that it was almost indecent to let a respectable woman's name march unaccompanied across the pages of a dictionary. Women were listed with male names whether or not the male contributed to the woman's reason for being in the dictionary or whether or not in his own right he was as famous as the woman. For example:

Charlotte Brontë = Mrs. Arthur B. Nicholls
Amelia Earhart = Mrs. George Palmer Putnam
Helen Hayes = Mrs. Charles MacArthur
Jenny Lind = Mme. Otto Goldschmit
Cornelia Otis Skinner = daughter of Otis
Harriet Beecher Stowe = sister of Henry Ward Beecher
Dame Edith Sitwell = sister of Osbert and Sacheverell

Only a small number of rebels and crusaders got into the dictionary without the benefit of a masculine escort: temperance leaders Frances Elizabeth Caroline Willard and Carry Nation, women's rights leaders Carrie Chapman Catt and Elizabeth Cady Stanton, birth control educator Margaret Sanger, religious leader Mary Baker Eddy, and slaves Harriet Tubman and Phillis Wheatley.

Etiquette books used to teach that if a woman had Mrs. in front of her name, then the husband's name should follow because Mrs. is an abbreviated form of Mistress and a woman couldn't be a mistress of herself. As with many arguments about "correct" language usage, this isn't very logical because Miss is also an abbreviation of Mistress. Feminists hoped to simplify matters by introducing Ms. as an alternative to both Mrs. and Miss, but what happened is that Ms. largely replaced Miss to become a catch-all business title for women. Many married women still prefer the title Mrs., and some even resent being addressed with the term Ms. As one frustrated newspaper reporter complained, "Before I can write about a woman I have to know not only her marital status but also her political philosophy." The result of such complications may contribute to the demise of titles, which are already being ignored by many writers who find it more efficient to simply use names; for example, in a business letter: "Dear Joan Garcia," instead of "Dear Mrs. Joan Garcia," "Dear Ms. Garcia," or "Dear Mrs. Louis Garcia."

Titles given to royalty show how males can be disadvantaged by the assumption that 25 they always play the more powerful role. In British royalty, when a male holds a title, his wife is automatically given the feminine equivalent. But the reverse is not true. For example, a count is a high political office with a countess being his wife. The same pattern holds true for a duke and a duchess and a king and a queen. But when a female holds the royal title, the man she marries does not automatically acquire the matching title. For example, Queen Elizabeth's husband has the title of prince rather than king, but when Prince Charles married Diana, she became Princess Diana. If they had stayed married and he had ascended to the throne, then she would have become Queen Diana. The reasoning appears to be that since masculine words are stronger, they are reserved for true heirs and withheld from males coming into the royal family by marriage. If Prince Phillip were called "King Phillip," British subjects might forget who had inherited the right to rule.

The names that people give their children show the hopes and dreams they have for them, and when we look at the differences between male and female names in a culture, we can see the cumulative expectations of that culture. In our culture girls often have names taken from small, aesthetically pleasing terms; for example, Ruby, Jewel, and Pearl. Esther and Stella mean "star," and Ada means "ornament." One of the few women's names that refers to strength is Mildred, and it means "mild strength." Boys often have names with meanings of power and strength; for example, Neil means "champion"; Martin is from Mars, the God of war; Raymond means "wise protection"; Harold means "chief of the army"; Ira means "vigilant"; Rex means "king"; and Richard means "strong king."

We see similar differences in food metaphors. Food is a passive substance just sitting there waiting to be eaten. Many people have recognized this and so no longer feel comfortable describing women as "delectable morsels." However, when I was a teenager, it was considered a compliment to refer to a girl (we didn't call anyone a "woman" until she was middle-aged) as a cute tomato, a peach, a dish, a cookie, honey, sugar, or sweetie-pie. When being affectionate, women will occasionally call a man honey or sweetie, but in general, food metaphors are used much less often with men than with women. If a man is called "a fruit" his masculinity is being questioned. But it's perfectly acceptable to use a food metaphor if the food is heavier and more substantive than that used for women. For example, pin-up pictures of women have long been known as "cheese-cake," but when Burt Reynolds posed for a nude centerfold, the picture was immediately dubbed "beefcake," that is, a hunk of meat. That such sexual references to men have come into the language is another reflection of how society is beginning to lessen the differences between their attitudes toward men and women.

Something similar to the fruit metaphor happens with references to plants. We insult a man by calling him a "pansy," but it wasn't considered particularly insulting to talk about a girl being a wallflower, a clinging vine, or a shrinking violet, or to give girls such names as Ivy, Rose, Lily, Iris, Daisy, Camelia, Heather, and Flora. A positive plant metaphor can be used with a man only if the plant is big and strong; for example, Andrew Jackson's nickname of Old Hickory. Also, the phrases *blooming idiots* and *budding geniuses* can be used with either sex, but notice how they are based on the most active thing a plant can do, which is bloom or bud.

Animal metaphors also illustrate the different expectations for males and females. Men are referred to as studs, bucks, and wolves, while women are referred to with such metaphors as kitten, bunny, beaver, bird, chick, and lamb. In the 1950s we said that boys went "tom catting," but today it's just "catting around," and both boys and girls do it. When the term foxy, meaning that someone was sexy, first became popular it was used only for females, but now someone of either sex can be described as a fox. Some animal metaphors that are used predominantly with men have negative connotations based on the size and/or strength of the animals; for example, beast, bullheaded, jackass, rat, loanshark, and vulture. Negative metaphors used with women are based on smaller animals; for example, social butterfly, mousey, catty, and vixen. The feminine terms connote action, but not the same kind of large scale action as with the masculine terms.

WOMEN ARE CONNECTED WITH NEGATIVE CONNOTATIONS; MEN WITH POSITIVE CONNOTATIONS

The final point that my note cards illustrated was how many positive connotations are as-   30
sociated with the concept of masculinity, while there are either trivial or negative connotations connected with the corresponding feminine concept. An example from the animal

metaphors makes a good illustration. The word *shrew* taken from the name of a small but especially vicious animal was defined in my dictionary as "an ill-tempered scolding woman," but the word *shrewd* taken from the same root was defined as "marked by clever, discerning awareness" and was illustrated with the phrase "a shrewd businessman."

Early in life, children are conditioned to the superiority of the masculine role. As child psychologists point out, little girls have much more freedom to experiment with sex roles than do little boys. If a little girl acts like a tomboy, most parents have mixed feelings, being at least partially proud. But if their little boy acts like a sissy (derived from *sister*) they call a psychologist. It's perfectly acceptable for a little girl to sleep in the crib that was purchased for her brother, to wear his hand-me-down jeans and shirts, and to ride the bicycle that he has outgrown. But few parents would put a boy baby in a white-and-gold crib decorated with frills and lace, and virtually no parents would have their little boy wear his sister's hand-me-down dresses, nor would they have their son ride a girl's pink bicycle with a flower-bedecked basket. The proper names given to girls and boys show this same attitude. Girls can have "boy" names—Cris, Craig, Jo, Kelly, Shawn, Teri, Toni, and Sam—but it doesn't work the other way around. A couple of generations ago, Beverly, Frances, Hazel, Marion, and Shirley were common boys' names. As parents gave these names to more and more girls, they fell into disuse for males, and some older men who have these names prefer to go by their initials or by such abbreviated forms as Haze or Shirl.

When a little girl is told to be a lady, she is being told to sit with her knees together and to be quiet and dainty. But when a little boy is told to be a man, he is being told to be noble, strong, and virtuous—to have all the qualities that the speaker looks on as desirable. The concept of manliness has such positive connotations that it used to be a compliment to call someone a he-man, to say that he was doubly a man. Today many people are more ambivalent about this term and respond to it much as they do to the word *macho*. But calling someone a manly man or a virile man is nearly always meant as a compliment. Virile comes from the Indo-European *vir*, meaning "man," which is also the basis of *virtuous*. Consider the positive connotations of both virile and virtuous with the negative connotations of hysterical. The Greeks took this latter word from their name for uterus (as still seen in *hysterectomy*). They thought that women were the only ones who experienced uncontrolled emotional outbursts, and so the condition must have something to do with a part of the body that only women have. But how word meanings change is regularly shown at athletic events where thousands of *virtuous* women sit quietly beside their *hysterical* husbands.

Differences in the connotations between positive male and negative female connotations can be seen in several pairs of words that differ denotatively only in the matter of sex. Bachelor as compared to spinster or old maid has such positive connotations that women try to adopt it by using the term *bachelor-girl* or *bachelorette*. Old maid is so negative that it's the basis for metaphors: pretentious and fussy old men are called "old maids," as are the leftover kernels of unpopped popcorn and the last card in a popular children's card game.

Patron and matron (Middle English for "father" and "mother") have such different levels of prestige that women try to borrow the more positive masculine connotations with the word *patroness*, literally "female father." Such a peculiar term came about because of the high prestige attached to patron in such phrases as *a patron of the arts* or *a patron saint*. Matron is more apt to be used in talking about a woman in charge of a jail or a public restroom.

When men are doing jobs that women often do, we apparently try to pay the men extra 35 by giving them fancy titles. For example, a male cook is more likely to be called a "chef" while a male seamstress will get the title of "tailor." The armed forces have a special problem in that they recruit under such slogans as "The Marine Corps builds men!" and "Join the Army! Become a Man." Once the recruits are enlisted, they find themselves doing much of the work that has been traditionally thought of as "women's work." The solution to getting the work done and not insulting anyone's masculinity was to change the titles as shown below:

waitress = orderly
nurse = medic or corpsman
secretary = clerk-typist
assistant = adjutant
dishwasher = KP (kitchen police) or kitchen helper

Compare *brave* and *squaw*. Early settlers in America truly admired Indian men and hence named them with a word that carried connotations of youth, vigor, and courage. But for Indian women they used an Algonquin slang term with negative sexual connotations that are almost opposite to those of brave. Wizard and witch contrast almost as much. The masculine *wizard* implies skill and wisdom combined with magic, while the feminine *witch* implies evil intentions combined with magic. When witch is used for men, as in witch-doctor, many mainstream speakers feel some carry-over of the negative connotations.

Part of the unattractiveness of both witch and squaw is that they have been used so often to refer to old women, something with which our culture is particularly uncomfortable, just as the Afghans were. Imagine my surprise when I ran across the phrases *grandfatherly advice* and *old wives' tales* and realized that the underlying implication is the same as the Afghan proverb about old men being worth listening to while old women talk only foolishness.

Other terms that show how negatively we view old women as compared to young women are *old nag* as compared to *filly, old crow* or *old bat* as compared to *bird*, and being *catty* as compared to being *kittenish*. There is no matching set of metaphors for men. The chicken metaphor tells the whole story of a woman's life. In her youth she is a chick. Then she marries and begins feathering her nest. Soon she begins feeling cooped up, so she goes to hen parties where she cackles with her friends. Then she has her brood, begins to henpeck her husband, and finally turns into an old biddy.

I embarked on my study of the dictionary not with the intention of prescribing language change but simply to see what the language would tell me about sexism. Nevertheless, I have been both surprised and pleased as I've watched the changes that have occurred over the past three decades. I'm one of those linguists who believes that new language customs will cause a new generation of speakers to grow up with different expectations. This is why I'm happy about people's efforts to use inclusive language, to say "he or she" or "they" when speaking about individuals whose names they do not know. I'm glad that leading publishers have developed guidelines to help writers use language that is fair to both sexes. I'm glad that most newspapers and magazines list women by their own names instead of only by their husbands' names. And I'm so glad that educated and thoughtful people no longer begin their business letters with "Dear Sir" or "Gentlemen," but instead use a memo form or begin with such salutations as "Dear Colleagues," "Dear Reader," or "Dear Committee Members." I'm also glad that such words as *poetess, authoress, conductress,* and *aviatrix* now sound quaint and old-fashioned and that *chairman* is giving way to *chair* or *head, mailman* to *mail carrier, clergyman* to *clergy,* and *stewardess* to *flight attendant.* I was also pleased when the National Oceanic and Atmospheric Administration bowed to feminist complaints and in the late 1970s began to alternate men's and women's names for hurricanes. However, I wasn't so pleased to discover that the change did not immediately erase sexist thoughts from everyone's mind, as shown by a headline about Hurricane David in a 1979 New York tabloid, "David Rapes Virgin Islands." More recently a similar metaphor appeared in a headline in the *Arizona Republic* about Hurricane Charlie, "Charlie Quits Carolinas, Flirts with Virginia."

What these incidents show is that sexism is not something existing independently in 40 American English or in the particular dictionary that I happened to read. Rather, it exists in people's minds. Language is like an X-ray in providing visible evidence of invisible thoughts. The best thing about people being interested in and discussing sexist language is that as they make conscious decisions about what pronouns they will use, what jokes they will tell or laugh at, how they will write their names, or how they will begin their letters, they are forced to think about the underlying issue of sexism. This is good because as a problem that begins in people's assumptions and expectations, it's a problem that will be solved only when a great many people have given it a great deal of thought.

Questions

1. Nilsen uses *ethos*, *pathos*, and *logos* to build her argument. Find an example of each of these techniques in the text.

2. How does Nilsen use her own story to introduce the greater issue at hand? In what types of writing is this sort of introduction effective? In which genres might it not be acceptable?

3. Pick a famous person, and write a paragraph describing them to an unfamiliar audience. Revise the paragraph and remove the gendered language.

Shelly Branch

One Term Says It All: "Shut Up!"

Journalist **Shelly Branch** is an expert in personal finance, a staff writer for the *Wall Street Journal*, and a frequent contributor to *Money's* Smart Spending column. She is the author of *Dollar Pinching: A Consumer's Guide to Smart Spending* (1996) and *What Would Jackie Do?: An Inspired Guide to Distinctive Living* (2005).

Her essay "One Term Says It All: 'Shut Up!'," taken from the *Wall Street Journal*, shows how the once negative term now has a positive spin, especially among the young and hip. The phenomenon of a word's losing its negative connotations is called *amelioration*.

As chief of staff to a California assemblyman, Bob Hartnagel chooses his words carefully—especially when his boss is around. But once the coast is clear, he can't resist tossing off a playful "Shut up!" to his colleagues. "It's kind of an exclamation point to whatever's going on," says Mr. Hartnagel, 32 years old. "If it's met with a smile, you proceed. If there's a gasp...you refrain."

Not too many years ago, the unrude use of "Shut up!" might have baffled linguists and just about everybody else. But the term has now made its way from schoolgirl chatter to adult repartee and into movies and advertising. People use it as much to express disbelief, shock and joy as to demand silence. In some circles, it has become the preferred way to say "Oh my God!" "Get out of town!" and "No way!" all at once.

A recent ad for Hyundai's Elantra shows a young woman sparring with a dealer. "Shut up!" screams the woman, who pokes the man in the chest each time he points out a feature that sounds too good to be true.

Editors of the *New Oxford American Dictionary* are considering a new entry for "Shut up!" in the next edition. "I think we should add it because it appears to be widespread," says senior editor Erin McKean. Already, she has mulled possible definitions: "used to express amazement or disbelief" and "oh, so true!"

Shut up! is the latest example of a linguistic phenomenon called amelioration, whereby 5
a word or phrase loses its negative associations over time. A classic example is "nice," which meant "stupid" up through the 13th century. Recent flip-flops include "bad" (as in good) and "dope" (as in great). "Words that were once considered rude are now included in regular conversation, but in a context that lets you know it's not impolite," says Connie Eble, professor of English at the University of North Carolina at Chapel Hill and the author of "Slang and Sociability." "They become so generalized that the shock value wears off."

Words with rich semantic connotations "typically have the possibility to mean their opposite when used in an ironic or joking context," adds Bert Vaux, an associate professor of linguistics at Harvard University.

In the case of the Elantra ad, copy writers at the Richards Group in Dallas settled on the line while cramming last Memorial Day weekend for snappy, youthful expressions. At first, they considered having the actress say something like, "no way," or "you're kidding," but were inspired by the irreverent lingo that staff people in their twenties had been shouting across the agency's open-office cubicles.

"There's a very fine line between being funny and obnoxious," says creative director Mike Malone, who was nervous about offending Hyundai's older dealers. "But every time we said

'Shut up!' it just sounded funnier." He knew he had a hit on his hands, he says, when the agency showed the TV spot to a group of Hyundai dealers in their fifties and they burst out laughing. "After the meeting, they were all walking around telling each other to shut up," says Mr. Malone.

To ensure the proper tone for their ad, writers for the Hyundai spot auditioned more than 200 actresses. "We were getting a really annoying read," says writer Kevin Paetzel, who wanted the character to have a more endearing quality. "The trick is to hit the 'sh' very hard."

The most effective enunciation also places a full stop between "shut and "up." Excitable 10 types pitch their voices higher on the word "up." (Mr. Hartnagel adds "right now!" when he's feeling acutely peppy.) Spoken in haste, the phrase loses what linguists call its "rhythmic features." Then, it can sound too much like an affront.

Once considered base, "shut up" has a long, distinguished history. According to the *Oxford English Dictionary*, an early documented use, in 16th-century England, was a figurative one, meaning "to withhold one's money or kindness from a person." In 1840, the *New Orleans Picayune* printed the first known slang/imperative use of "shut up," when a reporter referred to an officer's demand for a Dutchman to be quiet.

More recently, children's author Meg Cabot has given the phrase a literary twist. Her title character in "The Princess Diaries" favors it to express geeky teenage delight. Disney screenwriters were so fond of the princess's breezy use of the term that they wove it prominently into the movie adaptation. "Shut up!" even landed in the promotional trailer for the film. "I've had a lot of letters from parents thanking me sarcastically for introducing 'shut up!' to their kids' vocabulary," says Ms. Cabot.

The origins of the newest usage have fueled some debate. Ms. Cabot says she picked it up a few years ago from schoolgirls on Manhattan's Lower East Side. An earlier adopter of the phrase was the character Elaine on "Seinfeld." In a 1992 episode written by Larry David called "The Pez Dispenser," Jerry tells a story about a man who splashed Gatorade on his head, got pneumonia and dropped dead. Elaine responds: "Shut up!" In subsequent episodes, Elaine tells people to "Shut up!" all the time—but she really means it. Writers had her intone the hip version just twice, according to Paul McFedries, a language writer and founder of the online site "The Word Spy" who has studied the complete body of Seinfeld scripts.

The fact that "Shut up!" seems to resonate particularly with women doesn't surprise word whizzes. "Women tend to use more conversational movers than men," says dictionary editor Ms. McKean, who also edits "Verbatim," a language quarterly. "These are little phrases that help keep the dialogue going."

Though some people don't like the phrase ("I think it just sounds rude," says actress 15 Drew Barrymore), plenty of professional types are hooked. Says Dawn Jackson, a 32-year-old communications manager in San Francisco, "There are just times when nothing else can express the level of shock, surprise, you name it, that you're feeling."

Questions

1. What is the rhetorical reason for Branch beginning her essay with an anecdote about Bob Hartnagel, a chief of staff to a California assemblyman?

2. "Shut up!" is one example of amelioration. Consider other words that have lost their negative associations over time. Can you trace the history of why? Choose a word that has been ameliorated, and explain what it used to mean and what it means now.

Anne Lamott [b. 1954]

Shitty First Drafts

Born in San Francisco in 1954, **Anne Lamott** is the best-selling author of six novels and several works of nonfiction, including *Operating Instructions* (1993), a brutally honest account of motherhood in her son's first year of life; *Bird by Bird: Some Instructions on Writing and Life* (1994), a riotous handbook for aspiring writers; and *Traveling Mercies*, a collection of autobiographical essays on living with faith. The recipient of a Guggenheim Fellowship, a one-time food critic for *California* magazine and book reviewer for *Mademoiselle*, Lamott has taught at the University of California, Davis, and at numerous writers' conferences. "Word by Word," her biweekly personal reflections contributed to the online *Salon Magazine* from 1996 to 1999, were voted *The Best of the Web* by *Time* magazine. A self-identified recovering alcoholic and born-again Christian, Lamott's writing is frank, candid, and utterly sincere. Her sharp words and strong sense of humor make for a poignantly entertaining read.

"Shitty First Drafts," an excerpt from her book *Bird by Bird: Some Instructions on Writing and Life,* encourages writers to trust their writing processes. Lamott shares her own writing methods and drolly suggests ways of blocking out even the most annoying distractions.

For me and most of the other writers I know, writing is not rapturous. In fact, the only way I can get anything written at all is to write really, really crummy first drafts.

The first draft is the child's draft, where you let it all pour out and then let it romp all over the place, knowing that no one is going to see it and that you can shape it later. You just let this childlike part of you channel whatever voices and visions come through and onto the page. If one of the characters wants to say "Well, so what, Mr. Poopy Pants?" you let her. No one is going to see it. If the kid wants to get into really sentimental, weepy, emotional territory, you let him. Just get it all down on paper, because there may be something great in those six crazy pages that you would never have gotten to by more rational, grown-up means. There may be something in the very last line of the very last paragraph on page six that you just love, that is so beautiful or wild that you now know what you're supposed to be writing about, more or less, or in what direction you might go—but there was no way to get to this without first getting through the first five and a half pages.

I used to write food reviews for *California* magazine before it folded. (My writing food reviews had nothing to do with the magazine folding, although every single review did cause a couple of canceled subscriptions. Some readers took umbrage at my comparing mounds of vegetable puree with various ex-presidents' brains.) These reviews always took two days to write. First I'd go to a restaurant several times with a few opinionated, articulate friends in tow. I'd sit there writing down everything anyone said that was at all interesting or funny. Then on the following Monday I'd sit down at my desk with my notes, and try to write the review. Even after I'd been doing this for years, panic would set in. I'd try to write a lead, but instead I'd write a couple of dreadful sentences, XX them out, try again, XX everything out, and then feel despair and worry settle on my chest like an x-ray apron. It's over, I'd think, calmly. I'm not going to be able to get the magic to work this time. I'm ruined. I'm through. I'm toast. Maybe, I'd think, I can get my old job back as a clerk-typist. But probably not.

I'd get up and study my teeth in the mirror for a while. Then I'd stop, remember to breathe, make a few phone calls, hit the kitchen and chow down. Eventually I'd go back and sit down at my desk, and sigh for the next ten minutes. Finally I would pick up my one-inch picture frame, stare into it as if for the answer, and every time the answer would come: all I had to do was to write a really crummy first draft of, say, the opening paragraph. And no one was going to see it.

So I'd start writing without reining myself in. It was almost just typing, just making my fingers move. And the writing would be *terrible*. I'd write a lead paragraph that was a whole page, even though the entire review could only be three pages long, and then I'd start writing up descriptions of the food, one dish at a time, bird by bird, and the critics would be sitting on my shoulders, commenting like cartoon characters. They'd be pretending to snore, or rolling their eyes at my overwrought descriptions, no matter how hard I tried to tone those descriptions down, no matter how conscious I was of what a friend said to me gently in my early days of restaurant reviewing. "Annie," she said, "it is just a piece of *chicken*. It is just a bit of *cake*."

But because by then I had been writing for so long, I would eventually let myself trust 5 the process—sort of, more or less. I'd write a first draft that was maybe twice as long as it should be, with a self-indulgent and boring beginning, stupefying descriptions of the meal, lots of quotes from my black-humored friends that made them sound more like the Manson girls[*] than food lovers, and no ending to speak of. The whole thing would be so long and incoherent and hideous that for the rest of the day I'd obsess about getting creamed by a car before I could write a decent second draft. I'd worry that people would read what I'd written and believe that the accident had really been a suicide, that I had panicked because my talent was waning and my mind was shot.

The next day, though, I'd sit down, go through it all with a colored pen, take out everything I possibly could, find a new lead somewhere on the second page, figure out a kicky place to end it, and then write a second draft. It always turned out fine, sometimes even funny and weird and helpful. I'd go over it one more time and mail it in.

Then, a month later, when it was time for another review, the whole process would start again, complete with the fears that people would find my first draft before I could rewrite it.

Almost all good writing begins with terrible first efforts. You need to start somewhere. Start by getting something—anything—down on paper. A friend of mine says that the first draft is the down draft—you just get it down. The second draft is the up draft—you fix it up. You try to say what you have to say more accurately. And the third draft is the dental draft, where you check every tooth, to see if it's loose or cramped or decayed, or even, God help us, healthy.

What I've learned to do when I sit down to work on a crummy first draft is to quiet the voices in my head. First there's the vinegar-lipped Reader Lady, who says primly, "Well, *that's* not very interesting, is it?" And there's the emaciated German male who writes these Orwellian memos detailing your thought crimes. And there are your parents, agonizing over your lack of loyalty and discretion; and there's William Burroughs, dozing off or shooting up because he finds you as bold and articulate as a houseplant; and so on. And there are also the dogs: let's not forget the dogs, the dogs in their pen who will surely hurtle and snarl their

---

[*]**Manson girls:** Young, troubled members of a cult led by Charles Manson (b. 1934). In 1969 Manson and some of his followers were convicted of murder in California.

way out if you ever *stop* writing, because writing is, for some of us, the latch that keeps the door of the pen closed, keeps those crazy, ravenous dogs contained. [...]

Close your eyes and get quiet for a minute, until the chatter starts up. Then isolate one 10 of the voices and imagine the person speaking as a mouse. Pick it up by the tail and drop it into a mason jar. Then isolate another voice, pick it up by the tail, drop it in the jar. And so on. Drop in any high-maintenance parental units, drop in any contractors, lawyers, colleagues, children, anyone who is whining in your head. Then put the lid on, and watch all these mouse people clawing at the glass, jabbering away, trying to make you feel crummy because you won't do what they want—won't give them more money, won't be more successful, won't see them more often. Then imagine that there is a volume-control button on the bottle. Turn it all the way up for a minute, and listen to the stream of angry, neglected, guilt-mongering voices. Then turn it all the way down and watch the frantic mice lunge at the glass, trying to get to you. Leave it down, and get back to your crummy first draft.

A writer friend of mine suggests opening the jar and shooting them all in the head. But I think he's a little angry, and I'm sure nothing like this would ever occur to you.

Questions

1. How does Lamott's description of her writing process compare or contrast with your own? What mantras do you repeat to yourself? What voices do you silence?

2. Lamott provides her audience with a humorously precise step-by-step method for silencing the voices in one's head. Take a moment to brainstorm anxieties you experience when you are writing. Choose one of those anxieties, and like Lamott, create a humorous how-to detailing the steps toward quieting that anxiety.

Narratives and
Personal Essays

Junot Díaz [b. 1968]

The Money

Born in the Dominican Republic in 1968 and raised in New Jersey, **Junot Díaz** earned his bachelor's degree from Rutgers University and an M.F.A. in creative writing from Cornell University. He is the author of several works of fiction, including *Drown* (1996), *The Brief Wondrous Life of Oscar Wao* (2007), and *This Is How You Lose Her* (2012). The winner of many awards, including a Pulitzer Prize and MacArthur and Guggenheim Fellowships, Díaz is the fiction editor at *Boston Review* and the Rudge and Nancy Allen Professor of Writing at the Massachusetts Institute of Technology.

Background on Dominicans in the United States Dominicans living in the United States account for 3 percent of the U.S. Hispanic population; they numbered about 1.5 million when the Census Bureau made its American Community Survey in 2011. For many years, the northeast has been home to the majority of Dominicans in the United States. Although historically almost half settled in New York City, in recent years they have established sizable populations in several other northeastern states, such as New Jersey, Massachusetts, and Pennsylvania. Dominicans living in the United States are significantly more likely to have been born outside the United States, as Díaz was, than the general Hispanic population (56 percent versus 36 percent). The Dominican population also has a slightly higher poverty rate compared to all Hispanics; however, it can also claim a higher level of education. Dominicans have had an impact on American food, music, and culture, and they are an integral part of social and commercial life in the United States, where they are teachers, bankers, lawyers, small business owners, entrepreneurs, and workers. With a long history of activism, Dominicans have also begun to wield political influence as elected officials in U.S. state, city, and local governments.

All the Dominicans I knew in those days sent money home. My mother didn't have a regular job besides caring for us five kids, so she scrimped the loot together from whatever came her way. My father was always losing his forklift jobs, so it wasn't like she ever had a steady flow. But my grandparents were alone in Santo Domingo, and those remittances, beyond material support, were a way, I suspect, for Mami to negotiate the absence, the distance, caused by our diaspora. She chipped dollars off the cash Papi gave her for our daily expenses, forced our already broke family to live even broker. That was how she built the nut—two, maybe three hundred dollars—that she sent home every six months or so.

We kids knew where the money was hidden, but we also knew that to touch it would have meant a violent punishment approaching death. I, who could take the change out of my mother's purse without thinking, couldn't have brought myself even to look at that forbidden stash.

So what happened? Exactly what you'd think. The summer I was twelve, my family went away on a "vacation"—one of my father's half-baked get-to-know-our-country-better-by-sleeping-in-the-van extravaganzas—and when we returned to Jersey, exhausted, battered, we found our front door unlocked. My parents' room, which was where the thieves had concentrated their search, looked as if it had been tornado-tossed. The thieves had kept it simple; they'd snatched a portable radio, some of my Dungeons & Dragons hardcovers, and, of course, Mami's remittances.

It's not as if the robbery came as a huge surprise. In our neighborhood, cars and apartments were always getting jacked, and the kid stupid enough to leave a bike unattended for more than a tenth of a second was the kid who was never going to see that bike again. Everybody got hit; no matter who you were, eventually it would be your turn.

And that summer it was ours.   5

Still, we took the burglary pretty hard. When you're a recent immigrant, it's easy to feel targeted. Like it wasn't just a couple of assholes that had it in for you but the whole neighborhood—hell, maybe the whole country.

No one took the robbery as hard as my mom, though. She cursed the neighborhood, she cursed the country, she cursed my father, and of course she cursed us kids, swore that we had run our gums to our idiot friends and they had done it.

And this is where the tale should end, right? Wasn't as if there was going to be any "C.S.I."-style investigation or anything. Except that a couple of days later I was moaning about the robbery to these guys I was hanging with at that time and they were cursing sympathetically, and out of nowhere it struck me. You know when you get one of those moments of mental clarity? When the nictitating membrane obscuring the world suddenly lifts? That's what happened. I realized that these two dopes I called my friends had done it. They were shaking their heads, mouthing all the right words, but I could see the way they looked at each other, the Raskolnikov glances. I *knew*.

Now, it wasn't like I could publicly denounce these dolts or go to the police. That would have been about as useless as crying. Here's what I did: I asked the main dope to let me use his bathroom (we were in front of his apartment) and while I pretended to piss I unlatched the window. Then we all headed to the park as usual, but I pretended that I'd forgotten something back home. Ran to the dope's apartment, slid open the bathroom window, and in broad daylight wriggled my skinny ass in.

Where the hell did I get these ideas? I have not a clue. I guess I was reading way too   10 much Encyclopedia Brown and the Three Investigators in those days. And if mine had been a normal neighborhood this is when the cops would have been called and my ass would have been caught *burglarizing*.

The dolt and his family had been in the U.S. all their lives and they had a ton of stuff, a TV in every room, but I didn't have to do much searching. I popped up the dolt's mattress and underneath I found my D.&D. books and most of my mother's money. He had thoughtfully kept it in the same envelope.

And that was how I solved the Case of the Stupid Morons. My one and only case.

The next day at the park, the dolt announced that someone had broken into *his* apartment and stolen all his savings. This place is full of thieves, he complained bitterly, and I was, like, No kidding.

It took me two days to return the money to my mother. The truth was I was seriously considering keeping it. But in the end the guilt got to me. I guess I was expecting my mother to run around with joy, to crown me her favorite son, to cook me my favorite meal. Nada. I'd wanted a party or at least to see her happy, but there was nothing. Just two hundred and some dollars and fifteen hundred or so miles—that's all there was.

Questions

Comprehension

1. Díaz grew up poor. How does he communicate this fact to readers?

2. According to Díaz, why is the money in his mother's "forbidden stash" (2) different from the money in her purse? Do you think this distinction makes sense?

3. How did Díaz solve "the Case of the Stupid Morons" (12)?

4. What does Díaz mean when he says, "Just two hundred and some dollars and fifteen hundred or so miles—that's all there was" (14)?

Purpose and Audience

1. Even though Díaz uses a very informal style, full of slang expressions, he also uses words like *diaspora* (1) and expressions like "Raskolnikov glances" (8). What does this tell you about him—and about how he sees his audience?

2. This essay does not have a stated thesis. What is Díaz's main idea? Write a sentence that could serve as a thesis statement. Where in the essay could this sentence be added? *Should* such a sentence be added? Why or why not?

3. Does this essay have an informative or a persuasive purpose, or is Díaz just trying to share his memories with readers? Explain.

Style and Structure

1. Identify the one- and two-sentence paragraphs in this essay. Are these very brief paragraphs effective as they are, or should they be expanded or combined with other paragraphs? Explain.

2. This is a personal, informal essay, and it uses first person and contractions. It also includes a number of sentence fragments. Identify a few fragments, and try to turn each one into a complete sentence. Then, explain why you think Díaz used each fragment.

3. In paragraphs 3, 8, and 10, Díaz asks **rhetorical questions**. How would you answer these questions?

4. **Vocabulary Project.** What words, besides morons, does Díaz use to describe the thieves? Which word seems most appropriate to you? Why?

5. Like a crime story, Díaz's narrative moves readers through events from the crime itself to its impact to its final outcome. Identify each of these sections of the narrative.

Journal Entry

Do you think Díaz feels more angry at the "morons" or at himself? Does he also feel frustration? Disappointment? If so, with whom (or what)?

Writing Workshop

1.   Díaz mentions Encyclopedia Brown and the Three Investigators, fictional young detectives whose adventures he followed. When you were young, what was as important to you as these fictional characters were to Díaz? In a narrative essay, trace the development of your fascination with a particular fictional character, pastime, or hobby.

2.   When he returns the money to his mother, Díaz expects "a party or at least to see her happy" (14), but that isn't the reaction he gets. Write a narrative essay about a time when you expected a particular reaction or outcome but were disappointed or surprised.

3.   **Working with Sources.** Consult several dictionaries to find out what the term *diaspora* has meant throughout history. Then, write a narrative essay tracing your own family's diaspora, focusing on their movement from one country, region, or neighborhood to another. Include a definition from one of the dictionaries you consult, and be sure to include parenthetical documentation and a works-cited page.

Combining the Patterns

Díaz discusses both his family's life in a Dominican neighborhood in New York City and his relatives' lives back in Santo Domingo. If he wanted to write a **comparison-and-contrast** paragraph comparing his life to his relatives', what details might he include? Do you think he should add such a paragraph? If so, why—and where?

Alan Dean Foster [b. 1946]

Living with Fire

Fantasy and science-fiction writer **Alan Dean Foster** earned a B.A. and an M.F.A. from the University of California, Los Angeles. He has published dozens of novels and short stories, including books set in the Humanx Commonwealth Universe; the Spellsinger series; and novelizations of *Star Trek*, *Alien*, and *Transformers* films. He is also the author of many standalone novels, including *Kingdoms of Light* (2001) and *Sagramanda* (2006).

Background on wilderness fires. In this essay, Foster writes about the Yarnell Hill wildfire, near his home in Prescott, Arizona, which burned from June 28 to July 10 in 2013. Before it was over, the fire had burned 8,500 acres (over thirteen square miles), killed nineteen people, and destroyed many buildings and homes. Such fires have always been part of America's landscape: the Peshtigo wildfire of 1871 in Peshtigo, Wisconsin, burned 1.2 million acres and killed more than 1,500 people; in 1910, a fire in Montana killed eighty. High-profile disasters aside, fires are a natural part of the life cycle of wilderness areas, and they are often beneficial, clearing dead brush, wood, and undergrowth. But over the last several decades, the number—and the destructive power—of such fires has increased significantly. According to U.S. Forest Service Chief Thomas Tidwell, more than 9.3 million acres in the United States burned in 2012, and fifty-one wildfires exceeded 40,000 acres. Moreover, over the last forty years, the length of the fire season has increased by two months. Researchers cite several variables that may be contributing to this phenomenon, from irresponsible campers and changes in weather patterns to logging practices and the composition of insect populations, but two possible factors stand out. First, climate change may be leading to hotter, drier summers, as well as to shifts in regional weather in Western states such as Arizona and California. Second, as the population grows in the American South and West, homes are increasingly being built in areas prone to fires. Ironically, attempts to control and prevent forest and wilderness fires may actually be contributing to the problem as well because smaller, naturally occurring burns can often remove the deadwood and brush that could lead to much more devastating fires.

When you build a fire in a fireplace, you start with paper, add kindling, and finally arrange the larger logs on top. That perfectly describes the summertime environment in the southwestern mountains of the United States.

Yet many thousands of us choose to live here.

I live in Prescott, Arizona, where a wildfire called the Doce fire is now almost completely contained, after burning 6,767 tinder-dry acres. It started two weeks ago, six miles or so from the house where my wife and I have lived for more than thirty years.

We live in the bottom of a small canyon, and it took a moment for me to realize that the smoke I was seeing from the study window was all wrong. Distant fires, which we are used to, score the blue sky with a thin haze, like a watercolorist's brown wash. But this cloud was massive, a darker brown, moving too fast, and flush with orange.

I drove to the top of the highest hill behind our house and as I swung around the crest, 5 between homes with neat desert landscaping, a view opened before me that bordered on the apocalyptic. Someone had switched the channel of my life.

The mountains were on fire. At that moment the wind was so strong that much of the smoke was lying down, the flames blown almost parallel to the ground. It didn't look like a movie. I could smell it.

Confronted by the immediacy of destruction, technology is the first thing that flees. I was reduced to tossing bits of dried weed into the air to check the direction of the wind. You think: water, family, pets. What do I put in the car first? By then the mass of orange-brown smoke had taken over the north sky.

Move, your mind tells you. Yet you can't stop staring. If you stare at it long enough, perhaps it will go away.

But the monster doesn't go away. It burns north-northeast, luckily almost directly away from our house. It burns right into the backyards of some homes, but no structures are lost, no lives are lost, thanks to the coordination of multiple fire units.

Among the best of these, the front-line fighters, are the Hotshots. They're the best 10 trained, the best conditioned, the hardest working of all. They go right up to the fire line, and sometimes into it.

On Sunday they showed up to fight another fire, near the small, picturesque town of Yarnell, some thirty miles southwest of here. At first it wasn't a big fire, nor was it considered a dangerous one.

But a monsoon blew up. The southwest monsoon is not technically a monsoon, but that's what we call it. Rain poured down in Prescott—welcome, drenching rain. Out in front of the storm, however, winds rose, turned erratic.

The fire essentially flipped over a team of Hotshots, the Granite Mountain Hotshots, from Prescott. Nineteen of them died, the worst loss of firefighter life in a wildland fire in Arizona's history, the worst in the country in eighty years. The greatest tragedy to strike the firefighting profession since 9/11.

I did not know any of them personally, but based on the group photo that has been widely distributed, I think some of them went to my gym. It's strange to think I won't see them again. Small blank spaces in one's existence that used to be occupied by actual people.

Terrible calamity, the television anchors keep repeating. Horrible tragedy. If you live 15 here, you don't need those words. You call those you know to make sure they're O.K. You meet people in the drugstore, on the street. A knowing look, a regretful nod convey all that needs to be said. People living in proximity to disaster don't shout; they just prepare in case it turns and comes for them.

Two major fires in two weeks. Why stay there, people who live elsewhere must wonder as they watch such tragedies unfold. Why not move someplace where you don't spend every summer wondering if your house is going to burn down.

Why do humans live on the slopes of active volcanoes? Why do they live atop major earthquake faults? Why on earth do people continue to dwell, year after year, in a part of the country called Tornado Alley?

Because such places are beautiful, are peaceful, and, for better or worse, are home. No place is safe. Not on this planet. So you choose your home for what you love about it, and not what you fear. If we let fear dictate where we should live, we would all end up huddled together in one great shivering ball of humanity, and that wouldn't be safe, either.

The Doce fire could have been infinitely worse. All it would have taken was a shift in the wind. Yarnell is still burning. But I have to go feed the towhees and the hummingbirds, maybe shoo away a too-curious coyote. This is my home, and I'll deal with Mother Nature's dark side when and if it comes my way. As must we all.

Questions

Comprehension

1. Why was Foster confused when he first saw the fire from his study window?

2. In paragraph 7, Foster says, "Confronted by the immediacy of destruction, technology is the first thing that flees." What does he mean?

3. What immediate response did Foster have as he looked at the fire from the hill behind his house? In what sense is his reaction a **paradox**?

4. Who are the Granite Mountain Hotshots?

5. Foster observes that people who live "in proximity to disaster don't shout" (15). What do they do instead? Why?

6. According to Foster, why do people choose to live in areas that are prone to natural disasters?

Purpose and Audience

1. What is Foster's thesis? How would you restate it in your own words? What do you think he wants his essay to accomplish?

2. At several points in the essay, Foster asks rhetorical questions. What do these questions suggest about Foster's view of his audience?

3. Why do you think Foster includes the story of the Granite Mountain Hotshots? How does it support his overall purpose?

4. What do you think Foster hopes to accomplish in his essay's last two sentences? Do you think he is successful?

Style and Structure

1. Foster begins his essay with an **analogy**. Is this an appropriate opening strategy? Why or why not?

2. In paragraph 15, Foster writes, "If you live here, you don't need those words." To which words is he referring?

3. **Vocabulary Project.** When Foster sees the fire from a hill near his house, the view "bordered on the apocalyptic" (5). What does *apocalyptic* mean? Do you think the choice of this word is appropriate, or does the word seem overdramatic? Explain.

4. How would you describe Foster's attitude toward the fire and its consequences? Fearful? Angry? Exhilarated? How does he convey this attitude to the reader?

Journal Entry

In this essay, Foster writes about the experience of confronting the "immediacy of destruction" (7). Have you ever had an experience of this kind? Even if you have not witnessed disaster or tragedy on a grand scale, have you ever confronted a scene or situation that "switched the channel" (5) in your life? If so, how did you respond? Did you learn anything from the experience?

Writing Workshop

1. In paragraphs 16 and 17, Foster asks several rhetorical questions about people (like himself) who choose to live in areas prone to natural disasters. Consider the dangers—from nature or from other factors—that have threatened you (or that you think might threaten you in the future) in the place where you live. Then, write a narrative essay about a danger that you have faced (or might face) in your home or neighborhood.

2. **Working with Sources.** As the headnote explains, Foster is a fantasy and science-fiction writer. In what sense does this essay incorporate elements of fantasy or science fiction? How could the landscape it describes, and the central "apocalyptic" event, serve as background for a fantasy or science-fiction story? Write a fictional narrative that traces the events Foster describes. If you quote Foster's essay, be sure to cite your source and to include a works-cited page.

3. Think about the factors that Foster identifies as important: beauty, peacefulness, and the sense that some places are just "home" (18). Then, consider the power of a natural or man-made disaster to destroy that sense of home. In a narrative essay, write about a disaster that you witnessed or read about. How did this disaster shape (or change) what home means to you?

Combining the Patterns

How does Foster incorporate **description** into his narrative? Point to specific examples. Given the overall purpose of his essay, do you think Foster might want to limit his use of description and focus more on narrative action? Or should he do just the reverse?

Nancy Mairs [b. 1943]

On Being a Cripple

Born in 1943 in Long Beach, California, and raised north of Boston, Massachusetts, **Nancy Mairs** is a poet, essayist, and teacher. She has written memoirs and personal essays about women's issues, disability, and death in contemporary culture. In "On Being a Cripple," Mairs demonstrates the power of writing that confronts social issues through personal narrative as well as impersonal analysis. Starting with her blunt title, the piece offers an extended consideration of how we choose to name disability, and how that definition affects how we think about it. "I am not a disease," she writes (para. 23). Note other powerful moments in her essay when these two strands cross.

To escape is nothing. Not to escape is nothing.—LOUISE BOGAN

The other day I was thinking of writing an essay on being a cripple. I was thinking hard in one of the stalls of the women's room in my office building, as I was shoving my shirt into my jeans and tugging up my zipper. Preoccupied, I flushed, picked up my book bag, took my cane down from the hook, and unlatched the door. So many movements unbalanced me, and as I pulled the door open I fell over backward, landing fully clothed on the toilet seat with my legs splayed in front of me: the old beetle-on-its-back routine. Saturday afternoon, the building deserted, I was free to laugh aloud as I wriggled back to my feet, my voice bouncing off the yellowish tiles from all directions. Had anyone been there with me, I'd have been still and faint and hot with chagrin. I decided that it was high time to write the essay.

First, the matter of semantics. I am a cripple. I choose this word to name me. I choose from among several possibilities, the most common of which are "handicapped" and "disabled." I made the choice a number of years ago, without thinking, unaware of my motives for doing so. Even now, I'm not sure what those motives are, but I recognize that they are complex and not entirely flattering. People—crippled or not—wince at the word "cripple," as they do not at "handicapped" or "disabled." Perhaps I want them to wince. I want them to see me as a tough customer, one to whom the fates/gods/viruses have not been kind, but who can face the brutal truth of her existence squarely. As a cripple, I swagger.

But, to be fair to myself, a certain amount of honesty underlies my choice. "Cripple" seems to me a clean word, straightforward and precise. It has an honorable history, having made its first appearance in the Lindisfarne Gospel in the tenth century. As a lover of words, I like the accuracy with which it describes my condition: I have lost the full use of my limbs. "Disabled," by contrast, suggests any incapacity, physical or mental. And I certainly don't like "handicapped," which implies that I have deliberately been put at a disadvantage, by whom I can't imagine (my God is not a Handicapper General), in order to equalize chances in the great race of life. These words seem to me to be moving away from my condition, to be widening the gap between word and reality. Most remote is the recently coined euphemism "differently abled," which partakes of the same semantic hopefulness that transformed countries from "undeveloped" to "underdeveloped," then to "less developed," and finally to "developing" nations. People have continued to starve in those countries during the shift. Some realities do not obey the dictates of language.

Mine is one of them. Whatever you call me, I remain crippled. But I don't care what you call me, so long as it isn't "differently abled," which strikes me as pure verbal garbage designed, by its ability to describe anyone, to describe no one. I subscribe to George Orwell's thesis that "the slovenliness of our language makes it easier for us to have foolish thoughts." And I refuse to participate in the degeneration of the language to the extent that I deny that I have lost anything in the course of this calamitous disease; I refuse to pretend that the only differences between you and me are the various ordinary ones that distinguish any one person from another. But call me "disabled" or "handicapped" if you like. I have long since grown accustomed to them; and if they are vague, at least they hint at the truth. Moreover, I use them myself. Society is no readier to accept crippledness than to accept death, war, sex, sweat, or wrinkles. I would never refer to another person as a cripple. It is the word I use to name only myself.

I haven't always been crippled, a fact for which I am soundly grateful. To be whole of 5 limb is, I know from experience, infinitely more pleasant and useful than to be crippled; and if that knowledge leaves one open to bitterness at my loss, the physical soundness I once enjoyed (though I did not enjoy it half enough) is well worth the occasional stab of regret. Though never any good at sports, I was a normally active child and young adult. I climbed trees, played hopscotch, jumped rope, skated, swam, rode my bicycle, sailed. I despised team sports, spending some of the wretchedest afternoons of my life, sweaty and humiliated, behind a field-hockey stick and under a basketball hoop. I tramped alone for miles along the bridle paths that webbed the woods behind the house I grew up in. I swayed through countless dim hours in the arms of one man or another under the scattered shot of light from mirrored balls, and gyrated through countless more as Tab Hunter and Johnny Mathis gave way to the Rolling Stones, Creedence Clearwater Revival, Cream. I walked down the aisle. I pushed baby carriages, changed tires in the rain, marched for peace.

When I was twenty-eight I started to trip and drop things. What at first seemed my natural clumsiness soon became too pronounced to shrug off. I consulted a neurologist, who told me that I had a brain tumor. A battery of tests, increasingly disagreeable, revealed no tumor. About a year and a half later I developed a blurred spot in one eye. I had, at last, the episodes "disseminated in space and time" requisite for a diagnosis: multiple sclerosis. I have never been sorry for the doctor's initial misdiagnosis, however. For almost a week, until the negative results of the tests were in, I thought that I was going to die right away. Every day for the past nearly ten years, then, has been a kind of gift. I accept all gifts.

Multiple sclerosis is a chronic degenerative disease of the central nervous system, in which the myelin that sheathes the nerves is somehow eaten away and scar tissue forms in its place, interrupting the nerves' signals. During its course, which is unpredictable and uncontrollable, one may lose vision, hearing, speech, the ability to walk, control of bladder and/or bowels, strength in any or all extremities, sensitivity to touch, vibration, and/or pain, potency, coordination of movements—the list of possibilities is lengthy and, yes, horrifying. One may also lose one's sense of humor. That's the easiest to lose and the hardest to survive without.

In the past ten years, I have sustained some of these losses. Characteristic of MS are sudden attacks, called exacerbations, followed by remissions, and these I have not had. Instead, my disease has been slowly progressive. My left leg is now so weak that I walk with the aid of a brace and a cane; and for distances I use an Amigo, a variation on the electric wheelchair that looks rather like an electrified kiddie car. I no longer have much use of my left hand.

Now my right side is weakening as well. I still have the blurred spot in my right eye. Overall, though, I've been lucky so far. My world has, of necessity, been circumscribed by my losses, but the terrain left me has been ample enough for me to continue many of the activities that absorb me: writing, teaching, raising children and cats and plants and snakes, reading, speaking publicly about MS and depression, even playing bridge with people patient and honorable enough to let me scatter cards every which way without sneaking a peek.

Lest I begin to sound like Pollyanna, however, let me say that I don't like having MS. I hate it. My life holds realities—harsh ones, some of them—that no right-minded human being ought to accept without grumbling. One of them is fatigue. I know of no one with MS who does not complain of bone-weariness; in a disease that presents an astonishing variety of symptoms, fatigue seems to be a common factor. I wake up in the morning feeling the way most people do at the end of a bad day, and I take it from there. As a result, I spend a lot of time *in extremis* and, impatient with limitation, I tend to ignore my fatigue until my body breaks down in some way and forces rest. Then I miss picnics, dinner parties, poetry readings, the brief visits of old friends from out of town. The offspring of a puritanical tradition of exceptional venerability, I cannot view these lapses without shame. My life often seems a series of small failures to do as I ought.

I lead, on the whole, an ordinary life, probably rather like the one I would have led 10 had I not had MS. I am lucky that my predilections were already solitary, sedentary, and bookish—unlike the world-famous French cellist I have read about, or the young woman I talked with one long afternoon who wanted only to be a jockey. I had just begun graduate school when I found out something was wrong with me, and I have remained, interminably, a graduate student. Perhaps I would not have if I'd thought I had the stamina to return to a full-time job as a technical editor; but I've enjoyed my studies.

In addition to studying, I teach writing courses. I also teach medical students how to give neurological examinations. I pick up freelance editing jobs here and there. I have raised a foster son and sent him into the world, where he has made me two grandbabies, and I am still escorting my daughter and son through adolescence. I go to Mass every Saturday. I am a superb, if messy, cook. I am also an enthusiastic laundress, capable of sorting a hamper full of clothes into five subtly differentiated piles, but a terrible housekeeper. I can do italic writing and, in an emergency, bathe an oil-soaked cat. I play a fiendish game of Scrabble. When I have the time and the money, I like to sit on my front steps with my husband drinking Amaretto and smoking a cigar, as we imagine our counterparts in Leningrad and make sure that the sun gets down once more behind the sharp childish scrawl of the Tucson Mountains.

This lively plenty has its bleak complement, of course, in all the things I can no longer do. I will never run again, except in dreams, and one day I may have to write that I will never walk again. I like to go camping, but I can't follow George and the children along the trails that wander out of a campsite through the desert or into the mountains. In fact, even on the level I've learned never to check the weather or try to hold a coherent conversation: I need all my attention for my wayward feet. Of late, I have begun to catch myself wondering how people can propel themselves without canes. With only one usable hand, I have to select my clothing with care not so much for style as for ease of ingress and egress, and even so, dressing can be laborious. I can no longer do fine stitchery, pick up babies, play the piano, braid my hair. I am immobilized by acute attacks of depression, which may or may not be physiologically related to MS but are certainly its logical concomitant.

These two elements, the plenty and the privation, are never pure, nor are the delight and wretchedness that accompany them. Almost every pickle that I get into as a result of my weakness and clumsiness—and I get into plenty—is funny as well as maddening and some-times painful. I recall one May afternoon when a friend and I were going out for a drink after finishing up at school. As we were climbing into opposite sides of my car, chatting, I tripped and fell, flat and hard, onto the asphalt parking lot, my abrupt departure interrupting him in mid-sentence. "Where'd you go?" he called as he came around the back of the car to find me hauling myself up by the door frame. "Are you all right?" Yes, I told him, I was fine, just a bit rattly, and we drove off to find a shady patio and some beer. When I got home an hour or so later, my daughter greeted me with "What have you done to yourself?" I looked down. One elbow of my white turtleneck with the green froggies, one knee of my white trousers, one white kneesock were bloodsoaked. We peeled off the clothes and inspected the damage, which was nasty enough but not alarming. That part wasn't funny: The abrasions took a long time to heal, and one got a little infected. Even so, when I think of my friend talking earnestly, suddenly, to the hot thin air while I dropped from his view as though through a trap door, I find the image as silly as something from a Marx Brothers movie.

I may find it easier than other cripples to amuse myself because I live propped by the acceptance and the assistance and, sometimes, the amusement of those around me. Grocery clerks tear my checks out of my checkbook for me, and sales clerks find chairs to put into dressing rooms when I want to try on clothes. The people I work with make sure I teach at times when I am least likely to be fatigued, in places I can get to, with the materials I need. My students, with one anonymous exception (in an end-of-the-semester evaluation), have been unperturbed by my disability. Some even like it. One was immensely cheered by the information that I paint my own fingernails; she decided, she told me, that if I could go to such trouble over fine details, she could keep on writing essays. I suppose I became some sort of bright-fingered muse. She wrote good essays, too.

The most important struts in the framework of my existence, of course, are my husband and children. Dismayingly few marriages survive the MS test, and why should they? Most twenty-two- and nineteen-year-olds, like George and me, can vow in clear conscience, after a childhood of chicken pox and summer colds, to keep one another in sickness and in health so long as they both shall live. Not many are equipped for catastrophe: the dismay, the depression, the extra work, the boredom that a degenerative disease can insinuate into a relationship. And our society, with its emphasis on fun and its association of fun with physical performance, offers little encouragement for a whole spouse to stay with a crippled partner. Children experience similar stresses when faced with a crippled parent, and they are more helpless, since parents and children can't usually get divorced. They hate, of course, to be different from their peers, and the child whose mother is tacking down the aisle of a school auditorium packed with proud parents like a Cape Cod dinghy in a stiff breeze jolly well stands out in a crowd. Deprived of legal divorce, the child can at least deny the mother's disability, even her existence, forgetting to tell her about recitals and PTA meetings, refusing to accompany her to stores or church or the movies, never inviting friends to the house. Many do.

But I've been limping along for ten years now, and so far George and the children are still at my left elbow, holding tight. Anne and Matthew vacuum floors and dust furniture and haul trash and rake up dog droppings and button my cuffs and bake lasagna and Toll House cookies with just enough grumbling so I know that they don't have brain fever. And far from hiding me, they're forever dragging me by racks of fancy clothes or through teeming school corridors, or welcoming gaggles of friends while I'm wandering through the house in Anne's filmy pink babydoll pajamas. George generally calls before he brings someone home, but he does just as many dumb thankless chores as the children. And they all yell at me, laugh at some of my jokes, write me funny letters when we're apart—in short, treat me as an ordinary human being for whom they have some use. I think they like me. Unless they're faking....

Faking. There's the rub. Tugging at the fringes of my consciousness always is the terror that people are kind to me only because I'm a cripple. My mother almost shattered me once, with that instinct mothers have—blind, I think, in this case, but unerring nonetheless—for striking blows along the fault-lines of their children's hearts, by telling me, in an attack on my selfishness, "We all have to make allowances for you, of course, because of the way you are." From the distance of a couple of years, I have to admit that I haven't any idea just what she meant, and I'm not sure that she knew either. She was awfully angry. But at the time, as the words thudded home, I felt my worst fear, suddenly realized. I could bear being called selfish: I am. But I couldn't bear the corroboration that those around me were doing in fact what I'd always suspected them of doing, professing fondness while silently putting up with me because of the way I am. A cripple. I've been a little cracked ever since.

Along with this fear that people are secretly accepting shoddy goods comes a relentless pressure to please—to prove myself worth the burdens I impose, I guess, or to build a substantial account of goodwill against which I may write drafts in times of need. Part of the pressure arises from social expectations. In our society, anyone who deviates from the norm had better find some way to compensate. Like fat people, who are expected to be jolly, cripples must bear their lot meekly and cheerfully. A grumpy cripple isn't playing by the rules. And much of pressure is self-generated. Early on I vowed that, if I had to have MS, by God I was going to do it well. This is a class act, ladies and gentlemen. No tears, no recriminations, no faint-heartedness.

One way and another, then, I wind up feeling like Tiny Tim, peering over the edge of the table at the Christmas goose, waving my crutch, piping down God's blessing on us all. Only sometimes I don't want to play Tiny Tim. I'd rather be Caliban, a most scurvy monster. Fortunately, at home no one much cares whether I'm a good cripple or a bad cripple as long as I make vichyssoise with fair regularity. One evening several years ago, Anne was reading at the dining-room table while I cooked dinner. As I opened a can of tomatoes, the can slipped in my left hand and juice spattered me and the counter with bloody spots. Fatigued and infuriated, I bellowed, "I'm so sick of being crippled!" Anne glanced at me over the top of her book. "There now," she said, "do you feel better?" "Yes," I said, "yes, I do." She went back to her reading. I felt better. That's about all the attention my scurviness ever gets.

Because I hate being crippled, I sometimes hate myself for being a cripple. Over the years I have come to expect—even accept—attacks of violent self-loathing. Luckily, in general our society no longer connects deformity and disease directly with evil (though a charismatic once told me that I have MS because a devil is in me) and so I'm allowed to move largely at will, even among small children. But I'm not sure that this revision of attitude has been particularly helpful. Physical imperfection, even freed of moral disapprobation, still defies and violates the ideal, especially for women, whose confinement in their bodies as objects of desire is far from over. Each age, of course, has its ideal, and I doubt that ours is any better or worse than any other. Today's ideal woman, who lives on the glossy pages of

20

dozens of magazines, seems to be between the ages of eighteen and twenty-five; her hair has body, her teeth flash white, her breath smells minty, her underarms are dry; she has a career but is still a fabulous cook, especially of meals that take less than twenty minutes to prepare; she does not ordinarily appear to have a husband or children; she is trim and deeply tanned; she jogs, swims, plays tennis, rides a bicycle, sails, but does not bowl; she travels widely, even to out-of-the-way places like Finland and Samoa, always in the company of the ideal man, who possesses a nearly identical set of characteristics. There are a few exceptions. Though usually white and often blonde, she may be black, Hispanic, Asian, or Native American, so long as she is unusually sleek. She may be old, provided she is selling a laxative or is Lauren Bacall. If she is selling a detergent, she may be married and have a flock of strikingly messy children. But she is never a cripple.

Like many women I know, I have always had an uneasy relationship with my body. I was not a popular child, largely, I think now, because I was peculiar: intelligent, intense, moody, shy, given to unexpected actions and inexplicable notions and emotions. But as I entered adolescence, I believed myself unpopular because I was homely: my breasts too flat, my mouth too wide, my hips too narrow, my clothing never quite right in fit or style. I was not, in fact, particularly ugly, old photographs inform me, though I was well off the ideal; but I carried this sense of self-alienation with me into adulthood, where it regenerated in response to the depredations of MS. Even with my brace I walk with a limp so pronounced that, seeing myself on the videotape of a television program on the disabled, I couldn't believe that anything but an inch-worm could make progress humping along like that. My shoulders droop and my pelvis thrusts forward as I try to balance myself upright, throwing my frame into a bony S. As a result of contractures, one shoulder is higher than the other and I carry one arm bent in front of me, the fingers curled into a claw. My left arm and leg have wasted into pipestems, and I try always to keep them covered. When I think about how my body must look to others, especially to men, to whom I have been trained to display myself, I feel ludicrous, even loathsome.

At my age, however, I don't spend much time thinking about my appearance. The burning egocentricity of adolescence, which assures one that all the world is looking all the time, has passed, thank God, and I'm generally too caught up in what I'm doing to step back, as I used to, and watch myself as though upon a stage. I'm also too old to believe in the accuracy of self-image. I know that I'm not a hideous crone, that in fact, when I'm rested, well dressed, and well made up, I look fine. The self-loathing I feel is neither physically nor intellectually substantial. What I hate is not me but a disease.

I am not a disease.

And a disease is not—at least not singlehandedly—going to determine who I am, though at first it seemed to be going to. Adjusting to a chronic incurable illness, I have moved through a process similar to that outlined by Elisabeth Kübler-Ross in *On Death and Dying*. The major difference—and it is far more significant than most people recognize—is that I can't be sure of the outcome, as the terminally ill cancer patient can. Research studies indicate that, with proper medical care, I may achieve a "normal" life span. And in our society, with its vision of death as the ultimate evil, worse even than decrepitude, the response to such news is, "Oh well, at least you're not going to *die*." Are there worse things than dying? I think that there may be.

I think of two women I know, both with MS, both enough older than I to have served   25
me as models. One took to her bed several years ago and has been there ever since. Although

she can sit in a high-backed wheelchair, because she is incontinent she refuses to go out at all, even though incontinence pants, which are readily available at any pharmacy, could protect her from embarrassment. Instead, she stays at home and insists that her husband, a small quiet man, a retired civil servant, stay there with her except for a quick weekly foray to the supermarket. The other woman, whose illness was diagnosed when she was eighteen, a nursing student engaged to a young doctor, finished her training, married her doctor, accompanied him to Germany when he was in the service, bore three sons and a daughter, now grown and gone. When she can, she travels with her husband; she plays bridge, embroiders, swims regularly; she works, like me, as a symptomatic-patient instructor of medical students in neurology. Guess which woman I hope to be.

At the beginning, I thought about having MS almost incessantly and because of the unpredictable course of the disease, my thoughts were always terrified. Each night I'd get into bed wondering whether I'd get out again the next morning, whether I'd be able to see, to speak, to hold a pen between my fingers. Knowing that the day might come when I'd be physically incapable of killing myself, I thought perhaps I ought to do so right away, while I still had the strength. Gradually I came to understand that the Nancy who might one day lie inert under a bedsheet, arms and legs paralyzed, unable to feed or bathe herself, unable to reach out for a gun, a bottle of pills, was not the Nancy I was at present, and that I could not presume to make decisions for that future Nancy, who might well not want in the least to die. Now the only provision I've made for the future Nancy is that when the time comes— and it is likely to come in the form of pneumonia, friend to the weak and the old—I am not to be treated with machines and medications. If she is unable to communicate by then, I hope she will be satisfied with these terms.

Thinking all the time about having MS grew tiresome and intrusive, especially in the large and tragic mode in which I was accustomed to considering my plight. Months and even years went by without catastrophe (at least without one related to MS), and really I was awfully busy, what with George and children and snakes and students and poems, and I hadn't the time, let alone the inclination, to devote myself to being a disease. Too, the richer my life became, the funnier it seemed, as though there were some connection between largesse and laughter, and so my tragic stance began to waver until, even with the aid of a brace and a cane, I couldn't hold it for very long at a time.

After several years I was satisfied with my adjustment. I had suffered my grief and fury and terror, I thought, but now I was at ease with my lot. Then one summer day I set out with George and the children across the desert for a vacation in California. Part way to Yuma I became aware that my right leg felt funny. "I think I've had an exacerbation," I told George. "What shall we do?" he asked. "I think we'd better get the hell to California," I said, "because I don't know whether I'll ever make it again." So we went on to San Diego and then to Orange, up the Pacific Coast Highway to Santa Cruz, across to Yosemite, down to Sequoia and Joshua Tree, and so back over the desert to home. It was a fine two-week trip, filled with friends and fair weather, and I wouldn't have missed it for the world, though I did in fact make it back to California two years later. Nor would there have been any point in missing it, since in MS, once the symptoms have appeared, the neurological damage has been done, and there's no way to predict or prevent that damage.

The incident spoiled my self-satisfaction, however. It renewed my grief and fury and terror, and I learned that one never finishes adjusting to MS. I don't know now why I thought one would. One does not, after all, finish adjusting to life, and MS is simply a fact of my life—not my favorite fact, of course—but as ordinary as my nose and my tropical fish and my yellow Mazda station wagon. It may at any time get worse, but no amount of worry, or anticipation can prepare me for a new loss. My life is a lesson in losses. I learn one at a time.

And I had best be patient in the learning, since I'll have to do it like it or not. As any   30 rock fan knows, you can't always get what you want. Particularly when you have MS. You can't, for example, get cured. In recent years researchers and the organizations that fund research have started to pay MS some attention even though it isn't fatal; perhaps they have begun to see that life is something other than a quantitative phenomenon, that one may be very much alive for a very long time in a life that isn't worth living. The researchers have made some progress toward understanding the mechanism of the disease: It may well be an autoimmune reaction triggered by a slow-acting virus. But they are nowhere near its prevention, control, or cure. And most of us want to be cured. Some, unable to accept incurability, grasp at one treatment after another, no matter how bizarre: megavitamin therapy, gluten-free diet, injections of cobra venom, hypothermal suits, lymphocytopharesis, hyperbaric chambers. Many treatments are probably harmless enough, but none are curative.

The absence of a cure often makes MS patients bitter toward their doctors. Doctors are, after all, the priests of modern society, the new shamans, whose business is to heal, and many an MS patient roves from one to another, searching for the "good" doctor who will make him well. Doctors too think of themselves as healers, and for this reason many have trouble dealing with MS patients, whose disease in its intransigence defeats their aims and mocks their skills. Too few doctors, it is true, treat their patients as whole human beings, but the reverse is also true. I have always tried to be gentle with my doctors, who often have more at stake in terms of ego than I do. I may be frustrated, maddened, depressed by the incurability of my disease, but I am not diminished by it, and they are. When I push myself up from my seat in the waiting room and stumble toward them, I incarnate the limitation of their powers. The least I can do is refuse to press on their tenderest spots.

This gentleness is part of the reason that I'm not sorry to be a cripple. I didn't have it before. Perhaps I'd have developed it anyway—how could I know such a thing?—and I wish I had more of it, but I'm glad of what I have. It has opened and enriched my life enormously, this sense that my frailty and need must be mirrored in others, that in searching for and shaping a stable core in a life wrenched by change and loss, change and loss, I must recognize the same process, under individual conditions, in the lives around me. I do not deprecate such knowledge, however I've come by it.

All the same, if a cure were found, would I take it? In a minute. I may be a cripple, but I'm only occasionally a loony and never a saint. Anyway, in my brand of theology God doesn't give bonus points for a limp. I'd take a cure; I just don't need one. A friend who also has MS startled me once by asking, "Do you ever say to yourself, 'Why me, Lord?'" "No, Michael, I don't," I told him, "because whenever I try, the only response I can think of is 'Why not?'" If I could make a cosmic deal, who would I put in my place? What in my life would I give up in exchange for sound limbs and a thrilling rush of energy? No one. Nothing. I might as well do the job myself. Now that I'm getting the hang of it.

[1986]

Questions

1. *Cripple* is a loaded word. Did you agree with Mairs's use of the term *crippled*? How did this essay affect your understanding of the power of this and similar labels?

2. As a personal narrative, Mairs's essay frequently reflects on her individual experience as "a cripple." How does the introduction to this piece prepare the reader for the rest of the essay? What makes the introduction successful or effective? Refer to specific elements.

3. Following several anecdotes (short personal stories or excerpts), Mairs writes a paragraph or two explaining the larger context of her personal story. In small groups, select two or three anecdotes from "On Being a Cripple" and identify the "larger-context" paragraphs following the anecdotes. Why are these paragraphs necessary? Why doesn't Mairs simply write about personal experience? Note the language utilized in these larger-context paragraphs.

Chang-rae Lee [b. 1965]

Coming Home Again

An American novelist and professor of creative writing, **Chang-rae Lee** was born in Seoul, South Korea, on July 29, 1955. When he was three, Lee immigrated with his family to the United States, where his father studied and established a practice in psychiatry. A child of a self-proclaimed "standard suburban American upbringing," Lee attended the Phillips Exeter Academy in New Hampshire and, later, Yale University in Connecticut, where he earned his bachelor's degree in English. After graduating in 1987, Lee started work as an equities analyst on Wall Street—a short stint before beginning his master of fine arts degree the following year. His thesis the manuscript for his first novel, Lee graduated from the University of Oregon in 1993, and there began his teaching career as an assistant professor of creative writing. That same year, he married Michelle Branca, an architect, with whom he had two children. With the success of his first book, *Native Speaker* (1995), an exploration of identity and assimilation honored with the prestigious PEN/Hemingway Award for Debut Fiction and the American Book Award, Lee was appointed director of the creative writing program at Hunter College of the City University of New York. His second book, *A Gesture Life* (1999), earned him a spot on the *New Yorker*'s 1999 list of the twenty best American writers under forty, and another of his novels, *The Surrendered* (2010), was a finalist for the Pulitzer Prize for Fiction. Currently a professor in the Lewis Center for the Arts at Princeton University, Lee has also written short stories and essays that have seen publication in the *New Yorker*, *Granta*, and the *New York Times*, among other magazines and journals.

A tribute to his mother, Inja Hong Lee, who died of cancer, "Coming Home Again" was first published in the *New Yorker* in 1995. Lee recalls when he was young, watching his mother cook traditional Korean dishes, and how she learned to make typical American fare to appease his curiosity about the exotic cuisine of their new home. Food, he describes, became a central means by which he and his mother communicated their love for each other.

When my mother began using the electronic pump that fed her liquids and medication, we moved her to the family room. The bedroom she shared with my father was upstairs, and it was impossible to carry the machine up and down all day and night. The pump itself was attached to a metal stand on casters, and she pulled it along wherever she went. From anywhere in the house, you could hear the sound of the wheels clicking out a steady time over the grout lines of the slate-tiled foyer, her main thoroughfare to the bathroom and the kitchen. Sometimes you would hear her halt after only a few steps, to catch her breath or steady her balance, and whatever you were doing was instantly suspended by a pall of silence.

I was usually in the kitchen, preparing lunch or dinner, poised over the butcher block with her favorite chef's knife in my hand and her old yellow apron slung around my neck. I'd be breathless in the sudden quiet, and, having ceased my mincing and chopping, would stare blankly at the brushed sheen of the blade. Eventually, she would clear her throat or call out to say she was fine, then begin to move again, starting her rhythmic *ka-jug*; and only then could I go on with my cooking, the world of our house turning once more, wheeling through the black.

I wasn't cooking for my mother but for the rest of us. When she first moved downstairs she was still eating, though scantily, more just to taste what we were having than from any genuine desire for food. The point was simply to sit together at the kitchen table and array ourselves like a family again. My mother would gently set herself down in her customary chair near the stove. I sat across from her, my father and sister to my left and right, and crammed in the center was all the food I had made—a spicy codfish stew, say, or a casserole of gingery beef, dishes that in my youth she had prepared for us a hundred times.

It had been ten years since we'd all lived together in the house, which at fifteen I had left to attend boarding school in New Hampshire. My mother would sometimes point this out, by speaking of our present time as being "just like before Exeter," which surprised me, given how proud she always was that I was a graduate of the school.

My going to such a place was part of my mother's not so secret plan to change my char- 5
acter, which she worried was becoming too much like hers. I was clever and able enough, but without outside pressure I was readily given to sloth and vanity. The famous school—which none of us knew the first thing about—would prove my mettle. She was right, of course, and while I was there I would falter more than a few times, academically and otherwise. But I never thought that my leaving home then would ever be a problem for her, a private quarrel she would have even as her life waned.

Now her house was full again. My sister had just resigned from her job in New York City, and my father, who typically saw his psychiatric patients until eight or nine in the evening, was appearing in the driveway at four-thirty. I had been living at home for nearly a year and was in the final push of work on what would prove a dismal failure of a novel. When I wasn't struggling over my prose, I kept occupied with the things she usually did— the daily errands, the grocery shopping, the vacuuming and the cleaning, and, of course, all the cooking.

When I was six or seven years old, I used to watch my mother as she prepared our favorite meals. It was one of my daily pleasures. She shooed me away in the beginning, telling me that the kitchen wasn't my place, and adding, in her half-proud, half-deprecating way, that her kind of work would only serve to weaken me. "Go out and play with your friends," she'd snap in Korean, "or better yet, do your reading and homework." She knew that I had already done both, and that as the evening approached there was no place to go save her small and tidy kitchen, from which the clatter of her mixing bowls and pans would ring through the house.

I would enter the kitchen quietly and stand beside her, my chin lodging upon the point of her hip. Peering through the crook of her arm, I beheld the movements of her hands. For *kalbi*, she would take up a butchered short rib in her narrow hand, the flinty bone shaped like a section of an airplane wing and deeply embedded in gristle and flesh, and with the point of her knife cut so that the bone fell away, though not completely, leaving it connected to the meat by the barest opaque layer of tendon. Then she methodically butterflied the flesh, cutting and unfolding, repeating the action until the meat lay out on her board, glistening and ready for seasoning. She scored it diagonally, then sifted sugar into the crevices with her pinched fingers, gently rubbing in the crystals. The sugar would tenderize as well as sweeten the meat. She did this with each rib, and then set them all aside in a large shallow bowl. She minced a half-dozen cloves of garlic, a stub of gingerroot, sliced up a few scallions, and spread it all over the meat. She wiped her hands and took out a bottle of sesame oil, and, after pausing for a moment, streamed the dark oil in two swift circles around the bowl. After adding a few splashes of soy sauce, she thrust her hands in and kneaded the flesh, careful not to dislodge the bones. I asked her why it mattered that they remain connected. "The meat needs the bone nearby," she said, "to borrow its richness." She wiped her hands clean of the marinade, except for her little finger, which she would flick with her tongue from time to time, because she knew that the flavor of a good dish developed not at once but in stages.

Whenever I cook, I find myself working just as she would, readying the ingredients— a mash of garlic, a julienne of red peppers, fantails of shrimp—and piling them in little mounds about the cutting surface. My mother never left me any recipes, but this is how I learned to make her food, each dish coming not from a list or a card but from the aromatic spread of a board.

I've always thought it was particularly cruel that the cancer was in her stomach, and that   10 for a long time at the end she couldn't eat. The last meal I made for her was on New Year's Eve, 1990. My sister suggested that instead of a rib roast or a bird, or the usual overflow of Korean food, we make all sorts of finger dishes that our mother might fancy and pick at.

We set the meal out on the glass coffee table in the family room. I prepared a tray of smoked-salmon canapés, fried some Korean bean cakes, and made a few other dishes I thought she might enjoy. My sister supervised me, arranging the platters, and then with some pomp carried each dish in to our parents. Finally, I brought out a bottle of champagne in a bucket of ice. My mother had moved to the sofa and was sitting up, surveying the low table. "It looks pretty nice," she said. "I think I'm feeling hungry."

This made us all feel good, especially me, for I couldn't remember the last time she had felt any hunger or had eaten something I cooked. We began to eat. My mother picked up a piece of salmon toast and took a tiny corner in her mouth. She rolled it around for a moment and then pushed it out with the tip of her tongue, letting it fall back onto her plate. She swallowed hard, as if to quell a gag, then glanced up to see if we had noticed. Of course we all had. She attempted a bean cake, some cheese, and then a slice of fruit, but nothing was any use.

She nodded at me anyway, and said, "Oh, it's very good." But I was already feeling lost and I put down my plate abruptly, nearly shattering it on the thick glass. There was an ugly pause before my father asked me in a weary, gentle voice if anything was wrong, and I answered that it was nothing, it was the last night of a long year, and we were together, and I was simply relieved. At midnight, I poured out glasses of champagne, even one for my mother, who took a deep sip. Her manner grew playful and light, and I helped her shuffle to her mattress, and she lay down in the place where in a brief week she was dead.

My mother could whip up most anything, but during our first years of living in this country we ate only Korean foods. At my haranguelike behest, my mother set herself to learning how to cook exotic American dishes. Luckily, a kind neighbor, Mrs. Churchill, a tall, florid young woman with flaxen hair, taught my mother her most trusted recipes. Mrs. Churchill's two young sons, palish, weepy boys with identical crew cuts, always accompanied her, and though I liked them well enough, I would slip away from them after a few minutes, for I knew that the real action would be in the kitchen, where their mother was playing guide. Mrs. Churchill hailed from the state of Maine, where the finest Swedish meatballs and tuna casserole and angel-food cake in America are made. She readily demonstrated certain techniques—how to layer wet sheets of pasta for a lasagna or whisk up a simple roux, for example. She often brought gift shoeboxes containing curious ingredients like dried oregano, instant yeast, and cream-of-mushroom soup. The two women, though at ease and jolly with each other, had difficulty communicating, and this was made worse by the often confusing terminology of Western cuisine ("corned beef," "devilled eggs"). Although I was just learning the language myself, I'd gladly play the interlocutor, jumping back and forth between their places at the counter, dipping my fingers into whatever sauce lay about.

I was an insistent child, and, being my mother's firstborn, much too prized. My mother 15 could say no to me, and did often enough, but anyone who knew us—particularly my father and sister—could tell how much the denying pained her. And if I was overconscious of her indulgence even then, and suffered the rushing pangs of guilt that she could inflict upon me with the slightest wounded turn of her lip, I was too happily obtuse and venal to let her cease. She reminded me daily that I was her sole son, her reason for living, and that if she were to lose me, in either body or spirit, she wished that God would mercifully smite her, strike her down like a weak branch.

In the traditional fashion, she was the house accountant, the maid, the launderer, the disciplinarian, the driver, the secretary, and, of course, the cook. She was also my first basketball coach. In South Korea, where girls' high-school basketball is a popular spectator sport, she had been a star, the point guard for the national high-school team that once won the all-Asia championships. I learned this one Saturday during the summer, when I asked my father if he would go down to the school yard and shoot some baskets with me. I had just finished the fifth grade, and wanted desperately to make the middle-school team the coming fall. He called for my mother and sister to come along. When we arrived, my sister immediately ran off to the swings, and I recall being annoyed that my mother wasn't following her. I dribbled clumsily around the key, on the verge of losing control of the ball, and flung a flat shot that caromed wildly off the rim. The ball bounced to my father, who took a few not so graceful dribbles and made an easy layup. He dribbled out and then drove to the hoop for a layup on the other side. He rebounded his shot and passed the ball to my mother, who had been watching us from the foul line. She turned from the basket and began heading the other way.

"*Um-mah*," I cried at her, my exasperation already bubbling over, "the basket's over *here!*"

After a few steps she turned around, and from where the professional three-point line must be now, she effortlessly flipped the ball up in a two-handed set shot, its flight truer and higher than I'd witnessed from any boy or man. The ball arced cleanly into the hoop, stiffly popping the chain-link net. All afternoon, she rained in shot after shot, as my father and I scrambled after her.

When we got home from the playground, my mother showed me the photograph album of her team's championship run. For years, I kept it in my room, on the same shelf that housed the scrapbooks I made of basketball stars, with magazine clippings of slick players like Bubbles Hawkins and Pistol Pete and George (the Iceman) Gervin.

It puzzled me how much she considered her own history to be immaterial, and if she never patently diminished herself, she was able to finesse a kind of self-removal by speaking of my father whenever she could. She zealously recounted his excellence as a student in medical school and reminded me, each night before I started my homework, of how hard he drove himself in his work to make a life for us. She said that because of his Asian face and imperfect English, he was "working two times the American doctors." I knew that she was building him up, buttressing him with both genuine admiration and her own brand of anxious braggadocio, and that her overarching concern was that I might fail to see him as she wished me to—in the most dawning light, his pose steadfast and solitary.

In the year before I left for Exeter, I became weary of her oft-repeated accounts of my father's success. I was a teen-ager, and so ever inclined to be dismissive and bitter toward anything that had to do with family and home. Often enough, my mother was the object of my derision. Suddenly, her life seemed so small to me. She was there, and sometimes, I thought, *always* there, as if she were confined to the four walls of our house. I would even complain about her cooking. Mostly, though, I was getting more and more impatient with the difficulty she encountered in doing everyday things. I was afraid for her. One day, we got into a terrible argument when she asked me to call the bank, to question a discrepancy she had discovered in the monthly statement. I asked her why she couldn't call herself. I was stupid and brutal, and I knew exactly how to wound her.

"Whom do I talk to?" she said. She would mostly speak to me in Korean, and I would answer in English.

"The bank manager, who else?"

"What do I say?"

"Whatever you want to say."   25

"Don't speak to me like that!" she cried.

"It's just that you should be able to do it yourself," I said.

"You know how I feel about this!"

"Well, maybe then you should consider it *practice*," I answered lightly, using the Korean word to make sure she understood.

Her face blanched, and her neck suddenly became rigid, as if I were throttling her. 30
She nearly struck me right then, but instead she bit her lip and ran upstairs. I followed her, pleading for forgiveness at her door. But it was the one time in our life that I couldn't convince her, melt her resolve with the blandishments of a spoiled son.

When my mother was feeling strong enough, or was in particularly good spirits, she would roll her machine into the kitchen and sit at the table and watch me work. She wore pajamas day and night, mostly old pairs of mine.

She said, "I can't tell, what are you making?"

"*Mahn-doo* filling."

"You didn't salt the cabbage and squash."

"Was I supposed to?"   35

"Of course. Look, it's too wet. Now the skins will get soggy before you can fry them."

"What should I do?"

"It's too late. Maybe it'll be O.K. if you work quickly. Why didn't you ask me?"

"You were finally sleeping."

"You should have woken me."   40

"No way."

She sighed, as deeply as her weary lungs would allow.

"I don't know how you were going to make it without me."

"I don't know, either. I'll remember the salt next time."

"You better. And not too much."   45

We often talked like this, our tone decidedly matter-of-fact, chin up, just this side of being able to bear it. Once, while inspecting a potato-fritter batter I was making, she asked me if she had ever done anything that I wished she hadn't done. I thought for a moment, and told her no. In the next breath, she wondered aloud if it was right of her to have let me go to Exeter, to live away from the house while I was so young. She tested the batter's thickness with her finger and called for more flour. Then she asked if, given a choice, I would go to Exeter again.

I wasn't sure what she was getting at, and I told her that I couldn't be certain, but probably, yes, I would. She snorted at this and said it was my leaving home that had once so troubled our relationship. "Remember how I had so much difficulty talking to you? Remember?"

She believed back then that I had found her more and more ignorant each time I came home. She said she never blamed me, for this was the way she knew it would be with my wonderful new education. Nothing I could say seemed to quell the notion. But I knew that the problem wasn't simply the *education*; the first time I saw her again after starting school, barely six weeks later, when she and my father visited me on Parents Day, she had already grown nervous and distant. After the usual campus events, we had gone to the motel where they were staying in a nearby town and sat on the beds in our room. She seemed to sneak looks at me, as though I might discover a horrible new truth if our eyes should meet.

My own secret feeling was that I had missed my parents greatly, my mother especially, and much more than I had anticipated. I couldn't tell them that these first weeks were a mere blur to me, that I felt completely overwhelmed by all the studies and my much brighter friends and the thousand irritating details of living alone, and that I had really learned nothing, save perhaps how to put on a necktie while sprinting to class. I felt as if I had plunged too deep into the world, which, to my great horror, was much larger than I had ever imagined.

I welcomed the lull of the motel room. My father and I had nearly dozed off when my   50 mother jumped up excitedly, murmured how stupid she was, and hurried to the closet by the door. She pulled out our old metal cooler and dragged it between the beds. She lifted the top and began unpacking plastic containers, and I thought she would never stop. One after the other they came out, each with a dish that travelled well—a salted stewed meat, rolls of Korean-style sushi. I opened a container of radish kimchi and suddenly the room bloomed with its odor, and I reveled in the very peculiar sensation (which perhaps only true kimchi lovers know) of simultaneously drooling and gagging as I breathed it all in. For the next few minutes, they watched me eat. I'm not certain that I was even hungry. But after weeks of pork parmigiana and chicken patties and wax beans, I suddenly realized that I had lost all the savor in my life. And it seemed I couldn't get enough of it back. I ate and I ate, so much and so fast that I actually went to the bathroom and vomited. I came out dizzy and sated with the phantom warmth of my binge.

And beneath the face of her worry, I thought, my mother was smiling.

From that day, my mother prepared a certain meal to welcome me home. It was always the same. Even as I rode the school's shuttle bus from Exeter to Logan airport, I could already see the exact arrangement of my mother's table.

I knew that we would eat in the kitchen, the table brimming with plates. There was the *kalbi*, of course, broiled or grilled depending on the season. Leaf lettuce, to wrap the meat with. Bowls of garlicky clam broth with miso and tofu and fresh spinach. Shavings of cod dusted in flour and then dipped in egg wash and fried. Glass noodles with onions and shiitake. Scallion-and-hot-pepper pancakes. Chilled steamed shrimp. Seasoned salads of bean sprouts, spinach, and white radish. Crispy squares of seaweed. Steamed rice with barley and red beans. Homemade kimchi. It was all there—the old flavors I knew, the beautiful salt, the sweet, the excellent taste.

After the meal, my father and I talked about school, but of course I could never say enough for it to make any sense. My father would often recall his high-school principal, who had gone to England to study the methods and traditions of the public schools, and regaled students with stories of the great Eton man. My mother sat with us, paring fruit, not saying a word but taking everything in. When it was time to go to bed, my father said good night first. I usually watched television until the early morning. My mother would sit with me for an hour or two, perhaps until she was accustomed to me again, and only then would she kiss me and head upstairs to sleep.

During the following days, it was always the cooking that started our conversations. 55
She'd hold an inquest over the cold leftovers we ate at lunch, discussing each dish in terms of its balance of flavors or what might have been prepared differently. But mostly I begged her to leave the dishes alone. I wish I had paid more attention. After her death, when my father and I were the only ones left in the house, drifting through the rooms like ghosts, I sometimes tried to make that meal for him. Though it was too much for two, I made each dish anyway, taking as much care as I could. But nothing turned out quite right—not the color, not the smell. At the table, neither of us said much of anything. And we had to eat the food for days.

I remember washing rice in the kitchen one day, and my mother's saying in English, from her usual seat, "I made a big mistake."

"About Exeter?"

"Yes. I made a big mistake. You should be with us for that time. I should never let you go there."

"So why did you?" I said.

"Because I didn't know I was going to die." 60

I let her words pass. For the first time in her life, she was letting herself speak her full mind, so what else could I do?

"But you know what?" she spoke up. "It was better for you. If you stayed home, you would not like me so much now."

I suggested that maybe I would like her even more.

She shook her head. "Impossible."

Sometimes I still think about what she said, about having made a mistake. I would have 65
left home for college, that was never in doubt, but those years I was away at boarding school grew more precious to her as her illness progressed. After many months of exhaustion and pain and the haze of the drugs, I thought that her mind was beginning to fade, for more and more it seemed that she was seeing me again as her fifteen-year-old boy, the one she had dropped off in New Hampshire on a cloudy September afternoon.

I remember the first person I met, another new student, named Zack, who walked to the welcome picnic with me. I had planned to eat with my parents—my mother had brought a coolerful of food even that first day—but I learned of the cookout and told her that I should probably go. I wanted to go, of course. I was excited, and no doubt fearful and nervous, and I must have thought I was only thinking ahead. She agreed wholeheartedly, saying I certainly should. I walked them to the car, and perhaps I hugged them, before saying goodbye. One day, after she died, my father told me what happened on the long drive home to Syracuse.

He was driving the car, looking straight ahead. Traffic was light on the Massachusetts Turnpike, and the sky was nearly dark. They had driven for more than two hours and had not yet spoken a word. He then heard a strange sound from her, a kind of muffled chewing noise, as if something inside her were grinding its way out.

"So, what's the matter?" he said, trying to keep an edge to his voice.

She looked at him with her ashen face and she burst into tears. He began to cry himself, and pulled the car over onto the narrow shoulder of the turnpike, where they stayed for the next half hour or so, the blank-faced cars droning by them in the cold, onrushing night.

Every once in a while, when I think of her, I'm driving alone somewhere on the high- 70 way. In the twilight, I see their car off to the side, a blue Olds coupe with a landau top, and as I pass them by I look back in the mirror and I see them again, the two figures huddling together in the front seat. Are they sleeping? Or kissing? Are they all right?

Questions

1. In one sentence, describe the main point of "Coming Home Again." How do each of the individual narratives in the essay reinforce your sentence?

2. Lee uses dialogue in his narrative. Think about an important or memorable conversation in your life. Briefly describe the situation—who was part of the conversation and when and where it took place. What made it important or memorable? Are there other moments or conversations that came before or after that you can relate or connect to that conversation?

Susan Allen Toth [b. 1940]

Boyfriends

Born in the Midwestern United States, **Susan Allen Toth** earned her B.A. at Smith College, her M.A. from the University of California–Berkeley, and her Ph.D. from the University of Minnesota in 1969. Place plays a prominent role in Toth's writing, as evidenced from her autobiography *Blooming: A Small-Town Girlhood* (1981) and *Leaning into the Wind: A Memoir of Midwest Weather* (2003). Toth has written a few books on England, including *My Love Affair with England* (1992), *England As You Like It* (1995), and *England for All Seasons* (1997). She is a frequent contributor to such popular publications as the *New York Times*, the *Washington Post*, *Harper's*, *Ms.*, and *Vogue*.

In her essay "Boyfriends," which was excerpted from *Blooming*, Toth narrates her experiences with her first boyfriend in high school. The action culminates in her first kiss, which she returned with a lick on her astonished boyfriend's cheek.

Just when I was approaching sixteen, I found Peter Stone. Or did he find me? Perhaps I magicked him into existence out of sheer need. I was spooked by the boys who teased us nice girls about being sweet-sixteen-and-never-been-kissed. I felt that next to being an old maid forever, it probably was most demeaning to reach sixteen and not to have experienced the kind of ardent embrace Gordon MacRae periodically bestowed on Kathryn Grayson between choruses of "Desert Song." I was afraid I would never have a real boyfriend, never go parking, never know true love. So when Peter Stone asked his friend Ted to ask Ted's girl-friend Emily who asked me if I would ever neck with anyone, I held my breath until Emily told me she had said to Ted to tell Peter that maybe I would.

Not that Peter Stone had ever necked with anyone either. But I didn't realize that for a long time. High-school courtship usually was meticulously slow, progressing through in-quiry, phone calls, planned encounters in public places, double or triple dates, single dates, handholding, and finally a good-night kiss. I assumed it probably stopped there, but I didn't know. I had never gotten that far. I had lots of time to learn about Peter Stone. What I knew at the beginning already attracted me. He was a year ahead of me, vice-president of Hi-Y, a shot-putter who had just managed to earn a letter sweater. An older man, *and* an athlete. Tall, heavy, and broad-shouldered, Peter had a sweet slow smile. Even at a distance there was something endearing about the way he would blink nearsightedly through his glasses and light up with pleased recognition when he saw me coming toward him down the hall.

For a long while I didn't come too close. Whenever I saw Peter he was in the midst of his gang, a group of five boys as close and as self-protective as any clique we girls had. They were an odd mixture: Jim, an introspective son of a lawyer; Brad, a sullen hot-rodder; Ted, an unambitious and gentle boy from a poor family; Andy, a chubby comedian; and Peter. I was a little afraid of all of them, and they scrutinized me carefully before opening their circle to admit me, tentatively, as I held tight to Peter's hand. The lawyer's son had a steady girl, a fast number who was only in eighth grade but looked eighteen; the hot-rodder was reputed to have "gone all the way" with his adoring girl, a coarse brunette with plucked eyebrows; gentle Ted pursued my friend Emily with hangdog tenacity; but Peter had never shown real interest in a girlfriend before.

Although I had decided to go after Peter, I was hesitant about how to plot my way into the interior of his world. It was a thicket of strange shrubs and tangled branches. Perhaps I see it that way because I remember the day Peter took me to a wild ravine to shoot his gun. Girls who went with one of "the guys" commiserated with each other that their boyfriends all preferred two other things to them: their cars and their guns. Although Peter didn't hunt and seldom went to practice at the target range, still he valued his gun. Without permits, "the guys" drove outside of town to fire their guns illegally. I had read enough in my *Seventeen* about how to attract boys to know I needed to show enthusiasm about Peter's hobbies, so I asked him if someday he would take me someplace and teach me how to shoot.

One sunny fall afternoon he did. I remember rattling over gravel roads into a rambling   5 countryside that had surprising valleys and woods around cultivated farmland. Eventually we stopped before a barred gate that led to an abandoned bridge, once a railroad trestle, now a splintering wreck. We had to push our way through knee-high weeds to get past the gate. I was afraid of snakes. Peter took my hand; it was the first time he had ever held it, and my knees weakened a little. I was also scared of walking onto the bridge, which had broken boards and sudden gaps that let you look some fifty feet down into the golden and rust-colored brush below. But I didn't mind being a little scared as long as Peter was there to take care of me.

I don't think I had ever held a gun until Peter handed me his pistol, a heavy metal weapon that looked something like the ones movie sheriffs carried in their holsters. I was impressed by its weight and power. Peter fired it twice to show me how and then stood close to me, watching carefully, while I aimed at an empty beer can he tossed into the air. I didn't hit it. The noise of the gun going off was terrifying. I hoped nobody was walking in the woods where I had aimed. Peter said nobody was, nobody ever came here. When I put the gun down, he put his arm around me, very carefully. He had never done that before, either. We both just stood there, looking off into the distance, staring at the glowing maples and elms, dark red patches of sumac, brown heaps of leaves. The late afternoon sun beat down on us. It was hot, and after a few minutes Peter shifted uncomfortably. I moved away, laughing nervously, and we walked back to the car, watching the gaping boards at our feet.

What Peter and I did with our time together is a mystery. I try to picture us at movies or parties or somebody's house, but all I can see is the two of us in Peter's car. "Going for a drive!" I'd fling at my mother as I rushed out of the house; "rinking" was our high-school term for it, drawn from someone's contempt for the greasy "hoods" who hung out around the rollerskating rink and skidded around corners on two wheels of their souped-up cars. Peter's car barely made it around a corner on all four wheels. Though he had learned something about how to keep his huge square Ford running, he wasn't much of a mechanic. He could make jokes about the Ford, but he didn't like anyone else, including me, to say it looked like an old black hearse or remind him it could scarcely do forty miles an hour on an open stretch of highway. Highways were not where we drove, anyway, nor was speed a necessity unless you were trying to catch up with someone who hadn't seen you. "Rinking" meant cruising aimlessly around town, looking for friends in *their* cars, stopping for conversations shouted out of windows, maybe parking somewhere for a while, ending up at the A&W Root Beer Stand or the pizza parlor or the Rainbow Cafe.

Our parents were often puzzled about why we didn't spend time in each other's homes. "Why don't you invite Peter in?" my mother would ask a little wistfully, as I grabbed my billfold and cardigan and headed toward the door. Sometimes Peter would just pause in front of the house and honk; if I didn't come out quickly, he assumed I wasn't home and drove away. Mother finally made me tell him at least to come to the door and knock. I couldn't explain to her why we didn't want to sit in the living room, or go down to the pine-paneled basement at the Harbingers', or swing on the Harrises' front porch. We might not have been bothered at any of those places, but we really wouldn't have been alone. Cars were our private space, a rolling parlor, the only place we could relax and be ourselves. We could talk, fiddle with the radio if we didn't have much to say, look out the window, watch for friends passing by. Driving gave us a feeling of freedom.

Most of my memories of important moments with Peter center in that old black Ford. One balmy summer evening I remember particularly because my friend Emily said I would. Emily and Ted were out cruising in his rusty two-tone Chevy, the lawyer's son Jim and his girl had his father's shiny Buick, and Peter and I were out driving in the Ford. As we rumbled slowly down the Main Street, quiet and dark at night, Peter saw Ted's car approaching. We stopped in the middle of the street so the boys could exchange a few laconic grunts while Emily and I smiled confidentially at each other. We were all in a holiday mood, lazy and happy in the warm breezes that swept through the open windows. One of us suggested that we all meet later at Camp Canwita, a wooded park a few miles north of town. Whoever saw Jim would tell him to join us too. We weren't sure what we would do there, but it sounded like an adventure. An hour or so later, Peter and I bumped over the potholes in the road that twisted through the woods to the parking lot. We were the first ones there. When Peter turned off the motor, we could hear grasshoppers thrumming on all sides of us and leaves rustling in the dark. It was so quiet, so remote, I was a little frightened, remembering one of my mother's unnerving warnings about the dangerous men who sometimes preyed upon couples who parked in secluded places. We didn't have long to wait, though, before Ted's car coughed and sputtered down the drive. Soon Jim arrived too, and then we all pulled our cars close together in a kind of circle so we could talk easily out the windows. Someone's radio was turned on, and Frank Sinatra's mournful voice began to sing softly of passing days and lost love. Someone suggested that we get out of the cars and dance. It wouldn't have been Peter, who was seldom romantic. Ted opened his door so the overhead light cast a dim glow over the tiny area between the cars. Solemnly, a little self-consciously, we began the shuffling steps that were all we knew of what we called "slow dancing." Peter was not a good dancer, nor was I, though I liked putting my head on his bulky shoulder. But he moved me around the small lighted area as best he could, trying not to bump into Ted and Emily or Jim and his girl. I tried not to step on his toes. While Sinatra, Patti Page, and the Four Freshmen sang to us about moments to remember and Cape Cod, we all danced, one-two back, one-two back. Finally Emily, who was passing by my elbow, looked significantly at me and said, "This is something we'll be able to tell our grandchildren." Yes, I nodded, but I wasn't so sure. The mosquitoes were biting my legs and arms, my toes hurt, and I was getting a little bored. I think the others were too, because before long we all got into our cars and drove away.

Not all the time we spent in Peter's car was in motion. After several months, we did begin parking on deserted country roads, side streets, even sometimes my driveway, if my mother had heeded my fierce instructions to leave the light turned off. For a while we simply sat and talked with Peter's arm draped casually on the back of the seat. Gradually I moved a little closer. Soon he had his arm around me, but even then it was a long time before he managed to kiss me good-night. Boys must have been as scared as we girls were, though we   10 always thought of them as having much more experience. We all compared notes, shyly, about how far our boyfriends had gone; was he holding your hand yet, or taking you parking, or…? When a girl finally got kissed, telephone lines burned with the news next day. I was getting a little embarrassed about how long it was taking Peter to get around to it. My sixteenth birthday was only a few weeks away, and so far I had nothing substantial to report. I was increasingly nervous too because I still didn't know quite how I was going to behave. We girls joked about wondering where your teeth went and did glasses get in the way, but no one could give a convincing description. For many years I never told anyone about what *did* happen to me that first time. I was too ashamed. Peter and I were parked down the street from my house, talking, snuggling, listening to the radio. During a silence I turned my face toward him, and then he kissed me, tentatively and quickly. I was exhilarated but frightened. I wanted to respond in an adequate way but my instincts did not entirely cooperate. I leaned towards Peter, but at the last moment I panicked. Instead of kissing him, I gave him a sudden lick on the cheek. He didn't know what to say. Neither did I.

Next morning I was relieved that it was all over. I dutifully reported my news to a few key girlfriends who could pass it on to others. I left out the part about the lick. That was my last bulletin. After a first kiss, we girls also respected each other's privacy. What more was there to know? We assumed that couples sat in their cars and necked, but nice girls, we also assumed, went no farther. We knew the girls who did. Their names got around. We marveled at them, uncomprehending as much as disapproving. Usually they talked about getting married to their boyfriends, and eventually some of them did. A lot of "nice" girls suffered under this distinction. One of them told me years later how she and her steady boyfriend had yearned and held back, stopped just short, petted and clutched and gritted their teeth. "When we went together to see the movie *Splendor in the Grass*, we had to leave the theater," she said ruefully. "The part about how Natalie Wood and Warren Beatty wanted to make love so desperately and couldn't…. Well, that was just how we felt."

My mother worried about what was going on in the car during those long evenings when Peter and I went "out driving." She needn't have. Amazing as it seems now, when courting has speeded up to a freeway pace, when I wonder if a man who doesn't try to get me to bed immediately might possibly be gay, Peter and I gave each other hours of affection without ever crossing the invisible line. We sat in his car and necked, a word that was anatomically correct. We hugged and kissed, nuzzling ears and noses and hairlines. But Peter never put a hand on my breast, and I wouldn't have known whether Peter had an erection if it had risen up and thwapped me in the face. I never got that close. Although we probably should have perished from frustration, in fact I reveled in all that holding and touching. Peter seemed pleased too, and he never demanded more. Later, I suppose, he learned quickly with someone else about what he had been missing. But I remember with gratitude Peter's awkward tenderness and the absolute faith I had in his inability to hurt me.

After Peter graduated and entered the university, our relationship changed. Few high-school girls I knew went out with college men; it was considered risky, like dating someone not quite in your social set or from another town. You were cut off. At the few fraternity functions Peter took me to, I didn't know anyone there. I had no idea what to talk about or how to act. So I refused to go, and I stopped asking Peter to come with me to parties or dances at the high school. I thought he didn't fit in there either. When I was honest with myself, I admitted that romance had gone. Already planning to go away to college, I could sense new vistas opening before me, glowing horizons whose light completely eclipsed a boyfriend like Peter. When I got on the Chicago & Northwestern train to go east to Smith, I felt with relief that the train trip was erasing one problem for me. I simply rode away from Peter.

On my sixteenth birthday, Peter gave me a small cross on a chain. All the guys had decided that year to give their girlfriends crosses on chains, even though none of them was especially religious. It was a perfect gift, they thought, intimate without being soppy. Everyone's cross cost ten dollars, a lot of money, because it was real sterling silver. Long after Peter and I stopped seeing each other, I kept my cross around my neck, not taking it off even when I was in the bathtub. Like my two wooden dolls from years before, I clung to that cross as a superstitious token. It meant that someone I had once cared for had cared for me in return. Once I had had a boyfriend.

Questions

1. How does the narrator convince readers that Peter was more at fault for their breakup? What language and rhetorical strategies does she use to specifically try and convince the reader of this?

2. Imagine you are driving back to campus with a friend after seeing a movie in Christiansburg and you hit a lamppost. If you had to call and tell your parents about the accident, what would you say? How would you explain it to your friends? What about your insurance company? Which details would you emphasize in each version, and which would you leave out? How would your tone and language change for each audience? Why?

David Sedaris [b. 1956]
A Plague of Tics

Humorist and best-selling author **David Sedaris** was born on December 26, 1956, in Johnson City, New York, and raised in Raleigh, North Carolina. The second of six children, Sedaris was inclined to visual and performance arts as a boy and attended Western Carolina University and Kent State University before finally graduating from the School of the Art Institute of Chicago, where he later taught writing part time, in 1987. Discovered while reading from a diary in a Chicago club by radio personality Ira Glass, Sedaris debuted locally, on Chicago Public Radio, on Glass's *The Wild Room*, before gaining national attention for his original "SantaLand Diaries" essay on National Public Radio's Morning Edition on December 23, 1992. Since then, he has written and published at least forty essays for the *New Yorker*, as well as seven individual essay collections and one short story collection. Often written from a very personal perspective, though arguably with a heavy dose of creative license, Sedaris's essays expose a range of moments of his life, both trivial and profound, from growing up in the South with his family to living abroad in France and England with his partner Hugh Hamrick. His books include *Naked* (1997), *Me Talk Pretty One Day* (2000), *Dress Your Family in Corduroy and Denim* (2004), and *Let's Explore Diabetes with Owls* (2013). Beyond print, Sedaris frequently performs his shorter works for Chicago WBEZ's *This American Life*, also hosted by Ira Glass, and the audiobook for *Dress Your Family in Corduroy and Denim* was nominated for a Grammy Award for Best Spoken Word Album. Additionally, Sedaris has written several plays in collaboration with his sister, actress Amy Sedaris.

In "A Plague of Tics," a self-deprecating tale collected in *Naked*, Sedaris describes the many ways symptoms of obsessive-compulsive disorder manifested throughout his childhood and into his college years. Recounting interactions with teachers and family—and how they experienced his eccentricities—Sedaris struggles to reconcile his behaviors and quirks with those of others, including his parents and his college roommate.

When the teacher asked if she might visit with my mother, I touched my nose eight times to the surface of my desk.

"May I take that as a 'yes'?" she asked.

According to her calculations, I had left my chair twenty-eight times that day. "You're up and down like a flea. I turn my back for two minutes and there you are with your tongue pressed against that light switch. Maybe they do that where you come from, but here in my classroom we don't leave our seats and lick things whenever we please. That is Miss Chestnut's light switch, and she likes to keep it dry. Would you like me to come over to your house and put my tongue on *your* light switches? Well, would you?"

I tried to picture her in action, but my shoe was calling. *Take me off*, it whispered. *Tap my heel against your forehead three times. Do it now, quick, no one will notice.*

"Well?" Miss Chestnut raised her faint, penciled eyebrows. "I'm asking you a question. 5 Would you or would you not want me licking the light switches in your house?"

I slipped off my shoe, pretending to examine the imprint on the heel.

"You're going to hit yourself over the head with that shoe, aren't you?"

It wasn't "hitting," it was tapping; but still, how had she known what I was about to do?

"Heel marks all over your forehead," she said, answering my silent question.

"You should take a look in the mirror sometime. Shoes are dirty things. We wear them   10
on our feet to protect ourselves against the soil. It's not healthy to hit ourselves over the head
with shoes, is it?"

I guessed that it was not.

"Guess? This is not a game to be guessed at. I don't 'guess' that it's dangerous to run into
traffic with a paper sack over my head. There's no guesswork involved. These things are facts,
not riddles." She sat at her desk, continuing her lecture as she penned a brief letter. "I'd like
to have a word with your mother. You do have one, don't you? I'm assuming you weren't
raised by animals. Is she blind, your mother? Can she see the way you behave, or do you
reserve your antics exclusively for Miss Chestnut?" She handed me the folded slip of paper.
"You may go now, and on your way out the door I'm asking you please not to bathe my light
switch with your germ-ridden tongue. It's had a long day; we both have."

It was a short distance from the school to our rented house, no more than six hundred
and thirty-seven steps, and on a good day I could make the trip in an hour, pausing every
few feet to tongue a mailbox or touch whichever single leaf or blade of grass demanded my
attention. If I were to lose count of my steps, I'd have to return to the school and begin again.
"Back so soon?" the janitor would ask. "You just can't get enough of this place, can you?"

He had it all wrong. I wanted to be at home more than anything, it was getting there
that was the problem. I might touch the telephone pole at step three hundred and fourteen
and then, fifteen paces later, worry that I hadn't touched it in exactly the right spot. It needed
to be touched again. I'd let my mind wander for one brief moment and then doubt had set
in, causing me to question not just the telephone pole but also the lawn ornament back at
step two hundred and nineteen. I'd have to go back and lick that concrete mushroom one
more time, hoping its guardian wouldn't once again rush from her house shouting, "Get
your face out of my toadstool!" It might be raining or maybe I had to go to the bathroom,
but running home was not an option. This was a long and complicated process that demanded an oppressive attention to detail. It wasn't that I enjoyed pressing my nose against
the scalding hood of a parked car—pleasure had nothing to do with it. A person *had* to do
these things because nothing was worse than the anguish of not doing them. Bypass that
mailbox and my brain would never for one moment let me forget it. I might be sitting at the
dinner table, daring myself not to think about it, and the thought would revisit my mind.
Don't think about it. But it would already be too late and I knew then exactly what I had to
do. Excusing myself to go to the bathroom, I'd walk out the front door and return to that
mailbox, not just touching but jabbing, practically pounding on the thing because I thought
I hated it so much. What I really hated, of course, was my mind. There must have been an
off switch somewhere, but I was damned if I could find it.

I didn't remember things being this way back north. Our family had been transferred   15
from Endicott, New York, to Raleigh, North Carolina. That was the word used by the people
at IBM, *transferred*. A new home was under construction, but until it was finished we were
confined to a rental property built to resemble a plantation house. The building sat in a tree-
less, balding yard, its white columns promising a majesty the interior failed to deliver. The
front door opened onto a dark, narrow hallway lined with bedrooms not much larger than
the mattresses that furnished them. Our kitchen was located on the second floor, alongside

the living room, its picture window offering a view of the cinder-block wall built to hold back the tide of mud generated by the neighboring dirt mound.

"Our own little corner of hell," my mother said, fanning herself with one of the shingles littering the front yard.

Depressing as it was, arriving at the front stoop of the house meant that I had completed the first leg of that bitter-tasting journey to my bedroom. Once home I would touch the front door seven times with each elbow, a task made more difficult if there was someone else around. "Why don't you try the knob," my sister Lisa would say. "That's what the rest of us do, and it seems to work for us." Inside the house there were switches and doorstops to be acknowledged. My bedroom was right there off the hallway, but first I had business to tend to. After kissing the fourth, eighth, and twelfth carpeted stair, I wiped the cat hair off my lips and proceeded to the kitchen, where I was commanded to stroke the burners of the stove, press my nose against the refrigerator door, and arrange the percolator, toaster, and blender into a straight row. After making my rounds of the living room, it was time to kneel beside the banister and blindly jab a butter knife in the direction of my favorite electrical socket. There were bulbs to lick and bathroom faucets to test before finally I was free to enter my bedroom, where I would carefully align the objects on my dresser, lick the corners of my metal desk, and lie upon my bed, rocking back and forth and thinking of what an odd woman she was, my third-grade teacher, Miss Chestnut. Why come here and lick my switches when she never used the one she had? Maybe she was drunk.

Her note had asked if she might visit our home in order to discuss what she referred to as my "special problems."

"Have you been leaving your seat to lick the light switch?" my mother asked. She placed the letter upon the table and lit a cigarette.

"Once or twice," I said.   20

"Once or twice what? Every half hour? Every ten minutes?"

"I don't know," I lied. "Who's counting?"

"Well, your goddamned math teacher, for one. That's her *job*, to count. What, do you think she's not going to notice?"

"Notice what?" It never failed to amaze me that people might notice these things. Because my actions were so intensely private, I had always assumed they were somehow invisible. When cornered, I demanded that the witness had been mistaken.

"What do you mean, 'notice what?' I got a phone call just this afternoon from that lady 25 up the street, that Mrs. Keening, the one with the twins. She says she caught you in her front yard, down on your hands and knees kissing the evening edition of her newspaper."

"I wasn't kissing it. I was just trying to read the headline."

"And you had to get that close? Maybe we need to get you some stronger glasses."

"Well, maybe we do," I said.

"And I suppose this Miss..." My mother unfolded the letter and studied the signature. "This Miss Chestnut is mistaken, too? Is that what you're trying to tell me? Maybe she has you confused with the other boy who leaves his seat to lick the pencil sharpener or touch the flag or whatever the hell it is you do the moment her back is turned?"

"That's very likely," I said. "She's old. There are spots on her hands."   30

"How many?" my mother asked.

On the afternoon that Miss Chestnut arrived for her visit, I was in my bedroom, rocking. Unlike the obsessive counting and touching, rocking was not a mandatory duty but a voluntary and highly pleasurable exercise. It was my hobby, and there was nothing else I would rather do. The point was not to rock oneself to sleep: This was not a step toward some greater goal. It was the goal itself. The perpetual movement freed my mind, allowing me to mull things over and construct elaborately detailed fantasies. Toss in a radio, and I was content to rock until three or four o'clock in the morning, listening to the hit parade and discovering that each and every song was about me. I might have to listen two or three hundred times to the same song, but sooner or later its private message would reveal itself. Because it was pleasant and relaxing, my rocking was bound to be tripped up, most often by my brain, which refused to allow me more than ten consecutive minutes of happiness. At the opening chords of my current favorite song, a voice would whisper, *Shouldn't you be upstairs making sure there are really one hundred and fourteen peppercorns left in that small ceramic jar? And, hey, while you're up there, you might want to check the iron and make sure it's not setting fire to the baby's bedroom.* The list of demands would grow by the moment. *What about that television antenna? Is it still set into that perfect V, or has one of your sisters destroyed its integrity. You know, I was just wondering how tightly the lid is screwed onto that mayonnaise jar. Let's have a look, shall we?*

I would be just on the edge of truly enjoying myself, this close to breaking the song's complex code, when my thoughts would get in the way. The trick was to bide my time until the record was no longer my favorite, to wait until it had slipped from its number-one position on the charts and fool my mind into believing I no longer cared.

I was coming to terms with "The Shadow of Your Smile" when Miss Chestnut arrived. She rang the bell, and I cracked open my bedroom door, watching as my mother invited her in.

"You'll have to forgive me for these boxes." My mother flicked her cigarette out the door   35 and into the littered yard. "They're filled with crap, every last one of them, but God forbid we throw anything away. Oh no, we can't do that! My husband's saved it all: every last Green Stamp and coupon, every outgrown bathing suit and scrap of linoleum, it's all right here along with the rocks and knotted sticks he swears look just like his old department head or associate district manager or some goddamned thing." She mopped at her forehead with a wadded paper towel. "Anyway, to hell with it. You look like I need a drink, scotch all right?"

Miss Chestnut's eyes brightened. "I really shouldn't but, oh, why not?" She followed my mother up the stairs. "Just a drop with ice, no water."

I tried rocking in bed, but the sound of laughter drew me to the top of the landing, where from my vantage point behind an oversized wardrobe box, I watched the two women discuss my behavior.

"Oh, you mean the touching," my mother said. She studied the ashtray that sat before her on the table, narrowing her eyes much like a cat catching sight of a squirrel. Her look of fixed concentration suggested that nothing else mattered. Time had stopped, and she was deaf to the sounds of the rattling fan and my sisters' squabbling out in the driveway. She opened her mouth just slightly, running her tongue over her upper lip, and then she inched forward, her index finger prodding the ashtray as though it were a sleeping thing she was trying to wake. I had never seen myself in action, but a sharp, stinging sense of recognition told me that my mother's impersonation had been accurate.

"Priceless!" Miss Chestnut laughed, clasping her hands in delight. "Oh, that's very good, you've captured him perfectly. Bravo, I give you an A-plus."

"God only knows where he gets it from," my mother said. "He's probably down in his room right this minute, counting his eyelashes or gnawing at the pulls on his dresser. One, two o'clock in the morning and he'll still be at it, rattling around the house to poke the laundry hamper or press his face against the refrigerator door. The kid's wound too tight, but he'll come out of it. So, what do you say, another scotch, Katherine?"

Now she was Katherine. Another few drinks and she'd probably be joining us for our summer vacation. How easy it was for adults to bond over a second round of cocktails. I returned to my bed, cranking up the radio so as not to be distracted by the sound of their cackling. Because Miss Chestnut was here in my home, I knew it was only a matter of time before the voices would order me to enter the kitchen and make a spectacle of myself. Maybe I'd have to suck on the broom handle or stand on the table to touch the overhead light fixture, but whatever was demanded of me, I had no choice but to do it. The song that played on the radio posed no challenge whatsoever, the lyric as clear as if I'd written it myself. "Well, I think I'm going out of my head," the man sang, "yes, I think I'm going out of my head."

Following Miss Chestnut's visit, my father attempted to cure me with a series of threats. "You touch your nose to that windshield one more time and I'll guarantee you'll wish you hadn't," he said driving home from the grocery store with a lapful of rejected, out-of-state coupons. It was virtually impossible for me to ride in the passenger seat of a car and not press my nose against the windshield, and now that the activity had been forbidden, I wanted it more than anything. I tried closing my eyes, hoping that might eliminate my desire, but found myself thinking that perhaps *he* was the one who should close his eyes. So what if I wanted to touch my nose to the windshield? Who was it hurting? Why was it that he could repeatedly worry his change and bite his lower lip without the threat of punishment? My mother smoked and Miss Chestnut massaged her waist twenty, thirty times a day—and here *I* couldn't press my nose against the windshield of a car? I opened my eyes, defiant, but when he caught me moving toward my target, my father slammed on the brakes. "You like that, did you?" He handed me a golf towel to wipe the blood from my nose. "Did you like the feel of that?"

Like was too feeble for what I felt. I loved it. If mashed with the right amount of force, a blow to the nose can be positively narcotic. Touching objects satisfied a mental itch, but the task involved a great deal of movement: run upstairs, cross the room, remove a shoe. I soon found those same urges could be fulfilled within the confines of my own body. Punching myself in the nose was a good place to start, but the practice was dropped when I began rolling my eyes deep in their sockets, an exercise that produced quick jolts of dull, intoxicating pain.

"I know exactly what you're talking about," my mother said to Mrs. Shatz, my visiting fourth-grade teacher. "The eyes rolling every which way, it's like talking to a slot machine. Hopefully, one day he'll pay off, but until then, what do you say we have ourselves another glass of wine?"

"Hey, sport," my father said, "if you're trying to get a good look at the contents of your skull, I can tell you right now that you're wasting your time. There's nothing there to look at, and these report cards prove it."

He was right. I had my nose pressed to the door, the carpet, and the windshield but not, apparently, to the grindstone. School held no interest whatsoever. I spent my days waiting to return to the dark bedroom of our new house, where I could roll my eyes, listen to the radio, and rock in peace.

I took to violently shaking my head, startled by the feel of my brain slamming against the confines of my skull. It felt so good and took so little time; just a few quick jerks and I was satisfied for up to forty-five seconds at a time.

"Have a seat and let me get you something cool to drink." My mother would leave my fifth- and then my sixth-grade teachers standing in the breakfast nook while she stepped into the kitchen to crack open a tray of ice. "I'm guessing you're here about the head-shaking, am I right?" she'd shout. "That's my boy, all right, no flies on him." She suggested my teachers interpret my jerking head as a nod of agreement. "That's what I do, and now I've got him washing the dishes for the next five years. I ask, he yanks his head, and it's settled. Do me a favor, though, and just don't hold him after five o'clock. I need him at home to straighten up and make the beds before his father gets home."

This was part of my mother's act. She played the ringleader, blowing the whistle and 50 charming the crowd with her jokes and exaggerated stories. When company came, she often pretended to forget the names of her six children. "Hey, George, or Agnes, whatever your name is, how about running into the bedroom and finding my cigarette lighter." She noticed my tics and habits but was never shamed or seriously bothered by any of them. Her observations would be collected and delivered as part of a routine that bore little resemblance to our lives.

"It's a real stretch, but I'm betting you're here about the tiny voices," she said, offering a glass of sherry to my visiting seventh-grade teacher. "I'm thinking of either taking him to an exorcist or buying him a doll so he can bring home some money as a ventriloquist."

It had come out of nowhere, my desperate urge to summon high-pitched noises from the back of my throat. These were not words, but sounds that satisfied an urge I'd never before realized. The sounds were delivered not in my voice but in that of a thimble-sized, temperamental diva clinging to the base of my uvula. "Eeeeeeeee—ummmmmmmmm-mmm—ahhhh—ahhh—meeeeeeee." I was a host to these wailings but lacked the ability to control them. When I cried out in class, the teachers would turn from their blackboards with increasingly troubled expressions. "Is someone rubbing a balloon? Who's making that noise?"

I tried making up excuses, but everything sounded implausible. "There's a bee living in my throat." Or "If I don't exercise my vocal cords every three minutes, there's a good chance I'll never swallow again." The noise-making didn't replace any of my earlier habits, it was just another addition to what had become a freakish collection of tics. Worse than the constant yelps and twitchings was the fear that tomorrow might bring something even worse, that I would wake up with the urge to jerk other people's heads. I might go for days without rolling my eyes, but it would all come back the moment my father said, "See, I knew you could quit if you just put your mind to it. Now, if you can just keep your head still and stop making those noises, you'll be set."

Set for what? I wondered. Often while rocking, I would imagine my career as a movie star. There I was attending the premiere beneath a floodlit sky, a satin scarf tied just so around my throat. I understood that most actors probably didn't interrupt a love scene to press their noses against the camera or wail a quick "Eeeeeee—ahhhhhhh" during a dramatic monologue, but in my case the world would be willing to make an exception. "This is a moving and touching film," the papers would report. "An electrifying, eye-popping performance that has audiences squealing and the critics nodding, 'Oscar, Oscar, Oscar.'"

I'd like to think that some of my nervous habits faded during high school, but my class 55
pictures tell a different story. "Draw in the missing eyeballs and this one might not be so
bad," my mother would say. In group shots I was easily identified as the blur in the back
row. For a time I thought that if I accompanied my habits with an outlandish wardrobe, I
might be viewed as eccentric rather than just plain retarded. I was wrong. Only a confirmed
idiot would wander the halls of my high school dressed in a floor-length caftan; as for the
countless medallions that hung from around my neck, I might as well have worn a cowbell.
They clanged and jangled with every jerk of my head, calling attention when without them I
might have passed unnoticed. My oversized glasses did nothing but provide a clearer view of
my rolling, twitching eyes, and the clunky platform shoes left lumps when used to discreetly
tap my forehead. I was a mess.

I could be wrong, but according to my calculations, I got exactly fourteen minutes of
sleep during my entire first year of college. I'd always had my own bedroom, a meticulously
clean and well-ordered place where I could practice my habits in private. Now I would have
a roommate, some complete stranger spoiling my routine with his God-given right to exist.
The idea was mortifying, and I arrived at the university in full tilt.

"The doctors tell me that if I knock it around hard enough, there's a good chance the
brain tumor will shrink to the point where they won't have to operate," I said the first time
my roommate caught me jerking my head. "Meanwhile, these other specialists have me
doing these eye exercises to strengthen what they call the 'corneal fibers,' whatever that
means. They've got me coming and going, but what can you do, right? Anyway, you go
ahead and settle in. I think I'll just test this electrical socket with a butter knife and rearrange a few of the items on my dresser. Eeeee-sy does it. That's what I always s-ahhhhhhh."

It was hard enough coming up with excuses, but the real agony came when I was forced
to give up rocking.

"Give it a rest, Romeo," my roommate moaned the first night he heard my bedsprings
creak. He thought I was masturbating, and while I wanted to set the record straight, something told me I wouldn't score any points by telling him that I was simply rocking in bed,
just like any other eighteen-year-old college student. It was torture to lie there doing nothing. Even with a portable radio and earphones, there was no point listening to music unless
I could sway back and forth with my head on a pillow. Rocking is basically dancing in a
horizontal position, and it allowed me to practice in private what I detested in public. With
my jerking head, rolling eyes, and rapid stabbing gestures, I might have been a sensation if
I'd left my bed and put my tics to work on the dance floor. I should have told my roommate
that I was an epileptic and left it at that. He might have charged across the room every so
often to ram a Popsicle stick down my throat, but so what? I was used to picking splinters
out of my tongue. *What*, I wondered, *was an average person expected to do while stretched
out in a darkened room?* It felt pointless to lie there motionless and imagine a brighter life.
Squinting across the cramped, cinder-block cell, I realized that an entire lifetime of wishful
thinking had gotten me no further than this. There would be no cheering crowds or es-
teemed movie directors shouting into their bullhorns. I might have to take this harsh reality
lying down, but while attempting to do so, couldn't I rock back and forth just a little bit?

Having memorized my roommate's course schedule, I took to rushing back to the room 60
between classes, rocking in fitful spurts but never really enjoying it for fear he might return
at any moment. Perhaps he might feel ill or decide to cut class at the last minute. I'd hear his

key in the door and jump up from my bed, mashing down my wadded hair and grabbing one of the textbooks I kept on my prop table. "I'm just studying for that pottery test," I'd say. "That's all I've been up to, just sitting in this chair reading about the history of jugs." Hard as I tried, it always wound up sounding as if I were guilty of something secretive or perverse. *He* never acted in the least bit embarrassed when caught listening to one of his many heavy-metal albums, a practice far more shameful than anything I have yet to imagine. There was no other solution: I had to think of a way to get rid of this guy.

His biggest weakness appeared to be his girlfriend, whose photograph he had tacked in a place of honor above the stereo. They'd been dating since tenth grade, and while he had gone off to college, she'd stayed behind to attend a two-year nursing school in their home-town. A history of listening to Top 40 radio had left me with a ridiculous and clichéd notion of love. I had never entertained the feeling myself but knew that it meant never having to say you're sorry. It was a many-splendored thing. Love was a rose *and* a hammer. Both blind and all-seeing, it made the world go round.

My roommate thought that he and his girlfriend were strong enough to make it through the month without seeing each other, but I wasn't so sure. "I don't know that I'd trust her around all those doctors," I said. "Love fades when left untended, especially in a hospital environment. Absence might make the heart grow fonder, but love is a two-way street. Think about it."

When my roommate went out of town, I would spend the entire weekend rocking in bed and fantasizing about his tragic car accident. I envisioned him wrapped tight as a mummy, his arms and legs suspended by pulleys. "Time is a great healer," his mother would say, packing the last of his albums into a milk crate. "Two years of bed rest and he'll be as good as new. Once he gets out of the hospital, I figure I'll set him up in the living room. He likes it there."

Sometimes I would allow him to leave in one piece, imagining his joining the army or marrying his girlfriend and moving someplace warm and sunny, like Peru or Ethiopia. The important thing was that he leave this room and never come back. I'd get rid of him and then move on to the next person, and the one after that, until it was just me, rocking and jerking in private.

Two months into the semester, my roommate broke up with his girlfriend. "And I'm going to spend every day and night sitting right here in this room until I figure out where I went wrong." He dabbed his moist eyes with the sleeve of his flannel shirt. "You and me, little buddy. It's just you and me and Jethro Tull from here on out. Say, what's with your head? The old tumor acting up again?"   65

"College is the best thing that can ever happen to you," my father used to say, and he was right, for it was there that I discovered drugs, drinking, and smoking. I'm unsure of the scientific aspects, but for some reason, my nervous habits faded about the same time I took up with cigarettes. Maybe it was coincidental or perhaps the tics retreated in the face of an adversary that, despite its health risks, is much more socially acceptable than crying out in tiny voices. Were I not smoking, I'd probably be on some sort of medication that would cost the same amount of money but deny me the accoutrements: the lighters I can thoughtlessly open and close, the ashtrays that provide me with a legitimate reason to leave my chair, and the cigarettes that calm me down while giving me something to do with my hands and mouth. It's as if I had been born to smoke, and until I realized it, my limbs were left to search for some alternative. Everything's fine as long as I know there's a cigarette in my immediate future. The people who ask me not to smoke in their cars have no idea what they're in for.

"Remember when you used to roll your eyes?" my sisters ask. "Remember the time you shook your head so hard, your glasses fell into the barbeque pit?"

At their mention I sometimes attempt to revisit my former tics and habits. Returning to my apartment late at night, I'll dare myself to press my nose against the doorknob or roll my eyes to achieve that once-satisfying ache. Maybe I'll start counting the napkins sandwiched in their plastic holder, but the exercise lacks its old urgency and I soon lose interest. I would no sooner rock in bed than play "Up, Up, and Away" sixty times straight on my record player. I could easily listen to something else an equal number of times while seated in a rocking chair, but the earlier, bedridden method fails to comfort me, as I've forgotten the code, the twitching trick needed to decipher the lyrics to that particular song. I remember only that at one time the story involved the citizens of Raleigh, North Carolina, being herded into a test balloon of my own design and making. It was rigged to explode once it reached the city limits, but the passengers were unaware of that fact. The sun shone on their faces as they lifted their heads toward the bright blue sky, giddy with excitement.

"Beautiful balloon!" they all said, gripping the handrails and climbing the staircase to their fiery destiny. "Wouldn't you like to ride?"

"Sorry, folks," I'd say, pressing my nose against the surface of my ticket booth. "But I've got other duties." 70

[1997]

Questions

1. Titles can offer important clues about a text's purpose, tone, content, context, and intentions, yet we often overlook them. Consider the title of Sedaris's essay. What does this title suggest to you about Sedaris's intentions for this piece? What do you think you would have assumed about the tone, context, and content of the essay if you had only read the title? How does the title influence how you approach the essay as a reader?

2. How does Sedaris weave a narrative line through his observations of himself and others? Create an outline of Sedaris's piece. What do you notice?

Sandra Cisneros [b. 1954]

Only Daughter

Born in a Hispanic neighborhood in Chicago, **Sandra Cisneros** (b. 1954) spoke Spanish at home with her Mexican father, Chicana mother, and six brothers. At ten she began writing poetry, and soon experimented with other forms. In 1977, when she was studying in the M.F.A. program at the University of Iowa Writers' Workshop, she came to see herself as a Chicana writer. Cisneros has published three books of poems; a book of interrelated narratives, *The House on Mango Street* (1983); and a fiction collection, *Woman Hollering Creek and Other Stories* (1991).

Once, several years ago, when I was just starting out my writing career, I was asked to write my own contributor's note for an anthology I was part of. I wrote: "I am the only daughter in a family of six sons. *That* explains everything."

Well, I've thought about that ever since, and yes, it explains a lot to me, but for the reader's sake I should have written: "I am the only daughter in a *Mexican* family of six sons." Or even: "I am the only daughter of a Mexican father and a Mexican American mother." Or: "I am the only daughter of a working-class family of nine." All of these had everything to do with who I am today.

I was/am the only daughter and *only* a daughter. Being an only daughter in a family of six sons forced me by circumstance to spend a lot of time by myself because my brothers felt it beneath them to play with a *girl* in public. But that aloneness, that loneliness, was good for a would-be writer—it allowed me time to think and think, to imagine, to read and prepare myself.

Being only a daughter for my father meant my destiny would lead me to become someone's wife. That's what he believed. But when I was in fifth grade and shared my plans for college with him, I was sure he understood. I remember my father saying, "*Que bueno, mi'ja,* that's good." That meant a lot to me, especially since my brothers thought the idea hilarious. What I didn't realize was that my father thought college was good for girls—for finding a husband. After four years in college and two more in graduate school, and still no husband, my father shakes his head even now and says I wasted all that education.

In retrospect, I'm lucky my father believed daughters were meant for husbands. It 5 meant it didn't matter if I majored in something silly like English. After all, I'd find a nice professional eventually, right? This allowed me the liberty to putter about embroidering my little poems and stories without my father interrupting with so much as a "What's that you're writing?"

But the truth is, I wanted him to interrupt. I wanted my father to understand what it was I was scribbling, to introduce me as "My only daughter, the writer." Not as "This is my only daughter. She teaches." *El maestra*—teacher. Not even *profesora*.

In a sense, everything I have ever written has been for him, to win his approval even though I know my father can't read English words, even though my father's only reading includes the brown-ink *Esto* sports magazines from Mexico City and the bloody *¡Alarma!* magazines that feature yet another sighting of *La Virgen de Guadalupe* on a tortilla or a wife's revenge on her philandering husband by bashing his skull in with a *molcajete* (a kitchen mortar made of volcanic rock). Or the *fotonovelas,* the little picture paperbacks with tragedy and trauma erupting from the characters' mouths in bubbles.

My father represents, then, the public majority. A public who is uninterested in reading, and yet one whom I am writing about and for, and privately trying to woo.

When we were growing up in Chicago, we moved a lot because of my father. He suffered periodic bouts of nostalgia. Then we'd have to let go our flat, store the furniture with mother's relatives, load the station wagon with baggage and bologna sandwiches, and head south. To Mexico City.

We came back, of course. To yet another Chicago flat, another Chicago neighborhood,   10 another Catholic school. Each time, my father would seek out the parish priest in order to get a tuition break, and complain or boast: "I have seven sons."

He meant *siete hijos*, seven children, but he translated it as "sons." "I have seven sons." To anyone who would listen. The Sears Roebuck employee who sold us the washing machine. The short-order cook, where my father ate his ham-and-eggs breakfasts. "I have seven sons." As if he deserved a medal from the state.

My papa. He didn't mean anything by that mistranslation, I'm sure. But somehow I could feel myself being erased. I'd tug my father's sleeve and whisper: "Not seven sons. Six! and *one daughter*."

When my oldest brother graduated from medical school, he fulfilled my father's dream that we study hard and use this—our heads, instead of this—our hands. Even now my father's hands are thick and yellow, stubbed by a history of hammer and nails and twine and coils and springs. "Use this," my father said, tapping his head, "and not this," showing us those hands. He always looked tired when he said it.

Wasn't college an investment? And hadn't I spent all those years in college? And if I didn't marry, what was it all for? Why would anyone go to college and then choose to be poor? Especially someone who had always been poor.

Last year, after ten years of writing professionally, the financial rewards started to trickle   15 in. My second National Endowment for the Arts Fellowship. A guest professorship at the University of California, Berkeley. My book, which sold to a major New York publishing house.

At Christmas, I flew home to Chicago. The house was throbbing, same as always; hot *tamales* and sweet *tamales* hissing in my mother's pressure cooker, and everybody—mother, six brothers, wives, babies, aunts, cousins—talking too loud and at the same time, like in a Fellini film, because that's just how we are.

I went upstairs to my father's room. One of my stories had just been translated into Spanish and published in an anthology of Chicano writing, and I wanted to show it to him. Ever since he recovered from a stroke two years ago, my father likes to spend his leisure hours horizontally. And that's how I found him, watching a Pedro Infante movie on Galavision and eating rice pudding.

There was a glass filmed with milk on the bedside table. There were several vials of pills and balled Kleenex. And on the floor, one black sock and a plastic urinal that I didn't want to look at but looked at anyway. Pedro Infante was about to burst into song, and my father was laughing. I'm not sure if it was because my story was translated into Spanish, or because it was published in Mexico, or perhaps because the story dealt with Tepeyac, the *colonia* my father was raised in, but at any rate, my father punched the mute button on his remote control and read my story.

I sat on the bed next to my father and waited. He read it very slowly. As if he were 20
reading each line over and over. He laughed at all the right places and read lines he liked out
loud. He pointed and asked questions: "Is this So-and-so?" "Yes," I said. He kept reading.

When he was finally finished, after what seemed like hours, my father looked up and
asked: "Where can we get more copies of this for the relatives?"

Of all the wonderful things that happened to me last year, that was the most wonderful.

Questions

1. How does Cisneros transform from "only a daughter" to "only daughter" within the
    narrative? Why is the change significant?

2. What specifically does Cisneros's blend of English and Spanish help convey to her
    readers regarding her relationship with her family? If the piece were written entirely in
    English, how would that alter the effect of the piece?

3. Cisneros's use of specific details throughout the narrative gives her readers a deeper
    understanding of who or what she is describing (for instance, her father does not sim-
    ply read sports magazines, but "brown-ink *Esto* sports magazines from Mexico City"
    [para. 7]). Think of a unique person in your life, whether a family member or a close
    friend. Attempt to describe that person with the kind of precise detail Cisneros uses.

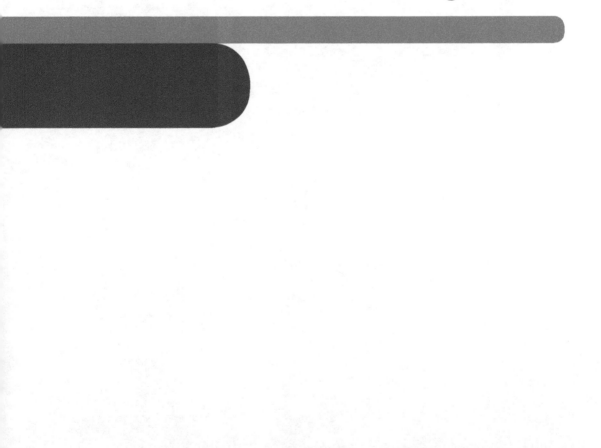

Rhetorical Analysis and Argument

Michael J. Arlen [b. 1930]

Ode to Thanksgiving

Essayist and nonfiction writer **Michael J. Arlen** was born in 1930 in France. His family moved to England in 1939, and then to the United States in 1941 to escape English intolerance of their Armenian heritage. Arlen's father, also named Michael, was a dandy of European high society who achieved wealth and fame with *The Green Hat* (1924), a work that captured the tumultuous postwar life of polite London society with its dry wit, jaded characters, and cynical outlook. Michael J. Arlen attended Harvard University and, following graduation, was employed as a writer for *Life* magazine. In 1966 his essays began appearing regularly in the *New Yorker*. Arlen's nonfiction includes *Exiles* (1970), a memoir of his family's early years in America and his father's grief over his fading literary career, *An American Verdict* (1973), and *Passage to Ararat* (1975), an exploration of Arlen's Armenian ancestry for which he was awarded a National Book Award. His essay collections, *Living-Room War* (1969), *View from Highway 1* (1976), and *The Camera Age* (1981), are entertaining and insightful.

Arlen's sardonic "Ode to Thanksgiving" pokes fun at the traditional American holiday with sarcastic jibes at the strain of family relations, the dreariness of November, and the "bowls of luridly colored yams." Arlen's satirical flippancy and fast-paced readability paint a colorful picture of Thanksgiving scenarios familiar to a great many Americans. This universality gives Arlen's cheeky performance its appeal.

It is time, at last, to speak the truth about Thanksgiving, and the truth is this. Thanksgiving is really not such a terrific holiday. Consider the traditional symbols of the event: Dried cornhusks hanging on the door! Terrible wine! Cranberry jelly in little bowls of extremely doubtful provenance which everyone is required to handle with the greatest of care! Consider the participants, the merrymakers: men and women (also children) who have survived passably well throughout the years, mainly as a result of living at considerable distances from their dear parents and beloved siblings, who on this feast of feasts must apparently forgather (as if beckoned by an aberrant Fairy Godmother), usually by circuitous routes, through heavy traffic, at a common meeting place, where the very moods, distempers, and obtrusive personal habits that have kept them all happily apart since adulthood are then and there encouraged to slowly ferment beneath the cornhusks, and gradually rise with the aid of the terrible wine, and finally burst forth out of control under the stimulus of the cranberry jelly! No, it is a mockery of a holiday. For instance: *Thank you, O Lord, for what we are about to receive.* This is surely not a gala concept. There are no presents, unless one counts Aunt Bertha's sweet rolls a present, which no one does. There is precious little in the way of costumery: miniature plastic turkeys and those witless Pilgrim hats. There is no sex. Indeed, Thanksgiving is the one day of the year (a fact known to everybody) when all thoughts of sex completely vanish, evaporating from apartments, houses, condominiums, and mobile homes like steam from a bathroom mirror.

Consider also the nowhereness of the time of year: the last week or so in November. It is obviously not yet winter: winter, with its death-dealing blizzards and its girls in tiny skirts pirouetting on the ice. On the other hand, it is certainly not much use to anyone as fall: no golden leaves or Oktoberfests, and so forth. Instead, it is a no-man's-land between the seasons. In the cold and sobersides northern half of the country, it is a vaguely unsettling interregnum of long, mournful walks beneath leafless trees: the long, mournful walks following the midday repast with the dread inevitability of pie following turkey, and the leafless trees looming or standing about like eyesores, and the ground either as hard as iron or slightly mushy, and the light snow always beginning to fall when one is halfway to the old green gate—flecks of cold, watery stuff plopping between neck and collar, for the reason that, it being not yet winter, one has forgotten or not chosen to bring along a muffler. It is a corollary to the long, mournful Thanksgiving walk that the absence of this muffler is quickly noticed and that four weeks or so later, at Christmastime, instead of the Sony Betamax one had secretly hoped the children might have chipped in to purchase, one receives another muffler: by then the thirty-third. Thirty-three mufflers! Some walk! Of course, things are more fun in the warm and loony southern part of the country. No snow there of any kind. No need of mufflers. Also, no long, mournful walks, because in the warm and loony southern part of the country everybody drives. So everybody drives over to Uncle Jasper's house to watch the Cougars play the Gators, a not entirely unimportant conflict which will determine whether the Gators get a Bowl bid or must take another postseason exhibition tour of North Korea. But no sooner do the Cougars kick off (an astonishing end-over-end squiggly thing that floats lazily above the arena before plummeting down toward K. C. McCoy and catching him on the helmet) than Auntie Em starts hustling turkey. Soon Cousin May is slamming around the bowls and platters, and Cousin Bernice is oohing and ahing about "all the fixin's," and Uncle Bob is making low, insincere sounds of appreciation: "Yummy, yummy, Auntie Em, I'll have me some more of these delicious yams!" Delicious yams? Uncle Bob's eyes roll wildly in his head. Billy Joe Quaglino throws his long bomb in the middle of Grandpa Morris saying grace, Grandpa Morris speaking so low nobody can hear him, which is just as well, since he is reciting what he can remember of his last union contract. And then, just as J. B. (Speedy) Snood begins his ninety-two-yard punt return, Auntie Em starts dealing everyone second helpings of her famous stuffing, as if she were pushing a controlled substance, which it well might be, since there are no easily recognizable ingredients visible to the naked eye.

Consider for a moment the Thanksgiving meal itself. It has become a sort of refuge for endangered species of starch: cauliflower, turnips, pumpkin, mince (whatever "mince" is), those blessed yams. Bowls of luridly colored yams, with no taste at all, lying torpid under a lava flow of marshmallow! And then the sacred turkey. One might as well try to construct a holiday repast around a fish—say, a nice piece of boiled haddock. After all, turkey tastes very similar to haddock: same consistency, same quite remarkable absence of flavor. But then, if the Thanksgiving *pièce de résistance* were a nice piece of boiled haddock instead of turkey, there wouldn't be all that fun for Dad when Mom hands him the sterling-silver, bone-handled carving set (a wedding present from her parents and not sharpened since) and then everyone sits around pretending not to watch while he saws and tears away at the bird as if he were trying to burrow his way into or out of some grotesque, fowllike prison.

What of the good side to Thanksgiving, you ask. There is always a good side to everything. Not to Thanksgiving. There is only a bad side and then a worse side. For instance, Grandmother's best linen tablecloth is a bad side: the fact that it is produced each year, in the manner of a red flag being produced before a bull, and then is always spilled upon by whichever child is doing poorest at school that term and so is in need of greatest reassurance. Thus:

"Oh, my God, *Veronica*, you just spilled grape juice [or plum wine or tar] on Grandmother's best linen tablecloth!" But now comes worse. For at this point Cousin Bill, the one who lost all Cousin Edwina's money on the car dealership three years ago and has apparently been drinking steadily since Halloween, bizarrely chooses to say: "Seems to me those old glasses are always falling over." To which Auntie Meg is heard to add: "Somehow I don't remember receivin' any of those old glasses." To which Uncle Fred replies: "That's because you and George decided to go on vacation to Hawaii the summer Grandpa Sam was dying." Now Grandmother is sobbing, though not so uncontrollably that she can refrain from murmuring: "I think that volcano painting I threw away by mistake got sent me from Hawaii, heaven knows why." But the gods are merciful, even the Pilgrim-hatted god of cornhusks and soggy stuffing, and there is an end to everything, even to Thanksgiving. Indeed, there is a grandeur to the feelings of finality and doom which usually settle on a house after the Thanksgiving celebration is over, for with the completion of Thanksgiving Day the year itself has been properly terminated: shot through the cranium with a high-velocity candied yam. At this calendrical nadir, all energy on the planet has gone, all fun has fled, all the terrible wine has been drunk.

But then, overnight, life once again begins to stir, emerging, even by the next morning,   5 in the form of Japanese window displays and Taiwanese Christmas lighting, from the primeval ooze of the nation's department stores. Thus, a new year dawns, bringing with it immediate and cheering possibilities of extended consumer debt, office-party flirtations, good—or, at least, mediocre—wine, and visions of Supersaver excursion fares to Montego Bay. It is worth noting, perhaps, that this true new year always starts with the same mute, powerful mythic ceremony: the surreptitious tossing out, in the early morning, of all those horrid aluminum-foil packages of yams and cauliflower and stuffing and red, gummy cranberry substance which have been squeezed into the refrigerator as if a reenactment of the siege of Paris were shortly expected. Soon afterward, the phoenix of Christmas can be observed as it slowly rises, beating its drumsticks, once again goggle-eyed with hope and unrealistic expectations.

Questions

1. Thanksgiving is a culturally specific holiday. What cultural references in Arlen's essay match your experiences? Which do not? Are any of these behaviors universal to your experience of holidays?

2. What type of tone does Arlen employ throughout the essay? Does his tone remain consistent or does it fluctuate? How? Why do you believe he selected this tone for this topic?

Jacob Neusner [b. 1932]

The Speech the Graduates Didn't Hear

Jacob Neusner, a renowned scholar and leader in the American study of Judaism, was born in Hartford, Connecticut. He attended Harvard, Oxford, and Columbia Universities as well as the Jewish Theological Seminary, where he was ordained a rabbi. As a professor, he has taught at several institutions including Columbia and Brown. He is also known as one of the most published scholars in academic history, having written or edited approximately one thousand publications. Neusner's contributions to the academic study of religion are considered profound by many, and he has won awards and received honorary degrees from institutions around the world. Neusner currently is a research professor of religion and theology at Bard College in New York.

Neusner addresses the quality of college academics in preparing students for the real world in his satirical speech "The Speech the Graduates Didn't Hear." Written while teaching at Brown University, his words are intended as an address to a graduating class on their commencement day. He bluntly tells students that professors indulged their mediocre work because "[they] did not want to be bothered" and that praise from professors, flexible deadlines, and good grades are all meaningless. He warns that college has not given students an education, but created a "forgiving world" that will fade after graduation. Although this speech was never delivered, it was published originally in Brown's *Daily Herald* on June 12, 1983.

We the faculty take no pride in our educational achievements with you. We have prepared you for a world that does not exist, indeed, that cannot exist. You have spent four years supposing that failure leaves no record. You have learned at Brown that when your work goes poorly, the painless solution is to drop out. But starting now, in the world to which you go, failure marks you. Confronting difficulty by quitting leaves you changed. Outside Brown, quitters are no heroes.

With us you could argue about why your errors were not errors, why mediocre work really was excellent, why you could take pride in routine and slipshod presentation. Most of you, after all, can look back on honor grades for most of what you have done. So, here grades can have meant little in distinguishing the excellent from the ordinary. But tomorrow, in the world to which you go, you had best not defend errors but learn from them. You will be ill-advised to demand praise for what does not deserve it, and abuse those who do not give it.

For four years we created an altogether forgiving world, in which whatever slight effort you gave was all that was demanded. When you did not keep appointments, we made new ones. When your work came in beyond the deadline, we pretended not to care.

Worse still, when you were boring, we acted as if you were saying something important. When you were garrulous and talked to hear yourself talk, we listened as if it mattered. When you tossed on our desks writing upon which you had not labored, we read it and even responded, as though you earned a response. When you were dull, we pretended you were smart. When you were predictable, unimaginative, and routine, we listened as if to new and wonderful things. When you demanded free lunch, we served it. And all this why?

Despite your fantasies, it was not even that we wanted to be liked by you. It was that we 5
did not want to be bothered, and the easy way out was pretense: smiles and easy Bs.

It is conventional to quote in addresses such as these. Let me quote someone you've never heard of: Professor Carter A. Daniel, Rutgers University (*Chronicle of Higher Education*, May 7, 1979):

> College has spoiled you by reading papers that don't deserve to be read, listening to comments that don't deserve a hearing, paying attention even to the lazy, ill-informed, and rude. We had to do it, for the sake of education. But nobody will ever do it again. College has deprived you of adequate preparation for the last fifty years. It has failed you by being easy, free, forgiving, attentive, comfortable, interesting, unchallenging fun. Good luck tomorrow.

That is why, on this commencement day, we have nothing in which to take much pride.

Oh, yes, there is one more thing. Try not to act toward your coworkers and bosses as you have acted toward us. I mean, when they give you what you want but have not earned, don't abuse them, insult them, act out with them your parlous relationships with your parents. This too we have tolerated. It was, as I said, not to be liked. Few professors actually care whether or not they are liked by peer-paralyzed adolescents, fools so shallow as to imagine professors care not about education but about popularity. It was, again, to be rid of you. So go, unlearn the lies we taught you. To Life!

[1983]

Questions

1. This essay is sometimes described as a satire. Define *satire*: What are the characteristics and purposes of satirical writing? Do you agree that this essay is satirical? Why or why not? How does labeling this essay as satire change the way we might approach and understand this piece? What is Neusner really arguing?

2. At first glance, Neusner's speech seems to be directed toward students who are about to leave college, but it actually has strong relevance for students—like you—who have just entered college. Write for ten minutes about your choice to go to college. Why did you choose college over other options? Did you even consider other options? Why did you choose this college in particular? What do you expect to get out of your time here? Do you think your expectations will be met? Why or why not?

Ishmael Reed [b. 1938]

America: The Multinational Society

Born in Chattanooga, Tennessee in 1938, **Ishmael Reed** grew up in Buffalo, New York, where he was compelled to drop out of the state college without a degree. Reed began to write and, after moving to New York in 1962, helped to establish the legendary *East Village Other*. In 1967, Reed published his first novel, *The Freelance Pallbearers*, and moved to California, where he released his second novel, *Yellow Back Radio Broke-Down* (1969), a satire of the traditional American western. The outspoken and at times controversial Reed was denied tenure at the University of California at Berkeley, but has taught at many other institutions, including Yale, and has published nine novels, six books of poetry, and four essay collections. For most of his career, Reed has represented one of the most convincing "alternative" voices. He has been a nominee for the Pulitzer Prize and has twice been a finalist for the National Book Award. Reed considers his most important achievement the establishment of the Before Columbus Foundation, a multiethnic group dedicated to promoting a pan-cultural view of America.

> *At the annual Lower East Side Jewish Festival yesterday, a Chinese woman ate a pizza slice in front of Ty Thuan Duc's Vietnamese grocery store. Beside her a Spanish-speaking family patronized a cart with two signs: "Italian Ices" and "Kosher by Rabbi Alper." And after the pastrami ran out, everybody ate knishes.*—NEW YORK TIMES, 23 JUNE 1983

On the day before Memorial Day, 1983, a poet called me to describe a city he had just visited. He said that one section included mosques, built by the Islamic people who dwelled there. Attending his reading, he said, were large numbers of Hispanic people, forty thousand of whom lived in the same city. He was not talking about a fabled city located in some mysterious region of the world. The city he'd visited was Detroit.

A few months before, as I was leaving Houston, Texas, I heard it announced on the radio that Texas's largest minority was Mexican American, and though a foundation recently issued a report critical of bilingual education, the taped voice used to guide the passengers on the air trams connecting terminals in Dallas Airport is in both Spanish and English. If the trend continues, a day will come when it will be difficult to travel through some sections of the country without hearing commands in both English and Spanish; after all, for some western states, Spanish was the first written language and the Spanish style lives on in the western way of life.

Shortly after my Texas trip, I sat in an auditorium located on the campus of the University of Wisconsin at Milwaukee as a Yale professor—whose original work on the influence of African cultures upon those of the Americas has led to his ostracism from some monocultural intellectual circles—walked up and down the aisle, like an old-time southern evangelist, dancing and drumming the top of the lectern, illustrating his points before some serious Afro-American intellectuals and artists who cheered and applauded his performance and his mastery of information. The professor was "white." After his lecture, he joined a group of Milwaukeeans in a conversation. All of the participants spoke Yoruban, though only the professor had ever traveled to Africa.

One of the artists told me that his paintings, which included African and Afro-American mythological symbols and imagery, were hanging in the local McDonald's restaurant. The next day I went to McDonald's and snapped pictures of smiling youngsters eating hamburgers below paintings that could grace the walls of any of the country's leading museums. The manager of the local McDonald's said, "I don't know what you boys are doing, but I like it," as he commissioned the local painters to exhibit in his restaurant.

Such blurring of cultural styles occurs in everyday life in the United States to a greater 5 extent than anyone can imagine and is probably more prevalent than the sensational conflict between people of different backgrounds that is played up and often encouraged by the media. The result is what the Yale professor, Robert Thompson, referred to as a cultural bouillabaisse, yet members of the nation's present educational and cultural Elect still cling to the notion that the United States belongs to some vaguely defined entity they refer to as "Western civilization," by which they mean, presumably, a civilization created by the people of Europe, as if Europe can be viewed in monolithic terms. Is Beethoven's Ninth Symphony, which includes Turkish marches, a part of Western civilization, or the late nineteenth- and twentieth-century French paintings, whose creators were influenced by Japanese art? And what of the cubists, through whom the influence of African art changed modern painting, or the surrealists, who were so impressed with the art of the Pacific Northwest Indians that, in their map of North America, Alaska dwarfs the lower forty-eight in size?

Are the Russians, who are often criticized for their adoption of "Western" ways by Tsarist dissidents in exile, members of Western civilization? And what of the millions of Europeans who have black African and Asian ancestry, black Africans having occupied several countries for hundreds of years? Are these "Europeans" members of Western civilization, or the Hungarians, who originated across the Urals in a place called Greater Hungary, or the Irish, who came from the Iberian Peninsula?

Even the notion that North America is part of Western civilization because our "system of government" is derived from Europe is being challenged by Native American historians who say that the founding fathers, Benjamin Franklin especially, were actually influenced by the system of government that had been adopted by the Iroquois hundreds of years prior to the arrival of large numbers of Europeans.

Western civilization, then, becomes another confusing category like Third World, or Judeo-Christian culture, as man attempts to impose his small-screen view of political and cultural reality upon a complex world. Our most publicized novelist recently said that Western civilization was the greatest achievement of mankind, an attitude that flourishes on the street level as scribbles in public restrooms: "White Power," "Niggers and Spics Suck," or "Hitler was a prophet," the latter being the most telling, for wasn't Adolf Hitler the archetypal monoculturalist who, in his pigheaded arrogance, believed that one way and one blood was so pure that it had to be protected from alien strains at all costs? Where did such an attitude, which has caused so much misery and depression in our national life, which has tainted even our noblest achievements, begin? An attitude that caused the incarceration of Japanese-American citizens during World War II, the persecution of Chicanos and Chinese Americans, the near-extermination of the Indians, and the murder and lynchings of thousands of Afro-Americans.

Virtuous, hardworking, pious, even though they occasionally would wander off after some fancy clothes, or rendezvous in the woods with the town prostitute, the Puritans are idealized in our schoolbooks as "a hardy band" of no-nonsense patriarchs whose discipline razed the forest and brought order to the New World (a term that annoys Native American historians). Industrious, responsible, it was their "Yankee ingenuity" and practicality that created the work ethic. They were simple folk who produced a number of good poets, and they set the tone for the American writing style, of lean and spare lines, long before Hemingway. They worshiped in churches whose colors blended in with the New England snow, churches with simple structures and ornate lecterns.

The Puritans were a daring lot, but they had a mean streak. They hated the theater   10 and banned Christmas. They punished people in a cruel and inhuman manner. They killed children who disobeyed their parents. When they came in contact with those whom they considered heathens or aliens, they behaved in such a bizarre and irrational manner that this chapter in the American history comes down to us as a late-movie horror film. They exterminated the Indians, who taught them how to survive in a world unknown to them, and their encounter with the calypso culture of Barbados resulted in what the tourist guide in Salem's Witches' House refers to as the Witchcraft Hysteria.

The Puritan legacy of hard work and meticulous accounting led to the establishment of a great industrial society; it is no wonder that the American industrial revolution began in Lowell, Massachusetts, but there was the other side, the strange and paranoid attitudes toward those different from the Elect.

The cultural attitudes of that early Elect continue to be voiced in everyday life in the United States: the president of a distinguished university, writing a letter to the *Times*, belittling the study of African civilizations; the television network that promoted its show on the Vatican art with the boast that this art represented "the finest achievements of the human spirit." A modern up-tempo state of complex rhythms that depends upon contacts with an international community can no longer behave as if it dwelled in a "Zion Wilderness" surrounded by beasts and pagans.

When I heard a schoolteacher warn the other night about the invasion of the American educational system by foreign curriculums, I wanted to yell at the television set, "Lady, they're already here." It has already begun because the world is here. The world has been arriving at these shores for at least ten thousand years from Europe, Africa, and Asia. In the late nineteenth and early twentieth centuries, large numbers of Europeans arrived, adding their cultures to those of the European, African, and Asian settlers who were already here, and recently millions have been entering the country from South America and the Caribbean, making Yale Professor Bob Thompson's bouillabaisse richer and thicker.

One of our most visionary politicians said that he envisioned a time when the United States could become the brain of the world, by which he meant the repository of all of the latest advanced information systems. I thought of that remark when an enterprising poet friend of mine called to say that he had just sold a poem to a computer magazine and that the editors were delighted to get it because they didn't carry fiction or poetry. Is that the kind of world we desire? A humdrum homogenous world of all brains but no heart, no fiction, no poetry; a world of robots with human attendants bereft of imagination, of culture? Or does North America deserve a more exciting destiny? To become a place where the cultures of the world crisscross. This is possible because the United States is unique in the world: The world is here.

Questions

1. Readers often skip over the biographies for essays, despite the important information they reveal about the author. How does Reed's biography contribute to or diminish his *ethos*/credibility? Why?

2. The beginning of this essay focuses on several examples of what Reed later refers to as a blurring of cultural styles, or "cultural bouillabaisse" (para. 5). Identify your own cultural affiliations, and write a paragraph on how your own experiences reflect Reed's "cultural bouillabaisse."

Natalie Angier [b. 1958]

One Thing They Aren't: Maternal

Born in New York, **Natalie Angier** graduated with high honors from Barnard College in 1978, having studied English, physics, and astronomy. A founding staff member of *Discover* magazine in 1980, Angier has also been a science writer for *Time* magazine, a professor in the Graduate Program in Science and Environmental Reporting at New York University, and a contributing writer for *Atlantic*, *Parade*, *Reader's Digest*, and the *Washington Monthly*, among others. Since 1990, Angier has been a science writer on staff at the *New York Times*. She has received numerous honors, including the Lewis Thomas Award for distinguished writing in the life sciences and the General Motors International Award for writing about cancer. Recognized for a variety of science-based feature stories, she won a Pulitzer Prize for beat reporting in 1991. Her book *Natural Obsessions* (1988) was named as both a *New York Times* Notable Book of the Year and an American Association for the Advancement of Science (AAAS) Notable Book of the Year. Since, Angier has also authored *The Beauty of the Beastly* (1995) and *Woman: An Intimate Geography* (2000).

In "One Thing They Aren't: Maternal," which originally appeared in the *New York Times*, Angier questions how deserving mothers are of our "admiration." In the weeks before Mother's Day in 2006, she considers the nesting and birthing habits of mothers of various species—including guinea hens, pandas, and rabbits.

Oh, mothers! Dear noble, selfless, tender and ferocious defenders of progeny all across nature's phylogeny: How well you deserve our admiration as Mother's Day draws near, and how photogenically you grace the greeting cards that we thrifty offspring will send in lieu of a proper gift.

Here is a mother guinea hen, trailed by a dozen cotton-ball chicks. Here a mother panda and a baby panda share a stalk of bamboo, while over there, a great black eagle dam carries food to her waiting young. We love you, Mom, you're our port in the storm. You alone help clip Mother Nature's bloodstained claws.

But wait. That guinea hen is walking awfully fast. In fact, her brood cannot quite keep up with her, and by the end of the day, whoops, only two chicks still straggle behind. And the mama panda, did she not give birth to twins? So why did just one little panda emerge from her den? As for the African black eagle, her nest is less a Hallmark poem than an Edgar Allan Poe. The mother has gathered prey in abundance, and has hyrax carcasses to spare. Yet she feeds only one of her two eaglets, then stands by looking bored as the fattened bird repeatedly pecks its starving sibling to death.

What is wrong with these coldhearted mothers, to give life then carelessly toss it away? Are they freaks or diseased or unnatural? Cackling mad like Piper Laurie in *Carrie*?

In a word—ha. As much as we may like to believe that mother animals are designed 5 to nurture and protect their young, to fight to the death, if need be, to keep their offspring alive, in fact, nature abounds with mothers that defy the standard maternal script in a raft of macabre ways. There are mothers that zestily eat their young and mothers that drink their young's blood. Mothers that pit one young against the other in a fight to the death and mothers that raise one set of their babies on the flesh of their siblings.

Among several mammals, including lions, mice and monkeys, females will either spontaneously abort their fetuses or abandon their newborns when times prove rocky or a new male swaggers into town.

Other mothers, like pandas, practice a postnatal form of family planning, giving birth to what may be thought of as an heir and a spare, and then, when the heir fares well, walking away from the spare with nary a fare-thee-well.

"Pandas frequently give birth to twins, but they virtually never raise two babies," said Scott Forbes, a professor of biology at the University of Winnipeg. "This is the dark side of pandas, that they have two and throw one away."

It is also something that zoos with ever-popular panda displays rarely discuss.

"They consider it bad P.R. for the pandas," Dr. Forbes said.   10

Researchers long viewed infanticide and similar acts of maternal skullduggery as pathological, a result of the mother's being under extreme stress. A farmer's child pokes around in a rabbit's nest, for example, and the mother rabbit responds by methodically consuming every one of her eight baby bunnies. By standard reckoning, it made little genetic sense for a mother to destroy her young, and maternal nurturing was assumed to be a hard-wired affair.

More recently, scientists have accrued abundant evidence that "bad" mothering is common in nature and that it is often a centerpiece of the reproductive game plan.

In the blockbuster movie *The March of the Penguins*, the emperor penguins were portrayed as fairy parents, loving every egg they laid and mourning every egg that cracked before its time. Among the less storied royal penguins, a mother lays two eggs each breeding season, the second 60 percent larger than the first. Just before the second egg is laid, the mother unsentimentally rolls the first egg right out of the nest.

In Magellanic penguins, the mother also lays two eggs and allows both to hatch; only then does she begin to discriminate. Of the fish she brings to the nest, she gives 90 percent to the larger chick, even as the smaller one howls for food. In the pitiless cold of the Southern Cone of South America, the underfed bird invariably dies.

Like penguins, many species that habitually jettison a portion of their progeny live in   15 harsh or uncertain environments, where young are easily lost and it pays to have a backup. At the same time, the harshness and uncertainty make it virtually impossible for a mother to raise multiples, so if the primary survives, the backup must go. Sometimes the mother does the dirty work herself. More often, she leaves it to her preferred young to dispatch of its understudy.

When Douglas W. Mock of the University of Oklahoma began studying egrets in Texas three decades ago, he knew that the bigger babies in a clutch would peck the smaller ones to death. Still, Dr. Mock was caught off guard by what he saw—or failed to see. He had assumed that the murderous attacks would surely take place while Mom and Dad egret were out fishing.

"I figured that, if the parents were around, they'd try to block these things," he said. "I have three older brothers, and I never would have made it if my parents hadn't interceded."

Instead, Dr. Mock witnessed utter parental indifference. The mother or father would stand by the side of the nest, doing nothing as one chick battered its sibling bloody. "The parent would yawn or groom itself and look completely blasé," said Dr. Mock, author of *More Than Kin and Less Than Kind: The Evolution of Family Conflict*. "In the 3,000 attacks that I witnessed, I never saw a parent try to stop one. It's as though they expect it to happen."

Since then, siblicide under parental supervision has been observed in many bird species, including pelicans, cranes, and blue-footed boobies.

One researcher watched a nest of African black eagles for three days as the larger ea- 20
glet alternated between tirelessly stabbing at its sibling and taking food from its solicitous mother's mouth. There was prey to spare, but the mother did not bother feeding the second, abused baby. When the eaglet's poor, tattered body was finally tossed to the ground, the researcher calculated that it had been pecked 1,569 times.

Pigs, too, have their own version of litter culling by sibling rivalry. Piglets are born with little eyeteeth that stick out sideways from their lower jaw, Dr. Mock said, and they use these teeth to slice at the faces of one another as they jockey for the best teats. The runt of the litter is so often sliced and bullied that it cannot get enough milk. It must spend every spare moment fighting to nurse and may get crushed by its mother. In other cases, mothers turn infanticidal because they are born optimists, ever tuned to the sunny expectation that good times lie ahead. Each year they breed for a banquet, producing a maximum of begging bairns as the season starts; and when there is plenty of food, they will provision every young.

If the feast does not materialize, however, they cut their losses. Kangaroos have an elaborate method for child rearing through fat and lean years. In a good season, a mother may care for three offspring simultaneously, each at a different stage of development: the eldest, already hopping around on its own but still nursing; the second, a joey, which lives in her pouch and breast-feeds; and the youngest, an embryo stashed internally in a state of suspended animation.

During a severe drought, the mother will first refuse her breast to the autonomous juvenile, leaving it to forage as best it can. If the drought continues, her milk dries up and the joey dies and falls from her pouch. At that point, the embryo kept in cold storage begins to develop toward joeyhood. Tomorrow will surely be a better, wetter day.

Some mother hawks and owls are practical optimists, not only halving their brood 25
when necessary but also eating them.

"Cannibalizing the victim serves the dual function of providing a timely meal and ensuring that there is one less mouth to feed," Dr. Forbes, the University of Winnipeg biologist, writes in his new book, *A Natural History of Families*.

A hungry mother can be the stuff of nightmares—especially if it is the mother next door. Chimpanzees are exemplary mothers when it comes to caring for their own, said Sarah Blaffer Hrdy, a primatologist and the author of *Mother Nature: A History of Mothers, Infants and Natural Selection*.

Unlike humans, Dr. Hrdy said, the apes never abandon or reject their young, no matter how diseased or crippled a baby may be. Yet because female chimpanzees live in troops with other nonrelated females, a ravenous, lactating mother feels little compunction about killing and eating the child of a group mate. "It's a good way to get lipids," Dr. Hrdy said.

As meal plans go, cannibalism can be no-muss, no-fuss. A mother nurse shark has two uteri in which her babies develop, safe from the ocean's predators. But the nurse shark is not a mammal, and she has no placenta. How to feed her fetal fish? On the fins and flesh of fellow fetal fish.

The mother incubates as many as 20 eggs per womb. The eggs hatch and start to grow, 30
and when their jaws are sufficiently mature, they commence feeding on one another. By gestation's end, just one sharklet emerges from each uterine chamber.

Extracting nutrients from one's offspring need not be fatal, though. Among ants of the rare genus *Adetomyrma*, Dr. Forbes writes, "queens chew holes in their larvae and then consume the oozing fluid," a practice that explains why the insects, found in Madagascar, are known as Dracula ants. The sampled larvae recover and mature into ants, but they bear lifelong scars of their early bloodletting.

There are voracious mothers and vampiric mothers, and then there are phantom mothers. In the annals of mammaldom, the maximal minimalist of a mother must surely be the rabbit. Only recently have scientists studied rabbit behavior closely enough to appreciate what a marvel of efficiency a breeding rabbit is, said Robyn Hudson of the National University of Mexico.

Rabbits live together in complex burrows, where an expecting female will build a little nest and line it with grass and fur that she plucks from her flank. When she is ready to give birth, she enters the chamber and in less than eight minutes plops out 10 pups, "like peas in a pod," Dr. Hudson said.

Without bestowing on the litter so much as a single welcoming lick, the mother hops back out, closes up the entrance and leaves the helpless, furless newborns to huddle among themselves in the dark. Over the next 25 days, the mother will return to the nest for a mere two minutes a day, during which she crouches over the pups and they frantically nurse.

"Her milk is under high pressure, and it's almost squirted into their mouths," Dr. 35
Hudson said. "You can see them visibly expand, like little grapes."

Two minutes are up, and she's out of there. On Day 26, she abandons them completely, and the bunnies must crawl from the nest and make their way in the world on their own.

The mother rabbit may seem awfully cold for a warmblood, but her aloofness makes sense. Rabbits are a highly popular prey, and many predators will pursue them into their burrows. To keep the fox from the nursery door, the mother rabbit shuns the room. Her absence may not make her pups' hearts grow fonder, but it may keep those hearts thumping a little longer.

[2006]

Questions

1. Angier never describes the significance of her argument. What is it and why does it matter?

2. Find an image that demonstrates the conception of motherhood. Does it fall into the clichés that Angier describes? Using what you have learned about visual analysis, analyze the claims made in your image.

Deb Aronson

The Nurture of Nature

Deb Aronson earned her B.A. in anthropology in 1983 from Harvard University and her M.A. in Middle Eastern archaeology in 1988 from Yale University. After having served as the senior news editor of the office of communications at Washington University in St. Louis from 1994 to 1996 and as a content coordinator for a new media company from 1996 to 1999, Aronson turned full-time to freelance writing and editing. She lives in Urbana, Illinois, and her essays and features have appeared in *Mary Englebreit Home Companion, Indy's Child*, the *Illinois Times*, the *University of Illinois Alumni Magazine*, and *Washington University Alumni Magazine*. Writing for the middle-school audience, Aronson has also authored a biography, *E. B. White*. She also belongs to the National Association of Science Writers.

   Originally appearing in the July/August 2003 issue of *Science and Spirit*, Deb Aronson's essay "The Nurture of Nature" speaks to the stress of our modern world and an unexpected and simple solution—nature. All our efforts to relieve anxiety and reinvigorate our spirits through exercise and meditation and medication may be better put to use in a greener environment. Citing various studies that look at the ameliorating effect of gardens on people living and working in depressing surroundings, Aronson points to the restorative quality of "involuntary attention," the relaxed state people assume when their attention need not be sharply focused on a given task.

Can contact with nature relieve anxiety and stress, aid healing, and increase concentration? It appears that it can, even when "contact" is defined in the loosest way. Some researchers now suggest that passive contact with nature, like looking at trees from a car, can be as therapeutic as a walk in the woods. It appears that nature can really provide nurture—for the young and old, healthy and sick, alike.

   Here's why.

   "We have two kinds of attention," says Andrea Faber Taylor, an environmental psychologist and postdoctoral research associate at the University of Illinois. The first is the "directed attention" we call on for tasks that require focus, like driving or doing our taxes. Directed attention tends to be tiring, however, and fatigue affects our ability to make good decisions and control destructive impulses. The best way to restore directed attention is to give it a rest by shifting to the second type, "involuntary attention," which we display when we watch a fire or meditate, for instance. Looking at nature is another activity that gives our directed attention a chance to recover.

   For example, Roger Ulrich and his colleagues at Texas A&M University found that people who commuted along scenic roads recovered more quickly from stressful driving conditions than those who saw billboards, buildings, and parking lots. Ulrich also noted something he termed an "inoculation" effect: Drivers who had taken the scenic route responded more calmly to stressful situations later on. Ulrich also looked at patients recovering from gallbladder surgery. The patients who could see trees from their hospital beds needed fewer painkillers and had shorter hospital stays than those who looked out on brick walls.

So, with all our efforts to alleviate stress—from aerobics and yoga to anti-anxiety pills— 5
maybe the key is as simple as a garden. In fact, even a little bit of green seems to make a
big impact. Some studies suggest that a houseplant or even a picture of nature can convey
similar benefits.

"It used to be that we looked at cataclysmic events, like divorce or loss of a job, as stressors," says Kathleen Wolf of the College of Forest Resources at the University of Washington.
"But now we are seeing that our daily lives have constant small stressors, and the cumulative
effect is significant. Consequently, even small, incremental contacts with nature in our daily
lives are beneficial."

In her study, Andrea Faber Taylor looked at children living in Chicago's notorious
Robert Taylor Homes housing project. The children she studied were all from the same
socioeconomic bracket; all were African American; all lived in virtually identical apartments
to which their families had been randomly assigned; and all lived on the second, third, or
fourth floors, the best levels for viewing nature. The only difference was that some apartments overlooked trees and grass while others overlooked pavement.

Girls who could see nature from their windows were better able to concentrate, and
to control impulsive behavior, as measured in standard psychological tests. These behaviors
tend to help children resist peer pressure and sexual pressure, and help in other challenging
situations.

"Our theory was that public housing is a very fatiguing environment," says Faber Taylor.
"It turns out that small amounts of greenery seem to make a big difference. You don't have to
live in Sherwood Forest to enjoy nature's benefits."

By creating more green spaces, particularly in urban areas, we could minimize, or at
least buffer, the stresses of everyday life and the long-term costs in mental and physical
health associated with stress. Now that's a magic bullet.

Questions

1. Look at the introduction to Aronson's essay. What is the thesis? How does the author
    try to get her audience to read further? What clues does the introduction give you
    about what the essay will discuss?

2. Analyze this essay thinking about audience, and write a description of who you believe
    to be the author's intended audience. Reference parts of the text that led you to your
    conclusions. It may be helpful to consider the questions about analyzing audience on
    pages 12–17, but do not let these limit your response.

Thomas H. Benton [b. 1968]

The Seven Deadly Sins of Students

Thomas H. Benton is the pen name of William Pannapacker, an associate professor of English at Hope College in Holland, Michigan. Born in New Jersey, Pannapacker received his Ph.D. in the history of American civilization from Harvard University in 1999 and has published widely on Walt Whitman. His published works include *Revised Lives: Walt Whitman and Nineteenth-Century Authorship* (2004), and he is currently working on a scholarly monograph entitled *Walt Whitman's Cities*, two chapters of which have been published as articles in *Leaves of Grass: The Sesquicentennial Essays* (2007) and *A Companion to Walt Whitman* (2005). Using his pseudonym, Pannapacker also publishes regularly in the *Chronicle of Higher Education* about life and careers in academia.

Using the traditional framework of the "Seven Deadly Sins," Pannapacker analyzes the troubling behavior he has witnessed of undergraduate students in his classes in the following purported sermon. He laments that the consumer mentality many students bring to the classroom is accompanied by a sense of entitlement, particularly in terms of their grades. Per Pannapacker's promise, this article was succeeded by "The Seven Deadly Sins of Professors," published in the *Chronicle of Higher Education* in May 2006.

I've been teaching for about 10 years now, and, of course, I was a student for 20 years before that. So I have some experience observing my students' sins, and perhaps even more experience committing them.

The sins that I see in the everyday life of the typical college student are not great ones. Most of the time, they don't seem like "sins" at all, even if one accepts the religious significance of the term. But they spring from thoughts and behaviors that, over time, become habits.

Enabled by institutions, students repeatedly take the path of least resistance, imagining they are making creative compromises with duty that express their unique talents. So they choose self-indulgence instead of self-denial and self-esteem instead of self-questioning. They do not understand that those choices will eventually cause more unhappiness than the more difficult paths they chose not to walk.

The traditional model of the "Seven Deadly Sins" provides a helpful means of categorizing—and perhaps simplifying—the complicated and cumulative experience I am trying to describe:

Sloth: Students often postpone required readings and assigned preparations, making 5
it hard for them to understand their classes the next day. Gradually, lectures and discussions that were once interesting start to seem boring and irrelevant, and the temptation to skip classes becomes greater and greater, especially when the classes are in the morning. Sometimes students arrive late with—in my opinion—insufficient shame, closing the door behind them with a bang. Slothful students regard themselves as full of potential, and so they make a bargain: "I will be lazy now, but I will work hard later." Like St. Augustine, students say to themselves, "Let me be chaste, but not yet." More on lust later.

Greed: Students often pursue degrees not for the sake of learning itself but with the aim of getting a better-paying job, so they can buy a bigger house and fancier cars than those owned by their parents and their neighbors. That often leads to greed for grades that they have not earned. Some students cheat on exams or plagiarize their papers; others, sometimes the most diligent, harass professors into giving them grades unjustified by their performance. The goal of such cheaters and grade-grubbers is not the reality of achievement but the appearance of it. They will then apply to graduate programs or entry-level jobs that they do not really desire and for which they are not really qualified. They want to be lawyers, but they are bored by law courses. They want to be doctors, but they do not care about healing people. They want to go into business, not to provide useful products and services, but to get rich by any means necessary. And so they come to believe that no one has integrity and that there is no basis—other than the marketplace—by which value can be judged.

Anger: Seemingly more often than in the past, professors encounter students who are angered by challenging assignments, which they label—with bureaucratic self-assurance—"unfair" or even "discriminatory." When students do not succeed, they sometimes conclude that their professors are "out to get them" because of some vague prejudice. Students feel entitled to deference by professors who "work for them and should act like it." They do not come to office hours for clarification about an A–; instead, they argue that they are paying a lot of money and, therefore, deserve a high grade, and, if you don't give it to them, they will "complain to management," as if they were sending back food in a restaurant. One hears rumors of cars and homes vandalized by angry students. But, perhaps, the easiest places to find uncensored student rage are the anonymous, libelous evaluations of faculty members found online at Web sites such as RateMyProfessors.com. Often those evaluations say less about the quality of a teacher than they do about the wounded pride of coddled students. More on that topic soon.

Lust: I have seen students come to classes barefoot, with bare midriffs and shoulders, in boxer shorts, bathing suits, and other kinds of clothes that, even by fairly casual standards, are more appropriate for street-walking than higher learning. When did liberation from uniforms transform itself into the social demand that one prepare to be ogled in the classroom? It is hardly a surprise that on RateMyProfessors.com, students are asked to rate their professors' "hotness"—in other words, the teachers' worthiness to be sexually fantasized about by bored students. Even in high-school classes, as an observer of novice teachers, I have overheard lewd remarks about female teachers from denizens of the back row who fear no rebuke because none is forthcoming from the current culture.

Gluttony: It hardly needs saying that most colleges struggle to control alcohol consumption by students and the embarrassing incidents and tragedies that result from it. But there are other manifestations of gluttony these days. For example, when did it become acceptable for students to eat and drink in class as if they were sitting in a cafeteria? Nowadays, I occasionally encounter a student who thinks it's OK to consume a large, messy, and odorous meal in class. I once saw a student eat an entire rotisserie chicken, a tub of mashed potatoes with gravy, several biscuits, and an enormous soft drink during the first 10 minutes of a lecture. I felt like a jester in the court of Henry VIII. It seems hard these days to find a student in class whose mouth is not stuffed with food. Such students will often say that they have no other time to eat, but previous generations—who were no less busy—managed to consume small snacks between classes. That is why colleges have vending machines.

Envy: I think competition is a good thing in education; up to a point, it encourages   10
students to work harder and excel. But the envious student, perhaps daunted by some temporary setback, comes to believe that education is "a rigged game." Envy is the voice of
resignation that cringes at the success of one's peers: "Listen to her, trying to impress the
teacher, like she's so brilliant. I hate her." Envy is the feeling that no one "earns" anything
because there are no objective criteria of accomplishment; and, as a result, success and failure
seem to be based on political and personal preferences. But envy is not limited to differences
in effort and ability. Even more pervasive is a sense of unjustified economic inequality, but,
it seems to me, the fashionable students in their convertibles who jeer the commuters at the
bus stop commit a greater sin than those who envy their money and status.

Pride: I once asked a group of 20 students how many thought they were "better than
their parents"? All of them raised their hands. I didn't ask, but I assume they all believed
they were better than their teachers too. They would rise higher, be more successful, and
transcend the limitations of their elders. We read this belief in our students' expressions:
"What you know is not worth learning. They're just your opinions anyway. I am young. I
have infinite potential. You are old. And you're just a college professor. But I will be rich and
famous someday." They have rarely been given a realistic assessment of their abilities and
prospects. Out of this pride—nurtured by the purveyors of unearned self-esteem, personal
grievance, dumbed-down courses, and inflated grades (often in the guise of liberality)—the
opportunity to earn an education is squandered by prideful students who can make a potential heaven seem like hell.

The concept of the "Seven Deadly Sins" comes out of the Christian tradition, but it also
has value as an ethical guide or at least as a means of avoiding unhappiness. Increasingly,
as a professor who teaches undergraduates, I believe that one of the paramount purposes
of a liberal-arts education is to help young people acquire the wisdom to escape those sins,
particularly the last one from which the others often spring.

A liberal-arts education, as I see it, is not about acquiring wealth and opportunities to
further indulge one's desires. Nor is it about cultivating in students an insular, idolatrous
view of their nation, ethnic group, gender, or religion. It is also not about celebrating the
so-called "great tradition" of authors, philosophers, and artists.

It is about the recognition, ultimately, of how little one really knows, or can know. A
liberal-arts education, most of all, fights unmerited pride by asking students to recognize
the smallness of their ambitions in the context of human history, and more. Whether it is
grounded in faith or not, a liberal-arts education should help students to combat the Seven
Deadly Sins with the "Seven Contrary Virtues" of diligence, generosity, patience, chastity,
moderation, contentment, and, most important of all, humility.

Of course, moral perfection seldom arrives at graduation, even in the best of cases. I   15
teach the courses, and yet I must present myself, at last, as the "Chief of Sinners." The behaviors I observe in students often reflect the deeper drives—the resentments and weaknesses—
of their teachers. Perhaps the impulse to identify the sins of others reflects a corruption more
serious than any I have described here. And that is why, next month, I will sermonize on the
"Seven Deadly Sins of Professors."

[2006]

Questions

1. In "How to Say Nothing in Five Hundred Words," Roberts uses headings to separate ideas. Benton uses a similar organizational method. How does Benton's structure inform his argument? What can you learn about structure from this argument?

2. The structure of the traditional "Seven Deadly Sins" comes with cultural connotations. How do these connotations affect how we approach and understand this piece?

Christopher Clausen [b. 1942]

Against Work

Christopher Clausen received his Ph.D. from Queen's University in Canada in 1972 and is now a retired professor of English at Pennsylvania State University. His research focuses on issues in philosophy, Victorian literature, and contemporary American society. Clausen's books include *The Place of Poetry: Two Centuries of an Art in Crisis* (1981), *The Moral Imagination: Essays on Literature and Ethics* (1986), *My Life with President Kennedy* (1994), and *Faded Mosaic: The Emergence of Post-Cultural America* (2000). He has also published poems and essays in the *Kenyon Review*, the *Virginia Quarterly Review*, and the *Sewanee Review*.

In his essay "Against Work," originally published in the *American Scholar* in September 2004, Clausen argues that Americans have an unhealthy relationship with their work. Tracing the etymology of the word "workaholism," he contends that, in comparison to those of other cultures, Americans pursue work and employment status almost religiously, often at the expense of happiness and other forms of fulfillment.

A history of my suburban early ambitions would sound utterly conventional. At the age of six I wanted to be a cowboy. At twelve I decided instead to become a professional football player, which, for someone who would never weigh more than a hundred and thirty pounds, was even more hopeless. In high school I made up my mind to be a writer. As in most such cases, it wasn't the work of writing that appealed to me. It was that, secretly, I never wanted to do any work at all. But teenagers are rarely of one mind, and their inconsistent wishes seldom come true in a recognizable way.

"What is the use of having money if you have to work for it?" Violet Malone disdainfully asks her father-in-law, a self-made Irish-American billionaire, in George Bernard Shaw's play *Man and Superman*. A century ago, when Shaw was writing, the different valuation that Americans and Europeans set on work as an abstract ideal was already evident to anyone who had a chance to compare them. By that time the "gospel of work" preached by Thomas Carlyle, who repeated endlessly that "work is alone noble," was a mid-Victorian relic.

To her perfectly reasonable question, the Englishwoman Violet receives no answer. She would be just as baffled a hundred years later. If humans are the only animal that doesn't think the purpose of life is to enjoy it, Americans are an especially hard case. Today those of us with full-time employment typically put in several hundred more hours per year than western Europeans—the equivalent of seven additional weeks, according to some surveys. Even the proverbially hardworking Germans spend only about three-quarters as many hours on the job and retire younger. Our disposable income is correspondingly higher, though when asked whether we would prefer more leisure to greater wealth, most of us opt for leisure. Statistics on voluntary overtime, however, suggest that we may not be telling the truth. A long American tradition leads people to define themselves not just by their occupations but also by the amount of labor they put in.

Captain John Smith's declaration that those who do not work shall not eat is the real national motto, ratified by subsequent authorities from Benjamin Franklin to Donald Trump. Rockefellers and Kennedys, whose international counterparts would spend all their time collecting works of art, instead work conspicuously hard at finance or politics. The American way is to prove one's worth by long hours, almost regardless of what one actually accomplishes. The fact that many people appear to work hard while actually coasting through the week merely confirms the gap between what they think they should be doing and their actual preferences.

Consider the fate of the word *workaholism*, coined by W. E. Oates in 1968 to identify a disturbing psychological obsession—an "addiction," a "compulsion"—that Oates had noticed around him. Others took up the new term enthusiastically. "The workaholic, as an addict is called, neglects his family, withdraws from social life, and loses interest in sex," the *Sydney Bulletin* explained ominously in 1973. But within a decade the term lost all connotation of pathology and became a compliment. "Unlike their workaholic American cousins," *Time* reported in 1981, "Europeans tend to see lengthy vacations as somehow part of the natural order of things." Today the word is most often heard in the proud boast "I'm a workaholic," recited ad nauseam by type A personalities in corporations, politics, and the professions. Carlyle lives, if only in America.

Why on earth do we do it? Do most of us really prefer to work—to spend our lives in labor as an end rather than as an unavoidable means to our own or others' happiness? Of course not. Most jobs are boring at best, with few psychic rewards. Nobody works on an assembly line or at Wal-Mart, or recites the weather on Channel 9, simply for lack of a pleasanter way to spend two thousand hours every year. It's true that the most energetic and gregarious of us, the kind who have been claiming since high school that they "want to work with people," often find even jobs like these a relief from loneliness. One suspects, though, that if they suddenly didn't need the money or respect, they would quickly turn to playing games instead, or traveling the world, or finding innovative new ways to cope. The upper-middle-class professions are supposed to be a different story. Doctors, lawyers, and college professors usually think of themselves as "committed," with the implication that there is nothing they would rather be doing.

Speaking from experience, I can attest that being a senior academic is one of the more privileged assignments in life, although anyone who thinks universities are relaxed, humane centers for the free play of intellect hasn't spent much time in one lately. Plenty of hard work goes into getting a Ph.D., achieving tenure, and practicing a profession that despite its flattering self-image involves as much stress, conformity, and tedium as other occupations. In response to charges made a few years ago that professors are slackers, the Department of Education released a survey concluding that the average full-time university faculty member puts in between forty-five and fifty-five hours a week. Some of what I do for a living is fun—though I discovered early that writing anything meant to be read by others involves a good deal of labor—and the rest is pleasanter than what many people have to do. But still. Most of your waking hours for forty years?

There is something deeply conflicted about the devotion to work, vocation, career as an ideal in any society, but especially in one that has zealously cast off so many of its other repressions. Americans at the beginning of the twenty-first century pursue pleasure with the same avid desperation as upscale high school students pursue getting into the right college—that is, with a hell of a lot of work. We have all been so over-socialized that an unnatural devotion to toil leaves its mark on every area of life. It could even be argued that the most highly prized pleasures have themselves become a form of work, complete with their own uniforms, disciplines, and special lingo.

My own conflicted attitude probably owes something to the fact that during the summer between high school and college, I worked as an information clerk for the National Heart Institute in a suburb of the capital. As a temporary, I spent my days keeping track of off-prints from medical journals, answering requests for the Heart Institute's own publications, and cleaning out the primitive photocopier. Much of the time there was not enough work to keep me busy, and like other low-level civil servants, I soon discovered that the Washington summer in a building with no air conditioning called for a relaxed approach to the public's business.

Most mornings I stayed in my office filling orders from schoolteachers for our most 10 popular publication, a garish poster titled "The Living Pump." Having answered the mail as best I could, I generally retreated in the heat of the afternoon to the comfortable underground vault where our own materials and hundreds of articles on heart disease were stored. This fastness lay beneath a building that had been constructed with nuclear attack in mind. In addition to a normal basement, it had four sub-basements reached by a freight elevator that no one else seemed to use. Once I got to the bottom, I made my way through nearly half a mile of corridors filled with abandoned office furniture. I never encountered another human being down there, just thousands of desks and chairs and filing cabinets that nobody wanted anymore. After several hours in this environment, it was easy to believe the world had ended, and all that was left of the United States government was one GS-2 surrounded by acres of junk five levels below ground zero. It seemed odd to me that reams of Living Pumps would survive Armageddon while the doctors who ran the National Institutes of Health turned into dust, but eighteen-year-olds have a high tolerance for irrationality. That's one reason they make good soldiers. I catalogued the contents of my bunker, restocked as necessary, composed juvenile light verse, and read a lot of novels in the cool silence. Some July afternoons I thought seriously about canceling my college plans and staying underground in the government forever.

The Department of Health, Education, and Welfare, as it was then called, had its headquarters on Independence Avenue in downtown Washington. Olive, a Southern widow who must have been in her fifties, presided over the Heart Institute's offices there. She had worked in similar offices since the New Deal and had seen bosses come and go. A slim woman of vast charm and presence, she liked young men who would spend Friday afternoons in her office drinking coffee and conversing. I retain only the general impression of an elegant lady from a different world where manners and human contact counted for nearly everything and bureaucratic procedures for nothing. Without ever saying so, she conveyed through her demeanor that the government was too absurd to worry about. My guess, although I really have no idea, is that Olive did her job very well, if in an unconventional fashion. Whoever was nominally her superior must have had a difficult time until he tacitly agreed that everything she did would be done her way.

As I look back, it's hard for me to believe what her way meant to my weekly routine. Every Thursday I would receive a slip entitling me to take a pickup truck out of the motor pool on Friday and drive it downtown to HEW. On alternate Friday mornings I would load the truck with publications from the bunker. Then I would have lunch, drive to Olive's office, unload the truck, and spend the afternoon listening, like a young man out of a Faulkner novel. The next Friday I would drive an empty truck to HEW, load it up with the same publications I had delivered the previous week, and return them to Bethesda. It sounds worse than it seemed at the time. Perhaps I'm forgetting some deliveries that served a real purpose beyond bringing me into Olive's presence. The possibility that my cheerful, unambitious colleagues would object to these excursions did not occur to me, and nobody ever did.

Everyone has met people who boast (sometimes repetitively) of loving their work so much that they rarely take vacations and can't bear the thought of retirement. Star athletes, successful artists, and research scientists are sometimes credible when they make these assertions. Occasionally an obstetrician goes on delivering babies into his nineties, and the local newspaper praises his enthusiasm for life. But who believes middle managers when they claim to spend the weekend looking forward to Monday? Who takes teachers seriously in June when they say they can't wait for September? If hypocrisy is the tribute vice pays to virtue, the oddity here is that so many people believe work as such, work divorced from any particular achievement, is especially virtuous. Working to earn one's bread is something few people can escape. Working out of moral vanity is sheer self-deception.

Of course Americans didn't invent the idea. As with so many things, we merely perfected it. To get people to do their best over a long period of time, it has always been necessary to make what they do seem both a duty and a pleasure, something like rearing children. Seneca assured affluent Roman parents, "Nothing is so certain as that the evils of idleness can be shaken off by hard work." In a similar vein, Voltaire wrote, "Work keeps us from three great evils, boredom, vice, and need." These are the homilies of the fortunate. Those who have been forced to work hard are often more realistic about what is at stake. "I don't like work—no man does," Joseph Conrad's alter ego Marlow announces in *Heart of Darkness*, and then adds, "—but I like what is in work—the chance to find yourself. Your own reality—for yourself, not for others—what no other man can ever know." The self-respect that comes from being financially self-supporting, as well as capable of some useful accomplishment for oneself or others, is a worthy goal for anyone. Fetishizing the labor itself is merely a form of bondage, workaholism in the true, perverse sense.

Because it serves so many different practical and psychic purposes, it's no wonder that, in the celebrated words of C. Northcote Parkinson, "work expands so as to fill the time available for its completion." Still, much can be said not just for the strenuous, cultivated leisure that hardworking professionals sometimes allow themselves to imagine as an alternative to virtuous toil, but for bone-idleness. There is in fact no indication that those who work are happier than those who choose not to. After surveying a mass of research on what it takes to make people happy, the psychologist David Watson declares, "With the notable exception of involuntary unemployment, we see little evidence that occupational and employment status have a major impact on well-being. Generally speaking, people in seemingly uninteresting, low-status jobs report levels of happiness and life satisfaction that are quite comparable to those of individuals in high-status occupations. Moreover, the employed and voluntarily unemployed report extremely similar levels of affect and well-being." He concludes, "One particularly interesting implication of this literature is that people apparently devote much of their lives to striving after things—education, marriage, money, and so on—that ultimately have little effect on their happiness." Although having some goals in life seems to work better than having none, "happiness is primarily a subjective phenomenon....not highly constrained by objective circumstances."

If your work won't make you or anyone else happier, why do more of it than you have to? Believers in the gospel of work typically consider happiness irrelevant. Deep down, they think we have a duty to be miserable. As usual, the bullying Carlyle put it most brutally:

15

"'Happy,' my brother? First of all, what difference is it whether thou art happy or not!...The only happiness a brave man ever troubled himself with asking much about was, happiness enough to get his work done. Not 'I can't eat!' but 'I can't work!' that was the burden of all wise complaining among men." Men must work, and women must weep, as Carlyle's friend Charles Kingsley decreed. Work itself, work as a sacred abstraction, had become a substitute for the God that Carlyle and many of his readers no longer believed in.

In America this grim pseudo-religion continues to draw worshippers on a scale no longer seen elsewhere in the Western world. The only major change is that women are now expected to work like men. We speak in reverent tones of the "work ethic"; politicians praise "working families" and, even in times of relatively low unemployment, make job creation an issue in every campaign. A few years ago, cutting the work week was a central promise in a French election, and the government actually passed laws on the subject. In the United States, by contrast, legislation has been introduced to make overtime easier for companies to afford. We abolished mandatory retirement in the 1980s. Despite the growth in productivity and affluence over the past decades, all the social pressures are for working longer hours and later in life rather than cashing in on the promise of greater leisure—partly to take some of the pressure off Social Security and Medicare, but mostly because work is such an ingrained American value.

I don't know about the civil service, but not many Olives are left in major universities. Sometimes I dream of my vault full of Living Pumps. A colleague and I recently passed the time by talking speculatively of retirement. "You wouldn't actually retire at sixty-five, would you?" this proud workaholic asked with incredulity.

"Of course," I gulped, suddenly and unexpectedly defensive about my secret plan to quit at sixty-two. "Why not?"

He shrugged disdainfully and went back to writing his next book on Chaucer. Truly, 20 we are the last Puritans.

[2004]

Questions

1. How does Clausen's sequencing and presentation of his evidence affect the rhetorical impact of his argument? For example, why does he spend so much time on the Olive story, and why does he place it where he does?

2. List the kinds of primary and secondary evidence (observations, personal anecdotes, statistics, etc.) Clausen uses to support his claim.

3. Imagine you have been asked to write a research paper using this essay as a starting point. With a partner, come up with as many research questions as you can that build on Clausen's ideas and concerns about work.

Paul M. Barrett

Muslims in America

New Jersey native **Paul M. Barrett** is a journalist, in his father's footsteps, and a graduate of Harvard Law School. For more than fifteen years, he worked as a reporter and editor at the *Wall Street Journal,* covering topics including legal issues and corporate culture. Barrett is now an assistant managing editor of investigative reporting for *Bloomberg Businessweek ,* and his contributions have earned the magazine several awards. Barrett also teaches as an adjunct professor at New York University's School of Law. He has authored several books including *The Good Black: A True Story of Race in America,* published in 1999, and *American Islam: The Struggle for the Soul of a Religion,* which was named among the best books of the year in 2007 by the *Washington Post* and *Publishers Weekly.*

In the following excerpt from *American Islam,* Barrett dispels many common stereotypes of and assumptions about Muslims in the United States through an objective presentation of factual data. American Muslims are, on average, highly educated and economically prosperous individuals, according to Barrett, and although the exact number of American Muslims is not known, the demographic is growing in numbers and gaining both cultural and political influence in the process.

Most American Muslims are not Arab, and most Americans of Arab descent are Christian, not Muslim. People of South Asian descent—those with roots in Pakistan, India, Bangladesh, and Afghanistan—make up 34 percent of American Muslims, according to the polling organization Zogby International. Arab-Americans constitute only 26 pecent, while another 20 percent are native-born American blacks, most of whom are converts. The remaining 20 percent come from Africa, Iran, Turkey, and elsewhere.

Muslims have no equivalent to the Catholic pope and his cardinals. The faith is decentralized in the extreme, and some beliefs and practices vary depending on region and sect. In America, Muslims do not think and act alike any more than Christians do. That said, all observant Muslims acknowledge Islam's "five pillars": faith in one God, prayer, charity, fasting during Ramadan, and pilgrimage to Mecca. Muslims are also united in the way they pray. The basic choreography of crossing arms, bowing, kneeling, and prostrating oneself is more or less the same in mosques everywhere.

The two major subgroups of Muslims, Sunni and Shiite, are found in the United States in roughly their global proportions: 85 percent Sunni, 15 percent Shiite. Ancient history still animates the rivalry, which began in the struggle for Muslim leadership after the Prophet Muhammad's death in 632. Shiites believe that Muhammad intended for only his blood descendants to succeed him. Muhammad's beloved cousin and son-in-law Ali was the only male relative who qualified. Ali's follower became known as Shiites, a derivation of the Arabic phrase for "partisans of Ali." Things did not go smoothly for them.

The larger body of early Muslims, known as Sunnis, a word related to Sunnah, or way of the Prophet, had a more flexible notion of who should succeed Muhammad. In 661, an extremist assassinated Ali near Najaf in what is now Iraq. Nineteen years later Sunnis killed his son, Hussein, not far away in Karbala. These deaths permanently divided the aggrieved Shiite minority from the Sunni majority.

Sunnis historically have afflicted the weaker Shiites, accusing them of shaping a blasphe-   5
mous cult around Ali and Hussein. At the Karbalaa Islamic Education Center in Dearborn,
Michigan, a large mural depicts mourning women who have encountered the riderless horse
of Hussein after his final battle. "You see our history and our situation in this," says Imam
Husham al-Husainy, a Shiite Iraqi émigré who leads the center. In Dearborn, Shiite Iraqis
initially backed the American invasion to depose Saddam Hussein, who persecuted Iraq's
Shiite majority. Most Sunnis in Dearborn condemned the war as an exercise in American
imperialism.

Sufism, another important strain of Islam, is also present in the United States. Sufis
follow a spiritual, inward-looking path. Only a tiny percentage of American Muslims would
identify themselves primarily as Sufis, in part because some more rigid Muslims condemn
Sufism as heretical. But Sufi ideas crop up among the beliefs of many Muslims without
being labeled as such. Sufism's emphasis on self-purification appeals to New Age seekers
and has made it the most common avenue into Islam for white American converts such as
Abdul Kabir Krambo of Yuba City, California. Krambo, an electrician who grew up in a
conservative German Catholic family, helped build a mosque amidst the fruit arbors of the
Sacramento Valley, only to see it burn down in a mysterious arson. Once rebuilt, the Islamic
Center of Yuba City was engulfed again, this time by controversy over whether Krambo and
his Sufi friends were trying to impose a "cult" on other worshipers.

Although there is a broad consensus that Islam is the fastest-growing religion in the
country and the world, no one has provable numbers on just how many American Muslims
there are. The Census Bureau doesn't count by religion, and private surveys of the Muslim
population offer widely disparate conclusions. A study of four hundred mosques nationwide
estimated that there are two million people in the United States "associated with" Islamic
houses of worship. The authors of the survey, published in 2001 under the auspices of the
Council on American Islamic Relations (CAIR), a Muslim advocacy group, employed a
common assumption that only one in three American Muslims associates with a mosque. In
CAIR's view, that suggests there are at least six million Muslims in the country. (Perhaps not
coincidentally the American Jewish population is estimated to be slightly below six million.)
Other Muslim groups put the number higher, seeking to maximize the size and influence of
their constituency.

Surveys conducted by non-Muslims have produced much lower estimates, some in the
neighborhood of only two million or three million. These findings elicit anger from Muslim
leaders, who claim that many immigrant and poor black Muslims are overlooked. On the
basis of all the evidence, a very crude range of three million to six million seems reasonable.
Rapid growth of the Muslim population is expected to continue, fueled mainly by immigration and high birthrates, and, to a lesser extent, by conversion, overwhelmingly by African-
Americans. In the next decade or two there probably will be more Muslims in the United
States than Jews. Worldwide, the Muslim head count is estimated at 1.3 billion, second
among religions only to the combined membership of Christian denominations.

American Muslims, like Americans generally, live mostly in cities and suburbs. Large
concentrations are found in New York, Detroit, Chicago, and Los Angeles. But they also
turn up in the Appalachian foothills and rural Idaho—the sites of two of the stories that
follow—among other surprising places. Often the presence of several hundred Muslims in
an out-of-the-way town can be explained by proximity to a large state university. Many of
these schools have recruited foreign graduate students, including Muslims, since the 1960s.

In the 1980s Washington doled out scholarships to Arab students as part of a campaign to counter the influence of the 1979 Iranian Revolution. Some of the Muslim beneficiaries have stayed and raised families.

In New York, Muslims are typecast as cab drivers; in Detroit, as owners of grocery stores   10 and gas stations. The overall economic reality is very different. Surveys show that the majority of American Muslims are employed in technical, white-collar, and professional fields. These include information technology, corporate management, medicine, and education. An astounding 59 percent of Muslim adults in the United States have college degrees. That compares with only 27 percent of all American adults. Four out of five Muslim workers earn at least twenty-five thousand dollars a year; more than half earn fifty thousand or more. A 2004 survey by a University of Kentucky researcher found that median family income among Muslims is sixty thousand dollars a year; the national median is fifty thousand. Most Muslims own stock or mutual funds, either directly or through retirement plans. Four out of five are registered to vote.

Relative prosperity, high levels of education, and political participation are indications of a minority population successfully integrating into the larger society. By comparison, immigrant Muslims in countries such as Britain, France, Holland, and Spain have remained poorer, less well educated, and socially marginalized. Western European Muslim populations are much larger in percentage terms. Nearly 10 percent of French residents are Muslim; in the United Kingdom the figure is 3 percent. In the more populous United States the Muslim share is 1 to 2 percent, depending on which Muslim population estimate one assumes. It's unlikely that American cities will see the sort of densely packed, volatile Muslim slums that have cropped up on the outskirts of Paris, for example.

America's social safety net is stingy compared with those of Western Europe, but there is greater opportunity for new arrivals to get ahead in material terms. This may attract to the United States more ambitious immigrants willing to adjust to the customs of their new home and eager to acquire education that leads to better jobs. More generous welfare benefits in Europe allow Muslims and other immigrants to live indefinitely on the periphery of society, without steady jobs or social interaction with the majority. Europeans, who for decades encouraged Muslim immigration as a source of menial labor, have shown overt hostility toward the outsiders and little inclination to embrace them as full-fledged citizens. Partly as a result, violent Islamic extremism has found fertile ground in Western Europe.

[2007]

Questions

1. Choosing statistics as support is a strategic approach. Rhetorically, why has Barrett chosen to do this?

2. Barrett uses statistics very effectively to support his claim. What is his claim?

3. When is it helpful to use statistics? Where do you see statistics being used the most? Why do we trust numbers so often? Should we?

Taylor Clark [b. 1979]

Meatless Like Me

A Pacific Northwest native, **Taylor Clark** is a journalist and freelance writer based in Portland, Oregon. Since his graduation from Dartmouth College in 2002, Clark has written for a variety of publications, including *GQ* and *Psychology Today*, and served as a staff writer for *Williamette Week*, Portland's alternative weekly newspaper. During his time at *Williamette Week*, he reported on local government, personalities, and popular culture. His books include *Starbucked: A Double Tall Tale of Caffeine, Commerce, and Culture* (2007), which chronicles Starbucks's expansion into and domination of the global coffee market, and *Nerve: Poise under Pressure, Serenity under Stress, and the Brave New Science of Fear and Cool* (2011).

In "Meatless Like Me," Clark addresses his omnivorous readers, explaining, in an attempt to debunk the stereotypes and misconceptions associated with vegetarianism, why he chooses not to eat meat. In his characteristic style, Clark uses humor as he attempts to foster mutual understanding between skeptical omnivores and his fellow herbivores.

Every vegetarian remembers his first time. Not the unremarkable event of his first meal without meat, mind you. No, I mean the first time he casually lets slip that he's turned herbivore, prompting everyone in earshot to stare at him as if he just revealed plans to sail his carrot- powered plasma yacht to Neptune. For me, this first time came at an Elks scholarship luncheon in rural Oregon when I was 18. All day, I'd succeeded at seeming a promising and responsible young man, until that fateful moment when someone asked why I hadn't taken any meat from the buffet. After I offered my reluctant explanation—and the guy announced it *to the entire room*—30 people went eerily quiet, undoubtedly expecting me to launch into a speech on the virtues of hemp. In the corner, an elderly, suited man glared at me as he slowly raised a slice of bologna and executed the most menacing bite of cold cut in recorded history. I didn't get the scholarship.

I tell this story not to win your pity but to illustrate a point: I've been vegetarian for a decade, and when it comes up, I still get a look of confused horror that says, "But you seemed so...*normal*." The U.S. boasts more than 10 million herbivores today, yet most Americans assume that every last one is a loopy, self-satisfied health fanatic, hellbent on draining all the joy out of life. Those of us who want to avoid the social nightmare have to hide our vegetarianism like an Oxycontin addiction, because admit it, omnivores: You know nothing about us. Do we eat fish? Will we panic if confronted with a hamburger? Are we dying of malnutrition? You have no clue. So read on, my flesh-eating friends—I believe it's high time we cleared a few things up.

To demonstrate what a vegetarian really is, let's begin with a simple thought experiment. Imagine a completely normal person with completely normal food cravings, someone who has a broad range of friends, enjoys a good time, is carbon-based, and so on. Now remove from this person's diet anything that once had eyes, and, *wham!*, you have yourself a vegetarian. Normal person, no previously ocular food, end of story. Some people call themselves vegetarians and still eat chicken or fish, but unless we're talking about the kind of salmon that comes freshly plucked from the vine, this makes you an omnivore. A select few herbivores go one step further and avoid *all* animal products—milk, eggs, honey, leather—and they call themselves *vegan*, which rhymes with "tree men." These people are intense.

Vegetarians give up meat for a variety of ethical, environmental, and health reasons that are secondary to this essay's goal of increasing brotherly understanding, so I'll mostly set them aside. Suffice it to say that one day, I suddenly realized that I could never look a cow in the eyes, press a knocking gun to her temple, and pull the trigger without feeling I'd done something cruel and unnecessary. (Sure, if it's kill the cow or starve, then say your prayers, my bovine friend—but for now, it's not quite a mortal struggle to subsist on the other five food groups.) I am well-aware that even telling you this makes me seem like the kind of person who wants to break into your house and liberate your pet hamster—that is, like a PETA activist. Most vegetarians, though, would tell you that they appreciate the intentions of groups like PETA but not the obnoxious tactics. It's like this: We're all rooting for the same team, but they're the ones in face paint, bellowing obscenities at the umpire and flipping over every car with a Yankees bumper sticker. I have no designs on your Camry or your hamster.

Now, when I say that vegetarians are normal people with normal food cravings, many 5 omnivores will hoist a lamb shank in triumph and point out that you can hardly call yourself normal if the aroma of, say, sizzling bacon doesn't fill you with deepest yearning. To which I reply: We're not *insane*. We *know* meat tastes good; it's why there's a freezer case at your supermarket full of woefully inadequate meat substitutes. Believe me, if obtaining bacon didn't require slaughtering a pig, I'd have a BLT in each hand right now with a bacon layer cake waiting in the fridge for dessert. But, that said, I can also tell you that with some time away from the butcher's section, many meat products start to seem gross. Ground beef in particular now strikes me as absolutely revolting; I have a vague memory that hamburgers taste good, but the idea of taking a cow's leg, mulching it into a fatty pulp, and forming it into a pancake makes me gag. And hot dogs…I mean, *hot dogs*? You *do* know what that is, right?

As a consolation prize we get tofu, a treasure most omnivores are more than happy to do without. Well, this may stun you, but I'm not any more excited about a steaming heap of unseasoned tofu blobs than you are. Tofu is like fugu blowfish sushi: Prepared correctly, it's delicious; prepared incorrectly, it's lethal. Very early in my vegetarian career, I found myself famished and stuck in a mall, so I wandered over to the food court's Asian counter. When I asked the teenage chief culinary artisan what was in the tofu stir-fry, he snorted and replied, "Shit." Desperation made me order it anyway, and I can tell you that promises have rarely been more loyally kept than this guy's pledge that the tofu would taste like shit. So here's a tip: Unless you know you're in expert hands (Thai restaurants are a good bet), don't even try tofu. Otherwise, it's your funeral.

As long as we're discussing restaurants, allow me a quick word with the hardworking chefs at America's dining establishments. We really appreciate that you included a vegetarian option on your menu (and if you didn't, is our money not green?), but it may interest you to know that most of us are not salad freaks on a grim slog for nourishment. We actually enjoy food, especially the kind that tastes good. So enough with the bland vegetable dishes, and, for God's sake, *please* make the Gardenburgers stop; it's stunning how many restaurants lavish unending care on their meat dishes yet are content to throw a flavorless hockey puck from Costco into the microwave and call it cuisine. Every vegetarian is used to slim pickings when dining out, so we're not asking for much—just for something *you'd* like to eat. I'll even offer a handy trick. Pretend you're trapped in a kitchen stocked with every ingredient imaginable, from asiago to zucchini, but with zero meat. With no flesh available, picture what you'd make for yourself; this is what we want, too.

For those kind-hearted omnivores who willingly invite feral vegetarians into their homes for dinner parties and barbecues (really! we do that, too!), the same rule applies—but also know that unless you're dealing with an herbivore who is a prick for unrelated reasons, we don't expect you to bend over backward for us. In fact, if we get the sense that you cooked for three extra hours to accommodate our dietary preferences, we will marvel at your considerate nature, but we will also feel insanely guilty. Similarly, it's very thoughtful of you to ask whether it'll bother me if I see you eat meat, but don't worry: I'm not going to compose an epic poem about your club sandwich.

Which leads me to a vital point for friendly omnivore-herbivore relations. As you're enjoying that pork loin next to me, *I am not silently judging you.* I realize that anyone who has encountered the breed of smug vegetarian who says things like, "I can hear your lunch screaming," will find this tough to believe, but I'm honestly not out to convert you. My girlfriend and my closest pals all eat meat, and they'll affirm that I've never even raised an eyebrow about it. Now, do I think it strange that the same people who dress their dogs in berets and send them to day spas are often unfazed that an equally smart pig suffered and died to become their McMuffin? Yes, I do. (Or, to use a more pressing example, how many Americans will bemoan Eight Belles' fatal Kentucky Derby injury tonight at the dinner table between bites of beef?) Would I prefer it if we at least raised these animals humanely? Yes, I would.

Let's be honest, though: I'm not exactly St. Francis of Assisi over here, tenderly minis-   10
tering to every chipmunk that crosses my path. I try to represent for the animal kingdom, but take a look at my shoes—they're made of leather, which, I am told by those with expert knowledge of the tanning process, comes from dead cows. This is the sort of revelation that prompts meat boosters to pick up the triumphant lamb shank once again and accuse us of hypocrisy. Well, *sort of.* (Hey, *you* try to find a pair of nonleather dress shoes.) My dedication to the cause might be incomplete, but I'd still say that doing something beats doing nothing. It's kind of like driving a hybrid: not a solution to the global-warming dilemma but a decent start. Let's just say that at the dinner table, I roll in a Prius.

Finally, grant me one more cordial request: Please don't try to convince us that being vegetarian is somehow wrong. If you're concerned for my health, that's very nice, though you can rest assured that I'm in shipshape. If you want to have an amiable tête-à-tête about vegetarianism, that's great. But if you insist on being the aggressive blowhard who takes meatlessness as a personal insult and rails about what fools we all are, you're only going to persuade me that you're a dickhead. When someone says he's Catholic, you probably don't start the stump speech about how God is a lie created to enslave the ignorant masses, and it's equally offensive to berate an herbivore. I know you think we're crazy. That's neat. But seeing as I've endured the hassle of being a vegetarian for several years now, perhaps I've given this a *little* thought. So let's just agree to disagree and get on with making fun of Hillary Clinton's inability to operate a coffee machine.

Because, really, peace and understanding are what it's all about: your porterhouse and my portobello coexisting in perfect harmony—though preferably not touching. We're actually not so different, after all, my omnivorous chums. In fact, I like to think that when an omnivore looks in the mirror, he just sees a vegetarian who happens to eat meat. Or, no, wait, maybe the *mirror* sees the omnivore through the *prism* of flesh and realizes we all have a crystalline animal soul, you know?

This is excellent weed, by the way, if you want a hit. Hey, while you're here: Have I ever told you about hemp?

[2008]

Questions

1. "Meatless Like Me" is framed as the truth about being a vegetarian. List some of the misconceptions with which Clark engages. Choose one you found compelling, and analyze Clark's argument. What was effective about it?

2. Choose an aspect of your identity you feel is often stereotyped. Imagine you are composing an argument in which you, like Clark, attempt to persuade someone who may subscribe to these stereotypical notions to view you through a more complex lens that recognizes your humanity. What rhetorical choices would you make to assert your humanity?

Philip Gefter

Photographic Icons: Fact, Fiction, or Metaphor?

Photography critic and writer **Philip Gefter** is a 1973 graduate of the Pratt Institute. After completing his fine arts degree in painting and photography, Gefter worked as a picture researcher for the Time-Life Picture Collection. Since, he has written about photography for publications including the *Daily Beast* and the *New York Times*, and he has also held the position of picture editor for the *New York Times*, *Aperture*, *Forbes*, *Fortune*, and the *San Francisco Examiner's* Sunday magazine. In 1991, Gefter was among the founding members of the National Lesbian and Gay Journalists Association, and in 2008, his writings on contemporary photography—critical reviews, essays, and even obituaries—were collected in the book *Photography after Frank* (2009). Gefter is currently working on a biography of art curator Sam Wagstaff, as well as producing a feature-length documentary about photographer Bill Cunningham of the *New York Times*.

In the following essay, originally published in *Aperture*, Gefter writes, "Truth-telling is the promise of a photograph…. A photograph comes as close as we get to witnessing an authentic moment with our own eyes while not actually being there." But, as he questions, what is truth, even in "real" photos that have not been altered or digitally enhanced? Gefter invites us to reevaluate a collection of famous images and ask: What is real? Are photographs facts? Fiction? Something in between?

Truth-telling is the promise of a photograph—as if fact itself resides in the optical precision with which the medium reflects our native perception. A photograph comes as close as we get to witnessing an authentic moment with our own eyes while not actually being there. Think of all the famous pictures that serve as both documentation and verification of historic events: Mathew Brady's photographs of the Civil War; Lewis Hine's chronicle of industrial growth in America; the birth of the Civil Rights movement documented in a picture of Rosa Parks on a segregated city bus in Montgomery, Alabama. Aren't they proof of the facts in real time, moments in history brought to the present?

Of course, just because a photograph reflects the world with perceptual accuracy doesn't mean it is proof of what spontaneously transpired. A photographic image might look like actual reality, but gradations of truth are measured in the circumstances that led up to the moment the picture was taken.

The viewer's expectation about a picture's veracity is largely determined by the context in which the image appears. A picture published in a newspaper is believed to be fact; an advertising image is understood to be fiction. If a newspaper image turns out to have been set up, then questions are raised about trust and authenticity. Still, somewhere between fact and fiction—or perhaps hovering slightly above either one—is the province of metaphor, where the truth is approximated in renderings of a more poetic or symbolic nature.

The impulse to define, perfect, or heighten reality is manifest in a roster of iconic photographs that have come to reside in the world as "truth." While Mathew Brady is known for his Civil War pictures, he rarely set foot on a battlefield. He couldn't bear the sight of dead bodies. In fact, most pictures of the battlefield attributed to Brady's studio were taken by his employees Alexander Gardner and Timothy O'Sullivan—both of whom were known to have moved bodies around for the purposes of composition and posterity.

In *Home of a Rebel Sharpshooter, Gettysburg* (1863), a picture by Gardner, the body of a 5 dead soldier lies in perfect repose. His head is tilted in the direction of the camera, his hand on his belly, his rifle propped up vertically against the rocks. There would be no question that this is a scene the photographer happened upon, if it weren't for another picture by Gardner of the same soldier, this time his face turned away from the camera and his rifle lying on the ground.

In the Library of Congress catalog, the photograph *Dead Soldiers at Antietam* (1862) is listed twice, under the names of both Brady and Gardner. In the image, approximately two dozen dead soldiers lie in a very neat row across the field. Could they possibly have fallen in such tidy succession? Knowing what we do about Gardner's picture of the rebel soldier, the possibility lingers that he moved some of these bodies to create a better composition. Or it could be that other soldiers had lined the bodies up before digging a mass grave for burial. But whatever the circumstances that led to this picture, it is verifiable that the battle of Antietam took place on this field. We know that numbers of soldiers were killed. Evidence of the battle remains—the soldiers that died on that date, the battlefield on which they fought, the clothes they wore, and so on. Just how much of the subject matter does the photographer have to change before fact becomes fiction, or a photograph becomes metaphor?

Mathew Brady/Alexander Gardner, *Bodies of Confederate Dead Gathered for Burial*, Battle of Antietam, September, 1862.
(Library of Congress Prints and Photographs Division, LC# B811-0557C.)

"Mathew Brady used art to forge a relationship between photography and history, but when the memory of Brady the artist vanished, we came to accept his images as fact," Mary Panzer wrote in her 1997 book *Mathew Brady and the Image of History*. "Acknowledged or not, Brady's careful manipulation of his subjects continues to influence our perception, and still shapes the way in which we see his era, and the story of the nation."

Lewis Hine's 1920 photograph of a powerhouse mechanic symbolizes the work ethic that built America. The simplicity of the photograph long ago turned it into a powerful icon, all the more poignant because of its "authenticity." But in fact, Hine—who was interested in the human labor aspect of an increasingly mechanized world, and once claimed that "there is an urgent need for intelligent interpretation of the world's workers"—posed this man in order to make the portrait. Does that information make the picture any less valid?

Lewis Hine, an early variant of his *Powerhouse Mechanic*.
(Courtesy George Eastman House.)

Lewis Hine, his final, iconic *Powerhouse Mechanic*, 1920.
(Courtesy George Eastman House.)

We see in the first shot that the worker's zipper is down. Isn't it a sad fact that the flaws in daily life should prevent reality from being the best version of how things really are? In our attempt to perfect reality, we aim for higher standards. A man with his zipper down is undignified, and so the famous icon, posed as he is, presents an idealized version of the American worker—dignity customized, but forever intact. Still, the mechanic did work in that powerhouse and his gesture is true enough to his labor. The reality of what the image depicts is indisputable, and whether Hine maintained a fidelity to what transpired in real time may or may not be relevant to its symbolic import.

Le Baiser de l'Hôtel de Ville (Kiss at the Hôtel de Ville, 1950) by Robert Doisneau, 10 despite its overexposure on posters and postcards, has long served as an example of how photography can capture the spontaneity of life. What a breezy testament to the pleasure of romance! How lovely the couple is, how elegant their gesture and their clothing, how delightful this perspective from a café in Paris! It makes you believe in romantic love: you want to be there, as if you, too, would surely witness love blossoming all around you—or even find it yourself—while sitting at a café in the City of Light.

But despite the story this picture seems to tell—one of a photographer who just happened to look up from his Pernod as the enchanted lovers walked by—there was no serendipity whatsoever in the moment. Doisneau had seen the man and woman days earlier, near the school at which they were studying acting. He was on assignment for *Life* magazine, for a story on romance in Paris, and hired the couple as models for the shot. This information was not brought to light until the early 1990s, when lawsuits demanding compensation were filed by several people who claimed to be the models in the famous picture. Does the lack of authenticity diminish the photograph? It did for me, turning its promise of romance into a beautifully crafted lie.

Ruth Orkin was in Florence, Italy, in the early 1950s when she met Jinx Allen, whom she asked to be the subject of a picture Orkin wanted to submit to the *Herald Tribune*. *American Girl in Italy* was conceived inadvertently when Orkin noticed the Italian men on their Vespas ogling Ms. Allen as she walked down the street. Orkin asked her to walk down the street again, to be sure she had the shot. Does a second take alter the reality of the phenomenon? How do you parse the difference between Doisneau's staged picture and Orkin's re-creation?

Ruth Orkin, *American Girl in Italy*, Florence, Italy, 1951.
(Copyright © Ruth Orkin 1951, 1980.)

Iwo Jima, Old Glory Goes Up on Mt. Suribachi was taken in 1945 by Joe Rosenthal, an Associated Press photographer. As documentation of a World War II victory, the picture immediately assumed symbolic significance—indeed, it won Rosenthal a Pulitzer Prize, and is one of the most enduring images of the twentieth century. For some time, it was considered a posed picture, but this was due to a misunderstanding. The famous image was the first of three pictures Rosenthal took of the flag being raised. For the last shot, he asked the soldiers to pose in front of the raised flag, thinking that the newspapers back home would expect a picture in which the soldiers' faces were visible. Later, asked if his picture of Iwo Jima was posed, he said yes—referring in his mind to that third frame, not the one that had been published. Still, that the moment captured in the well-known picture occurred just as we see it today surely confirms the truth-telling capability of photography.

Joe Rosenthal, *Flag-Raising on Iwo Jima*, 1945.
(Courtesy Joe Rosenthal/AP/Wide World Photos.)

The birth of the Civil Rights movement is often dated back to a moment in 1955 when Rosa Parks, a black woman, refused to give up her seat on a crowded city bus to a white man in Montgomery, Alabama. (While she was not the first black bus rider to refuse to give up her seat, her case became the one on which the legal challenge was based.) Many people assume that the famous picture of Parks sitting on a city bus is an actual record of that historic moment. But the picture was taken on December 21, 1956, a year after she refused to give up her seat, and a month after the U.S. Supreme Court ruled Montgomery's segregated bus system illegal. Before she died, Parks told Douglas Brinkley, her biographer, that she posed for the picture. A reporter and two photographers from *Look* magazine had seated her on the bus in front of a white man. Similar photo opportunities were arranged on the same day for other members of the Civil Rights community, including Martin Luther King. Here is a staged document that has become a historic reference point, and a revealing parable about the relationship of history to myth.

Rosa Parks, 1956. Rosa Parks sits at the front of a bus on December 21, 1956, the first day that the transportation system in Montgomery, Alabama, was integrated. Parks was arrested on December 1, 1955, for refusing to give up her seat in the front of a bus in Montgomery. The man sitting behind Parks in this photo is Nicholas C. Chriss, a reporter for United Press International out of Atlanta. (Bettmann/Corbis.)

As a witness to events, the photojournalist sets out to chronicle what happens in the world   15
as it actually occurs. A cardinal rule of the profession is that the presence of the camera must
not alter the situation being photographed. Four years ago, Edward Keating, among the best
staff photographers at the *New York Times*, was fired because of questions raised about one
picture he took that ended up in the newspaper. This correction was published in the Times
five days later:

> A picture in the early editions on September 20, 2002, showed a 6-year-old boy aiming
> a toy pistol alongside a sign reading "Arabian Foods" outside a store in Lackawanna,
> N.Y., near Buffalo. The store was near the scene of two arrests in a raid described by the
> authorities as a pre-emptive strike against a cell of Al Qaeda, and the picture appeared
> with an article recounting the life stories of the detainees. The picture was not relevant
> to the article and should not have appeared.

Edward Keating, *Boy with Pistol*, 2002.
(Edward Keating/The New York Times/Redux.)

The correction went on to say that photographers on the scene from other news organizations had reported that Keating asked the young boy to aim the toy pistol. Upon further inquiry and a full inspection of the images from the entire photo assignment, the "editors concluded, and Mr. Keating acknowledged, that the boy's gesture had not been spontaneous." Altering the reality of the situation is a violation of journalistic policy, and it turned Keating's image from fact to illustration—a potent editorial statement about the Arabic community at a highly sensitive moment.

Paradoxically, looking through the photography archives of the *New York Times*, one is struck by the numbers of prints in which one or more people have been airbrushed out of the picture. The technique has been used at times to highlight an individual relevant to a particular news story, or simply to sharpen a line for better reproduction on newsprint. Other pictures have red-pencil crop marks, with which the art director or picture editor isolated only that part of the image relevant to the news story. To be fair, these changes were made not for the sake of censorship, but rather as part of an editing process simply to filter out unwanted information—perhaps no more egregious than cutting down a subject's spoken quotation to its salient points.

In 1839, the invention of photography provided a revolutionary method of replicating reality in accurate visual terms. What a great tool for artists and painters to construct images with greater perceptual facility. The history of art is a continuum of constructed images that depict reality as it was truly, or else as it was imagined in ideal terms. Photography did not change that continuum; it only made the difference between perception and reality more difficult to determine.

[2006]

Questions

1. What does Gefter mean when he writes: "truth-telling is the promise of a photograph" (para. 1)? Can a photograph ever live up to that promise?

2. Choose one of the photographs Gefter mentions in this essay (Notice that not all the photographs he talks about are pictured in the text, but you may choose these as well). Analyze Gefter's discussion of your chosen photograph—what is the main point he is communicating? Find examples for how Gefter uses *logos, ethos,* and *pathos* in this discussion. How do the examples of *logos, ethos,* and *pathos* that you located make his argument more convincing?

3. Scan social media or a news outlet for an article that incorporates a photograph. Why was this photo chosen for the article? What message is it trying to convey? How does the photograph contribute to the purpose of the article?

Ariel Levy [b. 1974]

Women and the Rise of Raunch Culture

Raised in Larchmont, New York, **Ariel Levy** studied literature at Wesleyan University and worked briefly at Planned Parenthood prior to beginning her career as a journalist. Before becoming a staff writer for the *New Yorker* in 2008, she spent twelve years as a contributing editor for *New York* magazine. Her articles, which often focus on issues in American popular culture, have been published in the *New York Times*, the *Washington Post*, *Vogue*, and *Men's Journal*. Levy also authored the foreword to the twentieth-anniversary edition of Andrea Dworkin's *Intercourse* (2006) and was named as one of the *Advocate*'s "Forty under 40" in 2009. In *Female Chauvinist Pigs: Women and the Rise of Raunch Culture* (2005), focusing on the rise of such things as *Girls Gone Wild* and the Howard Stern radio show, Levy wonders about the new and troubling ways we have learned to think about gender equity, feminist politics, and the pursuit of civil rights.

In the following excerpt from *Female Chauvinist Pigs*, Levy chronicles the twenty-first-century rise of the raunch. She claims that female self-exhibition has become, more than a norm, a perverse kind of social ideal. Levy asks her readers to be critical of the overly sexual representations of women prevalent in contemporary American society, arguing that this postfeminist movement has embraced ideologies of women that feminists struggled to overcome.

I first noticed it several years ago. I would turn on the television and find strippers in pasties explaining how best to lap dance a man to orgasm. I would flip the channel and see babes in tight, tiny uniforms bouncing up and down on trampolines. Britney Spears was becoming increasingly popular and increasingly unclothed, and her undulating body ultimately became so familiar to me I felt like we used to go out.

Charlie's Angels, the film remake of the quintessential jiggle show, opened at number one in 2000 and made $125 million in theaters nationally, reinvigorating the interest of men and women alike in leggy crime fighting. Its stars, who kept talking about "strong women" and "empowerment," were dressed in alternating soft-porn styles—as massage parlor geishas, dominatrixes, yodeling Heidis in alpine bustiers. (The summer sequel in 2003—in which the Angels' perilous mission required them to perform stripteases—pulled in another $100 million domestically.) In my own industry, magazines, a porny new genre called the Lad Mag, which included titles like *Maxim*, *FHM*, and *Stuff*, was hitting the stands and becoming a huge success by delivering what *Playboy* had only occasionally managed to capture: greased celebrities in little scraps of fabric humping the floor.

This didn't end when I switched off the radio or the television or closed the magazines. I'd walk down the street and see teens and young women—and the occasional wild fifty-year-old—wearing jeans cut so low they exposed what came to be known as butt cleavage paired with miniature tops that showed off breast implants and pierced navels alike. Sometimes, in case the overall message of the outfit was too subtle, the shirts would be emblazoned with the Playboy bunny or say Porn Star across the chest.

Some odd things were happening in my social life, too. People I knew (female people) liked going to strip clubs (female strippers). It was sexy and fun, they explained; it was liberating and rebellious. My best friend from college, who used to go to Take Back the Night marches on campus, had become captivated by porn stars. She would point them out to me in music videos and watch their (topless) interviews on *Howard Stern*. As for me, I wasn't going to strip clubs or buying *Hustler* T-shirts, but I was starting to show signs of impact all the same. It had only been a few years since I'd graduated from Wesleyan University, a place where you could pretty much get expelled for saying "girl" instead of "woman," but somewhere along the line I'd started saying "chick." And, like most chicks I knew, I'd taken to wearing thongs.

What was going on? My mother, a shiatsu masseuse who attended weekly women's 5 consciousness-raising groups for twenty-four years, didn't own makeup. My father, whom she met as a student radical at the University of Wisconsin, Madison, in the sixties was a consultant for Planned Parenthood, NARAL, and NOW. Only thirty years (my lifetime) ago, our mothers were "burning their bras" and picketing *Playboy*, and suddenly we were getting implants and wearing the bunny logo as supposed symbols of our liberation. How had the culture shifted so drastically in such a short period of time?

What was almost more surprising than the change itself were the responses I got when I started interviewing the men and—often—women who edit magazines like *Maxim* and make programs like *The Man Show* and *Girls Gone Wild*. This new raunch culture didn't mark the death of feminism, they told me; it was evidence that the feminist project had already been achieved. We'd *earned* the right to look at *Playboy*; we were *empowered* enough to get Brazilian bikini waxes. Women had come so far, I learned, we no longer needed to worry about objectification or misogyny. Instead, it was time for us to join the frat party of pop culture, where men had been enjoying themselves all along. If Male Chauvinist Pigs were men who regarded women as pieces of meat, we would outdo them and be Female Chauvinist Pigs: women who make sex objects of other women and of ourselves.

When I asked female viewers and readers what they got out of raunch culture, I heard similar things about empowering miniskirts and feminist strippers, and so on, but I also heard something else. They wanted to be "one of the guys"; they hoped to be experienced "like a man." Going to strip clubs or talking about porn stars was a way of showing themselves and the men around them that they weren't "prissy little women" or "girly-girls." Besides, they told me, it was all in fun, all tongue-in-cheek, and for me to regard this bacchanal as problematic would be old-school and uncool.

I tried to get with the program, but I could never make the argument add up in my head. How is resurrecting every stereotype of female sexuality that feminism endeavored to banish *good* for women? Why is laboring to look like Pamela Anderson empowering? And how is imitating a stripper or a porn star—a woman whose *job* is to imitate arousal in the first place—going to render us sexually liberated?

Despite the rising power of Evangelical Christianity and the political right in the United States, this trend has only grown more extreme and more pervasive in the years that have passed since I first became aware of it. A tawdry, tarty, cartoonlike version of female sexuality has become so ubiquitous, it no longer seems particular. What we once regarded as a *kind* of sexual expression we now view as sexuality. As former adult film star Traci Lords put it to a reporter a few days before her memoir hit the bestseller list in 2003, "When I was in porn, it was like a back-alley thing. Now it's everywhere." Spectacles of naked ladies have moved from seedy side streets to center stage, where everyone—men and women—can watch them in broad daylight. *Playboy* and its ilk are being "embraced by young women in a curious way in a postfeminist world," to borrow the words of Hugh Hefner.

But just because we are post doesn't automatically mean we are feminists. There is a widespread assumption that simply because my generation of women has the good fortune to live in a world touched by the feminist movement, that means everything we do is magically imbued with its agenda. It doesn't work that way. "Raunchy" and "liberated" are not synonyms. It is worth asking ourselves if this bawdy world of boobs and gams we have resurrected reflects how far we've come, or how far we have left to go.

[2005]

Questions

1. This essay was published in 2005, and the pop culture references may have become outdated. Rewrite specific sections, updating these references. How are your references different? Does the argument change?

2. While Aronson's piece, "The Nurture of Nature," does not directly address the "So what?" question, Levy's does. How does Levy address the "So what?" question in her essay? Why is it important to discuss the implications of your argument?

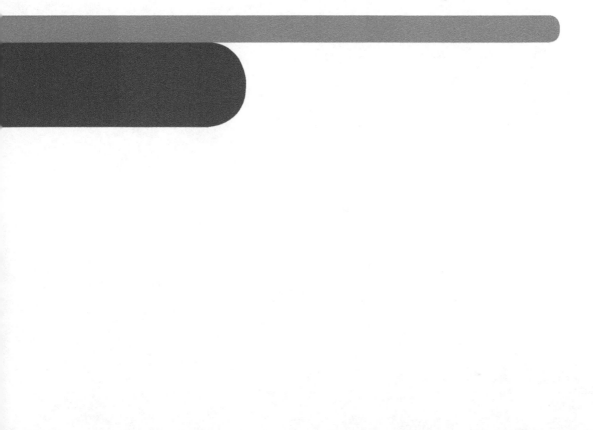

Advanced Rhetorical
Analysis and Argument

Charles Seife

The Loneliness of the Interconnected

I think it's a very firm part of human nature that if you surround yourself with like-minded people, you'll end up thinking more extreme versions of what you thought before.
—Cass Sunstein

Opinions are stubborn things. The firmest ones can weather for years a hailstorm of contrary facts, remaining nearly immutable in a flood of contrary evidence. Only slowly do they yield, eroded, bit by bit, by time as much as by the impositions of external reality.

The importance of a fact is measured not in absolute terms, but by judging it against the opinions it challenges. In the field known as information theory, the bits and bytes of an incoming message contain information only if the content is, to some degree, unexpected. If you can predict, with perfect confidence, what's inside an envelope without needing to open it, there's nothing to be gained by opening the envelope. It's the very unpredictability of the message—the fact that the reader doesn't know exactly what the letter contains—that gives the message any informational value at all. Information is that which defies expectation.

Information is not the barrage of facts that's pelting us from every direction. Information consists of those facts and messages that, in some way, shape our ideas. Information is the force that causes the erosion of our mental landscape, that undermines and reconstructs our perceptions of the world. Anything that does not affect our opinions is not information; it's noise.

As we grow and learn, the fragile and unsupported parts of our mental landscape are washed away, and we are left with some opinions that are as firm as bedrock—and just as difficult to move. And once in a great while, there is such a storm of hard, inescapable fact that it challenges to topple even one of our bedrock beliefs, and this causes a mental crisis.

In the 1950s, psychologist Leon Festinger sought to understand what happens at the 5 crisis moment—when an immovable object of a core belief comes into conflict with the irresistible force of an undeniable contrary fact. And he did it by making an inspired choice about whom to study: an apocalyptic cult.

Festinger decided that the ideal subjects to study would be the members of a small group of people led by a housewife in a Chicago suburb. This woman, Dorothy Martin, claimed to write letters under the direction of beings from the planet Clarion. These beings told her that early in the morning on December 21, 1955, there would be a tremendous cataclysm: Chicago would be destroyed, and much of the United states would be submerged in a great flood. But all was not lost: Martin learned from her spirit guide that as the clock tolled midnight in the last few hours before the disaster, a spaceman would knock on the door and lead Martin and her followers to a saucer that would whisk them to safety.

Festinger knew that for the cult's members, the belief in this disaster and salvation was incredibly deeply held. Many of the members of the cult had made large personal sacrifices because of their faith in Mrs. Martin's prophecy; one, a respected physician, had lost his job—and become a laughingstock—when he exposed his daft beliefs to the newspapers. The members of the cult were so sure of the coming day of reckoning that they were willing to isolate themselves, give away their worldly goods, and even tear apart their clothing (to remove metal zippers and snaps that could injure them aboard the flying saucer) based upon their confidence in Mrs. Martin's writings. Only a deep, firm belief could inspire people to make such sacrifices. Yet when the spaceman failed to knock at the door, the cult members would be faced with the inescapable fact that the prophecy had been false. Here was a clear-cut case of immovable belief versus irresistible fact—and it would happen on a schedule.

For Festinger, this was a perfect case study that would help him understand what he termed "cognitive dissonance"—a situation in which a person is forced to believe two mutually incompatible ideas at the same time. In particular, it would allow him to test a somewhat counterintuitive hypothesis: that when the spaceman failed to show up, Mrs. Martin and some of her followers would become even more fervent in their beliefs. in other words, the inescapable fact that the prediction failed wouldn't merely fail to shake some of Mrs. Martin's followers from their faith—it would even strengthen their fervor.

Festinger's theory was based upon the assumption that cognitive dissonance is intensely uncomfortable for most humans. When confronted with such pain, we attempt to resolve the dissonance through whatever mechanisms we have at hand. And when the dissonance-causing fact is as firm and unyielding as the continued existence of Chicago, there are only two basic approaches that one can take. First, a person can reshape the belief to accommodate the fact, or perhaps even discard the belief entirely. However, this would have been a very painful thing to do in this case, given how deeply held the belief was. The other alternative is to attempt to counter the weight of the oppressing fact by increasing one's conviction in the belief. Since this can't be done with facts, it's done with people. Specifically, Festinger argued that once Mrs. Martin's prophecy failed, some of the cult members would try to solve their cognitive dissonance by strengthening social bonds within the group and by attempting to gain more supporters. As Festinger puts it:

> It is unlikely that one isolated believer could withstand the kind of disconfirming evidence we have specified. If, however, the believer is a member of a group of convinced persons who can support one another, we would expect the belief to be maintained and the believers to attempt to proselyte or to persuade nonmembers that the belief is correct.

It happened, more or less, as Festinger thought it would. Mrs. Martin and many of the   10 die-hard believers weren't put off by the disconfirmation. Instead, she softened the blow by revealing new alien messages that would help explain the failed coming of the apocalypse. Even more telling, though, the group suddenly increased its attempts to proselytize—even to the point of issuing press releases to the media. The group would seek comfort by trying to increase its size.

The most potent weapon for fighting off uncomfortable facts is other people—a network of the faithful who are willing to believe with you. In the arms of fellow true believers, you can find solace from the brutal reality of disconfirmation.

This is just as true today as it was in the 1950s. We seek shelter from the harsh information that carves away our cherished beliefs by finding other people who share our convictions. Social ties reinforce our internal mental landscape so that it can better resist a blast of unwelcome facts. But now, with the advent of the digital age, our interconnectedness has increased almost without bound. We are able to communicate with peers all around the world as easily as—more easily than—visiting our next-door neighbor. With this tremendous interconnectedness comes the ability to build many more social ties, to weave a vaster web of personal bonds than ever before. and that means that the internet gives us much more raw social material than ever before to help us bolster our shaky prejudices and beliefs.

In a very real way, the internet is helping us preserve our mental landscape from the weathering effects of information. We are becoming ever more resistant to the effects of uncomfortable facts—and ever more capable of treating them as mere noise.

If you've ever been to London, there's a good chance you've visited the northeast edge of Hyde Park. It's a prime tourist attraction because, if you're interested in seeing the local wildlife, you can't do better than visiting Speakers' Corner on a gray Sunday afternoon. If you choose to go, you'll almost certainly be treated to a fine display: a dozen or so men (mostly) and a few women, perched on ladders and makeshift podiums, each bellowing out their complaints and exhortations to all passersby. There are Marxists on the left, apocalyptic Christians on the right, and all variety of true believers in between, haranguing the crowd—and one another—in hopes of winning a few converts. The best (or merely the most entertaining) among them can draw crowds of fifty or a hundred people or even more; even likelier is the chance to pick up a heckler or two who will fling verbal pies in hopes of catching a speaker square in the face.

Speakers' Corner is touted as a bastion of free speech—a place where Londoners and other Britons can come and air their grievances, no matter how absurd. But it's not really the prospect of free speech that draws so many speakers to that particular corner of Hyde Park every Sunday afternoon. After all, the vast majority of speakers are able to speak freely about their beliefs in plenty of other places, both public and private, without getting hauled off to jail. What brings them to Hyde Park on Sunday is not free speech, but a free audience. 15

What's so valuable to the speakers is that the Sunday-afternoon ritual is likely to draw a thousand or more curious people, tourists and locals alike, all of whom mill about in hopes of finding something worth listening to for a few brief moments. It's an opportunity to speak in front of a receptive crowd of a respectable size—a size that few speakers are dynamic and interesting enough to draw on their own. It's a tremendous amount of work to build up an audience as an orator, and Speakers' Corner is a way to reach far more people than an amateur could get any other way.

An audience used to be a precious and rare commodity. Generally, one could get it only through unusual eloquence, through power, or through money. The politician and the preacher build and wield their strength by gathering large audiences and influencing their thought. Conversely, certain offices automatically confer upon the holder massive, world-spanning audiences. The entire world hangs upon what the president or the pope has to say; before their elections, Barack Obama and Jorge Bergoglio had to struggle and shout to get significant numbers of people to pay attention—and they seldom had the opportunity to garner a large audience. Money, too, buys listeners; Michael Bloomberg and Rupert Murdoch, like William Randolph Hearst and Joseph Pulitzer before them, realized that nothing's better for reaching people than owning a media empire.

What opportunities were there for the rest of us? Barring an accident of fate that brings us into the public eye—as a witness or a victim or a bit player in a drama—we had to be content with writing the occasional angry letter to the editor of our local paper or joining forces with a handful of like-minded people who felt strongly about an issue dear to us. Perhaps we might try to attract the attention of somebody with his own audience, like a congressperson or a reporter. We could speak as freely as we wanted, but it made little difference if nobody heard what we were saying.

Then came the internet.

The audience problem had vanished. The internet's vast interconnectivity made it pos- 20
sible for everyone to hear everyone else—and to be heard by everyone else. This is perhaps
the most important and radical change wrought by digital information. every single person
hooked up to the web can instantly reach every other person. Your audience is potentially
the world.

Twitter is an international Speakers' Corner writ larger than anyone had ever imagined.
The speech isn't quite free, but the number of people listening is vast. You can say something
and, in theory, hundreds of millions of people on all seven continents are able to hear you
loud and clear—if you can convince them to tune in. As with Speakers' Corner, most orators
on Twitter and in other corners of the internet ramble and rave, sharing little of interest.
But there are enough virtual passersby that if you have a little eloquence and a little skill,
you can soon have your voice and even your image echoing around the globe. It's sometimes
stunning to see how easy it can be to become an international celebrity, if only for a short
time. Even against your will.

In 2002, Canadian high school student Ghyslain Raza videotaped himself swinging
a large pole around himself as if it were a kung fu weapon. Somewhat portly and terribly
uncoordinated, Raza cut a ridiculous figure—as many of us soon found out. For poor Raza
left the videotape where some of his fellow classmates could find it, and they uploaded it
to YouTube. It soon went viral; Ghyslain, dubbed "Star Wars Kid" for his very un-Jedi-like
martial-arts skills, had become an international celebrity. Within a short time, hundreds of
thousands of people had watched Raza's antics. As of 2013, the video had been viewed some
twenty-eight million times. (By way of comparison, I'll consider myself very, very lucky if
this book is read by a few hundred thousand.) Upload a cute enough video of a cat playing
a piano, or do something extraordinarily foolish like shoot yourself in the leg during a gun-
safety class, or create something goofy enough to tickle people's fancy—dancing hamsters
or dancing babies or dancing Gangnams—and there's a chance you'll get a brief adrenaline
burst of fame.

The point is not that you're guaranteed to be heard among the clatter and noise of the
internet; it's that, as small and insignificant as your voice might be, it is at least possible
that your voice can be perceived—and amplified—to the point that you're heard by an
international audience that would make any major broadcast network proud. The mob is
always there, listening, waiting to hear something interesting, and even without the power
of a president or the money of a Mort Zuckerman, for a short time, at least, you can have
a pulpit almost as bully as what they've got. This is free speech in the truest sense. It's not
just the freedom to speak out about anything; it's also the ability to be heard by everybody.

With the ability to be heard comes the ability to organize. The internet has made it
easier than ever to set up networks of like-minded people—to set up groups who have a
belief or an interest in common, no matter how unusual or bizarre that interest or belief
might be. Even the ideas on the very fringe of human thought—a notion that might be held
by only one in a million people—might find a devoted network of several hundred or even
a few thousand followers on the internet.

For example, in 2008, the Centers for Disease Control launched an investigation into a 25
new, horrific disease. Sufferers often feel a weird crawling or biting sensation underneath the
skin, and rashes and sores soon appear. Many people afflicted with the disease report pulling

thin, wormlike fibers from sores. Only a few years earlier had the ailment gotten a name: Morgellons disease.

The name Morgellons was coined by Mary Leitao, a mother who was increasingly frustrated at dermatologists' inability to find out what was wrong with her young son, who kept developing strange sores that had threads poking out of them. Using a word from an old French medical article that seemed to describe a similar ailment, Leitao gave the disease a concrete name and created a foundation to attempt to find the cause of the mysterious ailment. And a website.

Once that website was established, it became a focal point for people who felt they had similar problems. The word spread quickly, and hundreds of people with similar symptoms began contacting the foundation, as well as other authorities who might be able to help, such as the Mayo Clinic and the Centers for Disease Control. By 2007—just three years after the first report of Morgellons—the CDC received about twelve hundred reports of Morgellons, triggering the inquiry. This was quite remarkable, given that the disease doesn't really exist.

Morgellons appears to be a variant of a fairly well-known condition called "delusional parasitosis"—the false conviction that you've got bugs crawling under your skin. It's not uncommon in people who are taking cocaine or other drugs, and in those who have schizophrenia, and it can occasionally strike healthy (or healthy-seeming) people as well.

The CDC study was very gentle about dispelling the myth of Morgellons, saying only that it "shares a number of clinical and epidemiologic features" with delusional parasitosis, but the message was clear enough: the disease was in the patients' minds. The fibers they found—which were analyzed by researchers—were almost all skin fragments or cotton threads that likely came from clothing. There are no bugs or strange foreign-body-producing organisms under the skin. Nevertheless, the victims clearly suffer, even if the disease has no external cause.

Despite the findings of the study, many Morgellons sufferers are unshaken in their 30 belief that there really is something going on underneath their skin—whether it's parasites or, as a number of Morgellons theorists believe, alien DNA or self-replicating nanobots dumped by government airplanes. The deeper you delve into the internet literature on the subject, the stranger the ideas become. And looking into these ideas, it becomes clear that the internet is not just the repository in which these odd beliefs are archived and transmitted—it's also the medium that gives these ideas life in the first place. The fringe beliefs are birthed and nourished by the social connections that the internet makes possible. As two Canadian psychiatrists put it:

> a belief is not considered delusional if it is accepted by other members of an individual's culture or subculture. Although this may be appropriate in the context of spiritual or religious beliefs, the scenario in which a widely held belief is accepted as plausible simply because many people ascribe to it requires a revised conceptualization in our current era. That is, Internet technology may facilitate the dissemination of bizarre beliefs on a much wider scale than ever before.

Morgellons is an internet disease. It is a delusion that likely would have died out naturally, but thanks to its rapid spread on the internet, it took on a life of its own. Believers gathered around the banner of Morgellons, and the very size of that group convinced members that their collective delusion was, in fact, real. Soon there was a big community in which the bizarre belief—that there were unidentifiable little organisms crawling under your skin—was completely normal. The movement became strong enough that its members were able to compel the CDC to investigate their fictional disease.

It's not just Morgellons that has taken off in this way. A person's belief in any sort of fringe idea can gain strength—and become unshakable—thanks to social bonds with other true believers. Any idea, no matter how bizarre, can seem mainstream if you're able to find a handful of others who will believe along with you. And since we are all plugged in to the ultimate Speakers' Corner every hour of every day of every week, it's trivially easy to find a group of sympathetic souls. Those small groups are constantly forming and gathering strength, reinforcing the beliefs around which they're formed, no matter how outlandish.

There are the plushies (people who like to have sex with stuffed animals) and the furries (people who like to have sex while wearing animal costumes) and the object-sexuals (people who form sexual attachments to inanimate objects). There are groups devoted to exposing shape-shifting reptilian humanoids living among us, to revealing that the U.S. government brought down the twin towers on September 11, and to arguing that the IRS has no right to collect income taxes. There are fan groups devoted to time travelers, perpetual-motion-machine builders, and crackpot theorists of all varieties. It's not that these kinds of groups came into being with the internet; anyone who's met a follower of Lyndon LaRouche or a UFO nut or a moon hoaxer knows that strange, fringe ideas can catch on even in the absence of an internet. But before the digital web made society so interconnected, it was much harder to encounter such ideas—and it took active effort to engage with the communities that had fringe theories. Now even the craziest ideas are usually but a few mouse clicks away from confirmation and reinforcement by a band of fellow travelers.

It used to be that the roughest edges of people's odd beliefs would erode and crumble through simple isolation, through a lack of reinforcement with social bonds. Now isolation is nigh impossible, and those odd beliefs are sharpened and exaggerated when they are brought into the open in the company of a cozy group of like-minded individuals. In other words, the internet is amplifying our quirks and our odd ideas. Bit by bit, it is driving us toward extremism.

The trend is reflected in the media we consume. The fragmentation of the media, especially the broadcast media, began before digital information first came into our lives. It's been almost two generations since the day when three networks held captive Americans who wanted to watch television. After a slow start, cable TV took off in the 1980s, and no longer could CBS, NBC, and ABC control the majority of television programming in the United States. In 1980, roughly 90 percent of prime-time television watchers in the U.S. were tuned in to one of the Big Three networks. By 2005 that number had dropped to 32 percent, and it has continued to decline ever since. There are more choices out there, so the audience is spread more thinly. For TV news alone, CNN, Fox News, and MSNBC and various other spinoffs and subsidiaries provide direct competition to the evening newscasts of the major networks.

Then, when the internet came along, people could get their news—even news in video format—in innumerable new ways. It's not surprising that the Big Three's evening news programs have lost 55 percent of their viewers in the past thirty years. The surprise is that they've managed to hold on to that other 45 percent.

Back when the Big Three ruled the airwaves, the nightly news had to perform a delicate balancing act. A news program had to try to appeal to the entire television audience—it had to be, quite literally, a broad cast—if it was to compete with the other two networks that were taking the same strategy. This meant that the networks couldn't become too partisan or take an extreme position on anything, for fear of alienating its potential audience. If roughly half of the country was republican, you'd instantly alienate half your audience if your program began to seem like it was too tilted in favor of Democrats.

Then cable and the internet increased our choices. The Big Three kept trying to capture as big a slice of America as possible by staying centrist, but a couple of upstarts—particularly Fox News and MSNBC—realized that there was another possible strategy. Instead of trying to go after the entire American population with a broadly targeted program that appealed to everyone, you could go with a narrowly targeted program that appealed to only a subgroup of the population. Throw in your lot with, say, die-hard Republicans and give them coverage that makes them happy; you'll alienate Democrats and won't get them as viewers, but you can more than make up for that loss by gaining a devoted Republican fan base. This is exactly what Fox News did. Few liberals would tune in to watch Bill O'Reilly except out of grim amusement at how crazy the other side has become, but it's a program that makes the far right happy. MSNBC did exactly the reverse; by filling its schedule with shows that appeal to liberals, such as Keith Olbermann's show, it made a play for the leftist Democrats to the exclusion of the more centrist and right-leaning folks. These networks have given up on broadcasting; instead they're narrowcasting.

The more choices a consumer has on his TV, the more thinly spread the audience will be for each TV show, just because there's more competition. The more thinly spread the audience, the more it makes sense to drop the pretense of trying to appeal to everybody and to instead attempt to corner the market on one chunk of the population; and as choices increase and audiences dwindle, the proportion of the population it makes economic sense to go after becomes smaller. In this light, MSNBC and Fox make perfect sense; they are the natural consequence of the ever-increasing competition to get our attention. Narrowcasting is gradually beating out broadcasting, and the casts will get narrower and narrower as the audience becomes harder and harder to find. In effect, as audience becomes more narrowly defined, the viewer is getting more power about what kind of news and data are served up and what kind of news and data are ignored.

The internet is allowing narrowcasting on a scale never before dreamed of. When you go to CNN.com or BBC.com or PBS.org, the website is tracking which stories you read and which ones you don't. And they're using that information to make the website more appealing to you—you personally. Google News looks at your reading patterns and chooses to present you with news items that are likely to appeal to you based upon your location, your past reading choices, even your web history. It's not just Google News, in fact. Google itself—the web search engine—uses your search history and your past behavior to try to guess what kinds of links you're most likely to find useful. You might not even be conscious of it, but your online behavior is dictating what news you're exposed to, what data you're being served. In a very real sense, you are controlling which elements of the outside world you see and which you don't.

This is welcome news in many ways. We all have limited time to read, watch, or listen   40
to the news, and we can't waste our entire day searching for information on the internet.

The better the media outlets and search engines are at giving us the news we want, the more efficiently we can use our time. But at the same time, there's a very big downside. We tend to shy away from data that challenges our assumptions, that erodes our preconceptions. Getting rid of our wrong ideas is a painful and difficult process, yet it's that very process that makes data truly useful. A fact becomes information when it challenges our assumptions. These challenges are the raw material that forces our ideas to evolve, our tastes to change, our minds to grow.

The more power we have over the data that comes in, the better able we are to shelter ourselves from uncomfortable truths—from facts that challenge our preconceptions and misperceptions. If you have a steady diet of items from Fox News and *The Drudge Report*, your belief that Barack Obama is not a U.S. citizen will be perfectly safe. If you believe that vaccines cause autism, frequenting *The Huffington Post* and MSNBC will likely strengthen your conviction rather than weaken it. With news and data that is tailored to our prejudices, we deprive ourselves of true information. We wind up wallowing in our own false ideas, reflected back at us by the media. The news is ceasing to be a window unto the world; it is becoming a mirror that allows us to gaze only upon our own beliefs.[*]

Couple this dynamic with the microsociety-building power of the hyper-interconnected internet and you've got two major forces that are radicalizing us. Not only does the media fail to challenge our preconceptions—instead reinforcing them as media outlets try to cater to smaller audiences—but we all are able to find small groups of people who share and fortify the beliefs we have, no matter how quirky or out-right wrong they might be. Ironically, all this interconnection is isolating us. We are all becoming solipsists, trapped in worlds of our own creation.

Solipsism wouldn't be so bad but for the fact that the worlds we're creating around ourselves are not just fictions of the mind but have real, concrete consequences for other people who don't share the same delusions.

A bad idea, a wrong piece of information, a digital brain-altering virus can spread at the speed of light through the internet and quickly find a home among a dispersed but digitally interconnected group of true believers. This group acts as a reservoir for the bad idea, allowing it to gather strength and reinfect people; as the group grows, the belief, no matter how crazy, becomes more and more solidly established among the faithful.

Morgellons is a relatively benign example; other than the believers themselves, the only   45
people inconvenienced are physicians and insurers. Not so with real diseases. Since the late 1980s, Peter Duesberg, a biologist at Berkeley, has been arguing that AIDS is not caused by a virus, but instead is the product of using recreational drugs—or of taking the anti-HIV drugs that are used to keep the virus in check. It was a dubious belief even at the time Duesberg proposed it, and it quickly failed several tests in the early 1990s and was soundly rejected by the scientific community. Duesberg was pretty much banished from the better—and more widely read—scientific journals after that. In the days before the internet, that would have almost guaranteed that he would fade into obscurity; forced to the fringe, Duesberg would rant and rave in fourth-tier journals and be ignored by the rest of the world. But by the mid-1990s the web had come along, so Duesberg took to the internet and quickly found a large audience. Several HIV-denialist groups coalesced on the web, touting Duesberg's research as evidence that AIDS wasn't caused by a virus.

---

*Eli Pariser talks about this phenomenon in his book *The Filter Bubble*.

On October 28, 1999, Thabo Mbeki, then the president of South Africa, gave a controversial speech about AZT, the first anti-HIV drug. "Many in our country have called on the government to make the drug AZT available in our public health system," he said, but warned that "the toxicity of this drug is such that it is in fact a danger to health." It was astonishing that the president of South Africa would try to keep an anti-HIV drug out of his country, especially given that his country was ground zero for the epidemic. The incidence of HIV was skyrocketing— almost 13 percent of the population was infected by 1997—and the country was crying out for drugs that might help. AZT was in wide use to prevent pregnant mothers from transmitting the virus to children. Why was Mbeki so convinced that AZT would do more harm than good? He didn't go into detail, but he hinted at where he had gotten his information: online. "To understand this matter better," he said, "I would urge the honorable members of the National Council to access the huge volume of literature on this matter available on the internet."

Physicians and AIDS researchers in South Africa—and around the world—were shocked. The South African newspaper the *Sunday Independent* described the reaction:

> Mark Lurie, a Medical Research Council senior scientist based in Mtubatuba in KwaZulu-Natal, was "flabbergasted" by Mbeki's speech.
>
> "Here is a drug that cuts the rate of mother-to-child transmission by 50 percent. If the president is telling us that this drug doesn't work, where is his evidence for such a statement?"
>
> Mbeki's evidence seems to be the Internet, according to Tasneem Carrim, a media liaison officer for the presidency.
>
> "The president got a thick set of documents. He went into many sites, including the World Health Organisation's one. The president goes into the Net all the time," she said.

It soon became clear what sites Mbeki was visiting. The South African president had stumbled upon HIV-denialist websites and was soon consulting with them, and with Duesberg (whom Mbeki invited to South Africa). Mbeki was soon a true believer. He publicly questioned whether HIV caused AIDS, and engaged in political maneuvers to prevent the distribution of anti-HIV drugs—even ones donated for free. (Eventually the courts had to intervene to allow unfettered access to the lifesaving drugs.) The minister of health earned the scorn of the scientific world by extolling the virtues of beetroot, lemon, and garlic as better ways to prevent AIDS than the antiretroviral drugs her ministry was denying the sick and dying. A 2008 study in the *Journal of Acquired Immune Deficiency Syndromes* estimated that more than 300,000 people lost their lives between 2000 and 2005 because of Mbeki's obstinate refusal to allow his citizens to begin taking antiretroviral drugs.

Of course, volumes and volumes of HIV-denial literature are still just a Google search away.

Three hundred thousand deaths might be the most extreme consequence of a Google 50 search gone wrong. However, history is littered with examples of fringe beliefs—ones that the vast majority of people rejected—killing thousands upon thousands. For one, millions of people starved in the Soviet Union in part because Joseph Stalin embraced the wacky anti-Darwinist ideas of Trofim Lysenko, a man who believed that you could "train" crops to grow in the wrong seasons.

But comparing the Duesberg case with Lysenko's reveals just how much more potent fringe ideas become when they're digitized. Lysenko rose to power in part because he was of peasant stock, like his powerful benefactor, Stalin. And it was the fear of Stalin that allowed his ideas to grow and take hold. Scientists couldn't silence Lysenko; indeed, Lysenko silenced (and murdered) accomplished scientists who dared to say that Lysenkoism was nonsense. It's the opposite of what happened to Duesberg, who was shunted to the fringe and silenced by the scientific community. Had Duesberg lived in the time of Lysenko, his ideas would never have circulated around the United States, much less affected a government halfway around the world several years after he was discredited at home.

Yet because of the digital revolution, the has-been professor who was a laughingstock of his home country's scientific community was able to have a Lysenko-like influence without the backing of a Joseph Stalin. And Duesberg's ideas will last much longer than Lysenko's. Lysenkoism essentially died with Stalin. However, even if the HIV-denialist movement dies in South Africa, Duesberg's ideas will remain visible to everyone for years and years to come, ready to spark a new outbreak.

Because of the interconnectedness of the digital world and the transmissibility of even large volumes of work, the most absurd fringe idea can reach far beyond the fevered mind of its creator. Even the craziest notions can be heard and amplified and transmitted by virtual communities. The extremes of human thought are gathering strength.

As we sink into the comfortable monotony of constant reinforcement, as we spend an increasing amount of time listening to sources of information that are tailored to strengthen our mental fictions rather than challenge them, we are slowly being turned into cranks ourselves. And those who don't succumb are often at the mercy of those who do.

Questions

1. Given your experiences with social media culture, what do you make of Seife's suggestion that "anything that does not affect our opinions is not information; it's noise" (para. 3)? How much of what you encounter daily is information versus noise?

2. Seife's essay is long, which gives him the space to develop a more sophisticated argument. What is that argument, and what "subarguments" are used to develop it? How does Seife step the reader through his key points in the development of his argument?

3. In small groups, do an Internet search for Seife's book in which this essay is published, *Virtual Unreality: Just Because the Internet Told You, How Do You Know It's True?* Have each group member find a review of the book in a different source (Amazon, newspaper, academic journal, blog, etc.). Compare and contrast the opinions in these reviews. How many different opinions, understandings, and interpretations of this book can you find? How easy was it to find this information? Which kinds of reviews were more effectively constructed and researched? How does the source of the review reflect its content?

Amanda Hess

Why Women Aren't Welcome on the Internet

"Ignore the barrage of violent threats and harassing messages that confront you online every day." That's what women are told. But these relentless messages are an assault on women's careers, their psychological bandwidth, and their freedom to live online. We have been thinking about Internet harassment all wrong.

I was 12 hours into a summer vacation in Palm springs when my phone hummed to life, buzzing twice next to me in the dark of my hotel room. I squinted at the screen. it was 5:30 a.m., and a friend was texting me from the opposite coast. "Amanda, this twitter account. Freaking out over here," she wrote. "There is a twitter account that seems to have been set up for the purpose of making death threats to you."

I dragged myself out of bed and opened my laptop. a few hours earlier, someone going by the username "headlessfemalepig" had sent me seven tweets. "1 see you are physically not very attractive. Figured," the first said. Then: "You suck a lot of drunk and drug fucked guys cocks." As a female journalist who writes about sex (among other things), none of this feedback was particularly out of the ordinary. But this guy took it to another level: "I am 36 years old, I did 12 years for 'manslaughter,' I killed a woman, like you, who decided to make fun of guys cocks." and then: "Happy to say we live in the same state. im looking you up, and when I find you, im going to rape you and remove your head." There was more, but the final tweet summed it up: "You are going to die and I am the one who is going to kill you. I promise you this."

My fingers paused over the keyboard. I felt disoriented and terrified. Then embarrassed for being scared, and, finally, pissed. On the one hand, it seemed unlikely that I'd soon be defiled and decapitated at the hands of a serial rapist-murderer. On the other hand, headlessfemalepig was clearly a deranged individual with a bizarre fixation on me. I picked up my phone and dialed 911.

Two hours later, a Palm springs police officer lumbered up the steps to my hotel room, paused on the outdoor threshold, and began questioning me in a steady clip. I wheeled through the relevant background information: I am a journalist; I live in Los Angeles; sometimes, people don't like what I write about women, relationships, or sexuality; this was not the first time that someone had responded to my work by threatening to rape and kill me. The cop anchored his hands on his belt, looked me in the eye, and said, "What is Twitter?"

Staring up at him in the blazing sun, the best answer I could come up with was, "It's like 5 an e-mail, but it's public." What I didn't articulate is that Twitter is the place where I laugh, whine, work, schmooze, procrastinate, and flirt. It sits in my back pocket wherever I go and lies next to me when I fall asleep. And since I first started writing in 2007, it's become just one of the many online spaces where men come to tell me to get out.

The examples are too numerous to recount, but like any good journalist, I keep a running file documenting the most deranged cases. There was the local cable viewer who hunted down my email address after a television appearance to tell me I was "the ugliest woman he had ever seen." And the group of visitors to a "men's rights" site who pored over photographs of me and a prominent feminist activist, then discussed how they'd "spend the night with" us. ("Put em both in a gimp mask and tied to each other 69 so the bitches can't talk or move and go round the world, any old port in a storm, any old hole," one decided.) And the anonymous commenter who weighed in on one of my articles: "Amanda, I'll fucking rape you. How does that feel?"

None of this makes me exceptional. It just makes me a woman with an Internet connection. Here's just a sampling of the noxious online commentary directed at other women in recent years. To Alyssa Royse, a sex and relationships blogger, for saying that she hated *The Dark Knight*: "you are clearly retarded, i hope someone shoots then rapes you." To Kathy Sierra, a technology writer, for blogging about software, coding, and design: "i hope someone slits your throat and cums down your gob." To Lindy West, a writer at the women's website Jezebel, for critiquing a comedian's rape joke: "I just want to rape her with a traffic cone." To Rebecca Watson, an atheist commentator, for blogging about sexism in the skeptic community: "If I lived in Boston I'd put a bullet in your brain." To Catherine Mayer, a journalist at *Time* magazine, for no particular reason: "A BOMB HAS BEEN PLACED OUTSIDE YOUR HOME. IT WILL GO OFF AT EXACTLY 10:47 PM ON A TIMER AND TRIGGER DESTROYING EVERYTHING."

A woman doesn't even need to occupy a professional writing perch at a prominent platform to become a target. According to a 2005 report by the Pew research Center, which has been tracking the online lives of Americans for more than a decade, women and men have been logging on in equal numbers since 2000, but the vilest communications are still disproportionately lobbed at women. We are more likely to report being stalked and harassed on the Internet—of the 3,787 people who reported harassing incidents from 2000 to 2012 to the volunteer organization Working to halt Online abuse, 72.5 percent were female. Sometimes, the abuse can get physical: a Pew survey reported that five percent of women who used the Internet said "something happened online" that led them into "physical danger." And it starts young: Teenage girls are significantly more likely to be cyberbullied than boys. Just appearing as a woman online, it seems, can be enough to inspire abuse. In 2006, researchers from the University of Maryland set up a bunch of fake online accounts and then dispatched them into chat rooms. Accounts with feminine usernames incurred an average of 100 sexually explicit or threatening messages a day. Masculine names received 3.7.

There are three federal laws that apply to cyberstalking cases; the first was passed in 1934 to address harassment through the mail, via telegram, and over the telephone, six decades after Alexander Graham Bell's invention. Since the initial passage of the Violence Against Women Act, in 1994, amendments to the law have gradually updated it to apply to new technologies and to stiffen penalties against those who use them to abuse. Thirty-four states have cyberstalking laws on the books; most have expanded long-standing laws against stalking and criminal threats to prosecute crimes carried out online.

But making quick and sick threats has become so easy that many say the abuse has   10 proliferated to the point of meaninglessness, and that expressing alarm is foolish. Reporters who take death threats seriously "often give the impression that this is some kind of shocking event for which we should pity the 'victims,'" my colleague Jim Pagels wrote in *Slate* this fall, "but anyone who's spent 10 minutes online knows that these assertions are entirely toothless." On Twitter, he added, "When there's no precedent for physical harm, it's only baseless fear mongering." My friend Jen Doll wrote, at The Atlantic Wire, "it seems like that old 'ignoring' tactic your mom taught you could work out to everyone's benefit.... These people are bullying, or hope to bully. Which means we shouldn't take the bait." In the epilogue to her book *The End of Men*, Hanna Rosin—an editor at *Slate*—argued that harassment of women online could be seen as a cause for celebration. It shows just how far we've come. Many women on the Internet "are in positions of influence, widely published and widely read; if they sniff out misogyny, I have no doubt they will gleefully skewer the responsible sexist in one of many available online outlets, and get results."

So women who are harassed online are expected to either get over ourselves or feel flattered in response to the threats made against us. We have the choice to keep quiet or respond "gleefully."

But no matter how hard we attempt to ignore it, this type of gendered harassment—and the sheer volume of it—has severe implications for women's status on the Internet. Threats of rape, death, and stalking can overpower our emotional bandwidth, take up our time, and cost us money through legal fees, online protection services, and missed wages. I've spent countless hours over the past four years logging the online activity of one particularly committed cyberstalker, just in case. And as the Internet becomes increasingly central to the human experience, the ability of women to live and work freely online will be shaped, and too often limited, by the technology companies that host these threats, the constellation of local and federal law enforcement officers who investigate them, and the popular commentators who dismiss them—all arenas that remain dominated by men, many of whom have little personal understanding of what women face online every day.

This summer, Caroline Criado-Perez became the English-speaking Internet's most famous recipient of online threats after she petitioned the British government to put more female faces on its bank notes. (When the Bank of England announced its intentions to replace social reformer Elizabeth Fry with Winston Churchill on the £5 note, Criado-Perez made the modest suggestion that the bank make an effort to feature at least one woman who is not the Queen on any of its currency.) Rape and death threats amassed on her Twitter feed too quickly to count, bearing messages like "I will rape you tomorrow at 9 p.m....Shall we meet near your house?"

Then, something interesting happened. Instead of logging off, Criado-Perez retweeted the threats, blasting them out to her Twitter followers. She called up police and hounded Twitter for a response. Journalists around the world started writing about the threats. As more and more people heard the story, Criado-Perez's follower count skyrocketed to near 25,000. Her supporters joined in urging British police and Twitter executives to respond.

Under the glare of international criticism, the police and the company spent the next 15 few weeks passing the buck back and forth. Andy Trotter, a communications adviser for the British police, announced that it was Twitter's responsibility to crack down on the messages. Though Britain criminalizes a broader category of offensive speech than the U.S. does, the sheer volume of threats would be too difficult for "a hard-pressed police service" to investigate, Trotter said. Police "don't want to be in this arena." It diverts their attention from "dealing with something else."

Meanwhile, Twitter issued a blanket statement saying that victims like Criado-Perez could fill out an online form for each abusive tweet; when Criado-Perez supporters hounded Mark Luckie, the company's manager of journalism and news, for a response, he briefly shielded his account, saying that the attention had become "abusive." Twitter's official recommendation to victims of abuse puts the ball squarely in law enforcement's court: "If an interaction has gone beyond the point of name calling and you feel as though you may be in danger," it says, "contact your local authorities so they can accurately assess the validity of the threat and help you resolve the issue offline."

In the weeks after the flare-up, Scotland Yard confirmed the arrest of three men. Twitter—in response to several online petitions calling for action—hastened the rollout of a "report abuse" button that allows users to flag offensive material. And Criado-Perez went on receiving threats. Some real person out there—or rather, hundreds of them—still liked the idea of seeing her raped and killed.

The Internet is a global network, but when you pick up the phone to report an online threat, whether you are in London or Palm springs, you end up face-to-face with a cop who patrols a comparatively puny jurisdiction. And your cop will probably be a man: According to the U.S. Bureau of Justice statistics, in 2008, only 6.5 percent of state police officers and 19 percent of FBI agents were women. The numbers get smaller in smaller agencies. And in many locales, police work is still a largely analog affair: 911 calls are immediately routed to the local police force; the closest officer is dispatched to respond; he takes notes with pen and paper.

After Criado-Perez received her hundreds of threats, she says she got conflicting instructions from police on how to report the crimes, and was forced to repeatedly "trawl" through the vile messages to preserve the evidence. "I can just about cope with threats," she wrote on Twitter. "What I can't cope with after that is the victim-blaming, the patronising, and the police record-keeping." Last year, the American atheist blogger Rebecca Watson wrote about her experience calling a series of local and national law enforcement agencies after a man launched a website threatening to kill her. "Because I knew what town [he] lived in, I called his local police department. They told me there was nothing they could do and that I'd have to make a report with my local police department," Watson wrote later. "[I] finally got through to someone who told me that there was nothing they could do but take a report in case one day [he] followed through on his threats, at which point they'd have a pretty good lead."

The first time I reported an online rape threat to police, in 2009, the officer dispatched   20 to my home asked, "Why would anyone bother to do something like that?" and declined to file a report. In Palm Springs, the officer who came to my room said, "This guy could be sitting in a basement in Nebraska for all we know." That my stalker had said that he lived in my state, and had plans to seek me out at home, was dismissed as just another online ruse.

Of course, some people are investigated and prosecuted for cyberstalking. In 2009, a Florida college student named Patrick Macchione met a girl at school, then threatened to kill her on Twitter, terrorized her with lewd videos posted to YouTube, and made hundreds of calls to her phone. Though his victim filed a restraining order, cops only sprung into action after a county sheriff stopped him for loitering, then reportedly found a video camera in his backpack containing disturbing recordings about his victim. The sheriff's department later worked with the state attorney's office to convict Macchione on 19 counts, one of which was cyberstalking (he successfully appealed that count on grounds that the law hadn't been enacted when he was arrested); Macchione was sentenced to four years in prison. Consider also a recent high-profile case of cyberstalking investigated by the FBI.

In the midst of her affair with General David Petraeus, biographer Paula Broadwell allegedly created an anonymous email account for the purpose of sending harassing notes to Florida socialite Jill Kelley. Kelley reported them to the FBI, which sniffed out Broadwell's identity via the account's location-based metadata and obtained a warrant to monitor her email activity.

In theory, appealing to a higher jurisdiction can yield better results. "Local law enforcement will often look the other way," says Dr. Sameer Hinduja, a criminology professor at Florida Atlantic University and co-director of the Cyberbullying Research Center. "They don't have the resources or the personnel to investigate those crimes." County, state, or federal agencies at least have the support to be more responsive: "Usually they have a computer crimes unit, savvy personnel who are familiar with these cases, and established relationships with social media companies so they can quickly send a subpoena to help with the investigation," Hinduja says.

But in my experience and those of my colleagues, these larger law enforcement agencies have little capacity or drive to investigate threats as well. Despite his pattern of abusive online behavior, Macchione was ultimately arrested for an unrelated physical crime. When I called the FBI over headlessfemalepig's threats, a representative told me an agent would get in touch if the bureau was interested in pursuing the case; nobody did. And when Rebecca Watson reported the threats targeted at her to the FBI, she initially connected with a sympathetic agent—but the agent later expressed trouble opening Watson's file of screenshots of the threats, and soon stopped replying to her emails. The Broadwell investigation was an uncommon, and possibly unprecedented, exercise for the agency. As University of Wisconsin–Eau Claire criminal justice professor Justin Patchin told Wired at the time: "I'm not aware of any case when the FBI has gotten involved in a case of online harassment."

After I received my most recent round of threats, I asked Jessica Valenti, a prominent 25 feminist writer (and the founder of the blog Feministing), who's been repeatedly targeted with online threats, for her advice, and then I asked her to share her story. "It's not really one story. This has happened a number of times over the past seven years," she told me. When rape and death threats first started pouring into her inbox, she vacated her apartment for a week, changed her bank accounts, and got a new cell number. When the next wave of threats came, she got in touch with law enforcement officials, who warned her that though the men emailing her were unlikely to follow through on their threats, the level of vitriol indicated that she should be vigilant for a far less identifiable threat: silent "hunters" who lurk behind the tweeting "hollerers." The FBI advised Valenti to leave her home until the threats blew over, to never walk outside of her apartment alone, and to keep aware of any cars or men who might show up repeatedly outside her door. "It was totally impossible advice," she says. "You have to be paranoid about everything. You can't just not be in a public place."

And we can't simply be offline either. When *Time* journalist Catherine Mayer reported the bomb threat lodged against her, the officers she spoke to—who thought usernames were secret codes and didn't seem to know what an IP address was—advised her to unplug. "Not one of the officers I've encountered uses Twitter or understands why anyone would wish to do so," she later wrote. "The officers were unanimous in advising me to take a break from Twitter, assuming, as many people do, that Twitter is at best a time-wasting narcotic."

All of these online offenses are enough to make a woman *want* to click away from Twitter, shut her laptop, and power down her phone. Sometimes, we do withdraw: Pew found that from 2000 to 2005, the percentage of Internet users who participate in online chats and discussion groups dropped from 28 percent to 17 percent, "entirely because of women's fall off in participation." But for many women, steering clear of the Internet isn't an option. We use our devices to find supportive communities, make a living, and construct safety nets. For a woman like me, who lives alone, the Internet isn't a fun diversion—it is a necessary resource for work and interfacing with friends, family, and, sometimes, law enforcement officers in an effort to feel safer from both online and offline violence.

The Polish sociologist Zygmunt Bauman draws a distinction between "tourists" and "vagabonds" in the modern economy. Privileged tourists move about the world "on purpose," to seek "new experience" as "the joys of the familiar wear off." Disempowered vagabonds relocate because they have to, pushed and pulled through mean streets where they could never hope to settle down. On the Internet, men are tourists and women are vagabonds. "Telling a woman to shut her laptop is like saying, 'Eh! Just stop seeing your family,'" says Nathan Jurgenson, a social media sociologist (and a friend) at the University of Maryland.

What does a tourist look like? In 2012, Gawker unmasked "Violentacrez," an anonymous member of the online community Reddit who was infamous for posting creepy photographs of underage women and creating or moderating subcommunities on the site with names like "chokeabitch" and "rapebait." Violentacrez turned out to be a Texas computer programmer named Michael Brusch, who displayed an exceedingly casual attitude toward his online hobbies. "I do my job, go home, watch TV, and go on the Internet. I just like riling people up in my spare time," he told Adrian Chen, the Gawker reporter who outed him. "People take things way too seriously around here."

Abusers tend to operate anonymously, or under pseudonyms. But the women they target often write on professional platforms, under their given names, and in the context of their real lives. Victims don't have the luxury of separating themselves from the crime. When it comes to online threats, "one person is feeling the reality of the Internet very viscerally: the person who is being threatened," says Jurgenson. "It's a lot easier for the person who made the threat—and the person who is investigating the threat—to believe that what's happening on the Internet isn't real." 30

When authorities treat the Internet as a fantasyland, it has profound effects on the investigation and prosecution of online threats. Criminal threat laws largely require that victims feel tangible, immediate, and sustained fear. IN my home state of California, a threat must be "unequivocal, unconditional, immediate, and specific" and convey a "gravity of purpose and an immediate prospect of execution of the threat" to be considered a crime. If police don't know whether the harasser lives next door or out in Nebraska, it's easier for them to categorize the threat as non-immediate. When they treat a threat as a boyish hoax, the implication is that the threat ceases to be a criminal offense.

So the victim faces a psychological dilemma: How should she understand her own fear? Should she, as many advise, dismiss an online threat as a silly game, and not bother to inform the cops that someone may want to—ha, ha—rape and kill her? Or should she dutifully report every threat to police, who may well dismiss her concerns? When I received my most recent rape and death threats, one friend told me that I should rest assured that the anonymous tweeter was unlikely to take any physical action against me in real life; another noted that my stalker seemed like the type of person who would fashion a coat from my skin, and urged me to take any action necessary to land the stalker in jail.

Danielle Citron, a University of Maryland law professor who focuses on Internet threats, charted the popular response to Internet death and rape threats in a 2009 paper published in the Michigan Law Review. She found that Internet harassment is routinely dismissed as "harmless locker-room talk," perpetrators as "juvenile pranksters," and victims as "overly sensitive complainers." Weighing in on one online harassment case, in an interview on National Public Radio, journalist David Margolick called the threats "juvenile, immature, and obnoxious, but that is all they are…frivolous frat-boy rants."

Of course, the frat house has never been a particularly safe space for women. I've been threatened online, but I have also been harassed on the street, groped on the subway, followed home from the 7-Eleven, pinned down on a bed by a drunk boyfriend, and raped on a date. Even if I sign off Twitter, a threat could still be waiting on my stoop.

Today, a legion of anonymous harassers are free to play their "games" and "pranks" 35 under pseudonymous screen names, but for the women they target, the attacks only compound the real fear, discomfort, and stress we experience in our daily lives.

If American police forces are overwhelmingly male, the technology companies that have created the architecture of the online world are, famously, even more so. In 2010, according to the information services firm CB Insights, 92 percent of the founders of fledgling Internet companies were male; 86 percent of their founding teams were exclusively male. While the number of women working across the sciences is generally increasing, the percentage of women working in computer sciences peaked in 2000 and is now on the decline. In 2012, the Bureau of Labor Statistics found, women made up just 22.5 percent of American computer programmers and 19.7 percent of software developers. In a 2012 study of 400 California companies, researchers at the University of California–Davis, found that just seven percent of the highest-paid executives at Silicon Valley companies were women.

When Twitter announced its initial public offering in October, its filings listed an all-male board. Vijaya Gadde, Twitter's general counsel, was the only woman among its executive officers. When Vivek Wadhwa, a fellow at Stanford's Rock Center for Corporate Governance, suggested that the gender imbalance on Twitter's board was an issue of "elite arrogance" and "male chauvinistic thinking," Twitter CEO Dick Costolo responded with a joking tweet, calling Wadhwa "the Carrot Top of academic sources."

Most executives aren't intentionally boxing women out. But the decisions these men make have serious implications for billions of people. The gender imbalance in their companies compromises their ability to understand the lives of half their users.

Twitter "has a history of saying 'too bad, so sad'" when confronted with concerns about harassment on its platform, says Citron, the University of Maryland law professor who studies the emerging legal implications of online abuse against women. The culture of the platform has typically prioritized freewheeling discussion over zealous speech policing. Unlike Facebook, Twitter doesn't require people to register accounts under their real names. Users are free to enjoy the frivolity—and the protection—that anonymous speech provides. if a user runs afoul of Twitter's terms of service, he's free to create a new account under a fresh handle. And the Communications Decency Act of 1996 protects platforms like Twitter from being held legally responsible for what individuals say on the site.

The advent of the "report abuse" button is a development Citron finds "very hearten- 40 ing." Allowing people to block an abuser's account helps women avoid having to be faced with vile and abusive tweets. But our problems can't all be solved with the click of a button. In some cases, the report-abuse button is just a virtual Band-aid for a potentially dangerous real-world problem. it can undermine women by erasing the trail of digital evidence. And it does nothing to prevent these same abusers from opening a new account and continuing their crimes.

When I received those seven tweets in Palm springs, a well-meaning friend reported them as abusive through Twitter's system, hoping that action on the platform's end would help further my case. a few hours later, the tweets were erased from the site without comment (or communication with me). Headlessfemalepig's Twitter feed was replaced with a page noting that the account had been suspended. Luckily, I had taken screenshots of the tweets, but to the cops working with a limited understanding of the platform, their sudden disappearance only confused the issue. The detective assigned to my case asked me to send him links pointing to where the messages lived online—but absent a subpoena of Twitter's records, they were gone from law enforcement's view. If someone had reported the threats before I got a chance to see them, I might not even have been able to indicate their existence at all. Without a proper investigation, I am incapable of knowing whether headlessfemalepig is a one-time offender or the serial stalker who has followed me for many years. Meanwhile, nothing's stopping headlessfemalepig from continuing to tweet away under a new name.

It shouldn't be Twitter's responsibility to hunt down and sanction criminals who use its service—that's what cops are (supposedly) for. Twitter has to balance its interests in addressing abusive behavior with its interests in protecting our private information (or that of, say, political dissidents), which means keeping a tight lid on users' IP addresses and refusing to offer up deleted material to civilians. When I asked how Twitter balances those demands, Nu Wexler, who leads public policy communications for the company, pointed me to a chart published by the Electronic Frontier Foundation—an advocacy group dedicated to defending the free speech and privacy rights of Internet users—that illustrates the platform's "commitment to user privacy." The chart, titled "Who has Your Back: Which Companies help Protect Your Data from the Government?," awards Twitter high marks for fighting for users' privacy rights in court and publishing a transparency report about government data requests.

A high score awarded by the Electronic Frontier Foundation communicates to users that their Internet activity will be safe from overreaching government snoops—and post–Edward Snowden, that concern is more justified than ever. But in some cases, the impulse to protect our privacy can interfere with the law's ability to protect us when we're harassed. Last year, the Electronic Frontier Foundation came out against an amendment to the Violence Against Women Act. Until recently, the law criminalized abusive, threatening, and harassing speech conveyed over a telephone line, provided the abuser placed the call; the new law, passed in March, applies to any electronic harassment targeted at a specific person, whether it's made over the telephone or by another means. Critics of the legislation pulled out the trope that the Internet is less real than other means of communication. As the Foundation put it, "a person is free to disregard something said on Twitter in a way far different than a person who is held in constant fear of the persistent ringing of a telephone intruding in their home."

The Electronic Frontier Foundation—and the tech companies that benefit from its ratings—are undoubtedly committed to fighting government First Amendment abuses. But when they focus their efforts on stemming the spread of anti-harassment laws from outdated media, like landline telephones, to modern means like Twitter, their efforts act like a thumb on the scale, favoring some democratic values at the expense of others. "Silicon Valley has the power to shape society to conform to its values, which prioritize openness and connectivity," Jurgenson says. "But why are engineers in California getting to decide what constitutes harassment for people all around the world?"

Tech companies are, of course, fully aware that they need a broad base of users to flour- 45 ish as billion-dollar businesses. Today women have the bargaining power to draft successful petitions calling for "report abuse" buttons, but our corporate influence is limited, and alternative venues for action are few. Local police departments "have no money," Jurgenson says, and "it feels unlikely that the government is going to do more anytime soon, so we're forced to put more pressure on Twitter." And while an organized user base can influence the decisions of a public, image-conscious company like Twitter, many platforms—like the dedicated "revenge porn" sites that have proliferated on the Web—don't need to appease women to stay popular. "I call this the myth of the market," Citron says. "There's definitely a desire for anti-social behavior. There are eyeballs. And there are users who are providing the content. The market isn't self-correcting, and it's not going to make this go away."

In a 2009 paper in the Boston University Law Review, Citron proposed a new way of framing the legal problem of harassment on the Internet: she argued that online abuse constitutes "discrimination in women's employment opportunities" that ought to be better addressed by the U.S. government itself. Title VII of the Civil Rights Act of 1964, which outlawed discrimination based on race, religion, or gender, was swiftly applied to members of the Ku Klux Klan, who hid behind hoods to harass and intimidate black Louisianans from voting and pursuing work. Anonymous online harassment, Citron argued, similarly discourages women from "writing and earning a living online" on the basis of their gender. "It interferes with their professional lives. It raises their vulnerability to offline sexual violence. It brands them as incompetent workers and inferior sexual objects. The harassment causes considerable emotional distress."

On the Internet, women are overpowered and devalued. We don't always think about our online lives in those terms—after all, our days are filled with work to do, friends to keep up with, Netflix to watch. But when anonymous harassers come along—saying they would like to rape us, or cut off our heads, or scrutinize our bodies in public, or shame us for our sexual habits—they serve to remind us in ways both big and small that we can't be at ease online. It is precisely the banality of Internet harassment, University of Miami law professor Mary Anne franks has argued, that makes it "both so effective and so harmful, especially as a form of discrimination."

The personal and professional costs of that discrimination manifest themselves in very real ways. Jessica Valenti says she has stopped promoting her speaking events publicly, enlisted security for her public appearances, signed up for a service to periodically scrub the Web of her private information, invested in a post-office box, and begun periodically culling her Facebook friend list in an attempt to filter out readers with ulterior motives. Those efforts require a clear investment of money and time, but the emotional fallout is less directly quantifiable. "When people say you should be raped and killed for years on end, it takes a toll on your soul," she says. Whenever a male stranger approaches her at a public event, "the hairs on the back of my neck stand up." Every time we call the police, head to court to file a civil protection order, or get sucked into a mental hole by the threats that have been made against us, zeroes drop from our annual incomes. Says Jurgenson, "It's a monetary penalty for being a woman."

Citron has planted the seed of an emerging debate over the possibility of applying civil rights laws to ensure equal opportunities for women on the Internet. "There's no silver bullet for addressing this problem," Citron says. But existing legislation has laid the groundwork for potential future reforms. Federal civil rights law can punish "force or threat[s] of force" that interfere with a person's employment on the basis of race, religion, or national origin. That protection, though, doesn't currently extend to threats targeted at a person's gender. However, other parts of the Civil Rights Act frame workplace sexual harassment as discriminatory, and requires employers to implement policies to both prevent and remedy discrimination in the

office. And Title IX of the education amendments of 1972 puts the onus on educational institutions to take action against discrimination toward women. Because Internet harassment
affects the employment and educational opportunities of women, laws could conceivably be
amended to allow women to bring claims against individuals.

But it's hard to get there from here. As Citron notes, the Internet is not a school or a   50
workplace, but a vast and diffuse universe that often lacks any clear locus of accountability.
Even if online threats are considered a civil rights violation, who would we sue? Anonymous
tweeters lack the institutional affiliation to make monetary claims worthwhile. And there is
the mobbing problem: One person can send just one horrible tweet, but then many others
may pile on. A single vicious tweet may not clear the hurdle of discriminatory harassment
(or repetitive abuse). And while a mob of individuals each lobbing a few attacks clearly looks
and feels like harassment, there is no organized group to take legal action against. Bringing
separate claims against individual abusers would be laborious, expensive, and unlikely to
reap financial benefits. At the same time, amending the Communications Decency Act to
put the onus on Internet platforms to police themselves could have a serious chilling effect
on all types of speech, discriminatory or otherwise.

Citron admits that passing new civil rights legislation that applies to a new venue—the
Internet—is a potentially Sisyphean task. But she says that by expanding existing civil rights
laws to recognize the gendered nature of Internet threats, lawmakers could put more pressure on law enforcement agencies to take those crimes seriously. "We have the tools already,"
Citron says. "Do we use them? Not really." Prosecuting online threats as bias-motivated
crimes would mean that offenders would face stronger penalties, law enforcement agencies
would be better incentivized to investigate these higher-level crimes—and hopefully, the
Internet's legions of anonymous abusers would begin to see the downside of mouthing off.

Our laws have always found a way to address new harms while balancing long-standing
rights, even if they do it very slowly. Opponents of the Civil Rights Act of 1964 characterized
its workplace protections as unconstitutional and bad for business. Before workplace sexual
harassment was reframed as discriminatory under Title VII, it was written off as harmless
flirting. When Title IX was first proposed to address gender discrimination in education, a
senate discussion on the issue ended in laughter when one senator cracked a co-ed football
joke. Until domestic violence became a national policy priority, abuse was dismissed as a lovers' quarrel. Today's harmless jokes and undue burdens are tomorrow's civil rights agenda.

My serial cyberstalker began following me in 2009. I was on the staff of an alt-weekly
when a mini-controversy flared up on a blog. One of the blog's writers had developed a pattern of airing his rape fantasies on the site; I interviewed him and the site's other contributors
and published a story. Then I started receiving rape threats of my own. Their author posted
a photo of me on his blog and wrote, "Oh, sure, you might say she's pretty. Or you might
say she looks sweet or innocent. But don't let looks fool you. This woman is pure evil." (To
some harassers, you're physically not very attractive; to others, you're beautiful.) "I thought
I'd describe her on my blog as 'rape-worthy,' but ultimately decided against it," he added.
"Oops! I've committed another thought crime!"

In the comments section below the article, threats popped up under a dozen fake names
and several phony IP addresses—which usually point to a device's precise location, but can be
easily faked if you have the right software. "Amanda, I'll fucking rape you," one said. "How's
that feel? Like that? What's my IP address, bitch?" On his Twitter account, my stalker wrote

that he planned to buy a gun—apparently intending to defend his First Amendment rights by exercising the Second.

Then, one night when my boyfriend and I were in our apartment, my cell phone started 55 ringing incessantly. I received a series of voicemails, escalating in tone from a stern "You cut the shit right fucking now" to a slurred "You fucking dyke...I will fuck you up." For the first time ever, I called the police. When an officer arrived at my house, I described the pattern of abuse. He expressed befuddlement at the "virtual" crime, handed me his card, and told me to call if anyone came to my house—but he declined to take a report.

Without police support, I opted to file a civil protection order in family court. I posted a photograph of my stalker at my office's front desk. When the local sheriff's department failed to serve him court papers, I paid $100 for a private investigator to get the job done. It took me five visits to court, waiting for my case to be called up while sitting quietly across the aisle from him in the gallery as dozens of other local citizens told a domestic violence judge about the boyfriends and fathers and ex-wives who had threatened and abused them. These people were seeking protection from crowbar-wielding exes and gun-flashing acquaintances—more real crimes the justice system had failed to prosecute. By the time the judge finally called up my protection order for review, I had missed a half-dozen days of work pursuing the case. I was lucky to have a full-time job and an understanding boss—even if he didn't understand the threats on the same level I did. And because my case was filed under new anti-stalking protections—protections designed for cases like mine, in which I was harassed by someone I didn't have a personal relationship with—I was lucky to get a court-appointed lawyer, too. Most victims don't.

My harasser finally acquiesced to the protection order when my lawyer showed him that we knew the blog comments were coming from his computer—he had made a valiant attempt to obscure his comments, but he'd slipped up in a couple of instances, and we could prove the rape threats were his. When the judge approved the order, she instructed my harasser that he was not allowed to contact me in any way—not by email, Twitter, phone, blog comment, or by hiring a hot air balloon to float over my house with a message, she said. And he had to stay at least 100 feet away from me at all times. The restraining order would last one year.

Soon after the order expired, he sent an email to my new workplace. Every once in a while, he re-establishes contact. Last summer, he waded into the comments section of an article I wrote about sex website creator Cindy Gallop, to say, "I would not sacrifice the physiological pleasure of ejaculating inside the woman for a lesser psychological pleasure.... There is a reason it feels better to do it the right way and you don't see others in the ape world practicing this behavior." A few months later, he reached out via LinkedIn. ("Your stalker would like to add you to his professional network.") A few days before I received the threats in Palm Springs, he sent me a link via Twitter to a story he wrote about another woman who had been abused online. Occasionally, he sends his tweets directly my way—a little reminder that his "game" is back on.

It's been four years, but I still carry the case files with me. I record every tweet he sends me in a Word document, forward his emails to a dedicated account, then print them out to ensure I'll have them ready for police in analog form if he ever threatens me again (or worse). Whenever I have business travel to the city where he lives, I cart my old protection order along, even though the words are beginning to blur after a dozen photocopies. The stacks of paper are filed neatly in my apartment. My anxieties are harder to organize.

Questions

1. Much like Seife, Hess has written a long nuanced article. To see how she develops her argument, create an outline of her points, subpoints, and key sources of support.

2. Compare this essay to Nilsen's "Sexism in English: Embodiment and Language." How are the issues of female language and technology treated in each essay? Write one page about the essays' similarities and differences, paying attention to both the ideas of the writers and the writing itself. Provide at least one example of concrete textual evidence for each essay.

3. In small groups, find two articles from a mainstream news source on the same subject—one written by a man and one written by a woman—and compare the comments sections. What do you notice?

Michael J. Bamshad & Steve E. Olson

Does Race Exist?

Michael J. Bamshad is a professor of pediatrics and genome sciences in the University of Washington's School of Medicine and a member of Seattle Children's Hospital's Genetics Care Team. A recipient of the Society for Pediatric Research's Young Investigator Award, Bamshad is interested in the relationship between evolution and genetics. With colleagues Lynn B. Jorde and John C. Carey, Bamshad also coauthored the textbook *Medical Genetics*. **Steve E. Olson**, a graduate of Yale University with a degree in physics, is a freelance science and public policy writer based in Washington, D.C., and Seattle, Washington. Olson has written for various publications including the *Smithsonian*, the *Atlantic*, the *Washington Post*, and *Wired*. He also has served as a consultant writer for organizations such as the National Academy of Sciences and National Research Council, the White House Office of Science and Technology Policy, the National Institutes of Health, and the Institute for Genomic Research. Olson's books include the 2002 National Book Award finalist *Mapping Human History: Genes, Race, and Our Common Origins* (2003); *Count Down: Six Kids Vie for Glory at the World's Toughest Math Competition* (2004); and *Anarchy Evolution: Faith, Science, and Bad Religion in a World without God* (2010), which was coauthored with musician Greg Graffin.

First published in *Scientific American* in December 2003, "Does Race Exist?" explores both the social definitions and biological components of race. Examining implications for the diagnosis and treatment of diseases such as sickle cell anemia and AIDS, Bamshad and Olson consider four classifications of race based on genetics, as well as the risks and benefits of genetic testing and the controversy surrounding the use of race as a variable in scientific research.

Look around on the streets of any major city, and you will see a sampling of the outward variety of humanity: skin tones ranging from milk-white to dark brown; hair textures running the gamut from fine and stick-straight to thick and wiry. People often use physical characteristics such as these—along with area of geographic origin and shared culture—to group themselves and others into "races." But how valid is the concept of race from a biological standpoint? Do physical features reliably say anything informative about a person's genetic makeup beyond indicating that the individual has genes for blue eyes or curly hair?

The problem is hard in part because the implicit definition of what makes a person a member of a particular race differs from region to region across the globe. Someone classified as "black" in the U.S., for instance, might be considered "white" in Brazil and "colored" (a category distinguished from both "black" and "white") in South Africa.

Yet common definitions of race do sometimes work well to divide groups according to genetically determined propensities for certain diseases. Sickle cell disease is usually found among people of largely African or Mediterranean descent, for instance, whereas cystic fibrosis is far more common among those of European ancestry. In addition, although the results have been controversial, a handful of studies have suggested that African-Americans are more likely to respond poorly to some drugs for cardiac disease than are members of other groups.

Over the past few years, scientists have collected data about the genetic constitution of populations around the world in an effort to probe the link between ancestry and patterns of disease. These data are now providing answers to several highly emotional and contentious questions: Can genetic information be used to distinguish human groups having a common heritage and to assign individuals to particular ones? Do such groups correspond well to pre-defined descriptions now widely used to specify race? And, more practically, does dividing people by familiar racial definitions or by genetic similarities say anything useful about how members of those groups experience disease or respond to drug treatment?

In general, we would answer the first question yes, the second no, and offer a qualified 5 yes to the third. Our answers rest on several generalizations about race and genetics. Some groups do differ genetically from others, but how groups are divided depends on which genes are examined; simplistically put, you might fit into one group based on your skin-color genes but another based on a different characteristic. Many studies have demonstrated that roughly 90 percent of human genetic variation occurs within a population living on a given continent, whereas about 10 percent of the variation distinguishes continental populations. In other words, individuals from different populations are, on average, just slightly more different from one another than are individuals from the same population. Human populations are very similar, but they often can be distinguished.

CLASSIFYING HUMANS

As a first step to identifying links between social definitions of race and genetic heritage, scientists need a way to divide groups reliably according to their ancestry. Over the past 100,000 years or so, anatomically modern humans have migrated from Africa to other parts of the world, and members of our species have increased dramatically in number. This spread has left a distinct signature in our DNA.

To determine the degree of relatedness among groups, geneticists rely on tiny variations, or polymorphisms, in the DNA—specifically in the sequence of base pairs, the building blocks of DNA. Most of these polymorphisms do not occur within genes, the stretches of DNA that encode the information for making proteins (the molecules that constitute much of our bodies and carry out the chemical reactions of life). Accordingly, these common variations are neutral, in that they do not directly affect a particular trait. Some polymorphisms do occur in genes, however; these can contribute to individual variation in traits and to genetic diseases.

As scientists have sequenced the human genome (the full set of nuclear DNA), they have also identified millions of polymorphisms. The distribution of these polymorphisms across populations reflects the history of those populations and the effects of natural selection. To distinguish among groups, the ideal genetic polymorphism would be one that is present in all the members of one group and absent in the members of all other groups. But the major human groups have separated from one another too recently and have mixed too much for such differences to exist.

Polymorphisms that occur at different frequencies around the world can, however, be used to sort people roughly into groups. One useful class of polymorphisms consists of the Alus, short pieces of DNA that are similar in sequence to one another. Alus replicate occasionally, and the resulting copy splices itself at random into a new position on the original chromosome or on another chromosome, usually in a location that has no effect on the functioning of nearby genes. Each insertion is a unique event. Once an Alu sequence inserts itself, it can remain in place for eons, getting passed from one person to his or her descendants. Therefore, if two people have the same Alu sequence at the same spot in their genome, they must be descended from a common ancestor who gave them that specific segment of DNA.

One of us (Bamshad), working with University of Utah scientists Lynn B. Jorde, Stephen   10 Wooding, and W. Scott Watkins and with Mark A. Batzer of Louisiana State University, examined 100 different Alu polymorphisms in 565 people born in sub-Saharan Africa, Asia, and Europe.

First we determined the presence or absence of the 100 Alus in each of the 565 people. Next we removed all the identifying labels (such as place of origin and ethnic group) from the data and sorted the people into groups using only their genetic information.

Our analysis yielded four different groups. When we added the labels back to see whether each individual's group assignment correlated to common, predefined labels for race or ethnicity, we saw that two of the groups consisted only of individuals from sub-Saharan Africa, with one of those two made up almost entirely of Mbuti Pygmies. The other two groups consisted only of individuals from Europe and East Asia, respectively. We found that we needed 60 Alu polymorphisms to assign individuals to their continent of origin with 90 percent accuracy. To achieve nearly 100 percent accuracy, however, we needed to use about 100 Alus.

Other studies have produced comparable results. Noah A. Rosenberg and Jonathan K. Pritchard, geneticists formerly in the laboratory of Marcus W. Feldman of Stanford University, assayed approximately 375 polymorphisms called short tandem repeats in more than 1,000 people from 52 ethnic groups in Africa, Asia, Europe, and the Americas. By looking at the varying frequencies of these polymorphisms, they were able to distinguish five different groups of people whose ancestors were typically isolated by oceans, deserts or mountains: sub-Saharan Africans; Europeans and Asians west of the Himalayas; East Asians; inhabitants of New Guinea and Melanesia; and Native Americans. They were also able to identify subgroups within each region that usually corresponded with each member's self-reported ethnicity.

The results of these studies indicate that genetic analyses can distinguish groups of people according to their geographic origin. But caution is warranted. The groups easiest to resolve were those that were widely separated from one another geographically. Such samples maximize the genetic variation among groups. When Bamshad and his co-workers used their 100 Alu polymorphisms to try to classify a sample of individuals from southern India into a separate group, the Indians instead had more in common with either Europeans or Asians. In other words, because India has been subject to many genetic influences from Europe and Asia, people on the subcontinent did not group into a unique cluster. We concluded that many hundreds—or perhaps thousands—of polymorphisms might have to be examined to distinguish between groups whose ancestors have historically interbred with multiple populations.

THE HUMAN RACE

Given that people can be sorted broadly into groups using genetic data, do common notions of race correspond to underlying genetic differences among populations? In some cases they do, but often they do not. For instance, skin color or facial features—traits influenced by natural selection—are routinely used to divide people into races. But groups with similar physical characteristics as a result of selection can be quite different genetically. Individuals from sub-Saharan Africa and Australian Aborigines might have similar skin pigmentation (because of adapting to strong sun), but genetically they are quite dissimilar.

In contrast, two groups that are genetically similar to each other might be exposed to   15
different selective forces. In this case, natural selection can exaggerate some of the differences between groups, making them appear more dissimilar on the surface than they are underneath. Because traits such as skin color have been strongly affected by natural selection, they do not necessarily reflect the population processes that have shaped the distribution of neutral polymorphisms such as Alus or short tandem repeats. Therefore, traits or polymorphisms affected by natural selection may be poor predictors of group membership and may imply genetic relatedness where, in fact, little exists.

Another example of how difficult it is to categorize people involves populations in the U.S. Most people who describe themselves as African-American have relatively recent ancestors from West Africa, and West Africans generally have polymorphism frequencies that can be distinguished from those of Europeans, Asians, and Native Americans. The fraction of gene variations that African-Americans share with West Africans, however, is far from uniform, because over the centuries African-Americans have mixed extensively with groups originating from elsewhere in Africa and beyond.

Over the past several years, Mark D. Shriver of Pennsylvania State University and Rick A. Kittles of Howard University have defined a set of polymorphisms that they have used to estimate the fraction of a person's genes originating from each continental region. They found that the West African contribution to the genes of individual African-Americans averages about 80 percent, although it ranges from 20 to 100 percent. Mixing of groups is also apparent in many individuals who believe they have only European ancestors. According to Shriver's analyses, approximately 30 percent of Americans who consider themselves "white" have less than 90 percent European ancestry. Thus, self-reported ancestry is not necessarily a good predictor of the genetic composition of a large number of Americans. Accordingly, common notions of race do not always reflect a person's genetic background.

MEMBERSHIP HAS ITS PRIVILEGES

Understanding the relation between race and genetic variation has important practical implications. Several of the polymorphisms that differ in frequency from group to group have specific effects on health. The mutations responsible for sickle cell disease and some cases of cystic fibrosis, for instance, result from genetic changes that appear to have risen in frequency because they were protective against diseases prevalent in Africa and Europe, respectively. People who inherit one copy of the sickle cell polymorphism show some resistance to malaria; those with one copy of the cystic fibrosis trait may be less prone to the dehydration resulting from cholera. The symptoms of these diseases arise only in the unfortunate individuals who inherit two copies of the mutations.

Genetic variation also plays a role in individual susceptibility to one of the worst scourges of our age: AIDS. Some people have a small deletion in both their copies of a gene that encodes a particular cell-surface receptor called chemokine receptor 5 (CCR5). As a result, these individuals fail to produce CCR5 receptors on the surface of their cells. Most strains of HIV-1, the virus that causes AIDS, bind to the CCR5 receptor to gain entry to cells, so people who lack CCR5 receptors are resistant to HIV-1 infection. This polymorphism in the CCR5 receptor gene is found almost exclusively in groups from northeastern Europe.

Several polymorphisms in CCR5 do not prevent infection but instead influence the 20 rate at which HIV-1 infection leads to AIDS and death. Some of these polymorphisms have similar effects in different populations; others only alter the speed of disease progression in selected groups. One polymorphism, for example, is associated with delayed disease progression in European-Americans but accelerated disease in African-Americans. Researchers can only study such population-specific effects—and use that knowledge to direct therapy—if they can sort people into groups.

In these examples—and others like them—a polymorphism has a relatively large effect in a given disease. If genetic screening were inexpensive and efficient, all individuals could be screened for all such disease-related gene variants. But genetic testing remains costly. Perhaps more significantly, genetic screening raises concerns about privacy and consent: some people might not want to know about genetic factors that could increase their risk of developing a particular disease. Until these issues are resolved further, self-reported ancestry will continue to be a potentially useful diagnostic tool for physicians.

Ancestry may also be relevant for some diseases that are widespread in particular populations. Most common diseases, such as hypertension and diabetes, are the cumulative results of polymorphisms in several genes, each of which has a small influence on its own. Recent research suggests that polymorphisms that have a particular effect in one group may have a different effect in another group. This kind of complexity would make it much more difficult to use detected polymorphisms as a guide to therapy. Until further studies are done on the genetic and environmental contributions to complex diseases, physicians may have to rely on information about an individual's ancestry to know how best to treat some diseases.

RACE AND MEDICINE

But the importance of group membership as it relates to health care has been especially controversial in recent years. Last January the U.S. Food and Drug Administration issued guidelines advocating the collection of race and ethnicity data in all clinical trials. Some investigators contend that the differences between groups are so small and the historical abuses associated with categorizing people by race so extreme that group membership should play little if any role in genetic and medical studies. They assert that the FDA should abandon its recommendation and instead ask researchers conducting clinical trials to collect genomic data on each individual. Others suggest that only by using group membership, including common definitions of race based on skin color, can we understand how genetic and environmental differences among groups contribute to disease. This debate will be settled only by further research on the validity of race as a scientific variable.

A set of articles in the March 20 issue of the *New England Journal of Medicine* debated both sides of the medical implications of race. The authors of one article—Richard S. Cooper of the Loyola Stritch School of Medicine, Jay S. Kaufman of the University of North Carolina at Chapel Hill and Ryk Ward of the University of Oxford—argued that race is not an adequate criterion for physicians to use in choosing a particular drug for a given patient. They pointed out two findings of racial differences that are both now considered questionable: that a combination of certain blood vessel-dilating drugs was more effective in treating heart failure in people of African ancestry and that specific enzyme inhibitors (angiotensin converting enzyme, or ACE, inhibitors) have little efficacy in such individuals. In the second article, a group led by Neil Risch of Stanford University countered that racial or ethnic groups can differ from one another genetically and that the differences can have medical importance. They cited a study showing that the rate of complications from type 2 diabetes varies according to race, even after adjusting for such factors as disparities in education and income.

The intensity of these arguments reflects both scientific and social factors. Many bio- 25 medical studies have not rigorously defined group membership, relying instead on inferred relationships based on racial categories. The dispute over the importance of group membership also illustrates how strongly the perception of race is shaped by different social and political perspectives.

In cases where membership in a geographically or culturally defined group has been correlated with health-related genetic traits, knowing something about an individual's group membership could be important for a physician. And to the extent that human groups live in different environments or have different experiences that affect health, group membership could also reflect nongenetic factors that are medically relevant.

Regardless of the medical implications of the genetics of race, the research findings are inherently exciting. For hundreds of years, people have wondered where various human groups came from and how those groups are related to one another. They have speculated about why human populations have different physical appearances and about whether the biological differences between groups are more than skin deep. New genetic data and new methods of analysis are finally allowing us to approach these questions. The result will be a much deeper understanding of both our biological nature and our human interconnectedness.

Questions

1. As stated at the outset, this article examines notions of race primarily "from a biological standpoint" (para. 1). What do the article's conclusions suggest or argue about the scientific validity of established, culturally variant racial categories?

2. The article plainly presents its opinions and main points at the outset before going into more detail in subsequent sections. What are the advantages and disadvantages of such an approach?

3. What role does audience play in the choice of evidence used in this essay?

4. This essay is similar to the sort of writing you may be required to do in many of your classes. What makes this essay an academic piece? Consider language, tone, structure, and types of evidence. Why do you think this type of writing is privileged in academic settings?

William Zinsser [1922–2015]

College Pressures

William Zinsser was born in New York City, graduated from Princeton with a B.A. in 1944, and subsequently began a long association with the *New York Herald Tribune* as a writer, editor, and critic. He also contributed to *Life*, the *New Yorker*, and other magazines. His experience teaching writing at Yale (1970–1979) led to his classic guide *On Writing Well* (1976; sixth edition, 2000), which recounts his own struggles to master and to impart the writer's "craft." Zinsser's related textbooks include *Writing to Learn* (1988) and *Speaking of Journalism: 12 Writers and Editors Talk About Their Work* (1994), in which former students—now successful writers and editors—explain how they write feature articles, personal columns, and sports stories. Zinsser's 1989 *Spring Training* is about the Pittsburgh Pirates baseball team's preseason experiences in Florida. In *American Places* (1992), Zinsser describes his visits to American landmarks (including Mount Rushmore, the Alamo, and Disneyland), where he met rangers, custodians, and others, who agreed that such places satisfy visitors' patriotic and psychic needs. In *Writing about Your Life: A Journey into the Past* (2004), Zinsser guides writers of memoir to focus on small, authentic moments and to be themselves in their writing.

"College Pressures" first appeared in *Blair and Ketchum's Country Journal* in 1979.

Dear Carlos: I desperately need a dean's excuse for my chem midterm which will begin in about 1 hour. All I can say is that I totally blew it this week. I've fallen incredibly, inconceivably behind.

Carlos: Help! I'm anxious to hear from you. I'll be in my room and won't leave it until I hear from you. Tomorrow is the last day for...

Carlos: I left town because I started bugging out again. I stayed up all night to finish a take-home make-up exam & am typing it to hand in on the 10th. It was due on the 5th. P.S. I'm going to the dentist. Pain is pretty bad.

Carlos: Probably by Friday I'll be able to get back to my studies. Right now I'm going to take a long walk. This whole thing has taken a lot out of me.

Carlos: I'm really up the proverbial creek. The problem is I really bombed *the history final. Since I need that course for my major I...*

Carlos: Here follows a tale of woe. I went home this weekend, had to help my Mom, & caught a fever so didn't have much time to study. My professor...

Carlos: Aargh! Trouble. Nothing original but everything's piling up at once. To be brief, my job interview...

Hey Carlos, good news! I've got mononucleosis.

Who are these wretched supplicants, scribbling notes so laden with anxiety, seeking such miracles of postponement and balm? They are men and women who belong to Branford College, one of the twelve residential colleges at Yale University, and the messages are just a few of the hundreds that they left for their dean, Carlos Hortas—often slipped under his door at 4 A.M.—last year.

But students like the ones who wrote those notes can also be found on campuses from coast to coast—especially in New England and at many other private colleges across the country that have high academic standards and highly motivated students. Nobody could doubt that the notes are real. In their urgency and their gallows humor they are authentic voices of a generation that is panicky to succeed.

My own connection with the message writers is that I am master of Branford College. I live in its Gothic quadrangle and know the students well. (We have 485 of them.) I am privy to their hopes and fears—and also to their stereo music and their piercing cries in the dead of night ("Does anybody *ca-a-are* ?"). If they went to Carlos to ask how to get through tomorrow, they come to me to ask how to get through the rest of their lives.

Mainly I try to remind them that the road ahead is a long one and that it will have more unexpected turns than they think. There will be plenty of time to change jobs, change careers, change whole attitudes and approaches. They don't want to hear such liberating news. They want a map—right now—that they can follow unswervingly to career security, financial security. Social Security and, presumably, a prepaid grave.

What I wish for all students is some release from the clammy grip of the future. I wish 5 them a chance to savor each segment of their education as an experience in itself and not as a grim preparation for the next step. I wish them the right to experiment, to trip and fall, to learn that defeat is as instructive as victory and is not the end of the world.

My wish, of course, is naïve. One of the few rights that America does not proclaim is the right to fail. Achievement is the national god, venerated in our media—the million-dollar athlete, the wealthy executive—and glorified in our praise of possessions. In the presence of such a potent state religion, the young are growing up old.

I see four kinds of pressure working on college students today: economic pressure, parental pressure, peer pressure, and self-induced pressure. It is easy to look around for villains—to blame the colleges for charging too much money, the professors for assigning too much work, the parents for pushing their children too far, the students for driving themselves too hard. But there are no villains; only victims.

"In the late 1960s," one dean told me, "the typical question that I got from students was 'Why is there so much suffering in the world?' or 'How can I make a contribution?' Today it's 'Do you think it would look better for getting into law school if I did a double major in history and political science, or just majored in one of them?'" Many other deans confirmed this pattern. One said: "They're trying to find an edge—the intangible something that will look better on paper if two students are about equal."

Note the emphasis on looking better. The transcript has become a sacred document, the passport to security. How one appears on paper is more important than how one appears in person. *A* is for Admirable and *B* is for Borderline, even though, in Yale's official system of grading, *A* means "excellent" and *B* means "very good." Today, looking very good is no longer good enough, especially for students who hope to go on to law school or medical school. They know that entrance into the better schools will be an entrance into the better law firms and better medical practices where they will make a lot of money. They also know that the odds are harsh, Yale Law School, for instance, matriculates 170 students from an applicant pool of 3,700; Harvard enrolls 550 from a pool of 7,000.

It's all very well for those of us who write letters of recommendation for our students 10 to stress the qualities of humanity that will make them good lawyers or doctors. And it's nice to think that admission officers are really reading our letters and looking for the extra dimension of commitment or concern. Still, it would be hard for a student not to visualize these officers shuffling so many transcripts studded with *A*s that they regard a *B* as positively shameful.

The pressure is almost as heavy on students who just want to graduate and get a job. Long gone are the days of the "gentleman's C," when students journeyed through college with a certain relaxation, sampling a wide variety of courses—music, art, philosophy, classics, anthropology, poetry, religion—that would send them out as liberally educated men and women. If I were an employer I would rather employ graduates who have this range and curiosity than those who narrowly pursued safe subjects and high grades. I know countless students whose inquiring minds exhilarate me. I like to hear the play of their ideas. I don't know if they are getting As or Cs, and I don't care. I also like them as people. The country needs them, and they will find satisfying jobs. I tell them to relax. They can't.

Nor can I blame them. They live in a brutal economy. Tuition, room, and board at most private colleges now comes to at least $7,000, not counting books and fees. This might seem to suggest that the colleges are getting rich. But they are equally battered by inflation. Tuition covers only 60 percent of what it costs to educate a student, and ordinarily the remainder comes from what colleges receive in endowments, grants, and gifts. Now the remainder keeps being swallowed by the cruel costs—higher every year—of just opening the doors. Heating oil is up. Insurance is up. Postage is up. Health-premium costs are up. Everything is up. Deficits are up. We are witnessing in America the creation of a brotherhood of paupers—colleges, parents, and students, joined by the common bond of debt.

Today it is not unusual for a student, even if he works part time at college and full time during the summer, to accrue $5,000 in loans after four years—loans that he must start to repay within one year after graduation. Exhorted at commencement to go forth into the world, he is already behind as he goes forth. How could he not feel under pressure throughout college to prepare for this day of reckoning? I have used "he," incidentally, only for brevity. Women at Yale are under no less pressure to justify their expensive education to themselves, their parents, and society. In fact, they are probably under more pressure. For although they leave college superbly equipped to bring fresh leadership to traditionally male jobs, society hasn't yet caught up with this fact.

Along with economic pressure goes parental pressure. Inevitably, the two are deeply intertwined.

I see many students taking pre-medical courses with joyless tenacity. They go off to their 15 labs as if they were going to the dentist. It saddens me because I know them in other corners of their life as cheerful people.

"Do you want to go to medical school?" I ask them.

"I guess so," they say, without conviction, or "Not really."

"Then why are you going?"

"Well, my parents want me to be a doctor. They're paying all this money and…"

Poor students, poor parents. They are caught in one of the oldest webs of love and duty 20 and guilt. The parents mean well; they are trying to steer their sons and daughters toward a secure future. But the sons and daughters want to major in history or classics or philosophy—subjects with no "practical" value. Where's the payoff on the humanities? It's not easy to persuade such loving parents that the humanities do indeed pay off. The intellectual faculties developed by studying subjects like history and classics—an ability to synthesize and relate, to weigh cause and effect, to see events in perspective—are just the faculties that make creative leaders in business or almost any general field. Still, many fathers would rather put their money on courses that point toward a specific profession—courses that are pre-law, pre-medical, pre-business, or, as I sometimes heard it put, "pre-rich."

But the pressure on students is severe. They are truly torn. One part of them feels obligated to fulfill their parents' expectations; after all, their parents are older and presumably wiser. Another part tells them that the expectations that are right for their parents are not right for them.

I know a student who wants to be an artist. She is very obviously an artist and will be a good one—she has already had several modest local exhibits. Meanwhile she is growing as a well-rounded person and taking humanistic subjects that will enrich the inner resources out of which her art will grow. But her father is strongly opposed. He thinks that an artist is a "dumb" thing to be. The student vacillates and tries to please everybody. She keeps up with her art somewhat furtively and takes some of the "dumb" courses her father wants her to take—at least they are dumb courses for her. She is a free spirit on a campus of tense students—no small achievement in itself—and she deserves to follow her muse.

Peer pressure and self-induced pressure are also intertwined, and they begin almost at the beginning of freshman year.

"I had a freshman student I'll call Linda," one dean told me, "who came in and said she was under terrible pressure because her roommate, Barbara, was much brighter and studied all the time. I couldn't tell her that Barbara had come in two hours earlier to say the same thing about Linda."

The story is almost funny—except that it's not. It's symptomatic of all the pressures 25 put together. When every student thinks every other student is working harder and doing better, the only solution is to study harder still. I see students going off to the library every night after dinner and coming back when it closes at midnight. I wish they would sometimes forget about their peers and go to a movie. I hear the clacking of typewriters in the hours before dawn. I see the tension in their eyes when exams are approaching and papers are due: "*Will I get everything done?*"

Probably they won't. They will get sick. They will get "blocked." They will sleep. They will oversleep. They will bug out. *Hey Carlos, help*!

Part of the problem is that they do more than they are expected to do. A professor will assign five-page papers. Several students will start writing ten-page papers to impress him. Then more students will write ten-page papers, and a few will raise the ante to fifteen. Pity the poor student who is still just doing the assignment.

"Once you have twenty or thirty percent of the student population deliberately over-exerting," one dean points out, "it's bad for everybody. When a teacher gets more and more effort from his class, the student who is doing normal work can be perceived as not doing well. The tactic works, psychologically."

Why can't the professor just cut back and not accept longer papers? He can, and he probably will. But by then the term will be half over and the damage done. Grade fever is highly contagious and not easily reversed. Besides, the professor's main concern is with his course. He knows his students only in relation to the course and doesn't know that they are also overexerting in their other courses. Nor is it really his business. He didn't sign up for dealing with the student as a whole person and with all the emotional baggage the student brought along from home. That's what deans, masters, chaplains, and psychiatrists are for.

To some extent this is nothing new: a certain number of professors have always been 30 self-contained islands of scholarship and shyness, more comfortable with books than with people. But the new pauperism has widened the gap still further, for professors who actually like to spend time with students don't have as much time to spend. They also are overexerting. If they are young, they are busy trying to publish in order not to perish, hanging by their finger nails onto a shrinking profession. If they are old and tenured, they are buried under the duties of administering departments—as departmental chairmen or members of committees—that have been thinned out by the budgetary axe.

Ultimately it will be the students' own business to break the circles in which they are trapped. They are too young to be prisoners of their parents' dreams and their classmates' fears. They must be jolted into believing in themselves as unique men and women who have the power to shape their own future.

"Violence is being done to the undergraduate experience," says Carlos Hortas. "College should be open-ended: at the end it should open many, many roads. Instead, students are choosing their goal in advance, and their choices narrow as they go along. It's almost as if they think that the country has been codified in the type of jobs that exist—that they've got to fit into certain slots. Therefore, fit into the best-paying slot.

"They ought to take chances. Not taking chances will lead to a life of colorless mediocrity. They'll be comfortable. But something in the spirit will be missing."

I have painted too drab a portrait of today's students, making them seem a solemn lot. That is only half of their story; if they were so dreary I wouldn't so thoroughly enjoy their company. The other half is that they are easy to like. They are quick to laugh and to offer friendship. They are not introverts. They are unusually kind and are more considerate of one another than any student generation I have known.

Nor are they so obsessed with their studies that they avoid sports and extracurricular 35 activities. On the contrary, they juggle their crowded hours to play on a variety of teams, perform with musical and dramatic groups, and write for campus publications. But this in turn is one more cause of anxiety. There are too many choices. Academically, they have 1,300 courses to select from; outside class they have to decide how much spare time they can spare and how to spend it.

This means that they engage in fewer extracurricular pursuits than their predecessors did. If they want to row on the crew and play in the symphony they will eliminate one; in the '60s they would have done both. They also tend to choose activities that are self-limiting. Drama, for instance, is flourishing in all twelve of Yale's residential colleges as it never has before. Students hurl themselves into these productions—as actors, directors, carpenters, and technicians—with a dedication to create the best possible play, knowing that the day will come when the run will end and they can get back to their studies.

They also can't afford to be the willing slave of organizations like the *Yale Daily News*. Last spring at the one-hundredth anniversary banquet of that paper—whose past chairmen include such once and future kings as Potter Stewart, Kingman Brewster, and William F. Buckley, Jr.—much was made of the fact that the editorial staff used to be small and totally committed and that "newsies" routinely worked fifty hours a week. In effect they belonged to a club; Newsies is how they defined themselves at Yale. Today's student will write one or two articles a week, when he can, and he defines himself as a student. I've never heard the word Newsie except at the banquet.

If I have described the modern undergraduate primarily as a driven creature who is largely ignoring the blithe spirit inside who keeps trying to come out and play, it's because that's where the crunch is, not only at Yale but throughout American education. It's why I think we should all be worried about the values that are nurturing a generation so fearful of risk and so goal-obsessed at such an early age.

I tell students that there is no one "right" way to get ahead—that each of them is a different person, starting from a different point and bound for a different destination. I tell them that change is a tonic and that all the slots are not codified nor the frontiers closed. One of my ways of telling them is to invite men and women who have achieved success outside the academic world to come and talk informally with my students during the year. They are heads of companies or ad agencies, editors of magazines, politicians, public officials, television magnates, labor leaders, business executives, Broadway producers, artists, writers, economists, photographers, scientists, historians—a mixed bag of achievers.

I ask them to say a few words about how they got started. The students assume that they 40 started in their present profession and knew all along that it was what they wanted to do. Luckily for me, most of them got into their field by a circuitous route, to their surprise, after many detours. The students are startled. They can hardly conceive of a career that was not pre-planned. They can hardly imagine allowing the hand of God or chance to nudge them down some unforeseen trail

Questions

1. Zinsser first published "College Pressures" in 1979. Make a list of all the pressures Zinsser claims college students face. Do you find yourself facing similar pressures, over thirty years later? Are there pressures you think no longer apply or additional pressures you would add to the list? Given your response, do you think "College Pressures" is still relevant today?

2. What is Zinsser arguing in "College Pressures"? Choose a body paragraph of the essay that you think effectively advances or supports his argument. Break down the paragraph, and describe the purpose of each sentence.

Reg Weaver

No: NCLB's Excessive Reliance on Testing Is Unrealistic, Arbitrary, and Frequently Unfair

A thirty-year classroom veteran, **Reg Weaver** received his B.S. in special education at Illinois State University and his master's from Roosevelt University in Chicago. A long-time advocate of quality public education, he is involved in numerous advocacy groups on both the state and national levels. He has contributed articles to newspapers such as the *New York Times*, *USA Today*, and the *Washington Post* and to journals such as *Congressional Quarterly*, *Education Week*, and *Education Daily*. In addition, Weaver makes regular appearances on ABC's *World News Tonight*, CNN's *Headline News*, and C-Span's *Washington Journal*. He is currently serving his second term as president of the National Education Association.

In "No: NCLB's Excessive Reliance on Testing Is Unrealistic, Arbitrary, and Frequently Unfair," Reg Weaver discusses the weaknesses of the No Child Left Behind Act, especially its reliance on the concept of adequate yearly progress. Weaver argues that in its present state, the concept fails to increase school accountability, but that it could do so with such changes as following the progress of individual children and offering tutoring to struggling students.

As I travel around the country visiting schools and talking with National Education Association (NEA) members, I sense a growing concern among teachers and parents about the overwhelming emphasis given to standardized testing in America's schools. This concern is heightened when high stakes are attached to the outcomes of such tests. Teachers and parents worry that more and more of the important things that prepare us for life will be pushed off the curriculum plate to make room for test preparation.

According to a recent poll by Public Agenda, 88 percent of teachers say the amount of attention their school pays to standardized test results has increased during the last several years. And 61 percent agreed that teaching to the test "inevitably stifles real teaching and learning."

As any good teacher knows, there is no one-size-fits-all approach to either teaching or learning. In fact, we now have a solid body of research about cognition and learning styles that provides ample confirmation of this. Any good teacher also knows that proper assessment of learning is both complex and multifaceted. Tests—particularly paper and pencil tests that are standardized—are only one type of assessment. Good teachers make judgments about what has been learned on the basis of a variety of assessments. Finally, we know that what constitutes spectacular achievement for a child who suffers serious challenges may not equal the progress of his or her peers, but we honor this progress nonetheless.

The NEA has a proud history of supporting and nurturing our system of public education. When we are critical of the so-called No Child Left Behind (NCLB) Act, our interest is to fix those elements of the law that we see as destructive to public education and, ultimately, to the children we serve.

A consensus is emerging from coast to coast and across the political spectrum that this is   5
a law in need of repair. And the present definition of adequate yearly progress is at the heart of what is wrong with the law.

The concept of adequate yearly progress is relatively simple: Set a lofty goal, establish a time frame for accomplishing the goal, establish incremental targets or steps toward achieving the goal, and hold schools accountable for meeting the targets and, ultimately, the goal. The goal is 100 percent proficiency in reading and math, and all schools must meet it by 2014.

Wouldn't life, and particularly parenting and teaching, be simple if progress in learning were linear and time-sensitive? Parents, teachers and cognitive psychologists alike know that learning is anything but linear. And yet we now have a federal law that not only violates what we know to be true about human learning but says that unless schools achieve linear progress, the federal government will punish you.

Do we have a problem with this? You bet we do. Can it be fixed? We think so.

One of our state affiliates, the Connecticut Education Association (CEA), is a leader in recognizing and studying the problems with the federal definition of "adequate yearly progress" (AYP). Shortly after the law was adopted, the CEA had an independent economist develop a scenario based on existing test data in Connecticut in an attempt to visualize the impact of AYP in one of the highest achieving states in the nation. The initial results were shocking; however, because the law had yet to be implemented, the results were still hypothetical. Nonetheless, the prediction became reality last summer when nearly 25 percent of schools in Connecticut were identified as having failed to make AYP. An astonishing 155 elementary and middle schools and 88 high schools were identified as "in need of improvement" under the federal law.

More recently, armed with two years of test data, the CEA asked its economist, Ed   10 Moscovitch of Massachusetts, to update the scenarios. This time the CEA asked what failure rates might look like over the full 12 years of implementation. The new scenario, based on a model that allows for the rate of growth that students actually achieved in the last two years of testing, is very revealing. At the end of 12 years, 744 of 802 elementary and middle schools in Connecticut will have failed to make adequate yearly progress—that's 93 percent of its elementary and middle schools.

In the first year none of the schools identified had the white non-Hispanic subgroup failing to make AYP. In the final year 585 of the 744 schools will have the white subgroup failing to do so. Even the powerful combination of social capital and great schools in a state that is regarded nationally as a high performer is not adequate to meet the statistical demands of this law.

Only in Lake Wobegon, perhaps, where all the students are above average, is there a chance of meeting the requirements set forth in the so-called No Child Left Behind law.

The current formula for AYP fails to consider the difference between where you start and how quickly you must reach the goal. That is, in my opinion, irresponsible. It is particularly irresponsible as it applies to English-language learners and special-education subgroups. While the Department of Education (DOE) finally has acknowledged that students whose first language is not English may not perform well when given a test in English, it does not go far enough to correct the problem. With respect to special-education students, the DOE has granted some leeway for the small percentage of severely cognitively disabled students, but there are thousands of other students in this subgroup for whom the test is totally inappropriate and emotionally injurious.

What's more, while the department has acknowledged the unfairness of how English-language learners and students with disabilities were tested, it has refused to go back and reconsider schools labeled "in need of improvement" under the old procedures.

Is this all the law of unintended consequences? Or is there, as many believe, an insidious   15 intent to discredit public education, paving the way for a breakup of the current system—an opening of the door to a boutique system with increased privatization and government vouchers?

We believe that for every ideologue who wants to subject public education to market forces, there are scores of policymakers and political officials who supported this law based solely on its stated, laudable intent. Many of them still do not understand the full import of what they supported. So what do we believe needs to be done?

First, we need to ask whether the measurement of AYP is an accurate barometer of a student's progress or a school's effectiveness. We have urged the adoption of multiple indicators. Measuring this year's fourth-graders against next year's fourth-graders tells us little that we need to know about the improvement of individual students. Wouldn't it make more sense to follow the progress of individual children? We have called for this kind of cohort analysis, and recently 14 state superintendents asked for the same change in a meeting with President George W. Bush.

Second, is it fair to have the same starting point for all groups? We need to find a more rational way to acknowledge the dramatic gaps in performance among subgroups. As an example, high-achieving students in Connecticut wait for years for targeted low-achieving subgroups to catch up with their performance, while other groups are asked to fill an un-achievable gap in one year just to get to the starting gate. Yet the race begins at the same time and at the same pace for all. For certain subgroups, even dramatic increases in performance relative to their prior performance will only lead to failure. We need to acknowledge and honor progress.

Third, if we really have a goal of improving student achievement, shouldn't we offer tutoring to struggling students first? Right now NCLB adopts an "abandon ship" philoso-phy of allowing parents to change schools. The focus should be on helping the individual student in the subgroup in need of attention. And by the way, why is it less important to have a highly qualified tutor, or supplemental service provider, than it is to have a highly qualified teacher? Academic tutors should be certified, as well. Current law prohibits states from requiring that tutors be certified.

So in answer to the question "Does AYP increase school accountability?" our answer is   20 no. But it could with serious and thoughtful revision.

The NEA and its state affiliates have always supported high standards and account-ability. And we believe that no child should be left behind. We believe that every child in a public school should be taught by a highly qualified teacher in an atmosphere that is safe and conducive to learning, and all students should have access to a rich and deep curriculum. We also believe that each child is unique and brings to the classroom a variety of gifts and chal-lenges. We have built a system in the United States that has struggled to honor this notion of gifts and challenges—our doors are open to all—and we have huge systemic challenges in meeting this philosophical ideal. There's much more that the federal government must do to guarantee that No Child Left Behind is more than just an empty promise.

Questions

1. Considering Weaver's role as president of the National Education Association (NEA), what sort of bias might his critics accuse him of and why? How well does Weaver's argument forestall such claims of bias, and why?

2. Write a brief account of your personal experience with standardized testing, and compare that experience to the way Weaver describes such testing, especially its problems. How familiar to you are Weaver's concerns? Does his critique of high stakes testing ring true for you? Why or why not?

3. In small groups, find two recent articles that criticize President Obama's Race to the Top initiative for public education. Compare these critical articles to Weaver's article— how similar and different are the authors' concerns? Based on the similarities and differences you find, how much has changed in public education since Weaver wrote his article in 2004? How applicable is Weaver's critique to the present situation and why?

William Saletan [b. 1964]

Please Don't Feed the People

A native Texan and 1987 graduate of Swarthmore College, **William Saletan** is journalist and national correspondent, reporting on topics including politics, science,
technology, and bio- and sexual ethics. Saletan has been a contributing writer for the
Washington Post, the *New York Times*, the *Wall Street Journal*, the *National Review*,
Mother Jones, and *Slate.com*. He maintains a "Human Nature" column published
at *Slate.com* and is well known for his coverage of the 2004 Republican National
Convention, as well as the presidential election itself. In 2003, Saletan published his
first book, *Bearing Right: How Conservatives Won the Abortion War*.

Saletan's article "Please Don't Feed the People," first published in the *Washington
Post*, presents statistics that, at the end of the twentieth century, indicate a global
rise in obesity, especially for low-income families. He observes that technology is
largely to blame, particularly for its role in making fast food so readily accessible and
lifestyles increasingly sedentary. Ultimately, Saletan calls for global change, asking his
readers to take a critical look at their eating habits and, as a result, their bodies and
their health.

In 1894, Congress established a national Labor Day to honor those who "from rude nature
have delved and carved all the grandeur we behold." In the century since, the grandeur
of human achievement has multiplied. Over the past four decades, global population has
doubled, but food output, driven by increases in productivity, has outpaced it. Poverty,
infant mortality and hunger are receding. For the first time in our planet's history, a species
no longer lives at the mercy of scarcity. We have learned to feed ourselves.

We've learned so well, in fact, that we're getting fat. Not just the United States or
Europe, but the whole world. Egyptian, Mexican and South African women are now as fat as
Americans. Far more Filipino adults are now overweight than underweight. In China, one in
five adults is too heavy, and the rate of overweight children is 28 times higher than it was two
decades ago. In Kuwait, Thailand and Tunisia, obesity, diabetes and heart disease are soaring.

Hunger is far from conquered. But since 1990, the global rate of malnutrition has declined an average of 1.7 percent a year. Based on data from the World Health Organization
and the U.N. Food and Agriculture Organization, for every two people who are malnour-
ished, three are now overweight or obese. Among women, even in most African countries,
overweight has surpassed underweight. The balance of peril is shifting.

Fat is no longer a rich man's disease. For middle- and high-income Americans, the
obesity rate is 29 percent. For low-income Americans, it's 35 percent. Fourteen percent
of middle- and high-income kids age 15 to 17 are overweight. For low-income kids in the
same age bracket, it's 23 percent. Globally, weight has tended to rise with income. But a
recent study in Vancouver, Canada, found that preschoolers in "food-insecure" households
were twice as likely as other kids to be overweight or obese. In Brazilian cities, the poor have
become fatter than the rich.

Technologically, this is a triumph. In the early days of our species, even the rich starved.   5
Barry Popkin, a nutritional epidemiologist at the University of North Carolina, divides history into several epochs. In the hunter-gatherer era, if we didn't find food, we died. In the

agricultural era, if our crops perished, we died. In the industrial era, famine receded, but infectious diseases killed us. Now we've achieved such control over nature that we're dying not of starvation or infection, but of abundance. Nature isn't killing us. We're killing ourselves.

You don't have to go hungry anymore; we can fill you with fats and carbs more cheaply than ever. You don't have to chase your food; we can bring it to you. You don't have to cook it; we can deliver it ready to eat. You don't have to eat it before it spoils; we can pump it full of preservatives so it lasts forever. You don't even have to stop when you're full. We've got so much food to sell, we want you to keep eating.

What happened in America is happening everywhere, only faster. Fewer farmers markets, more processed food. Fewer whole grains, more refined ones. More sweeteners, salt and transfats. Cheaper meat, more animal fat. Less cooking, more eating out. Bigger portions, more snacks.

Kentucky Fried Chicken and Pizza Hut are spreading across the planet. Coca-Cola is in more than 200 countries. Half of McDonald's business is outside the United States. In China, animal fat intake has tripled in 20 years. By 2020, meat consumption in developing countries will grow by 106 million metric tons, outstripping growth in developed countries by a factor of more than five. Forty years ago, to afford a high-fat diet, your country needed a gross national product per capita of nearly $1,500. Now the price is half that. You no longer have to be rich to die a rich man's death.

Soon it'll be a poor man's death. The rich have Whole Foods, gyms and personal trainers. The poor have 7-11, Popeye's and streets unsafe for walking. When money's tight, you feed your kids at Wendy's and stock up on macaroni and cheese. At a lunch buffet, you do what your ancestors did: store all the fat you can.

That's the punch line: Technology has changed everything but us. We evolved to survive 10
scarcity. We crave fat. We're quick to gain weight and slow to lose it. Double what you serve us; we'll double what we eat.

Thanks to technology, the deprivation that made these traits useful is gone. So is the link between flavors and nutrients. The food industry can sell you sweetness without fruit, salt without protein, creaminess without milk. We can fatten and starve you at the same time.

And that's just the diet side of the equation. Before technology, adult men expended about 3,000 calories a day. Now they expend about 2,000. The folks fielding customer service calls in Bangalore are sitting at desks. Nearly everyone in China has a television set. Remember when Chinese rode bikes? In the past six years, the number of cars there has grown from 6 million to 20 million. More than one in seven Chinese has a motorized vehicle, and households with such vehicles have an obesity rate 80 percent higher than their peers.

The answer to these trends is simple. We have to exercise more and change the food we eat, donate and subsidize. Next year [in 2007], for example, the U.S. Women, Infants, and Children program, which subsidizes groceries for impoverished youngsters, will begin to pay for fruits and vegetables. For 32 years, the program has fed toddlers eggs and cheese but not one vegetable. And we wonder why poor kids are fat.

The hard part is changing our mentality. We have a distorted body image. We're so used to not having enough, as a species, that we can't believe the problem is too much. From China to Africa to Latin America, people are trying to fatten their kids. I just got back from a vacation with my Jewish mother and Jewish mother-in-law. They told me I need to eat more.

The other thing blinding us is liberal guilt. We're so caught up in the idea of giving that we can't see the importance of changing behavior rather than filling bellies. We know better than to feed buttered popcorn to zoo animals, yet we send it to a food bank and call ourselves humanitarians. Maybe we should ask what our fellow humans actually need.

[2006]

Questions

1. Saletan's use of third person suggests that he believes both himself and his readers are complicit in denying certain groups access to healthy food. To determine the veracity of his claim, locate a flier or Web site from a local food bank and look at what kind of items they need. Brainstorm a list of nutritious options for these items. Next, make a list of reasons that would make it difficult or less convenient for a shopper to donate such foods. Consider things like cost, availability, convenience, and perishability. Is it difficult or easy to donate nutritious foods to those in need? Does your work reveal that Saletan is right or has his claim been debunked?

2. In small groups, focus on the way individual paragraphs work with Saletan's argument in the essay. Read a paragraph at a time, and answer the following questions for each: What is the main point of this paragraph? What information or evidence does the author use to support his point in this paragraph? What is the function or purpose of this paragraph within the essay? Share your results with other groups to understand the organization of Saletan's essay as a whole. How does he use reversals and previously established claims to guide the reader to his argument?

Morgan Spurlock [b. 1970]

Do You Want Lies with That?

Born and raised in West Virginia, **Morgan Spurlock** is a journalist, documentary filmmaker, and television producer. As a graduate of New York University's acclaimed Tisch School of the Arts, Spurlock directed a full-length play entitled *The Phoenix*, which won awards at both the New York International Film Festival in 1999 and the Route 66 American Playwright Competition in 2000. During that year, he also created and hosted *I Bet You Will*, a Web cast that later aired as a television show on MTV. Spurlock is perhaps best known for his Academy Award–nominated *Super Size Me* (2004), in which he eats only McDonald's food for thirty days in order to determine the effect of fast food on his health. After the success of this documentary, Spurlock developed a television series called *30 Days*, in which he and others spend thirty days living the life of another. His latest project, released in October 2010, is a film adaptation of the book *Freakonomics* (2009) by Steven D. Levitt and Stephen J. Dubner. In 2007, Spurlock was named among the top ten best journalists in the world by *Time*.

In the following excerpt from *Don't Eat This Book: Fast Food and the Supersizing of America* (2005), Spurlock critiques the culture of mass consumption —of tobacco, automobiles, food—in contemporary American society. After considering examples of smoking and overeating through the lenses of personal and corporate responsibility, Spurlock ultimately blames corporations for the current trend of over-consumption.

Don't do it. Please. I know this book looks delicious, with its lightweight pages sliced thin as prosciutto and swiss, stacked in a way that would make Dagwood salivate. The scent of freshly baked words wafting up with every turn of the page. *Mmmm*, page. But don't do it. Not yet. Don't eat this book.

We turn just about everything you can imagine into food. You can eat coins, toys, cigars, cigarettes, rings, necklaces, lips, cars, babies, teeth, cameras, film, even underwear (which come in a variety of scents, sizes, styles and flavors). Why not a book?

In fact, we put so many things in our mouths, we constantly have to be reminded what *not* to eat. Look at that little package of silicon gel that's inside your new pair of sneakers. It says Do Not Eat for a reason. Somewhere, sometime, some genius bought a pair of sneakers and said, "Ooooh, look. They give you free mints with the shoes!"—soon followed, no doubt, by the lawsuit charging the manufacturer with negligence, something along the lines of, "Well, it didn't say *not* to eat those things."

And thus was born the "warning label." To avoid getting sued, corporate America now labels everything. Thank the genius who first decided to take a bath and blow-dry her hair at the same time. The Rhodes scholar who first reached down into a running garbage disposal. That one-armed guy down the street who felt around under his power mower while it was running.

Yes, thanks to them, blow-dryers now come with the label Do Not Submerge In   5
Water While Plugged In. Power mowers warn Keep Hands and Feet Away From Moving Blades. And curling irons bear tags that read For External Use Only.

And that's why I warn you—please!—do not eat this book. This book is FOR EXTERNAL USE ONLY. Except maybe as food for thought.

We live in a ridiculously litigious society. Opportunists know that a wet floor or a hot cup of coffee can put them on easy street. Like most of you, I find many of these lawsuits pointless and frivolous. No wonder the big corporations and the politicians they own have been pushing so hard for tort reform.

Fifty years ago it was a different story. Fifty years ago, adult human beings were presumed to have enough sense not to stick their fingers in whirring blades of steel. And if they did, that was their own fault.

Take smoking. For most of us, the idea that "smoking kills" is a given. My mom and dad know smoking is bad, but they don't stop. My grandfather smoked all the way up until his death at a grand old age, and my folks are just following in his footsteps—despite the terrifying warning on every pack.

They're not alone, of course. It's estimated that over a billion people in the world are   10 smokers. Worldwide, roughly 5 million people died from smoking in 2000. Smoking kills 440,000 Americans every year. All despite that surgeon general's warning on every single pack.

What is going on here? It's too easy to write off all billion-plus smokers as idiots with a death wish. My parents aren't idiots. I don't think they want to die. (When I was younger, there were times when I wanted to kill them, but that's different.) We all know that tobacco is extremely addictive. And that the tobacco companies used to add chemicals to make cigarettes even more addictive, until they got nailed for it. And that for several generations— again, until they got busted for it—the big tobacco companies aimed their marketing and advertising at kids and young people. Big Tobacco spent billions of dollars to get people hooked as early as they could, and to keep them as "brand-loyal" slaves for the rest of their unnaturally shortened lives. Cigarettes were cool, cigarettes were hip, cigarettes were sexy. Smoking made you look like a cowboy or a movie starlet.

And it worked. When my parents were young, everybody smoked. Doctors smoked. Athletes smoked. Pregnant women smoked. Their kids came out of the womb looking around the delivery room for an ashtray to ash their Lucky Strikes. Everyone smoked.

The change began in 1964, when the first surgeon general's warning about smoking and cancer scared the bejesus out of everybody. In 1971, cigarette ads were banned from TV, and much later they disappeared from billboards. Little by little, smoking was restricted in airplanes and airports, in public and private workplaces, in restaurants and bars. Tobacco sponsorship of sporting events decreased. Tighter controls were placed on selling cigarettes to minors. Everyone didn't quit overnight, but overall rates of smoking began to decrease— from 42 percent of adults in 1965 to 23 percent in 2000, and from 36 percent of high school kids in 1997 to 29 percent in 2001. The number of adults who have never smoked more than doubled from 1965 to 2000.

Big tobacco companies knew it was a war they couldn't win, but they didn't give up without a fight. They threw billions and billions of more dollars into making smoking look cool, hip, sexy—and safe. They targeted new markets, like women, who increased their rate of smoking 400 percent *after* the surgeon general's report. Yeah, you've come a long way, baby—all the way from the kitchen to the cancer ward. They expanded their markets in the Third World and undeveloped nations, getting hundreds of millions of people hooked; it's estimated that more than four out of five current smokers are in developing countries. As if people without a regular source of drinking water didn't have enough to worry about already. Big Tobacco denied the health risks of smoking, lied about what they were putting into cigarettes and lobbied like hell against every government agency or legislative act aimed at curbing their deadly impact.

Which brings me back to those "frivolous" lawsuits. Back when people were first suing 15
the tobacco companies for giving them cancer, a lot of folks scoffed. (And coughed. But they still scoffed.) Smokers knew the dangers of smoking, everyone said. If they decided to keep smoking for thirty, forty years and then got lung cancer, they couldn't blame the tobacco companies.

Then a funny thing happened. As the lawsuits progressed, it became more and more apparent that smokers did *not* know all the dangers of smoking. They couldn't know, because Big Tobacco was hiding the truth from them—lying to them about the health risks, and lying about the additives they were putting in cigarettes to make them more addictive. Marketing cigarettes to children, to get them hooked early and keep them puffing away almost literally from the cradle to the early grave, among other nefarious dealings.

In the mid-1990s, shouldering the crushing burden of soaring Medicare costs due to smoking-related illnesses, individual states began to imitate those "ambulance-chasers," bringing their own class-action lawsuits against Big Tobacco. In 1998, without ever explicitly admitting to any wrongdoing, the big tobacco companies agreed to a massive $246 billion settlement, to be paid to forty-six states and five territories over twenty-five years. (The other four states had already settled in individual cases.)

Two hundred and forty-six billion dollars is a whole lot of frivolous, man.

What these lawsuits drove home was the relationship between personal responsibility and corporate responsibility. Suddenly it was apparent that sticking a cigarette in your mouth was not *quite* the same thing as sticking those sneaker mints in your mouth. No one spent billions and billions of dollars in marketing, advertising, and promotions telling that guy those sneaker mints would make him cool, hip and sexy. Big Tobacco did exactly that to smokers.

Still, a lot of people were skeptical about those lawsuits. Are the big bad corporations 20
with all their big bad money and big bad mind-altering advertising really so powerful that we as individuals cannot think for ourselves anymore? Are we really so easily swayed by the simplest of pleasant images that we'll jump at the chance to share in some of that glorious, spring-scented, new and improved, because-you-deserve-it goodness, without a thought about what's best for us anymore?

You tell me. Every waking moment of our lives, we swim in an ocean of advertising, all of it telling us the same thing: Consume. Consume. And then consume some more.

In 2003, the auto industry spent $18.2 billion telling us we needed a new car, more cars, bigger cars. Over the last twenty-five years, the number of household vehicles in the United States has doubled. The rate of increase in the number of cars, vans, and SUVs for personal travel has been six times the rate of population increase. In fact, according to the Department of Transportation, there are now, for the first time in history, *more cars than drivers* in America. That's ridiculous!

Did we suddenly *need* so many more vehicles? Or were we sold the idea?

We drive everywhere now. Almost nine-tenths of our daily travel takes place in a personal vehicle. Walking, actually using the legs and feet God gave us, accounts for appallingly little of our day-to-day getting around. Even on trips of under one mile, according to the Department of Transportation, we walked only 24 percent of the time in 2001 (and rode a bike under 2 percent). Walking declined by almost half in the two decades between 1980 and 2000. In Los Angeles, you can get arrested for walking. The cops figure if you're not in a car you can't be up to any good. If you're not in a car, you're a vagrant. Same goes for the suburbs, where so many of us now live.

And what do you put inside that SUV, minivan or pickup truck you're driving every- 25
where, other than your kids? Well, lots of *stuff*, that's what. In 2002, the retail industry in this country spent $13.5 billion telling us what to buy, and we must have been listening, because in 2003 we spent nearly $8 *trillion* on all kinds of crap. That's right, trillion. How insane is that? We are the biggest consuming culture on the planet. We buy almost twice as much crap as our nearest competitor, Japan. We spend more on ourselves than the entire gross national product of any nation in the world.

And all that shopping—whew, has it made us hungry. Every year, the food industry spends around $33 billion convincing us that we're famished. So we all climb back into our giant vehicle filled with all our stuff from Wal-Mart, and we cruise to the nearest fast-food joint. If not McDonald's or Burger King or Taco Bell, then a "fast casual" restaurant like Outback Steakhouse or TGI Friday's or the Olive Garden, where they serve us portions larger than our smallest kid, with the calories to match.

What does all that consumption do for us? Does it make us happy? You tell me. If we were all so happy, would we be on so many drugs? Antidepressant use in the U.S. nearly *tripled* in the past decade. We've got drugs in America we can take for anything: if we're feeling too bad, too good, too skinny, too fat, too sleepy, too wide awake, too unmanly. We've got drugs to counteract the disastrous health effects of all our overconsumption—diet drugs, heart drugs, liver drugs, drugs to make our hair grow back and our willies stiff. In 2003, we Americans spent $227 billion on medications. That's a whole lot of drugs!

This is the power of advertising at work, of billions of hooks that've been cast into our heads in the last thirty years, billions of messages telling us what we want, what we need and what we should do to feel happy. We all buy into it to some degree, because none of us is as young as we'd like to be, or as thin, or as strong.

Yet none of the stuff we consume—no matter how much bigger our SUV is than our neighbor's, no matter how many Whoppers we wolf down, no matter how many DVDs we own or how much Zoloft we take—makes us feel full, or satisfied or happy.

So we consume some more. 30

And the line between personal responsibility and corporate responsibility gets finer and more blurred. Yes, you're still responsible for your own life, your own health, your own happiness. But your *desires*, the things you *want*, the things you think you *need*—that's all manipulated by corporate advertising and marketing that now whisper and shout and wink at you from every corner of your life—at home, at work, at school, at play.

Consume. Consume. Still not happy? Then you obviously haven't consumed enough.

Like this book, the epidemic of overconsumption that's plaguing the nation begins with the things we put in our mouths. Since the 1960s, everyone has known that smoking kills, but it's only been in the last few years that we've become hip to a new killer, one that now rivals smoking as the leading cause of preventable deaths in America and, if current trends continue, will soon be the leading cause: overeating.

Americans are eating themselves to death.

[2005]

Questions

1. Spurlock's article has a distinctive introduction. Why does he choose to begin this way? What does he expect such an introduction will do? Find a recent essay that you've already completed, and rewrite the introduction so that it mimics Spurlock's introduction.

2. In small groups, consider the way Spurlock uses outside sources. Spurlock's article includes many outside sources (though they're not cited), but his writing doesn't come across as a research text. Given his writing style, what sort of audience is he appealing to? How do you know? Provide textual evidence for your answer. Next, identify two more audiences that Spurlock could write to. What changes would he have to make—to style, content, and choice of supporting evidence—in order to appeal to these additional audiences?

3. In small groups, identify three specific outside statistics, facts, or claims referenced by Spurlock. Search online to find the likely source for each one. For example, what source might Spurlock have used to learn that Americans spent $227 billion on medications in 2003 (para. 27)?

Loretta Schwartz-Nobel

America's Wandering Families

A Pennsylvania writer and journalist, **Loretta Schwartz-Nobel** is best known for her advocacy of impoverished and disadvantaged American families. Her first article on hunger, for which she received national acclaim, appeared in 1974 in *Philadelphia* magazine. In 1981, she published a book on the issue called *Starving in the Shadow of Plenty*. Since, Schwartz-Nobel has authored numerous works of nonfiction, including *Engaged to Murder* (1987), *The Baby Swap Conspiracy* (1993), and *Poisoned Nation* (2007).

In her 2002 book *Growing Up Empty*, from which the following selection is excerpted, Schwartz-Nobel returns to the issue of hunger in America, seeking to explode the widespread, false conviction among many Americans that "nobody starves" in the United States. She takes her readers on a tour of one of our nation's many homeless shelters, relating her encounters with a handful of the thousands of Americans who depend on these places for their very survival.

Each night, when darkness falls, more than 100,000 American children have no home of their own to go back to. Some of them sleep in cars or abandoned buildings and eat whatever they can find. Some stay in over-crowded houses with friends or relatives. Others sleep in cheap run-down motels or overpriced residential hotels. The rest lay their heads down on the streets or in crowded, often dangerous shelters. Most move from place to place as they search for food and shelter. Every year their numbers increase.

These children and their parents signal the rise of a new, more desperate level of poverty and hunger in America. Twenty-five years ago, the homeless population was composed primarily of the mentally ill, the alcoholic, or the drug addicted. Now that underclass has increased from single people who were lost long before homelessness ruled their lives, to families who are lost because it does. "Today homeless families account for between 38 percent and 77 percent of the homeless population, depending on the area. Two-thirds of the people in these families are children."

In the year 2000, unemployment was lower than it had been in thirty years but hunger, poverty, and the number of children without homes was higher than it had been since the Depression of the 1930s.

Part of this was due to the increasing gap between the incomes of the working poor and the cost of living. More and more families who lived in wealthy cities like San Diego simply couldn't afford the rent and ended up on the street. Today, their children create an underclass of hungry street urchins who sometimes wander among the wealthy. Their need for emergency food assistance is often as urgent as their need for housing.

Like many cities, San Diego is a place where the well educated and highly skilled prosper while one in three children live in poverty.   5

St. Vincent de Paul Village, one of the largest and best-known shelters in the country, is only minutes from San Diego's upscale Gas Light District, where well-dressed tourists and residents eat expensive meals at lovely restaurants, but it is also a world away.

St. Vincent's rises like a giant hacienda out of the grim industrial section of town. The perimeter of the huge yellow brick building takes up an entire city block. The main two-door entrance is topped by a bell tower reminiscent of the old California missions. In the year 2000, St. Vincent de Paul Village had an annual budget of $9.5 million. It employed 180 people and had more than 500 volunteers. Each night, about 850 men, women and children slept at St. Vincent's and, each day, more than 2,000 hungry people were fed there. All this is relatively recent.

The Village began as a small breakfast feeding program for the homeless in 1982, when the late Bishop Maher of the Diocese of San Diego decided to respond to the growing needs of the homeless. A short time later, he asked Father Joe Carroll, a native of New York, to spearhead the new project. Father Joe had worked at jobs that ranged from bookstore manager to teacher before becoming an ordained Roman Catholic priest at the age of thirty-three. During his first eight years in the priesthood, he had developed a reputation for being a man who made things happen. Between 1982 and 1987, true to his reputation, Father Joe raised $11.5 million for St. Vincent's.

When he began fund-raising, he had three major objectives: the first was to create a facility that would last forever; the second was to make it a beautiful building that would enhance the self-esteem of the people it served, and the third was to provide comprehensive services. Father Joe designed what he called a campus or a "one stop shopping center" so that the homeless could get the food, shelter, health care, child care, education, counseling, public assistance, jobs, and permanent housing they needed. His unique concept became an internationally recognized model, but Father Joe still wasn't satisfied. He said he would not rest until all the homeless in downtown San Diego who wanted a bed had one. At that time there were over four thousand homeless people in San Diego. So, even feeding two thousand people a day and providing beds for eight hundred left him with a long way to go.

"The lunch line at St. Vincent's begins forming at nine A.M. each morning and stretches 10 around the block by ten. We feed five hundred to six hundred people an hour, every day, seven days a week," explained John Moore, the heavyset, cheerful retired military officer who serves as the director of volunteers. "Families always come first, and then the disabled, but the mass of people waiting for food includes the homeless and the working poor and the military families. Some come only occasionally but we can usually pick out a hundred or a hundred fifty regulars, people who come every day. We ask no questions because we don't want to make them feel uncomfortable about being here. We know that many of them are not homeless, at least not yet. So I always tell them, 'Save your money to pay your rent and your other bills and come here to eat with us. That way you won't become homeless.'

"We also provide medical help to anyone without insurance," Moore explained as we walked through the mission's kitchen, filled with gleaming pots, cooks learning their trade, and volunteers practicing their skills. It was noon now and the dining room was rapidly filling up. Hundreds of women and children were already sitting at long, narrow tables, so close together that they were almost elbow to elbow.

About two hundred more people with trays in their hands were walking along the rapidly moving line. A dozen or so of those had the dazed look in their eyes that comes with having been at the bottom too long. It was like nothing I had ever seen before but a lot like what I imagined a Red Cross relief effort might look like in a third world country during a famine or after a natural disaster. It seemed almost impossible to believe that this was actually San Diego. The hall was filled with a loud but indecipherable hum. There were so many people eating and talking at once that it was impossible to hear what anyone was saying.

A pretty, young blonde girl in a pink T-shirt and black shorts caught my eye. She was holding a baby and had been led to the front of the line. Both the mother and baby were stuffing food into their mouths as if they were starving.

"We'd rather be overcrowded like this than turn away someone who needs us in their moment of crisis," John said, speaking loudly and leaning close enough for me to hear. "Our determining factor is whether they are at risk. If there is a child involved like that one over there on the line, we always immediately assume that they are at risk."

As we watched the young woman and the baby, I couldn't help wondering where her 15 own mother and father were, what had gone wrong at home and how she and her little daughter had fallen through all the cracks in all the programs and wound up here.

"People are often starving when they first arrive at our door because they have waited too long to come to us," John said, as if he were reading my thoughts. "They have resisted us too hard. They are also often sick for the same reason. We have four volunteer doctors and nurses who see thirteen hundred to fifteen hundred patients every month. There is no charge to them. The only requirement is that they have no health insurance. We've had the American Medical Association visit us here to see how we do it. That's how amazed they are.

"Our biggest concern," John added as my eyes moved away from the baby and her mother out over the huge crowd, "is how we can help people get back on their feet. It starts with the simple gift of a meal. It's usually the hunger that brings them in, but the urgency of hunger provides us with the opportunity to address the deeper, longer-term series of needs. People usually want help, and after their second or third time eating here, they feel safe enough to start asking questions about our other services.

"Meeting their needs is a huge challenge. We know we can't do it all but we just keep trying. There were five or six thousand people on our streets last winter. They come because it's warm here. They often just don't realize how difficult it is to find work or affordable housing in San Diego. They also don't know how tough it can be to live without shelter even in a warm climate. We respect the fact that it's hard for them to come to us. A lot of people are very proud and they're afraid that if they show up here they will be considered incompetent. Some of them think that they might lose their kids. They are scared to death of that.

"One woman came here for lunch when her baby was only a few days old. She was living out on the street but she didn't tell us that, she just said she wanted food. We accepted that and sent her to the lunchroom. We deliberately don't have any caseworkers in the lunchroom because we don't want to frighten people like her away. We want them to feel comfortable coming here. We want them to know that they can eat with no questions asked and no downstream repercussions. Only when they ask do we tell them that we are a resource center in the fullest sense, a helping hand, not just a handout."

As John talked, the line of hungry people just kept coming and coming in what seemed 20 to be an almost endless procession.

"Do you ever run out of food?" I asked, glancing at the mother and baby again. They were finally about to sit down but a lot of the food on their tray had already disappeared. Some, I noticed, had been stuffed directly into the mother's pockets.

"Yes," John said. "We run out all the time. It's a constant turnover. The food comes in and it goes back out. We never know exactly how much we'll need or even how much we'll get. Even with our regular suppliers like Food Chain, it's hard to predict. Both the supply and the demand are always uncertain. The only thing we know is that we always need more. There is really never enough.

"But then sometimes, just when we're feeling most concerned, something amazing happens. Like last year, Bill Gates was planning a big party for two or three thousand people, and then the weather got bad. When the party was canceled, he donated the food to us. Bill Gates was personally out there along with Father Joe helping to unload the food. Can you imagine that? Bill Gates himself unloading all those crates of food for the hungry." John grinned broadly. "It renewed my faith.

"Father Joe doesn't run the Village like a priest," he explained, turning serious again. "He runs it like a businessman, like Gates himself might. He has to because, just to keep things going, he needs to raise $43,000 every day. We are on a $24-million-a-year non-profit budget. But at the same time, we're independent, at least in our thinking. We've turned down grants, big grants from the government, because Father Joe doesn't want them to control him. We could have grown bigger, quicker, but he wants to remain true to his vision and true to his dream. He's an organized man but he's also a man with a vision. To do what he's done, you need both. If you're not organized, you will simply be overwhelmed by the need that's out there. It would be like taking a bag of bread crumbs and throwing it up in the sky and all of a sudden there would be one hundred birds. You can't just say, 'Come and eat,' without a plan and without resources because you will be overwhelmed. They will want more than you have to give.

"Father Joe's a bubbly guy who gives parties and does a lot of entertaining to raise   25
money so we can keep on expanding. His entire job now is fund-raising. He signs one hundred fifty letters a day. He's turned over the daily operations to others. Some people think that's a shame, but after all, he's just one man, one man who doesn't know the word stop. Folks like me are here because we believe in Father Joe and we believe in his dream. His belief empowers us. Because of it, there is nothing we can't do. We can make the rules, we can bend the rules and we can break the rules. Our vision is to do what we can for everyone who is in need. It is a huge vision but it is also as individual as each person we serve."

I was still thinking about St. Vincent's the next day at lunchtime as I sat in my car in front of the Presbyterian Crisis Center. The modest, yellow clapboard house on Market Street was about as different from St. Vincent's in appearance as anything I could imagine. The clientele, however, were very similar. There were several mothers with small children, an elderly couple, and a father with two teenage daughters sitting on the porch eating oranges.

The place had the look of a cozy cottage that had been misplaced on a busy street in a poor neighborhood. The front porch was filled with white chairs and the low green fence was covered by creeping vines and bounded by a small city lot. The Crisis Center, which began in the late '80s, provides emergency food, clothing, transportation tokens and whatever other emergency assistance they can.

"We sit down with people," explained director Bill Radatz, the warm, articulate pastor who heads the Presbyterian Ministry, "and we say, 'Have you thought things through and figured out why you are in crisis?' We've got some folks who have been coming here every month for years and others who are in an acute state for the first time in their lives. We try not to enable them but, at the same time, we want to meet their needs. Sometimes, it's a delicate balance."

Then Bill stopped talking and leaned back in his chair. "On second thought, I'm not sure I really meant what I just said about it being a delicate balance. I think most of the people we see here really do want to be self-sufficient. We've moved more toward advocacy recently because so many people are just trapped in an economic situation where they can't earn enough to make it no matter what they do. Housing availability in San Diego is down to two percent and some people are spending between fifty and seventy percent of their income on a place to live. We know that they will never work their way out of poverty when that much of their income is spent on shelter.

"To barely get by, and I mean barely, a family of four needs to have someone who earns   30 eleven dollars an hour, forty hours a week plus benefits. So if it's five dollars and seventy-five cents an hour and there are no benefits, no matter how hard they are working, we know they are doomed. Our politicians don't have the political will to help these people by changing the system or even the minimum wage, at least not nearly enough. They'd rather pretend that the people had problems instead of admit that the system did."

Bill stood up, walked to his office door, and closed it for privacy. "The political will is to eliminate welfare, not to eliminate poverty," he said. "It's a very important distinction. They want to cover up the problem, not solve it. On the other hand, it is also true that a few of our clients are not highly motivated enough. I've had people come to me and say that they don't have time to work because getting food takes all day. After breakfast, they have to wait on the lunch line, then after lunch they have to get on the dinner line." He smiled. "I know it sounds like a joke and I personally don't accept it as a reason to give up on working, and yet I also know that there's more than a grain of truth to it."

"Yes," I said, as the memory of two thousand people stretched around several blocks came back. "The lunch line at St. Vincent's starts forming at nine A.M. and it's halfway around the block by ten. It takes three hours just to get lunch."

"You think that's difficult? Take a look at this free-meal announcement," Bill said as he handed me a sheet that listed other free-meal centers in the San Diego area.

I glanced down at the page:

- Breakfast—Lutheran Church, Third and Ash—9:00 A.M. *Fridays only*
- Lunch—Neil Good Day Center, 299 17th Street—1:30 P.M. *Wednesdays only*
- Dinner—Vacant lot, 13th and Broadway—4:30 P.M. *Thursdays only*

There were a half dozen more meal sites on the list that were scattered throughout the   35 city but many served one meal only, one day a week. I thought about how tough it would be to get to the right place at the right time on the right day for the right meal without any money or transportation, and how difficult the logistics might get if you were also working part- or full-time but didn't earn enough for food. To make it even more complicated there was a note at the bottom of the page that said you must attend church services to receive certain meals at certain sites. In some cases you also had to attend services at one specific address or on one specific day to get a ticket to eat your meal at another site on another day. When I pointed this out to Bill, he nodded and said, "Yes, I know, and some people have to figure out how to get over here to the crisis center first to get a free bus token to take them over there."

When I turned the sheet over, I saw that in order to get a free token, a client had to remember to bring valid identification or a birth certificate. In some cases, they also needed a social security card and appropriate clothing. Even then, the tokens were strictly limited to six per month.

As we talked, Bill led me into the small client waiting room. I immediately spotted the same mother and baby I had seen eating so quickly the day before on the lunch line at St. Vincent's. I smiled at the mother and thought I saw a flash of recognition in her eyes.

"I saw you yesterday at St. Vincent's," I ventured, stooping down to greet the baby, who was sitting in a small, portable plaid stroller with red plastic wheels.

"Yes. I remember you," she said shyly. Her smile was beautiful. Her eyes were pale blue and shining.

Everything about her, even her voice, her pink T-shirt, her short, blonde hair, and her 40 perfect teeth made her seem more like a mid-western high school cheerleader than a hungry, homeless mother.

"Do you live around here?" I asked while the baby squeezed my index finger. She laughed, nervously.

"I don't know where I live right now," she said, seeming to take my question literally. "It's like I really don't live anywhere. I mean I don't have a place. That's why I'm here."

"I'm sorry," I said, hoping I hadn't embarrassed her.

"That's OK," she answered, sweetly. "I just said that, I don't know why. I know what you meant. I grew up in Michigan then one of my brothers invited me to move to Arizona. While I was there, I met an ex-Marine. We're still best friends but we got divorced when he moved back to New York to finish college. Things have been pretty bad ever since."

I settled down in the chair next to her, told her about the book I was writing, and asked 45 if she'd like to be part of it.

"Wow, me in a book? Sure, that's cool. But why would anyone care about me?" She tilted her head and smiled her beautiful smile again. "My father never did. My stepfather never did. I thought my husband was different till he started hitting me and messing around with other girls, but I think that's because we were too young for a committed relationship."

"Were you abused?" I asked, thinking of Bertha and the statistics on poverty and homelessness.

First, she shrugged and said, "No, not really," then the story poured out. "He beat me up a couple of times but he was always sorry. Now he's gone back to his old girlfriend but I don't think it will work out for the two of them. My mother always said an X is an X for some reason and I believe that. My mom's still in Michigan with my stepfather. I really miss her a lot. I came out here with my mother-in-law. It's kind of a screwed-up situation. See, she's HIV positive because her husband was on drugs. She needed care and she couldn't get it in Arizona, so we came out here together with a hundred fifty dollars after bus fare. We got a room at the Y but then she got real sick and went into the hospital. I ran out of money. My real mom always said I was impulsive and I guess I didn't think this thing through very well.

"I get three hundred fifty dollars a month from my husband whenever he remembers. It goes directly into my checking account. I think it will come soon but it's not here yet. I only had twenty-nine cents left yesterday and we were really hungry. I mean like really hungry. We hadn't eaten in two days. That's when you saw me. Right after lunch, I applied for welfare. I hate the idea of getting welfare and if I didn't have a baby, I'd rather live on the beach. But the baby needs food and shelter and stuff."

As Tina spoke, I was struck again by the fluctuations in her tone, which wavered be- 50 tween childishness and maturity, depression and cheerfulness, hope and fear.

She picked her baby up. "You can't live on the beach," she cooed. "No. No. It's too hot and you're too little." She kissed the baby then put her back in the stroller.

"So, I told the caseworker that we were homeless and we needed help right away and she gave us this hotel voucher for one night. But what good is a one-night voucher when another night's coming in just a few hours?"

Then Jean, an attractive, well-dressed, middle-aged caseworker, came over to us. "Tina," she said softly, "I've pulled some strings and gotten you and April into St. Vincent's. Be there at the front desk at 4:30. No later." She stroked the baby's hair and continued without waiting for an answer. "They're strict, and if you're late you can lose your place. They'll keep you there for ninety days and then you can apply for transitional housing."

Tina's eyes widened. Her face turned crimson. "Wow. Ninety days, ninety whole days," she said. "That's ninety days I don't have to worry."

She started to laugh with childlike delight then suddenly she was crying. 55

"I knew something good was going to happen when I walked in here today," she said, hugging Jean. "I could just feel it. Thank you sooo much. How did you do it? How'd you ever get me in?"

"I pulled all the strings," Jean answered gently. "We're small and they're big but they owe us, and every once in a while when I really need a favor, I remind them of that."

Tina was still laughing and crying. "I just know we're gonna be safe there. We were at their food line yesterday. I was so hungry that I was about to faint. The place was jam-packed. It was the longest food line I've ever seen in my whole life and I thought, how am I ever gonna stand here on this line and wait my turn, but guess what? They saw me holding my baby and they came right over and led us to the front of the line, I mean the very front, and then they gave us all this food. They didn't just give us a little. They gave us a lot, a whole lot. I'm not used to eating very much anymore 'cause for a long time I've just been eating a little here and there and giving the rest to my baby, but at St. Vincent's there was so much that I filled up both of my pockets and we ate some for dinner last night and some for breakfast this morning."

She sniffed then laughed again. "Boy, I still can't believe it. No more going hungry for ninety whole days. I've been hungry a lot lately. Even when I got my child support, it was only three hundred fifty dollars, and my rent was two hundred ninety-five dollars including utilities, so that left just fifty-five dollars a month for food and everything else. We haven't had a phone for two years. But I sure learned how to shop. I bought a lot of rice and beans and Bisquick mix. I bought big bags of cereal for two dollars and powdered milk because it is cheaper and it lasts longer. I almost never bought meat." She shook her head incredulously again. "I still can't get over this. I feel like I've just been rescued. I thought about asking the people yesterday at St. Vincent's if we could stay there, but when I saw how many people they had on that line, I said to myself, 'No way. Never. There's no room for us here.'"

Another flood of tears poured down Tina's cheeks. "I'm not sure why I can't stop cry- 60 ing," she said, laughing again. "I'm just so happy. I think it's because this is the start of something good. I think my luck is finally going to change. I can just sort of like feel it."

She wiped her eyes with the bottom of her pink T-shirt then tucked the shirt into her shorts. "I want to go back to college so much." She sniffled. "And I want to major in business and then someday, I want to own a chain of hotels." Tina was talking quickly now and her flawless young face was a brighter pink than her shirt. She looked pretty and buoyant. She raised her shoulders, let them drop again and wrinkled her nose. "Well, maybe it won't be a chain exactly," she said, making the compromise with herself out loud. "But it has to be at least two hotels. If you're rich and you're mean, you will go to the expensive hotel. If you're nice, you can go to the free hotel even if you have money.

"You know," she added reflectively. "In a weird way, it's a funny thing that I'm homeless, me of all people, because ever since I was a little girl and I saw this huge farmhouse one day, my whole focus has been on housing. I couldn't have been more than four but I can still remember exactly how that farmhouse looked. It had three stories and it had to have at least ten bedrooms. I told my momma that I wanted to buy it and paint it blue, not just any blue but cobalt blue with a fluorescent pink door. Then I wanted my whole broken-up family to come and live there all together in that one farmhouse. See, my stepbrothers lived with their mother and I only got to see them once in a while. My stepdad had five kids from before and one little girl with my mom. That's my little sister. I'd kill for her. She was two and a half years younger than me and I always protected her. If she was bad, which was pretty often, my stepdad would whip out his big black belt with the brass buckle, but, I'd always run in front of her and say, 'I did it, Dad. I did it. It was me.' So I'd get hit, of course.

"My husband said I was abused. I never thought of it that way. I thought it was just another whopping. Anyhow, it was my idea, my dream that we'd all come together in this one big house and my stepfather would have to leave because there would be no whopping allowed. Then we'd be a real family and live happily ever after.

"My real father died when I was very little. I don't remember him. My stepfather works for General Motors. My mom's a school cook."

Some more tears leaked out of Tina's eyes and landed on her shorts. 65

"I'm sorry I'm so emotional today and I know I'm talking too fast and too much. I'm just so relieved. See, I would never ask my mom to send me any money because I know she would do it and then she'd get in trouble with my stepdad and he'd wop her. I've always taken the fall for her too, for her and for my little sister. I never want her to ask him for anything that will bring a whopping down on her. That's why I never want her to have to send money."

"Why'd you always take the fall, honey?" a very thin, sallow-skinned woman who introduced herself as Melissa asked. "Why do you think it's your place to get punished?"

I had noticed the woman watching and listening to us a few minutes before but I had been too captivated by Tina's breathless speech to think much about it. I looked at her more carefully now. She had a sad face. Her forehead was high and deeply creased. She was much thinner than she was meant to be and her teeth were brown and rotted.

Tina shrugged. "I don't know why I took the fall," she answered, looking confused and a little uncomfortable. "I guess it's just the way I am. But I better get going now so I won't be late for the shelter." She hugged me and invited me to stop by and see her once she was settled.

"My son Shad's a bright boy," Melissa said even before Tina was out the door, "but he 70 was failing in school because he was always hungry. Now, he gets As and Bs because I go to the store almost every day and steal food for him so he can concentrate. We've talked about it together, my son and me. I'm not proud of it but I'm not ashamed either. It's just something I have to do to take care of my boy. I tried all the other options first and they didn't work."

She leaned closer. There was an odor I recognized but couldn't name. I'd smelled it before in urban tenements and in rural shacks but I had never known if it was the smell of illness, of hunger, or of simply being unwashed. A wave of nausea swept over me and I felt myself moving back a little.

"I always tell my boy never to steal. If there is anyone getting caught and getting in trouble, I want it to be me."

I looked up and nodded to indicate that I understood the fierce protective instinct.

"I go in with my purse and my backpack, then I get a shopping cart," Melissa explained. "I put the things I'm going to buy into the big part and, in the little part where the baby's supposed to sit, I put the things that I'm going to steal. I keep my purse open and I put some small things in there. I also put some flat items like cheese and lunch meat under my sweatshirt, which has a tight band at the bottom. I wait till I get to an aisle where there are no cameras or people before I take the things from the top part of the cart and put them into my backpack."

Melissa looked at me again to check my reaction.   75

"There are two tricks to not getting caught," she said, solemnly. "The first is to make sure everyone there thinks you're a regular customer. The second is to always buy a couple of items."

She paused again. "Food is the only thing I have ever stolen. I still steal it because I have no choice. I have to do it or my son and I will both go without eating. There is nothing and nobody that's going to tear us apart. Over the past year, I've done it a lot. This month, we got thirty-seven dollars in food stamps. Thirty-seven dollars spread over four weeks. You know how far that goes? Usually, for me personally, I only take what I consider to be the necessities, but last week I stole some coffee for myself and a candy bar to go with it. I knew I shouldn't have done it because they were luxuries that I didn't have to have. I think I just needed to pamper myself and I gave in to it." Her face colored. "For Shad, it's a different story. He's a growing boy. He has to eat. Last week, I stole meat and a lot of other things he enjoys. When I got home, I dumped out the backpack and the purse I was carrying and I compared everything I bought with everything I had stolen. It was fifty-eight dollars that I stole and ten dollars that I bought. There's just no other way. Fruit is too expensive, even milk. Meat is way too high.

"Yesterday, I bought a couple of potatoes and some macaroni and cheese, the cheap things to go with dinner, but all the rest I stole."

Melissa straightened up and folded her arms defensively across her chest.

"What the hell else am I supposed to do with thirty-seven dollars in food stamps, a   80 growing teenage boy and a boss who doesn't pay me? Whenever I go to the store, I take a little something. Lately, I almost feel like it's our right because I work hard. I've worked hard ever since I was a young girl and it never got me anywhere."

She slumped down in her chair again.

"I prefer to be honest," she said. "I'm really trying to make it without stealing. Today I got three bags of food from the Salvation Army but we get so tired of eating that stuff. I know the poor aren't supposed to care what they eat, but they do just like everyone else, especially the kids. You don't get any fresh meat or even sandwich meat. I've tried everything else and I've resigned myself to the fact that the only way to eat right when you are poor is to take what you can't afford to buy.

"My welfare check was five hundred forty dollars a month. Then, Welfare to Work came along. They hooked me up with a job and my stamps were cut. My job was cleaning empty apartments so they could be rented. It was hard work with mops and brooms, vacuums and scrub buckets, bending over half the day with a bad back. I was supposed to be paid six dollars and twenty-five cents an hour once a month, but that's not how it went. I worked for one month, then on payday my boss told me that I had to work another month. I said, 'Wait a minute. I started May thirteenth and now it's June seventeenth. In my book that's more than a month.' He said, 'No, love. That's not how it works. One month is always withheld.' Meanwhile, welfare thought I'd been paid and they cut all my benefits.

"I brought my boss a paper saying he hadn't paid me and I asked him to sign it so I could keep getting my welfare. 'Not now, love,' he said. 'But they're cutting me off welfare,' I told him. He didn't care. He didn't give a damn. He wasn't signing anything. I couldn't pay my rent so I lost my apartment. I was still working full-time but now I was homeless and hungry. I was desperate and panicked. I was half out of my mind when I finally came to the crisis center with my son. They put us up in a cheap motel, and that's where we are now.

"A month later my boss finally gave me a hundred dollars just to get me off his back 85 because he knew it was illegal. He said, 'This is all I have now. Call me in a couple of days, love, and I'll have some more.' I called his cell phone, his pager, his home phone. He had caller ID, and when he saw it was me, he wouldn't answer.

"I had no choice but to steal food," she said, sighing deeply. "If I waited for him to pay me, hell would freeze over and my son would starve. Five or six days later, I called from a pay phone. He didn't recognize it and he answered, saying, 'Hello. How can I help you?' I said, 'This is Melissa.' He said, 'Who?' Then the phone clicked dead, so I went to the supermarket and took our dinner. I'm trying to get our benefits back but in the meantime..." Melissa shrugged, then said a little nervously, "There's only one thing worrying me. I've heard that stealing is a felony and that in California if you have three felony convictions you can get a life sentence. It's called the three-strikes law. Can you imagine that, a life sentence for feeding your kids? Thank God I've never been caught, because if you get caught stealing food even once, you're no longer eligible for food stamps or any kind of aid.

"It's ironic, isn't it? You steal food because your children are hungry and you don't have enough food stamps to feed them. You get caught and you lose the few food stamps you had, so naturally you need to steal again. Pretty soon, you've eaten it all up, you're hungry. After all, people have to eat. Then what happens? It's your third offense, so they can put you in jail for life where they have to feed you and house you until you die. They put your kid in foster care where they have to pay a stranger to house him and feed him. They break up your family. They take away your freedom. They spend a fortune punishing you, so why not just give you and your kid the food you need to stay alive in the first place?"

[2002]

Questions

1. Reading just the biographical excerpt on the author at the beginning of the essay, what do you assume Schwartz-Nobel's claim is? How do you anticipate that she will support this claim? What do you think she will use for data, and why might she choose such evidence?

2. Discuss how Schwartz-Nobel's use of St. Vincent's shelter as a specific example of hunger in America attempts to illustrate the problem's complexity. Give specific examples.

3. "America's Wandering Families" is taken from a book that Schwartz-Nobel published in 2002. In small groups, collect more recent research and data to confirm or refute the claim she is making.

Sherry Turkle [b. 1948]

How Computers Change the Way We Think

Sherry Turkle is the Abby Rockefeller Mauzé Professor of the Social Studies of Science and Technology at the Massachusetts Institute of Technology (MIT) as well as the director and founder of MIT's Initiative on Technology and Self. A licensed clinical psychologist, Turkle holds a joint doctorate in sociology and personality psychology from Harvard University. She is the author of several books, including *Life on the Screen: Identity in the Age of the Internet* (1997) and *Falling for Science: Objects in Mind* (2008).

In "How Computers Change the Way We Think," Turkle suggests that technology is changing how we understand and interact with the world—not necessarily for the better. As an example, Turkle notes how the ease of online friendships makes face-to-face interaction all the more difficult. She also argues that computers have become a mode for thinking and knowledge. Because of this, she believes there are few left who are not "computer people."

The tools we use to think change the ways in which we think. The invention of written language brought about a radical shift in how we process, organize, store, and transmit representations of the world. Although writing remains our primary information technology, today when we think about the impact of technology on our habits of mind, we think primarily of the computer.

My first encounters with how computers change the way we think came soon after I joined the faculty at the Massachusetts Institute of Technology in the late 1970s, at the end of the era of the slide rule and the beginning of the era of the personal computer. At a lunch for new faculty members, several senior professors in engineering complained that the transition from slide rules to calculators had affected their students' ability to deal with issues of scale. When students used slide rules, they had to insert decimal points themselves. The professors insisted that that required students to maintain a mental sense of scale, whereas those who relied on calculators made frequent errors in orders of magnitude. Additionally, the students with calculators had lost their ability to do "back of the envelope" calculations, and with that, an intuitive feel for the material.

That same semester, I taught a course in the history of psychology. There, I experienced the impact of computational objects on students' ideas about their emotional lives. My class had read Freud's essay on slips of the tongue, with its famous first example: the chairman of a parliamentary session opens a meeting by declaring it closed. The students discussed how Freud interpreted such errors as revealing a person's mixed emotions. A computer-science major disagreed with Freud's approach. The mind, she argued, is a computer. And in a computational dictionary—like we have in the human mind—"closed" and "open" are designated by the same symbol, separated by a sign for opposition. "Closed" equals "minus open." To substitute "closed" for "open" does not require the notion of ambivalence or conflict.

"When the chairman made that substitution," she declared, "a bit was dropped; a minus sign was lost. There was a power surge. No problem."

The young woman turned a Freudian slip into an information-processing error. An explanation in terms of meaning had become an explanation in terms of mechanism. 5

Such encounters turned me to the study of both the instrumental and the subjective sides of the nascent computer culture. As an ethnographer and psychologist, I began to study not only what the computer was doing *for* us, but what it was doing *to* us, including how it was changing the way we see ourselves, our sense of human identity.

In the 1980s, I surveyed the psychological effects of computational objects in everyday life— largely the unintended side effects of people's tendency to project thoughts and feelings onto their machines. In the twenty years since, computational objects have become more explicitly designed to have emotional and cognitive effects. And those "effects by design" will become even stronger in the decade to come. Machines are being designed to serve explicitly as companions, pets, and tutors. And they are introduced in school settings for the youngest children.

Today, starting in elementary school, students use e-mail, word processing, computer simulations, virtual communities, and PowerPoint software. In the process, they are absorbing more than the content of what appears on their screens. They are learning new ways to think about what it means to know and understand.

What follows is a short and certainly not comprehensive list of areas where I see information technology encouraging changes in thinking. There can be no simple way of cataloging whether any particular change is good or bad. That is contested terrain. At every step we have to ask, as educators and citizens, whether current technology is leading us in directions that serve our human purposes. Such questions are not technical; they are social, moral, and political. For me, addressing that subjective side of computation is one of the more significant challenges for the next decade of information technology in higher education. Technology does not determine change, but it encourages us to take certain directions. If we make those directions clear, we can more easily exert human choice.

THINKING ABOUT PRIVACY

Today's college students are habituated to a world of online blogging, instant messaging, and Web browsing that leaves electronic traces. Yet they have had little experience with the right to privacy. Unlike past generations of Americans, who grew up with the notion that the privacy of their mail was sacrosanct, our children are accustomed to electronic surveillance as part of their daily lives.

I have colleagues who feel that the increased incursions on privacy have put the topic more in the news, and that this is a positive change. But middle-school and high-school students tend to be willing to provide personal information online with no safeguards, and college students seem uninterested in violations of privacy and in increased governmental and commercial surveillance. Professors find that students do not understand that in a democracy, privacy is a right, not merely a privilege. In ten years, ideas about the relationship of privacy and government will require even more active pedagogy. (One might also hope that increased education about the kinds of silent surveillance that technology makes possible may inspire more active political engagement with the issue.)

AVATARS OR A SELF?

Chat rooms, role-playing games, and other technological venues offer us many different contexts for presenting ourselves online. Those possibilities are particularly important for adolescents because they offer what Erik Erikson described as a moratorium, a time out or safe space for the personal experimentation that is so crucial for adolescent development. Our dangerous world—with crime, terrorism, drugs, and AIDS—offers little in the way of safe spaces. Online worlds can provide valuable spaces for identity play.

But some people who gain fluency in expressing multiple aspects of self may find it harder to develop authentic selves. Some children who write narratives for their screen avatars may grow up with too little experience of how to share their real feelings with other people. For those who are lonely yet afraid of intimacy, information technology has made it possible to have the illusion of companionship without the demands of friendship.

FROM POWERFUL IDEAS TO POWERPOINT

In the 1970s and early 1980s, some educators wanted to make programming part of the regular curriculum for K–12 education. They argued that because information technology carries ideas, it might as well carry the most powerful ideas that computer science has to offer. It is ironic that in most elementary schools today, the ideas being carried by information technology are not ideas from computer science like procedural thinking, but more likely to be those embedded in productivity tools like PowerPoint presentation software.

PowerPoint does more than provide a way of transmitting content. It carries its own 15 way of thinking, its own aesthetic—which not surprisingly shows up in the aesthetic of college freshmen. In that aesthetic, presentation becomes its own powerful idea.

To be sure, the software cannot be blamed for lower intellectual standards. Misuse of the former is as much a symptom as a cause of the latter. Indeed, the culture in which our children are raised is increasingly a culture of presentation, a corporate culture in which appearance is often more important than reality. In contemporary political discourse, the bar has also been lowered. Use of rhetorical devices at the expense of cogent argument regularly goes without notice. But it is precisely because standards of intellectual rigor outside the educational sphere have fallen that educators must attend to how we use, and when we introduce, software that has been designed to simplify the organization and processing of information.

In *The Cognitive Style of PowerPoint* (Graphics Press, 2003), Edward R. Tufte suggests that PowerPoint equates bulleting with clear thinking. It does not teach students to begin a discussion or construct a narrative. It encourages presentation, not conversation. Of course, in the hands of a master teacher, a PowerPoint presentation with few words and powerful images can serve as the jumping-off point for a brilliant lecture. But in the hands of elementary-school students, often introduced to PowerPoint in the third grade, and often infatuated with its swooshing sounds, animated icons, and flashing text, a slide show is more likely to close down debate than open it up.

Developed to serve the needs of the corporate boardroom, the software is designed to convey absolute authority. Teachers used to tell students that clear exposition depended on clear outlining, but presentation software has fetishized the outline at the expense of the content.

Narrative, the exposition of content, takes time. PowerPoint, like so much in the computer culture, speeds up the pace.

WORD PROCESSING VERSUS THINKING

The catalog for the Vermont Country Store advertises a manual typewriter, which the adver-   20
tising copy says "moves at a pace that allows time to compose your thoughts." As many of us
know, it is possible to manipulate text on a computer screen and see how it looks faster than
we can think about what the words mean.

Word processing has its own complex psychology. From a pedagogical point of view,
it can make dedicated students into better writers because it allows them to revise text,
rearrange paragraphs, and experiment with the tone and shape of an essay. Few professional
writers would part with their computers; some claim that they simply cannot think without
their hands on the keyboard. Yet the ability to quickly fill the page, to see it before you can
think it, can make bad writers even worse.

A seventh grader once told me that the typewriter she found in her mother's attic is
"cool because you have to type each letter by itself. You have to know what you are doing in
advance or it comes out a mess." The idea of thinking ahead has become exotic.

TAKING THINGS AT INTERFACE VALUE

We expect software to be easy to use, and we assume that we don't have to know how a
computer works. In the early 1980s, most computer users who spoke of transparency meant
that, as with any other machine, you could "open the hood" and poke around. But only a
few years later, Macintosh users began to use the term when they talked about seeing their
documents and programs represented by attractive and easy-to-interpret icons. They were
referring to an ability to make things work without needing to go below the screen surface.
Paradoxically, it was the screen's opacity that permitted that kind of transparency. Today,
when people say that something is transparent, they mean that they can see how to make
it work, not that they know how it works. In other words, transparency means epistemic
opacity.

The people who built or bought the first generation of personal computers understood
them down to the bits and bytes. The next generation of operating systems were more
complex, but they still invited that old-time reductive understanding. Contemporary information technology encourages different habits of mind. Today's college students are already
used to taking things at (inter)face value; their successors in 2014 will be even less accustomed to probing below the surface.

SIMULATION AND ITS DISCONTENTS

Some thinkers argue that the new opacity is empowering, enabling anyone to use the most   25
sophisticated technological tools and to experiment with simulation in complex and creative
ways. But it is also true that our tools carry the message that they are beyond our understanding. It is possible that in daily life, epistemic opacity can lead to passivity.

I first became aware of that possibility in the early 1990s, when the first generation of
complex simulation games were introduced and immediately became popular for home as
well as school use. SimLife teaches the principles of evolution by getting children involved
in the development of complex ecosystems; in that sense it is an extraordinary learning tool.

During one session in which I played SimLife with Tim, a thirteen-year-old, the screen before us flashed a message: "Your orgot is being eaten up." "What's an orgot?" I asked. Tim didn't know. "I just ignore that," he said confidently. "You don't need to know that kind of stuff to play."

For me, that story serves as a cautionary tale. Computer simulations enable their users to think about complex phenomena as dynamic, evolving systems. But they also accustom us to manipulating systems whose core assumptions we may not understand and that may not be true.

We live in a culture of simulation. Our games, our economic and political systems, and the ways architects design buildings, chemists envisage molecules, and surgeons perform operations all use simulation technology. In ten years the degree to which simulations are embedded in every area of life will have increased exponentially. We need to develop a new form of media literacy: readership skills for the culture of simulation.

We come to written text with habits of readership based on centuries of civilization. At the very least, we have learned to begin with the journalist's traditional questions: who, what, when, where, why, and how. Who wrote these words, what is their message, why were they written, and how are they situated in time and place; politically and socially? A central project for higher education during the next ten years should be creating programs in information-technology literacy, with the goal of teaching students to interrogate simulations in much the same spirit, challenging their built-in assumptions.

Despite the ever-increasing complexity of software, most computer environments put 30 users in worlds based on constrained choices. In other words, immersion in programmed worlds puts us in reassuring environments where the rules are clear. For example, when you play a video game, you often go through a series of frightening situations that you escape by mastering the rules—you experience life as a reassuring dichotomy of scary and safe. Children grow up in a culture of video games, action films, fantasy epics, and computer programs that all rely on that familiar scenario of almost losing but then regaining total mastery: there is danger. It is mastered. A still-more-powerful monster appears. It is subdued. Scary. Safe.

Yet in the real world, we have never had a greater need to work our way out of binary assumptions. In the decade ahead, we need to rebuild the culture around information technology. In that new sociotechnical culture, assumptions about the nature of mastery would be less absolute. The new culture would make it easier, not more difficult, to consider life in shades of gray, to see moral dilemmas in terms other than a battle between Good and Evil. For never has our world been more complex, hybridized, and global. Never have we so needed to have many contradictory thoughts and feelings at the same time. Our tools must help us accomplish that, not fight against us.

Information technology is identity technology. Embedding it in a culture that supports democracy, freedom of expression, tolerance, diversity, and complexity of opinion is one of the next decade's greatest challenges. We cannot afford to fail.

When I first began studying the computer culture, a small breed of highly trained technologists thought of themselves as "computer people." That is no longer the case. If we take the computer as a carrier of a way of knowing, a way of seeing the world and our place in it, we are all computer people now.

[2004]

Questions

1. What evidence does Turkle use to support her claim that computers change the way we think? Considering your own experience with computers (including mobile devices), why do you find Turkle's argument convincing or unconvincing?

2. Divide into small groups. Each group should choose a different area where Turkle claims "technology encourages changes in thinking" (e.g., "Thinking about Privacy," "Avatars or a Self?"). Describe how she sees a particular change occurring, and then identify personal experiences that either confirm or challenge that change.

3. Both Turkle's essay and Eric Schmidt and Jared Cohen's "Our Future Selves" deal with the role of technology in our lives, while making very different claims, utilizing different evidence for support, and employing different rhetorical strategies. Write a short essay that compares and contrasts one particular rhetorical strategy used by each author.

danah boyd [b. 1977]

Inequality: Can Social Media Resolve Social Divisions?

In a school classroom in Los Angeles, Keke sat down, crossed her arms defensively, and looked at me with suspicion. After an hour of short, emotionless responses to my questions about her daily life and online activities, I hit a nerve when I asked the black sixteen-year-old to explain how race operated in her community. I saw her fill with rage as she described how gang culture shaped her life. "We can't have a party without somebody being a Blood or somebody being a Crip and then they get into it and then there's shooting. Then we can't go to my friend's house because it's on the wrong side of [the street]. You know what I'm saying? It's the Mexican side." Los Angeles gang culture forces her to think about where she goes, who she spends time with, and what she wears.

> We can't go places because of gangs…. We can't go to the mall, can't be a whole bunch of black people together…. I hate not being able to go places. I hate having to be careful what color shoes I'm wearing or what color is in my pants or what color's in my hair….
> I just hate that. It's just not right.

When each color represents a different gang, the choice to wear red or blue goes beyond taste and fashion.

Although Keke understood the dynamics of gang culture in her community and was respected by the gang to which members of her family belonged, she despised the gangs' power. She hated the violence. And she had good reason to be angry. Only a few weeks before we met, Keke's brother had been shot and killed after crossing into the turf of a Latino gang. Keke was still in mourning.

Though almost sixty years had passed since the US Supreme Court ruled that segregation of public high schools is unconstitutional, most American high schools that I encountered organized themselves around race and class through a variety of social, cultural, economic, and political forces. The borders of school districts often produce segregated schools as a byproduct of de facto neighborhood segregation. Students find themselves in particular classrooms—or on academic tracks—based on test scores, and these results often correlate with socioeconomic status.

Friend groups are often racially and economically homogenous, which translates into segregated lunchrooms and segregated online communities.

The most explicit manifestation of racial segregation was visible to me in schools like Keke's, where gangs play a central role in shaping social life. Her experiences with race and turf are common in her community. The resulting dynamics organize her neighborhood and infiltrate her school. When I first visited Keke's school, I was initially delighted by how diverse and integrated the school appeared to be. The majority of students were immigrants, and there was no dominant race or nationality. More than other schools I visited, classrooms looked like they were from a Benetton ad or a United Nations gathering, with students from numerous racial backgrounds sitting side by side. Yet during lunch or between classes, the school's diversity dissolved as peers clustered along racial and ethnic lines. As Keke explained,

This school is so segregated. It's crazy. We got Disneyland full of all the white people....
The hallways is full of the Indians, and the people of Middle Eastern descent....The
Latinos, they all lined up on this side. The blacks is by the cafeteria and the quad.
Then the outcasts, like the uncool Latinos or uncool Indians. The uncool whites, they
scattered.

Every teen I spoke with at Keke's school used similar labels to describe the different   5
shared spaces where teens cluster. "Disneyland" was the section in the courtyard where white
students gathered, while "Six Flags" described the part occupied by black students. When I
tried to understand where these terms came from, one of Keke's classmates—a fifteen-year-
old Latina named Lolo—explained, "It's just been here for, I think, generations. (Laughs)
I'm sure if you're a ninth grader, you might not know until somebody tells you. But I did
know 'cause my brother told me." Those same identifiers bled into nearby schools and were
used when public spaces outside of school were identified. No one knew who created these
labels, but they did know that these were the right terms to use. Each cohort had to learn
the racial organization of the school, just as they had to learn the racial logic of their neigh-
borhoods. They understood that flouting these implicit rules by crossing lines could have
serious social and physical consequences.

Although Keke's experience of losing a family member to gang violence is uncommon,
death is not that exceptional in a community where gun violence is pervasive. Gang members may know one another at school, but the tense civility they maintain in the hallways
does not carry over to the streets. Teens of different races may converse politely in the classroom, but that doesn't mean they are friends on social media. Although many teens connect
to everyone they know on sites like Facebook, this doesn't mean that they cross unspoken
cultural boundaries. Communities where race is fraught maintain the same systems of segregation online and off.

What struck me as I talked with teens about how race and class operated in their communities was their acceptance of norms they understood to be deeply problematic. In a
nearby Los Angeles school, Traviesa, a Hispanic fifteen-year-old, explained, "If it comes
down to it, we have to supposedly stick with our own races....That's just the unwritten code
of high school nowadays." Traviesa didn't want to behave this way, but the idea of fighting
expectations was simply too exhausting and costly to consider. In losing her brother, Keke
knew those costs all too well, and they made her deeply angry. "We all humans," she said.
"Skin shouldn't separate nobody. But that's what happens." Although part of Keke wanted to
fight back against the racial dynamics that had killed her brother, she felt powerless.

As I watched teens struggle to make sense of the bigotry and racism that surrounded
them in the mid- to late 2000s, the American media started discussing how the election of
Barack Obama as the president of the United States marked the beginning of a "postracial"
era. And because social media supposedly played a role in electing the first black US president, some in the press argued that technology would bring people together, eradicate social
divisions in the United States, and allow democracy to flourish around the world.[1] This
utopian discourse did not reflect the very real social divisions that I watched emerge and
persist in teens' lives.[2]

THE BIASES IN TECHNOLOGY

Society has often heralded technology as a tool to end social divisions. In 1858, when the Atlantic Telegraph Company installed the first transatlantic cable, many imagined that this new communication device would help address incivility. As authors Charles Briggs and Augustus Maverick said of the telegraph: "This binds together by a vital cord all the nations of the earth. It is impossible that old prejudices and hostilities should longer exist, while such an instrument has been created for an exchange of thought between all the nations of the earth."[3] New communication media often inspire the hope that they can and will be used to bridge cultural divides. This hope gets projected onto new technologies in ways that suggest that the technology itself does the work of addressing cultural divisions.

As I describe throughout this book, the mere existence of new technology neither creates nor magically solves cultural problems. In fact, their construction typically reinforces existing social divisions. This sometimes occurs when designers intentionally build tools in prejudicial ways. More often it happens inadvertently when creators fail to realize how their biases inform their design decisions or when the broader structural ecosystem in which a designer innovates has restrictions that produce bias as a byproduct.

In 1980, technology studies scholar Langdon Winner published a controversial essay entitled, "Do Artifacts Have Politics?" In it, he points to the case of urban planner Robert Moses as an example of how biases appear in design. In the mid-twentieth century, Moses was influential in designing roads, bridges, and public housing projects in New York City and neighboring counties. In planning parkways on Long Island, Moses designed bridges and overpasses that were too low for buses and trucks to pass under. Buses, for example, could not use the parkway to get to Jones Beach, a major summer destination. Winner argues that these design decisions excluded those who relied on public transportation—the poor, blacks, and other minorities and disadvantaged citizens—from getting to key venues on Long Island. He suggests that Moses incorporated his prejudices into the design of major urban infrastructures.

This parable is contested. Responding to Winner's essay, technology scholar Bernward Joerges argues in "Do Politics Have Artefacts?" that Moses's decisions had nothing to do with prejudice but rather resulted from existing regulatory restrictions limiting the height of bridges and the use of parkways by buses, trucks, and commercial vehicles. Joerges suggests that Winner used haphazard information to advance his argument. Alternatively, one could read the information that Joerges puts forward as reinforcing Winner's broader conceptual claim. Perhaps Robert Moses did not intentionally design the roadways to segregate Long Island racially and socioeconomically, but his decision to build low overpasses resulted in segregation nonetheless. In other words, the combination of regulation and design produced a biased outcome regardless of the urban planner's intention.

Companies often design, implement, and test new technologies in limited settings. Only when these products appear in the marketplace do people realize that aspects of the technology or its design result in biases that disproportionately affect certain users. For example, many image-capture technologies have historically had difficulty capturing darker-skinned people because they rely on light, which reflects better off of lighter objects. as a result, photography and film better capture white skin while transforming black skin in unexpected ways.[4] This same issue has reemerged in digital technologies like Microsoft's Kinect, an interactive gaming platform that relies on face recognition. Much to the frustration of many early adopters, the system often fails to recognize dark-skinned users.[5] In choosing to use image capture to do face recognition, the Kinect engineers built a system that is technically—and thus socially—biased in implementation. In other technologies, biases may emerge as a byproduct of the testing process. Apple's voice recognition software, Siri, has difficulty with some accents, including Scottish, Southern US, and Indian.[6] Siri was designed to recognize language iteratively. Because the creators tested the system primarily in-house, the system was better at recognizing those American English accents most commonly represented at Apple.

The internet was supposed to be different from previous technologies. Technology pundits and early adopters believed that the internet would be a great equalizer—where race and class wouldn't matter—because of the lack of visual cues available.[7] But it turns out that the techno-utopians were wrong. The same biases that configure unmediated aspects of everyday life also shape the mediated experiences people have on the internet. Introducing their book *Race in Cyberspace*, scholars Beth Kolko, Lisa Nakamura, and Gilbert Rodman explain that "race matters in cyberspace precisely because all of us who spend time online are already shaped by the ways in which race matters offline and we can't help but bring our own knowledge, experiences, and values with us when we log on."[8]

Cultural prejudice permeates social media. Explicit prejudice bubbles up through the 15 digital inscription of hateful epithets in comments sections and hatemongering websites, while the social networks people form online replicate existing social divisions. Some youth recognize the ways their experiences are constructed by and organized around cultural differences; many more unwittingly calcify existing structural categories.

How American teens use social media reflects existing problems in society and reinforces deep-seated beliefs. This may seem like a let-down to those who hoped that technology could serve as a cultural panacea. But the implications of this unfulfilled potential extend beyond disappointment. Because prominent figures in society—including journalists, educators, and politicians—consider social media to be a source of information and opportunity, our cultural naïveté regarding the ways social and cultural divisions are sewn into our mediated social fabric may have more damaging costs in the future. In order to address emerging inequities, we must consider the uneven aspects of the social platforms upon which we are building.

Social media—and the possibility of connecting people across the globe through communication and information platforms—may seem like a tool for tolerance because technology enables people to see and participate in worlds beyond their own. We often identify teens, in particular, as the great beneficiaries of this new cosmopolitanism.[9] However, when we look at how social media is adopted by teens, it becomes clear that the internet doesn't level inequality in any practical or widespread way. The patterns are all too familiar: prejudice, racism, and intolerance are pervasive. Many of the social divisions that exist in the offline world have been replicated, and in some cases amplified, online. Those old divisions shape how teens experience social media and the information that they encounter. This is because while technology does allow people to connect in new ways, it also reinforces existing connections. It does enable new types of access to information, but people's experiences of that access are uneven at best.

Optimists often point out that all who get online benefit by increased access to information and expanded connections, while pessimists often point to the potential for increased levels of inequality.[10] Both arguments have merit, but it's also important to understand how inequalities and prejudices shape youth's networked lives. Existing social divisions—including racial divisions in the United States—are not disappearing simply because people have access to technology. Tools that enable communication do not sweep away distrust, hatred, and prejudice. Racism, in particular, takes on new forms in a networked setting. Far from being a panacea, the internet simply sheds new light on the divisive social dynamics that plague contemporary society.

The internet may not have the power to reverse long-standing societal ills, but it does have the potential to make them visible in new and perhaps productive ways. When teens are online, they bring their experiences with them. They make visible their values and attitudes, hopes and prejudices. Through their experiences living in a mediated world in which social divisions remain salient, we can see and deal realistically with their more harmful assumptions and prejudices.

RACISM IN A NETWORKED AGE

In 1993, the *New Yorker* published a now infamous cartoon showing a big dog talking to a   20
smaller dog in front of a computer monitor.[11] The caption reads, "On the Internet, no one knows you're a dog." Over the years, countless writers commenting on social issues have used this cartoon to illustrate how privacy and identity operate positively and negatively online. One interpretation of this cartoon is that embodied and experienced social factors—race, gender, class, ethnicity—do not necessarily transfer into the mediated world. As discussed earlier in the chapter on identity, many people hoped that, by going online, they could free themselves of the cultural shackles of their embodied reality.

When teens go online, they bring their friends, identities, and network with them. They also bring their attitudes toward others, their values, and their desire to position themselves in relation to others. It is rare for anyone to be truly anonymous, let alone as disconnected from embodied reality as the *New Yorker* cartoon suggests.[12] Not only do other people know who you are online; increasingly, software engineers are designing and building algorithms to observe people's practices and interests in order to model who they are within a broader system. Programmers implement systems that reveal similarity or difference, common practices or esoteric ones. What becomes visible—either through people or through algorithms—can affect how people understand social media and the world around them. How people respond to that information varies.

During the 2009 Black Entertainment Television (BET) Awards, thousands of those watching from home turned to Twitter to discuss the various celebrities at the ceremony. The volume of their commentary caused icons of the black community to appear in Twitter's "Trending Topics," a list of popular terms representing topics users are discussing on the service at any given moment. Beyoncé, Ne-Yo, Jamie Foxx, and other black celebrities all trended, along with the BET Awards themselves. The visibility of these names on the Trending Topics prompted a response from people who were not watching the award ceremony. In seeing the black names, one white teenage girl posted, "So many black people!" while a tweet from a young-looking white woman stated: "Why are all these black people on trending topics? Neyo? Beyonce? Tyra? Jamie Foxx? Is it black history month again? LOL." A white boy posted, "Wow!! too many negros in the trending topics for me. I may be done with this whole twitter thing." Teens were not the only ones making prejudicial remarks. A white woman tweeted, "Did anyone see the new trending topics? I dont think this is a very good neighborhood. Lock the car doors kids." These comments—and many more—provoked outrage, prompting the creation of a blog called "omgblackpeople" and a series of articles on race in Twitter.[13]

Unfortunately, what happened on the night of the BET Awards is not an isolated incident. In 2012, two athletes were expelled from the London Olympics after making racist comments on Twitter.[14] Racism is also not just an issue only on Twitter, where black internet users are overrepresented compared with their online participation on other sites.[15] The now defunct site notaracistbut.com collected hundreds of comments from Facebook that began with "I'm not a racist, but…" and ended with a racist comment. For example, one Facebook status update from a teen girl that was posted to the site said, "Not to be a racist, but I'm starting to see that niggers don't possess a single ounce of intellect." While creators of sites like notaracistbut.com intend to publicly shame racists, racism remains pervasive online.

In countless online communities, from YouTube to Twitter to World of Warcraft, racism and hate speech run rampant.[16] Messages of hate get spread both by those who agree with the sentiment and also by those who critique it. After the critically acclaimed movie *The Hunger Games* came out, countless fans turned to Twitter to comment on the casting of Rue, a small girl described in the book as having "dark brown skin and eyes." Tweets like "Call me a racist but when I found out rue was black her death wasn't as sad" and "Why does rue have to be black not gonna lie kinda ruined the movie" sparked outrage among antiracists who forwarded the messages to call attention to them, thereby increasing the visibility of this hostility.[17] On one hand, calling attention to these messages shames those who contributed them. On the other, it incites a new type of hate, which continues to reinforce structural divides.

Annoyed with what she perceived to be a lack of manners among Asian and Asian American students at her school, Alexandra Wallace posted a racist tirade on YouTube mocking students of Asian descent at UCLA in March 2011. The video depicts Wallace, a white blond-haired girl, criticizing Asian students for not being considerate of others. The central message of the video focuses on her complaint that Asian students are rude because they talk on their cell phones in the library. To emphasize her point, she pretends to speak in a speech pattern that she believes sounds Asian, saying, "Ching chong ling long ting tong," in a mocking tone.

The video—"Asians in the library"—quickly attracted attention and spread widely, prompting an outpouring of angry comments, reaction videos, and parodies. For example, comedic singer-songwriter Jimmy Wong produced a video in which he sang a mock love song called "Ching Chong!" in response to Wallace's video. Hundreds of videos—with millions of views—were designed to publicly shame her and others with similar racist attitudes. A college lifestyle blog dug up bikini pictures of Wallace and posted them under the title "Alexandra Wallace: Racist UCLA Student's Bikini Photos Revealed."[18] Meanwhile, Wallace—and her family—began receiving death threats, prompting her to drop out of UCLA and seek police protection. As one of her professors explained to the UCLA newspaper, "What Wallace did was hurtful and inexcusable, but the response has been far more egregious. She made a big mistake and she knows it, but they responded with greater levels of intolerance."[19]

Social media magnifies many aspects of daily life, including racism and bigotry. Some people use social media to express insensitive and hateful views, but others use the same technologies to publicly shame, and in some cases threaten, people who they feel are violating social decorum.[20] By increasing the visibility of individuals and their actions, social media doesn't simply shine a spotlight on the problematic action; it enables people to identify and harass others in a very public way. This, in turn, reinforces social divisions that plague American society.

SEGREGATION IN EVERYDAY LIFE

In the United States, racism is pervasive, if not always visible. Class politics intertwine with race, adding another dimension to existing social divisions. Teens are acutely aware of the power of race and class in shaping their lives, even if they don't always have nuanced language to talk about it; furthermore, just because teens live in a culture in which racism is ever present doesn't mean that they understand how to deal with its complexities or recognize its more subtle effects. Some don't realize how a history of racism shapes what they observe. Heather, a white sixteen-year-old from Iowa, told me,

> I don't want to sound racist, but it is the black kids a lot of times that have the attitudes and are always talking back to the teachers, getting in fights around the school, starting fights around the school. I mean yeah, white kids of course get into their fights, but the black kids make theirs more public and so it's seen more often that oh, the black kids are such troublemakers.

In examining high school dynamics in the 1980s, linguist Penelope Eckert argued that schools are organized by social categories that appear on the surface to be about activities but in practice are actually about race and class.[21] I noticed this as I went through the rosters of various sports teams at a school in North Carolina. At first, when I asked students about why different sports seemed to attract students of one race exclusively, they told me that it was just what people were into. Later, one white boy sheepishly explained that he liked basketball but that, at his school, basketball was a black sport and thus not an activity that he felt comfortable doing. As a result of norms and existing networks, the sports teams in many schools I visited had become implicitly coded and culturally divided by race. Many teens are reticent to challenge the status quo.

Even in schools at which teens prided themselves on being open-minded, I found that they often ignorantly reproduced racial divisions. For example, in stereotypical fashion, teens from more privileged backgrounds would point to having friends of different races as "proof" of their openness.[22] When I asked about racial divisions in more privileged schools or in schools situated in progressive communities, I regularly heard the postracial society mantra, with teens initially telling me that race did not matter in friend groups at their school. And then we'd log in to their Facebook or Myspace page and I would find clues that their schools were quite segregated. For example, I'd find that friend networks within diverse schools would be divided by race. When I'd ask teens to explain this, they'd tell me that the divisions I was seeing were because of who was in what classes or who played what sport, not realizing that racial segregation played a role in those aspects of school life, too.

While on a work trip in Colorado, I met a group of privileged teens who were in town because their parents were at the meeting I was attending. Bored with the adult conversations, I turned to the teens in a casual manner. I started talking with Kath, a white seventeen-year-old who attended an east coast private school renowned for its elite student body and its phenomenal diversity program. Our casual conversation turned to race dynamics in schools; she was a passionate, progressive teen who took the issue of race seriously. Curious to see how this played out in her community, I asked her if we could visit her Facebook page together. I offered her my computer, and she gleefully logged into her account. Given the small size of her school, I wasn't surprised that she was friends with nearly everyone from her grade and many students from other grades. I asked her to show me her photos so that we could look at the comments on them. Although her school had recruited students from diverse racial and ethnic backgrounds, most of those who had left comments on her profile were white. I pointed this out to her and asked her to bring up profiles of other students in her grade from different racial and ethnic backgrounds. In each case, the commenters were predominantly of the same broad racial or ethnic background as the profile owner. Kath was stunned and a bit embarrassed. In her head, race didn't matter at her school. But on Facebook people were spending their time interacting with people from similar racial backgrounds.

When I analyzed friending patterns on social network sites with youth, I consistently found that race mattered. In large and diverse high schools where teens didn't befriend everyone in their school, their connections alone revealed racial preference. In smaller diverse schools, the racial dynamics were more visible by seeing who commented on each other's posts or who appeared tagged together in photographs. Only when I visited schools with low levels of diversity did race not seem to matter in terms of online connections. For example, in Nebraska, I met a young Muslim woman of Middle Eastern descent in a mostly white school. She had plenty of friends online and off, and not surprisingly, all were white. Of course, this did not mean that she was living in a world where ethnic differences didn't matter. Her classmates posted many comments about Middle Eastern Muslim terrorists on Facebook with caveats about how she was different.

Birds of a feather flock together, and personal social networks tend to be homogeneous, as people are more likely to befriend others like them.[23] Sociologists refer to the practice of connecting with like-minded individuals as *homophily*. Studies have accounted for homophily in sex and gender, age, religion, education level, occupation, and social class. But nowhere is homophily more strongly visible in the United States than in the divides along racial and ethnic lines. The reasons behind the practice of homophily and the resultant social divisions are complex, rooted in a history of inequality, bigotry, oppression, and structural constraints in American life.[24]

it's easy to lament self-segregation in contemporary youth culture, but teens' choice to connect to people like them isn't necessarily born out of their personal racist beliefs. In many cases, teens reinforce homophily in order to cope with the racist society in which they live. In *Why Are All the Black Kids Sitting Together in the Cafeteria?* psychologist Beverly Tatum argues that self-segregation is a logical response to the systematized costs of racism. For teens who are facing cultural oppression and inequality, connecting along lines of race and ethnicity can help teens feel a sense of belonging, enhance identity development, and help them navigate systematic racism. Homophily isn't simply the product of hatred or prejudice. It is also a mechanism of safety. Seong, a seventeen- year-old from Los Angeles, echoed this sentiment when she told me, "In a way we connect more 'cause we see each other and we're like, oh." Familiarity mattered to Seong because, as a Korean immigrant, she feels isolated and confused by American norms that seem very foreign to her. She doesn't want to reject her non-Korean peers, but at times, she just wants to be surrounded by people who understand where she comes from. Still, teens' willingness to accept—and thus *expect*—self-segregation has problematic roots and likely contributes to ongoing racial inequality.[25]

Race-based dynamics are a fundamental part of many teens' lives—urban and subur-   35 ban, rich and poor. When they go online, these fraught dynamics do not disappear. Instead, teens reproduce them. Although the technology makes it possible *in principle* to socialize with anyone online, in practice, teens connect to the people that they know and with whom they have the most in common.

MYSPACE VS. FACEBOOK

In a historic small town outside Boston, I was sitting in the library of a newly formed charter school in the spring of 2007. One of the school's administrators had arranged for me to meet different students to get a sense of the school dynamics. Given what I knew about the school, I expected to meet with a diverse group of teens, but I found myself in a series of conversations with predominantly white, highly poised, academically motivated teens who were reluctant to talk about the dynamics of inequality and race at their school.

After I met a few of her peers, Kat, a white fourteen-year-old from a comfortable background, came into the library, and we started talking about the social media practices of her classmates. She made a passing remark about her friends moving from MySpace to Facebook, and I asked to discuss the reasons. Kat grew noticeably uncomfortable. She began simply, noting that "MySpace is just old now and it's boring." But then she paused, looked down at the table, and continued. "It's not really racist, but I guess you could say that. I'm not really into racism, but I think that MySpace now is more like ghetto or whatever." Her honesty startled me so I pressed to learn more. I asked her if people at her school were still using MySpace and she hesitantly said yes before stumbling over her next sentence. "The people who use MySpace—again, not in a racist way—but are usually more like ghetto and hip-hop rap lovers group." Probing a little deeper, Kat continued to stare at and fiddle with her hands as she told me that everyone who was still using MySpace was black, whereas all of her white peers had switched to Facebook.[26]

During the 2006–2007 school year, when MySpace was at its peak in popularity with American high school students, Facebook started to gain traction. Some teens who had never joined MySpace created accounts on Facebook. Others switched from MySpace to Facebook. Still others eschewed Facebook and adamantly stated that they preferred MySpace. The presence of two competing services would not be particularly interesting if it weren't for the makeup of the participants on each site. During that school year, as teens chose between MySpace and Facebook, race and class were salient factors in describing which teens used which service. The driving force was obvious: teens focused their attention on the site where their friends were socializing.[27] In doing so, their choices reified the race and class divisions that existed within their schools. As Anastasia, a white seventeen-year-old from New York, explained in a comment she left on my blog:

> My school is divided into the "honors kids," (I think that is self-explanatory), the "good not-so-honors kids," "wangstas," (they pretend to be tough and black but when you live in a suburb in Westchester you can't claim much hood), the "latinos/hispanics," (they tend to band together even though they could fit into any other groups) and the "emo kids" (whose lives are alllllways filled with woe). We were all in MySpace with our own little social networks but when Facebook opened its doors to high schoolers, guess who moved and guess who stayed behind…. The first two groups were the first to go and then the "wangstas" split with half of them on Facebook and the rest on MySpace…. I shifted with the rest of my school to Facebook and it became the place where the "honors kids" got together and discussed how they were procrastinating over their next AP English essay.

When I followed up with Anastasia, I learned that she felt as though it was taboo to talk about these dynamics. She stood by her comment but also told me that her sister said that she sounded racist. Although the underlying segregation of friendship networks defined who chose what site, most teens didn't use the language of race and class to describe their social network site preference. Some may have recognized that this was what was happening, but most described the division to me in terms of personal preference.

My interviews with teens included numerous descriptive taste-based judgments about each site and those who preferred them. Those who relished MySpace gushed about their ability to "pimp out" their profiles with "glitter," whereas Facebook users viewed the resultant profiles as "gaudy," "tacky," and "cluttered." Facebook fans relished the site's aesthetic minimalism, while MySpace devotees described Facebook profiles as "boring," "lame," "sterile," and "elitist." Catalina, a white fifteen-year-old from Austin, told me that Facebook is better because "Facebook just seems more clean to me." What Catalina saw as cleanliness, Indian-Pakistani seventeen-year-old Anindita from Los Angeles labeled "simple." She recognized the value of simplicity, but she preferred the "bling" of MySpace because it allowed her to express herself.

In differentiating Facebook and MySpace through taste, teens inadvertently embraced and reinforced a host of cultural factors that are rooted in the history of race and class. Taste is not simply a matter of personal preference; it is the product of cultural dynamics and social structure. In *Distinction*, philosopher Pierre Bourdieu describes how one's education and class position shape perceptions of taste and how distinctions around aesthetics and tastes are used to reinforce class in everyday life. The linguistic markers that teens use to describe Facebook and MySpace—and the values embedded in those markers—implicitly mark class and race whether teens realize it or not.

Just as most teens believe themselves to be friends with diverse groups of people, most   40 teens give little thought to the ways in which race and class connect to taste. They judge others' tastes with little regard to how these tastes are socially constructed. Consider how Craig, a white seventeen-year-old from California, differentiated MySpace and Facebook users through a combination of social and cultural distinctions:

> The higher castes of high school moved to Facebook. It was more cultured, and less cheesy. The lower class usually were content to stick to MySpace. Any high school student who has a Facebook will tell you that MySpace users are more likely to be barely educated and obnoxious. Like Peet's is more cultured than Starbucks, and Jazz is more cultured than bubblegum pop, and like Macs are more cultured than PC's, Facebook is of a cooler caliber than MySpace.

In this 2008 blog post entitled "Myface; Spacebook," Craig distinguished between what he saw as highbrow and lowbrow cultural tastes, using consumption patterns to differentiate classes of people and describe them in terms of a hierarchy. By employing the term "caste," Craig used a multicultural metaphor with ethnic and racial connotations that runs counter to the American ideal of social mobility. In doing so, he located his peers in immutable categories defined by taste.

Not all teens are as articulate as Craig with regard to the issue of taste and class, but most recognized the cultural distinction between MySpace and Facebook and marked users according to stereotypes that they had about these sites. When Facebook became more broadly popular, teens who were early adopters of Facebook started lamenting the presence of "the MySpace people." Again, Craig described this dynamic:

> Facebook has become the exact thing it tried to destroy. Like Anikin Sky walker, who loved justice so much, and he decided to play God as Darth Vader, Facebook has lost its identity and mission. It once was the cool, cultured thing to do, to have a Facebook, but now its the same. Girls have quizzes on their Facebooks: "Would you like to hook up with me? Yes, No" without a shred of dignity or subtlety. Again, I must scroll for 5 minutes to find the comment box on one's Facebook. The vexation of bulletins of MySpace are now replaced by those of applications. It alienated its "cultured" crowd by the addition of these trinkets.

From Craig's perspective, as Facebook became popular and main-stream, it, too, became lowbrow. The cultural distinction that existed during the 2006–2007 school year had faded, and now both sites felt "uncivilized" to Craig. He ended his post with a "desperate" plea to Google to build something "cultured."

In differentiating MySpace and Facebook as distinct cultural spaces and associating different types of people with each site, teens used technology to reinforce cultural distinctions during the time in which both sites were extraordinarily popular. These distinctions, far from being neutral, are wedded to everyday cultural markers. In constituting an "us" in opposition to "them," teens reinforce social divisions through their use of and attitudes toward social media. Even as teens espouse their tolerance toward others with respect to embodied characteristics, they judge their peers' values, choices, and tastes along axes that are rooted in those very characteristics.

The racial divide that these teens experienced as they watched their classmates choose between MySpace and Facebook during the 2006–2007 school year is one that happens time and again in technology adoption. In some cases, white teens use different technologies than teens of color. For example, Black and Latino urban youth embraced early smartphones like the sidekick, but the device had limited traction among Asian, white, and suburban youth. In other cases, diverse populations adopt a particular tool, but practices within the service are divided along race and class lines. Such was the case in 2013 on both Facebook and Twitter, where teens' linguistic and visual conventions—as well as their choice of apps—were correlated with their race.[28]

People influence the technology practices of those around them. Because of this, the diffusion of technology often has structural features that reflect existing social networks. As teens turn to social media to connect with their friends, they consistently reproduce networks that reflect both the segregated realities of everyday life and the social and economic inequalities that exist within their broader peer networks. Teens go online to hang out with their friends, and given the segregation of American society, their friends are quite likely to be of the same race, class, and cultural background.

NETWORKS MATTER

The fact that social media reproduces—and makes visible—existing social divisions within American society should not be surprising, but it does challenge a persistent fantasy that the internet will dissolve and dismantle inequalities and create new opportunities to bring people together across race and class lines. In 2010, Secretary of State Hillary Rodham Clinton espoused such idealism in a speech at the Newseum in which she argued: "The internet can serve as a great equalizer. By providing people with access to knowledge and potential markets, networks can create opportunity where none exists.... Information networks have become a great leveler, and we should use them to help lift people out of poverty."[29] This rhetoric assumes that, because the internet makes information more readily available to more people than ever before, access to the internet will address historical informational and social inequities. Yet just because people have access to the internet does not mean that they have equal access to information. Information literacy is not simply about the structural means of access but also about the experience to know where to look, the skills to interpret what's available, and the knowledge to put new pieces of information into context. In a world where information is easily available, strong personal networks and access to helpful people often matter more than access to the information itself.[30]

In a technological era defined by social media, where information flows through networks and where people curate information for their peers, who you know shapes what you know. When social divisions get reinforced online, information inequities also get reproduced. When increased access to information produces information overload, sifting through the mounds of available information to make meaning requires time and skills. Those whose networks are vetting information and providing context are more privileged in this information landscape than those whose friends and family have little experience doing such information work.[31]

For many information needs, people turn to people around them. Sociologists have shown that social networks affect people's job prospects, health, and happiness.[32] Opportunities for social and economic support depend heavily on personal connections. Teens turn to their networks to learn about college opportunities. They also develop a sense of what's normative by watching those who surround them. When it comes to information and opportunity, who youth know matters. Just because teens can get access to a technology that can connect them to anyone anywhere does not mean that they have equal access to knowledge and opportunity.[33]

In his famous trilogy *The Information Age*, sociologist Manuel Castells argued that the industrial era is ending and that an information age has begun. His first volume—*The Rise of the Network Society*—makes the case for the power of networks as the organizational infrastructure of an economy based on information. Technology plays a central role in the network society that Castells recognizes is unfolding, and he documents the technological divide that put certain cities in better or worse positions to leverage the economic changes taking place. Although critics have accused Castells of technological determinism, Castells's analysis is more fruitfully understood as a critical accounting of what economic and cultural

45

shifts are possible because of technology and why not everyone will benefit equally from these shifts.[34] In short, not everyone will benefit equally because networks—both social and technical—are neither evenly distributed nor meritocratic.

Social media does not radically rework teens' social networks. As a result, technology does not radically reconfigure inequality. The transformative potential of the internet to restructure social networks in order to reduce structural inequality rests heavily on people's ability to leverage it to make new connections. This is not how youth use social media. Not only are today's teens reproducing social dynamics online, but they are also heavily discouraged from building new connections that would diversify their worldviews. The "stranger danger" rhetoric discussed in the chapter on danger doesn't just affect teens' interactions with adults; many teens are actively discouraged from developing relationships with other teens online for fear that those teens may turn out to be adults intending to harm them.

Not all teens buy into this moral panic, but when teens do make connections online, they focus on engaging with people who share their interests, tastes, and cultural background. For these teens, turning to people who seem familiar allows them to feel safe, confident, and secure. They reinforce the homophilous social networks they inhabit instead of using technology to connect across lines of difference. Access to a wide range of people does not guarantee a reconfiguration of social connections.

The limited scope of teens' engagement with people from diverse backgrounds—and the pressure that they receive to not engage with strangers—is particularly costly for less privileged youth. Although everyone benefits from developing a heterogeneous social network, privileged youth are more likely to have connections to people with more privilege and greater access to various resources, opportunities, and types of information. When information opportunities are tethered to social networks, how social relations are constructed matters for every aspect of social equality. When social divisions are reinforced—and inequities across social networks reproduced—there are material, social, and cultural consequences. 50

The issue of inequality gets realized when information is structured to flow only to certain groups of people. During the 2006–2007 school year—the period when teens were segmenting themselves into Facebook and Myspace—many college admissions officers also started using social media for college recruitment. They created online profiles, produced spreadable videos, and invited high school students to talk with them and student representatives. Although millions of teenagers were active exclusively on MySpace, most of the colleges tailored their recruitment efforts to Facebook. When I asked admissions officers about their decision to focus on Facebook, they invariably highlighted a lack of resources and a need to prioritize. Universally, when I pointed out that black and Latino youth were more likely to be on MySpace and that their decision was effectively targeting primarily white and Asian students, they were stunned. They had never considered the cultural consequences of their choices.

At the time of this book's writing, it's quite common for companies to turn to LinkedIn, a professional social network site, to recruit college interns and new graduates. Recruiters typically prioritize candidates who already have contacts to the company as performed through social media. Some even explicitly ask applicants to list everyone they know who already works at the company. Those who don't know anyone at the company are disadvantaged as candidates. This tends to reinforce same-ness because people's social networks are rarely diverse. This also provides an additional obstacle for under-represented minorities, those who come from less advantaged communities, and people who generally lack social capital.

We don't live in a postracial society, and social media is not the cultural remedy that some people hoped it would become. Today's youth live in a world with real and pervasive social divisions. Those dynamics are reproduced online and have significant implications for how teens make sense of public life. People help define what's normative for their friends and contacts. And everyone's opportunities are dependent on whom they know. Having access to the information available through the internet is not enough to address existing structural inequities and social divisions. The internet will not inherently make the world more equal, nor will it automatically usher today's youth into a tolerant world. Instead, it lays bare existing and entrenched social divisions.

Notes

1.   The rhetoric used by the US media to suggest that social media could democratize the world took a more magnificent form in January 2011. As citizens throughout the Middle East began challenging authoritarian regimes, the media described the uprisings of the Arab Spring as being a product of social media. The news media began extolling social media as being the source of the various Middle East revolutions. This narrative has been widely critiqued, but it reveals prevalent notions of how technology can do cultural work to eradicate inequalities and injustices.

2.   In *Digitizing Race*, Lisa Nakamura has pointed out that many technological discourses, particularly those involving the digital divide, have envisioned or positioned users of color as technologically limited and/or uninvolved.

3.   Briggs and Maverick quoted in Carey, "Technology and Ideology," 160–161.

4.   For a discussion of whiteness and photography, see Dyer, "Lighting for Whiteness."

5.   Sinclair, "Kinect Has Problems Recognizing Dark-Skinned Users?"

6.   Zax, "Siri, Why Can't You Understand Me?"

7.   Kendall, "Meaning and Identity in 'Cyberspace'"; Kolko, Nakamura, and Rodman, "Race in Cyberspace."

8.   Kolko, Nakamura, and Rodman, "Race in Cyberspace," 4–5.

9.   Ethan Zuckerman talks extensively about the "imaginary cosmopolitanism" and the fallacy of social media as an inherently democratizing force in *Rewire*. Although his focus is global in scope, the same issues he highlights internationally also play out domestically. And the challenges that he highlights in describing how adults negotiate differences are also true of teenagers.

10.   Warschauer, *Technology and Social Inclusion*; Drori, *Global E-litism*.

11.   Steiner, "On the Internet, Nobody Knows You're a Dog."

12.   Christopherson, "The Positive and Negative Implications of Anonymity in Internet Social Interactions."

13.   The "omgblackpeople" blog was originally hosted on Tumblr, but as of 2013, it is no longer available. The content was reposted on: http://omgblack-people.wordpress.com/. For a blog post covering the racist tweets surrounding the BET awards, see http://www.blackweb20.com/2009/06/29/bet-awards-dominate-twitter-causes-racist-backlash/#.UVB-flv5ms8.

14.   Smith, "Twitter Update 2011."

15.   Saraceno, "Swiss Soccer Player Banned from Olympics for Racist Tweet."

16.   For an analysis of racism online, see Daniels, *Cyber Racism*; and Nakamura, "Don't Hate the Player, Hate the Game."

17.   For a write-up of racist commentary following the casting of *The Hunger Games*, see D. Stewart, "Racist Hunger Games Fans Are Very Disappointed."

18.   CoEd Staff, "Alexandra Wallace."

19.   Mandell, "Alexandra Wallace, UCLA Student."

20.   At times, self-appointed norm protectors seek to regulate online decorum by engaging in digital vigilantism. See Phillips and Miltner, "Internet's Vigilante Shame Army"; and Norton, "Anonymous 101."

21.   Eckert, *Jocks and Burnouts.*

22.   The tendency for people to downplay racism by talking about how they have friends of different races is so common that it is a frame through which people look at cross-race connections. In the 2012 book *Some of My Best Friends Are Black*, Tanner Colby describes the challenges of racial integration in the United States through four different case studies. In a more comedic treatment of the same issue, comedian Baratunde Thurston dedicates an entire chapter in *How to Be Black* to "how to be the black friend." He offers entertaining advice to black readers on how they can make white people feel comfortable by taking concrete steps to be a "good" black friend.

23.   For a discussion of homophily, including how American society is divided along racial and ethnic lines, see McPherson, Smith-Lovin, and Cook, "Birds of a Feather."

24.   See Lin, "Inequality in Social Capital."

25.   Bonilla-Silva, *Racism Without Racists.*

26.   For a more detailed analysis of the division that emerged in the 2006–2007 school year between Facebook and MySpace, see boyd, "White Flight in Networked Publics?" Craig Watkins also documents the racialized tension between these sites in his work on youth and social media. Watkins, *The Young and the Digital.*

27.   As Siân Lincoln points out in *Youth Culture and Private Space*, teenagers use whatever platform their friends use, even if they personally prefer other platforms.

28.   Black and African American individuals are overrepresented on Twitter compared to their participation online more generally. Scholars have begun analyzing a practice known colloquially as "Black Twitter," referring both to the significant presence of black users as well as how practices and norms in Twitter appear to differ across race lines. See Brock, "From the Blackhand Side"; and Florini, "Tweets, Tweeps, and Signifyin'."

29.   Clinton, "Internet Freedom."

30.   Scholars and government agencies have pointed out that technology uptake is often dependent on contextual relevance. When it comes to information and communication technologies, people are often more likely to appreciate their value when they see others use them in beneficial ways. If people's personal networks aren't using particular technologies, they often see no reason to use them. See Haddon, "Social Exclusion and information and Communication Technologies"; and Federal Communications Commission, *National Broadband Plan.*

31.   Hargittai, "Digital Reproduction of Inequality."

32.   For a sampling of relevant studies on social networks, see Fischer, *To Dwell Among Friends*; Granovetter, "Strength of Weak Ties"; Lin, *Social Capital*; and Wellman, *Networks in the Global Village.*

33.   in *Invisible Users*, Jenna Burrell makes the issues of structural inequality especially visible in her study of Ghanaian youth. Although these youth have access to information technologies, the social networks in which they operate—and the norms that exist in their home communities—complicate their ability to connect successfully and meaningfully with more powerful users.

34.   Webster, *Theories of the Information Society*; Webster, "Information and Urban Change"; Garnham, *Information Society Theory as Ideology.*

Bibliography

Bonilla-Silva, Eduardo. *Racism Without Racists: Color-Blind Racism and the Persistence of Racial Inequality in America.* Lanham, MD: Rowman and Littlefield, 2006.

boyd, danah, "White Flight in Networked Publics? How Race and Class Shaped American Teen Engagement with MySpace and Facebook." In *Race After the Internet*, ed. Lisa Nakamura and Peter Chow-White, 203–222. New York: Routledge, 2011.

Briggs, Charles F., and Augustus Maverick. *The Story of the Telegraph and a History of the Great Atlantic Cable*. New York: Rudd and Carleton, 1858.

Brock, André. "From the Blackhand Side: Twitter as a Cultural Conversation." *Journal of Broadcasting and Electronic Media* 56 (2012): 529–549.

Burrell, Jenna. *Invisible Users: Youth in the Internet Cafes of Urban Ghana*. Cambridge, MA: MIT Press, 2012.

Carey, James W. "Technology and Ideology: The Case of the Telegraph." *Communication as Culture: Essays on Media and Society*. New York: Routledge, 1992.

Christopherson, Kimberly M. "The Positive and Negative Implications of Anonymity in Internet Social Interactions: 'On the Internet, Nobody Knows You're a Dog.'" *Computers in Human Behavior* 23 (2007): 3038–3056.

Clinton, Hillary Rodham. "Internet Freedom." Speech presented at the Newseum, January 21, 2010, http://www.foreignpolicy.com/articles/2010/01/21/ internet_freedom.

CoEd staff. "Alexandra Wallace: Racist UCLA Student's Bikini Photos Revealed." *CoEd Magazine*, March 14, 2011, http://coedmagazine. com/2011/03/14/alexandra-wallace-racist-ucla-students-bikini-photos-revealed-26-pics/.

Colby, Tanner. *Some of My Best Friends Are Black*. New York: Viking, 2012.

Daniels, Jessie. *Cyber Racism: White Supremacy Online and the New Attack on Civil Rights*. Lanham, MD: Rowman and Littlefield, 2009.

Dyer, Richard. "Lighting for Whiteness." in *White*, 89–103. London: Routledge, 1997.

Eckert, Penelope. *Jocks and Burnouts: Social Categories and Identity in High School*. New York: Teachers College Press, 1989.

Federal Communications Commission. *The National Broadband Plan: Connecting America*. Washington, DC: Federal Communications Commission, 2010.

Fischer, Claude S. *To Dwell Among Friends: Personal Networks in Town and City*. Chicago: University of Chicago Press, 1982.

Florini, Sarah. "Tweets, Tweeps, and Signifyin': Communication and Cultural Performance on 'Black Twitter.'" *Television New Media*, March 7, 2013, http://tvn.sagepub.com/content/early/2013/03/07/1527476413480247.

Garnham, Nicholas. "Information Society Theory as Ideology." In *The Information Society Reader*, ed. Frank Webster et al., 165–182. New York: Routledge, 2004.

Granovetter, Mark. "The Strength of Weak Ties." *American Journal of Sociology* 78 (1973): 1360–1380.

Haddon, Leslie. "Social Exclusion and Information and Communication Technologies: Lessons from Studies of Single Parents and the Young Elderly." *New Media and Society* 2 (2000): 387–406.

Hargittai, Eszter. "The Digital Reproduction of Inequality." In *Social Stratification*, ed. David Grusky, 936–944. Boulder, CO: Westview, 2008.

Kendall, Lori. "Meaning and Identity in 'Cyberspace': The Performance of Gender, Class, and Race." *Symbolic Interaction* 21, no. 2 (1998): 129–153.

Kolko, Beth E., Lisa Nakamura, and Gilbert B. Rodman. "Race in Cyberspace: An Introduction." In *Race in Cyberspace*, ed. Beth E. Kolko, Lisa Nakamura, and Gilbert B. Rodman, 1–14. New York: Routledge, 2000.

Lin, Nan. "Inequality in Social Capital." *Contemporary Sociology* 29, no. 6 (2000): 785–795.

———. *Social Capital: A Theory of Social Structure and Action*. Cambridge: Cambridge University Press, 2002.

Lincoln, Siân. *Youth Culture and Private Space*. London: Palgrave Macmillan, 2012.

Mandell, Nina. "Alexandra Wallace, UCLA Student Who Created Offensive Viral Video, Withdrawing from School." *NYDailyNews.com*, March 19, 2011, http://nydailynews.com/news/national/alexandra-wallace-ucla-student-created-offensive-viral-video-withdrawing-school-article-1.119105.

McPherson, Miller, Lynn Smith-Lovin, and James M. Cook. "Birds of a Feather: Homophily in Social Networks." *Annual Review of Sociology* 27 (2001): 415–444.

Nakamura, Lisa. *Digitizing Race: Visual Cultures of the Internet.* Minneapolis: University of Minnesota Press, 2008.

———. "Don't Hate the Player, Hate the Game: The Racialization of Labor in World of Warcraft." *Critical Studies in Media Communication* 26, no. 2 (2009): 128–144.

Norton, Quinn. "Anonymous 101: Introduction to the Lulz." *Wired*, November 8, 2011, http://www.wired.com/threatlevel/2011/11/ anonymous-101/.

OMG Black People, http://omgblackpeople.wordpress.com/.

Phillips, Whitney, and Kate Miltner. "The Internet's Vigilante Shame Army." *Awl*, December 19, 2012, http://www.theawl.com/2012/12/the-internets-vigilante-shame-army.

Saraceno, Jon. "Swiss Soccer Player Banned from Olympics for Racist Tweet." *USA Today*, July 30, 2012, http://www.usatoday.com/sports/olympics/london/soccer/story/2012–07–30/swiss-athlete-banned-michel-morganella-olympics/56591966/1.

Sinclair, Brendan, "Kinect Has Problems Recognizing Dark-Skinned Users? *Gamespot*, November 3, 2010, http://www.gamespot.com/articles/kinect-has-problems-recognizing-dark-skinned-users/1100-6283514/.

Smith, Aaron. "Twitter Update 2011." Pew Internet and American Life Project, June 1, 2011, http://pewresearch.org/pubs/2007/twitter-users-cell-phone-2011-demographics.

Steiner, Peter. "On the Internet, Nobody Knows You're a Dog." Cartoon, *New Yorker*, July 5, 1993.

Stewart, Dodai. "Racist Hunger Games Fans Are Very Disappointed." *Jezebel*, March 26, 2012, http://jezebel.com/5896408/racist-hunger-games-fans-dont-care-how-much-money-the-movie-made.

Thurston, Baratunde. *How to Be Black.* New York: HarperCollins, 2012.

Warschauer, Marc. *Technology and Social Inclusion: Rethinking the Digital Divide.* Cambridge, MA: MIT Press, 2003.

Watkins, Craig S. *The Young and the Digital: What the Migration to Social Network Sites, Games, and Anytime, Anywhere Media Means for Our Future.* Boston: Beacon, 2009.

Webster, Frank. "Information and Urban Change: Manuel Castells." In *Manuel Castells*, vol. 2, ed. Frank Webster and Basil Dimitriou, 15–39. London: Sage, 2004.

———. *Theories of the Information Society.* 2nd ed. New York: Routledge, 2002.

Wellman, Barry. *Networks in the Global Village: Life in Contemporary Communities.* Boulder, CO: Westview, 1999.

Zax, David. "Siri, Why Can't You Understand Me?" *Fast Company*, December 7, 2011, http://www.fastcompany.com/1799374/siri-why-cant-you-understand-me.

Zuckerman, Ethan. *Rewire: Digital Cosmopolitans in the Age of Connection.* New York: W. W. Norton, 2013.

Questions

1. In small groups, diagram (e.g., using an outline, map, or clustering) the organizational development of boyd's essay. What are its key components? Which ones are connected and why? How does the understanding of a specific aspect of the piece lead the reader to another understanding and ultimately to key assumptions?

2. How does boyd use data to support her arguments throughout the text? Why is her use of data effective or ineffective?

3. Choose three claims that boyd makes in her essay, and analyze the rhetorical strategies that she employs in each. How effective are those strategies and why?

Eric Schmidt & Jared Cohen [b. 1955, b. 1981]

Our Future Selves

Soon everyone on Earth will be connected. With five billion more people set to join the virtual world, the boom in digital connectivity will bring gains in productivity, health, education, quality of life and myriad other avenues in the physical world—and this will be true for everyone, from the most elite users to those at the base of the economic pyramid. But being "connected" will mean very different things to different people, largely because the problems they have to solve differ so dramatically. What might seem like a small jump forward for some—like a smart phone priced under $20—may be as profound for one group as commuting to work in a driverless car is for another. People will find that being connected virtually makes us feel more equal—with access to the same basic platforms, information and online resources—while significant differences persist in the physical world. Connectivity will not solve income inequality, though it will alleviate some of its more intractable causes, like lack of available education and economic opportunity. So we must recognize and celebrate innovation in its own context. Everyone will benefit from connectivity, but not equally, and how those differences manifest themselves in the daily lives of people is our focus here.

INCREASED EFFICIENCY

Being able to do more in the virtual world will make the mechanics of our physical world more efficient. As digital connectivity reaches the far corners of the globe, new users will employ it to improve a wide range of inefficient markets, systems and behaviors, in both the most and least advanced societies. The resulting gains in efficiency and productivity will be profound, particularly in developing countries where technological isolation and bad policies have stymied growth and progress for years, and people will do more with less.

The accessibility of affordable smart devices, including phones and tablets, will be transformative in these countries. Consider the impact of basic mobile phones for a group of Congolese fisher women today. Whereas they used to bring their daily catch to the market and watch it slowly spoil as the day progressed, now they keep it on the line, in the river, and wait for calls from customers. Once an order is placed, a fish is brought out of the water and prepared for the buyer. There is no need for an expensive refrigerator, no need for someone to guard it at night, no danger of spoiled fish losing their value (or poisoning customers), and there is no unnecessary overfishing. The size of these women's market can even expand as other fishermen in surrounding areas coordinate with them over their own phones. As a substitute for a formal market economy (which would take years to develop), that's not a bad work-around for these women or the community at large.

Mobile phones are transforming how people in the developing world access and use information, and adoption rates are soaring. There are already more than 650 million mobile-phone users in Africa, and close to 3 billion across Asia. The majority of these people are using basic-feature phones—voice calls and text messages only—because the cost of data service in their countries is often prohibitively expensive, so that even those who can buy web-enabled phones or smart phones cannot use them affordably. This will change, and when it does, the smartphone revolution will profoundly benefit these populations.

Hundreds of millions of people today are living the lives of their grandparents, in coun-   5
tries where life expectancy is less than sixty years, or even fifty in some places, and there is no
guarantee that their political and macroeconomic circumstances will improve dramatically
anytime soon. What is new in their lives and their futures is connectivity. Critically, they
have the chance to bypass earlier technologies, like dial-up modems, and go directly to high-
speed wireless connections, which means the transformations that connectivity brings will
occur even more quickly than they did in the developed world. The introduction of mobile
phones is far more transformative than most people in modern countries realize. As people
come online, they will quite suddenly have access to almost all the world's information in
one place in their own language. This will even be true for an illiterate Maasai cattle herder
in the Serengeti, whose native tongue, Maa, is not written—he'll be able to verbally inquire
about the day's market prices and crowd-source the whereabouts of any nearby predators,
receiving a spoken answer from his device in reply. Mobile phones will allow formerly isolated people to connect with others very far away and very different from themselves. On
the economic front, they'll find ways to use the new tools at their disposal to enlarge their
businesses, make them more efficient and maximize their profits, as the fisherwomen did
much more locally with their basic phones.

What connectivity also brings, beyond mobile phones, is the ability to collect and use
data. Data itself is a tool, and in places where unreliable statistics about health, education,
economics and the population's needs have stalled growth and development, the chance to
gather data effectively is a game-changer. Everyone in society benefits from digital data, as
governments can better measure the success of their programs, and media and other nongovernmental organizations can use data to support their work and check facts. For example,
Amazon is able to take its data on merchants and, using algorithms, develop customized bank
loans to offer them—in some cases when traditional banks have completely shut their doors.
Larger markets and better metrics can help create healthier and more productive economies.

And the developing world will not be left out of the advances in gadgetry and other
high-tech machinery. Even if the prices for sophisticated smart phones and robots to perform household tasks like vacuuming remain high, illicit markets like China's expansive
"*shanzhai*" network for knock-off consumer electronics will produce and distribute imita-
tions that bridge the gap. and technologies that emerged in first-world contexts will find
renewed purpose in developing countries. in "additive manufacturing," or 3-D printing,
machines can actually "print" physical objects by taking three-dimensional data about an
object and tracing the contours of its shape, ultra-thin layer by ultra-thin layer, with liquid
plastic or other material, until the whole object materializes. such printers have produced a
huge range of objects, including customized mobile phones, machine parts and a full-sized
replica motorcycle. These machines will definitely have an impact on the developing world.
Communal 3-D printers in poor countries would allow people to make whatever tool or
item they require from open-source templates—digital information that is freely available in
its edited source—rather than waiting on laborious or iffy delivery routes for higher-priced
premade goods.

In wealthier countries 3-D printing will be the perfect partner for advanced manufacturing. New materials and products will all be built uniquely to a specification from the
Internet and on demand by a machine run by a sophisticated, trained operator. This will not
replace the acres of high-volume, lowest-cost manufacturing present in many industries, but
it will bring an unprecedented variety to the products used in the developed world.

As for life's small daily tasks, information systems will streamline many of them for people living in those countries, such as integrated clothing machines (washing, drying, folding, pressing and sorting) that keep an inventory of clean clothes and algorithmically suggest outfits based on the user's daily schedule. Haircuts will finally be automated and machine-precise. And cell phones, tablets and laptops will have wireless recharging capabilities, rendering the need to fiddle with charging cables an obsolete nuisance. Centralizing the many moving parts of one's life into an easy-to-use, almost intuitive system of information management and decision making will give our interactions with technology an effortless feel. As long as safeguards are in place to protect privacy and prevent data loss, these systems will free us of many small burdens—including errands, to-do lists and assorted "monitoring" tasks—that today add stress and chip away at our mental focus throughout the day. Our own neurological limits, which lead us to forgetfulness and oversights, will be supplemented by information systems designed to support our needs. Two such examples are memory prosthetics—calendar reminders and to-do lists—and social prosthetics, which instantly connect you with your friend who has relevant expertise in whatever task you are facing.

By relying on these integrated systems, which will encompass both the professional and the personal sides of our lives, we'll be able to use our time more effectively each day— whether that means having the time to have a "deep think," spending more time preparing for an important presentation or guaranteeing that a parent can attend his or her child's soccer game without distraction. Suggestion engines that offer alternative terms to help a user find what she is looking for will be a particularly useful aid in efficiency by consistently stimulating our thinking, processes, ultimately enhancing our creativity, not pre-empting it. Of course, the world will be filled with gadgets, holograms that allow a virtual version of you to be somewhere else, and endless amounts of content, so there will be plenty of ways to procrastinate, too—but the point is that when you choose to be productive, you can do so with greater capacity.

Other advances in the pipeline in areas like robotics, artificial intelligence and voice recognition will introduce efficiency into our lives by providing more seamless forms of engagement with the technology in our daily routines. Fully automated human-like robots with superb AI abilities will probably be out of most people's price range for some time, but the average American consumer will find it affordable to own a handful of different multipurpose robots fairly soon. The technology in iRobot's Roomba vacuum cleaner, the progenitor of this field of consumer "home" robots (first introduced in 2002), will only become more sophisticated and multipurpose in time. Future varieties of home robots should be able to handle other household duties, electrical work and even plumbing issues with relative ease.

We also can't discount the impact that superior voice-recognition software will have on our daily lives. Beyond searching for information online and issuing commands to your robots (both of which are possible today), better voice recognition will mean instant transcription of anything you produce: e-mails, notes, speeches, term papers. Most people speak much faster than they type, so this technology will surely save many of us time in our daily affairs—not to mention helping us avoid cases of carpal tunnel syndrome. A shift toward voice-initiated writing may well change our world of written material. Will we learn to speak in paragraphs, or will our writing begin to mirror speech patterns?

Everyday use of gesture-recognition technology is also closer than we think. Microsoft's Kinect, a hands-free sensor device for the Xbox 360 video-game console that captures and integrates a player's motion, set a world record in 2011 as the fastest selling consumer-electronics device in history, with more than eight million devices sold in the first sixty days on the market. Gestural interfaces will soon move beyond gaming and entertainment into more functional areas; the futuristic information screens displayed so prominently in the film *Minority Report*—in which Tom Cruise used gesture technology and holographic images to solve crimes on a computer—are just the beginning. In fact, we've already moved beyond that—the really interesting work today is building "social robots" that can recognize human gestures and respond to them in kind, such as a toy dog that sits when a child makes a command gesture.

And, looking further down the line, we might not need to move physically to manipulate those robots. There have been a series of exciting breakthroughs in thought-controlled motion technology—directing motion by thinking alone—in the past few years. In 2012, a team at a robotics laboratory in Japan demonstrated successfully that a person lying in an fMRI machine (which takes continuous scans of the brain to measure changes in blood flow) could control a robot hundreds of miles away just by imagining moving different parts of his body. The subject could see from the robot's perspective, thanks to a camera on its head, and when he thought about moving his arm or his legs, the robot would move correspondingly almost instantaneously. The possibilities of thought-controlled motion, not only for "surrogates" like separate robots but also for prosthetic limbs, are particularly exciting in what they portend for mobility-challenged or "locked in" individuals—spinal-cord-injury patients, amputees and others who cannot communicate or move in their current physical state.

MORE INNOVATION, MORE OPPORTUNITY

That the steady march of globalization will continue apace, even accelerate, as connectivity   15
spreads will come as no surprise. But what might surprise you is how small some of the advances in technology, when paired with increased connection and interdependence across countries, will make your world feel. Instant language translation, virtual-reality interactions and real-time collective editing—most easily understood today as wikis—will reshape how firms and organizations interact with partners, clients and employees in other places. While certain differences will perhaps never be fully overcome—like cultural nuance and time zones—the ability to engage with people in disparate locations, with near-total comprehension and on shared platforms, will make such interactions feel incredibly familiar.

Supply chains for corporations and other organizations will become increasingly disaggregated, not just on the production side but also with respect to people. More effective communication across borders and languages will build trust and create opportunities for hardworking and talented individuals around the world. It will not be unusual for a French technology company to operate its sales team from Southeast Asia, while locating its human-resources people in Canada and its engineers in Israel. Bureaucratic obstacles that prevent this level of decentralized operation today, like visa restrictions and regulations around money transfers, will become either irrelevant or be circumvented as digital solutions are discovered. Perhaps a human-rights organization with staff living in a country under heavy diplomatic sanctions will pay its employees in mobile money credits, or in an entirely digital currency.

As fewer jobs require a physical presence, talented individuals will have more options available to them. Skilled young adults in Uruguay will find themselves competing for certain types of jobs against their counterparts in Orange County. Of course, just as not all jobs can or will be automated in the future, not every job can be conducted from a distance—but more can than you might think. And for those living on a few dollars per day, there will be endless opportunities to increase their earnings. In fact, Amazon Mechanical Turk, which is a digital task-distribution platform, offers a present-day example of a company outsourcing small tasks that can be performed for a few cents by anyone with an Internet connection. As the quality of virtual interactions continues to improve, a range of vocations can expand the platform's client base; you might retain a lawyer from one continent and use a Realtor from another. Globalization's critics will decry this erosion of local monopolies, but it should be embraced, because this is how our societies will move forward and continue to innovate. Indeed, rising connectivity should *help* countries discover their competitive advantage—it could be that the world's best graphic designers come from Botswana, and the world just doesn't know it yet.

This leveling of the playing field for talent extends to the world of ideas, and innovation will increasingly come from the margins, outside traditional bastions of growth, as people begin to make new connections and apply unique perspectives to difficult problems, driving change. New levels of collaboration and cross-pollination across different sectors internationally will ensure that many of the best ideas and solutions will have a chance to rise to the top and be seen, considered, explored, funded, adopted and celebrated. Perhaps an aspiring Russian programmer currently working as a teacher in Novosibirsk will discover a new application of the technology behind the popular mobile game Angry Birds, realizing how its game framework could be used to improve the educational tools he is building to teach physics to local students. He finds similar gaming software that is open source and then he builds on it. As the open-source movement around the world continues to gain speed (for governments and companies it is low cost, and for contributors the benefits are in recognition and economic opportunities to improve and enlarge the support ecosystems), the Russian teacher-programmer will have an enormous cache of technical plans to learn from and use in his own work. In a fully connected world, he is increasingly likely to catch the eyes of the right people, to be offered jobs or fellowships, or to sell his creation to a major multinational company. At a minimum, he can get his foot in the door.

Innovation can come from the ground up, but not all local innovation will work on a larger scale, because some entrepreneurs and inventors will be building for different audiences, solving very specific problems. This is true today as well. Consider the twenty-four-year-old Kenyan inventor Anthony Mutua, who unveiled at a 2012 Nairobi science fair an ultrathin crystal chip he developed that can generate electricity when put under pressure. He placed the chip in the sole of a tennis shoe and demonstrated how, just by walking, a person can charge his mobile phone. (It's a reminder of how bad the problems of reliable and affordable electricity, and to a lesser extent short battery life, are for many people—and how some governments are not rushing to fix the electricity grids—that innovators like Mutua are designing microchips that turn people into portable charging stations.) Mutua's chip is now set to go into mass production, and if that successfully brings down the cost, he will have invented one of the cleverest designs that no one outside the developing world will ever use, simply because they'll never need to. Unfortunately, the level of a population's access to technology is often determined by external factors, and even if power and electricity problems are eventually solved (by the government or by citizens), there is no telling what new roadblocks will prevent certain groups from reaching the same level of connectivity and opportunity as others.

The most important pillar behind innovation and opportunity—education—will see tre- 20
mendous positive change in the coming decades as rising connectivity reshapes traditional
routines and offers new paths for learning. Most students will be highly technologically
literate, as schools continue to integrate technology into lesson plans and, in some cases,
replace traditional lessons with more interactive workshops. Education will be a more flexible experience, adapting itself to children's learning styles and pace instead of the other way
around. Kids will still go to physical schools, to socialize and be guided by teachers, but as
much, if not more, learning will take place employing carefully designed educational tools
in the spirit of today's Khan Academy, a nonprofit organization that produces thousands
of short videos (the majority in science and math) and shares them online for free. With
hundreds of millions of views on the Khan Academy's YouTube channel already, educators
in the United States are increasingly adopting its materials and integrating the approach of
its founder, Salman Khan—modular learning tailored to a student's needs. Some are even
"flipping" their classrooms, replacing lectures with videos watched at home (as homework)
and using school time for traditional homework, such as filling out a problem set for math
class. Critical thinking and problem-solving skills will become the focus in many school
systems as ubiquitous digital-knowledge tools, like the more accurate sections of Wikipedia,
reduce the importance of rote memorization.

For children in poor countries, future connectivity promises new access to educational
tools, though clearly not at the level described above. Physical classrooms will remain dilapi-
dated; teachers will continue to take paychecks and not show up for class; and books and
supplies will still be scarce. But what's new in this equation—connectivity—promises that
kids with access to mobile devices and the Internet will be able to experience school physically *and* virtually, even if the latter is informal and on their own time.

In places where basic needs are poorly met by the government, or in insecure areas, basic
digital technologies like mobile phones will offer safe and inexpensive options for families
looking to educate their children. A child who cannot attend school due to distance, lack of
security or school fees will have a lifeline to the world of learning if she has access to a mobile
phone. Even for those children without access to data plans or the mobile web, basic mobile
services, like text messages and IVR (interactive voice response, a form of voice-recognition
technology), can provide educational outlets. Loading tablets and mobile phones with high-
quality education applications and entertainment content before they are sold will ensure
that the "bandwidth poor," who lack reliable connectivity, will still benefit from access to
these devices. And for children whose classrooms are overcrowded or understaffed, or whose
national curriculum is dubiously narrow, connectivity through mobile devices will supplement their education and help them reach their full potential, regardless of their origins.
Today numerous pilot projects exist in developing countries that leverage mobile technology
to teach a wide range of topics and skills, including basic literacy for children and adults, second languages and advanced courses from universities. In 2012, the MIT Media lab tested
this approach in Ethiopia by distributing preloaded tablets to primary-age kids without
instructions or accompanying teachers. The results were extraordinary: within months the
kids were reciting the entire alphabet and writing complete sentences in English. Without
the connectivity that will be ubiquitous in the future, there are limits to what any of these
efforts can accomplish today.

Just imagine the implications of these burgeoning mobile or tablet-based learning platforms for a country like Afghanistan, which has one of the lowest rates of literacy in the

world. Digital platforms, whether presented in simple mobile form or in more sophisticated ways online, will eventually be able to withstand any environmental turbulence (political instability, economic collapse, perhaps even bad weather) and continue to serve the needs of users. So while the educational experience in the physical world will remain volatile for many, the virtual experience will increasingly become the more important and predictable option. And students stuck in school systems that teach narrow curriculums or only rote memorization will have access to a virtual world that encourages independent exploration and critical thinking.

A BETTER QUALITY OF LIFE

In tandem with the wide variety of functional improvements in your daily life, future connectivity promises a dazzling array of "quality of life" improvements: things that make you healthier, safer and more engaged. As with other gains, there remains a sliding scale of access here, but that doesn't make them any less meaningful.

The devices, screens and various machines in your future apartment will serve a purpose   25 beyond utility—they will offer entertainment, wanted distraction, intellectual and cultural enrichment, relaxation and opportunities to share things with others. The key advance ahead is personalization. You'll be able to customize your devices—indeed, much of the technology around you—to fit your needs, so that your environment reflects your preferences. People will have a better way to curate their life stories and will no longer have to rely on physical or online photo albums, although both will still exist. Future videography and photography will allow you to project any still or moving image you've captured as a three-dimensional holograph. Even more remarkable, you will be able to integrate any photos, videos and geographic settings that you choose to save into a single holographic device that you will place on the floor of your living room, instantaneously transforming the space into a memory room. A couple will be able to re-create their wedding ceremony for grandparents who were too ill to attend.

What you can watch on your various displays (high-quality LCD—liquid crystal display—screens, holographic projections or a handheld mobile device) will be determined by you, not by network-television schedules. At your fingertips will be an entire world's worth of digital content, constantly updated, ranked and categorized to help you find the music, movies, shows, books, magazines, blogs and art you like. Individual agency over entertainment and information channels will be greater than ever, as content producers shift from balkanized protectiveness to more unified and open models, since a different business model will be necessary in order to keep the audience. Contemporary services like Spotify, which offers a large catalog of live-streaming music for free, give us a sense of what the future will look like: an endless amount of content, available anytime, on almost any device, and at little or no cost to users, with copyrights and revenue streams preserved. Long-standing barriers to entry for content creators are being flattened as well; just as YouTube can be said to launch careers today* (or at least offer fleeting fame), in the future, even more platforms will offer artists, writers, directors, musicians and others in every country the chance to

---

*The Korean K-pop star Psy's fame reached global proportions almost overnight as the video he created for his song "Gangnam style" became the most-watched YouTube video ever within a span of three months.

reach a wider audience. It will still require skill to create quality content, but it will also be easier to assemble a team with the requisite skills to do this—say, an animator from South Korea, a voice actor from the Philippines, a storyboarder from Mexico and a musician from Kenya—and the finished product may have the potential to reach as wide an audience as any Hollywood blockbuster.

Entertainment will become a more immersive and personalized experience in the future. Integrated tie-ins will make today's product placements seem passive and even clumsy. If while watching a television show you spot a sweater you want or a dish you think you'd like to cook, information including recipes or purchasing details will be readily available, as will every other fact about the show, its story lines, actors and locations. If you're feeling bored and want to take an hour-long holiday, why not turn on your holograph box and visit Carnival in Rio? Stressed? Go spend some time on a beach in the Maldives. Worried your kids are becoming spoiled? Have them spend some time wandering around the Dharavi slum in Mumbai. Frustrated by the media's coverage of the Olympics in a different time zone? Purchase a holographic pass for a reasonable price and watch the women's gymnastics team compete right in front of you, live. Through virtual-reality interfaces and holographic-projection capabilities, you'll be able to "join" these activities as they happen and experience them as if you were truly there. Nothing beats the real thing, but this will be a very close second. And if nothing else, it will certainly be more affordable. Thanks to these new technologies, you can be more stimulated, or more relaxed, than ever before.

You'll be safer, too, at least on the road. While some of the very exciting new possibilities in transportation, like supersonic tube commutes and suborbital space travel, are still far in the distance, ubiquitous self-driving cars are imminent. Google's fleet of driverless cars, built by a team of Google and Stanford University engineers, has logged hundreds of thousands of miles without incident, and other models will soon join it on the road. Rather than replacing drivers altogether, the liminal step will be a "driver-assist" approach, where the self-driving option can be turned on, just as an airline captain turns on the autopilot. Government authorities are already well versed on self-driving cars and their potential—in 2012, Nevada became the first state to issue licenses to driverless cars, and later that same year California also affirmed their legality. Imagine the possibilities for long-haul truck-driving. Rather than testing the biological limits of human drivers with thirty-hour trips, the computer can take over primary responsibility and drive the truck for stretches as the driver rests.

The advances in health and medicine in our near future will be among the most significant of all the new game-changing developments. And thanks to rising connectivity, an even wider range of people will benefit than at any other time in history. Improvements in disease detection and treatment, the management of medical records and personal-health monitoring promise more equitable access to health care and health information for potentially billions more people when we factor in the spread of digital technology.

The diagnostic capability of your mobile phone will be old news. (Of course you will 30 be able to scan body parts the way you do bar codes.) But soon you will be benefiting from a slew of physical augmentations designed to monitor your well-being, such as microscopic robots in your circulatory system that keep track of your blood pressure, detect nascent heart disease and identify early-stage cancer. Inside your grandfather's new titanium hip there will be a chip that can act as a pedometer, monitor his insulin levels to check for the early stages of diabetes, and even trigger an automated phone call to an emergency contact if he takes a particularly hard fall and might need assistance. A tiny nasal implant will be available to you that will alert you to airborne toxins and early signs of a cold.

Eventually these accoutrements will be as uncontroversial as artificial pacemakers (the first of which was implanted in the 1950s). They are the logical extensions of today's personal-health-tracking applications, which allow people to use their smart phones to log their exercise, track their metabolic rates and chart their cholesterol levels. Indeed, ingestible health technology already exists—the Food and Drug Administration (FDA) approved the first electronic pill in 2012. Made by a California-based biomedical firm called Proteus Digital Health, the pill carries a tiny sensor one square millimeter in size, and once the pill is swallowed, stomach acid activates the circuit and sends a signal to a small patch worn outside the body (which then sends its data to a mobile phone). The patch can collect information about a patient's response to a drug (monitoring body temperature, heart rate and other indicators), relay data about regular usage to doctors and even track what a person eats. For sufferers of chronic illnesses and the elderly particularly, this technology will allow for significant improvements: automatic reminders to take various medications, the ability to measure directly how drugs are reacting in a person's body and the creation of an instant digital feedback loop with doctors that is personalized and data-driven. Not everyone will want to actively oversee their health to this degree, let alone the even more detailed version of the future, but they probably will want their doctor to have access to such data. "Intelligent pills" and nasal implants will be sufficiently affordable so as to be as accessible as vitamins and supplements. In short order, we will have access to personal health-care systems run off of our mobile devices that will automatically detect if something is wrong with us based on data collected from some of the above-mentioned augmentations, prompt us with appointment options for a nearby doctor and subsequently (with consent) send all of the relevant data about our symptoms and health indicators to the doctor being consulted.

Tissue engineers will be able to grow new organs to replace patients' old or diseased ones, using either synthetic materials or a person's own cells. At the outset, affordability will limit the use. Synthetic skin grafts, which exist today, will give way to grafts made from burn victims' own cells. Inside hospitals, robots will take on more responsibilities, as surgeons increasingly let sophisticated machines handle difficult parts of certain procedures, where delicate or tedious work is involved or a wider range of motion is required.[*]

Advances in genetic testing will usher in the era of personalized medicine. Through targeted tests and genome sequencing (decoding a person's full DNA), doctors and disease specialists will have more information about patients, and what might help them, than ever before. Despite steady scientific progress, severe negative reactions to prescribed drugs remain a leading cause of hospitalization and death. Pharmaceutical companies traditionally pursue a "one-size-fits-all" approach to drug development, but this is due to change as the burgeoning field of pharmacogenetics continues to develop. Better genetic testing will reduce the likelihood of negative reactions, improve patients' chances and provide doctors and medical researchers with more data to analyze and use. Eventually, and initially only for the wealthy, it will be possible to design pharmaceutical drugs tailored to an individual's genetic structure. But this too will change as the cost of DNA sequencing drops below $100 and almost everything biological is sequenced, making it possible for a much broader segment of the world's population to benefit from highly specific, personalized diagnoses.

---

[*] Robotic surgical suites are already in operation in hospitals in the United States and Europe.

For those living in developing countries, basic connectivity and access to the virtual world will offer a resource they can leverage to improve their own quality of life, and no-where more so than in the area of health. Even though their environment in the physical world is colored by inadequate care, lack of available vaccines and medicines, broken health systems and other exogenous factors that create health crises (like conflict-related internal migration), many important gains in health care will be driven by innovative uses of mobile phones, largely by individuals and other nongovernmental actors who seize the opportunity to drive change in an otherwise stagnant system. We already see this happening. Across the developing world today, the "mobile health" revolution—mobile phones used as tools to connect patients to doctors, to monitor drug distribution and to increase the reach of health clinics—is responsible for a number of improvements as a range of technology start-ups, nonprofits and entrepreneurs tackle difficult problems with technology-first solutions. Mobile phones are now used to track drug shipments and verify their authenticity, to share basic health information that isn't available locally, to send reminders about medication and appointments to patients, and to gather data about health indicators that government officials, NGOs and other actors can use to design their programs. The central problems in health sectors in poor places, like understaffed clinics, under-served patients in remote places, too few medications or inefficient distribution of them, and misinformation about vaccines and disease prevention, will all find at least partial solutions through connectivity.

At the very least, the adoption of mobile phones gives people a new level of agency over 35 their personal health, even though the devices themselves, of course, can't cure illness. People can use their phones to access information about preventative health care or recovery. They can use basic diagnostic tools embedded in their phones—maybe not X-rays, but cameras and audio recordings. A woman can take a picture of a lesion, or a recording of a cough, and send that information to a doctor or health professional, whom she can then interact with remotely, efficiently, affordably and privately. Digital solutions like these are not a perfect substitute for a properly functioning health sector, but in the meantime, they can offer new information and interactions that at a minimum will chip away at a larger and more entrenched multigenerational problem.

THE UPPER BAND

Connectivity benefits everyone. Those who have none will have some, and those who have a lot will have even more. To demonstrate that, imagine you are a young urban professional living in an American city a few decades from now. An average morning might look something like this:

There will be no alarm clock in your wake-up routine—at least, not in the traditional sense. Instead, you'll be roused by the aroma of freshly brewed coffee, by light entering your room as curtains open automatically, and by a gentle back massage administered by your high-tech bed. You're more likely to awake refreshed, because inside your mattress there's a special sensor that monitors your sleeping rhythms, determining precisely when to wake you so as not to interrupt a REM cycle.

Your apartment is an electronic orchestra, and you are the conductor. With simple flicks of the wrist and spoken instructions, you can control temperature, humidity, ambient music and lighting. You are able to skim through the day's news on translucent screens while a freshly cleaned suit is retrieved from your automated closet because your calendar indicates an important meeting today. You head to the kitchen for breakfast and the translucent news display follows, as a projected hologram hovering just in front of you, using motion detection, as you walk down the hallway. You grab a mug of coffee and a fresh pastry, cooked to perfection in your humidity-controlled oven—and skim new e-mails on a holographic "tablet" projected in front of you. Your central computer system suggests a list of chores your house-keeping robots should tackle today, all of which you approve. It further suggests that, since your coffee supply is projected to run out next Wednesday, you consider purchasing a certain larger-size container that it noticed currently on sale online. Alternatively, it offers a few recent reviews of other coffee blends your friends enjoy.

As you mull this over, you pull up your notes for a presentation you'll give later that day to important new clients abroad. All of your data—from your personal and professional life—is accessible through all of your various devices, as it's stored in the cloud, a remote digital-storage system with near limitless capacity. You own a few different and interchangeable digital devices; one is the size of a tablet, another the size of a pocket watch, while others might be flexible or wearable. All will be lightweight, incredibly fast and will use more powerful processors than anything available today.

You take another sip of coffee, feeling confident that you'll impress your clients. You already feel as if you know them, though you've never met in person, since your meetings have been conducted in a virtual-reality interface. You interact with holographic "avatars" that exactly capture your clients' movements and speech. You understand them and their needs well, not least because autonomous language-translation software reproduces the speech of both parties in perfect translations almost instantly. Real-time virtual interactions like these, as well as the ability to edit and collaborate on documents and other projects, makes the actual distance between you seem negligible. 40

As you move about your kitchen, you stub your toe, hard, on the edge of a cabinet—ouch! You grab your mobile device and open the diagnostics app. Inside your device there is a tiny microchip that uses low-radiation submillimeter waves to scan your body, like an X-ray. A quick scan reveals that your toe is just bruised, not broken. You decline the invitation your device suggests to get a second opinion at a nearby doctors office.

There's a bit of time left before you need to leave for work—which you'll get to by driverless car, of course. Your car knows what time you need to be in the office each morning based on your calendar and, after factoring in traffic data, it communicates with your wristwatch to give you a sixty-minute countdown to when you need to leave the house. Your commute will be as productive or relaxing as you desire.

Before you head out, your device reminds you to buy a gift for your nephew's upcoming birthday. You scan the system's proposed gift ideas, derived from anonymous, aggregated data on other nine-year-old boys with his profile and interests, but none of the suggestions inspire you. Then you remember a story his parents told you that had everyone forty and older laughing: Your nephew hadn't understood a reference to the old excuse "A dog ate my homework"; how could a dog eat his cloud storage drive? He had never gone to school before digital textbooks and online lesson plans, and he had used paper to do his homework so rarely—and used cloud storage so routinely—that the notion that he would somehow "forget" his homework *and* come up with an excuse like that struck him as absurd. You do a quick search for a robotic dog and buy one with a single click, after adding a few special touches he might like, such as a reinforced titanium skeleton so that he can ride on it. In the card input, you type: "Just in case." It will arrive at his house within a five-minute window of your selected delivery time.

You think about having another cup of coffee, but then a haptic device ("haptic" refers to technology that involves touch and feeling) that is embedded in the heel of your shoe gives you a gentle pinch—a signal that you'll be late for your morning meeting if you linger any longer. Perhaps you grab an apple on the way out, to eat in the backseat of your car as it chauffeurs you to your office.

If you are a part of the world's upper band of income earners (as most residents of 45 wealthy Western countries are), you will have access to many of these new technologies directly, as owners or as friends of those who own them. You probably recognize from this morning routine a few things you have already imagined or experienced. Of course, there will always be the super-wealthy people whose access to technology will be even greater— they'll probably eschew cars altogether and travel to work in motion-stabilized automated helicopters, for example.

We will continue to encounter challenges in the physical world, but the expansion of the virtual world and what is possible online—as well as the inclusion of five billion more minds— means we will have new ways of getting information and moving resources to solve those problems, even if the solutions are imperfect. While there will remain significant differences between us, more opportunities to interact and better policy can help blur the edges.

The advance of connectivity will have an impact far beyond the personal level; the ways that the physical and virtual worlds coexist, collide and complement each other will greatly affect how citizens and states behave in the coming decades. And not all the news is good. The coming chapters delve into how everyone—individuals, companies, nongovernmental organizations (NGOs), governments and others—will handle this new reality of existing in both worlds, and how they will leverage the best and worst of what each world has to offer in the new digital age. Each individual, state and organization will have to discover its own formula, and those that can best navigate this multi-dimensional world will find themselves ahead in the future.

Questions

1. How do the writers organize and develop their argument? In other words, what is their claim, and what supports do the writers provide and why?

2. Discuss the effectiveness of these supports in light of the audience, purpose, and (what you deduce is) the exigence of the piece.

3. While presenting many of the "advantages" of a more connected world, Schmidt and Cohen state the following: "The advance of connectivity will have an impact far beyond the personal level; the ways that the physical and virtual worlds coexist, collide and complement each other will greatly affect how citizens and states behave in the coming decades. And not all the news is good" (para. 47). Discuss the ways such connectivity might be bad news for individuals, companies, governments, and nongovernmental organizations.

Lee Ann Fisher Baron

The Influence of "Junk Science" and the Role of Science Education

Lee Ann Fisher Baron graduated with a B.A. from Wittenberg University in 1977 and an M.S. and Ph.D. from the University of Michigan in 1979 and 1984, respectively. She is currently the Savona Professor of Natural Sciences and Professor of Chemistry at Hillsdale College, where she has been teaching since 1989. A pioneer in science education, Baron has developed science programs intended to attract middle-school girls to futures in scientific fields, study guides for high school summer science camps, and science curricula for elementary schools. She has been honored with numerous awards for teaching, including an Emily Daugherty Award for Teaching Excellence, a Lubrizol Award, a Paul F. Bagley Fellowship, and a Dow Chemical Foundation Fellowship, along with membership in the Phi Lambda Upsilon and Sigma Zeta Honorary societies and the American Chemical Society. Baron earned acclaimed recognition in the 2000 edition of *Who's Who among America's Teachers*.

Baron's "The Influence of 'Junk Science' and the Role of Science Education," first published in *Imprimis*, the monthly journal of Hillsdale College, mourns the failure of the American educational system to maintain high standards in science instruction. Baron criticizes the food industry and homeopathists for knowingly misleading "unwary consumers" who buy into the claims of "junk science." More emphatically, however, she stresses the necessity for all citizens to possess a working knowledge of the scientific method in order to make wise choices regarding their physical health.

Science is exciting partly because single discoveries can change the course of history. Think of the effects on human health and longevity of the discovery of antibiotics, the multi-faceted impact on our lives of the discovery of polymers, or the far-reaching importance of the Human Genome Project. Unfortunately, however, most of the "revolutionary discoveries" made throughout history have turned out to be wrong.

Error is a regular part of science. That is why reports of new findings or discoveries, no matter where or how widely they are reported, should be regarded with healthy skepticism. The proper scientific approach to such claims involves a set of procedures called the scientific method. This method requires the design of tests or experiments that can be repeated with the same results by anyone. These tests must also contain controls to ensure that the results are statistically significant.

Let me illustrate the importance of controls by describing briefly an experiment in which my daughter participated as a subject some years ago at the University of Michigan Medical School. Its purpose was to determine whether the vaccine for tuberculosis could lengthen the interval during which newly-diagnosed type 1 diabetics do not experience severe high or low blood sugar. The subjects were divided into a group of those who received the vaccine and a control group of those who received a placebo. The subjects did not know who got the vaccine and, just as importantly, neither did the researchers—a type of control referred to as a "double-blind." By using two groups, the researchers were able to measure the "placebo effect"—a phenomenon in which patients improve because they falsely believe that they are receiving medicine. And by keeping themselves ignorant of the breakdown of the groups, the researchers were prevented from reading their hypotheses into the results.

"JUNK SCIENCE"

Most erroneous conclusions by scientists are discovered during the process of publishing their research. Other scientists review submitted articles, often repeating any relevant tests or experiments and always evaluating the conclusions that have been drawn from them. So-called "junk science" bypasses this system of peer review. Presented directly to the public by people variously described as "experts" or "activists," often with little or no supporting evidence, this "junk science" undermines the ability of elected representatives, jurists, and others—including everyday consumers—to make rational decisions.

An example of "junk science" I like to use with my students is the myth of "fat-free   5 foods" invented by the food industry with the help of federal regulators. By regulatory definition, these foods may contain monoglycerides and diglycerides, but not triglycerides. From the point of view of solid science this definition makes no practical sense, given that the body metabolizes mono-, di- and triglycerides in essentially the same way. Meanwhile unwary consumers take the "fat-free" label as a license to eat these foods to excess, and Americans are more obese now than ever before.

A more amusing example is "Vitamin O," a wonder supplement advertised to "maximize your nutrients, purify your blood stream, and eliminate toxins and poisons—in other words, [to supply] all the processes necessary to prevent disease and promote health." It was described on its label as "stabilized oxygen molecules in a solution of distilled water and sodium chloride." In other words, the 60,000 consumers purchasing "Vitamin O"—to the tune of $20 a month—were taking salt water! Although this product was legally exempted from certain FDA requirements by virtue of its status as a "natural" diet supplement, the FTC was able to file a complaint against it in 1999, based on false claims by its promoters that it was being used by NASA astronauts. Otherwise "Vitamin O" would still be one of the world's best-selling placebos.

The potential lasting power of "junk science" is demonstrated by the story of German physician Samuel Hahnemann, who took quinine back in 1776 to investigate its use against malaria. After taking the quinine he experienced chills and fever, which are the symptoms of malaria. For this he concluded, wrongly, that "likes cure likes," i.e., that diseases should be treated with medicines that produce similar symptoms to the diseases. In the course of testing this theory with other herbal remedies, Hahnemann discovered that many "natural" herbs are toxic and made his patients worse. To reduce the toxic effects, he diluted the remedies until they seemed to be working. On that basis he formulated a "law of infinitesimals" stating that higher dilutions of herbal cures increase their medicinal benefits. To be fair, Hahnemann conducted these experiments more than 70 years before scientists understood that a dilution weaker than one part in 6.02×10^{23} may not contain even a single molecule of the dissolved substance. Thus he did not realize that upon administering to his patients 30x preparations—dilutions of one part herb to 10^{30} parts water—the placebo effect was all that was really left to measure.

Incredibly, homeopathic medicine today still relies on Hahnemann's theories. Not only does it often come in 30x preparations, it comes in 200c dilutions—solutions of one part herb to 100 parts of water 200 times, resulting in one molecule of the herb per 10^{400} molecules of water! Modern homeopathists obviously can't deny that such preparations are beyond the dilution limit, but they insist that the dilutions still work because their water or alcohol/water mixtures somehow "remember" the herbs. Despite this preposterous claim, the market for these remedies is enormous.

Just as many homeopathic preparations are diluted to the point that they are nothing but water, many "natural" herbs on the market contain drugs and chemicals which interact with the human body like prescription drugs. For example, Echinacea stimulates the immune system, which could prove harmful to people with type 1 diabetes, rheumatoid arthritis, or other autoimmune diseases. It is therefore unwise—to put it gently—to take herbal remedies or supplements of any kind without consulting a doctor and/or the *Physician's Desk Reference for Herbal Medicines*. But many Americans do so, equating "natural" with "harmless" and "good."

CAUSE AND SOLUTION

I have addressed here the corrupting influence of "junk science" in the area of consumer foods, vitamins and diet supplements. The same dynamic increasingly affects other aspects of our individual and collective lives as well. But I believe the root cause is the same: Americans are losing the common-sense skepticism toward scientific claims that animates the scientific method itself. And one of the reasons for this is a slow but steady degradation of our educational system. In short, as Charles J. Sykes explains in *Dumbing Down Our Kids*, theories such as "outcome-based education," "cooperative learning," and "maximization of self-esteem" are fast replacing reading, writing, and arithmetic as the goals of education. 10

Anecdotal evidence of this trend is vast and compelling. For instance, when average SAT math scores fell from 500 to 424, the College Board responded by allowing the use of calculators. When that didn't work, they "recentered" the test by adding approximately 20 points to the math scores (while also adding 80 points on the verbal side, for a total of 100), regardless of achievement. At the state level, many high school competency exams are written at an eighth-grade level. And coloring for credit in elementary-level math classes is now fairly common. Is it any wonder that so many of the kids we now graduate from high school enter the workforce unable to add in their heads or make correct change, or arrive at college incapable of solving the simplest equations?

The situation is no better in the sciences. Students at a Seattle middle school spend two weeks studying the eating habits of birds by trying to pick up Cheerios with tongue depressors, toothpicks, spoons, and clothes-pins between their teeth. "Educationalists" call this creative and engaging. But it doesn't create useful or important knowledge. And surely it is not true that such activity is more engaging than learning about Newton's Laws or DNA.

A popular high school chemistry book moves from "Supplying Our Water Needs," which includes a discussion of acid rain, to "Chemistry and the Atmosphere," which addresses the ozone layer. This approach would not be all bad if the chemistry behind these issues was rigorously taught and if important topics unrelated to social controversies were also included. Unfortunately they are not. When I called the American Chemical Society— which, sadly, produced this textbook—one of those responsible justified its approach by pointing out that most high school graduates don't pursue science in college. Furthermore, he said, students introduced to chemistry in this way enjoy it more and find it easier to handle, resulting in higher self-esteem. I asked if it had occurred to him that perhaps students don't pursue college science because they don't obtain the requisite skills or knowledge in high school. Regardless, when the American Chemical Society endorses a high school science text that doesn't even list the scientific method in its index, we shouldn't be surprised that so many Americans gorge themselves on "fat-free foods," throw their money at "Vitamin O," or risk their health by taking "natural" herbs without investigating their effects.

The solution to the problem I have outlined is easy to see, and is by no means impossible to accomplish. Individually, we must be careful to take our bearings from the scientific method when confronted with scientific claims, employing healthy skepticism and asking questions before believing what we hear or read. Together, we must work diligently to revive real standards in primary and secondary science education.

Questions

1. Lee Ann Fisher Baron uses anecdotes, quotations, and outside sources for a variety of purposes in her essay. How does Baron's discussion of Samuel Hahnemann's experimentations affect her own *ethos*? What purpose does the anecdote serve in her essay?

2. What purpose does the anecdote of her discussion with the American Chemical Society serve in her argument?

3. Thinking ahead to your research paper for the course, list the types of outside sources that you think would best contribute to your argument, and explain why they are effective.

Nicholas Carr [b. 1959]

iGod

In the summer of 2004, Google's founders, Larry Page and Sergey Brin, nearly sabotaged their own company. They sat down for a long interview with *Playboy*, and the magazine published the transcript in early August, just days before Google's scheduled debut on the NASDAQ stock exchange. The appearance of the interview roiled Wall Street, as it seemed to violate the Securities and Exchange Commission's prohibition on unauthorized disclosures of information during the "quiet period" leading up to an IPO. Investors feared that the SEC might force the company to cancel its stock offering. But after Google hurriedly distributed a revised prospectus, including the entire text of the *Playboy* interview as an appendix, the SEC cleared the stock sale, and on August 19 Google became a public company.

Lost in the hubbub was the interview itself, which provided a fascinating look into the thoughts and motivations of a pair of brilliant young mathematicians who were about to join the ranks of the world's wealthiest and most powerful businessmen. Toward the end of the interview, Page and Brin gave voice to their deepest ambition. They weren't just interested in perfecting their search engine, they said. What they really looked forward to was melding their technology with the human brain itself. "You want access to as much [information] as possible so you can discern what is most relevant and correct," explained Brin. "The solution isn't to limit the information you receive. Ultimately you want to have the entire world's knowledge connected directly to your mind."

The interviewer was taken aback. "Is that what we have to look forward to?" he asked.

"I hope so," said Brin. "At least a version of that. We probably won't be looking up everything on a computer."

The interviewer probed again: "Is your goal to have the entire world's knowledge con-   5 nected directly to our minds?"

"To get closer to that—as close as possible," replied Brin. "The smarter we can make the search engine, the better. Where will it lead? Who knows? But it's credible to imagine a leap as great as that from hunting through library stacks to a Google session, when we leap from today's search engines to having the entirety of the world's information as just one of our thoughts."

It wasn't the first time that Brin and Page had talked about their desire to tinker with the human brain—and it wouldn't be the last. In fact, the creation of an artificial intelligence that extends or even replaces the mind is a theme they return to again and again. "Every time I talk about Google's future with Larry Page," reports Steve Jurvetson, a prominent Silicon Valley venture capitalist, "he argues that it will become an artificial intelligence." During a question-and-answer session after a presentation at his alma mater, Stanford University, in May 2002, Page said that Google would fulfill its mission only when its search engine was "AI-complete." "You guys know what that means?" he quizzed the audience of students. "That's artificial intelligence."

In another presentation at Stanford a few months later, Page reiterated the goal: "The ultimate search engine is something as smart as people—or smarter.... For us, working on search is a way to work on artificial intelligence." Around the same time, in an interview on public television's *NewsHour*, Brin explained that the "ultimate search engine" would resemble the talking supercomputer HAL in the movie *2001: A Space Odyssey*. "Now, hopefully," said Brin, "it would never have a bug like HAL did where he killed the occupants of the spaceship. But that's what we're striving for, and I think we've made it a part of the way there."

In July 2003, during a talk at a technology conference, Brin and Page went into more detail about their aspiration to use artificial intelligence to make us smarter. Brin suggested, according to a report from a member of the audience, that "wireless brain appliances" might be used to automate the delivery of information. Page elaborated on that idea in a February 2004 interview with Reuters, saying, "On the more exciting front, you can imagine your brain being augmented by Google. For example you think about something and your cell phone could whisper the answer into your ear."

Brin also discussed Google's progress toward its ultimate goal in an interview with   10 *Newsweek* writer Steven Levy. "I think we're pretty far along [with Internet searching] compared to ten years ago," he said. "At the same time, where can you go? Certainly if you had all the world's information directly attached to your brain, or an artificial brain that was smarter than your brain, you'd be better off. Between that and today, there's plenty of space to cover." David Vise relates a similar remark by Brin in his 2005 book *The Google Story*. "Why not improve the brain?" Brin muses at one point. "Perhaps in the future, we can attach a little version of Google that you just plug into your brain."

At a London conference in May 2006, Larry Page again spoke of Google's pursuit of artificial intelligence. "We want to create the ultimate search engine," he said. "The ultimate search engine would understand everything in the world." A year later, in February 2007, he told a group of scientists that Google has a team of employees who are "really trying to build an artificial intelligence and to do it on a large scale." The fulfillment of their goal, he said, is "not as far off as people think."

In taking a transcendental view of information technology, seeing it as a way to overcome what they perceive to be the physical limitations of the human brain, Brin and Page are expressing a desire that has long been a hallmark of the mathematicians and computer scientists who have devoted themselves to the creation of artificial intelligence. It's a desire that, as David Noble notes in *The Religion of Technology*, can be traced all the way back to the seventeenth-century French philosopher René Descartes, who argued that "the body is always a hindrance to the mind in its thinking" and saw in mathematics a model for "pure understanding." The Cartesian ideal runs through the work of mathematicians like George Boole, Alfred North Whitehead, and Alan Turing, whose breakthroughs in algebraic logic set the stage for the modern binary computer.

In her 1979 book *Machines Who Think*, Pamela McCorduck wrote that artificial intelligence promises to provide "an extension of those human capacities we value most." She quoted MIT professor Edward Fredkin's claim that "artificial intelligence is the next step in evolution." Danny Hillis, whose pioneering work in parallel computing paved the way for Google's systems, argued in a 1992 interview that AI could provide a means of remedying man's mental shortcomings, of fixing the "bugs left over history, back from when we were animals," and lead to the creation of beings who are "better than us." In "Reinventing Humanity," a 2006 article, the acclaimed inventor and author Ray Kurzweil predicted that artificial intelligence "will vastly exceed biological intelligence by the mid-2040s," resulting in "a world where there is no distinction between the biological and the mechanical, or between physical and virtual reality."

To most of us, the desire of the AI advocates to merge computers and people, to erase or blur the boundary between man and machine, is troubling. It's not just that we detect in their enthusiasm a disturbing misanthropy—Hillis dismisses the human body as "the monkey that walks around," while Marvin Minsky, the former director of MIT's artificial intelligence program, calls the human brain a "bloody mess of organic matter"—it's also that we naturally sense in their quest a threat to our integrity as freethinking individuals. Even Bill Gates finds the concept discomforting. In a 2005 talk in Singapore, he discussed the possibility of connecting people's bodies and brains directly to computers. One of his Microsoft colleagues, he told the audience, "always says to me, 'I'm ready, plug me in.'" But Gates said that he was wary of the idea: "I don't feel quite the same way. I'm happy to have the computer over there and I'm over here."

In addition to finding the prospect of being turned into computer enhanced cyborgs 15 unsettling, we also tend to be skeptical of the idea. It seems far-fetched, even ludicrous—like something out of a particularly fanciful piece of science fiction. Here, though, we part company with Gates. In that same speech, he made it clear that he believes the blending of computers and people is inevitable, that we will, in the foreseeable future, come to be augmented by digital processors and software. "We will have those capabilities," he declared. And evidence suggests that Microsoft, like Google, aims to be a pioneer in creating human-computer interfaces for commercial gain. In 2004, the company was granted a patent for a "method and apparatus for transmitting power and data using the human body." In its filing, Microsoft described how it is developing technology that will turn skin into a new kind of electrical conduit, or "bus," that can be used to connect "a network of devices coupled to a single body." It also noted that "the network can be extended by connecting multiple bodies through physical contact [such as] a handshake. When two or more bodies are connected physically, the linked bodies form one large bus over which power and/or communications signals can be transmitted."

Microsoft's patent is just one manifestation of the many corporate and academic research programs that are aimed at merging computers and people and, in particular, at incorporating human beings more fully into the Internet's computing web. A 2006 study sponsored by the British government's Office of Science and Innovation surveyed some of the most promising of these initiatives. In addition to confirming that our bodies are fated to become data-transmission buses—leading to the rise of "computing on the human platform"—the study's authors document the rapid advances taking place in the melding of the real and virtual worlds. New "ambient displays," they write, promise to make computing "ubiquitous," surrounding us with data and software everywhere we go: "In ubiquitous computing, the physical location of data and processing power is not apparent to the user. Rather, information is made available to the user in a transparent and contextually relevant manner." Within ten years, we won't even have to use keystrokes and mouse clicks to tell computers what we want them to do. There will be "new ways of interacting with computers in which delegated systems perform tasks proactively on users' behalf, tuned precisely to the momentary requirements of time and place."

The researchers also predict that the Google founders' dream of a direct link between the brain and the Internet should become a reality by 2020. That's when we're likely to see "the first physical neural interface," providing "a direct connection between a human or animal brain and nervous system and a computer or computer network." At that point, we'll be able "to interact directly with computers by merely thinking." Such a neural interface promises to be a blessing to many people afflicted with severe disabilities. It could help the blind to see and the paralyzed to move. But its applications go well beyond medicine, the researchers note. It also offers the "potential for outside control of human behavior through digital media." We will become programmable, too.

The Internet doesn't just connect information-processing machines. It connects people. It connects us with each other, and it connects us with the machines. Our intelligence is as much a part of the power of the World Wide Computer as the intelligence embedded in software code or microchips. When we go online, we become nodes on the Internet. That's not just a metaphor. It's a reflection of the hyperlinked structure that has from the beginning defined the Web and our use of it. The Internet, and all the devices connected to it, is not simply a passive machine that responds to our commands. It's a thinking machine, if as yet a rudimentary one, that actively collects and analyzes our thoughts and desires as we express them through the choices we make while online—what we do, where we go, whom we talk to, what we upload, what we download, which links we click on, which links we ignore. By assembling and storing billions upon billions of tiny bits of intelligence, the Web forms what the writer John Battelle calls "a database of human intentions." As we spend more time and transact more of our commercial and social business online, that database will grow ever wider and deeper. Figuring out new ways for people—and machines—to tap into the storehouse of intelligence is likely to be the central enterprise of the future.

On November 2, 2005, we got a glimpse of what lies ahead for the World Wide Computer when Amazon.com began testing a new service with a strange name: Mechanical Turk. The name, it turned out, was borrowed from an infamous chess-playing "automaton" that was built in 1770 by a Hungarian baron named Wolfgang von Kempelen. The wooden machine, fashioned to look like a Turkish sorcerer sitting in front of a large cabinet, appeared to play chess automatically, using an elaborate system of gears and levers to move the pieces. In its debut, at the Schönbrunn/Palace in Vienna, the Mechanical Turk quickly dispatched its first opponent, a Count Cobenzl, to the delight of the assembled courtiers: News of the remarkably intelligent robot spread rapidly, and von Kempelen took the Turk on a tour of Europe, where it defeated a series of famous challengers, including Napoleon Bonaparte and Benjamin Franklin. It was not until years later, after von Kempelen's death, that the hoax was revealed. Hidden inside the cabinet had been a chess master, who used a system of magnets to follow opponents' moves and make his own. The player had been simulating an artificial intelligence.

Amazon's Mechanical Turk accomplishes a similar feat. It "hides" people inside a soft- 20 ware program, using them to carry out tasks that computers aren't yet very good at. Say, for example, that a programmer is writing an application that includes, as one of its steps, the identification of buildings in digital photographs—a job that baffles today's computers but is easy for people to do. Using the Mechanical Turk service, the programmer can write a few simple lines of code to tap into the required intelligence. At the designated point in the running of the program, a request to carry out the "human task" automatically gets posted on Amazon's Turk site, where people compete to perform it for a fee set by the programmer.

As Amazon explains on its Web site, Mechanical Turk stands the usual relationship between computers and people on its head: "When we think of interfaces between human beings and computers, we usually assume that the human being is the one requesting that a task be completed, and the computer is completing the task and providing the results. What if this process were reversed and a computer program could ask a human being to perform a task and return the results?" That's exactly what Mechanical Turk does. It turns people's actions and judgments into functions in a software program. Rather than the machine working for us, we work for the machine.

We play a similar role, without even realizing it, in the operation of Google's search engine. At the heart of that engine is the Page-Rank algorithm that Brin and Page wrote while they were graduate students at Stanford in the 1990s. They saw that every time a person with a Web site links to another site, he is expressing a judgment. He is declaring that he considers the other site important. They further realized that while every link on the Web contains a little bit of human intelligence, all the links combined contain a great deal of intelligence—far more, in fact, than any individual mind could possibly possess. Google's search engine mines that intelligence, link by link, and uses it to determine the importance of all the pages on the Web. The greater the number of links that lead to a site, the greater its value. As John Markoff puts it, Google's software "systematically exploits human knowledge and decisions about what is significant." Every time we write a link, or even click on one, we are feeding our intelligence into Google's system. We are making the machine a little smarter—and Brin, Page, and all of Google's shareholders a little richer.

In Mechanical Turk and the Google search engine, we begin to see the human mind merging into the artificial mind of the World Wide Computer. In both services, people become subservient to the machine. With Mechanical Turk, we're incorporated into a software program, carrying out a small function without being aware of the greater purpose—just as manual laborers became cogs in long assembly lines. In Google's search engine, our contributions are made unconsciously. Brin and Page have programmed their machine to gather the crumbs or intelligence that we leave behind on the Web as we go about our everyday business.

As the computing cloud grows, as it becomes ubiquitous, we will feed ever more intelligence into it. Using global positioning satellites and tiny radio transmitters, it will track our movements through the physical world as meticulously as it today tracks our clicks through the virtual world. And as the types of commercial and social transactions performed through the Internet proliferate, many more kinds of data will be collected, stored, analyzed, and made available to software programs. The World Wide Computer will become immeasurably smarter. The transfer of our intelligence into the machine will happen, in other words, whether or not we allow chips or sockets to be embedded in our skulls.

Computer scientists are now in the process of creating a new language for the Internet 25 that promises to make it a far more sophisticated medium for expressing and exchanging intelligence. In creating Web pages today, programmers have limited options for using codes, or tags, to describe text, images, and other content. The Web's traditional hypertext markup language, or HTML, concentrates on simple formatting commands—on instructing, for instance, a Web browser to put a line of text into italics or to center it on a page. The new language will allow programmers to go much further. They'll be able to use tags to describe the meaning of objects like words and pictures as well as the associations between different objects. A person's name, for instance, could carry with it information about the person's address and job, likes and dislikes, and relationships to other people. A product's name could have tags describing its price, availability, manufacturer, and compatibility with other products.

This new language, software engineers believe, will pave the way for much more intelligent "conversations" between computers on the Internet. It will turn the Web of information into a Web of meaning—a "Semantic Web," as it's usually called. HTML's inventor, Tim Berners-Lee, is also spearheading the development of its replacement. In a speech before the 2006 International World Wide Web Conference in Scotland, he said that "the Web is only going to get more revolutionary" and that "twenty years from now, we'll look back and say this was the embryonic period." He foresees a day when the "mechanisms of trade, bureaucracy and our daily lives will be handled by machines talking to machines."

At the University of Washington's Turing Center, a leading artificial intelligence laboratory, researchers have already succeeded in creating a software program that can, at a very basic level, "read" sentences on Web pages and extract meaning from them—without requiring any tags from programmers. The software, called TextRunner, scans sentences and identifies the relationships between words or phrases. In reading the sentence "Thoreau wrote *Walden* after leaving his cabin in the woods," for instance, TextRunner would recognize that the verb "wrote" describes a relationship between "Thoreau" and "*Walden*." As it scans more pages and sees hundreds or thousands of similar constructions, it would be able to hypothesize that Thoreau is a writer and *Walden* is a book. Because TextRunner is able to read at an extraordinary rate—in one test, it extracted a billion textual relationships from 90 million Web pages—it can learn quickly. Its developers see it as a promising prototype of "machine reading," which they define as "the automatic, unsupervised understanding of text" by computers.

Scientists are also teaching machines how to see. Google has been working with researchers at the University of California at San Diego to perfect a system for training computers to interpret photographs and other images. The system combines textual tag describing an image's contents with a statistical analysis of the image. A computer is first trained to recognize an object—a tree, say—by being shown many images containing the object that have been tagged with the description "tree" by people. The computer learns to make an association between the tag and a mathematical analysis of the shapes appearing in the images. It learns, in effect, to spot a tree, regardless of where the tree happens to appear in a given picture. Having been seeded with the human intelligence, the computer can then begin to interpret images on its own, supplying its own tags with ever increasing accuracy. Eventually, it becomes so adept at "seeing" that it can dispense with the trainers altogether. It thinks for itself.

In 1945, the Princeton physicist John von Neumann sketched out the first plan for building an electronic computer that could store in its memory the instructions for its use. His plan became the blueprint for all modern digital computers. The immediate application of von Neumann's revolutionary machine was military—designing nuclear bombs and other weapons—but the scientist knew from the start that he had created a general purpose technology, one that would come to be used in ways that could not be foretold. "I am sure that the projected device, or rather the species of devices of which it is to be the first representative, is so radically new that many of its uses will become clear only after it has been put into operation," he wrote to Lewis Strauss, the future chairman of the Atomic Energy Commission, on October 24, 1945. "Uses which are likely to be the most important are by definition those which we do not recognize at present because they are farthest removed from our present sphere."

We are today at a similar point in the history of the World Wide Computer. We have 30 built it and are beginning to program it, but we are a long way from knowing all the ways it will come to be used. We can anticipate, however, that unlike von Neumann's machine, the World Wide Computer will not just follow our instructions. It will learn from us and, eventually, it will write its own instructions.

George Dyson, a historian of technology and the son of another renowned Princeton physicist, Freeman Dyson, was invited to Google's headquarters in Mountain View, California, in October 2005 to give a speech at a party celebrating the sixtieth anniversary of von Neumann's invention. "Despite the whimsical furniture and other toys," Dyson would later recall of his visit, "I felt I was entering a 14th-century cathedral—not in the 14th century but in the 12th century, while it was being built. Everyone was busy carving one stone here and another stone there, with some invisible architect getting everything to fit. The mood was playful, yet there was a palpable reverence in the air." After his talk, Dyson found himself chatting with a Google engineer about the company's controversial plan to scan the contents of the world's libraries into its database. "We are not scanning all those books to be read by people," the engineer told him. "We are scanning them to be read by an AI."

The visit inspired Dyson to write an essay for the online journal *Edge*, in which he argues that we've reached a turning point in the history of computing. The computer we use today, von Neumann's computer, uses a physical matrix as its memory. Each bit of data is stored in a precise location on that matrix, with a unique address, and software consists of a set of instructions for finding bits of data at specified addresses and doing something with them. It's a process that, as Dyson explains, "translates informally into 'DO THIS with what you find HERE and go THERE with the result.' Everything depends not only on precise instructions, but on HERE, THERE, and WHEN being exactly defined."

As we know today—and as von Neumann foresaw in 1945—this machine can be programmed to perform an amazing variety of tasks. But it has a fundamental limitation: it can only do what it's told. It depends entirely on the instructions provided by the programmer, and hence it can only perform tasks that a programmer can conceive of and write instructions for. As Dyson writes, "Computers have been getting better and better at providing answers—but only to questions that programmers are able to ask."

That's very different from how living systems, such as our brains, process information. As we navigate our lives, our minds devote most of their time and energy to computing answers to questions that haven't been asked, or at least haven't been asked in precise terms. "In the real world, most of the time," Dyson explains, "finding an answer is easier than defining the question. It's easier to draw something that looks like a cat, for instance, than to describe what, exactly, makes something look like a cat. A child scribbles indiscriminately, and eventually something appears that resembles a cat. A solution finds the problem, not the other way around." What makes us so smart is that our minds are constantly providing answers without knowing the questions. They're making sense rather than performing calculations.

For a machine to demonstrate, or at least simulate, that kind of intelligence, it cannot 35 be restricted to a set of unambiguous instructions for acting on a rigidly defined set of data. It needs to be freed from its fixed memory. It needs to lose its machine-ness and begin acting more like a biological system. That is exactly what's becoming possible as the Internet itself becomes a computer. Suddenly, rather than having a finite set of data arrayed precisely in a matrix, we have a superfluity of data floating around in a great unbounded cloud. We have, to switch metaphors, a primordial soup of information that demands to be made sense of. To do that, we need software that acts more like a sense-making brain than like von Neumann's calculating machine—software with instructions that, as Dyson writes, "say simply 'DO THIS with the next copy of THAT which comes along.'"

We see this new kind of software, in embryonic form, in Google's search engine and in other programs designed to mine information from the Web. Google's engineers recognize that, as Dyson puts it, "a network, whether of neurons, computers, words, or ideas, contains solutions, waiting to be discovered, to problems that need not be explicitly defined." The algorithms of the company's search engine already do a very good job of drawing out of the Internet answers to questions that we pose, even when we phrase our questions in ambiguous terms. We don't always know precisely what we're looking for when we do a Google search, but we often find it nonetheless. If the World Wide Computer is a new kind of computer, then the Google search engine is a preview of the new kind of software that will run on it.

Eric Schmidt has said that the company's ultimate product, the one he's "always wanted to build," would not wait to respond to his query but would "tell me what I should be typing." It would, in other words, provide the answer without hearing the question. The product would be an artificial intelligence. It might even be, to quote Sergey Brin again, "an artificial brain that was smarter than your brain."

And what of our brains? As we come to rely ever more heavily on the Internet's vast storehouse of information as an extension of or even a substitute for our own memory, will it change the way we think? Will it alter the way we conceive of ourselves and our relationship to the world? As we put ever more intelligence into the Web, will we, individually, become more intelligent, or less so?

In describing the future of the World Wide Computer—the "Machine," in his terminology—Kevin Kelly writes, "What will most surprise us is how dependent we will be on what the Machine knows—about us and about what we want to know. We already find it easier to Google something a second or third time rather than remember it ourselves. The more we teach this megacomputer, the more it will assume responsibility for our knowing. It will become our memory. Then it will become our identity. In 2015 many people, when divorced from the Machine, won't feel like themselves—as if they'd had a lobotomy."* Kelly welcomes the prospect. He believes that the submergence of our minds and our selves into a greater intelligence will mark the fulfillment of our destiny. The human race, he says, finds itself today at a new beginning, a moment when "the strands of mind, once achingly isolated, have started to come together."

Others are less sanguine about our prospects. In early 2005, the playwright Richard 40 Foreman staged his surrealist drama *The Gods Are Pounding My Head* on a stage at St. Mark's Church in Manhattan. It was a bleak work, featuring two exhausted lumberjacks wandering through a wasteland of cultural detritus—a "paper-thin world," as one character puts

---

*Kelly's description of man's growing dependency on computers carries a disquieting, if inadvertent, echo of a passage in the notorious manifesto written by Theodore Kaczynski, the Unabomber. "[As] machines become more and more intelligent," Kaczynski wrote, "people will let machines make more of their decisions for them, simply because machine-made decisions will bring better results than man-made ones. Eventually a stage may be reached at which the decisions necessary to keep the system running will be so complex that human beings will be incapable of making them intelligently. At that stage the machines will be in effective control. People won't be able to just turn the machines off, because they will be so dependent on them that turning them off would amount to suicide." What was for Kaczynski a paranoia-making nightmare is for Kelly a vision of Utopia.

it—and muttering broken, incoherent sentences. In a note to the audience, Foreman described the inspiration for his "elegiac play" "I come from a tradition of Western culture," he wrote, "in which the ideal (my ideal) was the complex, dense and 'cathedral-like' structure of the highly educated and articulate personality—a man or woman who carried inside themselves a personally constructed and unique version of the entire heritage of the West." He feared, however, that this tradition is fading, that it is being erased as we come to draw more of our sense of the world not from the stores of our memory but from the databases of the Internet: "I see within us all (myself included) the replacement of complex inner density with a new kind of self—evolving under the pressure of information overload and the technology of the 'instantly available.'" As we are emptied of our "inner repertory of dense cultural inheritance," Foreman concluded, we seem to be turning into "pancake people—spread wide and thin as we connect with that vast network of information accessed by the mere touch of a button."

It will be years before there are any definitive studies of the effect of extensive Internet use on our memories and thought processes. But anyone who has spent a lot of time online will likely feel at least a little kinship with Foreman. The common term "surfing the Web" perfectly captures the essential superficiality of our relationship with the information we find in such great quantities on the Internet. The English biologist J. Z. Young, in his Reith Lectures of 1950, collected in the book *Doubt and Certainty in Science*, eloquently described the subtle ways our perceptions, ideas, and language change whenever we begin using a new tool. Our technologies, he explained, make us as surely as we make our technologies. That's been true of the tools we use to process matter and energy, but it's been particularly true of the tools we use to process information, from the map to the clock to the computer.

The medium is not only the message. The medium is the mind. It shapes what we see and how we see it. The printed page, the dominant information medium of the past 500 years, molded our thinking through, to quote Neil Postman, "its emphasis on logic, sequence, history, exposition, objectivity, detachment, and discipline." The emphasis of the Internet, our new universal medium, is altogether different. It stresses immediacy, simultaneity, contingency, subjectivity, disposability, and, above all, speed. The Net provides no incentive to stop and think deeply about anything, to construct in our memory that "dense repository" of knowledge that Foreman cherishes. It's easier, as Kelly says, "to Google something a second or third time rather than remember it ourselves." On the Internet, we seem impelled to glide across the slick surface of data as we make our rushed passage from link to link.

And this is precisely the behavior that the Internet, as a commercial system, is designed to promote. We are the Web's neurons, and the more links we click, pages we view, and transactions we make—the faster we fire—the more intelligence the Web collects, the more economic value it gains, and the more profit it throws off. We feel like "pancake people" on the Web because that's the role we are assigned to play. The World Wide Computer and those who program it have little interest in our exhibiting what Foreman calls "the thick and multi-textured density of deeply evolved personality." They want us to act as hyperefficient, data processors, as cogs in an intellectual machine whose workings and ends are beyond us. The most revolutionary consequence of the expansion of the Internet's power, scope, and usefulness may not be that computers will start to think like us but that we will come to think like computers. Our consciousness will thin out, flatten, as our minds are trained, link by link, to "DO THIS with what you find HERE and go THERE with the result." The artificial intelligence we're creating may turn out to be our own.

A hundred years ago, the utility executives and electrical engineers who joined the Jovian Society saw themselves as the architects of a new and more perfect world. To them, God was "the Great Electrician," animating the universe with an invisible but all-powerful spirit. In pursuing their work they were doing His work as well; His designs were their designs. "The idea of electricity," the Jovians announced, is "binding the world together in a body of brotherhood."

Many of the computer scientists and software engineers who are building the great   45 computing grid of the twenty-first century share a similar sense of the importance—and the beneficence—of their work. It's only the metaphor that has changed. God is no longer the Great Electrician. He has become the Great Programmer. The universe is not the emanation of a mysterious spirit. It is the logical output of a computer. "As soon as the universe began, it began computing," writes MIT professor Seth Lloyd in his 2006 book *Programming the Universe*. "Life, language, human beings, society, culture—all owe their existence to the intrinsic ability of matter and energy to process information." "All living creatures are information-processing machines at some level," argues Charles Seife in another, similarly titled 2006 book, *Decoding the Universe*. "In a sense, the universe as a whole is behaving like a giant information processor—a computer."

Our past and our destiny are inscribed in software code. And now, as all the world's computers are wired together into one machine, we have finally been given the opportunity, or at least the temptation, to perfect the code.

Questions

1. How does the title "iGod" connect to the claim(s) Nicholas Carr makes in the essay?

2. Explain how Carr uses discussions of artificial intelligence, Google, and Amazon to develop his argument.

3. Why do you think that Carr uses so many and such a range of supports to develop key points in his essay?

4. In small groups, diagram (e.g., using an outline, map, or clustering) the organizational development of Carr's essay. What are its key components? Which ones are connected and why? How does the understanding of a specific aspect of the piece lead the reader to another understanding and ultimately to key assumptions?

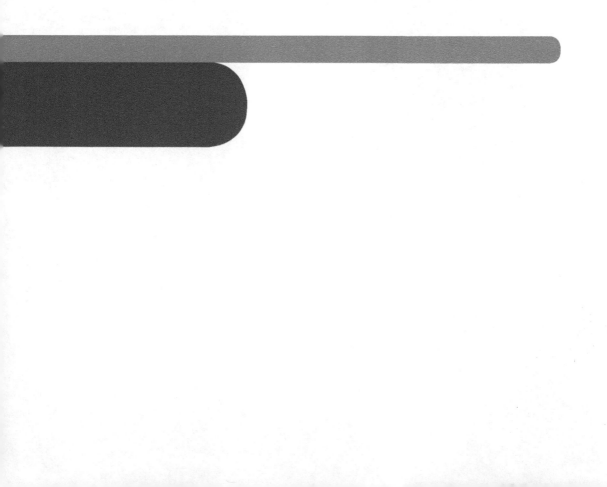

Research Writing

Trip Gabriel [b. 1955]

Plagiarism Lines Blur for Students in Digital Age

At Rhode Island College, a freshman copied and pasted from a Web site's frequently asked questions page about homelessness—and did not think he needed to credit a source in his assignment because the page did not include author information.

At DePaul University, the tip-off to one student's copying was the purple shade of several paragraphs he had lifted from the Web; when confronted by a writing tutor his professor had sent him to, he was not defensive—he just wanted to know how to change purple text to black.

And at the University of Maryland, a student reprimanded for copying from *Wikipedia* in a paper on the Great Depression said he thought its entries—unsigned and collectively written—did not need to be credited since they counted, essentially, as common knowledge.

Professors used to deal with plagiarism by admonishing students to give credit to others and to follow the style guide for citations, and pretty much left it at that.

But these cases—typical ones, according to writing tutors and officials responsible for 5 discipline at the three schools who described the plagiarism—suggest that many students simply do not grasp that using words they did not write is a serious misdeed.

It is a disconnect that is growing in the Internet age as concepts of intellectual property, copyright, and originality are under assault in the unbridled exchange of online information, say educators who study plagiarism.

Digital technology makes copying and pasting easy, of course. But that is the least of it. The Internet may also be redefining how students—who came of age with music file-sharing, *Wikipedia*, and Web-linking—understand the concept of authorship and the singularity of any text or image.

"Now we have a whole generation of students who've grown up with information that just seems to be hanging out there in cyberspace and doesn't seem to have an author," said Teresa Fishman, director of the Center for Academic Integrity at Clemson University. "It's possible to believe this information is just out there for anyone to take."

Professors who have studied plagiarism do not try to excuse it—many are champions of academic honesty on their campuses—but rather try to understand why it is so widespread.

In surveys from 2006 to 2010 by Donald L. McCabe, a co-founder of the Center 10 for Academic Integrity and a business professor at Rutgers University, about 40 percent of 14,000 undergraduates admitted to copying a few sentences in written assignments.

Perhaps more significant, the number who believed that copying from the Web constitutes "serious cheating" is declining—to 29 percent on average in recent surveys from 34 percent earlier in the decade.

Sarah Brookover, a senior at the Rutgers campus in Camden, N.J., said many of her classmates blithely cut and paste without attribution.

"This generation has always existed in a world where media and intellectual property don't have the same gravity," said Ms. Brookover, who at 31 is older than most undergraduates. "When you're sitting at your computer, it's the same machine you've downloaded music with, possibly illegally, the same machine you streamed videos for free that showed on HBO last night."

Ms. Brookover, who works at the campus library, has pondered the differences between researching in the stacks and online. "Because you're not walking into a library, you're not physically holding the article, which takes you closer to 'this doesn't belong to me,'" she said. Online, "everything can belong to you really easily."

A University of Notre Dame anthropologist, Susan D. Blum, disturbed by the high 15 rates of reported plagiarism, set out to understand how students view authorship and the written word, or "texts" in Ms. Blum's academic language.

She conducted her ethnographic research among 234 Notre Dame undergraduates. "Today's students stand at the crossroads of a new way of conceiving texts and the people who create them and who quote them," she wrote last year in the book *My Word! Plagiarism and College Culture*, published by Cornell University Press.

Ms. Blum argued that student writing exhibits some of the same qualities of pastiche that drive other creative endeavors today—TV shows that constantly reference other shows or rap music that samples from earlier songs.

In an interview, she said the idea of an author whose singular effort creates an original work is rooted in Enlightenment ideas of the individual. It is buttressed by the Western concept of intellectual property rights as secured by copyright law. But both traditions are being challenged. "Our notion of authorship and originality was born, it flourished, and it may be waning," Ms. Blum said.

She contends that undergraduates are less interested in cultivating a unique and authentic identity—as their 1960s counterparts were—than in trying on many different personas, which the Web enables with social networking.

"If you are not so worried about presenting yourself as absolutely unique, then it's O.K. 20 if you say other people's words, it's O.K. if you say things you don't believe, it's O.K. if you write papers you couldn't care less about because they accomplish the task, which is turning something in and getting a grade," Ms. Blum said, voicing student attitudes. "And it's O.K. if you put words out there without getting any credit."

The notion that there might be a new model young person, who freely borrows from the vortex of information to mash up a new creative work, fueled a brief brouhaha earlier this year with Helene Hegemann, a German teenager whose best-selling novel about Berlin club life turned out to include passages lifted from others.

Instead of offering an abject apology, Ms. Hegemann insisted, "There's no such thing as originality anyway, just authenticity." A few critics rose to her defense, and the book remained a finalist for a fiction prize (but did not win).

That theory does not wash with Sarah Wilensky, a senior at Indiana University, who said that relaxing plagiarism standards "does not foster creativity, it fosters laziness."

"You're not coming up with new ideas if you're grabbing and mixing and matching," said Ms. Wilensky, who took aim at Ms. Hegemann in a column in her student newspaper headlined "Generation Plagiarism."

"It may be increasingly accepted, but there are still plenty of creative people—authors 25 and artists and scholars—who are doing original work," Ms. Wilensky said in an interview. "It's kind of an insult that that ideal is gone, and now we're left only to make collages of the work of previous generations."

In the view of Ms. Wilensky, whose writing skills earned her the role of informal editor of other students' papers in her freshman dorm, plagiarism has nothing to do with trendy academic theories.

The main reason it occurs, she said, is because students leave high school unprepared for the intellectual rigors of college writing.

"If you're taught how to closely read sources and synthesize them into your own original argument in middle and high school, you're not going to be tempted to plagiarize in college, and you certainly won't do so unknowingly," she said.

At the University of California, Davis, of the 196 plagiarism cases referred to the disciplinary office last year, a majority did not involve students ignorant of the need to credit the writing of others.

Many times, said Donald J. Dudley, who oversees the discipline office on the campus   30 of 32,000, it was students who intentionally copied—knowing it was wrong—who were "unwilling to engage the writing process."

"Writing is difficult, and doing it well takes time and practice," he said.

And then there was a case that had nothing to do with a younger generation's evolving view of authorship. A student accused of plagiarism came to Mr. Dudley's office with her parents, and the father admitted that he was the one responsible for the plagiarism. The wife assured Mr. Dudley that it would not happen again.

Questions

1. Gabriel ends his article by referencing UC Davis's plagiarism cases in 2009, citing a discipline office official who explained that the cases often involved "students who intentionally copied—knowing it was wrong—who were 'unwilling to engage the writing process'" (paras. 29–30). How does this concluding material affect the way we understand Gabriel's overall discussion? How does it compare, for instance, to the ideas of anthropologist Susan D. Blum, which are presented earlier in the article?

2. How has your own understanding of authorship and plagiarism been shaped? What do you think counts as authorship and plagiarism, and what has led you to these conclusions?

3. Gabriel's article presents the idea that present-day concepts of authorship are different, and looser, from those held previously. But understanding authorship as somewhat fluid is by no means a new thing. Picasso famously and pithily stated that "Good artists copy, great artists steal." Copying the work of others has a long history in art, especially when it comes to an artist's early development: One of Beethoven's earliest piano sonatas opens with a theme he copied verbatim from Mozart. And Stravinsky's famous *Firebird* ballet includes passages that he lifted from his teacher, Nikolai Rimsky-Korsakov. So what is "true" authorship? In small groups, discuss the idea of authorship, and then take a position on what counts as true authorship. Develop several supporting arguments for your position, provide evidence for your stance, and make use of your rhetorical knowledge. Each group should present and debate their positions on authorship.

Elizabeth Minkel

Too Hard *Not* to Cheat in the Internet Age?

A deeply troubling article sat atop the *New York Times'* most-emailed list yesterday (no, not the one about catching horrible diseases at the gym). "Plagiarism Lines Blur for Students in Digital Age," the headline proclaimed, pinpointing a problem, weaving a theory, and excusing youthful copycats in one fell swoop. The story here is that a large number of college students today are acting as college students always have—baldly lifting whole passages for their term papers from other sources. But it's the Digital Age now, and between unverifiable, unattributed information sitting around online and the general ease with which young people obtain, alter, and share creative content on the Internet, students can't seem to figure out that cheating on a paper is wrong. In fact, a lot of them can't even tell that they're cheating, and the Internet is to blame.

Really? When I was in college (I graduated three years ago), I was well aware of the necessity of avoiding minefields of unattributed—and often incorrect—information on the Web. *Wikipedia* was never an acceptable source, perhaps because my professors knew they'd get students like the one from the University of Maryland who, when "reprimanded for copying from *Wikipedia*…said he thought its entries—unsigned and collectively written—did not need to be credited since they counted, essentially, as common knowledge." There are probably only two types of people pulling these excuses: the crafty, using the Digital Age argument to their advantage, and the completely clueless, who, like plenty in preceding generations, just don't understand the concept of plagiarism. The *Times* asked current students to weigh in (helpfully labelling them "Generation Plagiarism"), and one wrote:

"I never 'copy and paste' but I will take information from the Internet and change out a few words then put it in my paper. So far, I have not encountered any problems with this. Thought [*sic*] the information/words are technically mine because of a few undetectable word swaps, I still consider the information to be that of someone else."

The student goes on to say that, "In the digital age, plagiarism isn't and shouldn't be as big of a deal as it used to be when people used books for research." The response leaves me just as confused as I believe he is, but I'm pretty convinced that he'd still be fuzzy on plagiarism if he'd lived back when people actually used books. But what I've found most frustrating in the ensuing debate is the assertion that these students are a part of some new *Reality Hunger*–type wave of open-source everything—if every song is sampled, why shouldn't writers do the same? The question is interesting, complicated, and divisive, but it has little bearing on a Psych 101 paper.

Excusing plagiarism as some sort of modern-day academic mash-up won't teach students anything more than how to lie and get away with it. We should be teaching students how to produce original work—and that there's plenty of original thinking across the Internet—and leave the plagiarizing to the politicians.

Questions

1. Minkel's essay is a refutation of Trip Gabriel's article (p. 465), whose headline she accuses of "pinpointing a problem, weaving a theory, and excusing youthful copycats in one fell swoop" (para. 1). Do you agree that Gabriel's article excuses plagiarism, or do you think it simply identifies a problem? Explain.

2. In paragraph 1, Minkel summarizes Gabriel's article. Is this a fair summary?

3. How would you characterize Minkel's tone? For example, is she angry? Frustrated? Condescending? Annoyed? Is this tone appropriate for her audience? (Note that this essay first appeared in the *New Yorker*, a magazine likely to be read by educated readers.)

4. In paragraph 2, Minkel identifies herself as a recent college graduate. Why? Is she appealing here to *ethos*, *pathos*, or *logos*?

5. Evaluate Minkel's last paragraph, particularly her concluding statement. Does this paragraph accurately express her reasons for criticizing Gabriel's article? What, if anything, do you think she should add to her conclusion? Why?

WPA Outcomes Statement for First-Year Composition (v3.0)

(adopted 17 July 2014)

Introduction

This Statement identifies outcomes for first-year composition programs in U.S. postsecondary education. It describes the writing knowledge, practices, and attitudes that undergraduate students develop in first-year composition, which at most schools is a required general education course or sequence of courses. This Statement therefore attempts to both represent and regularize writing programs' priorities for first-year composition, which often takes the form of one or more required general education courses. To this end it is not merely a compilation or summary of what currently takes place. Rather, this Statement articulates what composition teachers nationwide have learned from practice, research, and theory.[1] It intentionally defines only "outcomes," or types of results, and not "standards," or precise levels of achievement. The setting of standards to measure students' achievement of these Outcomes has deliberately been left to local writing programs and their institutions.

In this Statement "composing" refers broadly to complex writing processes that are increasingly reliant on the use of digital technologies. Writers also attend to elements of design, incorporating images and graphical elements into texts intended for screens as well as printed pages. Writers' composing activities have always been shaped by the technologies available to them, and digital technologies are changing writers' relationships to their texts and audiences in evolving ways.

These outcomes are supported by a large body of research demonstrating that the process of learning to write in any medium is complex: it is both individual and social and demands continued practice and informed guidance. Programmatic decisions about helping students demonstrate these outcomes should be informed by an understanding of this research.

As students move beyond first-year composition, their writing abilities do not merely improve. Rather, their abilities will diversify along disciplinary, professional, and civic lines as these writers move into new settings where expected outcomes expand, multiply, and diverge. Therefore, this document advises faculty in all disciplines about how to help students build on what they learn in introductory writing courses.

---

1 This Statement is aligned with the *Framework for Success in Postsecondary Writing*, an articulation of the skills and habits of mind essential for success in college, and is intended to help establish a continuum of valued practice from high school through to the college major.

Rhetorical Knowledge

Rhetorical knowledge is the ability to analyze contexts and audiences and then to act on that analysis in comprehending and creating texts. Rhetorical knowledge is the basis of composing. Writers develop rhetorical knowledge by negotiating purpose, audience, context, and conventions as they compose a variety of texts for different situations.

By the end of first-year composition, students should
- Learn and use key rhetorical concepts through analyzing and composing a variety of texts
- Gain experience reading and composing in several genres to understand how genre conventions shape and are shaped by readers' and writers' practices and purposes
- Develop facility in responding to a variety of situations and contexts calling for purposeful shifts in voice, tone, level of formality, design, medium, and/or structure
- Understand and use a variety of technologies to address a range of audiences
- Match the capacities of different environments (e.g., print and electronic) to varying rhetorical situations

Faculty in all programs and departments can build on this preparation by helping students learn
- The expectations of readers in their fields
- The main features of genres in their fields
- The main purposes of composing in their fields

Critical Thinking, Reading, and Composing

Critical thinking is the ability to analyze, synthesize, interpret, and evaluate ideas, information, situations, and texts. When writers think critically about the materials they use—whether print texts, photographs, data sets, videos, or other materials—they separate assertion from evidence, evaluate sources and evidence, recognize and evaluate underlying assumptions, read across texts for connections and patterns, identify and evaluate chains of reasoning, and compose appropriately qualified and developed claims and generalizations. These practices are foundational for advanced academic writing.

By the end of first-year composition, students should
- Use composing and reading for inquiry, learning, critical thinking, and communicating in various rhetorical contexts

- Read a diverse range of texts, attending especially to relationships between assertion and evidence, to patterns of organization, to the interplay between verbal and nonverbal elements, and to how these features function for different audiences and situations

- Locate and evaluate (for credibility, sufficiency, accuracy, timeliness, bias and so on) primary and secondary research materials, including journal articles and essays, books, scholarly and professionally established and maintained databases or archives, and informal electronic networks and Internet sources

- Use strategies—such as interpretation, synthesis, response, critique, and design/redesign—to compose texts that integrate the writer's ideas with those from appropriate sources

Faculty in all programs and departments can build on this preparation by helping students learn

- The kinds of critical thinking important in their disciplines

- The kinds of questions, problems, and evidence that define their disciplines

- Strategies for reading a range of texts in their fields

Processes

Writers use multiple strategies, or *composing processes*, to conceptualize, develop, and finalize projects. Composing processes are seldom linear: a writer may research a topic before drafting, then conduct additional research while revising or after consulting a colleague. Composing processes are also flexible: successful writers can adapt their composing processes to different contexts and occasions.

By the end of first-year composition, students should

- Develop a writing project through multiple drafts

- Develop flexible strategies for reading, drafting, reviewing, collaborating, revising, rewriting, rereading, and editing

- Use composing processes and tools as a means to discover and reconsider ideas

- Experience the collaborative and social aspects of writing processes

- Learn to give and to act on productive feedback to works in progress

- Adapt composing processes for a variety of technologies and modalities

- Reflect on the development of composing practices and how those practices influence their work

Faculty in all programs and departments can build on this preparation by helping students learn

- To employ the methods and technologies commonly used for research and communication within their fields

- To develop projects using the characteristic processes of their fields

- To review work-in-progress for the purpose of developing ideas before surface-level editing

- To participate effectively in collaborative processes typical of their field

Knowledge of Conventions

Conventions are the formal rules and informal guidelines that define genres, and in so doing, shape readers' and writers' perceptions of correctness or appropriateness. Most obviously, conventions govern such things as mechanics, usage, spelling, and citation practices. But they also influence content, style, organization, graphics, and document design.

Conventions arise from a history of use and facilitate reading by invoking common expectations between writers and readers. These expectations are not universal; they vary by genre (conventions for lab notebooks and discussion-board exchanges differ), by discipline (conventional moves in literature reviews in Psychology differ from those in English), and by occasion (meeting minutes and executive summaries use different registers). A writer's grasp of conventions in one context does not mean a firm grasp in another. Successful writers understand, analyze, and negotiate conventions for purpose, audience, and genre, understanding that genres evolve in response to changes in material conditions and composing technologies and attending carefully to emergent conventions.

By the end of first-year composition, students should

- Develop knowledge of linguistic structures, including grammar, punctuation, and spelling, through practice in composing and revising

- Understand why genre conventions for structure, paragraphing, tone, and mechanics vary

- Gain experience negotiating variations in genre conventions

- Learn common formats and/or design features for different kinds of texts

- Explore the concepts of intellectual property (such as fair use and copyright) that motivate documentation conventions

- Practice applying citation conventions systematically in their own work

Faculty in all programs and departments can build on this preparation by helping students learn

- The reasons behind conventions of usage, specialized vocabulary, format, and citation systems in their fields or disciplines

- Strategies for controlling conventions in their fields or disciplines

- Factors that influence the ways work is designed, documented, and disseminated in their fields

- Ways to make informed decisions about intellectual property issues connected to common genres and modalities in their fields.

Acknowledgements

Text Credits

Angier, Natalie, "One Thing They Aren't: Maternal." From the *New York Times*, May 9, 2006. Copyright © 2006 by the *New York Times*. All rights reserved. Reprinted by permission and protected by the Copyright Law of the United States. The printing, copying, redistribution, or retransmission of the material without express written permission is prohibited.

Arlen, Michael, "Ode to Thanksgiving" from *Camera Age: Essays on Television* by Michael J. Arlen. Copyright © 1981 by Michael J. Arlen. Reprinted by permission of Donadio & Olson, Inc.

Aronson, Deb, "The Nurture of Nature," *Science & Spirit* magazine, Volume 14, issue 4, July–August 2003. Reprinted with permission of the author.

Bamshad, Michael J. and Steve E. Olson, "Does Race Exist?" Copyright © 2003 by *Scientific American*, a division of Nature America, Inc. All rights reserved. Reproduced by permission.

Baron, Lee Ann Fisher. "The Influence of 'Junk Science' and the Role of Science Education." Copyright © 2001. Reprinted by permission from *IMPRIMIS*, the national speech digest of Hillsdale College, www.hillsdale.edu.

Benton, Thomas H., "The Seven Deadly Sins of Students." From the *Chronicle of Higher Education*, April 14, 2006. Copyright © 2006 by William Pannapacker. Reprinted by permission of the author.

boyd, danah. "Inequality: Can Social Media Resolve Social Divisions?" from I*t's Complicated: The Social Lives of Networked Teens*. Copyright (c) 2014 by Yale University Press. Used with permission.

Branch, Shelly, "One Term Says It All: 'Shut Up!'" from the *Wall Street Journal*, May 1, 2003. Copyright © 2003 by Shelly Branch. Reprinted with permission of Dow Jones via Copyright Clearance Center. www.copyright.com.

Carr, Nicholas. "iGod," from *The Big Switch: Rewiring the World, from Edison to Google* by Nicholas Carr. Copyright © 2008 by Nicholas Carr. Used by permission of W.W. Norton & Company, Inc.

Cisneros, Sandra, "Only Daughter" by Sandra Cisneros. Copyright © 1990 by Sandra Cisneros. First published in *Glamour*, November 1990. By permission of Susan Bergholz Literary Services, New York, NY and Lamy, NM. All rights reserved.

Clausen, Christopher, "Against Work." From the *American Scholar*, Volume 73, No. 4, Autumn 2004. Copyright © 2004 by Christopher Clausen. Reprinted by permission of the author.

Spurlock, Morgan, "Do You Want Lies with That?" From *Don't Eat This Book: Fast Food and the Supersizing of America*, pp. 1–8. Copyright © 2005 by Morgan Spurlock. Used by permission of G. P. Putnam's Sons, an imprint of Penguin Publishing Group, a division of Penguin Random House LLC.

Toth, Susan Allen, "Boyfriends" from *Blooming: A Small-Town Girlhood*. Reprinted by permission of the author.

Turkle, Sherry, "How Computers Change the Way We Think" from the *Chronicle of Higher Education*, January 30, 2004. Reprinted by permission of the author.

Weaver, Reg, "No: NCLB's Excessive Reliance on Testing Is Unrealistic, Arbitrary, and Frequently Unfair" from *Insight*, May 11–24, 2004. Used with permission from the author.

Zinsser, William K., "College Pressures" from *Blair & Ketchum's Country Journal*, vol. 6, no. 4, Apr. 1979. Copyright © 1979 by William K. Zinsser. Reprinted by permission of the author.

Art Credits